THE VERSATILE MICROCOMPUTER

ROY W. GOODY
Mission College, Santa Clara, California

THE VERSATILE MICROCOMPUTER
The Motorola Family

SRA

SCIENCE RESEARCH ASSOCIATES, INC.
Chicago, Henley-on-Thames, Sydney, Toronto

A Subsidiary of IBM

Acquisition Editor	Alan W. Lowe
Project Editor	Gretchen Hargis
Compositor	Graphic Typesetting Service
Illustrator	John Foster
Text Designer	Judith Olson

Library of Congress Cataloging in Publication Data

Goody, Roy W.
   The versatile microcomputer.

   Includes index.
   1. Microcomputers.   2. Motorola computers.
I. Title.
QA76.5.G628   1984   001.64   83-20211
ISBN 0-574-21595-6

Portions of this book were previously published in *The Intelligent Microcomputer* by Roy W. Goody, © 1982 by Science Research Associates, Inc.

Copyright © Science Research Associates, Inc. 1984, 1982.
All rights reserved.

Printed in the United States of America.

10 9 8 7 6 5 4 3 2 1

To George and June Goody

preface

If learning the complex subject of microcomputers can be compared to scaling a high peak, then this book is written as a staircase. It is designed to provide the beginning-to-intermediate technician or industrial-engineering student a gradual, step-by-step, upward learning path, eliminating the sharp rises and gaps that often impede progress. The Contents lists the steps in the staircase and divides the material into 25 easily digested chapters. Depending on the pace of presentation, these chapters might be divided appropriately into two sections for a two-semester or two-quarter series.

Emphasizing the major aspects of hardware design (configuring), program development, interfacing, and applications, we base the material in this book on the inventor's approach. That is, on successful completion of the material, you will be able to design and troubleshoot a simple microprocessor-based system starting completely from scratch. As an added bonus, you will learn to choose the best type of Motorola microprocessor for the job and to configure the system in the most cost-effective way. The scope and depth are sufficient for both the technician, who must test and troubleshoot the system, and the engineer, who must design and develop the system.

Little or no previous knowledge of computers is required. Prerequisites are a basic background in ac/dc and semiconductor electronics, experience in the use of the hexadecimal number system, and a working knowledge of digital circuits and gates. No review of basic digital concepts and number systems is included: it is assumed that you have completed a course in basic digital before entering microcomputer studies. Those with some miocrocomputer background may wish only to skim the early chapters.

This book is based on the popular Motorola family of microprocessors (the 6800, 6801, 6809, and 68000, to name the most prominent). The study of real devices and real systems, whose characteristics can be reproduced in the laboratory, is deemed to be the most effective way to focus the mind on this complex subject. The basic principles gained from a study of the Motorola family can, of course, be easily applied to any comparable microprocessor on the market. (*The Intelligent Microcomputer* is an Intel 8080/8085-based version of this text.)

The Motorola microprocessor family includes over 40 members, from the basic 8-bit 6800 (introduced in 1974) to the advanced 32-bit 68020 (introduced in 1982). In this book we will emphasize the leading processor from each of the three major categories: the 6800 from the 8-bit general-purpose group (and upon which this presentation concentrates); the 6801 from the single-chip group; and the 68000 from the 16/32-bit group. A full discussion of the dozens of chips forming the Motorola family can be found in the *Motorola Microprocessors Data Manual* and other Motorola literature.

Although the basic 6800 microprocessor has long been eclipsed by the more advanced 6801 and 6809, we can nevertheless maintain a state-of-the-art presentation with emphasis on the 6800 because all the newer-generation 8-bit microprocessor chips from Motorola are software-compatible, and to varying degrees hardware-compatible, with the 6800. In other words, the 6800 is the model for the entire Motorola 8-bit line.

To enhance the software development skills of the student, the Questions and Problems sections suggest nearly 60 programs (in addition to those presented in the text) that can be written and tested. The solutions to all suggested programs are given in the *Instructor's Guide*.

To summarize, the *content* of this book is grounded in fundamentals: design, troubleshooting, and interfacing in a balanced hardware/software environment. The *theme* of this book, however, is quite different, for it keeps an eye on the future, and in the future one subject will dominate the field of computers: *artificial intelligence*.

Therefore, to further increase enthusiasm and to make the material more readable, this book takes full advantage of the notion of the computer as an intelligent machine (an android). Indeed, if you set out to build a functioning intelligent machine, what major steps would you follow? First you would fashion the anatomy of the system (assemble the hardware). Next you would study its basic bodily processes and metabolism (basic processing action). You would then bring it to life (initiate processor action), send it off to school to be taught (programmed) many useful skills, and finally train it to live successfully in the real world (interfacing and applications). These are also the steps in the staircase along which this book is organized.

Also within the theme of artificial intelligence (AI), the text makes occasional reference to the evolutionary parallel between human and computer. The author has chosen this parallel as a natural way to introduce a number of computer concepts. No attempt is made to convince you that a machine will someday be the equal of a human being. The subjects of artificial intelligence and natural selection are used primarily as vehicles to motivate your interest and perhaps to make the material more exciting and fascinating. On the other hand, the similarities between computers and people should in no way be construed as mere fantasy; moreover, it is predicted that after completing this book you will come to regard your home computer a little more like your family pet (a living creature) and a little less like your family car (a simple tool).

Roy W. Goody

contents

1 **The Microcomputer: An Overview**   1
    The Microcomputer Revolution   1
    Microprocessors and Existing Systems   1
    Microprocessor Design   1
    Microprocessors and Microcomputers Defined   1
    Microcomputer Applications   2
    A Brief History   2
    The Fundamental Principles of Computer Action   5
    Beyond the Fundamental Concepts   7
    Questions and Problems   7

**PART I   Hardware:
The Anatomy of a Computer**   9

2 **The Bus System**   10
    The Bus Concept   10
    Bus-System Categories   11
    Tristate Circuits   11
    Examples of Tristate Circuits   12
    Common Bus Standards   12
    Buffering the Bus Lines   14
    Intelligent-Machine Design   14
    Questions and Problems   15

3 **Input and Output Ports**   16
    The Input Port   16
    The Output Port   20
    Intelligent-Machine Update   21
    Questions and Problems   22

4 **Introduction to Memory/Memory Hierarchy**   24
    Memory Hierarchy   24
    The Microcomputer Memory Spectrum   25
    Virtual Memory   26
    The Memory Map   26
    Intelligent-Machine Update   27
    Questions and Problems   27

5 **Primary Memory**   28
    RAM vs ROM   28
    Static RAM   28
    Dynamic RAM   40
    Magnetic-Core RAM   42
    Read-Only Memory   43
    Nonvolatile Static RAMs   48
    Bytewide Pin-Out Standards   50
    A RAM/ROM System   51
    Logic Arrays   51
    Intelligent-Machine Update   55
    Questions and Problems   56

6 **Secondary and Backup Memory**   57
    Thin-Film Magnetic Technology   57
    Secondary Memory Systems   63
    Backup Storage Devices   70
    Selecting the Right Secondary/Backup Combination   73
    Intelligent-Machine Update   74
    Questions and Problems   74

7 **The Central Processing Unit: Introduction to Processing Action**   76
    A Computer Analogy   76
    Processing Action   82
    Intelligent-Machine Update   82
    Questions and Problems   82

**PART II   Basic Processing Action:
The Metabolism of a Computer**   83

8 **Introduction to Programming and Program Processing**   84
    Writing a Program   84
    Writing the Simple Mimic Program   85

Teaching the Mimic Task	91	
Performing the Mimic Task	91	
Intelligent-Machine Update	93	
Questions and Problems	93	

9 Timing and Processor Cycles

The System Clock	94
6800 Timing Cycles	94
Genealogy of the 6800 Family	99
Intelligent-Machine Update	103
Questions and Problems	104

PART III Software: The Spark of Life 105

10 The Data-Transfer Group 106

Data-Transfer Verbs	106
Data-Transfer Addressing Modes	107
Instruction Types	111
A Data-Transfer Example	111
Intelligent-Machine Update	113
Questions and Problems	114

11 The Arithmetic Group 115

The Group 2 Verbs	115
Positive and Negative Numbers	116
Arithmetic Instruction Examples	118
An Arithmetic Program	122
Extended VS Indexed Addresing	122
High-Level and Low-Level Flowcharting	122
Additional Study	124
Intelligent-Machine Update	124
Questions and Problems	125

12 The Logical Group 127

The Elements of Logic	127
The Logical Group Verbs	127
Boolean Operations	129
Solving the Mystery	131
Bit Manipulation	132
Bit Change of State	135
Op Code Organization	135
Intelligent-Machine Update	136
Questions and Problems	136

13 Loops and Jumps: Introduction to Assembly-Language Programming 138

Loops and Jumps	138
Jump Instruction Processing	140
Assembly-Language Programming	140
Program Assembly	142
Intelligent-Machine Update	146
Questions and Problems	146

14 Reasoning: The Conditional Jump 147

The Elements of Reasoning	147
A Decision-Making Example	151
Machine-Assembly Update I	153
The Test and Bit-Test Instructions	153
Greater - Than/Less - Than Decisions	155
The Conditional Branch Clues	157
Multipronged Forks in the Road	158
The Delay Loop	158
Nesting	159
Program Timing	159
Loops and Indexed Addressing	161
Computer Music	162
Machine-Assembly Update II	162
Intelligent-Machine Update	162
Questions and Problems	162

15 Subroutines, Calls, and Stacks 167

Subroutines	167
The JSR and BSR Instructions	167
A Subroutine Example	171
Nesting Subroutines	172
The PUSH and PULL Instructions	172
When to CALL	174
Parameter Passing	175
Machine-Assembly Update	177
Intelligent-Machine Update	181
Questions and Problems	181

16 Interrupts 184

An Everyday Example	184
6800 Interrupt Processing	184
A Simple Interrupt Test Program	189
Additional Interrupt Considerations	189
A 6800 Interrupt Design Example	195
Machine-Assembly Update	195
Heathkit ET-3400A Interrupt Processing	195
Intelligent-Machine Update	196
Questions and Problems	196

PART IV Applications and Interfacing: Living in a Real World 199

17 Mathematical Refinement 200

Multiple-Precision Numbers	200
Multiplication	200

Division	202	
Processing Negative Numbers	202	
BCD Addition	206	
Fractions	207	
Floating-Point Numbers	208	
LSI Mathematical Processors	209	
Data Structures	209	
Strings	210	
Machine-Assembly Update	210	
Intelligent-Machine Update	211	
Questions and Problems	213	

18 Basic I/O and Interfacing Techniques — 214

Synchronous vs Asynchronous	214
Requirements of Asynchronous Transmission	214
Handshaking	214
Programmed I/O vs Interrupt I/O	216
DMA I/O	216
Digital-to-Analog Conversion	217
Analog-to-Digital Conversion	219
Keyboard Input	222
Touch-Screen Displays	224
The Mouse	225
Display Multiplexing	225
Monitor Programs	227
Video Display	227
Graphics	228
Data Acquisition	233
Machine-Assembly Update	233
Intelligent-Machine Update	234
Questions and Problems	234

19 Programmable Peripheral Chips — 237

Basics of Programmable Peripheral Chips	237
The 6821 Peripheral Interface Adapter	239
The Standard Microcomputer System	245
The 6828 Priority Interrupt Controller	245
A Final Word	250
Intelligent-Machine Update	250
Questions and Problems	250

20 Controllers — 252

Cybernetics	252
A Computerized Temperature-Control System	253
Single-Chip Microcontrollers: Intelligent Machines on a Chip	255
Single-Chip Temperature Control	257
Temperature Control Using the MC146805G2	259
Stepper Motor	260
Robotics	262

Intelligent-Machine Update	268
Questions and Problems	268

21 Data Communication — 269

Synchronous vs Asynchronous	269
Simplex/Duplex Transmission	270
Transmission Codes	270
Bus and Communication Standards	271
The 6850 Asynchronous Communication Interface Adapter (ACIA)	274
Basic Description	275
Communication Protocols	282
Local Area Networks (LANs)	283
Telecommunications	285
Fiber-Optic Digital Highways	291
Speech Synthesis	291
Intelligent-Machine Update	294
Questions and Problems	294

22 Product Development — 295

Hardware/Software Development	295
Troubleshooting	302
Development Systems	310
CAD/CAM	315
Operating Systems	316
Intelligent-Machine Update	319
Questions and Problems	319

23 The 8-Bit Family of Microprocessors — 321

The Intel Group	321
The Zilog Group	329
Bit-Slice Processors	333
Intelligent-Machine Update	333
Questions and Problems	334

24 Putting It All Together: An Application — 335

Lunar-Landing Simulator	335
Intelligent-Machine Update	339
Questions and Problems	340

PART V Advanced Processors: The Newest Generation — 343

25 The 68000 16-bit Microprocessor — 344

The 68000 at a Glance	344
68000 Bus Interfacing	344
Privilege States	350

Exception Processing		350
The 68000 Instruction Set		350
The 68000 Family		351
Intelligent-Machine Update: A Final Word		354
Questions and Problems		355

Glossary   357

Appendixes

I	Dictionary of Executable Instructions	362
II	6800 Instruction Set—Motorola Classifications	372
III	6800 Instruction Set—Author Classifications	375
IV	6800 Instruction Set—Cycle-by-Cycle Operation	377
V	Design Suggestions for Lunar Landing Simulator	381
Index		383

THE VERSATILE MICROCOMPUTER

chapter 1

The Microcomputer: An Overview

The microcomputer has flourished because—like its animal-kingdom counterpart—it found a fertile niche in the electronic environment and survived by being the fittest of the species.

In this chapter we will look at the historical development of the microcomputer and examine its fundamental nature. As you will see, we can learn a great deal about the computer by studying ourselves.

THE MICROCOMPUTER REVOLUTION

By the turn of this century the first industrial revolution, which began in England around 1720, was well under way, and machine power was replacing muscle power at an ever-increasing pace. Since the early 1970s a second and far more profound industrial revolution has gathered strength. This time, however, machine power will enhance and replace not the muscle power of the human species but the *brain* power.

The machine we are talking about is, of course, the computer. But computers are not all that new. Why then has the microprocessor—essentially a computer on a chip—ushered in the second industrial revolution?

Strangely enough, the answer to this question can be found on the Salisbury Plain in southwest England—the site of Stonehenge. This curious arrangement of 30-ton stones, each hewn from a distant quarry and transported hundreds of miles, is actually an ancient neolithic computer, constructed 500 years after the Egyptian pyramids to predict eclipses and other celestial events. Clearly, if today's computers were of Stonehenge design—requiring 30-ton components and hundreds of years to design and construct, fashioned from hard-to-get materials, dedicated to a single purpose, slow, inaccurate, and very limited in power—the second industrial revolution would not be taking place. But today's microprocessor-based computers are just the opposite. They are inexpensive, ultrasmall, lightweight, multipurpose, highly accurate, breathtakingly fast, and incredibly powerful—and the second industrial revolution is under way.

MICROPROCESSORS AND EXISTING SYSTEMS

To be more specific, microcomputers are successfully filling a wide gap in the eletronic-design spectrum between ordinary arrays of gates and registers (called *combinational* or *random logic*) and minicomputers. Toward one end of the gap, microcomputers are replacing hardware with software, and toward the other end, they are replacing numerous discrete computer components with a handful of very large scale integrated (VLSI) chips, each containing 50,000 or more transistors on a single chip of silicon. Any combinational-logic circuit of 30 or more gates is a prime candidate to be replaced by a microprocessor, and any computer system of today—including mainframe computers—may soon be replaced by a handful of VLSI blocks.

MICROPROCESSOR DESIGN

Microprocessors are unique in the world of electronic design because successful designers and users must have a balanced knowledge of hardware, programming, and interfacing. No longer do we have the luxury of specializing either in hardware design or pure programming. Sometimes a design problem is best solved with extensive programming, using only the simplest of external hardware. At other times a careful combination of VLSI blocks will provide the best overall solution. Once this balanced approach is accepted, the rewards will be faster, more powerful, and less costly system designs.

MICROPROCESSORS AND MICROCOMPUTERS DEFINED

In a single sentence, a *microcomputer* is a system containing a *microprocessor*. A *microprocessor* is a VLSI programmable logic device on a single silicon chip, less than $\frac{1}{4}$ inch on a side, usually containing all necessary computer components except memory and input/output (I/O) ports. A *microcomputer* is an entire computer system, including a microprocessor, external memory, and I/O devices. Occasionally, the entire computer system is integrated on a single chip (the 6801 family), although means are usually provided for adding extra memory and I/O ports.

Compared to mini- and mainframe computers, a microcomputer is usually smaller and less expensive, and often does not include the wide variety of expensive peripherals, such as cathode-ray tube (CRT) or disk memory. Microcomputers normally require less memory, are slower, and often are dedicated to a specific task, whereas mini- and mainframe computers are usually very high speed, general-purpose systems. However, the realm of the microcomputer overlaps into the area now dominated by the minicomputer, and soon will push into the area occupied by mainframe systems. Clearly it is difficult to define a system that is constantly changing; and, compared to human beings, computers are changing and adapting at an explosive pace!

MICROCOMPUTER APPLICATIONS

Even more important than the replacement of existing circuits and systems are the thousands of applications lying within the design gap between combinational-logic arrays and minicomputers—applications only the microprocessor can bring to life. The applications are so vast that the microprocessor revolution has already spawned an electronic age, in which an army of willing servants watches over us from morning to night. We wake up to a microprocessor-controlled alarm clock, read a newspaper that was edited and printed by a microcomputer-based word processor, and watch the morning news on television as a microprocessor fine-tunes the picture. We leave our homes guarded by a microprocessor "watchman," drive to work as a microprocessor instantly adjusts the car's timing and fuel/air mixture for optimum performance, and converse over a microprocessor-controlled CB radio. Our commute is speeded up by microprocessor-based traffic-control systems, our on-the-job productivity is increased by computerized inventory systems, and our workrooms are environmentally controlled by a microprocessor. We shop at a store where an intelligent (microprocessor-controlled) cash register inputs data to a central computer system that automatically inventories and orders merchandise. We go out for dinner and have our meal ordered and cooked under microprocessor control, and our drinks dispensed with a microcomputerized mixing machine. Then we go to bed and dream.

When we wake up it will be the future and our alarm will talk to us in perfect English. Our home computer will accurately forecast the weather and diagnose our ailments. We will realize how much we have come to rely on our computer for its *judgment* as well as its knowledge, and it will be hard to tell whether we are still dreaming.

A BRIEF HISTORY

Like most inventions, the microprocessor resulted from the gradual blend of many scientific trends. Those most important to the development of the microprocessor were the mathematical, electronic, and computer trends. As shown in Figure 1.1, several important milestones finally led to today's advanced microprocessor.

- *The early days:* The first calculations were done on the human hand. From this simple beginning the familiar decimal, binary, and hexadecimal number systems eventually evolved. The first mechanical device to make use of number systems was the *abacus,* a calculating device that dates back before the birth of Christ and is still used today.

- *1642—Calculating machine:* Blaise Pascal invented the first "desk calculator." It was strictly a mechanical device, using systems of gears to add and subtract. Since the precision machining of parts was still many years away, the idea slowly died. (But Pascal's name did not die away, for a popular high-level computer language is named after him.)

- *1801—Automatic loom:* Joseph Jacquard's idea revolutionized the weaving industry and was destined to resurface many years later in the computer industry. It was an automatic loom that used punched cards (IBM cards!) to control the pattern.

- *1833—"Analytical engine":* Charles Babbage, more than any other computer pioneer, deserves the title "father of modern digital computers." His "analytical engine," developed to calculate and print mathematical tables, incorporated many of the principles of modern digital computers. Babbage was the first to envision the stored-program concept, in which all numbers *and* instructions were read before calculations began. In other words, once programmed, the machine worked without human intervention. Unfortunately, for a number of practical reasons that plague all inventions ahead of their time, it was never developed beyond the prototype stage.

- *1854—Boolean algebra:* Can formal logic be described mathematically? George Boole discovered that it could, and he developed a symbolic form of logic called *Boolean algebra,* a subject familiar to every student of digital electronics. The door to computer design was now wide open.

- *1890—Electric tabulating machine:* Herman Hollerith developed the first true data-processing machine. Using

Chapter 1 / The Microcomputer: An Overview   **3**

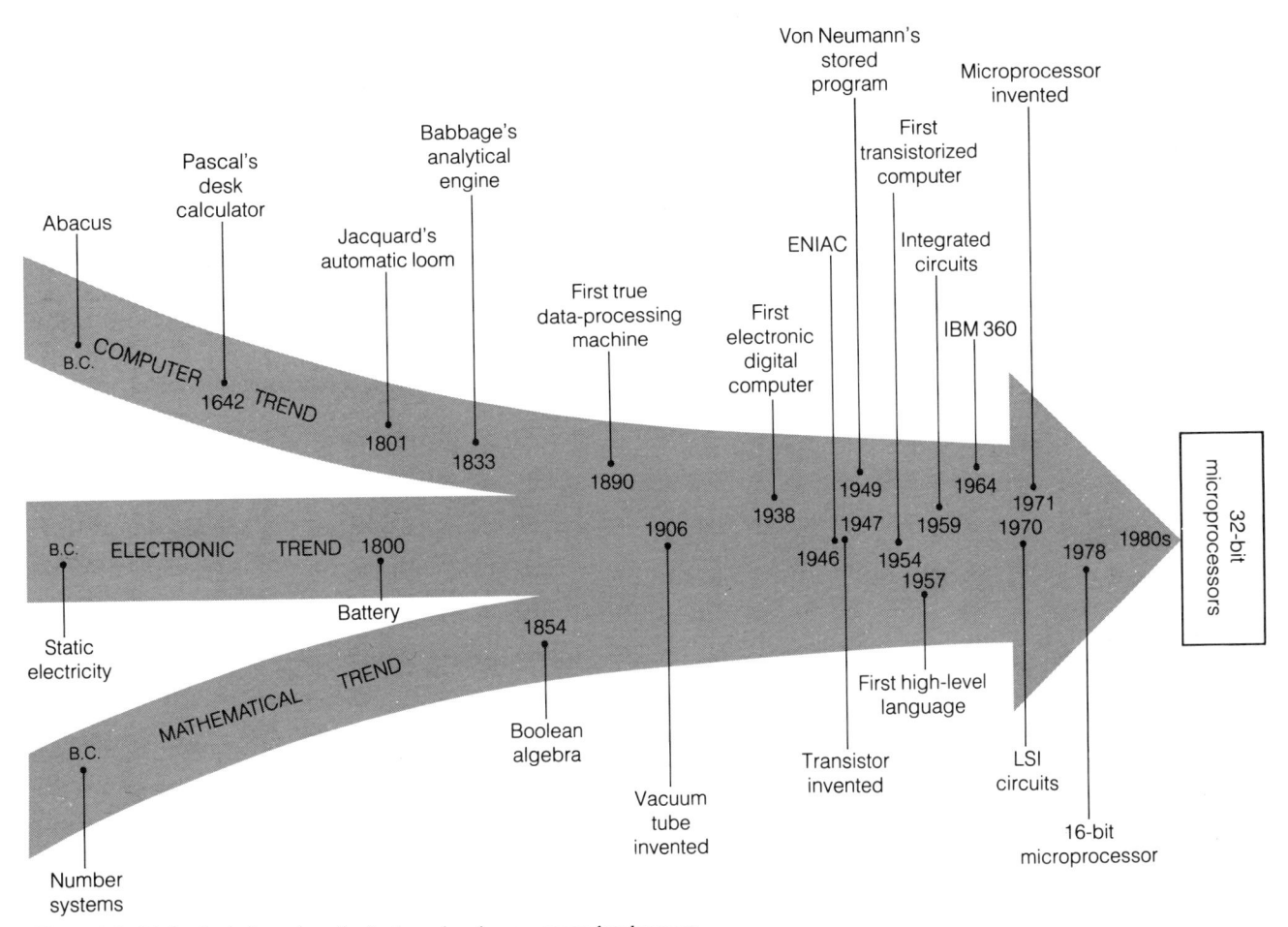

Figure 1.1 Technological trends and milestones in microprocessor development.

his machine, the task of tabulating the 1890 census was reduced from 20 to 3 years.

- *1906—Vacuum tube:* The electronic pathway began in earnest with the application of the triode vacuum tube, invented by Lee De Forest in 1906. Mathematical manipulations could now be done electronically rather than mechanically, with a quantum jump from seconds to milliseconds in processing speed.

- *1938—Electronic digital computer:* John V. Atanasoff formulated the basic ideas for computer memory and associated logic, and built the first electronic digital computer. Based on vacuum tubes, it paved the way for all work to follow.

- *1946—Large-scale electronic digital computer:* Prompted by the wartime need to calculate ballistic tables to produce trajectories for artillery and bombing, the U.S. Army funded the Electronic Numerical Integrator and Calculator (ENIAC) project. Completed in 1946, ENIAC was the first large-scale electronic digital calculating machine. By today's standards it was a monster. Composed of 18,000 vacuum tubes, it weighed in at 30 tons, occupied 1,500 square feet, and consumed 130,000 watts of power. However, it could multiply two numbers in about 3 milliseconds, a thousand times faster than ever before—and without the use of a single moving part. It was turned off for the last time in 1955.

- *1949—Stored-program computer:* Although ENIAC could perform individual mathematical operations at high speed, it had to wait for each instruction to be entered by its human operators. Intent on removing this human factor, John von Neumann picked up on the stored-program concept first conceived by Babbage and proposed placing computer instructions as well as data in the computer's memory. Whenever a sequence of instructions was to be performed, the computer could read in each instruction from memory without waiting for human intervention. Storing the program inside the computer along with the data allows today's computers to operate at high speed (and distinguishes a computer from a calculator).

With the stored-program concept, the last major hurdle to modern computer design was crossed, and in May of 1949 the first digital computer based on the stored-program concept went into operation. Named the Electronic Delay Storage Automatic Calculator (EDSAC), it set the stage for all computers to follow.

- *1954—Transistorized computer:* Although based on electronics, ENIAC and EDSAC were still of "Stonehenge" design—far too big, bulky, and power consuming to command widespread attention. In 1947, however, a breakthrough was made that can only be described in fairy-tale terms, for like Alice in Wonderland, the solid-state research it set in motion was destined to shrink the size of computers a thousandfold and more. Invented by John Bardeen, W. H. Brattain, and W. B. Shockley at Bell Laboratories in 1947, the transistor was the seed from which the second industrial revolution sprouted.

  The first product of this seed sprouted in 1954 with the introduction of the TRAnsistor DIgital Computer (TRADIC). By 1960 hundreds of transistorized computers were in operation, processing data faster and at lower cost than ever before. The days of the vacuum tube were numbered.

- *1957—High-level language:* Primarily because of their awesome size, the early vacuum-tube computers quickly acquired a public image of "giant brains," fearsome machines to be viewed with apprehension and mistrust. This image was largely undeserved, of course, for these early computers were very crude, and in one area in particular—languages—they were downright primitive. The only language these early machines understood was machine language—the language of ones and zeros—a language that made programming a cumbersome, error-prone, and difficult endeavor.

  The first major breakthrough in language development was made by an IBM research team headed by John Backus. Primarily interested in developing a language to solve mathematical calculations, the team devised a way of writing a program using mathematical notation instead of machine language. Using common typewriter symbols to write and enter the program, the computer would then translate (compile) the sequence of symbols into the required machine-language instructions.

  Introduced in 1957, the language was called *FORTRAN* (for FORmula TRANslation) and is still in widespread use today. By 1960 numerous high-level languages were in use, including COBOL (COmmon Business-Oriented Language), which gave the business community many of the same advantages that FORTRAN gave the scientific community.

- *1959—Integrated circuit:* By applying the principles of photolithography to flat surfaces of silicon, and by developing the method of solid-state diffusion for introducing the impurities that create p and n regions, engineers found they could construct entire circuits, consisting of many transistors, on a single chip of silicon. This was the basis of the integrated circuit, a technology that was to show the same explosive growth in sophistication as took place in the human brain during the end of the last ice age.

- *1964—Integrated-circuit computer:* On April 7, 1964, IBM introduced the standard mainframe computer, the System/360 (called 360 because the system was said to encompass the full range of scientific and business applications). Using highly reliable, mass-produced, integrated circuits, it could perform in 1 second nearly a half million computations at a cost of less than 10 cents. The System/360, designed for both business and scientific use, also introduced a number of new input/output and auxiliary storage devices.

- *1970—Large-scale integrated (LSI) circuit:* From the early 1960s to the early 1970s, the maximum complexity of integrated circuits doubled approximately every 18 months. By 1970 more than 15,000 transistors could be etched onto a single chip of silicon, an achievement that made the handheld calculator feasible.

- *1971 to present—era of the microprocessor:* In 1971 the computer, electronic, and mathematical trends came together in a unique way, and the microprocessor emerged on the scene—initially with little fanfare. In less than 10 years, though, it went from a simple 4-bit LSI device developed for calculators (the Intel 4004), to the MC68020, a 32-bit SLSI (super large scale integrated) enhanced 68000 microprocessor that forms the heart of a system resembling a mainframe computer.

- *Sometime in the future—first true intelligent machine:* In the field of microprocessors, the future blends with the past so quickly that no historical survey would be complete without a word about what lies ahead. Most far-reaching of all is a fourth scientific trend that is now merging with the ongoing development of the microprocessor. This fourth trend, known as *artificial intelligence,* will combine with the microprocessor to produce the true intelligent machine. Unlike the human brain, which must depend on the relatively slow process of biological change, the intelligent machine made of silicon is under no such restrictions. We can only wonder where the new technology will lead us. Soon a true learning machine will emerge, *one able to modify its program based on learning experience.* What would be the result if we taught two such learning machines to play chess, and what if they were pitted against each other, playing games at the speed of light for a month or a year? At the end of that time, what would we find? Perhaps a new way of thinking, or a new philosophy, or a new mathematics—or perhaps something we would not be able to understand at all!

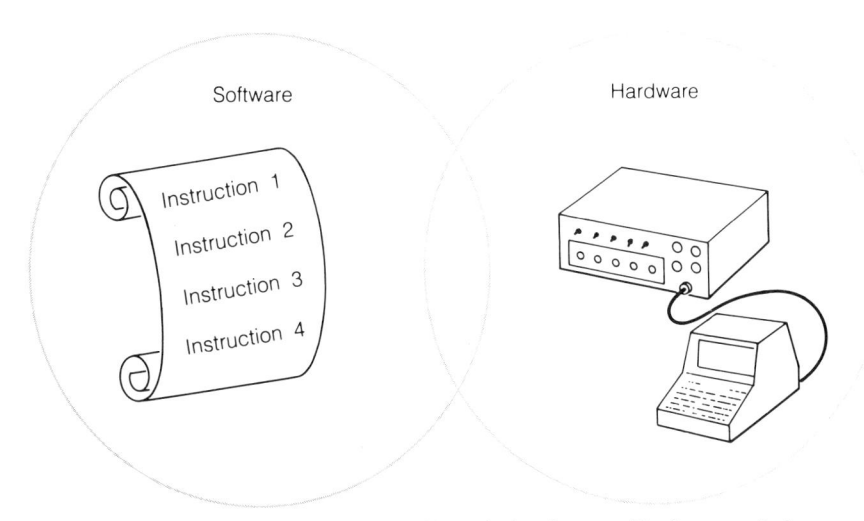

Figure 1.2 A computerized solution to a problem—both software and hardware required.

THE FUNDAMENTAL PRINCIPLES OF COMPUTER ACTION

The apparent similarity between people and computers presents us with an exciting possibility: If computers and humans do things in a similar way, then to develop the more basic concepts of computer action perhaps we can begin by studying ourselves.

What separates us and other members of the animal kingdom from the world of inanimate objects? The answer is very straightforward: we perform tasks; we do things.

To use an everyday example, consider a major-league outfielder catching a baseball. Even the most cursory analysis of this simple task reveals that it is composed of individual steps, taken in sequential order:

> Track ball
> Run under ball
> Raise glove
> Catch ball

Each step in the sequence commands a specific operation. In computer terminology, each command is called an *instruction*. To complete the task of catching a baseball, then, we simply go through the instructions in order. *A computer performs a task in precisely the same way.* Therefore, by studying our own actions, we already have uncovered perhaps the most fundamental of all computer concepts. Seven of these concepts are described below.

1. *A computer performs a task by processing a sequential list of instructions.*

Of course, it is important for us to write the list of instructions in the proper order. If any of the steps is incorrectly listed, the task probably could not be completed.

2. *To carry out a task by way of computer action, we require both the list of instructions (the software) and the physical circuitry (the hardware).*

To catch a baseball, we require two major items: the list of instructions and the collection of physical components (player, baseball, and glove). When applied to computers, the sequential list of instructions is known as *software*; the physical computer circuitry and peripheral components are known as *hardware* (see Figure 1.2).

3. *Each instruction given to a computer generally consists of a verb portion (the operation code) and an object portion (the operand).*

As listed below, each instruction written for a person is made up of two parts—a verb or action portion and a noun or object portion:

Verb	Object
track	ball
run under	ball
raise	glove
catch	ball

Each instruction written for a computer follows the same format. The verb portion of each instruction is known as the *operation code* (or *op code*), and the object portion is known as the *operand*.

4. *As each instruction is carried out (executed), the operation code (verb) directs the activities of the operand (object).*

As each instruction of our baseball routine is processed, the verb or action portion directs the activities of the object portion, and the instruction is carried out—or *executed*. Since this is true of all instructions carried out by people, it is also true of all instructions carried out by computers.

5. *Programming a computer means entering the proper sequence of instructions into its memory.*

During training, a baseball player quickly commits to memory the sequence of instructions for catching a baseball. In other words, the player has *learned* the sequence of steps. In computer terminology, learning is known as *programming,* and it consists of storing the sequence of instructions in memory. As previously noted, the concept of a stored program—that is, placing the instructions in memory before they are needed—was one of the great historical advances made in computer technology.

6. *A computer consists of five basic hardware blocks: input, output, memory, arithmetic/logic unit (ALU), and control unit.*

We know that the system software—or program—can be broken down into a sequence of instructions. Can the system hardware, for both human being and computer, also be broken down into a number of individual blocks? For people we find that it can, and catching a baseball puts five major parts of anatomy (hardware) into play:

- The *eye* (input port) tracks the flight of the ball.
- The *voice* (output port) calls for the ball.
- The *memory* holds the sequence of instructions.
- The *computation and logic area of the brain* (arithmetic/logic unit, or ALU) computes the ball's trajectory.
- The *central nervous system* (control unit) times and sequences the overall process.

As shown in Figure 1.3, these five basic hardware elements are also common to every computer.

The control unit and the ALU are often combined in a single unit known as the *central processing unit*—or simply CPU (the CPU is often a single microprocessor chip, such as the 6800).

7. *The basic processing cycle of a computer system consists of input of data, manipulation of data, and output or display of result.*

Human beings generally interact with their environment in a three-step process: we take in information, manipulate it mentally, and output the result. The overall processing cycle of a computer follows the same pattern: input, process, and output.

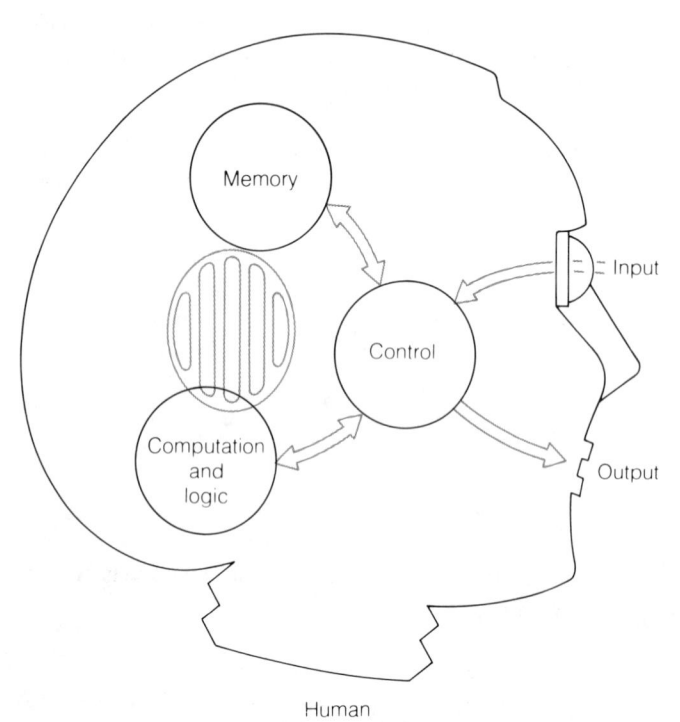

Figure 1.3 The five basic hardware blocks for both human being and computer.

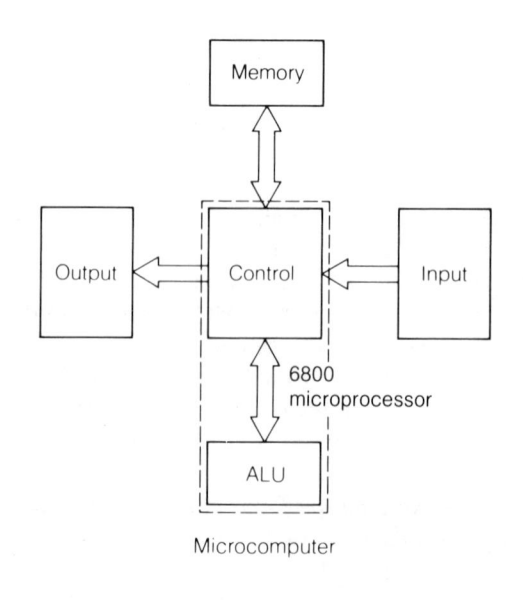

BEYOND THE FUNDAMENTAL CONCEPTS

When described in their most basic terms—as we have done in this chapter—the actions that human beings take to catch a baseball or perform other common tasks do not seem complex. It appears we use our marvelous mental machines with little regard for the intricate operations involved. Unfortunately, we cannot take computers so lightly, for to design and troubleshoot computer systems we must understand precisely how every component functions and interacts, and how every signal and waveform carries forward the processing cycle. The tasks before us are clear:

- The five blocks of the computer system must be opened up and the inner workings revealed.
- The processing action itself must be studied in detail.
- The computer's vocabulary (all the instructions it can follow) must be learned, and all instructions must be converted to a form the computer will understand (English will not do). In addition, the computer must be taught (programmed) to perform simple tasks.
- All the factors allowing a computer to operate efficiently in a real-world environment must be covered.
- More advanced, later-generation computer systems must be introduced.

Each of these tasks corresponds closely to Parts I, II, III, IV, and V of this book.

QUESTIONS AND PROBLEMS

1. List some ways in which you think people and computers are alike, and list ways in which they are not.
2. What is the difference between a microprocessor and a microcomputer?
3. What does VLSI stand for?
4. When a combinational-logic array is replaced by a microprocessor, why can the chip count usually be reduced?
5. What significant computer development do we owe to Charles Babbage?
6. List some of the microprocessor/microcomputer applications you have recently encountered.
7. Name several characteristics of a *high-level* language.
8. What is the major difference between a computer and a calculator?
9. Name the first and most fundamental of all computer concepts.
10. What is each step in a program called?
11. Why is it important to list the steps in a program in proper sequence?
12. What is the difference between *hardware* and *software*?
13. In technical terms, what do the (a) "verb" and (b) "object" of each instruction correspond to?
14. Programming a computer corresponds to what process in human beings?
15. What are the five major hardware blocks of a computer? To what human anatomical feature does each correspond, and what is the basic function of each?
16. How is a recipe like a computer program?

part I

Hardware: The Anatomy of a Computer

Armed with a knowledge of the most fundamental principles of computer action, we will now construct an intelligent machine from scratch.

In Part I, we will assemble, one at a time, the five hardware blocks that constitute the *anatomy* of the computer. The computer's anatomy is often called its *architecture*—the total collection of circuits, registers, and interconnecting lines that make up the physical system. When we have added all five components—and have completed Part I—the system will resemble the diagram of the intelligent machine that appears on the front cover of this book.

chapter 2

The Bus System

"Beauty of style and harmony and grace and good rhythm depend on simplicity." (Plato, *The Republic,* 4th century B.C.) This remarkable insight by Plato might be called the *designer's creed*. If our computer system is going to perform with style and harmony, it must be simple.

Unfortunately, the potential for complexity is enormous. A single CPU, for example, may be called on to communicate with hundreds of peripheral circuits. Imagine the overall complexity of such a system if we must provide a *unique* path between the CPU and every peripheral. Before microcomputers could evolve, this data roadblock had to be cleared away.

THE BUS CONCEPT

As with so many contemporary problems, the solution had already been demonstrated—it merely had to be applied to computers. Simply look at the neighborhood you live in. Your community may be a small one, with just five homes, but providing a *unique* roadway between each home results in a system of great complexity (see Figure 2.1a). As demonstrated by Figure 2.1b, the solution is well known: interconnect the five homes with a single intersection.

An intersection is a *common* area fed by all pathways, and its use results in a simpler system. To avoid conflicts, of course, we have to take great care that vehicles traveling on separate pathways do not attempt to use the intersection at the same time. In other words, they must take turns using the common medium, a process known as *time multiplexing*.

Microcomputers have adopted this hardware-saving configuration. The single transmission medium, known as a *bus,* consists of an array of *common* conductors into which all circuit elements tap. The bus concept allows for a very simple arrangement of components (see Figure 2.2).

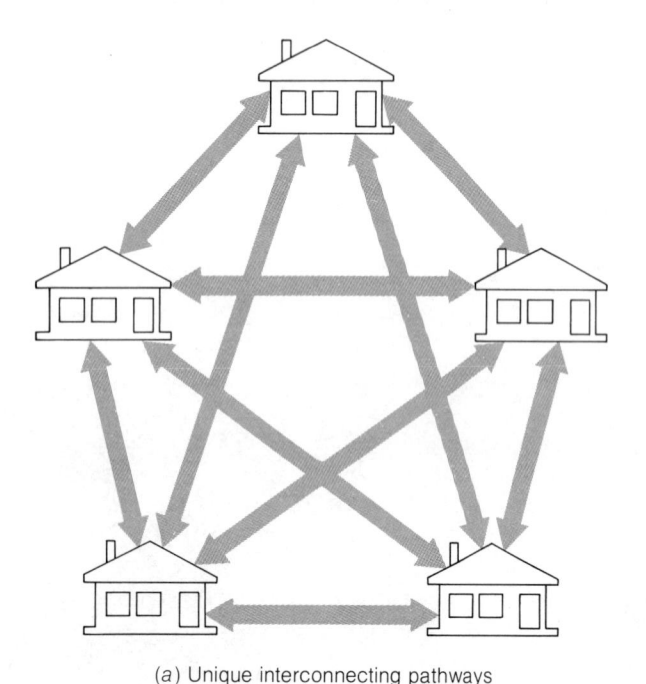

(a) Unique interconnecting pathways that result in complex system

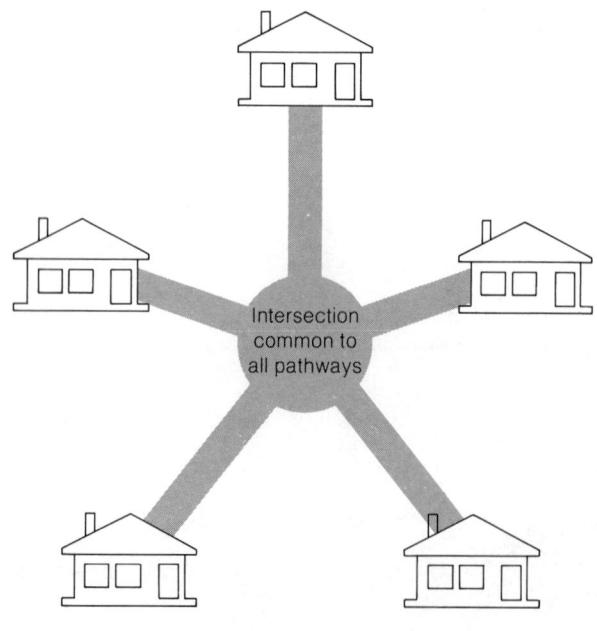

(b) A common intersection that simplifies the system

Figure 2.1 The bus concept.

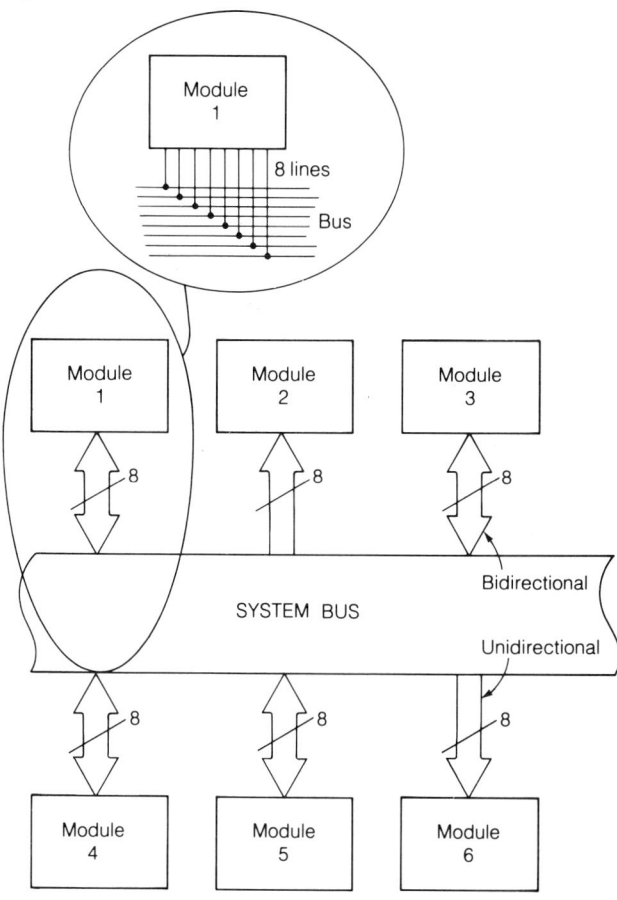

Figure 2.2 A bus-organized system.

Of course, all peripheral modules feeding the common bus system will have to share its use through the process of time multiplexing. First, one peripheral circuit transmits its data with full and exclusive use of the transmitting medium; then, in the next time slot, another peripheral circuit has full use of the common bus system. *Clearly, only one circuit module at a time can transmit data onto the common bus.*

BUS-SYSTEM CATEGORIES

Because it greatly simplifies the overall system, all 8-bit microcomputers use the bus concept. Furthermore, all microcomputers break down the bus system into four bus-strip categories. Each bus-strip category in turn consists of a number of "parallel" conductors:

- *Data bus*—The data bus consists of eight bidirectional conductors and carries data and instructions back and forth between the various circuit locations. The eight parallel data lines, carrying eight bits of information simultaneously, make the 6800 microprocessor a parallel processor. These 8-bit words are known as *bytes*.

- *Address bus*—The address bus consists of 16 lines and is used to locate data within memory or I/O ports. Since 65,536 different binary numbers can be specified with 16 bits (2^{16} = 65,536), the address bus can locate, or point out, one particular byte of data among 65,536 possible locations (65,536 = 64K, where 1K = 1,024).

- *Control bus*—The control bus carries the various timing signals used to regulate and sequence the transfer of data and to carry out various processes. The number of lines is arbitrary because the control bus is a catchall bus—that is, it contains signals that do not fit into the other bus-strip categories.

- *Power bus*—The power bus for most microcomputers consists of two lines: +5 volts and ground. Occasionally, for older microprocessors and components, additional lines are needed. For instance, the 8080 microprocessor requires −5 and +12-volt supplies in addition to the standard +5 volts. Component manufacturers clearly intend to produce circuits which run on a single +5-volt supply and which are fully TTL compatible. (To simplify future diagrams, the power bus usually will be deleted.)

TRISTATE CIRCUITS

The bus concept and time multiplexing go hand in hand. When one roadway is transmitting vehicles into an intersection, all others must be isolated. Traffic signals provide the necessary isolation by giving the green light to only one roadway at a time.

In electronics, the tristate circuit acts as the traffic signal, controlling the flow of data onto the data bus. It must have a transmitting state (green light) and an isolation state (red light). When in the transmitting state, either a logic 1 or a logic 0 can pass through to the data bus. When in the isolation state, the output floats and enters a high-impedance (Z) condition. Since three states are possible, we call the circuit a *tristate circuit*. The three states are:

0	transmitting state (logic 0)
1	transmitting state (logic 1)
high Z	isolation state

A high-impedance state accomplishes the necessary isolation since it does not prevent the single actively transmitting circuit from driving the data-bus lines high or low, as required. Devices receiving information from the data bus, on the other hand, need not be tristated, for conflicts of information between receiving circuits are not possible (once you leave an intersection, there is no need for further traffic control). However, the output circuits should present to the bus a reasonably high input impedance to avoid overloading the bus lines.

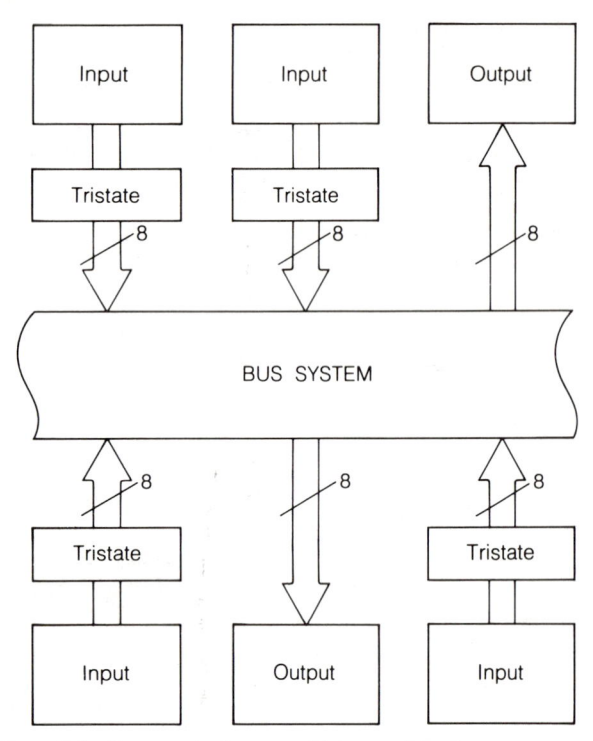

Figure 2.3 Bus-organized system with inputs tristated.

When tristate circuits are added to all input devices, notice how simple a bus-organized system becomes (Figure 2.3). The beauty of the bus system lies in the ease with which new circuits or modules can be added into the computer system. Simply tie the address, data, control, and power lines directly into the system bus.

EXAMPLES OF TRISTATE CIRCUITS

To implement a time-multiplexed bus system, a whole family of tristate circuits has evolved. We will look at three examples:

- The CD4016 quad bilateral switch shown in Figure 2.4a is a set of four analog switches that can be used for tristate functions. The circuit operation is very simple. When any given control line is high, the circuit is transmitting information, and the output state equals the input state. When the control line goes low, the circuit assumes the high-impedance state and does not prevent another circuit from transmitting onto the bus. The inherent high input impedance and low power drain of this chip simplify the job of the designer.

- The 74LS241 octal buffer (tristate) is similar to the CD4016. However, the 74LS241 integrates eight buffers within a single chip and, and as a member of the TTL family, has different I/O characteristics (see Figure 2.4b).

- The MC6882B octal tristate buffer/latch is a member of the newer family of tristate circuits and can be configured for either input or output operation (see Figure 2.4c). Eight tristate buffers are included within each chip, making the 6882B specifically designed for use with 8-bit microprocessors. For added flexibility, a D latch is paired with each tristate buffer. $\overline{\text{Output}}$ $\overline{\text{Enable}}$ controls the tristate buffers, and $\overline{\text{Latch}}$ clocks data through the D latches. We will be using the 6882B shortly, when the first two hardware blocks are added to our intelligent-machine system.

COMMON BUS STANDARDS

Standardization eliminates redundancy and improves efficiency. The English language, for example, is a standard form of communication, used by a great number of diverse peoples. For the same reasons, a number of widely adopted bus standards presently are found in the microcomputer world (with several others under development). We will examine a few of the more popular bus standards.

S-100 Bus

Like so many standards, the S-100 bus was not originally designed to be a standard. It was developed by MITS, Inc., in 1975 for their 8080-based Altair computer. Others soon adopted the S-100 format, and it quickly became an industry standard.

The S-100 bus is a collection of 100 data, address, control, and power signals. Its major appeal was the adoption of the "motherboard" concept. A motherboard is a printed-circuit board holding 100 parallel foil strips, with several 100-pin edge connectors soldered to the foil. Circuit boards (10 by 5.5 inches) are added to the system by merely plugging them into the edge connectors. Consequently, a flood of S-100 compatible modules—memory boards, I/O boards, and others—soon became available.

However, the original S-100 bus—developed in an era when 16-bit processors, multiprocessing, and megabyte memories were unheard of—was unable to keep up with new developments. To maintain the popular S-100 concept, yet meet the needs of modern systems, the IEEE-696 standard was developed. Among its improved features are a 24-bit address bus (16 megabytes), 16-bit data bus, 11 interrupt inputs, and provisions for multiprocessing. This new general-purpose interface system should ensure compatibility with present and future S-100 computer systems.

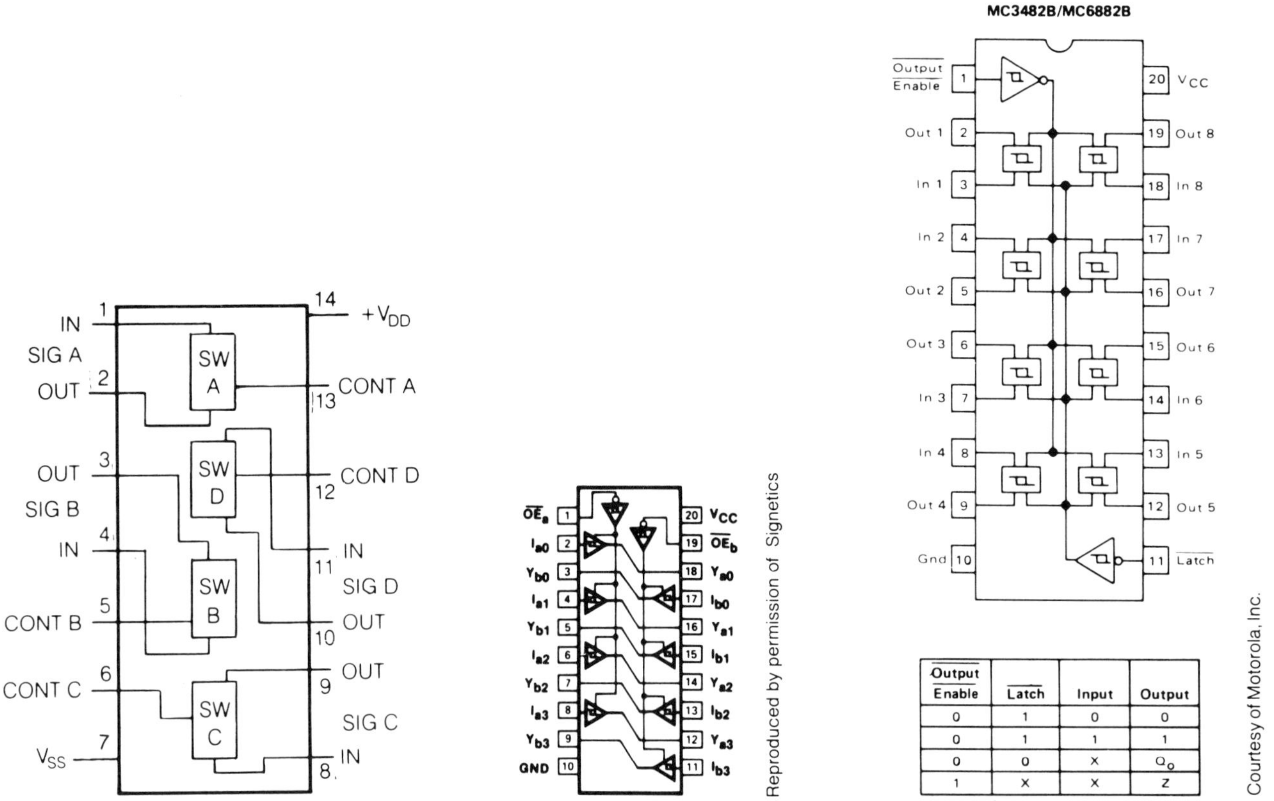

(a) The CD4016 quad analog switch (b) The 74LS241 octal buffer (3-state) (c) The MC6882B octal tristate buffer/latch

Figure 2.4 Three typical tristate circuits.

Multibus

Like the new S-100 standard, the recently developed Multibus standard is specifically designed to accept a wide variety of system modules (in this case, "multi" means multimodule). A variety of 6.75- by 12-inch CPU, memory, and I/O boards can be quickly assembled by plugging them into a Multibus card cage. These modules usually have a master/slave relationship. The master controls the bus, transmitting address and command signals; the slave merely receives signals.

A Multibus system may have a number of bus masters. Since only one bus master can control the bus at one time, bus arbitration logic (consisting of priority in and out lines) is included within the Multibus scheme.

The Multibus standard provides for 86 lines, with an optional 60-line system for carrying auxiliary bus signals. The 86 lines include 22 address lines, 16 data lines (bidirectional), 8 multilevel interrupt lines, a number of redundant power and ground lines, and an extensive control array.

The Intel-developed Multibus (officially designated IEEE-796) has gained widespread acceptance in the microcomputer industry.

The STD Bus

The increasingly popular Pro-Log/Mostek-inspired STD bus—smaller in scope than the S-100 or Multibus—touts its high degree of modularity (because it is smaller, you pay only for those features you need) as its major advantage. The STD bus is based on 56 pins, divided into five categories:

- 6 regular data
- 8 bidirectional data
- 16 address
- 22 control
- 4 power

The STD bus is also based on a motherboard accepting edge-connector cards. Compared to the large Multibus, however, the STD's edge-connected cards are tiny, measuring only 4.5 by 6.5 inches.

Unlike the S-100 and Multibus systems, the STD bus is universal and can handle any popular 8-bit microprocessor with equal ease. That is, all STD bus lines are fully defined, assuring us that any STD card from any manufacturer will fit into our system without modification (this total bus definition does result in some lack of flexibility).

VERSAbus

When 16-bit microprocessors (such as the 68000) were introduced, it became apparent that buses inspired by 8-bit microprocessors would not always suffice. The VERSAbus, introduced by Motorola, was designed with 16- and 32-bit microprocessors in mind. To accommodate all 16- and 32-bit systems, it is processor independent, with features based on system-level requirements.

To allow each plug-in circuit board to be an independent subsystem, the designers chose a relatively large format—9.25 by 14.5 inches. The 140 available lines support 32-bit data and address spaces, five-level bus arbitration, seven levels of interrupt, and other control and status features.

To meet the need for smaller, more modular, and rugged circuit boards, the VMEbus—a subset of VERSAbus—was introduced in 1981.

BUFFERING THE BUS LINES

For a small, single-board system, the current drive capability of the 6800 (a single TTL load) is adequate. For large multiboard systems, however, MOS and CMOS microprocessors and circuits often lack the required power to drive the system bus, and a *buffer* or *driver* must be interfaced between the CPU and system bus. If memory and I/O ports are MOS or CMOS devices, they too may require buffering.

Buffer/drivers fall into one of three categories:

1. *Transmitters,* which buffer the signals sent to the bus
2. *Receivers,* which buffer the signals sent from the bus
3. *Transceivers,* which perform both of the above processes

The MC6882B octal tristate buffer/latch introduced earlier is a typical buffer/driver, offering high input impedance, high output-drive capability, and tristate outputs. The 6882B can serve as either transmitter or receiver depending on how it is configured. The 6880A quad bus transceiver of Figure 2.5a provides back-to-back buffer/drivers for bidirectional operation.

As shown in Figure 2.5b, the 6882B transmitter buffers the unidirectional address and control lines, while the 6880A transceiver buffers the bidirectional data lines.

INTELLIGENT-MACHINE DESIGN

With an appreciation of the advantages of a bus-organized system, we can now begin the design of our intelligent machine.

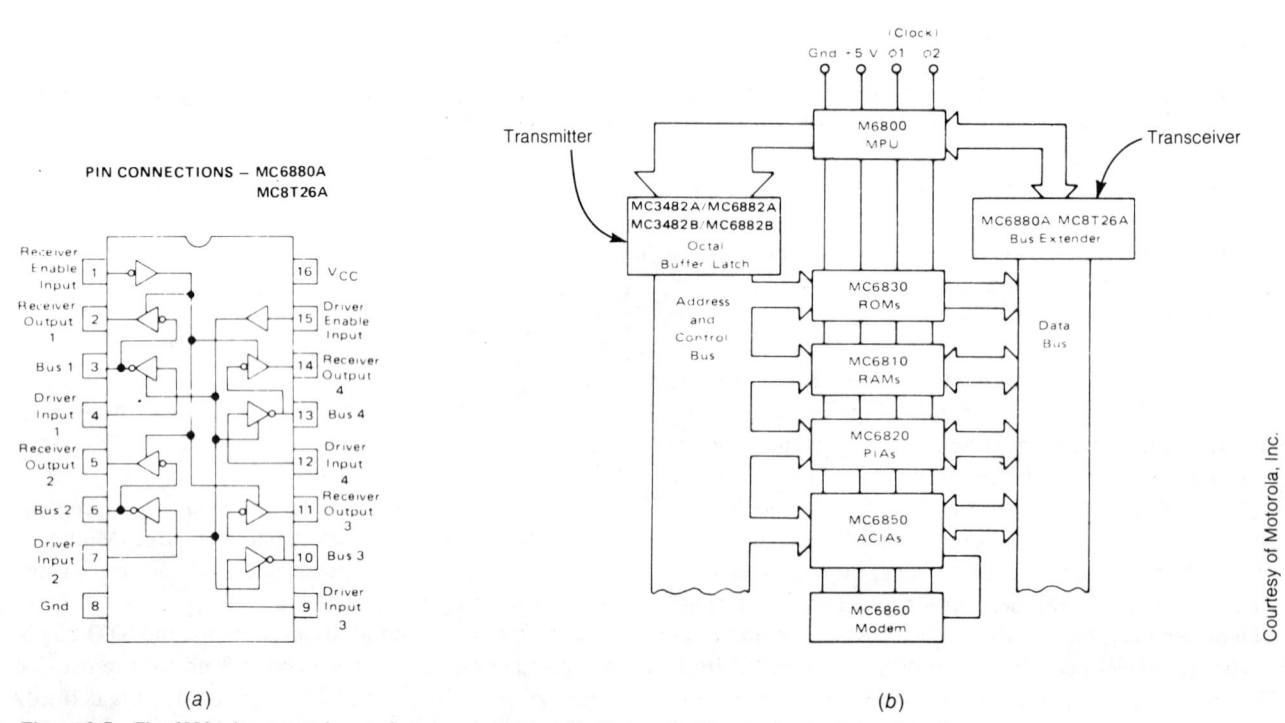

Figure 2.5 The 6880A bus transceiver—pin connections (a) and buffering of address/control and data lines (b).

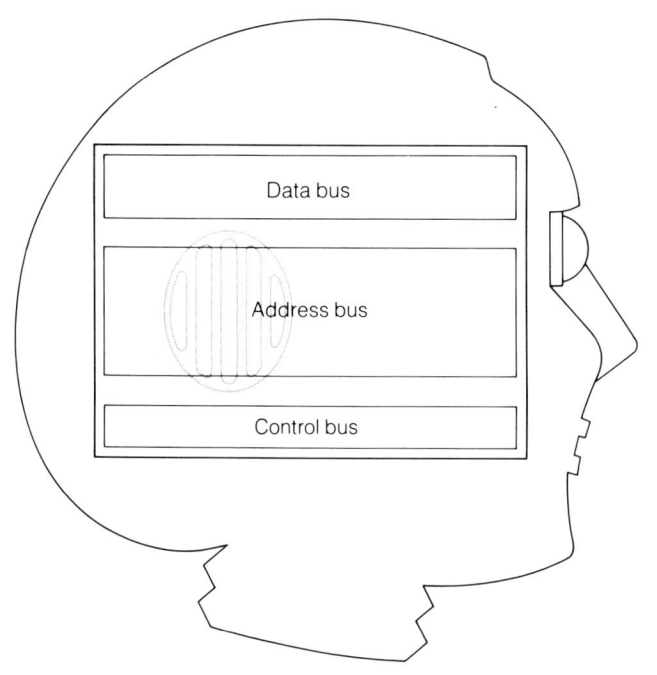

Figure 2.6 Thinking-machine design under way.

Adding a bus system to simplify the overall computer architecture sets our system on its way (Figure 2.6). So far it is a system that Plato would have approved of; it is a system that will lead to inherent simplicity.

QUESTIONS AND PROBLEMS

1. How does the *bus* concept simplify the overall hardware configuration of a computer?
2. What is another term for *time multiplexing?*
3. How many circuit modules are allowed to transmit data *onto* the bus at the same time?
4. What are the four bus-strip categories of a microcomputer bus system, and what general function is provided by each?
5. What does the term *floating* mean?
6. What are the three states of a *tristate* circuit?
7. What functions are performed by the $\overline{\text{Output Enable}}$ and $\overline{\text{Latch}}$ inputs to the MC6882B?
8. What is a *motherboard?*
9. Why is it sometimes necessary to buffer the bus lines?
10. What does *bidirectional* mean?
11. *Theoretically,* how many modules can simultaneously *receive* information from the common bus?
12. Why is it a simple process to add new modules to a bus-organized system?
13. The S-100 bus, unlike the STD bus, leaves a number of lines undefined. What are the advantages and disadvantages of each technique?
14. What is a transceiver?

chapter 3

Input and Output Ports

At the very beginnings of brain development, when the Earth belonged to tiny multicellular organisms, the first nervous systems were simple sensory receptors designed to sense the heat, light, and chemical makeup of their ocean environment and to respond by simple reflex action.

In this chapter we will follow the pattern of nature and make the first circuits added to our intelligent machine its "eyes," "ears," and "voice"—simple *input ports* and simple *output ports*. (More complex I/O circuits and techniques will be introduced in future chapters.)

THE INPUT PORT

An input port is a conduit for channeling information from the outside world to the internal data bus. As we learned in the previous chapter, however, all information transmitted onto the data bus must be tristated; otherwise, data from two sources would collide on the data bus, and the information would be garbled.

The MC6882B octal tristate buffer/latch has built-in tristate buffers and will satisfy all the requirements for input port operation (see Figure 3.1). When we examine the internal circuitry of the 6882B, we find all eight tristate buffers controlled by the active-low $\overline{\text{Output Enable}}$ line. When $\overline{\text{Output Enable}}$ is pulled low, the data present at the output of the latches pass through the port and appear on the eight output lines. When the $\overline{\text{Output Enable}}$ control line is inactive (high), the output lines are driven to their high-impedance state. Since simple input ports generally do not require latches, the eight D latches are made transparent to the incoming data by placing a high on the $\overline{\text{Latch}}$ line. (The D latches are level active, passing the input to the output when $\overline{\text{Latch}}$ is high, and latching the data on the high-to-low transition.)

Adding two 6882Bs to our system endows our thinking machine with sensory inputs (see Figure 3.2). When the computer wishes to "read," it pulls port 1's $\overline{\text{Output Enable}}$ line low. Information flows from the outside world to the data bus. When this $\overline{\text{Output Enable}}$ line is high and the output buffers are in their high-impedance state, port 2 can take its turn at transmitting data onto the data bus. By taking turns, all input ports can share the common data bus.

Our developing system can now read and listen at various times—by time multiplexing. But how does it choose what it wants to do—say, if it wants to read rather than listen? How does it single out the one correct input port from all the others in the system? Moreover, once it has found the right input port, how does it know precisely *when* to activate the port?

A careful look at the process of *data transfer* will help provide the answers. After all, reading and listening are nothing more than data-transfer operations.

Data Transfer

Suppose you plan to travel by air between San Francisco and New York. When you purchase your plane ticket, you must be able to answer two important questions:

1. *Where* am I now and *where* am I going?
2. *When* will I leave?

In short, traveling from one location to another is a *where/when* operation. First you specify your source and destination, and then you pinpoint the exact time of your trip.

Data-transfer operations within a computer system are also where/when operations:

1. *Where:* With the help of signals on the address and control buses, both the source and the destination of the data transfer are determined.
2. *When:* Control-bus signals then open the gates of the selected source and destination, allowing the data to flow between source and destination.

These considerations lead to the standard idealized Motorola-based waveforms for data transfer (Figure 3.3). The waveforms constitute a where/when data-transfer operation and must occur whenever information is transferred from

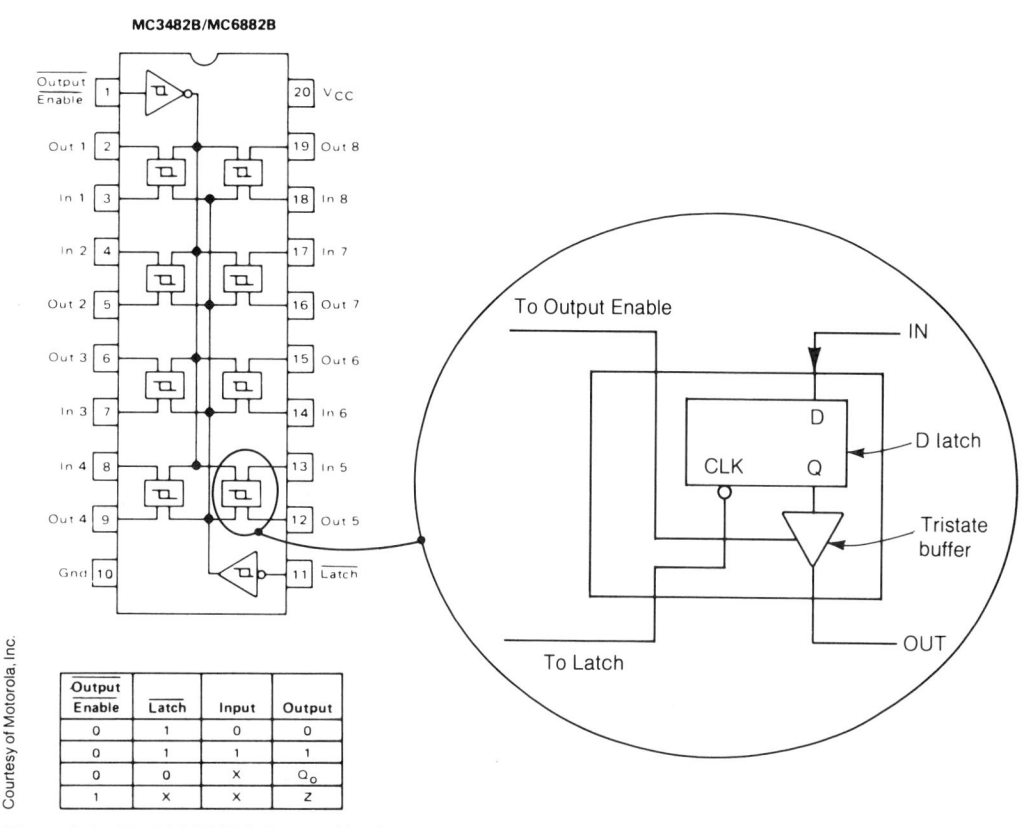

Figure 3.1 The MC6882B I/O port with tristate outputs.

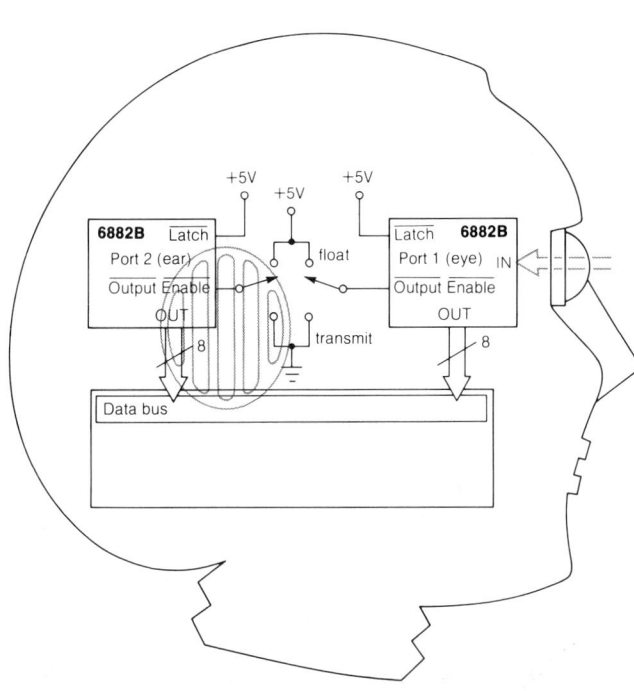

Figure 3.2 Sensory input ports added to intelligent machine.

one computer location to another. Since these waveforms are the key to unlocking the mysteries of basic processing action, we had better go over them in detail.

First, let's examine the *where* group of signals, sent by the CPU to determine source and destination of the data transfer. The 16-line address bus pinpoints a specific memory or port location among the 65,536 possibilities. The single line R/$\overline{\text{W}}$ (Read/$\overline{\text{Write}}$) signal determines the direction of travel (read into the CPU when high; write from the CPU when low). Finally, the VMA (valid memory address) output line indicates to peripheral devices that there is a valid address on the address bus. (During certain internal CPU operations—when VMA is low—the address transmitted from the CPU may be invalid.)

The *when* part of the data-transfer operation consists of a single line, the active-high ϕ_2 output, which is a basic clock signal sent throughout the system to time all data-transfer operations.

Note that the *when* part of the operation occurs within the time of the *where* part. This all-important address/control timing assures us that the address will have time to stabilize before data flows and will remain stable throughout the transfer process. (Imagine the confusion if data were allowed to flow

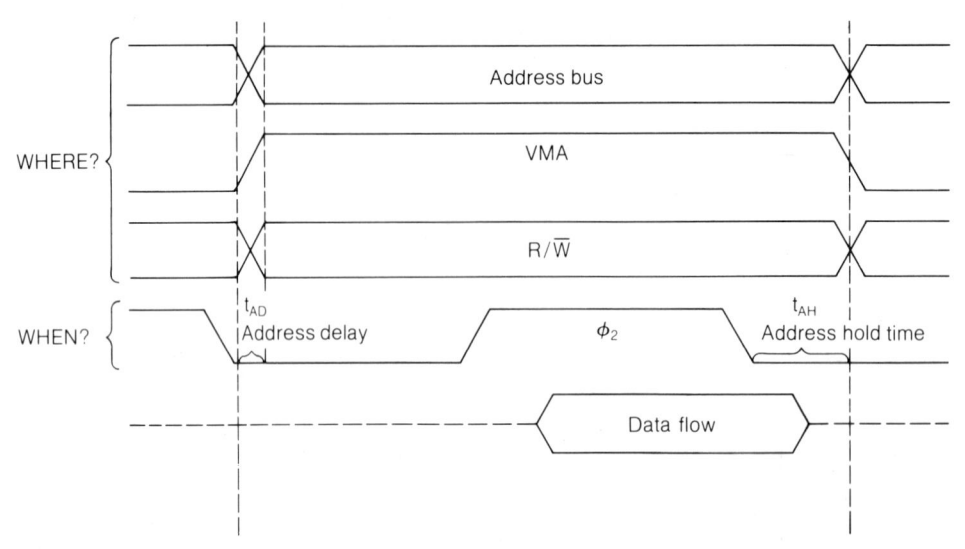

Figure 3.3 Standard (idealized) where/when data-transfer waveforms.

before the changing address bus settled down to point to a single memory or port location.) Also shown in Figure 3.3 are the two major 6800 specifications for address/control timing (t_{AD} is typically over 150 ns, and t_{AH} is typically under 100 ns).

By convention the crisscrossing lines of the address and R/$\overline{W}$ waveforms simply indicate a change from one address/control state to the next. That is, whenever an address changes, some of the address bits will go high, some will go low, and some will remain unchanged. The dotted lines of the data waveforms indicate a floating or high-impedance state.

Looking over the standard Motorola-based waveforms of Figure 3.3, we note that no distinction is made between a memory location and an I/O port location. This is because the Motorola family of microprocessors uses what is known as *memory-mapped I/O* exclusively, and *I/O port locations are addressed as if they were memory locations*. The Intel and Zilog microprocessor families, on the other hand, use *isolated I/O* techniques and have special control signals that differentiate between the memory space of addressable locations and the I/O port space of addressable locations. The distinctions between an isolated I/O system and a memory-mapped I/O system will crop up several times in future chapters.

6882B Bus Interfacing

To summarize our progress to date, we have our 6882B 8-bit input-port chip with its $\overline{\text{Output}}$ $\overline{\text{Enable}}$ line to allow the flow of information through the chip when pulled active low. We also know that any transfer of data must follow a where/when process using signals from the address and control bus. Are we now ready to complete the design and tie in the 6882B to the system bus, adding any necessary interfacing circuitry?

First, we must ask ourselves how the generalized where/when data-transfer waveforms of Figure 3.3 will behave during a specific operation—an input-port data transfer. The following will occur:

Where

- The address of the input port will appear on the address bus.
- VMA will go active high to indicate that a valid address appears on the address bus.
- R/$\overline{W}$ will go high to indicate a read operation (data flowing into the system).

When

- ϕ_2 will cycle active high to time the data transfer.

The Final Input-Port Design

Blending all the information, we arrive at the final input-port design for 6800-based systems (Figure 3.4).

To read in information through the input port to the data bus, simply sequence the address/control lines according to the where/when waveforms. (The arrows on the input waveforms indicate a cause/effect relationship—the control bus causes data to flow.) Two higher-order address signals—an active high A_{13} and an active low A_{12}—are all we require to address the input port. As we will see in Chapter 5, when addressing techniques will be covered in detail, this "partial decoding" method is a reasonable approach for small to

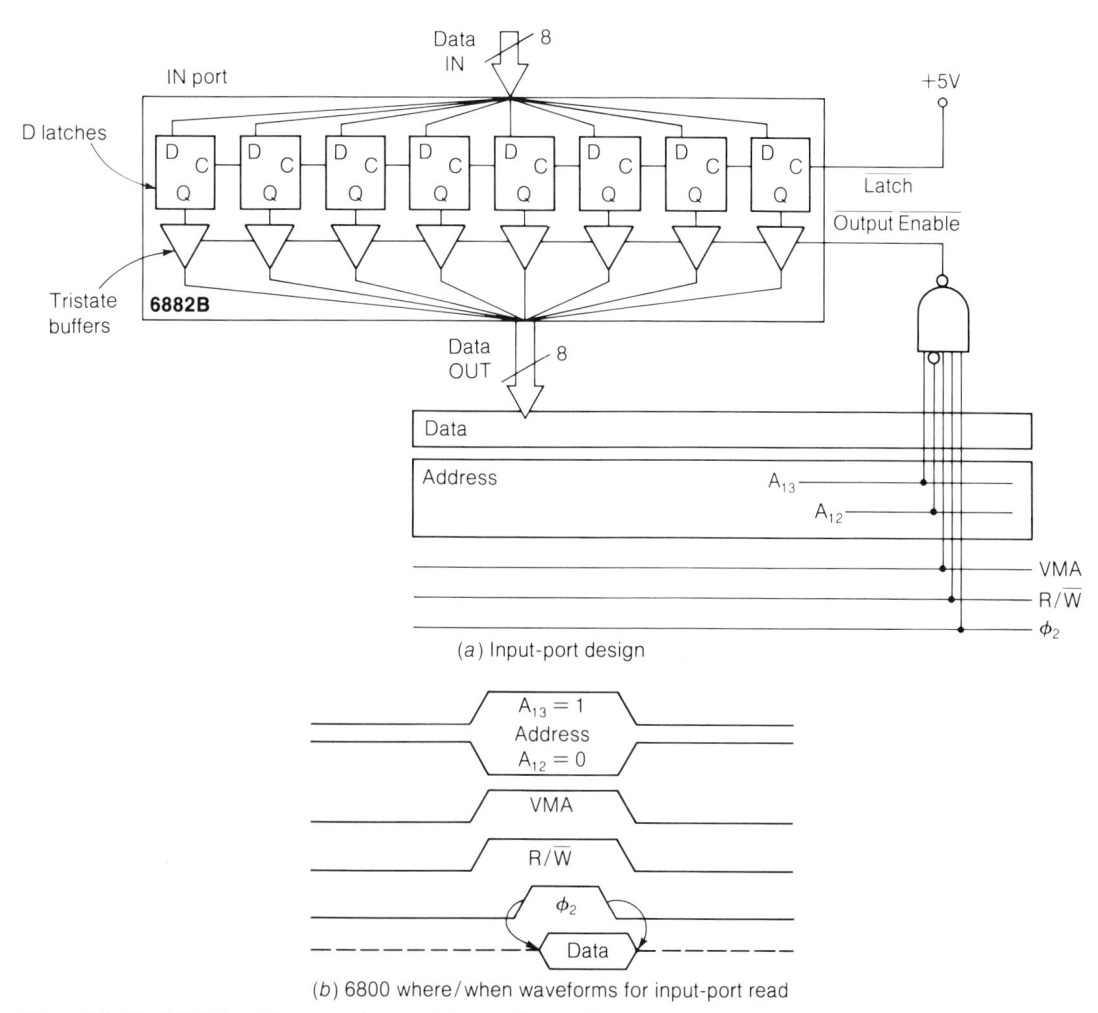

Figure 3.4 Final 6800-based input-port design and data-transfer waveforms.

(a) Input-port design

(b) 6800 where/when waveforms for input-port read

moderate-sized systems. (Although our address line selection is somewhat arbitrary, it will make it possible to interface all external circuits and run all programs presented in Parts I, II, and III on the Heathkit ET-3400A trainer.)

Interfacing Additional Input Ports

Interfacing additional 6882B-based input ports to the bus system is quite simple since there is only one difference in interfacing circuitry between the various input ports: *each interfacing circuit will be enabled by a different address*. With each input port receiving a unique address, the computer will easily be able to distinguish between them.

General Input-Port Design

Although our input-port design was developed around a specific chip—the 6882B—the basic principles must hold for all input ports:

- All input ports must include tristate buffers in order to implement the requirements of time multiplexing.
- All input-port operations must be controlled by a where/when operation.
- All input ports must include the interfacing circuitry required to correctly enable the tristate buffers when fed the proper address and control signals.

The Input Port in Action

With two input ports now added to our intelligent machine, it now possesses the ability to "see" and "hear" (Figure 3.5). As a final test of our input-port design, hold up a data word to the machine's "eyes" and follow through the where/when sequence as it reads the word to the internal data bus:

1. The where process begins with the address of input port 1 (eye) appearing on the address bus ($A_{12} = 0$; $A_{13} = 1$). Simultaneously, VMA and R/$\overline{W}$ go high.

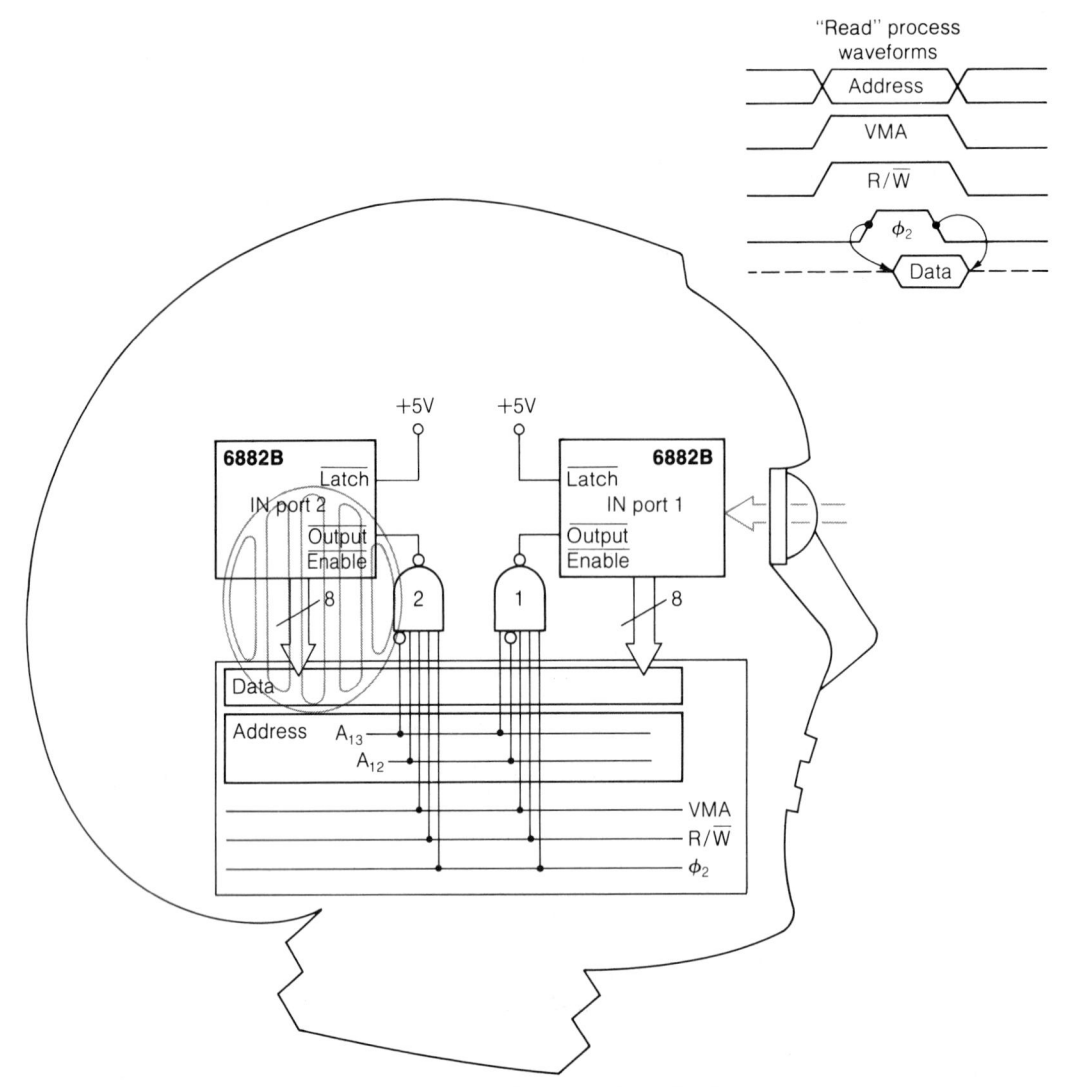

Figure 3.5 6800-based intelligent machine with sensory input ports (eye and ear).

2. After the address, VMA, and R/$\overline{\text{W}}$ lines have been given time to fully stabilize (t_{AD}), the ϕ_2 control (clock) line goes active high, completely enabling NAND gate 1 and driving the $\overline{\text{Output}}$ $\overline{\text{Enable}}$ line active low.
3. The data word flows from the outside world, through the selected 6882B input port, and onto the data bus.
4. The ϕ_2 control line goes low, shutting off the flow of data.
5. To make sure the tristate buffers are fully disabled before the address is changed, an additional address-stability period (t_{AH}) is provided after the ϕ_2 control line goes inactive.

THE OUTPUT PORT

Our computer system is now endowed with simple input ports and has the means to sense its environment. That, however, is not enough. It must also be able to respond to the information it has taken in. In other words, it must be given a voice—an *output port*.

Comparison of Input and Output Ports

Since both reading and speaking involve a simple transfer of data, the structure of both input and output ports will be similar. For example, the output port will also use the 6882B chip.

An output port, however, differs from an input port in two ways. First, an output port does not need tristate buffers. Remember, when information is *received* from the data bus, rather than being *transmitted* onto it, there can be no conflict of data. Therefore, the tristate buffers (which now interface the "outside world") are permanently enabled by grounding the $\overline{\text{Output}}$ $\overline{\text{Enable}}$ line.

Figure 3.6 Final 6800-based output-port design and data-transfer waveforms.

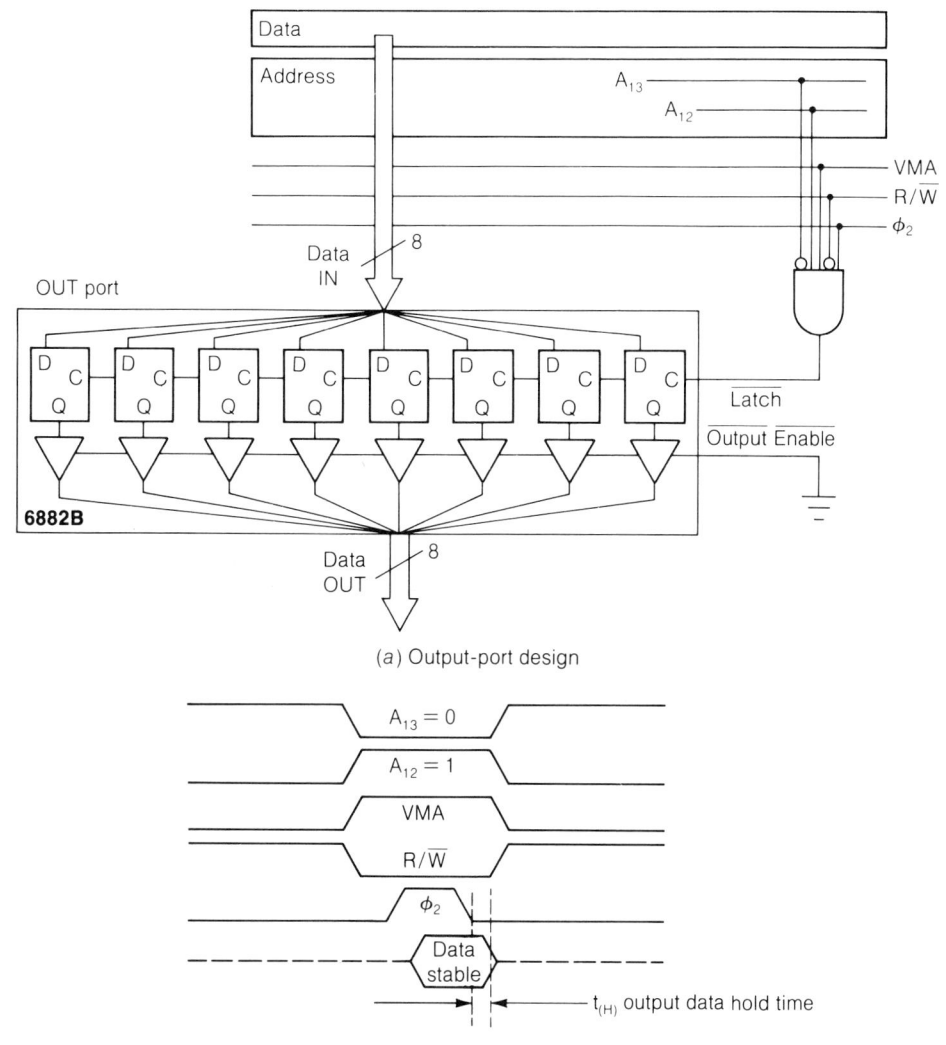

(a) Output-port design

(b) 6800 where/when waveforms for output-port write

The second significant difference between an input port and an output port is the presence of latches to catch and hold the outported information. Latches are especially important when the computer is speaking to people, for we need time to take in the information. In addition, clocked latches provide a means of passing to the outside world only the data-bus information of interest. (If we ask the computer to add two numbers, we are usually interested in only the final answer, not the intermediate information appearing on the data bus.)

These two differences between input and output ports also will require a slight change in the interfacing circuitry between the 6882B and the bus system.

The Complete Output-Port Design

The final output-port design is shown in Figure 3.6. The high-impedance D-latch inputs of the 6882B interface the data bus. By driving the $\overline{\text{Latch}}$ line with the combined bus signals, we can properly clock the output data into the latches. (Again, remember, we permanently enabled the tristate buffers by tying the output-enable line low.)

To transfer data from the data bus to the output-port latches, simply sequence the proper address/control bus lines according to the where/when data-transfer format. (Note the differences between the output and input waveforms: to output data, the R/$\overline{\text{W}}$ control line goes low, and the information on the data bus must be stable before the ϕ_2 control line goes low.)

INTELLIGENT-MACHINE UPDATE

As shown in Figure 3.7, our computer system now has (at least physically) an "eye" and a "voice"—an *input port* and an *output port*. But it cannot see and it cannot speak—at

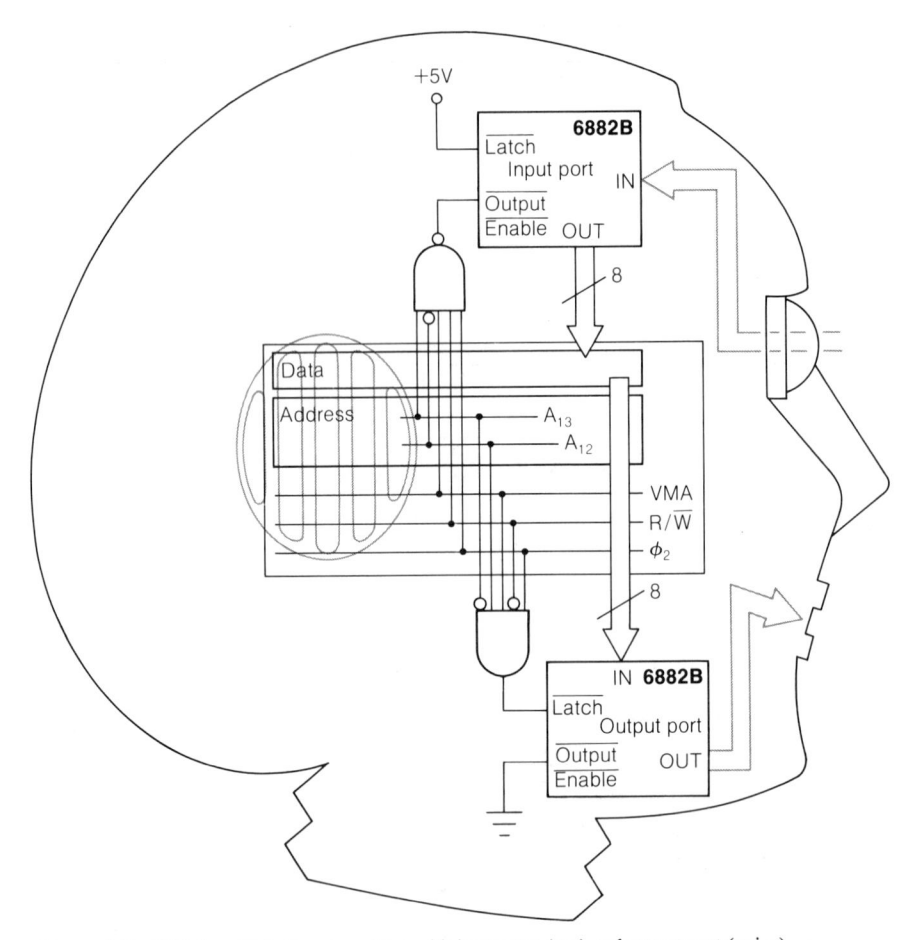

Figure 3.7 6800-based intelligent machine with input port (eye) and output port (voice).

least on its own—for that requires additional circuitry to control and time the input and output processes. This additional circuitry will be added in a future chapter. First, we must endow our intelligent machine with a memory.

QUESTIONS AND PROBLEMS

1. What is the purpose of an input port? Of an output port?
2. Why must an input port be tristated?
3. $\overline{\text{Output Enable}}$ ($\overline{\text{OE}}$) controls what internal circuits within the 6882B? $\overline{\text{Latch}}$ controls what internal circuits?
4. What two steps are involved in all data-transfer processes?
5. What is the function of the address bus in a data-transfer operation? Of the control bus?
6. Go through the precise steps required in a 6800-based system to both input and output data.
7. How are additional ports (input or output) added to a computer system?
8. Name three general principles that must hold for all input ports.
9. Why is the ϕ_2 control line active for a shorter period of time than the address lines?
10. Why is *read* a particularly appropriate term for the input-port operation? Why is *write* a reasonable term to use for the output-port operation?
11. How are ports addressed in a memory-mapped system?
12. Why can both an input port and an output port share the same address?
13. Why is it more important for the address to be stable prior to activation of ϕ_2 for a write operation than for a read operation?
14. Although latches are not essential for input-port operation, under what conditions might they be used?
15. Redraw the idealized input-port read waveforms of Figure 3.4, showing the effects of propagation delay (delay between control-line switching and data flow). By researching the specifications of the input-port circuitry, determine an expected value of the propagation delay.

16. Referring to Figure 3.6, why is it important for the data to be stable when the ϕ_2 control line goes low? What is the purpose of $t_{(H)}$ (output data hold time)?
17. What ranges of addresses will enable the input port of Figure 3.7?
18. To address the ports of Figure 3.7, could we have just as easily made use of address lines A_{14} and A_{15}? Could we have used just one address line? Could we have used more than two?
19. Redesign the system of Figure 3.7 using a single 8205 (3205) decoder instead of the AND/NAND gates (additional inverters may be required).

chapter 4

Introduction to Memory/Memory Hierarchy

There exists in this world a memory of remarkable properties. Its retention ability is so vast that 1,000 bits of information can be absorbed every second for more than one hundred years and still not overflow its capacity. It accepts information of various word lengths—sometimes up to thousands of bits per word. It functions reliably for many decades, weighs no more than 3 pounds, is very compact, and is so structured that the failure of one small part does not prevent the overall system from functioning.

Such a memory, of course, is our own!

Even though we cannot hope to equal the power and complexity of the human mind soon, we will find once again that the computer's memory needs and our own memory needs are closely related.

MEMORY HIERARCHY

Our own memory is hierarchical. Short-term memory (memory at the tip of our tongues) resides in electrical activity. If the idea to be remembered is important enough and persists long enough, however, the electrical activity is thought to give rise to protein synthesis, a more permanent form of memory.

Computer memory systems are also hierarchical and consist of up to three levels:

- Primary, or main
- Secondary, or auxiliary
- Backup

All microcomputer systems contain primary memory, but the need for secondary and backup systems depends on the specific application. As always, the goal is to optimize performance and cost.

Primary Memory

Primary memory is closely matched to the CPU and is available for instant communication. To qualify for primary status, therefore, the memory must be fast—fast enough to keep up with today's state-of-the-art microprocessors. As we will see in the following chapter, primary memory's high speed results from its parallel, random-access organization. Most small-scale, dedicated microcomputer systems (those designed for a specific task) contain only primary memory. For larger systems in which additional storage capacity is required, however, primary memory becomes a financial burden and we must look elsewhere.

Secondary Memory

By a change in technology and an increase in capacity, secondary memory stores information at a lower cost per bit. To achieve these features, secondary memory adds aspects of *sequential* or *serial* access (one bit follows another in a fixed order). Using part random-access and part sequential-access organization, secondary memory operates at moderate speed.

Secondary memory (also called *storage*) serves as a readily accessible data library. Since data and programs of immediate use are always stored in primary memory, blocks of data are transferred back and forth as required between primary and secondary memory.

Backup Memory

In a perfect world in which equipment failures and operator errors are unknown, the need for backup memory would be greatly reduced. In the real world, however, systems crash and mistakes are made. Despite the very high data-reliability specifications of today's secondary systems, many computer operators will not be satisfied until their data are resting securely on a nonvolatile backup shelf. A common mode of operation is for the database in primary or secondary memory to be moved to backup at regular intervals.

In addition, many computer applications generate continuous blocks of new data that must be periodically stored away, giving rise to the need for a high-capacity, low-cost, long-term, permanent storage medium (archival storage).

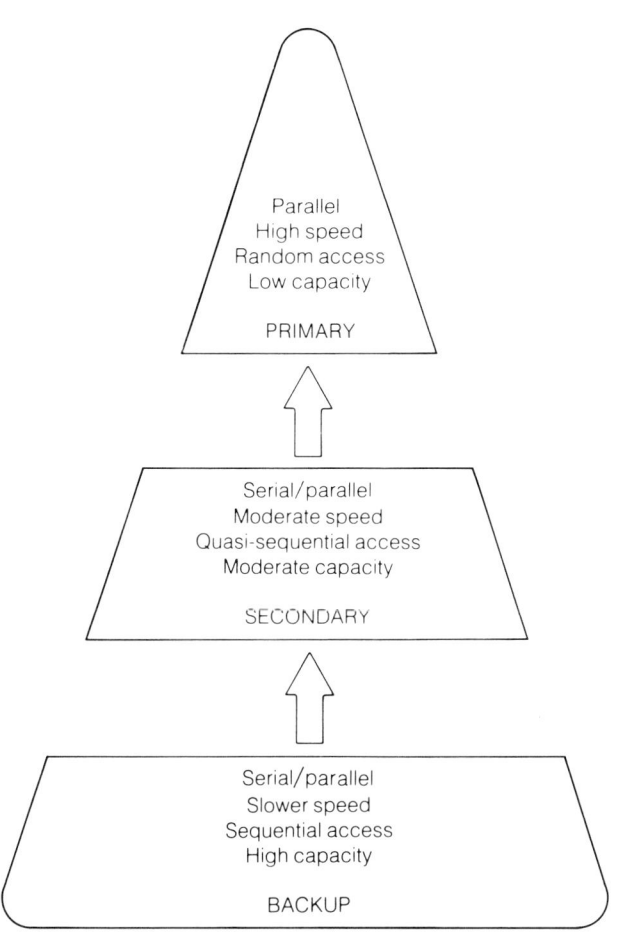

Figure 4.1 Primary/secondary/backup memory hierarchy.

Since speed is not a critical factor with such a backup system, further relaxing the access time has allowed the development of high-capacity, low-cost backup storage systems. Figure 4.1 diagrams the memory hierarchy of a microcomputer system.

THE MICROCOMPUTER MEMORY SPECTRUM

At each hierarchical level, the microcomputer designer is faced with a wide choice (only those memory systems generally associated with microcomputers have been included in the list):

Primary	*Secondary*	*Backup*
Static	Floppy disk	Floppy disk
Dynamic	Winchester disk	Magnetic tape
Magnetic core	Bubble	Magnetic cartridge
		Video tape

Each of these memory types will be discussed in detail in the following two chapters, so only a few general comments will be made here.

Three important factors entering into the selection of a memory type are access time (speed), capacity, and cost. Figure 4.2 shows the tradeoffs involved in these three factors for the various categories of memory.

For 6800-based systems, primary memory is generally limited to 64K—a tiny memory space all but swallowed up by the 200K to 500-megabyte capacity of secondary and backup storage systems. Remember, however, that the price you pay for large storage capacity is speed. Primary memory is the only hierarchical level the CPU can "converse with" at its own natural high rate of speed.

All memory systems, of course, are application dependent. A microcomputer controller assigned the task of regulating the fuel/air mixture of an automobile under varying load conditions will use only primary memory. (Controllers are the subject of Chapter 20.)

On the other hand, a word processor may require copious amounts of storage space to file away the many pages of material produced each day. At regular intervals, selected material may be copied onto the backup device.

Only when the application is known is it possible to recommend a particular memory ensemble.

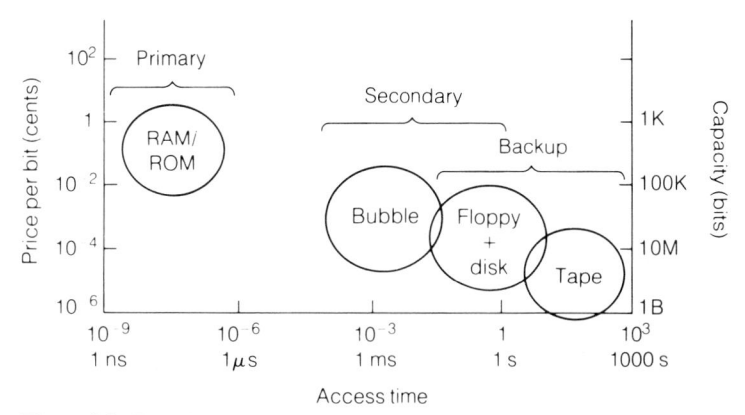

Figure 4.2 Primary/secondary/backup comparison.

VIRTUAL MEMORY

Memory management, even for large systems, would be a simple process if all memory were of the high-speed primary variety. Of necessity, however, much of the data and programs must be stored in the lower-cost, high-capacity secondary systems. Since the computer usually works directly on primary memory only, it is obvious that some fancy data exchanges between primary and secondary memory will have to take place.

The problem was solved in the late 1950s with a concept called *virtual memory*. The programmer writes programs as if the entire memory space were primary memory. When the virtual-memory management system finds a requested address unavailable in primary memory, it automatically initiates a swap procedure and exchanges a block of primary memory with a block of secondary memory.

Through the use of *cache memory*, even primary memory itself can be enhanced using virtual-memory concepts. Cache memory is a small block of ultrahigh-speed primary memory interposed between the CPU and the basic main (primary) memory. Through buffer action the processor "sees" a main memory system of near cache speed.

Virtual memory is an example of a mainframe concept gradually working its way into the micro world. (Some newer 16-bit and 32-bit microprocessors, such as the Motorola 68010 and Intel 80286, have included provisions for virtual-memory management.)

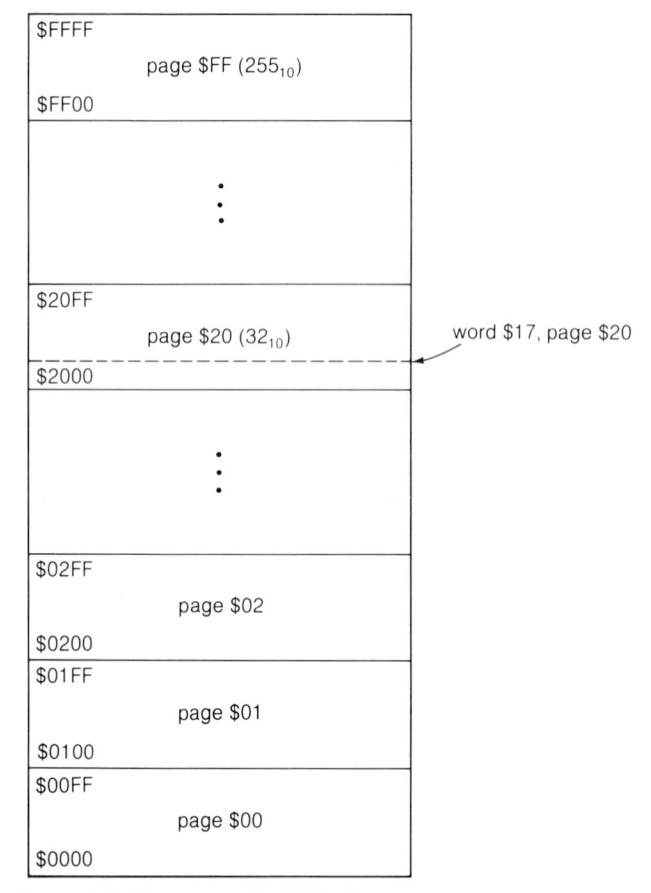

Figure 4.3 Memory map for 64K system.

THE MEMORY MAP

Books are a convenient way of storing information. One advantage is that information can be categorized according to page and chapter. Given the page on which it is contained, information can be located quickly. These techniques can be carried over to any memory system.

Consider the entire 64K of 6800-based primary memory space to be a book. Further, imagine the book to have 256 pages. Each page contains 256 words, and each word is made up of 8 letters. If we apply this convention to 8-bit microcomputers and say that a byte of data is word $17 on page $20, we have an instant feeling for the data location among the full 64K of memory space. (Using the Motorola convention, hexadecimal numbers are preceded by a $ sign to prevent confusion with decimal numbers. An alternative, widely used technique is to place an H after all hexadecimal numbers.)

To make the analogy more graphic, the 256 pages are often shown on a chart called a *memory map* (Figure 4.3). The pages can be designated by decimal numbers, but more commonly are given in hexadecimal form. A memory map is therefore a linear arrangement of memory pages. Quite often the pages are grouped together in sizes (chapters, perhaps) to match the memory chips used with the system.

The concept of pages is particularly well suited to 16-bit addresses. As diagrammed below, the pages and words are split evenly between the two highest-order hex digits and the two lowest-order hex digits:

$$A_{15}A_{14}A_{13}A_{12}A_{11}A_{10}A_9A_8 \quad A_7A_6A_5A_4A_3A_2A_1A_0$$
$$0\ 0\ 1\ 0\ 0\ 0\ 0\ 0 \quad 0\ 0\ 0\ 1\ 0\ 1\ 1\ 1$$
$$\underbrace{\qquad\qquad\qquad}_{\text{page \$20}} \quad \underbrace{\qquad\qquad\qquad}_{\text{word \$17}}$$

The memory-map convention can easily be carried over to large-scale memory systems. For example, a 20-bit address, constituting a megabyte of memory (1,048,576 locations) contains 4K *pages*, designated by the three highest-order hexadecimal digits:

$$A_{19}\ \ldots\ A_8 \quad A_7\ldots A_0$$
$$000000100000 \quad 00010111$$
$$\underbrace{\qquad\qquad}_{\text{page \$020}} \quad \underbrace{\qquad\qquad}_{\text{word \$17}}$$

INTELLIGENT-MACHINE UPDATE

Nature long ago realized that one type of memory was insufficient to enable its more intelligent forms of life to survive and prosper in a complex world. We now know that the same holds true for our intelligent machine, and with the following two chapters we will make sure that an inadequate memory system will not hold it back from evolving into a higher form of intelligence.

QUESTIONS AND PROBLEMS

1. What are the three levels in the memory hierarchy of a microcomputer?
2. What one characteristic, more than any other, distinguishes primary memory?
3. List the three hierarchical levels of memory in terms of (a) speed and (b) capacity.
4. What is *archival storage*?
5. The data and programs that the computer is currently working on are most likely contained in what hierarchical level of memory?
6. How does virtual memory make the programmer's job easier?
7. Draw a memory map for a 64K system consisting of 4K memory modules. How many pages are contained within each module?
8. Write the hexadecimal address of page 102_{10} word 17_{10}.
9. What is the difference between *random* and *sequential* memory organization?
10. What is *cache* memory?

chapter 5

Primary Memory

Evidence suggests that our minds store large amounts of information in the form of holograms or vast interconnecting neuronal patterns. Since the same neuron assemblies are involved in the storage of many different ideas (only the interconnecting patterns differ), many thoughts require approximately the same period of time to retrieve. This *random-access* technique was chosen by nature to speed up the process of recall.

The same random-access techniques (every storage location accessed in the same period of time), coupled with parallel architecture (all 8 bits are moved about and processed simultaneously as a unit), have produced memory systems fast enough to keep pace with the central processing unit. These are called *primary memory systems*.

Four types of primary memory, all found in microcomputer systems, will be covered in this chapter:

- Static RAM
- Dynamic RAM
- Magnetic-core RAM
- ROM

RAM VS ROM

To survive, we require two distinct types of memory. First, we require at birth a permanent memory to regulate the automatic processes of breathing and heartbeat. Second, we need memory space to receive new information that comes to us through our life experiences. Otherwise, we could never learn anything new—such as how to multiply or how to ride a bicycle.

These same two categories of memory are found in computer systems and are known as *RAM* and *ROM*. Unfortunately, the strict definitions of RAM and ROM do not always match conventional usage. The definitions that follow appear to be the most universally accepted:

- *RAM (Random-Access Memory):* a parallel memory unit composed of integrated-circuit memory chips that are truly random access in nature, have both read and write capability, and are usually volatile (stored information is lost when the power is removed).
- *ROM (Read-Only Memory):* a memory array composed of integrated-circuit memory chips that are truly random access in nature, possess only the read capability, and are nonvolatile (stored information is protected when the power is removed).

Clearly, based on the above definitions, RAM and ROM usually refer to *primary* memory components. No universally accepted definitions of RAM and ROM exist, however, and the final determination must be based on the context in which they are used.

STATIC RAM

Perhaps the most popular form of primary memory for small systems, and the one we will give the greatest coverage, is *static* RAM (memory requiring only dc power supplies). Following the conventional description of RAM, it is a parallel, read/write, random-access, volatile memory, available in standard dual-in-line, integrated-circuit packages (DIP).

One way to approach the study of static RAM is to follow the lead of nature again. Nature designs living systems by natural selection, beginning with the simple and gradually building to the more complex. Our study of static RAM will follow the same approach. Always keep in mind that the internal RAM circuits developed here will show only the essential features and may not necessarily be the precise circuitry used in an actual static-RAM device.

The Basic RAM Memory Cell

From a "primeval ocean" of simple electronic components emerged the basic static-RAM memory cell shown in Figure 5.1. Already it possesses several human characteristics: it can remember, recall, and learn a single bit of information. In memory terminology, these properties are known as *store*, *read*, and *write*.

The design is simple and efficient. A flip-flop stores the

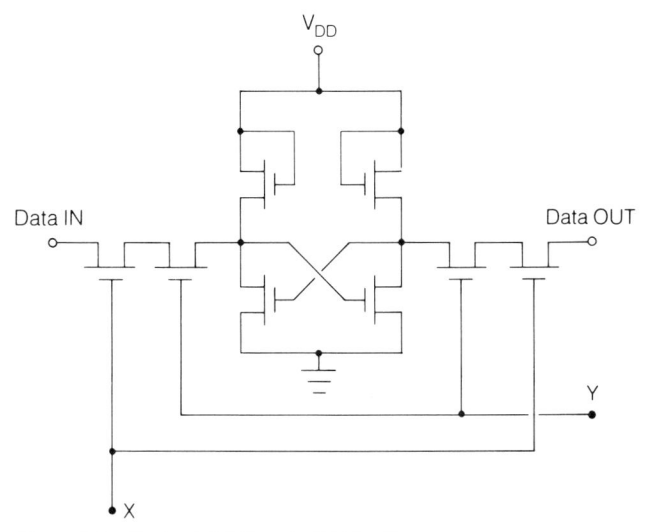

Figure 5.1 The basic MOS static-RAM cell.

logic 1 or logic 0 by way of positive-feedback latching action. To extract (read) the logic state of the cell, simply sense the drain voltage of either transistor. To set (write) a logic value into the cell, simply gain control over either gate. The AND gate barriers, spliced into both the data-in and data-out lines, provide a means for addressing the cell. To select (address) the memory cell, both X *and* Y lines must be high. If either X *or* Y is low, the information is blocked. The upper two transistors are active loads, and are substituted for resistors because they require less physical space. (However, a new polysilicon technology, promising high resistance in IC dimensions, may reverse the trend.)

Adding bus-interface circuitry, we arrive at the system of Figure 5.2. The data-out line ultimately will transmit information onto the data bus and is therefore time-multiplexed with a tristate buffer. The tristate buffer in the data-in line isolates the memory cell, except during the time information is written into the cell. The data-in and data-out lines join together and form a single line to the data bus.

A Multicelled 4 × 1 Static RAM

With the power of addressability, our one-celled memory unit can now evolve into a multicelled system—one capable of remembering many bits of information. We will begin our design with a four-celled memory system that can store, read, and write four separate unique bits of information. Such a system is known as a *4 × 1 static RAM*. The first number specifies the number of individually addressable memory locations, and the second number specifies the number of bits stored in each addressable location. Therefore, a 4 × 1 static RAM has four addressable memory

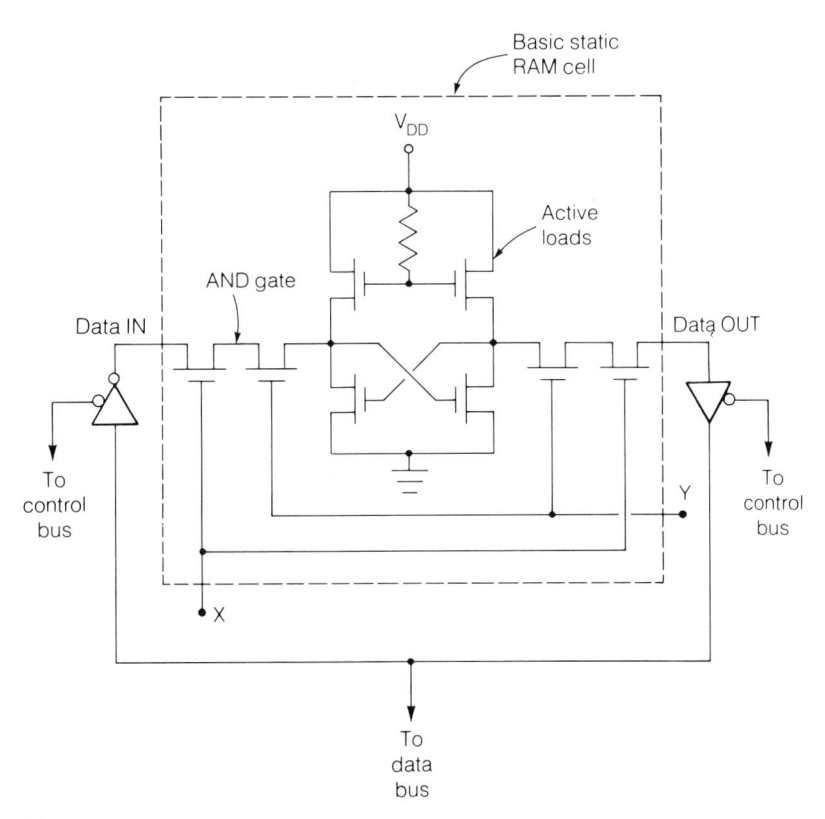

Figure 5.2 Static-RAM cell with bus-interface circuitry added.

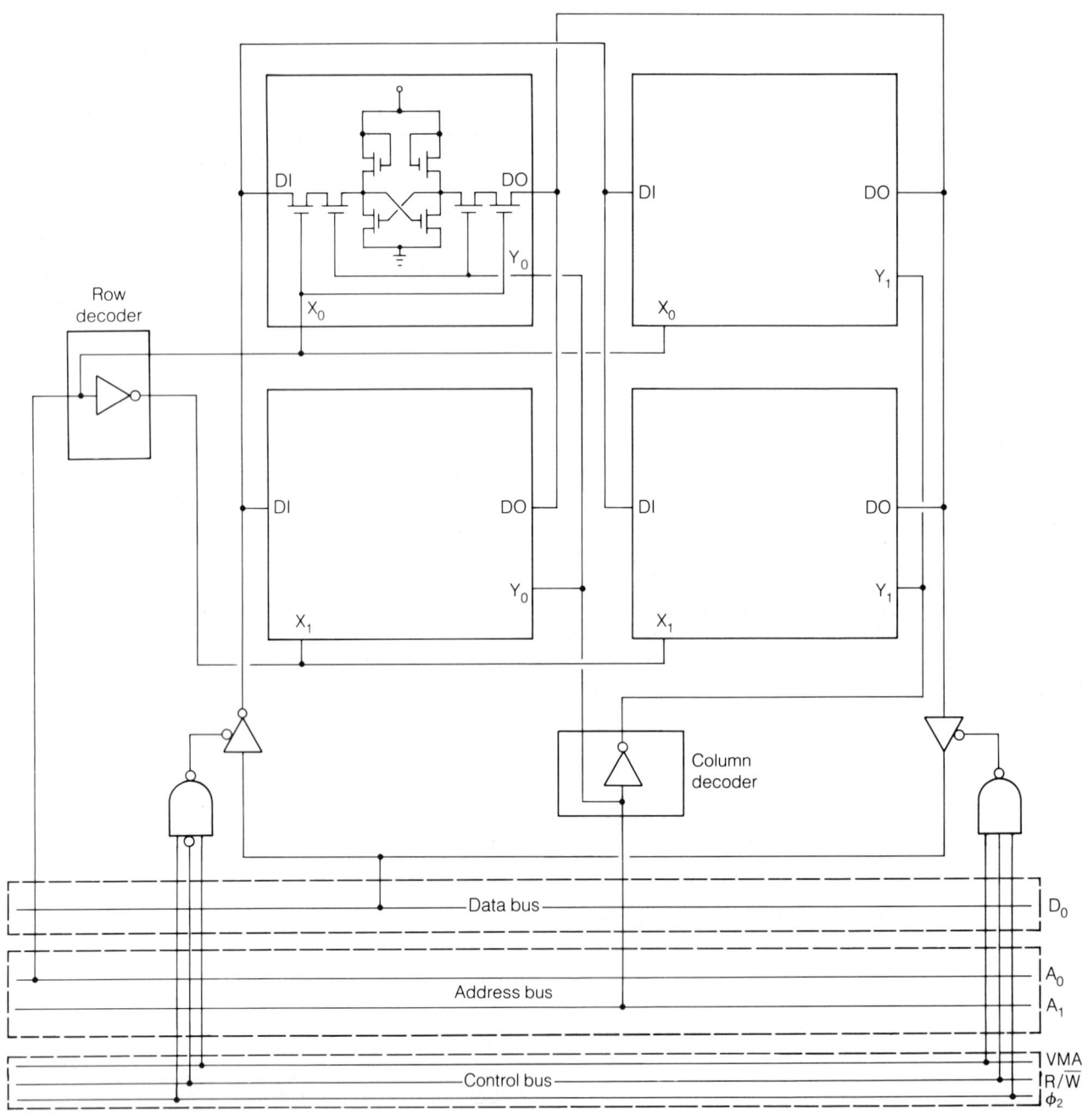

Figure 5.3 4 × 1 static RAM interfaced with 6800 bus.

locations, each storing one bit of information. (Of course, such a small RAM system would find little acceptance on the open market, but it does illustrate the principles involved.)

A complete 4 × 1 static RAM—tied into a 6800-based bus system—is shown in Figure 5.3. To simplify the diagram, three of the memory cells are shown purely in block form.

The 4 × 1 static-RAM system is involved in two activities:

- Memory *write into* the selected (addressed) cell
- Memory *read from* the selected (addressed) cell

Since both activities are merely data-transfer operations, we can immediately write the where/when data-transfer waveforms required to carry out each process (Figure 5.4).

To see how the memory system works, let us go through the read process, using the simple two-step where/when sequence (refer to Figures 5.3 and 5.4).

- Step 1—A memory cell is addressed. The address of the selected memory cell (00, 01, 10, or 11) is placed on the address bus. Address bit A_0 goes to the row decoder and address bit A_1 goes to the column decoder. It is the func-

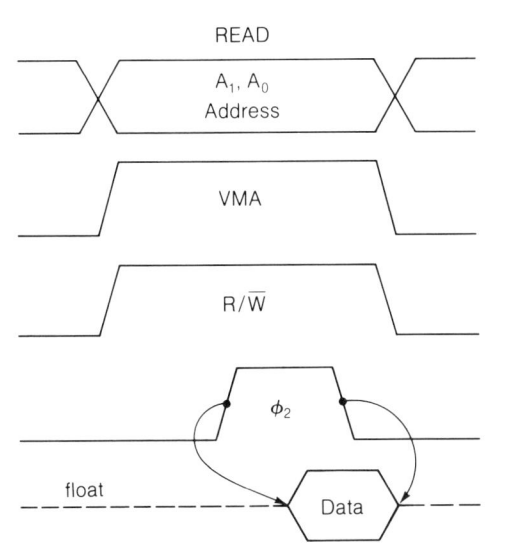

Figure 5.4 6800-based read/write waveforms for 4 × 1 RAM.

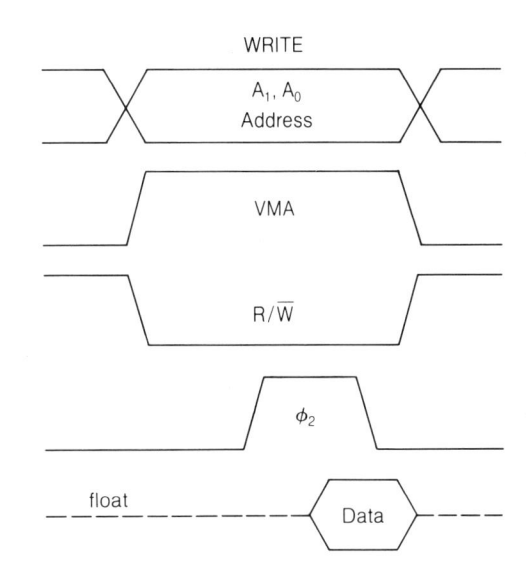

tion of the decoders (simple 1-in/2-out inverters in this case) to select one particular row and one particular column out of all the rows and columns that interlace the array of memory cells, a process known as *coincident-selection addressing*. Clearly, only the memory cell where the selected row and column cross is fully enabled. VMA goes active high to indicate a valid memory address, and R/$\overline{W}$ goes high to set up the system for a read process.

- Step 2—The ϕ_2 control line goes active high. When ϕ_2 is cycled active high (after the address has fully stabilized), the data bit stored in the addressed memory cell passes through the tristate buffers and onto the data bus.

An analysis of the memory write process for our 4 × 1 RAM is left as an exercise.

A 4 × 4 Static RAM

So far our simple 4 × 1 RAM system can remember only two-valued data: Is it hot or cold, night or day, high or low? To remember the actual temperature, or time, or elevation, we must increase the bit size of our memory words. Four bits per word, for example, would give us 16 value levels to choose from.

To expand our 4 × 1 RAM into a 4 × 4 RAM is simple. All we need to do is clone four identical 4 × 1 systems and arrange them side by side in planes, as shown in Figure 5.5.

Each memory operation will now involve a half byte (a nibble). The two address lines are simply extended to include the three additional 4 × 1 planes, and an address appearing on the address bus will enable four like cells, one in each plane. Although the address lines are common to all four

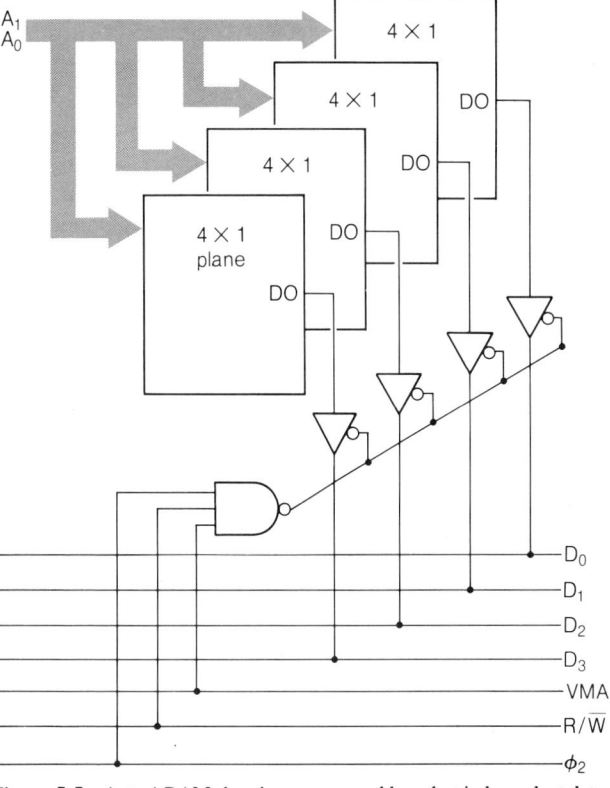

Figure 5.5 4 × 4 RAM showing common address but independent data lines.

planes, the four independent data lines are not; and as shown, each plane feeds a unique data-bus line. When a read or write control line is activated, information will flow 4 bits at a time onto or from the four-line data bus.

The MCM6810

By extending the size of each plane from 4 bits to 128 bits, and doubling the number of planes from 4 to 8, we create the MCM6810, a 128 × 8 static RAM. Although small and slow by today's standards, the MCM6810 is still used in small-scale hobby systems. Historically, the MCM6810 helped make the 6800 microprocessor popular, and it still is one of the few static RAMs based on a bytewide format.

Referring to Figure 5.6, the memory array, address decoders, and tristate buffers are apparent. With a single R/$\overline{\text{W}}$ input, it is designed to be directly compatible with the 6800 microprocessor. The numerous CS (Chip Select) inputs, some active high and others active low, provide great flexibility in addressing.

The MCM2114 Static RAM

Further increasing the size of each plane from 128 to 1024 bits, but reverting back to four planes to improve speed (the time it takes to read information from or write information to the RAM chip), we create the 1024 × 4 static RAM, the size of the MCM2114—a popular commercially available static RAM (Figure 5.7a). Figure 5.7b details the read/write waveforms for the 2114. Basically, they are standard where/when data-transfer waveforms, showing the effects of propagation delay. To read, $\overline{\text{S}}$ is pulled low and $\overline{\text{W}}$ remains high; to write, both $\overline{\text{S}}$ and $\overline{\text{W}}$ are pulled low. A detailed account of the many specifications can be found in the *Motorola Memory Data Manual* and other Motorola literature.

Larger RAM Systems

By expanding the number of memory planes and the number of addressable locations within each plane, it appears we could continue this process of RAM evolution indefinitely. In fact, this evolutionary expansion is going on continuously, and 64K × 8 and even larger RAMs will soon be commonplace. (Even though bytewide RAMs are more convenient, they are presently slower than nibblewide or especially bitwide formats. For this reason, the very highest speed static RAMs usually are offered in a bitwide format.)

The memory-addressing capabilities of the microprocessor chip are expanding even faster, however. Just when we satisfy the 64K × 8 needs of the 6800 family, we must look toward the 68000 with its 16-megabyte addressing capability (the 68000 16-bit microprocessor can directly address 16,777,216 words of data). The conclusion is inescapable:

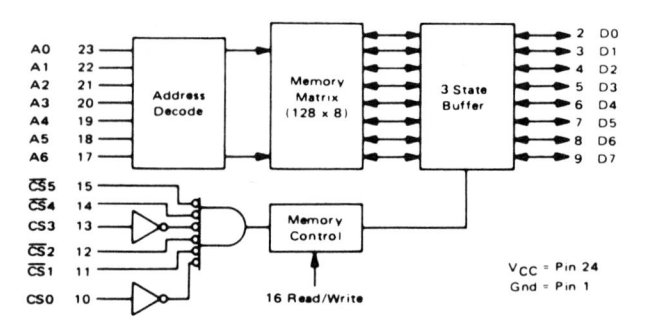

Courtesy of Motorola, Inc.

Figure 5.6 The 6810 128 × 8 static RAM pin-out and block diagram.

to build very large primary memory arrays, we will have to combine existing RAM chips.

Memory Arrays

The 2114 will serve as an example of how to form large memory arrays by combining individual static chips. First of all, to satisfy the need for an 8-bit memory system, two 1K × 4 RAM chips are placed in tandem to produce a 1K × 8 RAM module (Figure 5.8). With the address lines tied in common, an address sent to the memory module will point to the same 4-bit word location within each chip. One chip then handles the low-order 4 bits of data while the other handles the high-order 4 bits. Our task is to combine these 1K × 8 RAM modules to form large arrays—perhaps as large as 64K × 8.

A question naturally arises whenever a memory system contains more than one memory module. For example, if all RAM modules consist of 2114s in tandem, then all modules must be fed the identical address lines A_0 through A_9 ($2^{10} = 1,024$) in order to single out the correct memory location from the 1,024 possible locations. But the memory location we wish to access lies within a *particular* RAM module. How can the computer single out this one particular 1K × 8 RAM module from all the others in the system?

The problem is not at all unique to electronics. Most large cities, for example, contain a street named Broadway. How does the post office select the correct Broadway from among the hundreds available? By adding town information to the street address, of course. In like manner the 16-line address bus can be divided into two sections (Figure 5.9).

- The *high-level* address lines A_{10} through A_{15}, which can be termed *town* addressing lines, are used to single out one particular 1K × 8 memory module from all the others in the system.

- The *low-level* address lines A_0 through A_9, which can be termed *street* addressing lines, are used to single out the correct one of 1,024 memory locations within the selected town module.

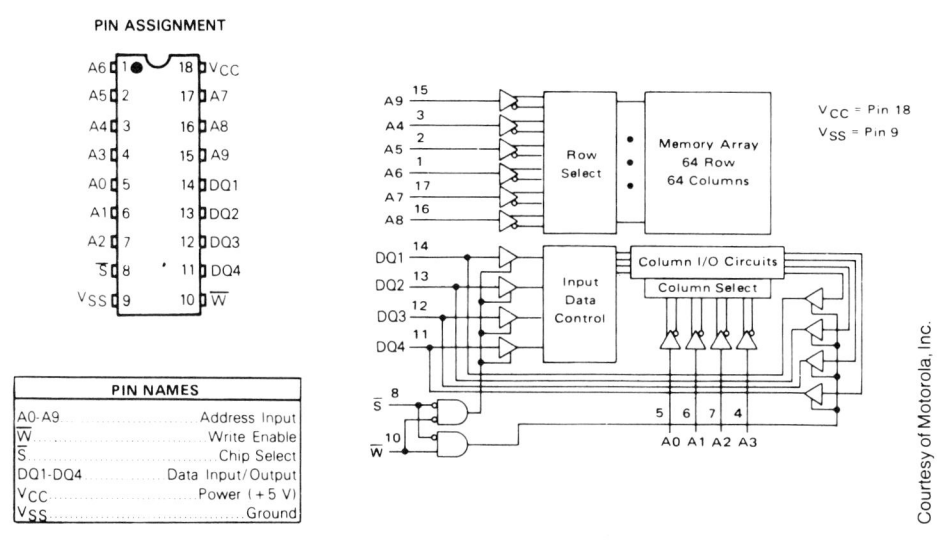

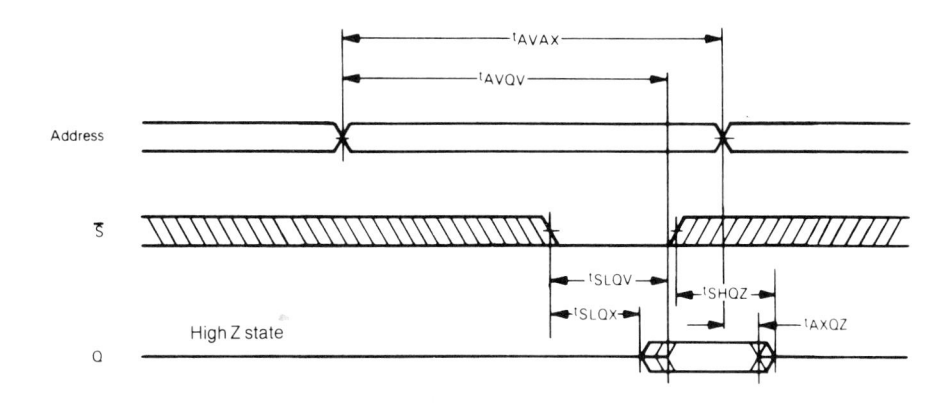

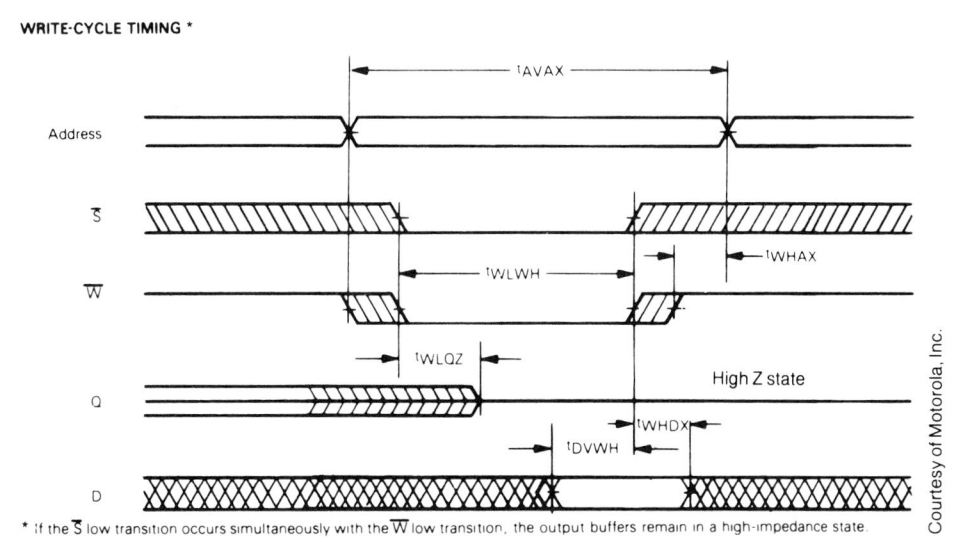

Figure 5.7 The MCM2114 1K × 4 static RAM.

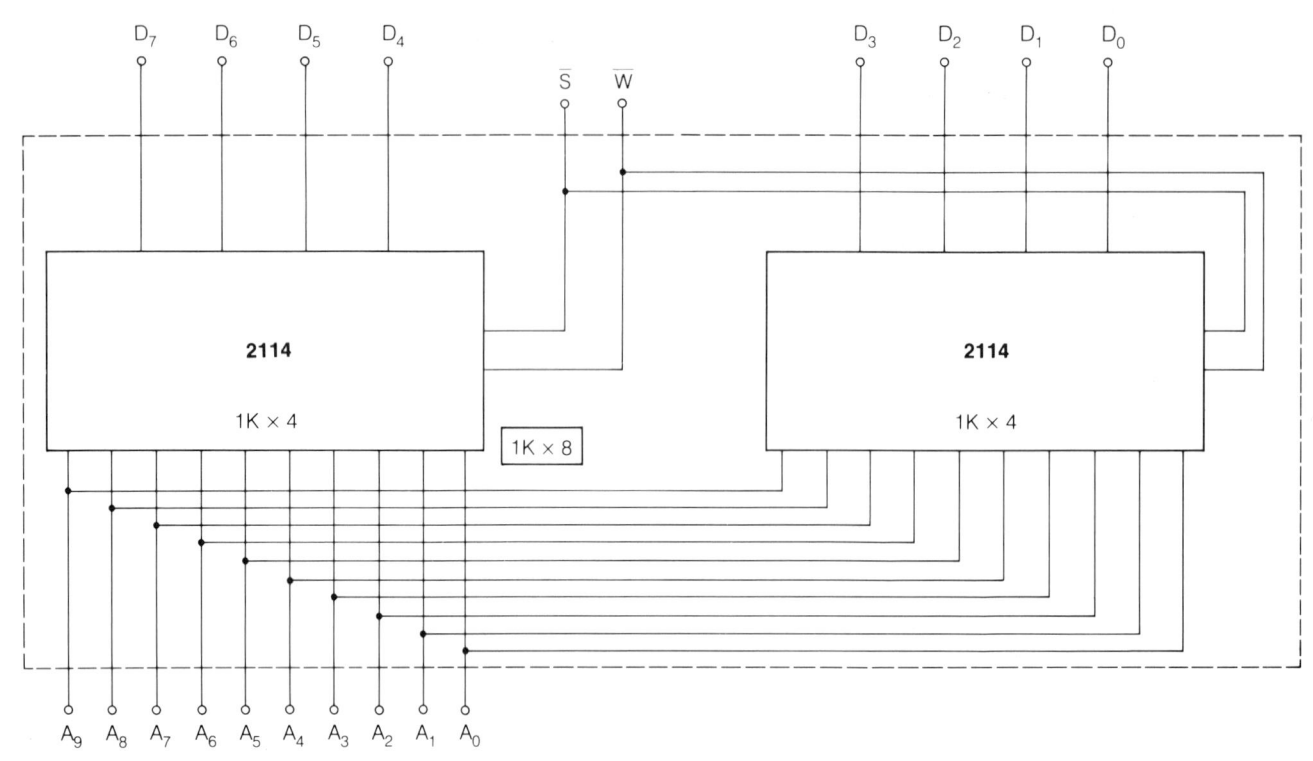

Figure 5.8 A 1K × 8 RAM module formed by combining two 1K × 4 2114 chips.

The exact dividing line between *high-level* (town) and *low-level* (street) address lines depends on the size of the memory modules used.

At the chip level, high-level addressing is handled by the *Select* ($\overline{S}$) input to the 2114. All memory chips contain one or more *Chip Select* (CS) input pins (sometimes they are called *Chip Enable,* or CE), and their purpose is to enable the entire chip. Referring to Figure 5.7a, locate the two AND gates fed by the $\overline{S}$ input. In a sense, the two AND gates are "guarding the gates" to the memory array. Unless $\overline{S}$ is active low, the entire chip is tristated and no read/write control information can flow to the internal circuitry (and hence no data information can pass through the tristate buffers). When $\overline{S}$ is pulled active low, the AND gates are enabled and data can flow to or from the memory array (depending on the state of $\overline{W}$):

- If $\overline{W}$ (write) is active low, the upper AND gate is fully enabled and data flow through the input tristate buffers to the addressed memory cells (a *write* operation).

- If $\overline{W}$ is high, the lower AND gate becomes fully enabled and data flow through the output tristate buffers from the addressed memory cells and onto the data bus (a *read* operation).

Linear vs Decoded High-Level Addressing

For our 2114-based RAM system, so far we know the following: the chip-select inputs to each 1K × 8 RAM module will be attached to high-level address lines A_{10} through A_{15}. The next question is: Exactly how will the tie-in be made? The simplest method, if we anticipate no more than six 1K × 8 modules in our system, is to assign each memory module its own unique "town" address line. This hardware-saving technique is called *linear addressing*; with six high-level address lines available, it can support up to six 1K × 8 RAM modules to form a 6K × 8 system. If additional memory is required, the high-level address lines can be decoded, allowing up to 64 1K × 8 memory modules, for a grand total of 64K (65,536) memory locations (more than enough for most medium-scale applications). Figure 5.10 compares the linear and partially decoded addressing schemes for a memory system consisting of two 1K × 8 RAM modules.

Very Large Memory Arrays

A full 64K × 8 RAM system, the largest that a 6800-based system can directly address, can be called a *very large mem-*

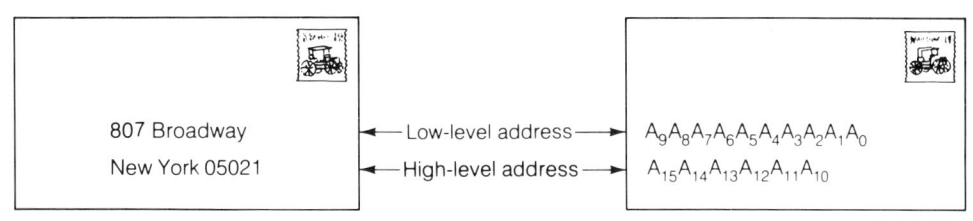

Figure 5.9 High-level/low-level addressing for 1K × 8 modules.

ory array. To provide high-level addressing for the required 64 1K × 8 RAM modules, we must fully decode the high-level address lines, making use of all address combinations. The following decoder chips are readily available:

$$
\begin{array}{ll}
74155 & \text{2-in/4-out} \\
8205 & \text{3-in/8-out} \\
74154 & \text{4-in/16-out}
\end{array}
$$

Unfortunately, the list does not include a 6-in/64-out decoder, precisely what we need to select one out of 64 RAM modules (the chip would have an unconventionally large number of pins). Perhaps we can arrange an array of decoders—say the popular 8205s—and simulate our unavailable 1-of-64 decoder. We can, and the technique is closely related to the U.S. Postal Service's Zip Code.

Looking over the solution (Figure 5.11), we note how it takes on a three-tiered pyramid structure. Let's see how a data "letter" winds its way through the decoder array to a single address.

First, we split the 16-bit binary address into the high-level (town) and low-level (street) portions. The six town binary address bits (A_{15}–A_{10}) are analogous to the postal service's Zip Code, for they will route the data to the correct memory module from among the 64 possible choices. The 10 "street" binary address bits (A_9–A_0) will then complete the job and route the data to the correct 1-of-1024 locations within the selected "town" module.

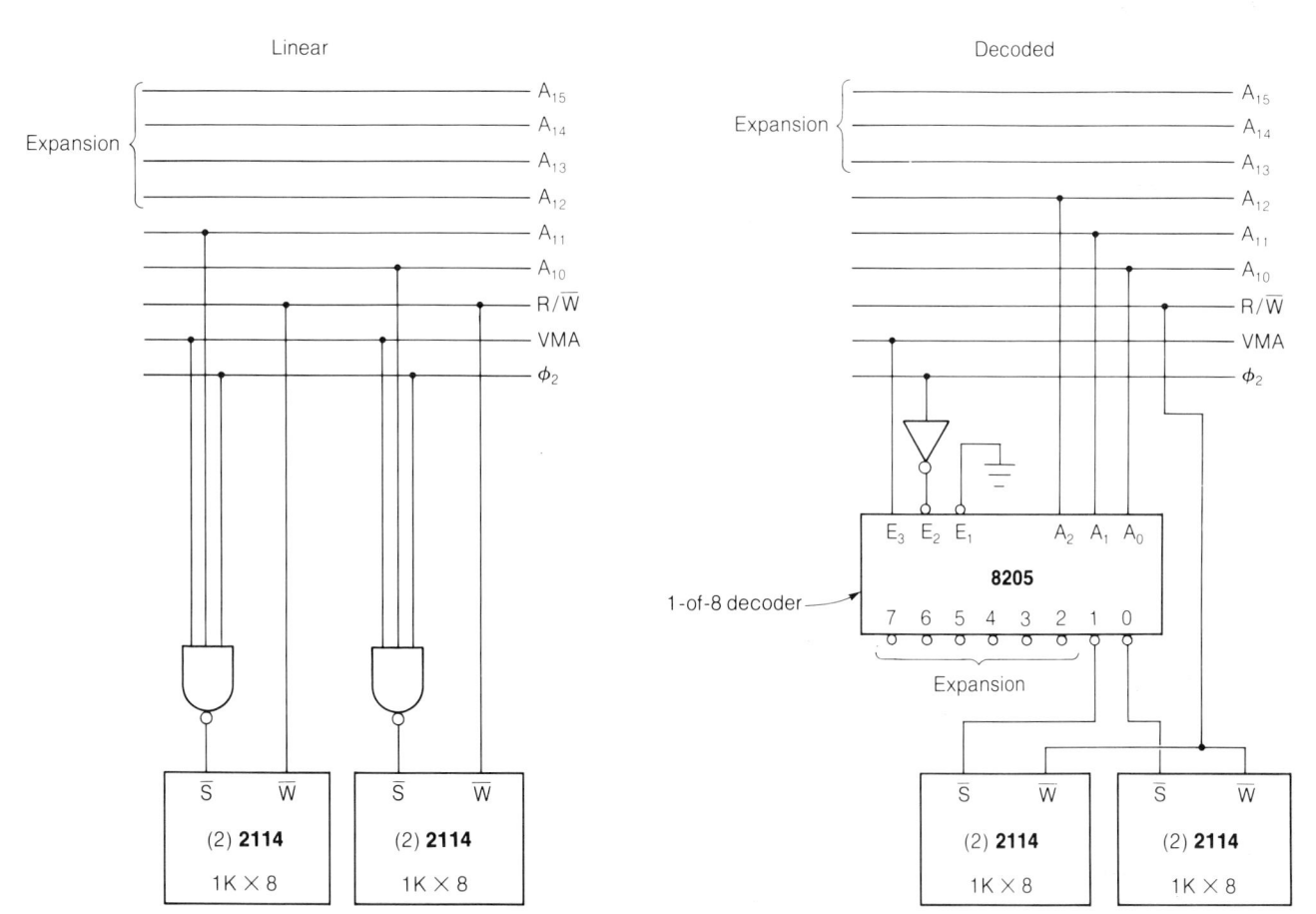

Figure 5.10 Comparison of linear and decoded addressing (6800 system).

The three highest-order address bits (A_{15}, A_{14}, and A_{13}) go to the top of the 8205 pyramid and are analogous to the leftmost numbers of the Zip Code. These three binary numbers select one of the eight 8205s in the second tier, and subdivide the entire 64K memory space into 1-of-8 8K subspaces. (In like manner the leftmost digit in the Zip Code subdivides the entire United States into 10 subregions.)

The next three address lines (A_{12}, A_{11}, and A_{10}) are analogous to the lowest numbers of the Zip Code and activate one of the eight outputs of the enabled 8205, which in turn selects one of the 64 1K RAM modules. Note how the Zip Code technique homes in on the correct module by successive subdivisions of the total address space. Low-level address lines A_0 through A_9 then finish the job by addressing the correct single-word location within the selected RAM module.

To avoid the two-tiered array of decoders, with their built-in complexity and propagation delay, we might select larger memory chips. For example, using the popular 16K × 1 RAM chips to form 16K × 8 modules, our full 64K system requires only four modules and takes on the simpler arrangement of Figure 5.12. (Note that only address lines A_{14} and A_{15} are high level.)

On those rare occasions when 64K of primary memory would be insufficient (for an 8-bit system), we can employ *bank-switching* tactics and obtain additional high-level address lines from output ports. Figure 5.13a shows how to expand our 64K system to 128K (two 64K banks) by outporting the additional address line A_{16}. The price we pay for bank switching is increased software complexity and slower speed. (The system must always be aware of which 64K bank it is presently accessing.)

Another popular technique of expanding primary memory beyond the normal 64K limits is known as *mapping RAM*, and is illustrated in Figure 5.13b. First, the microprocessor initializes the 8 × 8 mapping RAM by sending 8 bytes of address information via the data bus. When generating an address during a memory access, the upper 3 address bits (A_{13}, A_{14}, and A_{15}) are sent to the mapping RAM. The 8 output lines are then merged with address lines A_0 to A_{12} to form a 21-line address (2 megabytes). Since any data from 00 to $FF can be written to the mapping RAM, both megabytes are accessible. The MC6829 *Memory Management Unit* uses mapping RAM techniques to manage large-scale primary memory systems.

We have now completed our RAM evolution, from a simple one-celled memory unit to a jellyfishlike large memory array of 2M locations. Since most primary memory systems lie between these two extremes, it is the responsibility of the design engineer to produce the most efficient RAM system for the application at hand. Clearly, the job of the designer will be simplified as the newer high-density (64K, 128K, 256K) chips become available.

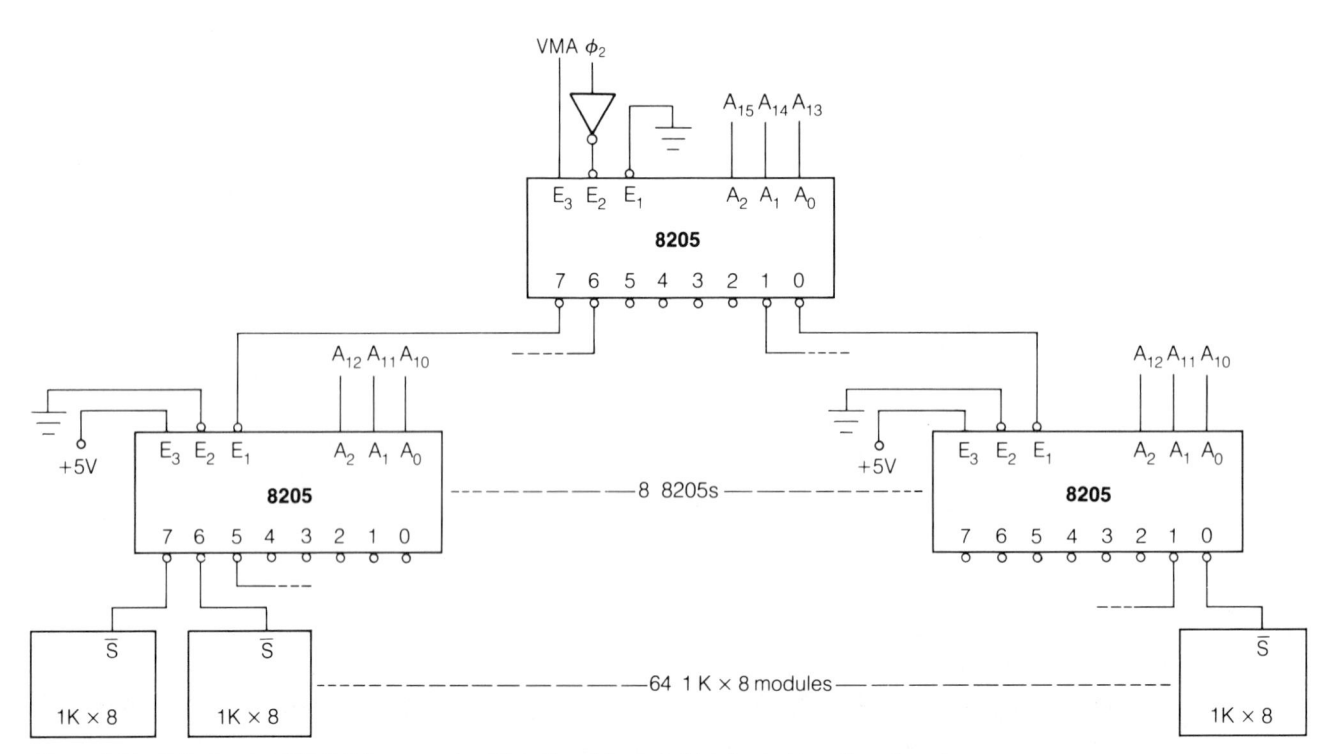

Figure 5.11 Fully decoded 64K RAM system using 1K × 8 modules (only high-level address lines shown).

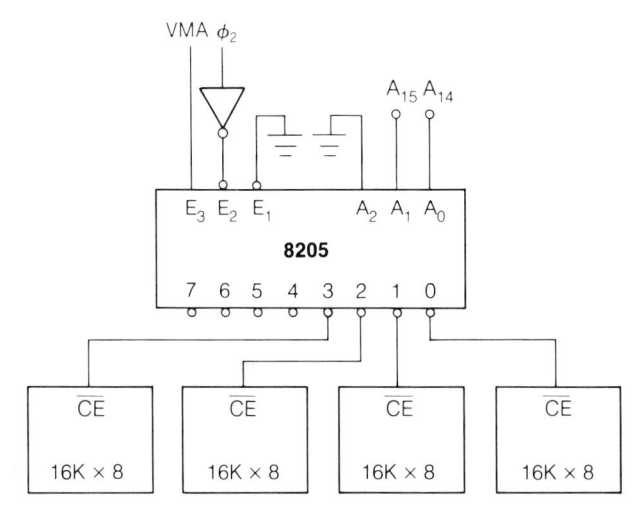

Figure 5.12 Simplified 64K RAM system using 16K × 8 modules (only high-level address lines shown).

RAM Performance

Cost, reliability, availability, size (density), and speed are the five factors most important to the acceptance of a RAM chip on the marketplace—and progress is occurring on all fronts. It is in speed, however, that the real horse race is taking place. As microprocessors become faster and faster, RAM cannot afford to be the weak link in the speed chain. (Many 16-bit processors—the 68000 for example—use techniques such as asynchronous bus control and instruction prefetching to reduce the need for superfast RAM.)

Referring back to Figure 5.7b, the following terms describing speed are most commonly seen (of these, *access time* is the most widely used):

- *Access time* (t_{AVOV}—Address Valid to Output Valid): The time span from the start of the read cycle (address applied) to the time when valid data are available at the output pins.
- *Read-cycle time/Write-cycle time* (t_{AVAX}—Address Valid to Address Don't Care): Total time span required for a read/write operation, from beginning to end.

For the 2114, the *access* and *cycle* times, in nanoseconds, vary, depending on the version chosen:

	Access (max)	Cycle (min)
MCM2114–20	200	200
MCM2114–25	250	250
MCM2114–30	300	300
MCM2114–45	450	450

An interesting feature of the performance specifications of the 2114—a RAM only recently introduced to the market—is that it is quite slow by state-of-the-art standards. HMOS II, CMOS, and Hi-CMOS are all technologies taking dead aim at an access time of 15 ns, clearly encroaching into areas once the sole property of bipolar technology. Using ECL technology, access times below 10 ns are inevitable, and gallium arsenide (GaAs) technology, with a fivefold improvement in electron mobility, promises to surpass the 1 ns barrier.

Still faster times are promised with the still-experimental *Josephson-junction* semiconductors. An OR gate fashioned with this superconducting technology could have a switching speed of 10 picoseconds! (A picosecond is to 1 second as 1 second is to 32,000 years.)

The ultimate technology for speed, if you include those still on the drawing board, is based on *light*. These all-optical speed-of-light devices, capable of operating at 5 gigabits per second, are based on a resonance/threshold effect. To provide the AND function, for example, two light beams

Foldback Memory

Foldback memory is an unavoidable trait of linear addressing. To see how memory is folded back, imagine a single 2114 1K × 8 RAM module linearly addressed by tying its active-high chip select to address line A_{15} (Figure 5.14). If you were asked to list the four pages of memory occupied by this RAM module, perhaps you would respond with 80, 81, 82, and 83 (all in hexadecimal). And you would be right—those four pages of memory extend from 8000 to 83FF.

But when you move on to the next word past location 83FF—to the first word of page 84—address line A_{15} is still high, so the first location in the RAM module is again addressed. In other words, page 84 is an exact copy of page 80. For that matter, page 85 is an exact copy of page 81, page 86 an exact copy of 82, page 87 an exact copy of page 83; the entire last half of the memory book, pages 80 to FF, consists of exact copies spaced four pages apart. The reason is that address line A_{15} is high for all those pages, and therefore the 1K × 8 RAM module is always selected.

It follows that no other RAM modules may be placed at these "folded-back" pages; therefore, in a sense, the folded-back pages are wasted (unavailable). For small systems, however, you can afford to waste memory space; and since linear addressing saves hardware (decoders), it is often the preferable technique. (To avoid folding back memory locations, the high-level address lines must be fully decoded.)

Figure 5.15 illustrates how the Heathkit ET-3400A microprocessor trainer addresses its 512 × 8 RAM block. It is left as an exercise to determine the addressing technique, as well as the location of the RAM block in the memory map.

38 Part I / Hardware: The Anatomy of a Computer

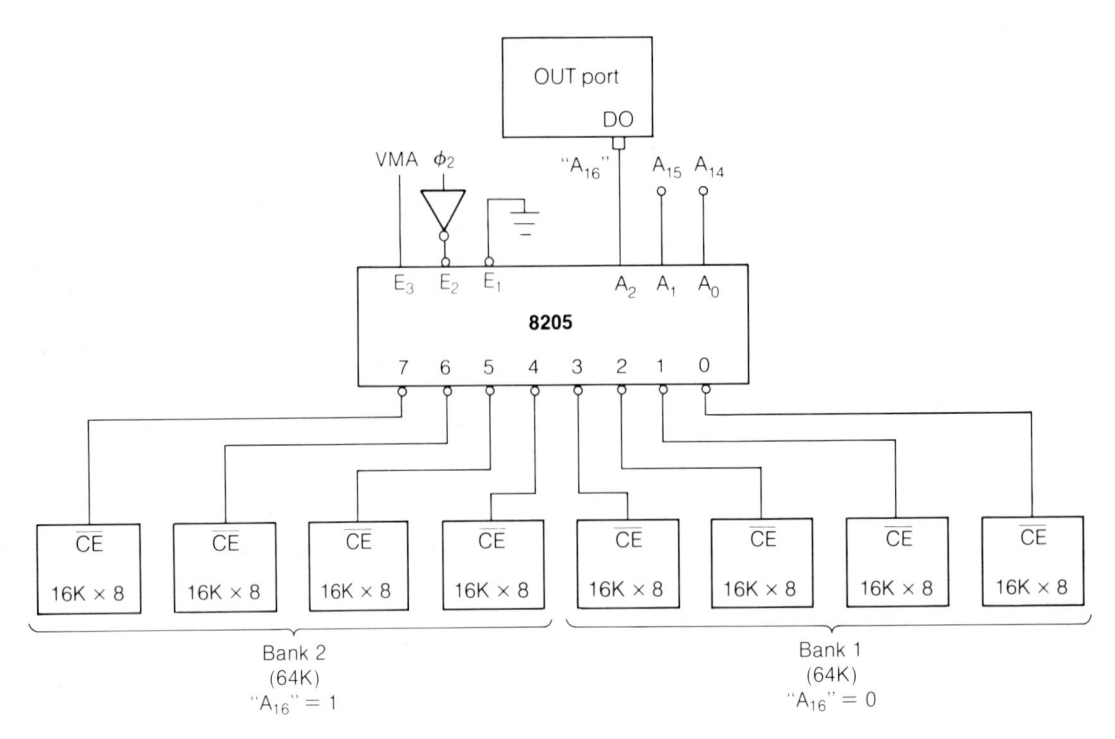

(a) Using bank switching to double the primary memory to 128K × 8

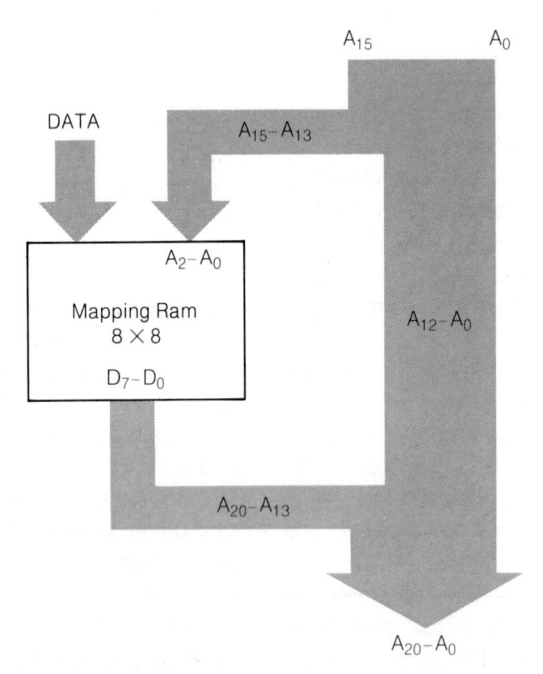

(b) Using mapping RAM to create a 2M memory system

Figure 5.13 Memory expansion techniques.

Chapter 5 / Primary Memory 39

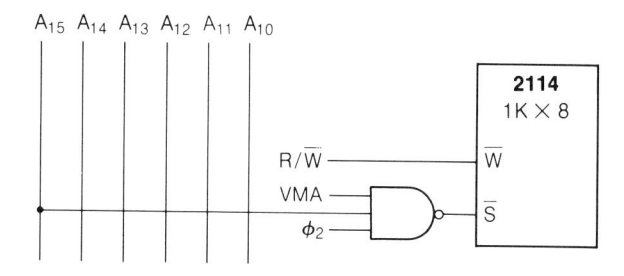

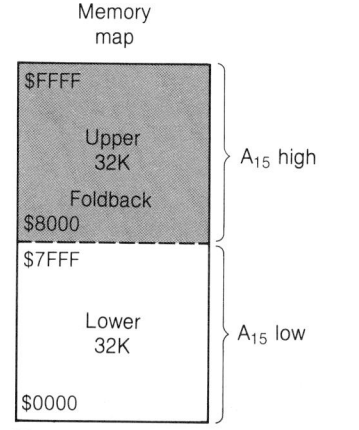

Figure 5.14 Linear addressing scheme resulting in four-page foldback over entire upper 32K of memory space.

are combined. Only when both light inputs are present will the input exceed a threshold and enter a resonator circuit to be amplified.

When matching a RAM chip to a computer, however, access time is not the only consideration. Inherent in the interface between RAM and CPU is propagation delay, composed of logic delay, capacitive-loading delay, and transit-time delay. Logic delay is the time it takes a signal to pass through the various decoders and buffers standing between CPU and RAM. Capacitive-loading delay is a function of the distributed capacitive-loading effects throughout the system. Transit-time delay is the time required to traverse the printed-circuit traces. As RAM access times fall, these once insignificant delay factors become of major importance.

Another factor related to RAM performance is power drain, and here CMOS technology is the recognized leader. No technology can match its automatic power-down feature and ultralow standby power drain. Sixteen-K static-RAM CMOS chips have been tested with a standby power draw of a mere 1 microwatt! For battery-powered operation, CMOS is the logical choice. Because of its many advantages (low power consumption, noise immunity, for example), CMOS may someday become the reigning technology of the computer industry.

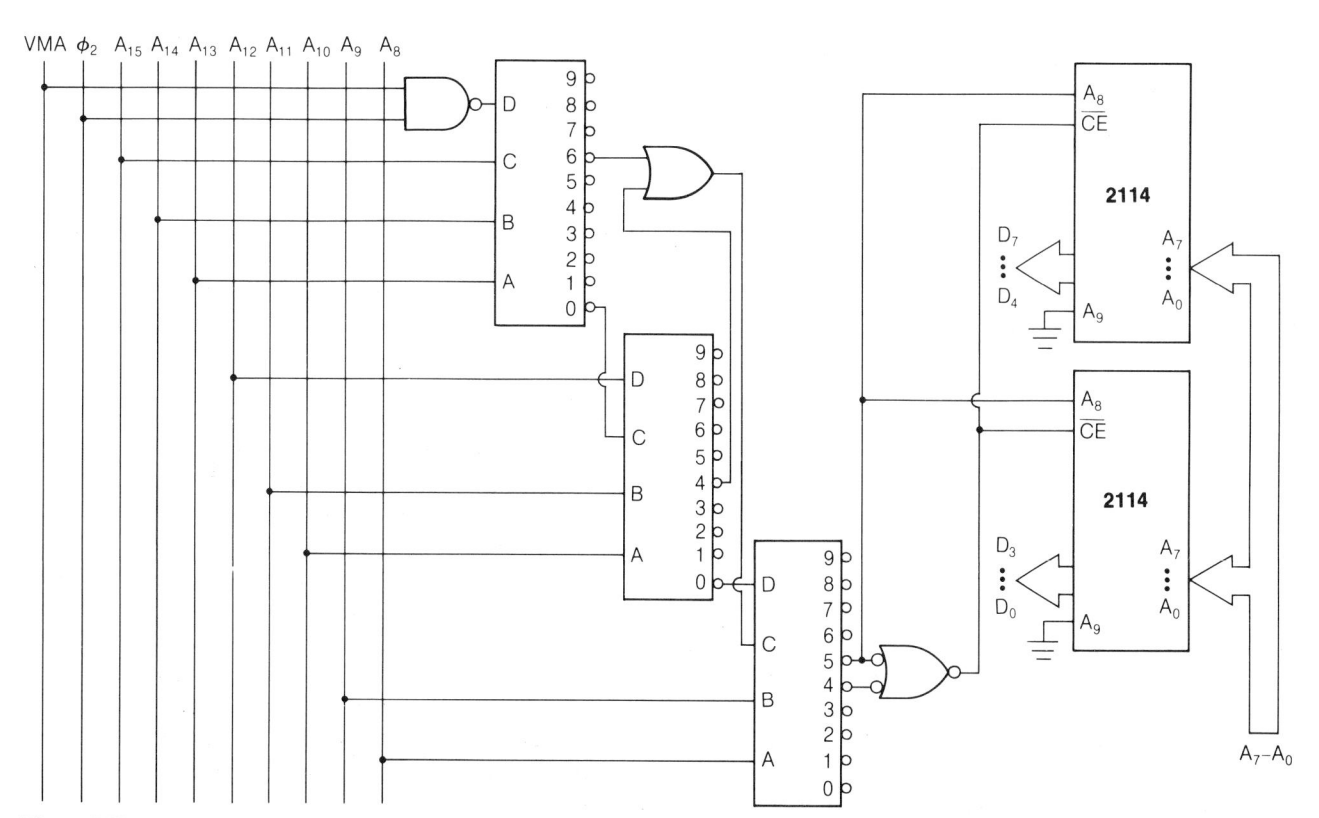

Figure 5.15 High-level RAM addressing used by the Heathkit ET-3400A microprocessor trainer.

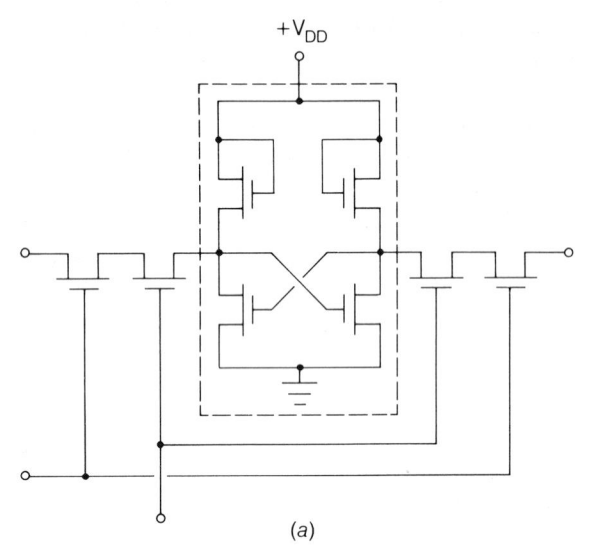

Figure 5.16 Comparison of static (*a*) and dynamic (*b*) RAM cells.

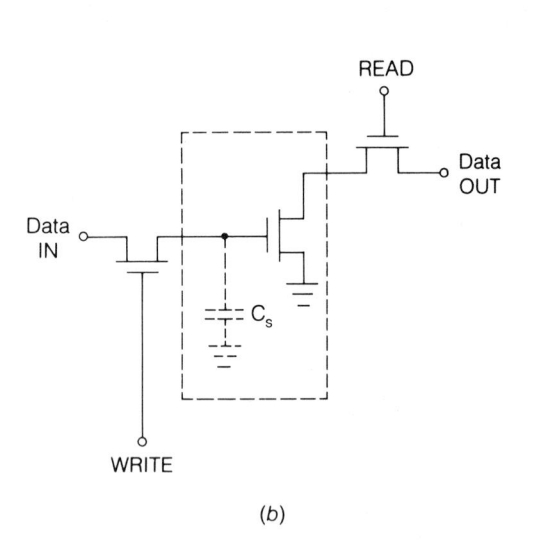

DYNAMIC RAM

Compared to static RAM, dynamic RAM (DRAM) seems to take a step backward, for the logic state is retained in the oldest electronic storage device known: the capacitor. But the key to the success of dynamic RAM is simplicity (Plato's creed), and it clearly shows up in Figure 5.16 when a dynamic-RAM cell is compared side by side to a static-RAM cell (C_s, the storage capacitor, is actually the 10^{-15} farad built-in gate to substrate capacitance).

One immediate benefit of simplicity is density, since many more memory cells can be etched on a single silicon chip (which is why ultrahigh-density memory chips—such as the recently announced 256K × 1—are generally DRAMs). When the density goes up, the cost per cell is greatly reduced. Dynamic RAM is fast, with access times as low as 50 ns, and it offers a low-power quiescent state (10 mW standby and 150 mW active are typical). In addition, dynamic RAMs now available require only a single +5-volt power supply, rather than the usual three voltages. These are the major reasons why dynamic RAM generally outsells static RAM by a wide margin.

Nevertheless, static RAM is preferred for small-sized computer systems, and for good reason. The problem with storing information by capacitors is that they leak. In fact, they leak so badly that, unless precautions are taken, all the information will drain away in just a couple of milliseconds. (Static RAM, remember, uses positive-feedback latching action to store information and in no way is subject to loss of data through capacitive leakage.)

We cannot prevent the storage capacitors from discharging, but we can periodically renew their state—a process called *refreshing*. Using the 6665A 64K dynamic RAM (Figure 5.17*b*) as an example, special refresh amplifiers (called *column amplifiers*) integrated within the chip sample each memory cell to determine its state, and then write this state back into each cell—a thousand times each second. Since each column in the memory array is supplied with its own refresh amplifier, refreshing is performed by rows, one row at a time. Refreshing can take place by the burst mode (all cells refreshed during a single time period) or by cycle stealing (refreshing done in small intervals between normal memory operations).

The problem for designers is that the proper address sequence involved in refreshing must be supplied externally. To speed the design along, most dynamic-RAM manufacturers offer special refresh-controller chips, designed to satisfy the address-sequencing needs of dynamic RAM.

Once refreshing is taken care of, the basic read/write waveform profiles for dynamic RAM vary widely depending on the chip and the manufacturer. Some chips—for example, the 6665—multiplex their address inputs (low-order and high-order address bits timeshare the same pins) in order to address 64K locations with only eight pins. During read or write operations, two 8-bit address words are latched into the 6665 by the two control inputs, Row Address Strobe ($\overline{RAS}$) and Column Address Strobe ($\overline{CAS}$) (see Figure 5.17*c*). Other dynamic RAMs require a precharge pulse before the read/write operations to charge up the output capacitors. (A full discussion of the many specifications can be found in the *Motorola Memory Data Manual*.)

Regardless of the refreshing mode, when the once-every-1-ms refresh time is compared with a typical 300 ns read/write cycle time, it is clear that refreshing takes up only a small fraction of a DRAM's available access time (more than 3,000 read/write cycles can fit into 1 ms). All external

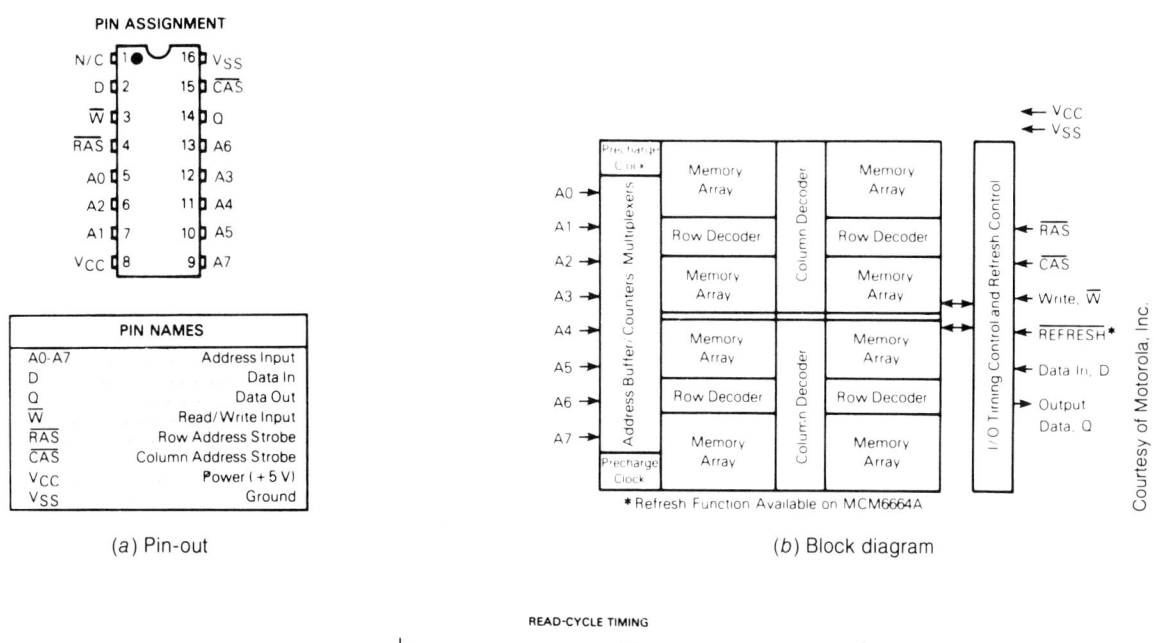

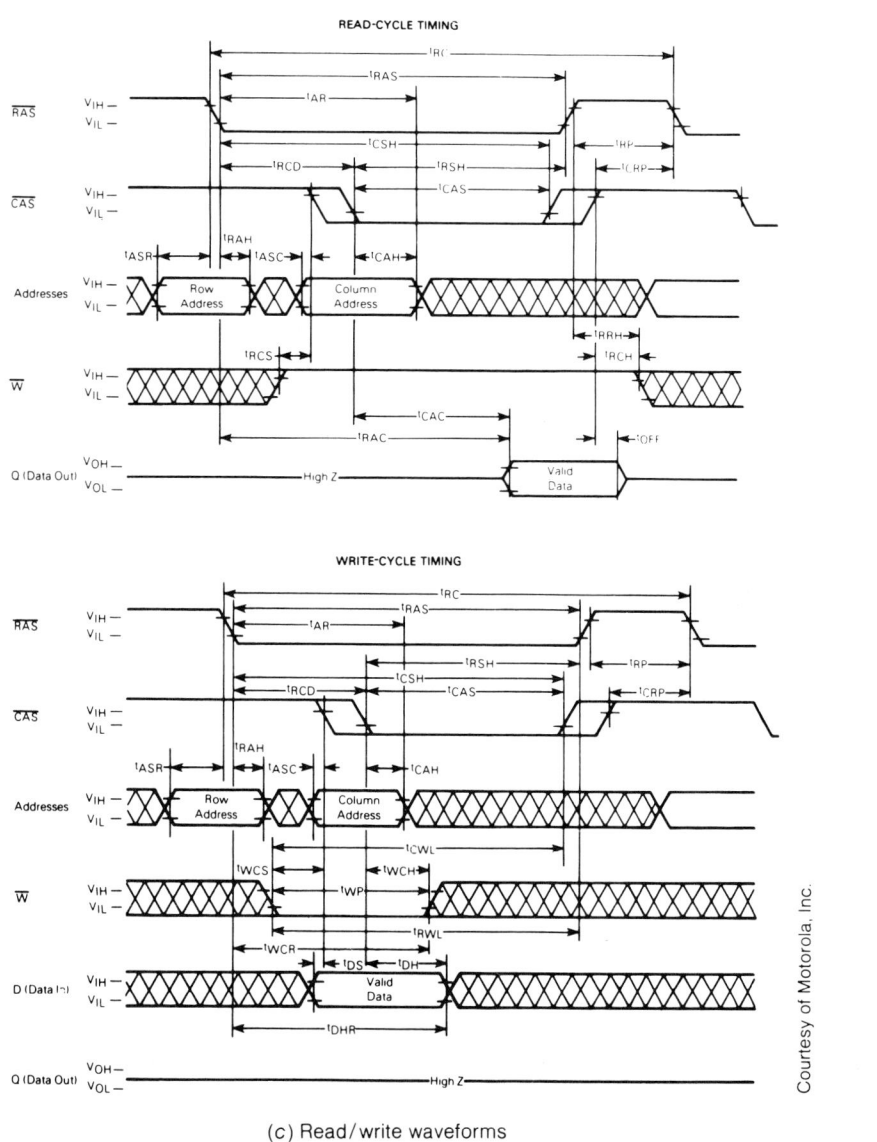

Figure 5.17 The 6665A 64K × 1 dynamic RAM.

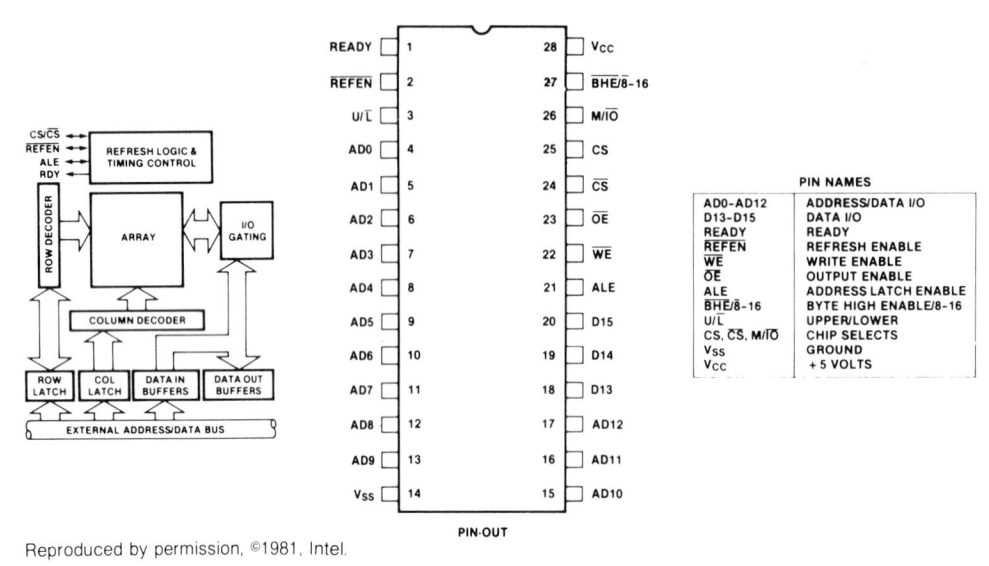

Figure 5.18 Intel's 21D1 pseudostatic RAM.

refreshing schemes, however, will soon be a thing of the past as intelligent dynamic RAMs (or *pseudostatic* RAMs) become readily available. Such devices incorporate all peripheral refresh circuitry on chip (they are self-refeshing), and look to the user as if they are nearly static. Intel's 4K × 8 21D1 (Figure 5.18) is a pseudostatic RAM incorporating the refresh address counting and multiplexing, interval timing, and request arbitration on chip. The 21D1 combines the convenience of a static RAM with the high density and low cost of dynamic RAM. For added convenience the 21D1 offers bytewide organization and a single supply voltage. Using a multiplexed address/data bus, the 21D1 is designed to interface with the Intel 8086 microprocessor.

As the various manufacturers unveil their entries in the quasi-static race for market position, look for each company to offer its own scheme for hiding the refreshing action from the user. One interesting scheme will offer a "very smart" dynamic RAM to interface automatically with all popular 8-bit microprocessors. By looking at the address, data, and control timing, the DRAM will determine which microprocessor it is connected to and thus the times it is safe to perform refreshing.

MAGNETIC-CORE RAM

It is surprising, considering the rapid advance of memory technology, to find magnetic-core memory still available—surprising since this type of RAM was among the very first developed. However, it has a combination of characteristics found nowhere else: nonvolatility coupled with 1 μs access times. Magnetic-core memory also is rugged and highly resistant to extremes in temperature and radiation, making it appropriate for military applications.

Data storage takes place in tiny ferromagnetic doughnuts (toroids) called *magnetic cores*. When the magnetic domains are lined up in one direction (and latched in place by self-reinforcing action), a logic 1 is stored; when latched in the opposite direction, a logic 0. If sufficient current is sent through the center of the core, it will flip from one state to the next (obeying the well-known hysteresis curve).

Addressing

A core is addressed by threading wires through the array in the manner of cross streets (see Figure 5.19a). Each wire carries only half the amount of current required to rotate the magnetic domains. To address memory core 3, for example, wires X_1 and Y_0 are activated. Only at the intersection of X_1 and Y_0 is there sufficient current to rotate the magnetic domains from one state to another (this condition is known as *coincident current selection*). Combined XY current in one direction produces the logic 1 state; combined XY current in the reverse direction causes the domains to flip, resulting in the reverse logic state.

Reading and Writing

The read and write processes rely on a single sense wire and a single inhibit wire threaded through the entire array (Figure 5.19b), as if forming a string of beads. The memory-read

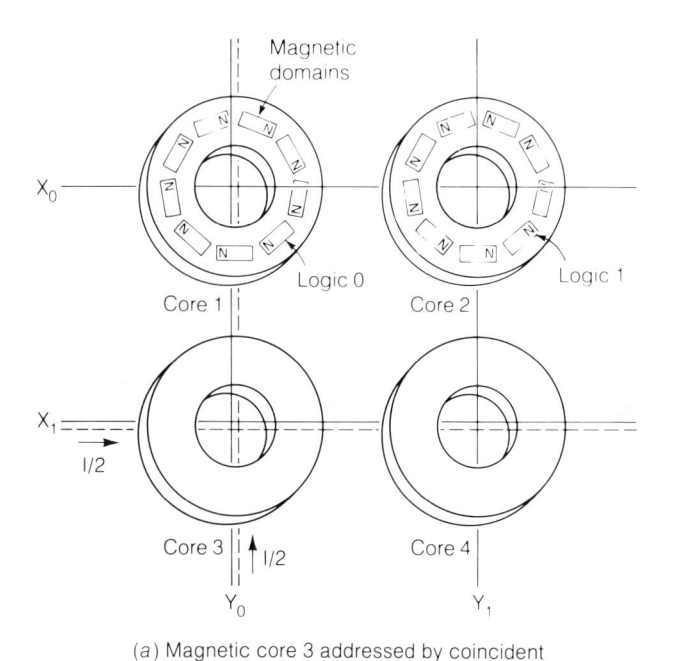

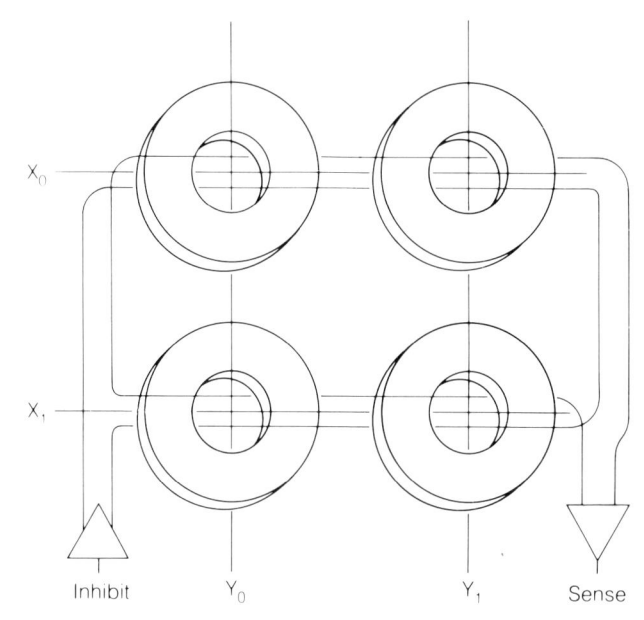

(a) Magnetic core 3 addressed by coincident current on lines X_1 and Y_0

(b) Read/write/addressing technique

Figure 5.19 Magnetic-core RAM.

and memory-write processes are unusual because each involves a full read/write sequence. To read out the contents of a memory location, we first force the selected core to the logic 0 state by sending current through the proper XY cross wires in the logic 0 direction. If the core was initially in the logic 1 state, a change occurred in the magnetic flux and, following Faraday's law (voltage is proportional to rate of change of magnetic flux), the sense wire received a voltage pulse indicating a logic 1 was indeed stored in the cell. However, the process of accessing the memory cell was destructive—we destroyed the logic 1 initially stored in the cell. We therefore reverse the current in the selected XY wires and write the logic 1 back into the cell, thereby restoring the cell to its original logic state.

If the core was initially in the logic 0 state, however, no change occurred in the magnetic flux and the sense wire received no voltage pulse (indicating a logic 0 was stored in the cell). This time, when the XY current is reversed, we activate the inhibit wire and prevent the writing of a logic 1 into the cell, thereby preserving the original logic 0 condition.

The memory-write process also consists of a read/write sequence, but it is much simpler. First, the selected cell is forced to the zero state. The XY current is reversed and logic 1 current sent through the selected cell. If a logic 1 is to be written into the cell, the inhibit wire is not activated. If a logic 0 is to be written, the inhibit wire is activated. Although magnetic-core memory is still being used, its high cost and low density make it unsuitable for most applications.

READ-ONLY MEMORY

Read-only memory (ROM), the second major category of primary memory, is associated with *instincts*—behavioral actions developed over thousands of years and passed along from one generation to the next. Instincts represent those programs that we simply cannot afford to forget or to have altered in any way, and ROM holds those programs the *computer* cannot afford to "forget" or to have altered in any way.

Because microcomputers are often dedicated to a specific purpose, they have a strong need for ROM. To use an everyday example, the typical camera now on the market is a "smart" camera. It can automatically determine the correct lens settings (and even the correct focus) to give the best picture in any given environment. As expected, it is controlled by a microcomputer—a miniature brain doing the work for us. In a sense, the camera knows what to do instinctively, and the program that makes this possible certainly cannot be lost when the camera is stored on the shelf. So the camera must have a permanent memory.

ROM Properties

ROM is a memory array whose contents, once programmed, are permanently fixed and cannot be altered by the microprocessor using the memory. (Here the term *ROM* refers to the entire family of read-only memory. But that is not always

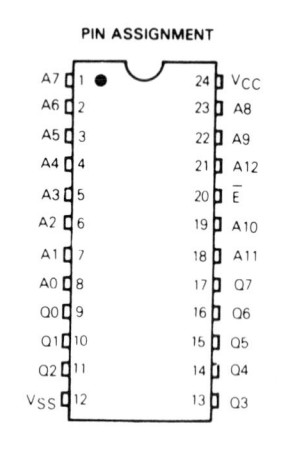

Figure 5.20 The MCM68364 factory-programmed ROM.

so. Sometimes ROM refers to a certain type of read-only memory. The context in which it is used will tell you what the term means.) In other words, ROM memory is nonvolatile, and its contents remain fixed, even when the power is removed. In addition, following the earlier definition of ROM, all ROM devices introduced in this chapter are integrated-circuit, high-speed, random-access, parallel devices—properties well suited to the requirements of a "smart" camera.

Programs stored in ROM have properties of hardware because they are permanent and based on internal physical connections. But, since they are programs, they also must have properties of software. Since programs stored in ROM have properties of both hardware and software, a new term was coined: *firmware*. Firmware refers to software instructions permanently contained in a ROM.

ROM Categories

The two major categories of read-only memory are ROM and PROM. ROM is custom-programmed read-only memory, meaning the programming is done at the factory during the manufacturing process. (Here the term *ROM* is more restrictive and refers only to the specific category of read-only memory that is custom-programmed at the factory.)

PROM (programmable read-only memory) must be programmed by the customer after the manufacturing process is complete (in the field).

Which read-only memory should we choose for our product—ROM or PROM? It depends on where we are in the manufacturing process. Suppose our product is the "smart" camera mentioned earlier. There are two major stages of manufacturing: development and production. We will consider them in reverse order.

The prototype model works as expected, and the software has been fully debugged. Development complete, you are ready to go into production, expecting to produce at least 100,000 camera units a year. Now—which memory category should you choose? Which one goes hand in hand with production? The answer is ROM.

Factory-Programmed ROM

ROM is the best choice for the production phase for a very important reason: less cost per unit. The process of manufacturing and ordering a ROM will tell us why.

Since a ROM is programmed at the factory, we must supply a program listing when placing our order. Acceptable formats include floppy disk, magnetic tape, a master ROM or PROM from which to copy, or computer punched cards. The 68364, shown in Figure 5.20, is a popular 8K × 8 factory-programmed ROM (it is common for ROMs to be available in bytewide format).

When the order arrives at the factory, a batch of 8K × 8 silicon chips, in which all but the very last manufacturing step has been completed, is taken off the shelf. The only missing step is to connect (or leave floating) the gate of each transistor according to the program ordered by the customer. This is accomplished in the final manufacturing step when a mask is prepared from the customer's order sheet and used

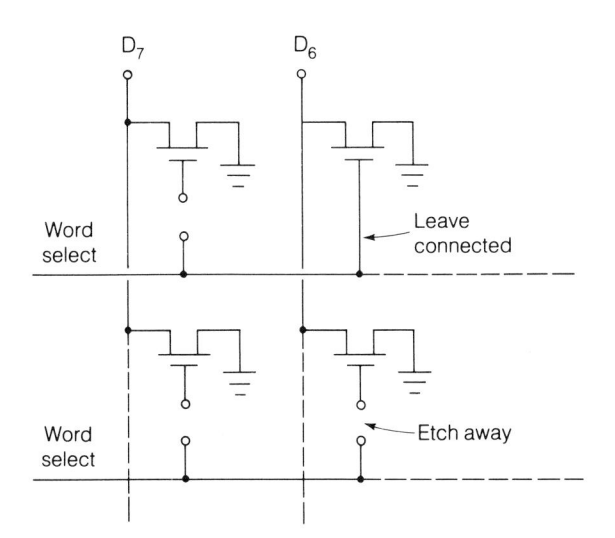

Figure 5.21 A portion of a factory-programmed MOS ROM.

to selectively etch away a layer of aluminum, leaving the correct interconnecting pattern (see Figure 5.21). For this reason, factory-programmed ROM is also called *mask-programmable ROM*.

Note how simple the entire structure is: one transistor per cell keeps the cost down and the density high. Leaving only the last manufacturing step undone until the customer's order arrives reduces the turnaround time. There is no question that ROMs are best for large-volume orders when the software has been fully tested.

Large-density MOS ROMs (16K and up) are available that access in less than 80 ns, and super-density 256K and larger ROMs will soon be commonplace.

Now let us back up to the development stage, when the entire manufacturing process is in a state of constant flux, and changes and improvements in both hardware and software occur quite often. Clearly, ROM would be inappropriate, for its cost is low only when large orders are placed, and the turnaround time, although short by manufacturing standards, is too long by development standards.

PROM

For development work, the logical choice is PROM, or programmable read-only memory. The crucial difference is that the programming of the chip is not tied to the manufacturing process. It can be done by the customer, often with relatively simple equipment. The only problem in the use of PROMs is the large variety available:

- EPROM
- Bipolar PROM
- CMOS PROM
- EE-PROM

This really is no problem at all, however, for until the recent development of the EE-PROM (to be covered shortly), one type on the PROM menu has all but captured the market. It is the first one on the list, EPROM, which stands for erasable programmable read-only memory.

EPROM EPROMs are nearly the ultimate in convenience. They can be programmed and erased by the customer over and over again, more than a hundred times, as the software undergoes development. No wonder the EPROM has become such a vital tool in the development phase of microcomputer products.

Structurally, each EPROM memory cell is similar to that of a ROM with one major exception: an additional floating gate is placed in the insulating material separating the select gate and the drain/source connection (see Figure 5.22). As with the ROM, the select gate is activated when the cell is addressed.

In order to turn on the memory-cell transistor, both the select gate *and* the floating gate must be charged. If the floating gate is devoid of charges, the cell cannot turn on, even when the select gate is activated. Therefore, the presence of charges on the floating gate is equivalent to one logic state (usually a zero), and the absence of charge stores the alternate logic state (usually a one). It follows that an EPROM cell is programmed by either forcing charges on the floating gate or leaving it uncharged, according to the requirements of the program.

To place a charge on the floating gate and program the cell with a logic 0, a high voltage is placed on the select gate, sufficient to force electrons across the insulating barrier by avalanche breakdown (as shown in Figure 5.23a). The process can best be explained by referring to the classic potential-well diagrams of Figure 5.23b.

The amount of energy required to overcome the insulating energy barrier, called E_p, is supplied by the programmer in the form of a dc voltage. After each electron is forced over this energy hump, it is attracted to the floating gate and falls into the deep potential well, where it becomes trapped. So deep is this potential-well trap that some EPROM manufacturers claim memory-retention capabilities superior to even

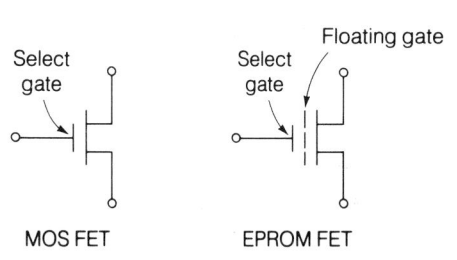

Figure 5.22 An EPROM memory cell, formed by adding an extra floating gate to the basic MOS cell.

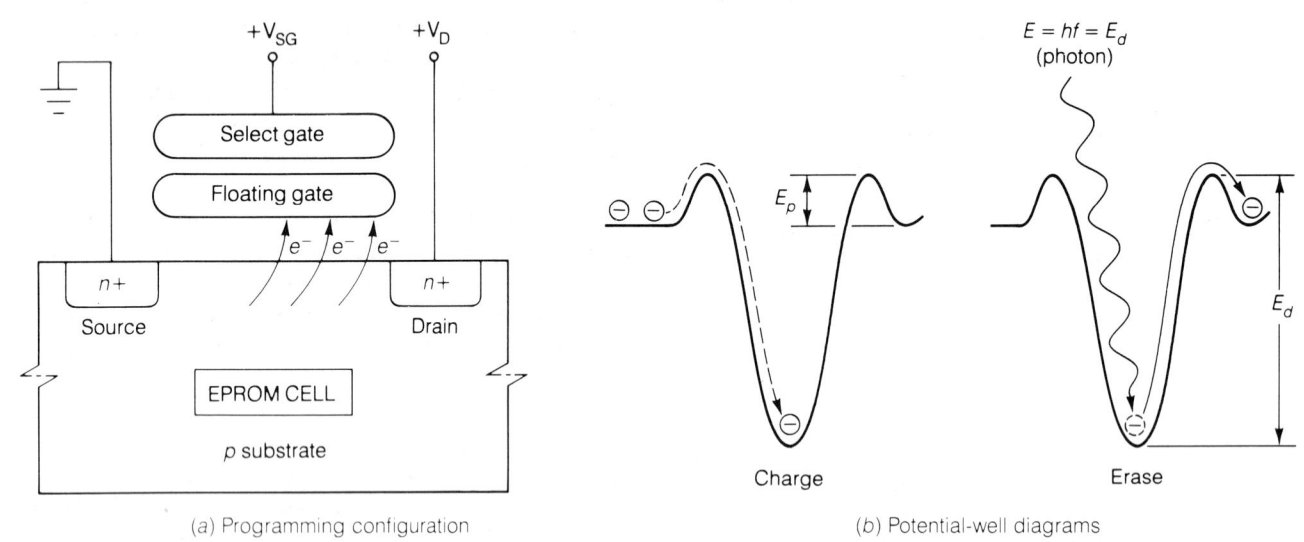

Figure 5.23 Programming the EPROM.

(a) Programming configuration

(b) Potential-well diagrams

---

an elephant's, with the charge remaining on the floating gate for more than a hundred years.

To erase the memory cell, the stored charges must be pulled out of the potential well—and that takes energy, an amount equal to E_d. This energy is supplied by ultraviolet photons of the proper frequency (energy). It is light, then—ultraviolet light—that erases EPROMs. The process is simple, quick, and clean.

MCM 68764 EPROM The 68764 EPROM is a widely used state-of-the-art device. It is a static $8K \times 8$ ultraviolet erasable EPROM, featuring a single 5-V supply, simple programming requirements, and an access time of about 350 ns (see Figure 5.24). Furthermore, the 68764 is pin compatible with the 68364 ROM of Figure 5.20, allowing for fast switchover when moving from development to production. We will follow the role of the 68764 as it might be used

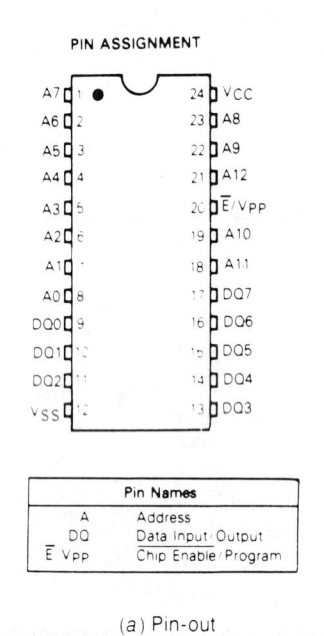

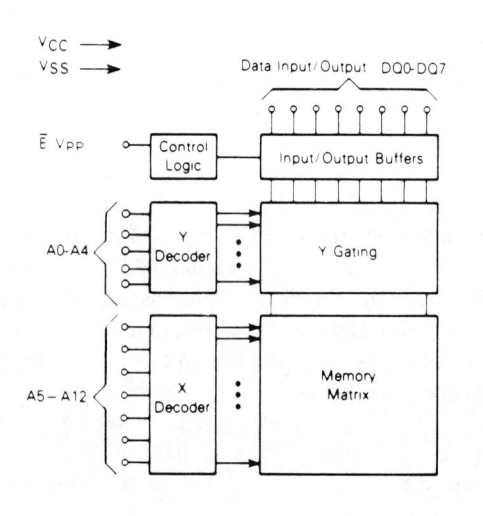

(a) Pin-out

(b) Block diagram

Figure 5.24 The MCM68764 $8K \times 8$ ultraviolet erasable PROM (EPROM).

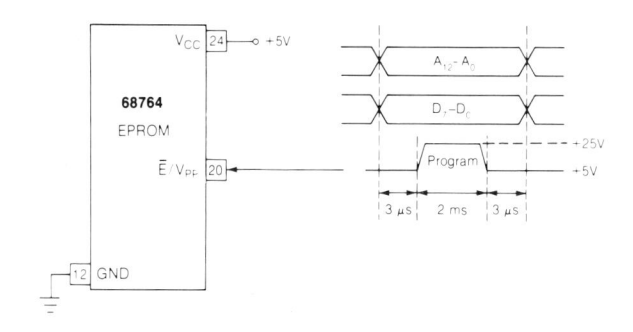

(a) Programming configuration

Figure 5.25 The 68764 EPROM.

Mode	Pin Number			
	9-11, 13-17, DQ	12 V_{SS}	20 $\overline{E}/V_{PP}$	24 V_{CC}
Read	Data out	V_{SS}	V_{IL}	V_{CC}
Output Disable	High-Z	V_{SS}	V_{IH}	V_{CC}
Standby	High-Z	V_{SS}	V_{IH}	V_{CC}
Program	Data in	V_{SS}	Pulsed V_{ILP} to V_{IHP}	V_{CC}

Courtesy of Motorola, Inc.

(b) Mode selection

to develop a smart camera program. Remember, we are in the development phase and have just written an improved program we wish to try out.

First, erase the old program by exposing the quartz see-through window to ultraviolet light of the proper wavelength. Inexpensive EPROM erasers are on the market and readily available. Even sunlight and fluorescent light will erase EPROMs if they are exposed long enough, so it is best to cover the window if the EPROM contains valid information.

Referring to Figure 5.25, we program the EPROM with our newly developed camera routine by first placing the dc voltages at the pins shown. Then, pulse the address, data, and program pins following the timing requirements provided by the manufacturer (also shown in Figure 5.25). With the 68764, you can program any location at any time, either individually, sequentially, or at random. To speed up the process of programming PROMs, portable field programmers are available (Figure 5.26).

Once programming is complete, tie in the 68764 to the system bus following the rules developed earlier in this chapter (see Figure 5.27). As shown, we have adopted linear addressing techniques and have tied chip enable to high-level address line A_{15}, placing our 8K of EPROM at pages $80 through $9F and folded back over the upper 32K of memory space. (For large-scale EPROM systems, decoding techniques would be adopted.) Note that no connection to the $R/\overline{W}$ line is necessary because data can only be read from an EPROM (or ROM).

As always, the ϕ_2 input is used to prevent *bus contention*. That is, if the ϕ_2 control line were not present, it would be possible for two EPROM chips to be enabled simultaneously during address switching, both chips sending information to the data bus at the same time. The two EPROM chips would then be in bus contention, with the possibility of voltage and current spikes (glitches). The ϕ_2 line qualifies the read process and allows the address time to stabilize.

EPROM access times By virtue of their design, EPROMs are inherently the slowest of all MOS technologies, typically about 350 to 450 ns. To satisfy the needs of today's superfast processors, however, EPROMs are now available with access times of 200 ns. As with all memory categories, there is every reason to believe that the advance of solid-state

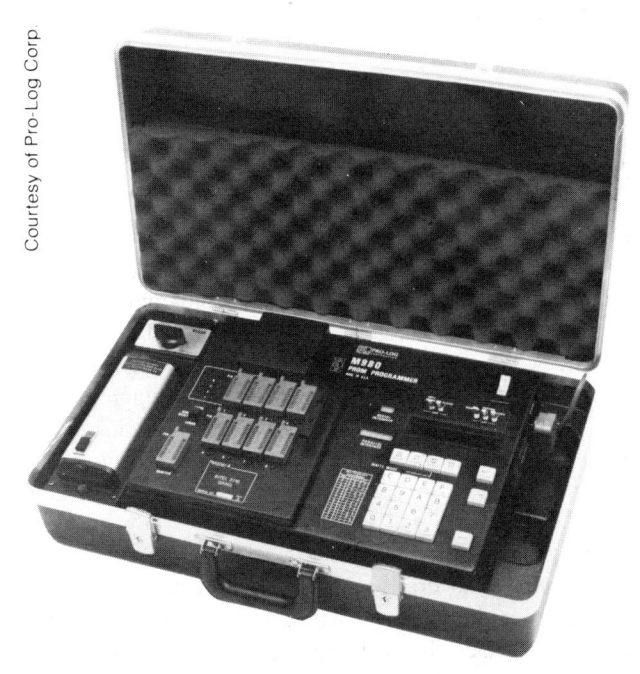

Figure 5.26 A portable PROM programmer.

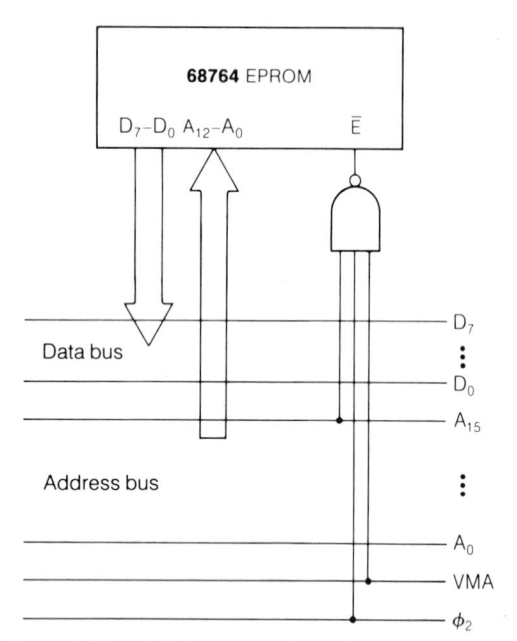

Figure 5.27 68764 bus-system tie-in (6800 bus).

technology will sweep the EPROM into the sub-100-ns range and beyond, even with devices as large as 64K.

ROMs vs EPROMs As the price differential between ROMs and EPROMs narrows (today, EPROMs cost no more than twice as much as ROMs), and as the higher-density 256K (32K × 8) EPROMs fall in price, the more flexible EPROM will be used even in the production phase. One obvious advantage of EPROMs over ROMs is that last-minute software changes can be incorporated into the product shortly before shipment.

Bipolar PROM At the present time, bipolar technology is the answer for sheer speed, with access times approaching 20 ns. High speed must be important enough, however, to compensate for several disadvantages. First of all, bipolar PROMs are lower-density devices and hence more expensive. In addition, the program cannot be erased and the PROM reused. If you make a mistake in programming, you buy a new PROM. Bipolar PROMs also would not be suitable for battery operation because of their high current draw.

Bipolar PROMs work on the fusible-link principle and are very easy to program (see Figure 5.28). To program a logic 1, the fuse is left intact. To program a logic 0, the metal fuse is blown away by a high-current external programming pulse.

Many cell designs and fuse materials are presently in use. To overcome the drawbacks of low density, stacked-fuse bipolar technology using a polysilicon fuse looks the most promising. Stacked-fuse technology should be capable of producing a 64K, 25 ns bipolar PROM.

CMOS PROM Where low-power operation is a must, the CMOS PROM is the answer. A typical 256 × 4 field-programmable CMOS PROM dissipates just 25 mW during low-power operation and 500 μW during low-power standby. CMOS PROMs are ideal for portable, battery-operated products where low current draw is essential (as in our intelligent camera).

EE-PROM Electrically erasable PROMs (EE-PROMs or E^2PROMs) are the sleepers of the PROM family. When they fully awaken, they will do so with a flourish, eventually surpassing the EPROM in popularity.

The advantages of erasing PROMs electrically rather than by ultraviolet light are many: programs can be altered remotely (by phone), the expensive quartz window can be eliminated, and computer systems will be able to adjust their own "permanent" programs without removing the chip from its system environment (thereby taking a major step ahead of the animal kingdom). The technical and manufacturing problems are many, and some rather exotic technology is going into the effort of solving them. For example, the floating gates are both erased and programmed by electron tunneling (quantum-mechanical penetration of an energy barrier).

The Motorola MCM2816 is a 2K × 8 EE-PROM featuring a 400 ns access time and a 100 ms erase time. As shown in Figure 5.29, it is pin compatible with the 2716, allowing easy system upgrade from EPROM to EE-PROM.

Although the internal cell structure of the two devices shows a great deal of similarity, the technique for forcing electrons across the silicon-dioxide insulating barrier had to be radically different for the EE-PROM. Avalanche injection, as used by the 2716, forced electrons *onto* the gate, but the process could not be reversed, and therefore the 2716 cannot be electrically erased. Electron tunneling is reversible, however, and when the oxide layer between gate and substrate was reduced to below 200 angstroms, bidirectional tunneling took place—and the EE-PROM was born. The next generation of EE-PROMs is sure to provide for erasure of individual bytes—a feature not presently found on the 2816. Figure 5.30 depicts the EE-PROM structure as well as the write/erase processes and the required voltage formats. (Future EE-PROMs will require only 5 volts for writing and erasing.)

NONVOLATILE STATIC RAMS

The 2816 EE-PROM, with its fast read but slow write times, is the precursor of a major goal of memory research: the nonvolatile static RAM. On drawing boards today are nonvolatile static RAMs (fast EE-PROMs) with write and erase times below 100 ns and offering billions of cycles of endurance (number of erase cycles possible before chip becomes unusable). Until such a technology comes of age, we will

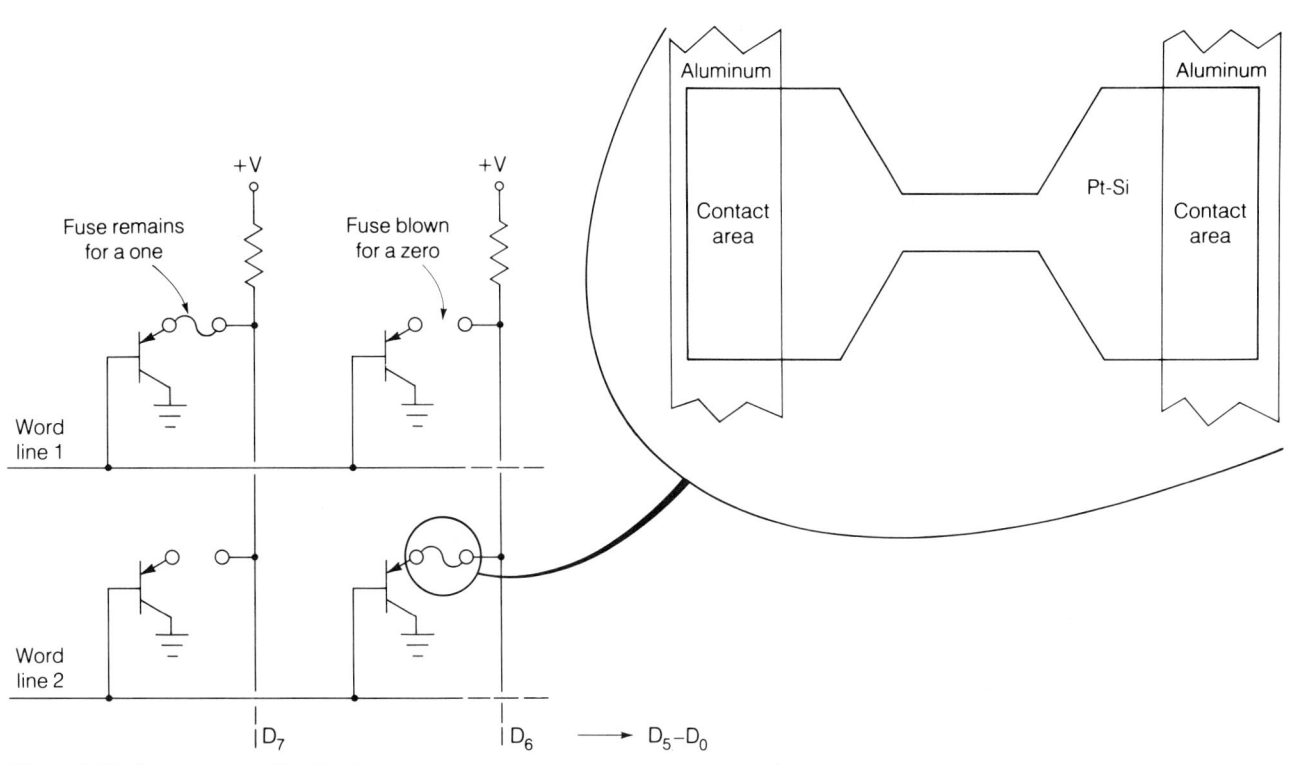

Figure 5.28 Programmed fusible-link PROM.

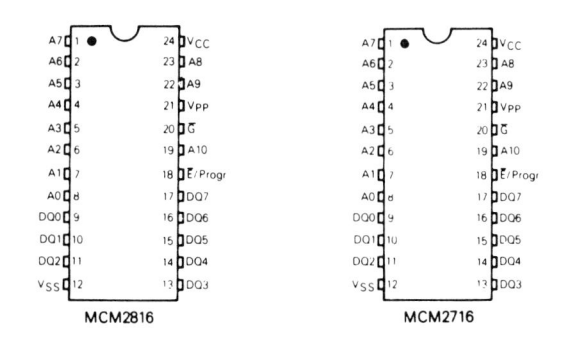

(a) Pin compatibility with 2716 EPROM

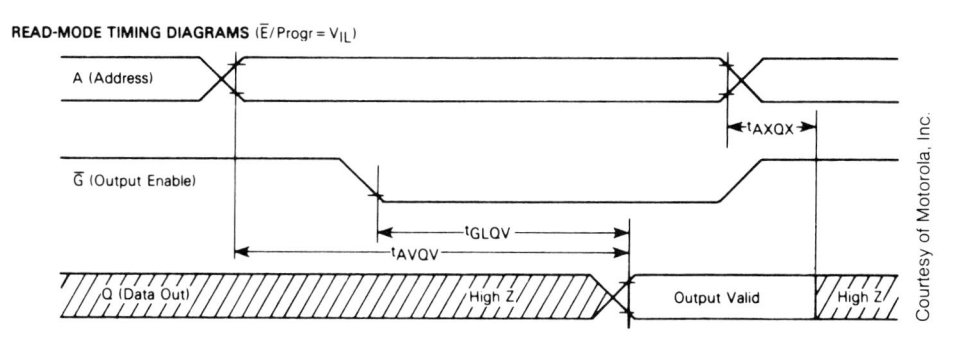

READ-MODE TIMING DIAGRAMS ($\overline{E}$/Progr = V_{IL})

(b) Read-mode timing diagram

Figure 5.29 The 2816 EE-PROM.

see many compromise nonvolatile solutions appearing on the market.

By adopting the "best of both worlds" philosophy, for example, the Xicor X2201 merges EE-PROM technology with static-RAM technology to provide a nonvolatile, 5-volt 1K × 1 static RAM. As diagrammed in Figure 5.31, a conventional 250 ns static RAM is overlaid bit for bit with a nonvolatile EE-PROM. By sending simple 5-volt signals to the X2201, data can be transferred back and forth between RAM and EE-PROM.

With a RAM-to-backup time of 2 ms, the X2201 will flourish in an environment where power failure is possible, where remote coding is required, and in general, wherever the convenience of a nonvolatile RAM is an important factor. (Nibble and bytewide devices should soon be widely available.)

An even more direct nonvolatile solution is offered by Mostek's 16K MK48202 *Zeropower RAM*. Lithium cells are piggybacked on a conventional CMOS static RAM. When power goes down, the chip automatically switches to its built-in battery backup—and, if necessary, will retain the data for a decade!

BYTEWIDE PIN-OUT STANDARDS

As we move from development to production, we generally replace EPROMs with less-expensive ROMs. As higher-density chips become available, we may replace 2K × 8 chips with 8K × 8 chips. Also, as newer technologies mature, we may eventually replace EPROMs with EE-PROMs. To make such memory-system upgrading quick and efficient, the Joint Electron Device Engineering Council (JEDEC) has approved standard 24-pin and 28-pin DIP sites for bytewide memories from 16K (2K × 8) to 256K (32K × 8) bits. All devices belonging to this compatible pin-out family can be used interchangeably in the same socket, including EPROMs, ROMs, EE-PROMs, bytewide static and dynamic RAMs, and quasi-static RAMs. The JEDEC standard even provides for memory densities not yet widely available (32K × 8 devices).

The 24/28-pin JEDEC standard is based on the Intel 2764 8K × 8 EPROM. As an example of the convenience of the standard, Figure 5.32 shows a possible density-upgrade path for EPROMs. Anticipating the need for this density upgrading, the manufacturer can fit all memory boards with JEDEC-approved 28-pin sites. The lower-capacity 24-pin 2716 (2K × 8) would initially be inserted into each 28-pin site, leaving the upper four pins unoccupied. As the need for larger-density devices arises, they are substituted with direct replacement. (When passing from the 2716 to the 2532, a jumper must be included to accommodate the $\overline{E}/A_{11}$ changeover.)

Although not all manufacturers have adopted the JEDEC standard, it is clearly desirable to have a standard pin-out format for all bytewide memories. However, when changing

(a) Writing a logic 1

(b) Erasing the cell

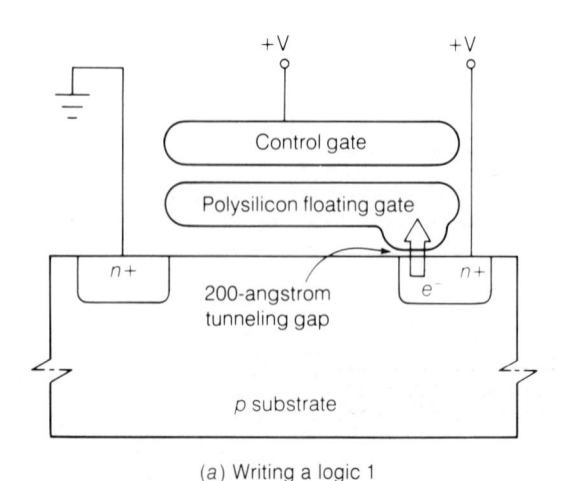

Figure 5.30 EE-PROM tunneling processes.

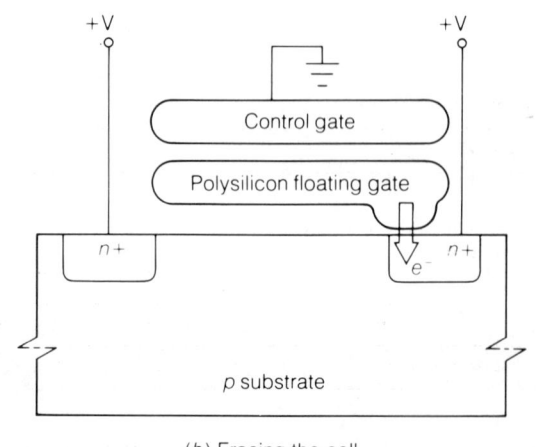

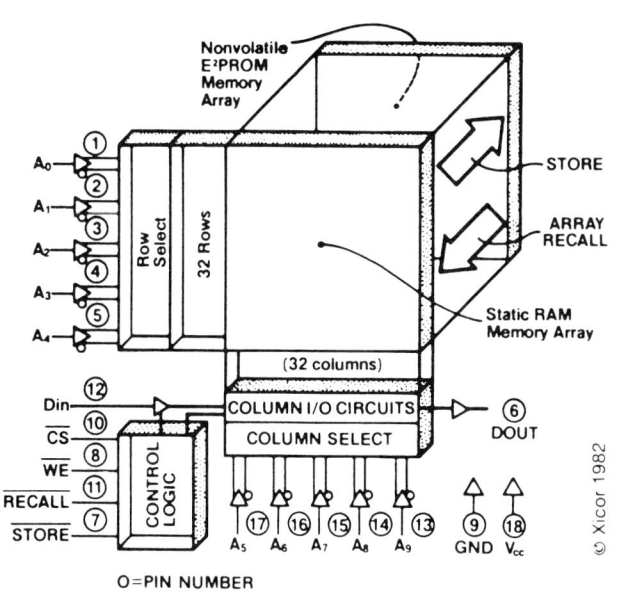

Figure 5.31 EE-PROM and static RAM combined to produce a nonvolatile static RAM.

over to higher-density memory devices, the decoding scheme must allow for easy page-boundary adjustments. For example, when we convert from the 32K 2532 to the 64K 68764, all page boundaries have to be doubled. To provide the decoding flexibility, a PROM is used as the decoding device. In practice, the PROM is programmed with a special decoding map, and a DIP switch feeds selected address inputs. A mode-selection table relates switch positions to device density. When a newer, higher-density device becomes available, the older devices are removed and the newer devices placed into the JEDEC 28-pin sites. To adjust the page boundaries, the DIP-switch input is set to a new value.

A RAM/ROM SYSTEM

A real microprocessor-based product—such as a "smart" camera—will contain a blend of both RAM and ROM. The main purpose of ROM will be to hold the permanent stored program that runs the exposure process. ROM will also hold lookup tables and other constants (such as the value of pi) that do not change and must always be available. RAM (usually smaller in size) will be used as a scratchpad memory, storing temporary, intermediate calculations during mathematical operations or other processes.

Figure 5.33 depicts a typical 6800-based RAM/ROM system. To give 1K of RAM, the 2114s are placed in tandem and addressed simultaneously. The bytewide PROMs, on the other hand, are fed by separate decoder output lines. Note again that the R/$\overline{\text{W}}$ line interfaces only the RAMs.

LOGIC ARRAYS

Logic arrays represent the third phase of logic design. Although logic arrays are not classified strictly as memory devices, they are included here because they have several similarities with primary memory.

The first phase of logic design was the use of the conventional 54/74 family of TTL/CMOS-logic chips, with their quad OR and AND gates and hex inverters. This design approach was relatively expensive and consumed large amounts of PC board space.

The second phase, starting in the early 1970s, was the development of the microprocessor, in which logic operations were performed sequentially under the direction of software. Here, one VLSI chip (the microprocessor) replaced many discrete-logic chips. However, sequential logic is relatively slow. Furthermore, VLSI was its own worst enemy. As density rises from MSI to VLSI, the integrated circuit becomes more specialized and unique. Only memories, microprocessors, and some peripheral chips have generated sufficient volume to bring the cost per chip to acceptable levels. Fully custom ICs, therefore, proved to be too expensive for many applications.

The third phase, combining the speed and flexibility of dedicated logic with the savings of VLSI circuitry, produced the logic array. A logic array is a semicustom array of logic devices fabricated on an MSI to VLSI base, in which interconnections between the components are specified by the customer. The various devices are interconnected either during the manufacturing process or in the field by selectively blowing fuse links (following the concept of ROM vs PROM). For large-scale, high-density arrays, computer-aided design (CAD) is the only way to achieve low-cost production. In practice, semicustom logic arrays occupy the middle ground between high-volume, low-cost, standard-logic chips and expensive, handcrafted, custom ICs.

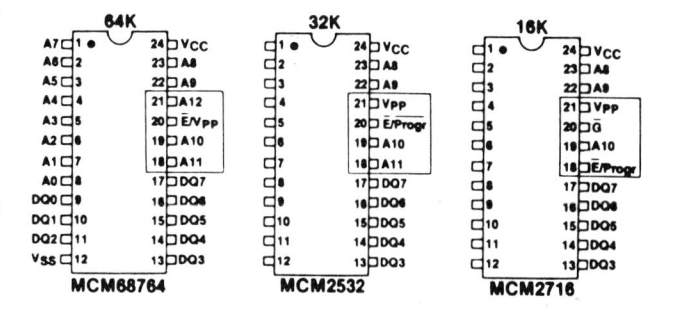

Figure 5.32 The JEDEC standard, showing ROM/EPROM density upgrading.

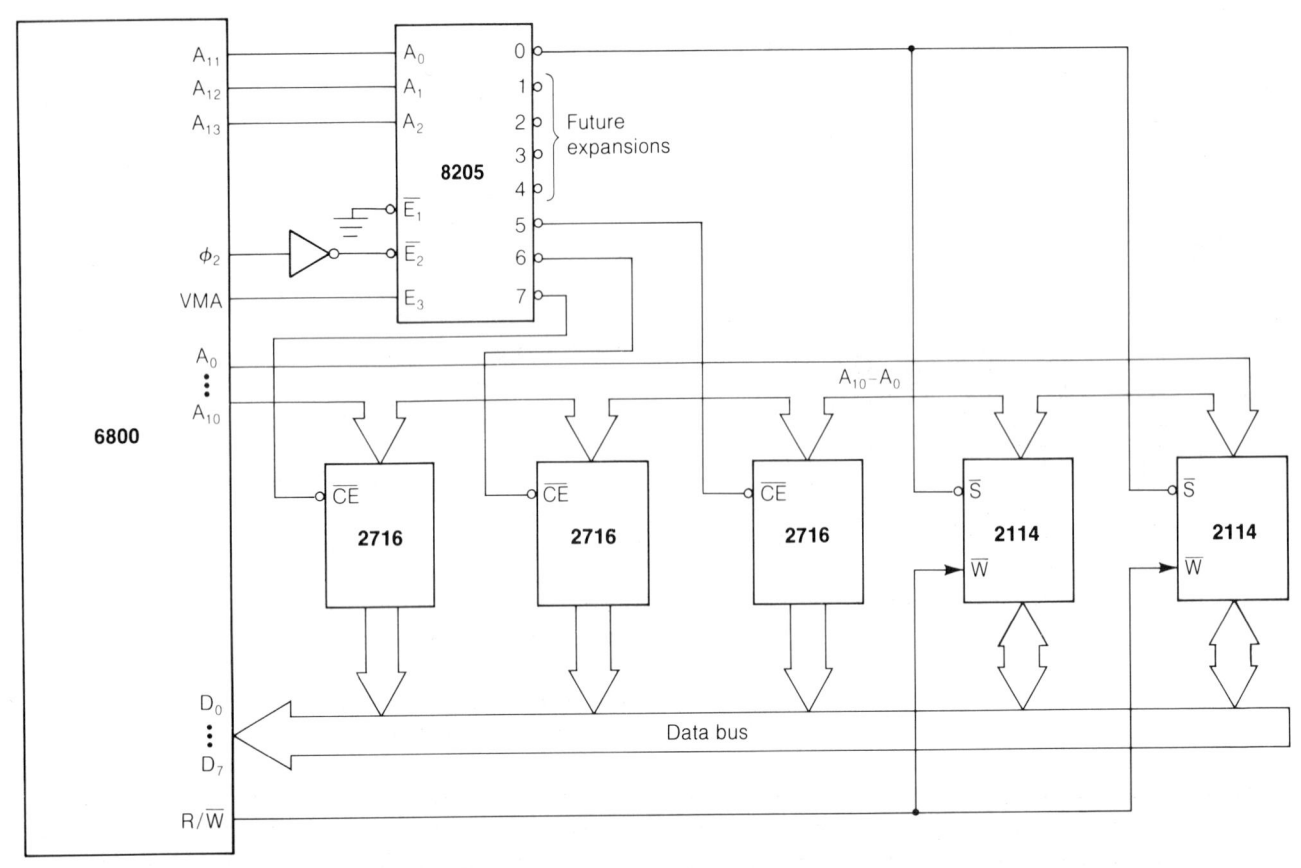

Figure 5.33 A typical 6800-based RAM/PROM system.

Logic Array Categories

The three general categories of logic arrays are:

- Programmable array logic (PAL) and programmable logic array (PLA)
- Gate arrays
- Standard cells

The PAL and PLA Since the distinctions between the PAL and PLA are quite subtle, Figure 5.34 compares them both with the more familiar PROM. All three arrays implement the familiar sum-of-products logic, used to express any Boolean transfer function.

- The PROM consists of a fixed AND array whose outputs feed a programmable OR array. It is low cost and easy to program.
- The PLA offers the designer a programmable AND array, feeding a fully programmable OR array. Full programmability of all interconnections allows the ultimate in flexibility. However, this increased generality makes PLAs relatively expensive.
- The PAL consists of a programmable AND array feeding a fixed OR array. PALs occupy the middle ground between PROMs and PLAs—they are more flexible than PROMs but less expensive than PLAs. PALs can replace up to 90% of the entire 54/74 S and LS series logic. Look for newer PALs to have additional devices beyond the simple sum-of-products format, giving future PALs the ability to perform, for example, complex arithmetic functions.

Gate arrays Gate arrays (or master slices), on the other hand, are not based on the sum-of-products format and are more generalized in concept. Furthermore, unlike (field-programmable) FPLAs and FPALs, which are user programmable, gate arrays are usually medium- to large-scale semicustom arrays in which the circuit interconnections are made during manufacturing, often using computer-aided design.

The most basic and general form of the master slice is an array of transistor cells. A typical medium-scale CMOS gate array, composed of approximately 100 array cells (also called *composite* cells), is shown in Figure 5.35.

Each array cell contains either two or three pairs of NMOS

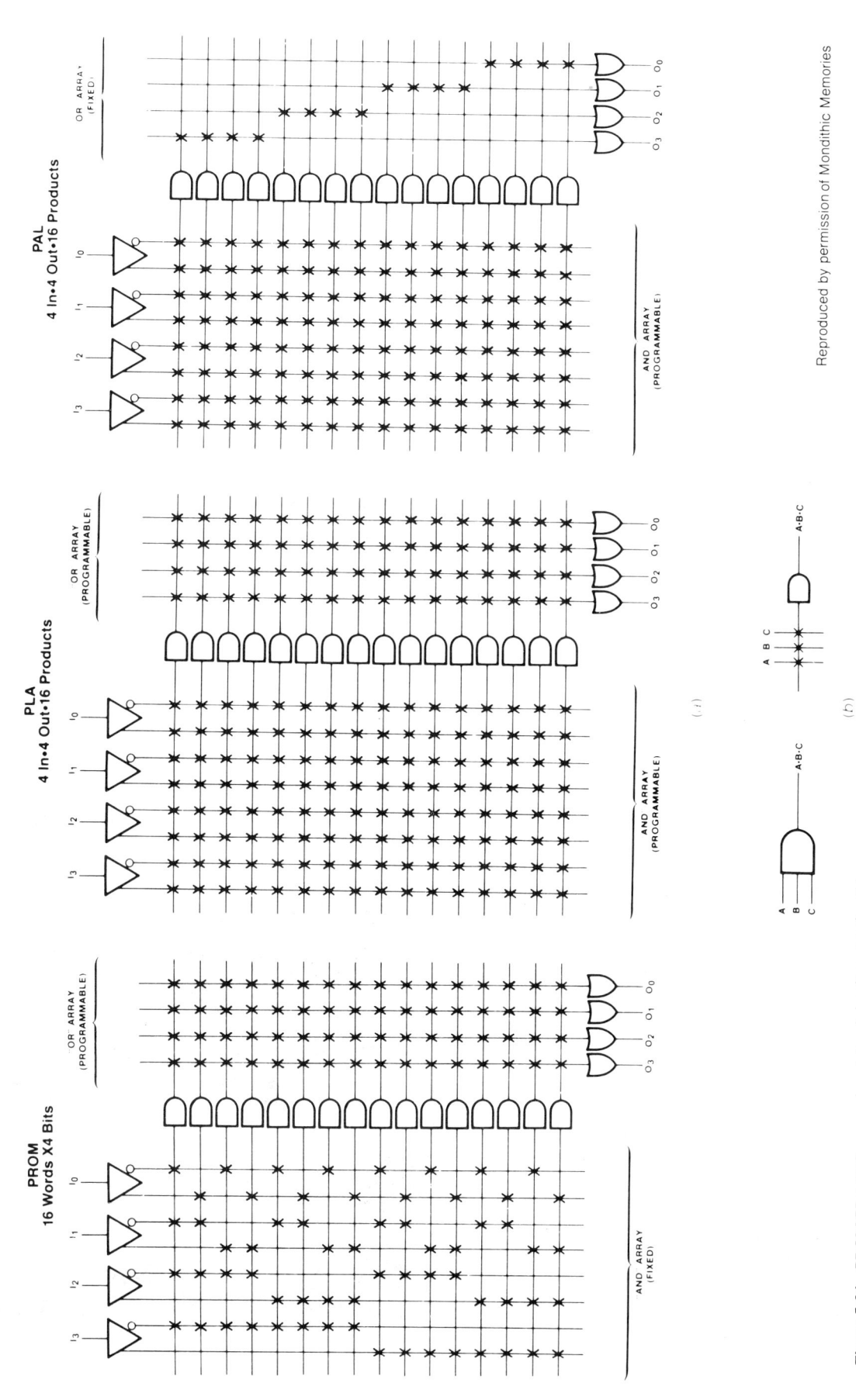

Figure 5.34 PROM/PLA/PAL comparison (*a*) and circuit convention (*b*).

Courtesy of Interdesign, Inc.

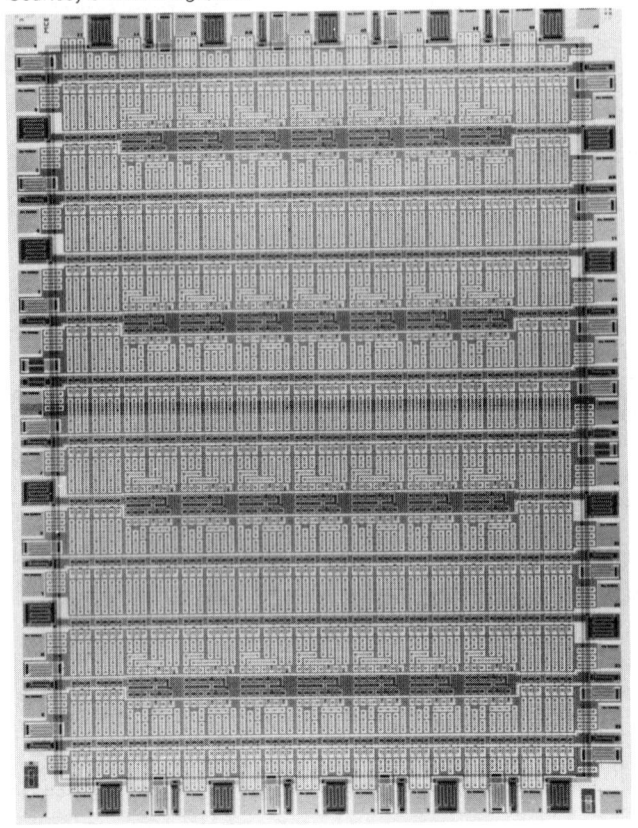

Figure 5.35 A typical medium-scale CMOS gate array.

In addition to the composite cell array of Figure 5.35, gate arrays encompass a large variety of approaches, giving the designer a continuum of options between standard logic chips and VLSI custom ICs. A less basic gate array may consist of more than 1,000 uncommitted NAND gates, with up to 10 inputs and 4 outputs per gate. To this, various manufacturers may include additional gates, flip-flops, drivers, counters, arithmetic circuits, and even RAM. These additional functions reduce generality but increase efficiency and density for those applications requiring the added devices. For arrays of more than 500 gates, the only efficient approach is computer-aided design, in which arrays of 4,000 or more gates can be interconnected (meaning a single master slice can replace more than 200 small-scale and MSI TTL chips).

Besides CMOS technology, TTL, I^2L, MOS, and ECL gate arrays are available, with ECL used primarily in high-speed mainframe computers. (Using ECL arrays, gate delays below 0.5 ns have been achieved.)

Standard cells As circuit complexity increases, gate arrays—known for fast turnaround time and low development cost—become more and more impractical (i.e., they require a great deal of silicon area). An alternative, before resorting to the expensive full-custom approach, is the *standard cell*.

and PMOS devices, with ample interconnection areas surrounding the cells. Through appropriate interconnections, each cell can be transformed into various logic functions. Interconnecting the various logic functions creates a custom integrated circuit to meet specific system requirements.

Designing with gate arrays is a three-step process. First, using standard CMOS ICs, you design and breadboard your circuit, determining the size of the array required. Second, you transform the circuit logic to conform to the array format. A design kit, such as that of Figure 5.36, will provide the necessary guidelines.

Third, using adhesive overlays, you lay out the circuit and interconnect the cell structures on an enlarged color-coded sheet of the array. When the layout sheet arrives at the factory, a photographic master is taken and used to etch the correct interconnect pattern. After testing and mounting in DIP packages, the finished circuits are shipped to the customer.

As CAD/CAM (computer-aided design/computer-aided manufacturing) systems lower in cost, all three steps, from initial layout to final photographic mask, will be fully computerized. Even prototype breadboarding and testing will be done by computer simulation. (CAD/CAM systems are discussed in Chapter 22.)

Courtesy of Interdesign, Inc.

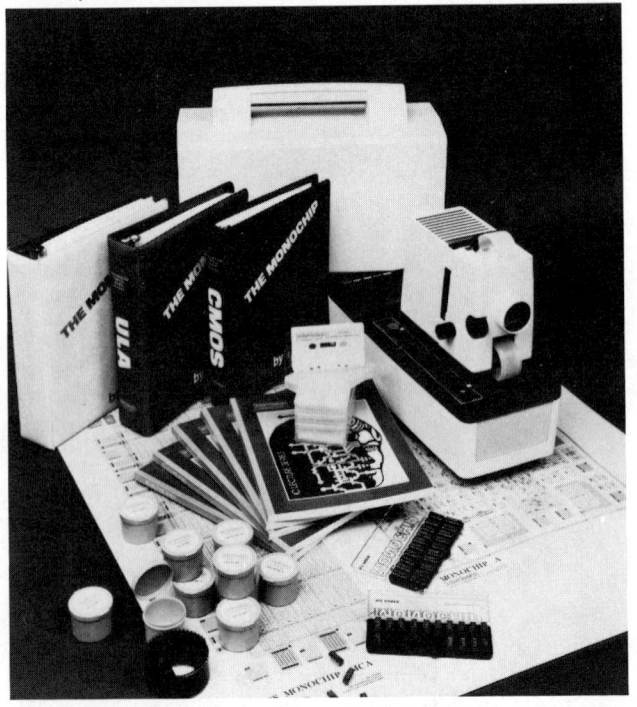

Figure 5.36 Gate-array design, simplified by kits supplying all required materials.

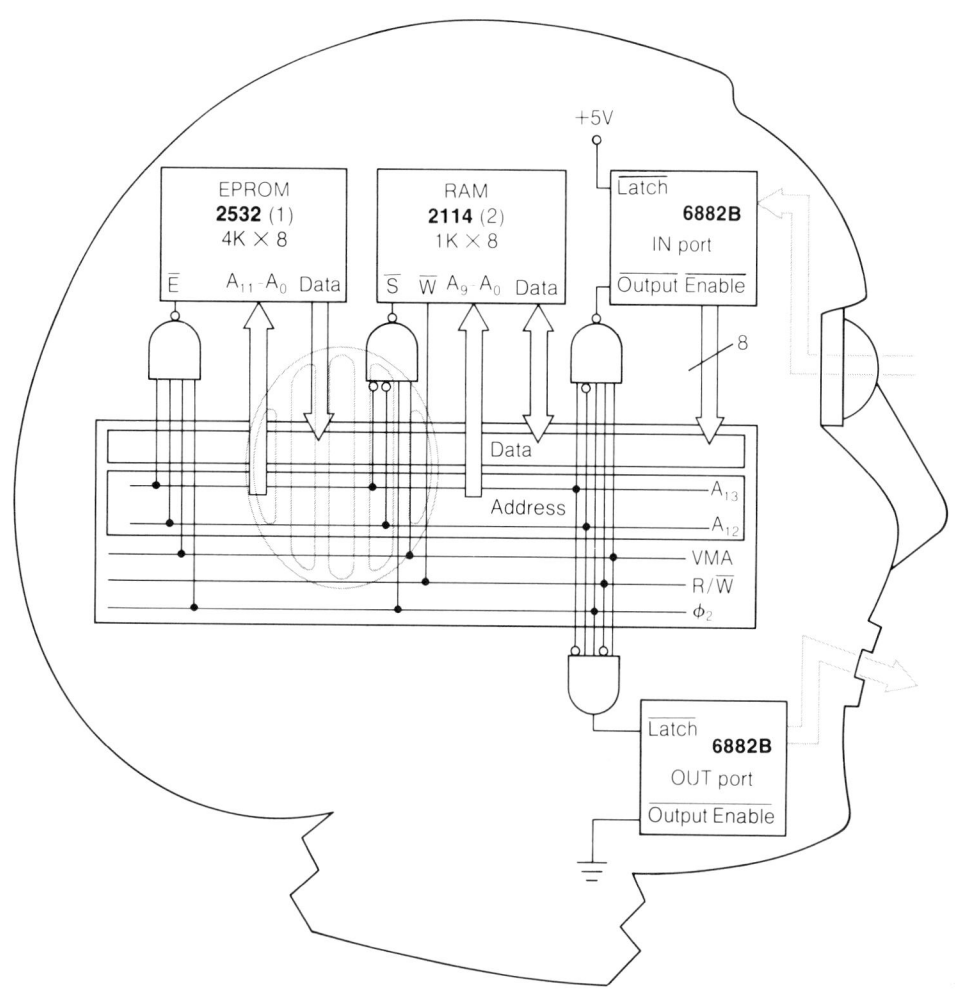

Figure 5.37 Intelligent machine with I/O ports, RAM, and PROM (eyes, voice, memory, and instincts).

Standard cell design is the hardware counterpart to modular software design. Unlike gate arrays, in which all but the last mask layer is predefined, a standard cell does not predefine any mask layers. Instead, a fully customized set of masks is created from "building blocks" (cells). Each cell—represented by a set of masks in a cell library—is a full-custom "standard" circuit, ranging from simple gates to UARTs (universal asynchronous receiver/transmitters), DACs (digital-to-analog converters), ALUs, etc. Supported by CAD techniques, the mask sets for each cell are combined (interconnected) to create a custom set of masks for the full circuit.

Logic Arrays vs Microprocessors

To the designer, the various forms of logic arrays—in competition with microprocessors—may seem quite confusing. Which approach is best? As usual, it depends on all the factors that go into bringing a product to market. For artificial intelligence applications, the flexibility of software programmed logic (the microprocessor) is ideal. For moderate volume, semicustom systems comprised of standard computer subcircuits, the standard cell approach may be most attractive. If low cost and fast turnaround are more important than high circuit density, the designer can look to the gate array. The full-custom approach—which maximizes use of silicon area—may be best when the high front-end cost is overcome by high production volume. For purely low-end logic-replacement applications, however, the low-cost field-programmable PAL or PLA may be the best choice. Clearly, only a thorough investigation and comparison of all options will yield the most suitable approach.

INTELLIGENT-MACHINE UPDATE

When primary memory—RAM and PROM—is added to our intelligent machine (Figure 5.37), it takes yet another step toward its human creators. It can remember, recall, and learn—and with the addition of permanent memory (ROM), it is endowed with instincts. Still, for all its impressive memory capabilities, it is only an inanimate object, incapable of actions on its own. Clearly, the biggest step (bringing the computer "to life") has yet to be taken.

QUESTIONS AND PROBLEMS

1. List the major features normally found in a primary-memory system.
2. List the major features normally associated with (a) a RAM system, and (b) a ROM system.
3. A static-RAM cell uses what process to store information?
4. What is the difference between *static* and *dynamic* RAM?
5. How is an individual static-RAM memory cell addressed?
6. For a 6800-based system, draw the where/when waveforms for both the memory-read and memory-write processes.
7. With regard to a 2K × 8 RAM, what do the numbers 2K and 8 mean?
8. What is the purpose of a high-level address line?
9. What is the dividing line between high-level and low-level address lines for a system composed exclusively of 4K × 8 modules?
10. What is *coincident address selection*? What part do decoders play in the addressing process?
11. What is the difference between *linear* and *decoded* addressing?
12. Using linear addressing, place a 2K × 8 RAM module at page 40 (hex).
13. Design a memory system in which two 1K × 8 RAM modules occupy pages $80 to $87 consecutively.
14. Figure 5.15 depicts the 512 × 8 memory system of the 6800-based Heathkit ET-3400A single-board microcomputer. What addressing technique is used? By tracing through the high-level address lines, at what pages is the memory located? To what locations (if any) is it folded back?
15. Draw the where/when diagram for the memory-read process and show what is meant by *access time*.
16. List the steps required for a memory-write process to the 2114 (see Figure 5.7*b*).
17. For large-scale systems, why is dynamic RAM preferred over static RAM?
18. What is *refreshing*?
19. What advantage does quasi-static RAM have over conventional dynamic RAM?
20. How is addressing done in magnetic-core memory?
21. What is the difference between PROM and ROM? Which one is used during the development stage of a new product?
22. How is information stored in an EPROM?
23. Why is it not possible to reprogram bipolar PROM?
24. What is the difference between an EPROM and an EE-PROM?
25. What property of electron tunneling directly resulted in the EE-PROM cell?
26. For a battery-powered system, what memory technology is preferred?
27. What is the difference between a *gate array* and a *standard cell*?
28. Draw a memory map of the RAM/PROM system of Figure 5.33.
29. A single 1K × 8 RAM module is linearly addressed by tying CE to line A_{14}. Draw the memory map, showing all addressed and foldback locations.
30. Show how a magnitude comparator (such as the 7485) might be used to provide "user selectable" decoding for a memory module.
31. Referring to Figure 5.10, draw a memory map (including foldback) for the linear and decoded 2K × 8 memory systems.
32. Draw a complete memory map of Figure 5.37, showing all RAM, ROM, and I/O port locations (include all foldback locations).
33. Redesign the system of Figure 5.37 using two 8205 decoders (and inverters) instead of the four AND/NAND gates. (*Hint:* Use one 8205 for the ports and the other for the memory chips.)
34. Under what circumstances might you *purposely* include the R/$\overline{W}$ line into the decoding circuitry of a ROM or PROM?

chapter 6

Secondary and Backup Memory

Secondary and backup memory act as vast data warehouses. Their function is much like that of an ordinary library. A library is an information storehouse consisting of thousands of books. However, a person can actively read only a single book at a time. When one book is finished, it is placed back on the shelf and another is retrieved. Writers may even add to the information storehouse from time to time. For convenience and protection, all the information contained in the library (as well as books and newspapers no longer in circulation) is available on microfilm.

A microcomputer's memory is also an information library organized along similar lines. Primary memory corresponds to the single book that one is actively reading. Secondary memory is analogous to the thousands of readily available books stored on the shelves, and backup memory serves the same purpose as archives of securely stored rolls of microfilm.

By switching from random to sequential organization, secondary- and backup-memory systems have sacrificed speed to produce nonvolatile data libraries of high capacity and low cost. Although such systems cannot approach the mega-megaword capacity of the human mind, the secondary and backup systems coming into the market give all the capacity and power a microcomputer system is likely to require.

In this chapter we will cover the following types of secondary and backup memory:

Secondary	*Backup*
Floppy disk	Magnetic tape
Winchester disk	Cartridge tape
Bubble	Cassette tape
Charge-coupled device	Video tape

THIN-FILM MAGNETIC TECHNOLOGY

With the exception of bubble and optical memory, all secondary- and backup-memory systems store information in a similar manner. The storage medium is a thin layer of iron oxide. Suspended within this magnetic slurry are billions of tiny magnetic, needlelike particles a thousand times thinner than a human hair. Each iron atom in the particle exhibits its own earthlike magnetic field. The iron atoms tend to align themselves along the axis of the elongated particle, turning each particle into a tiny bar magnet.

During manufacture of the memory element, the iron-oxide liquid is spread thinly on the surface of a disk or tape support material in the presence of an external magnetic field. When the iron-oxide slurry has dried, all magnetic particles will be aligned in the same north-south direction. Since the magnetic field strength in the critical region just above the magnetic film is the sum of all magnetic particles beneath, this mutual alignment assures the strongest possible field strength. (To reduce noise, some magnetic systems use a random alignment of magnetic particles.)

The whole system is useful as a memory device because of two distinct magnetic configurations. As seen in Figure 6.1, the iron atoms can align and latch themselves in one of two states. (Remember, only the magnetic state of the iron atoms turns, not the magnetic particles themselves.) Digital information is stored by a linear pattern of these two states of magnetic alignment.

Once the pattern has been established, the hysteresis properties of the magnetic material guarantee that the pattern will remain locked in place for long periods of time.

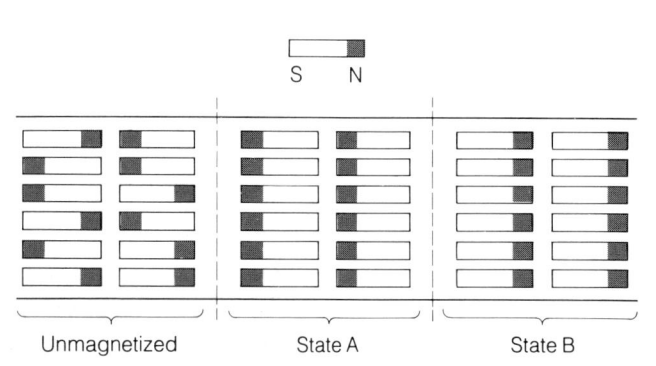

Figure 6.1 Digital two-valued storage in a magnetic medium.

Reading and Writing

Reading information from the magnetic medium takes place by passing the linear patterns of magnetic alignment under a magnetic head (see Figure 6.2). A coil of wire on the magnetic head senses the changing magnetic pattern by the principle of induction (a voltage pulse appears whenever the magnetic alignment *changes*). The resulting voltage waveform is decoded by logic circuitry to recreate the serial pattern of ones and zeros originally stored on the magnetic medium.

The same magnetic head (known as the *read/write head*) can be used in the write mode. Sufficient current is forced through the loops of wire to create a magnetic field. The direction of the magnetic field can be switched by changing the direction of the current flow. This switching magnetic field lays down the required pattern of magnetization as the magnetic medium passes beneath.

Recording Modes

It seems logical that magnetic alignment in one direction would store the logic 1 state, and magnetic alignment in the opposite direction would correspond to the logic 0 state. However, magnetic induction produces a voltage only when a *change* in magnetism is encountered. Following this constraint, a logic 1 is usually represented as a magnetic reversal, and a logic 0 as no reversal. Furthermore, most encoding schemes use the nonreturn-to-zero (NRZ) technique, in which the recording medium is always saturated in one direction or the other. In a return-to-zero (RZ) format, parts of the serial data track are left unmagnetized. Finally, most encoding schemes include timing signals in the data flow to provide synchronization.

Historically, the first major data-encoding scheme was called *frequency modulation* (FM). As shown in Figure 6.3a, the presence of a logic pulse stores a logic 1, and the absence

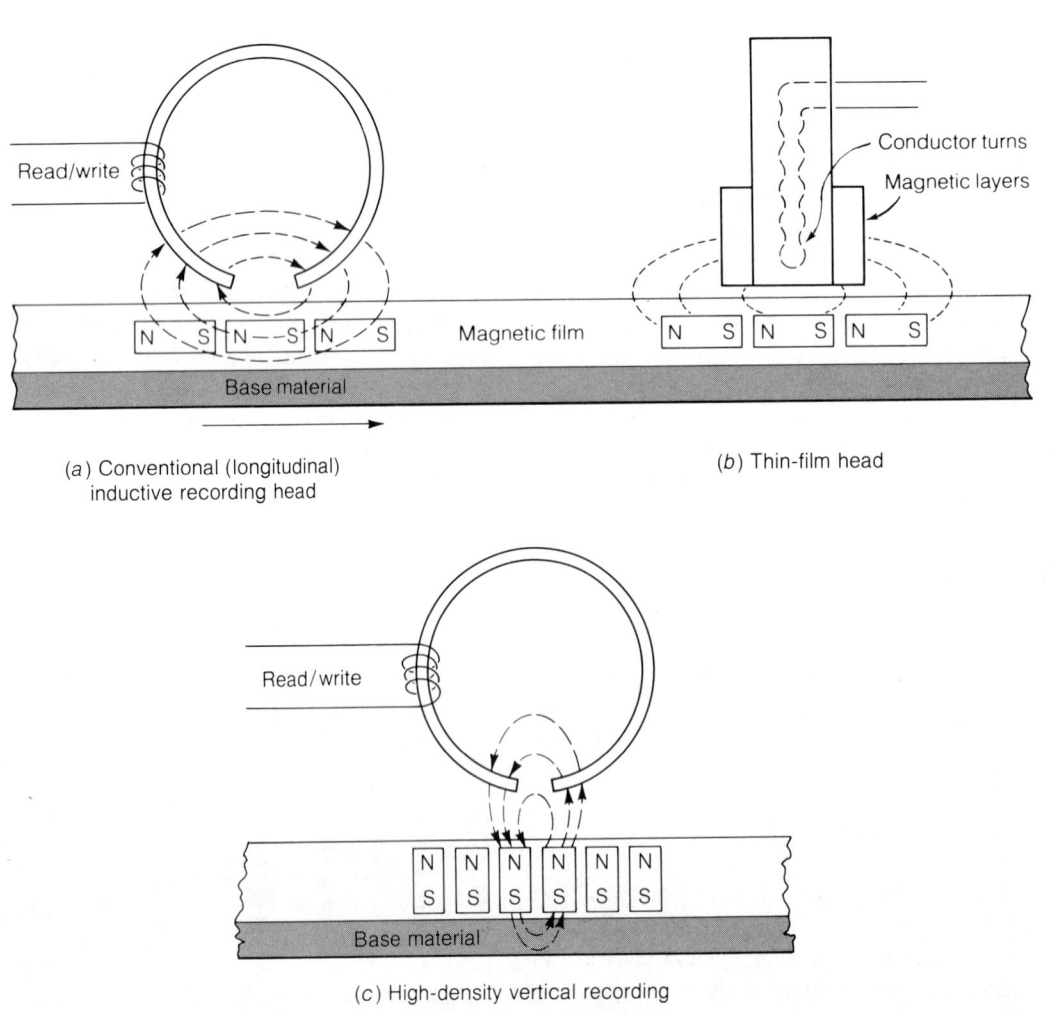

(a) Conventional (longitudinal) inductive recording head

(b) Thin-film head

(c) High-density vertical recording

Figure 6.2 Sensing (reading) and setting (writing) the magnetic domains.

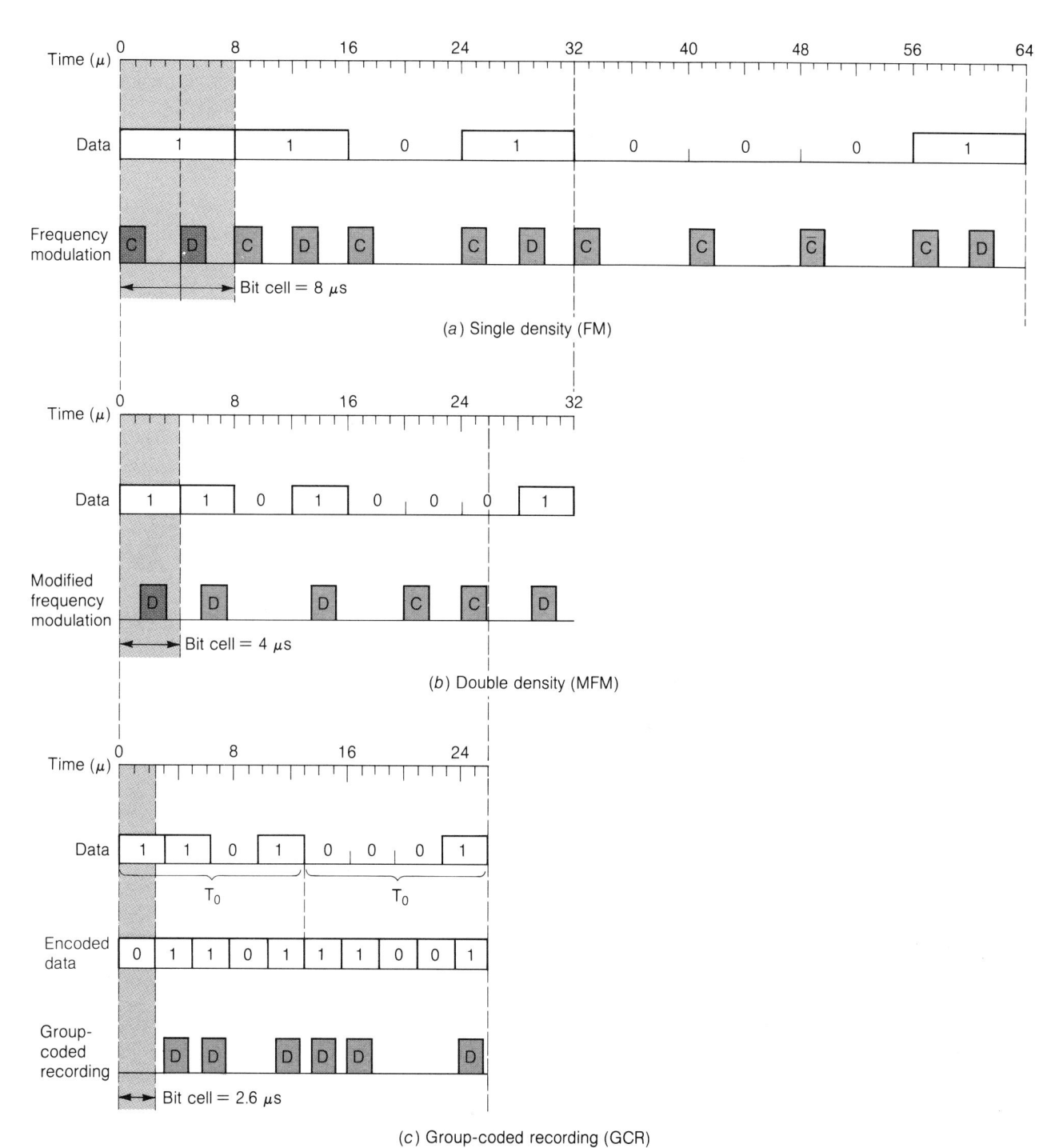

Figure 6.3 Major encoding techniques.

of a pulse stores the logic 0. The technique is called frequency modulation because a sequence of all zeros has frequency f, and a sequence of all ones has a frequency of $2f$. The problem with this "single-density" technique is inefficiency; one-half of the available 8-microsecond space (based on typical floppy disk speed) is used up by clock bits.

By using so-called "double-density" techniques, twice the information can be packed into the same space. Modified frequency modulation—the simplest and most popular double-density technique—is demonstrated in Figure 6.3b. Clock bits are written into the data stream only if data bits have not been written into both the preceding and present bit cells.

Because at no time will a bit cell contain both a clock and a data bit, each cell can be made half as large (4 microseconds).

Since each clock pulse, present or not, still requires space (a clock window) on the recording medium, we can increase density further by totally eliminating the clock pulses. However, suppose we have a long string of zeros; how will we maintain synchronization? The answer is *group-coded recording* (GCR). By means of GCR (Figure 6.3c), each byte of data to be written to the disk is divided into two nibbles. Each nibble is translated into 5-bit codes *including at least one flux reversal to maintain synchronization*. Upon reading from the disk, the process is reversed. GCR encoded data uses approximately 65% of the space required for double-density recording (2.6 microseconds).

Formatting

In any storage medium, identification of the data, synchronization between memory and CPU, and detection of errors are just as important as the information itself. Therefore, data stored on a magnetic medium usually are cradled in a complex format that allows for identification, synchronization, buffering, and error detection. Figure 6.4 shows a typical format in which the data have been divided into a number of sectors. Each sector is identical in form and contains the following fields: marks, gaps, addresses, error-detection bytes, and data.

The gaps act as buffer zones between information-containing areas and allow time for such actions as head movement, switching between read and write modes, and compensation for slight differences between read and write speeds of the magnetic medium. The marks (often consisting of a series of ones) signal the start of address and data fields and provide synchronization between the data medium and the internal electronics. The address field gives the address of each sector and allows the system to verify the address of each data field. Space is provided in both the address and data fields to check for errors. Many variations of this basic format are possible.

Error Detection

The error checks in both the address and data fields can be simple parity checks in which an extra parity bit is added to each data word so the total number of ones is even (for even parity) or odd (for odd parity). Periodic checking of the parity will reveal if a data bit has been inadvertently switched.

A more efficient method, which uses less overall space, is called the *checksum* method. All the data bytes in a data field are added and any carries beyond two bytes are ignored. At any time, the data bytes can be added again and the new checksum compared with the original. If no errors have accrued, the two sums will agree.

Nearly the ultimate in error-checking sophistication is known as *cyclic redundancy checking* (CRC). This method is particularly well suited to the detection of multiple bit errors that occur in bursts—a common problem in data communication.

The CRC method is based on simple mathematical theory. First of all, we must understand how a block of digital data can be written as a polynomial. Arbitrarily choosing the data word 10011, we see how a polynomial is formed from the data word by using the data bits as coefficients for each term:

$$
\begin{array}{lccccc}
 & 1 & 0 & 0 & 1 & 1 \\
\text{Step 1:} & a_4 x^4 & + a_3 x^3 & + a_2 x^2 & + a_1 x & + a_0 \\
\text{Step 2:} & 1x^4 & + 0x^3 & + 0x^2 & + 1x & + 1 \\
\text{Step 3:} & x^4 & & & + x & + 1 \\
\end{array}
$$

Therefore, $10011 = x^4 + x + 1$.

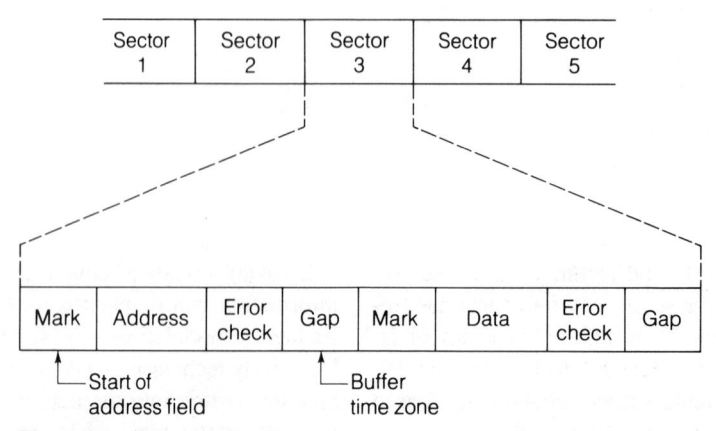

Figure 6.4 Formatting serial data.

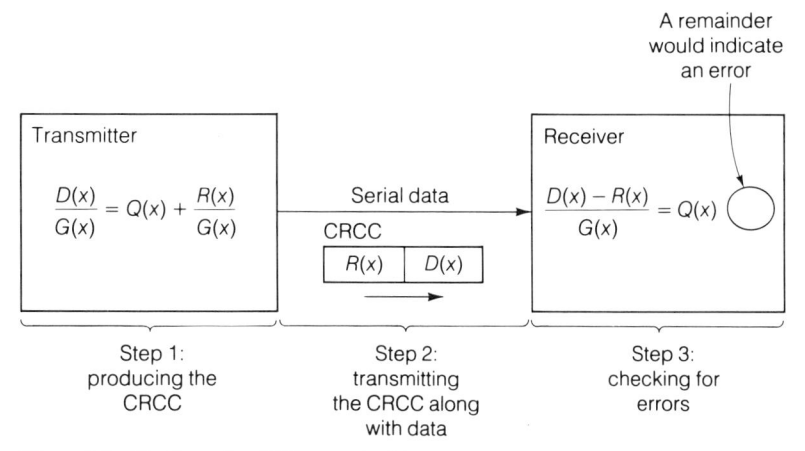

Figure 6.5 The three-step CRC error-checking process.

When this data polynomial (*Dx*) is divided by a generator polynomial (*Gx*), a remainder (*Rx*) is formed:

$$\frac{D(x)}{G(x)} = Q(x) + \frac{R(x)}{G(x)} \quad \text{where } R(x) = \text{CRCC}$$

The remainder, which is shorter than the original polynomial, will be a unique number for each data block. The remainder is known as a *cyclic-redundancy-check character* (CRCC). Rewriting the equation, we see how errors are revealed:

$$\frac{D(x) - R(x)}{G(x)} = Q(x) + 0$$

That is, if the remainder is subtracted from the data polynomial and the result divided by the generator polynomial, the division takes place an even number of times and *no remainder will be generated*. This fact forms the basis of the CRC method.

As shown by Figure 6.5, three steps are involved in the CRC process:

- *Step 1—Generation of the CRCC*. The data polynomial is divided by the generator polynomial to produce the CRCC (remainder polynomial).
- *Step 2—Transmission*. The CRCC is included with the data and transmitted.
- *Step 3—Error checking*. The CRCC remainder polynomial is subtracted from the data polynomial, and the result is divided by the same generator polynomial. If the remainder is zero, the message was transmitted without error. If a remainder appears, it tells us the data stream picked up an error.

A popular generator polynomial is:

$$G(x) = x^{16} + x^{15} + x^5 + 1$$

The higher the order of the generator polynomial, the greater the probability of detecting an error, but the more difficult the implementation.

Error-Checking-and-Correcting (ECC) Codes

The spread of microcomputer systems to critical real-time operations—such as banking and process control—demands that errors be automatically detected *and* corrected. The CRCC method, highly effective in detecting errors, is not so effective in correcting them.

For intermittent errors, most often occurring in semiconductor memories, the *Hamming code* is the most common error-correcting code. By processing parity bits interspersed with data bits, an incorrect bit can be located and automatically toggled to the correct value. Figure 6.6 details the process for a 4-bit word. Let's follow the action and see how the number 9 (1001), which picked up an error in bit position 3 and incorrectly became a $B, is automatically corrected back to a 9.

The process begins with parity-bit generation. As shown in Figure 6.6*a*, three parity bits are generated from exclusive-OR combinations of the 4 data bits and added to the data word at selected locations. During data storage in semiconductor memory, the data/parity word picked up an error in position 6 (perhaps due to an alpha particle). When the data word is read, the position of the error is obtained by exclusive-OR combinations of the data and parity bits. Once the error location is pinpointed, it is toggled to the correct value by a final exclusive-OR process (see Figure 6.6*b*).

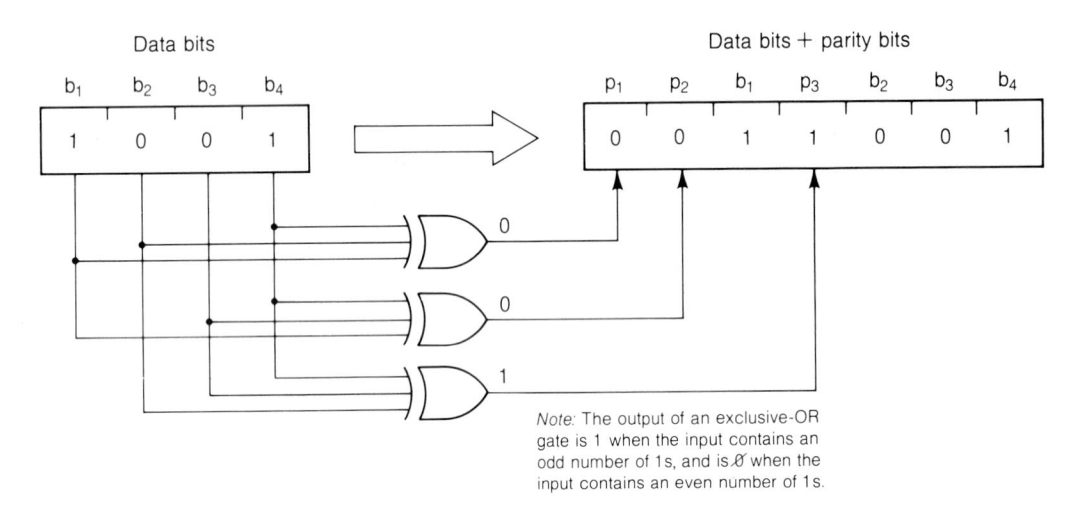

(a) Parity bit generation for number 9

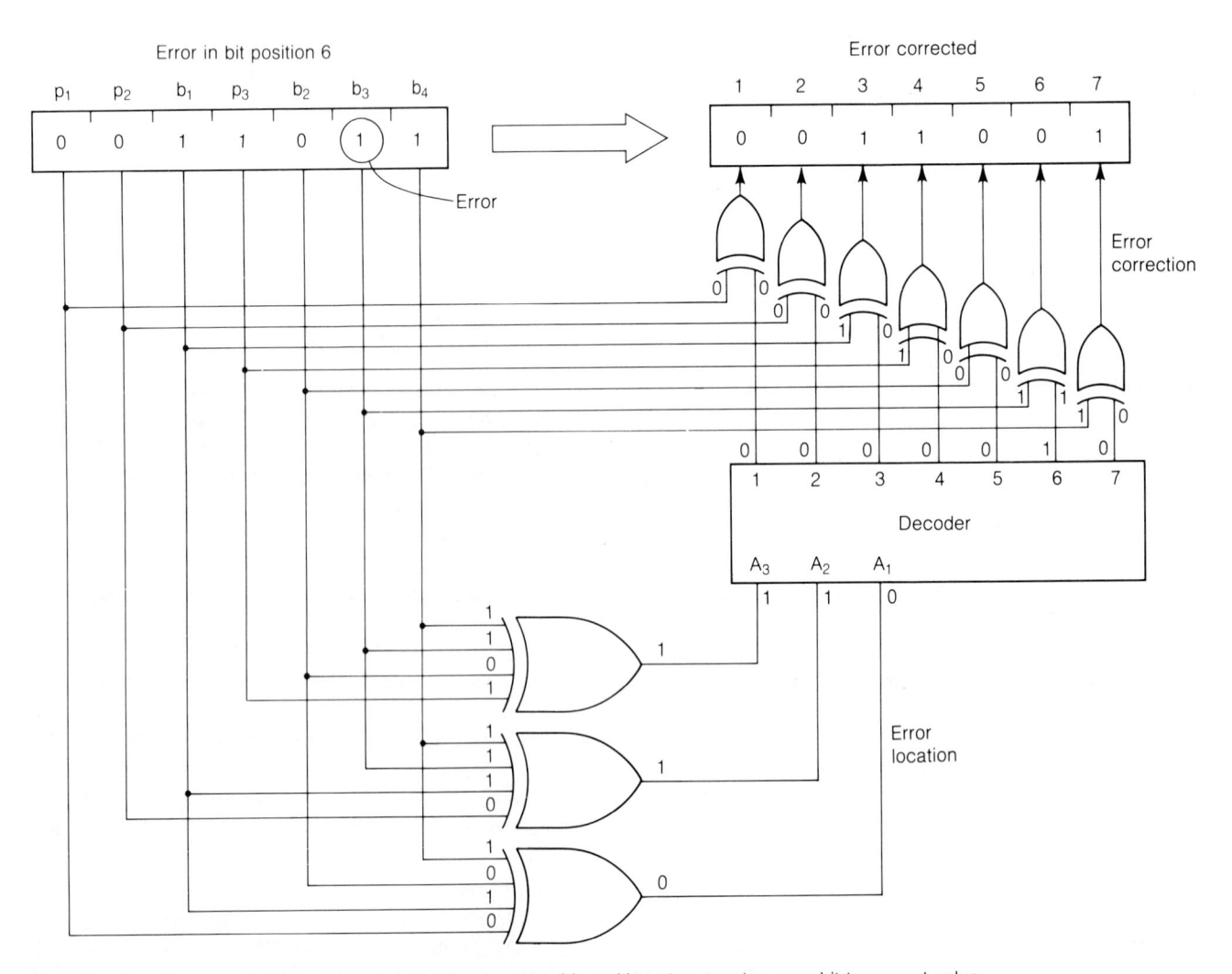

Note: The output of an exclusive-OR gate is 1 when the input contains an odd number of 1s, and is 0 when the input contains an even number of 1s.

(b) Error correction first locates error bit position, then toggles error bit to correct value

Figure 6.6 Hamming error correction.

Although error-correcting codes, such as the Hamming code, are bit wasteful and require complex on-board circuitry, memory boards with built-in ECC circuits can be 300 times more reliable than conventional memory boards.

ECC codes will come into widespread use as microcomputers take on more and more tasks in which high reliability is essential.

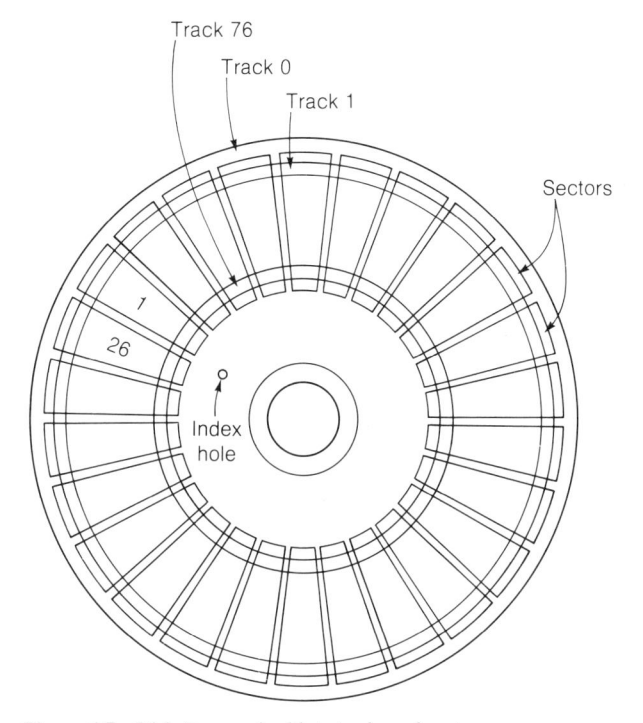

Figure 6.7 Diskette organized into tracks and sectors.

SECONDARY MEMORY SYSTEMS

Floppy Disks (300 RPM)

Convenience is the reason floppy-disk technology is such a popular form of auxiliary and backup storage for microcomputers. It is convenient to store music on records, and it is convenient to store binary data on floppy disks—a storage medium remarkably close in structure to an ordinary 45-rpm record. Flexibility of the recording medium (called a *diskette*) is achieved by the use of a thin section of Mylar as the base material on which the iron oxide is coated. Data are organized on the diskette in concentric tracks, each divided into a number of sectors (similar to a dart board). The standard 8-inch diskette illustrated in Figure 6.7 has 77 tracks and 26 sectors per track.

As shown in Figure 6.8, the diskette is contained within an envelope and is simply plugged into the record/play unit. During read or write activity, the diskette rotates within the low-friction plastic case at approximately 360 rpm. The radially shaped access slot allows the read/write head to move to the proper track and scan the surface of the disk. The large center hole allows the disk to be spun, and the small index hole is used to locate the first sector.

Figure 6.9 shows how the read/write head is positioned quickly and accurately within the access slot by the use of a stepper motor. Each circular step is translated into one track-to-track distance by a steel band wound over the motor's pulley. A more direct method is to rotate a head screw with a stepper motor, causing the read/write head to move in and out.

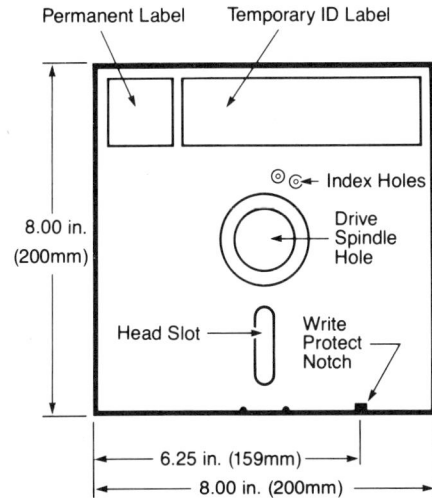

Figure 6.8 Floppy-disk envelope (left) plugged into record/play unit (right).

Addressing A floppy disk is a semi-random-access device. To go from one track/sector location to another, it is not necessary to pass through all intermediate locations.

When an address is sent to the floppy disk system, the read/write head is positioned over the correct track. The system then locates the first sector by waiting for the index hole to pass between the light-source/photodetector combination. By counting sectors from that time, the drive circuitry can determine which sector is passing under the read/write head. To verify that the correct sector has been reached, each track can be formatted to contain the complete track/sector address. Because the IBM 3740 floppy-disk format is in such widespread use, it is presented in Figure 6.10. It includes the expected marks, gaps, addresses, error detection, and data fields.

A newly purchased disk usually is unformatted (blank). Most microcomputers (e.g., Apple II, IBM PC) provide a simple means for formatting blank disks. While running under the *Disk Operating System* (DOS) program, simply type a command such as:

>FORMAT A: (Carriage Return)

The FORMAT *utility* (program contained in DOS) carries out the format operation on the disk stored in drive A, and a track format similar to that of Figure 6.10 is written onto the floppy disk (of course the data fields are left blank). When track and sector identification is prerecorded by the manufacturer, the diskette is called *preformatted*.

Soft-sectored vs hard-sectored format The soft-sectored format just covered relies on a single index hole and software formatting to locate and verify data sectors. Hard sectoring includes up to 32 sector holes (in addition to the index hole) evenly spaced about the diskette to locate up to 32 corresponding sectors. Because the need for address bytes has been largely eliminated, six additional sectors can be added to each track. (Since addresses cannot be verified, the price you pay for these six additional sectors is reduced reliability.)

Capacity Using 73 tracks (four tracks normally contain no data), with 26 sectors per track and 128 bytes of data per sector, a quick calculation will show that the typical diskette can store nearly 250,000 bytes of information. Double-density disks, which make use of the MFM encoding technique of Figure 6.3*b*, can double this figure. And by using double-sided, double-density diskettes (which require a special double-sided head assembly), we approach the magic 1-megabyte figure. Continued increases in bit density and improvements in head-positioning systems should soon provide the 10-megabyte, 8-inch floppy.

Speed and reliability On the average it requires approximately one-fifth of a second to position the read/write head over the correct sector (this is known as a *seek operation*). Such a relatively long time is misleading, however, because information is usually stored in large sequential blocks. Once the correct starting sector has been located, data can be read from the diskette at the rate of approximately 200K bits/s.

The term most commonly used to specify overall speed is *average access time,* the average amount of time required to access data from the beginning of a read operation to the end. For floppy disks, average access times of 150 to 250 ms are typical (a million times slower than primary memory).

Reliability of magnetic-based systems is determined by the average number of bits that can be read from the system before one bit is found to be in error. For a soft-sectored floppy-disk system, a typical reliability value lies between 1 error per 10^8 and 1 error per 10^{10} bits read. Since physical contact is made between diskette and read/write head, the magnetic medium is subject to wear. Therefore, another important reliability specification is mean time between failures (MTBF)—typically 8,000 hours under normal usage.

Disk controller and operating system A floppy-disk controller is the interface electronics between the floppy-disk system and the CPU. It must perform a wide variety of tasks:

- Read and write operations
- Parallel-to-serial and serial-to-parallel conversions
- Seek operations and other control commands
- Address verification
- CRC error detection
- Overall synchronization between CPU and floppy

These various functions are divided between hardware (disk-controller board) and software (Disk Operating System). The primary function of the DOS is to manage the transfer of data between primary and secondary memory.

As explained in greater depth in Chapter 22, modern Disk Operating Systems—which are usually stored on floppy disk—go beyond simple disk I/O operations, and allow the operator to perform a variety of operations on *files* (a named program stored on a floppy disk).

The Minifloppy

Also popular among microcomputer users is the Minifloppy™, a less-expensive, scaled-down version of the full-size floppy system. The disk size is reduced from 8 to $5\frac{1}{4}$ inches and the number of tracks from 77 to 40, with a comparable reduction in total storage capacity (approximately

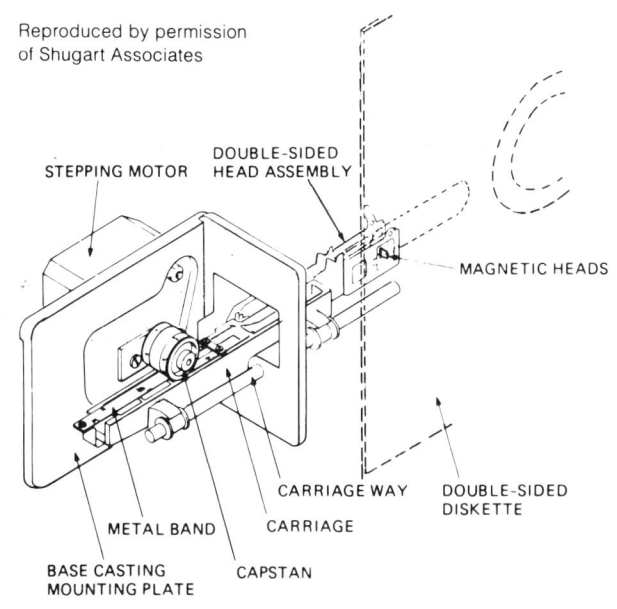

Figure 6.9 Linear-band head-positioning mechanism.

100 kbytes using formatted single density). Word processors, personal computers, and intelligent terminals are typical applications for the Minifloppy.

The Microfloppy

The newly emerging 3- to 4-inch *microfloppy* will further reduce the size of personal computers, and may spearhead a number of significant departures from conventional design.

For example, using recently developed vertical recording techniques (Figure 6.2c), in which the magnetic particles are aligned at right angles to the floppy disk surface rather than horizontal to the surface, a 3.5-inch platter should be capable of storing 3 megabytes on each side (with 100 megabytes possible!).

For greater protection, the recording medium may be enclosed in a rigid plastic case and can be fitted with a head-slot shield which automatically recedes when the disk is inserted.

The microfloppy is smaller, sturdier, and easier to handle than the mini and full-size floppy; it should make steady inroads into the conventional $5\frac{1}{4}$ and 8-inch floppy markets. Since the Microfloppy Industry Committee (MIC) has given its blessing to the $3\frac{1}{2}$-inch system, this intermediate size should gain favored market acceptance and emerge as the de facto standard.

RAM Disk

A basic tenet of memory hierarchy is that memory price is directly related to its speed. That is why a large program is broken into parts when stored on floppy disk; each piece loaded into main (primary) memory prior to its processing turn and after execution that portion of primary memory used by the program section is freed for other purposes (a technique known as *folding* or *overlaying*). Using *virtual memory* techniques, the computer automatically folds programs and data between primary and secondary memory.

However, with the dramatic drop in primary memory prices (approaching that of a floppy system), the *ramdisk* has emerged. A ramdisk is a circuit board of RAM chips that the computer treats as a disk drive. To use a ramdisk, simply transfer the information from floppy to ramdisk, and tell the computer (through special software) to access the ramdisk rather than the floppy disk. When finished, copy to ramdisk back to the floppy to save any updates. The primary advantage of a ramdisk is a 50-fold improvement in speed over the floppy.

Winchester Disks

Disk memories strongly resemble floppy-disk systems (Figure 6.11). The major difference is that the iron-oxide recording medium is coated onto a rigid aluminum base rather than flexible Mylar. In general, disk systems represent a general upgrading in precision, performance, and price (although the cost per bit usually is lower than for a floppy system).

Like the floppy system, information is stored serially in concentric tracks (typically, 1,000 per surface) on the magnetic-film medium. The disk is spun at high speeds (3,600 rpm), and a precision stepper motor positions the read/write head over the proper track. Sophisticated controller circuitry accepts the commands from the CPU and directs and activates the read/write head.

Winchester technology, introduced by IBM in 1973, is a package of refinements to this basic disk system. It is now spreading throughout the microcomputer industry as fast as its namesake, the Winchester rifle, spread through the early West. (In its conceptual stage, the Winchester disk was a dual-drive, 30-megabyte system. Although no longer in use, this "30-30" arrangement accounts for the code name "Winchester.")

Included in the Winchester technology package are:

- A lightweight, aerodynamic read/write head that floats on an air cushion a mere half micrometer above the surface of the spinning disk.
- Sealed disk environment.
- Filtered internal atmosphere.
- Very thin magnetic-oxide coating.
- Very high reliability (1 bit in 10^{11}).
- High track and bit densities (over 1,000 tracks/in and over 10,000 bits/in are projected).
- Read/write head rests on lubricated disk surface when

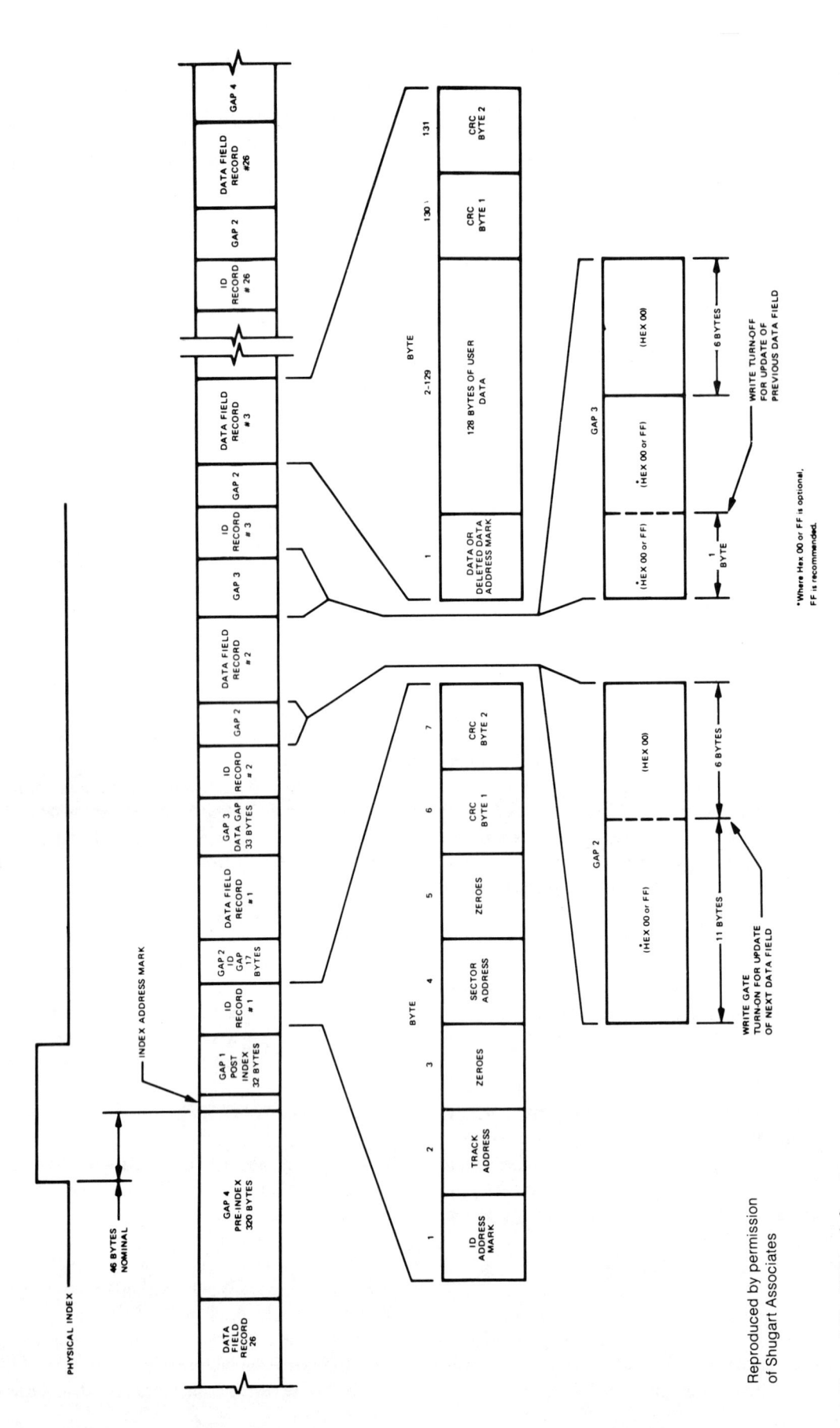

Figure 6.10 IBM track format.

not in operation, thereby eliminating head "crashes" (catastrophic collision of head and disk).

A key feature of Winchester technology is the small gap between the read/write head and rotating disk. The smaller the gap, the greater the data density. When you realize that a fingerprint would deposit a "mountain" of oil some five times higher than the half-micrometer flying height of the read/write head, you begin to realize why the head/disk assembly operates in a hermetically sealed, filtered environment.

Disk sizes range from the recently available 3.5 and 3.9 inches (100 mm), to the floppy-compatible $5\frac{1}{4}$ and 8 inches, to the large-scale 14-inch unit, covering the capacity spectrum from 5 to 600 megabytes and more. The $5\frac{1}{4}$-inch micro-Winchester (Figure 6.12) should prove popular with the microcomputer set. It is the same size as the Minifloppy, yet can store a respectable 6–15 megabytes of unformatted data. (Be aware that the $5\frac{1}{4}$-inch floppy is called a *Mini*-floppy and the $5\frac{1}{4}$-inch Winchester is known as a *micro*-Winchester.)

With an average access time approaching 25 ms and transfer rates exceeding 5 megabits per second (Mb/s), the Winchester far outstrips the floppy in performance.

Even the major drawback of the conventional Winchester when compared with the floppy (the permanently sealed Winchester disk cannot be removed and therefore offers no

Courtesy of PRIAM Associates

Figure 6.11 A 70-megabyte, 8-inch Winchester showing aerodynamic head and head-positioning assembly.

Courtesy of Seagate Associates

Figure 6.12 The Shugart micro-Winchester.

I/O capability) is overcome by the *removable* hard-disk cartridge. The removable Winchester disk offers all the advantages of the floppy, but with vastly increased storage capacity, access speed, reliability, and convenience of use.

Although removable hard disks are available in all four popular sizes (3.9, $5\frac{1}{4}$, 8, and 14 inches), only the more inexpensive 3.9-inch hard-disk cartridge is in a position to compete with the floppy disk. Only time will tell if the removable hard disk will relegate the floppy to the same fate as the nearly obsolete punched card and cassette tape.

Figure 6.13 compares the major characteristics of the floppy disk with the Winchester disk. All specifications will vary with time.

The popularity of the Winchester guarantees that a steady stream of improvements and modifications will appear on the market. Two recent innovations include *thin-film heads* and *servo positioners*. Thin-film heads (Figure 6.2b), which allow track/head distance to be reduced, will speed the micro-Winchester toward the 40-megabyte capacity, the 8-inch to the 400-megabyte, and the 14-inch to the 2.5-gigabyte. (Using vertical recording techniques, even these remarkable capacities will soon be far surpassed.) Servo positioners, which locate tracks by reading location information preset into the disk, will both increase density and decrease access times—all at reduced cost.

Bubble Memory

Although several companies have dropped out of the bubble-memory race, it still remains the rising star of secondary storage. Its major advantages over all other forms of sec-

	Capacity Mbytes	Cost/ Kbytes	Avg. Access	Data Rate Mbits/sec	AC Req'd	Voltages Required	Physical Size	Power Dissipation
Micro-Winchester (ST500)*	6.38	.144¢	170ms	5.0	no	+12 +5	5¾ X 3¼ X 8	30 watts
Double-sided minifloppy (SA450)**	.437	.744¢	298ms	.25	no	+12 +5	5¾ X 3¼ X 8	14.5 watts
8-inch Winchester (SA1000)**	5.33	.187¢	70ms	4.34	yes	+24 +5 −5	4.62 X 8.55 X 14.5	150 watts
Double-sided floppy (SA851)**	1.60	.368¢	91ms	.5	yes	+24 +5 −5	4.62 X 8.55 X 14.25	57 watts

*Shugart Technology
**Shugart Associates

Figure 6.13 Comparison of floppy disks and Winchesters.

Reproduced by permission of Shugart Associates

ondary storage are its compact size and complete absence of mechanical moving parts. Like other secondary storage devices, it is nonvolatile.

Magnetic bubbles are tiny cylindrical regions of magnetic domains, aligned in opposite polarity to the magnetic domain about them. When viewed under polarized light, they resemble liquid bubbles. They are created by applying a strong magnetic field perpendicular to a thin sheet of magnetic material. Most of the magnetic dipoles will line up with the external magnetic field, but some will not. As the external field grows in strength, the opposing regions will shrink to less than one-millionth of a meter in diameter and become true magnetic bubbles. (If the external magnetic field is increased further, the bubbles will eventually disappear.) The presence of a bubble stores a logic 1, and the absence stores a logic 0. An external permanent magnet supplies the static field required to retain the data when power is removed.

Like liquid bubbles, magnetic bubbles can be made to propagate through their medium. To provide the moving force, various magnetic-alloy patterns (often called *chevrons* because of their early shape) are placed on top of the film layer (Figure 6.14a). Rotating magnetic fields, produced by external orthogonal (right-angle) current-carrying coils, move the bubbles from chevron to chevron in shift-register fashion.

When in active storage, bubbles are synchronously circulated about in many small storage loops, like the rapidly moving teeth of a chain saw. As illustrated by Figure 6.14b, input and output tracks interconnect all the loops and provide a mainline pathway for the input and output of data. (Using many minor loops, rather than a single large storage loop, allows the addressed bubbles to circulate for a shorter average distance before they are read out, thereby greatly improving access times.)

The write process takes place when bubbles are injected into the input track and routed to the proper storage loop. (A bubble generator produces bubbles by replicating an existing bubble within the generator.) Reading takes place as the bubbles released to the output track pass beneath a special pattern of linked chevrons that detect a bubble by changing magnetoresistive properties.

The rotating storage loops give bubble memory its sequential characteristics and relatively slow access time (compared to primary memory) of approximately 5 to 40 ms. Once a block of data is in position, however, it streams out at the rate of over 200 kilobits per second (kb/s). And when several units are operated in parallel, transfer rates of over 100 Mb/s are possible. (In general, bubbles have faster access times than disks, but slower transfer rates.)

Nonvolatility, high storage capacity, fast access, compact size, and ruggedness are the properties that will guarantee bubble memory a place in the marketplace. Perhaps the first task assigned to bubble memory will be to reduce equipment size. Single devices storing 5 to 10 megabytes, in a medium no larger than the size of a postage stamp, should soon be commonplace. Although the interfacing problems have been challenging, single-board bubble-memory systems are now available that include all interfacing electronics.

Recently introduced to the market are bubble cassette systems, bringing I/O capability to the bubble world. A compact read/write unit accepts magnetic bubble cartridges (tiny modules of plug-in bubble memory), filling the need for a removable, nonvolatile, solid-state memory of exceptional durability (no moving parts).

Problems still remain with bubble-memory technology, but if past history is any guide, all eventually will be overcome. It remains to be seen if the price/performance ratio

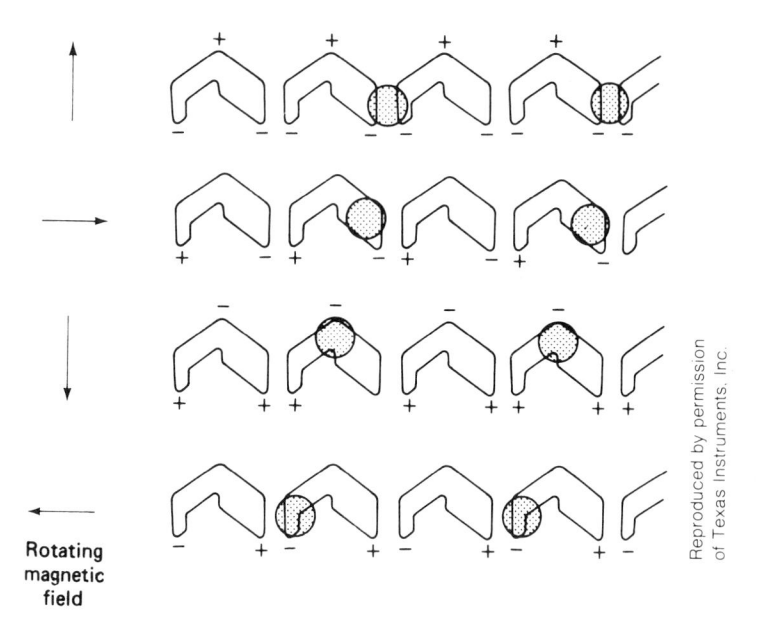

(a) Bubble propagated by rotating magnetic field

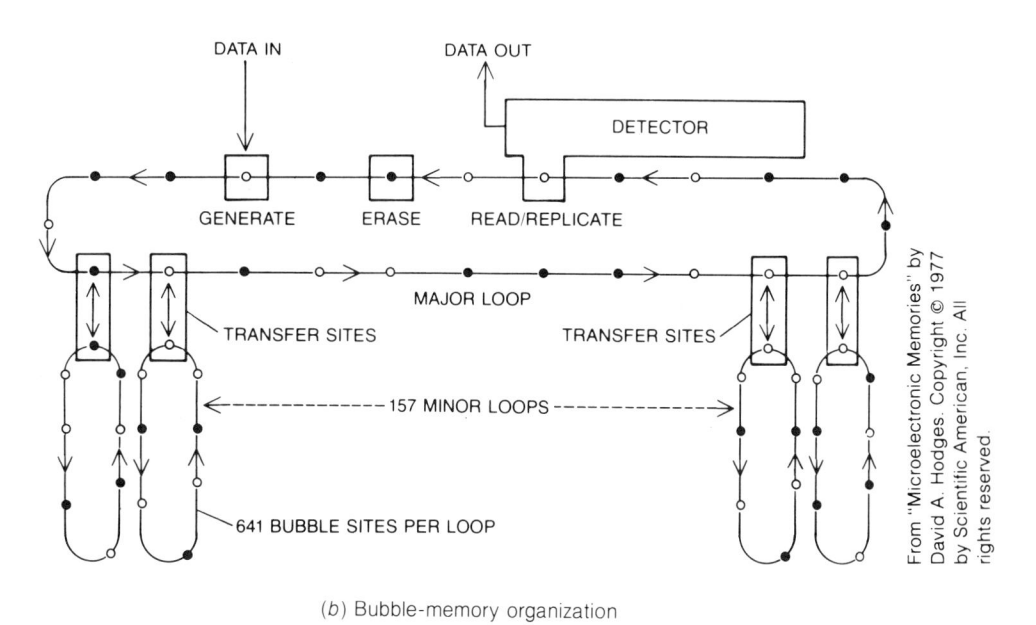

(b) Bubble-memory organization

Figure 6.14 Bubble memory.

of bubble memory will significantly displace the market position of floppy and Winchester disk systems.

Charge-Coupled-Devices (CCD)

In basic terms, a CCD memory is a large-capacity, very fast, serial-shift register. Because data bits are stored and transferred in serial format, CCD memory is conceptually similar to bubble memory. The major difference lies in the method of bit storage and transfer.

Figure 6.15 shows the basic structure of a CCD. The source and drain of an MOS transistor are pulled apart and a long string of gates placed between. By applying carefully phased pulses to alternate gates, charge packets injected at the source can be passed bucket-brigade fashion from transistor to transistor. A typical CCD memory array may have 4,096 storage cells with bits circulating at 5 million cycles per second.

Charge-coupled-device memories arrived on the scene with a great deal of fanfare, but have failed to live up to expec-

From "Microelectronic Circuit Elements" by James D. Meindl. Copyright © 1977 by Scientific American, Inc. All rights reserved.

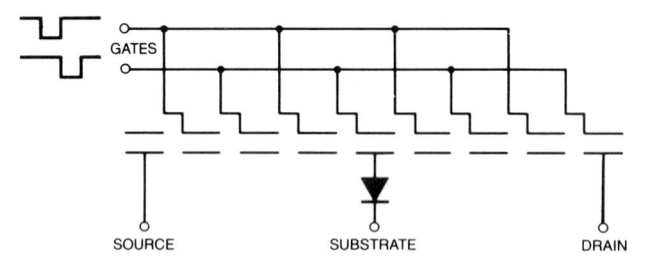

Figure 6.15 Internal structure of charge-coupled device (CCD).

tations. Charge-coupled technology, however, will "live on" because of its applications in imaging and filtering, where a repeating linear pattern of data is required.

BACKUP STORAGE DEVICES

The word *backup* implies protection, and indeed backup devices are often used to save data in the event of catastrophic failure. However, backup memory is more than a simple protection system. Since the spread of Winchester devices, with their typically nonremovable disks, the responsibility for program interchange and updates, exchange of data-bases, and archival storage has passed on to the backup system. To provide these services, backup memory systems must have the capacity for storing large amounts of information at low cost.

Backup memory for microcomputers includes those listed below (note that floppy-disk storage can serve as both backup and secondary storage):

- Half-inch magnetic tape
- Quarter-inch magnetic cartridge
- Floppy disk
- Cassette tape
- Video tape

Magnetic Tape

For proven reliability and low cost, magnetic-tape memory systems have few equals. They have provided reliable data storage for many years and have established an impressive track record of success.

The major advantage of magnetic-tape backup systems is their ability to store large amounts of information at low cost per bit. The major disadvantage is their slow access speed. Using sequential address exclusively, the tape is obliged to pass through all intermediate locations in order to arrive at the desired destination.

Present-day tape systems usually provide 2, 4, or 9 tracks (with future generation tape drives having up to 18 tracks), allowing information to be stored in parallel or serial (9 and 18 tracks allow room for parity bits). Data transfer to and from the tape system also can be either parallel or serial, depending on the interface.

Magnetic-tape drives come in either the conventional *start-stop* version or the newer *streaming-tape* option—the "talk of the town" in magnetic tape technology. Like Winchester technology, streaming-tape technology includes a package of features specifically designed to match well with today's high-speed computer systems. As the name implies, streaming-tape drives are designed to operate at full speed, with the need for frequent starts and stops largely overcome. Reading and writing is designed to take place "on the fly." By reducing the number of starts and stops, transfer rates above 150 kbytes/s are standard. Developed specifically for backup applications, streaming-tape technology has lowered the cost and improved the efficiency of both half-inch and quarter-inch tape systems.

Streaming operation depends on a double-buffering technique (Figure 6.16), which follows the classic producer/consumer problem. In the diagram, the Winchester disk is the producer, sending data to the ring of memory buffers, and the tape is the consumer, receiving information from the buffers. During data-transfer operations, the producer (disk) fills the first-in/first-out buffers from one end, while the tape (consumer) empties the buffers from the other. When

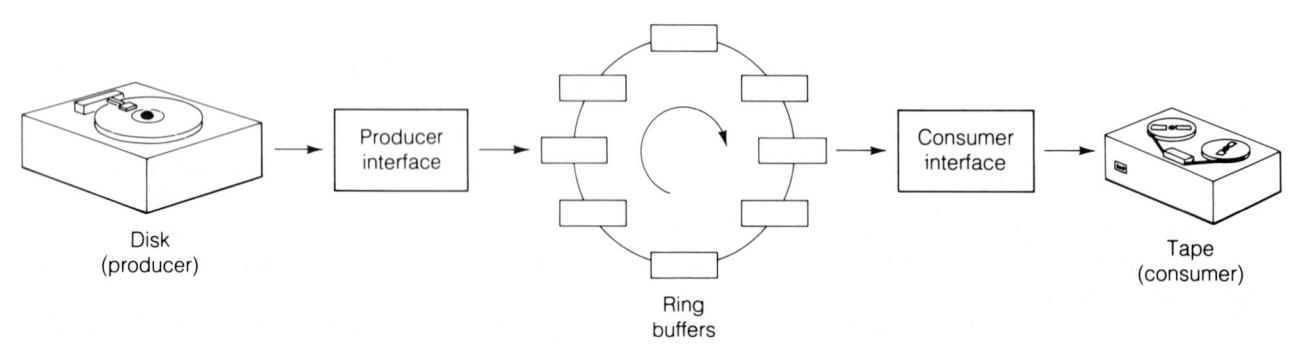

Figure 6.16 Double-buffering technique, which maintains data "streaming" to "consumer" at a steady rate.

data are to be written back into the Winchester from the tape, the roles of producer and consumer are reversed. The operation can be likened to filling a bucket in spurts, but allowing the water to flow out a hole in the bottom in a steady *stream* (of course, the bucket cannot be allowed either to overflow or to empty).

A disadvantage of streaming-tape drives is that the data on the tape cannot be directly accessed by the CPU. Start/stop tape drives, which store data in typically 4-kilobyte individually addressable blocks, overcome this drawback, but at much greater cost. Required to stop and start between each block of data, a high-torque motor is required to accelerate the tape to read/write speed in the required intergap distance.

Half-Inch Magnetic Tape

For very high-capacity backup storage at minimum cost, the half-inch streaming-tape systems have few equals (Figure 6.17). Nearly 50 Mbytes of data can be stored on a single reel of magnetic tape costing less than $10; 150-Mbyte storage on a single 7-inch reel is a realistic prediction. A complete half-inch system is no larger than the Winchester device it must back up, and great strides have been made in easing the once painful task of interfacing the tape drive to the computer system. Most half-inch systems are IBM compatible and are formatted accordingly. With a transfer rate of over 1 Mb/s, the half-inch streaming-tape system is effective backup for secondary systems of more than 30 or 40 Mbytes. With error rates of 10^{10} or better, the user can expect only a single error in 200 $10\frac{1}{2}$-inch reels of tape. With fully automatic loading, reels of tape can be interchanged quickly and easily, offering excellent I/O capability.

Quarter-Inch Cartridge Tape

When it comes to ease of handling and loading, quarter-inch cartridge-tape systems are unsurpassed. Operated as easily

Courtesy of Cipher Data Products, Inc.

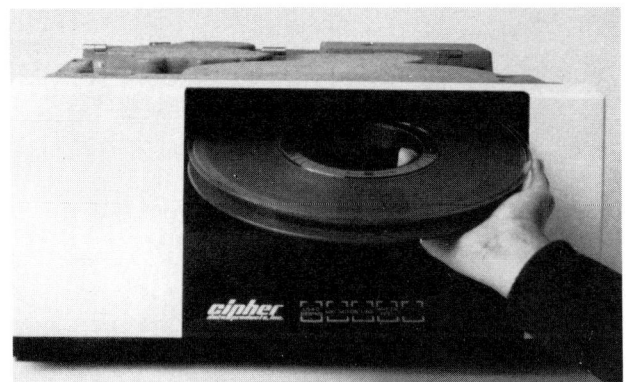

Figure 6.17 Cipher half-inch streaming-tape drive.

Courtesy of Data Electronics

Figure 6.18 Quarter-inch cartridge-tape system.

as a stereo or video-tape system, few memory devices so closely resemble a common consumer item (Figure 6.18). The tape is environmentally protected, compact, easily stored and transported, and can be used with no special training. Its 2- to 75-Mbyte capacity range is well matched to the Winchester disk and other midsized secondary systems, and its transfer rate is approaching a healthy 1 Mb/s (allowing a typical Winchester to be backed up in minutes). It offers a reliability approaching that of the Winchester (10^{10} bits), and is available in conventional start/stop action or the new high-speed streaming action.

Disk-Drive Controllers

To ease the task of interfacing an array of secondary/backup systems with the CPU, the *universal disk-drive controller* is the answer. The SA1400 disk-drive controller from Shugart Associates (Figure 6.19) is a typical system, performing control functions and data transfers between CPU and a mixture of up to four Winchester, floppy, and quarter-inch cartridge drives.

As intelligent peripheral devices flourish, the need for a more sophisticated interface grows. The goal is universal mutual compatibility between all peripheral devices, allowing full intermixing of disk drives, tapes, printers, and all other popular intelligent peripherals—regardless of manufacturer and without modification to system software or hardware.

Although such an ideal situation probably will never materialize (too many opposing viewpoints), when the dust

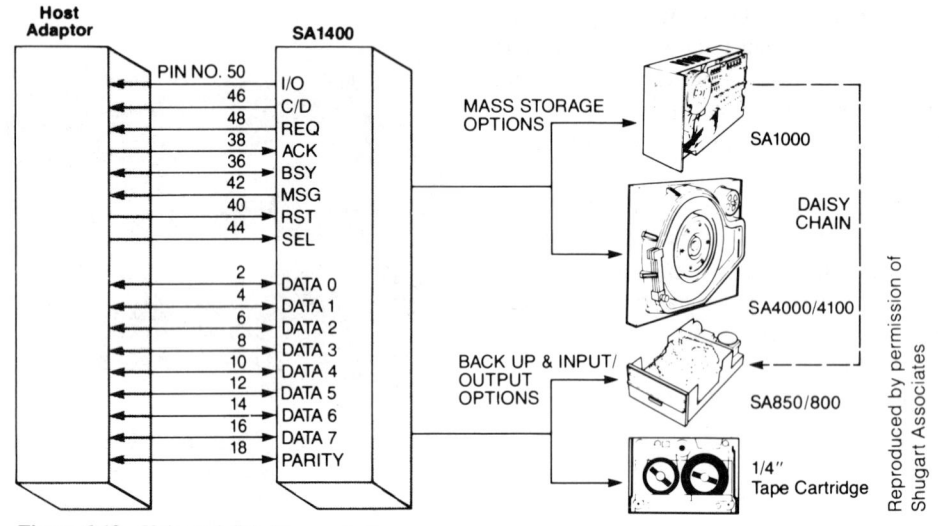

Figure 6.19 Universal disk-drive controller.

settles any proposed ANSI (American National Standards Institute) standard will most certainly resemble one of the following:

- Shugart Associates System Interface (SASI)
- Small Computer System Interface (SCSI)
- Intelligent Standard Interface (ISI)
- Intelligent Peripheral Interface (IPI)

Audio-Cassette Recording

Audio-cassette recording has prospered because it excels in one vital area: cost. To attain storage at ultralow cost, nearly all other factors had to be sacrificed. Although a cassette can store up to 1 Mbyte of data, the data-transfer rate is only 150 bytes/s and the average access time can be several minutes. The tape is subject to wear from high frictional contact with the head, and the reliability is low (1 bit in 10^8). Furthermore, the operator must perform manually many of the control operations done automatically by other systems.

As with all magnetic-based systems, the digital information must be encoded into a form the recording medium can accept. Because low-cost recorders are plagued by limited frequency response (300 to 3000 Hz) and poor tape-speed control, any encoding scheme would have to account for these limitations. The most popular encoding technique used with cassette tapes is the hobbyist-oriented *Kansas City standard* (formulated by a committee that met in Kansas City in November 1975). Using frequency-shift-keying (FSK) techniques, the system converts each logic 1 bit to 8 cycles of 2400 Hz and each logic 0 bit to 4 cycles of 1200 Hz. Therefore, as shown in Figure 6.20, a Kansas City storage system consists of three components. The *modulator* converts the digital stream of highs and lows (ones and zeros) to 2400 and 1200 Hz tones—which are recorded by the cassette deck. When the data are to be read back from the

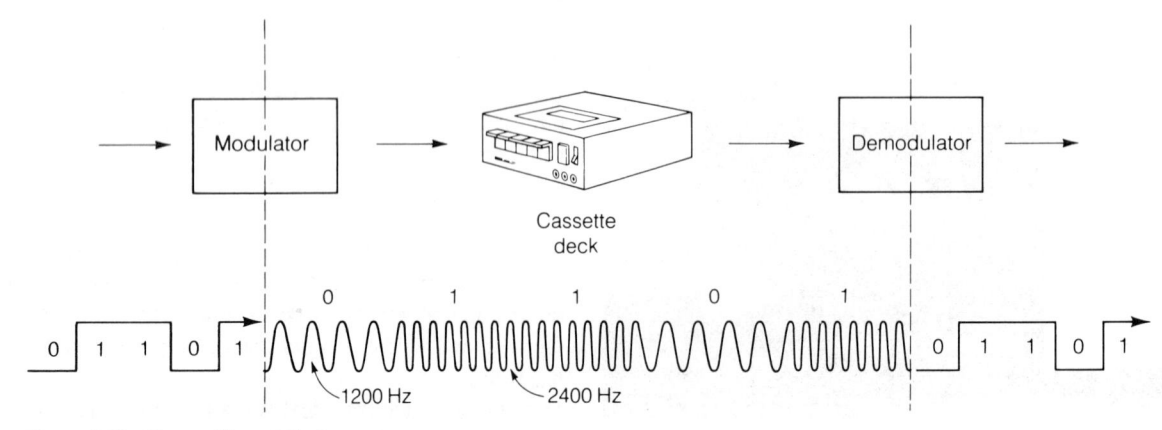

Figure 6.20 Kansas City standard cassette storage.

tape decks, the tones are converted back into high and low voltages (*demodulated*).

Video-Cassette Recording

Accompanying the growing popularity of commercial videotape recorders (VTRs) are techniques for storing digital data on video cassettes. An inexpensive system is shown in Figure 6.21. Called the *Corvus mirror*, it interfaces between the Winchester disk and VTR and converts digital signals to video signals, suitable for recording directly onto a commercially available video recorder. It has a capacity of 100 million bytes and, using CRC techniques, an estimated nonrecoverable error rate of one error per 15,000 hours. Data transfers at approximately 1.1 Mbauds, allowing the contents of an entire 10-Mbyte hard disk to be dumped to the VTR in 10 minutes.

Optical Storage

Since low cost per bit, high storage capacity, and I/O capability are the prime attributes of backup memory, optical storage systems should soon be prominent features on the backup storage "landscape."

The simplest optical (beam-addressed) memory device employs a laser beam to burn holes (1 micrometer in diameter) in the coating of a disk. A hole burned may be equivalent to a logic 1, and a hole not burned may be equivalent to a logic 0. During readout, another laser beam (of lower power) is positioned over the proper track of the disk, and it determines the logic value by reflected laser light—that is, if a hole is present, the light is transmitted; if not, the light is reflected.

Courtesy of Corvus Systems, Inc.

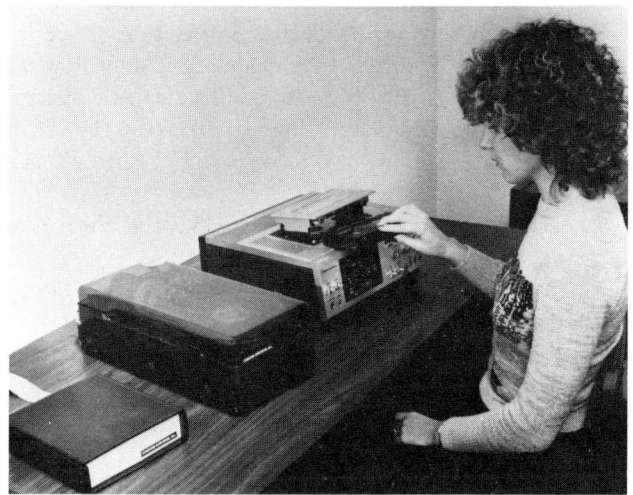

Figure 6.21 The Corvus mirror, a low-cost, large-capacity, videotape backup for Winchester disk systems.

An amazing 1.3 billion letters or numbers (words) can be stored on a single "platter" no more than 5 or 6 inches in diameter, and at much lower cost than a magnetic system. Its attractive price tag and its ability to store large amounts of data at high density make the optical disk ideal for archival storage.

The new home-use videodisk systems are also emerging as a means of gigabyte data storage. A pulse-width encoded signal is used to modulate a laser focused on a glass disk. The laser etches tiny pits into the surface of the disk. During playback, reflected laser light is broken by the pits to reconstruct the original signal.

The only major drawback to optical storage at the present time is that it is a read-only technology; the data, once written, cannot be changed. However, renewed efforts into erasable optical media—involving such exotic subjects as magneto-optic materials and amorphous-to-crystalline phase transitions—should soon result in read/write optical storage systems that will give all-magnetic technology a run for its money.

Secondary/Backup Hybrid Systems

When we combine the precision and capacity of the Winchester disk with the convenience and low cost of the cartridge backup, we create the fixed-disk/removable-cartridge memory system. It provides both secondary and backup capabilities in a single package.

A typical system may employ both fixed and removable Winchester disks in the same system. The removable cartridge is inserted above the fixed disks and engages with the drive-motor spindle and head-actuator assembly. When looking at this option, the user must weigh the relatively higher cost of the cartridges (compared to floppy and tape) against the precision, speed, and convenience of Winchester technology.

Another option (dubbed the "Flinchester" storage system) combines an 8-inch Winchester with a double-sided floppy-disk system. Also available in the area of hybrid secondary/backup systems is an 8-inch Winchester disk drive with an integrated cartridge-tape backup (Figure 6.22). We can expect the number of hybrid offerings to greatly increase in the years ahead.

SELECTING THE RIGHT SECONDARY/BACKUP COMBINATION

Although the concept of backup is hardly a new idea, the spread of Winchester storage—the little giant of the secondary world—has reopened the entire question: What secondary/backup combination will best fit my needs? It is not an easy question to answer. The following list includes just

Figure 6.22 Hybrid Winchester/tape storage system.

a few of the considerations leading to the correct secondary/backup choice:

- Do I need backup at all when using Winchester technology with its spectacular 1×10^{11} data-reliability specification?
- Must my entire database be backed up each day? Would it be efficient for me to back up an 80-Mbyte Winchester with a 1-Mbyte floppy, or should I choose the higher-capacity streaming-tape drives?
- Do I need I/O capability?
- How much access time do I need? For transitional (frequent) backup, the higher access times of the floppy are attractive. For daily backup, the lower-cost magnetic- or video-tape approach may be best.
- Who is going to use my system? Should I go for the convenience and ease of the quarter-inch cartridge?
- Can I easily integrate a backup device into my existing system? From the standpoint of file management and interfacing, the floppy is practically a twin of the Winchester. Is there a disk-drive controller to meet my needs?
- Are tape systems better for archival storage?
- Will I be transporting data (through the mail, for example)? If so, cartridge and floppy are excellent transportable mediums.
- Will the new removable hard-disk systems solve all my secondary/backup problems?
- How much can I afford to spend?
- How available are the various options?
- Should I opt for the newer video backup techniques, even though they are not yet in widespread use?

Clearly, those shopping for the right secondary/backup combination should carefully consider their overall needs and not be persuaded solely on the basis of one or two outstanding features of each system.

INTELLIGENT-MACHINE UPDATE

With access to secondary and backup memory systems, our intelligent machine now has a vast data library at its disposal. No longer is it restricted to a small primary memory book of 256 pages. Now, with Winchester storage and archival backup, it has quick and easy access to the entire collected works of its software library. Endowed with ports to the outside world, and with a memory system of great speed, capacity, and flexibility, it is now ready for the final step—its passage into the second industrial revolution, the era of the true intelligent machine.

QUESTIONS AND PROBLEMS

1. Is secondary-memory access *random* or *sequential*? Are the data stored in a *parallel* or *serial* manner?
2. How is digital information stored in a thin-film magnetic system?
3. As the read/write head scans over a magnetic pattern, exactly when are voltage pulses produced?
4. Using modified frequency modulation, show how the hexadecimal word C2 is stored in a magnetic pattern.
5. In a formatted storage medium, what is the purpose of each of the following: marks, gaps, addresses, and error-detection bytes?
6. Which rotates faster, a floppy disk or a Winchester disk?
7. Which stores information at a greater density, a floppy disk or a Winchester disk?
8. What is the difference between a soft-sectored and a hard-sectored format?
9. Why is the access time of secondary memory slower than that of primary memory?
10. Name three functions of a floppy-disk controller.
11. List three aspects of Winchester technology.
12. What is a micro-Winchester?

13. What is a magnetic bubble?
14. How are magnetic bubbles propagated through a medium?
15. Why do memory systems often contain backup memory?
16. What is streaming-tape technology?
17. Of the three types of memory—primary, secondary, and backup—which stores information at the lowest cost per bit?
18. Name two advantages (a) of floppy-disk backup over tape backup; (b) of tape backup over floppy backup.
19. Generate a data polynomial for the data word 1101101.
20. Sometimes we can remember a section of a long composition only by going back to the beginning and leading up to the desired section. Does this mean our memories also exhibit (besides random-access properties) properties of serial or sequential access—similar to secondary-memory systems? Discuss.
21. Why does *vertical recording* increase storage density?
22. What is the major drawback to present-day all-optical storage systems?

chapter 7

The Central Processing Unit: Introduction to Processing Action

For all its input/output and memory powers, our intelligent machine is only a puppet, with the outside world pulling on its bus-system strings—for as yet it can do nothing on its own. In this chapter all that will change, for we will add the final architectural block, the computer's *central processing unit* (CPU)—its central nervous system—the device that will control, sequence, and coordinate all activities. In our system, the central processing unit is the 6800 microprocessor, consisting of the control unit (CU) and the arithmetic/logic unit (ALU) integrated within its 40-pin package (see Figure 7.1).

Since the CPU (also known as the *microprocessing unit, or MPU*) is by far the most complex module we will add to the system, this chapter will introduce only the most basic aspects of CPU architecture and processing action, leaving the many refinements to be added throughout the remainder of the book.

Based on an analogy using understandable, easy-to-read material, this brief chapter is designed to bring computer action alive and to pave the way into the complex world of computer architecture and processing action that lies ahead.

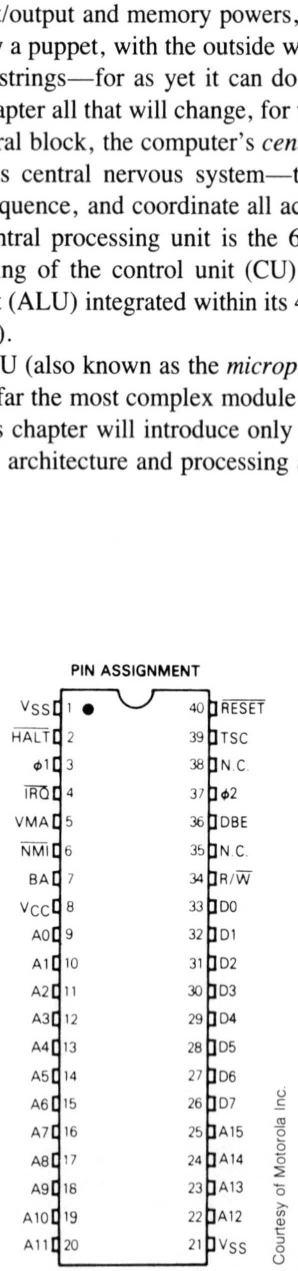

A COMPUTER ANALOGY

"All perception of truth is the detection of an analogy" (Thoreau, 1851). To truly understand a complex subject is to see an analogy within it. In this chapter we will bring out an everyday analogy that lies embedded in computer architecture and processing action. The analogy will provide a framework on which to build a complete, functioning microcomputer system.

To analogize a computer is to find something that is like a computer—something familiar to all of us, and something that can be described in familiar terms. And here it is: *an army base is like a computer*. The analogy is not at all farfetched when you realize that the fundamental principle of computer action—a computer works by processing a sequential list of instructions—is also true of an army base. To perform any task on an army base is to process a sequential list of instructions. For example, a typical process that takes place many times each day, and certainly involves a sequential list of instructions, is the task of transporting supplies from one location to another:

>Load truck
>Add fuel
>Transfer supplies

Load, add, and *transfer,* all verbs belonging to the 6800 instruction set, will be studied in detail in Part III when the emphasis shifts to software.

The task before us is to build an army base from scratch—from the ground up—and to examine carefully its architecture, for it should look a great deal like the architecture of

Figure 7.1 The 6800 CPU (MPU) pin assignment.

a microcomputer. We then will go through the process of transporting the supplies, watching carefully the steps that take place, for they should closely resemble basic processing action.

Ten Bright Ideas

The commanding officer, who is responsible for designing and operating the army base, gets a series of 10 bright ideas. After these 10 bright ideas are implemented, the base will be constructed, and it will carry out the task at hand. As an added bonus, it will run itself with the greatest of efficiency, for therein will be distilled the essence of 150 years of computer technology.

Bright idea #1 Delegate authority.

The commanding officer cannot personally issue all the commands required to run an army base—that is obvious. So, to perform the task of transporting the supplies, he summons to the base three sergeants, each a specialist at issuing one particular command. Each sergeant, therefore, represents one *instruction:*

Sergeant 1—Load truck
Sergeant 2—Add fuel
Sergeant 3—Transfer supplies

These three sergeants, not the commanding officer, will ultimately issue the three sequential commands for carrying out the task. The three sergeants will live in a special housing area. Within a computer system this special housing area is the *stored program* in ROM (or RAM).

As noted in Chapter 1, each instruction consists of two parts. The verb part (load, add, transfer) we call the *operation code,* and the object part (truck, fuel, supplies) we call the *operand*.

Bright idea #2 House the sergeants in the same sequential order in which they will be giving their instructions.

If the sergeants live next to each other, in the same order in which they issue their commands, the sequencing process is greatly simplified.

Bright idea #3 Assign each housing unit a sequential house number.

Each sergeant can now be identified not by *who* he is, but by *where* he is (his address). That is, the commanding officer need no longer remember the contents of each house—only the addresses.

By assigning an address to each memory location, computers also can identify instructions by "pointing to them" with an address. (The results of the first three bright ideas are summarized in Figure 7.2.)

Bright idea #4 To sequence through the task, start at the lowest-numbered house address and count upward.

This bright idea leads to a genuine revelation, for *we can process through a list of instructions by simply counting!*

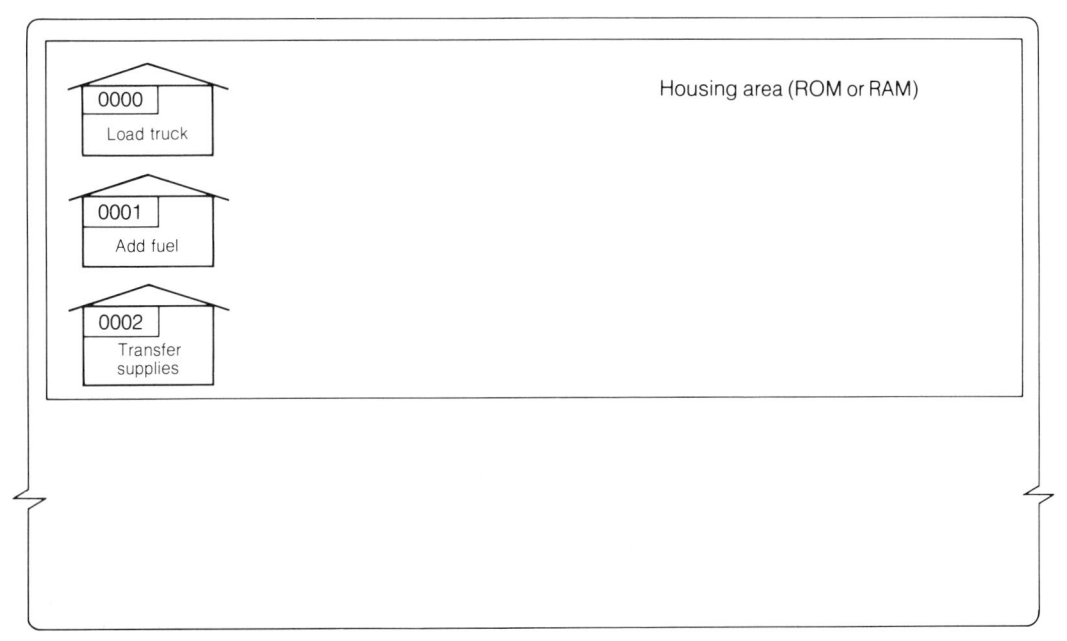

Figure 7.2 Army base/computer analogy.

And what are we counting? *Addresses*—an increasing sequence of housing unit addresses. It follows that the central authority for the entire army base—the headquarters of the whole operation—is a counter, not very different from the odometer in your car.

In a computer, this central authority, called the *program counter* (PC), is a 16-bit counter inside the 6800 microprocessor chip (Figure 7.3). The program counter holds the memory address of the instruction currently being processed. (Technically speaking, as we will see in future chapters, the present memory address in the program counter is latched into an internal bus-interfacing register early in each instruction-fetch operation, thereby freeing the program counter to look ahead to the next instruction byte to be fetched.)

Think of the program counter as an incrementing *memory pointer*, tying into the address bus and locating each instruction in sequential order. Note the common pathways (buses) interconnecting all sections of the base.

Bright idea #5 Separate the object of each instruction from the verb and place them into succeeding memory locations.

This action greatly increases efficiency since one sergeant can now direct the activities of many different objects. Likewise, in computers, one operation code can direct the activities of many different operands.

Bright idea #6 To process an instruction, bring both the verb (operation code) and object (operand) onto the main base (6800 microprocessor chip) where the verb can direct the activities of the object and the instruction can be carried out (executed).

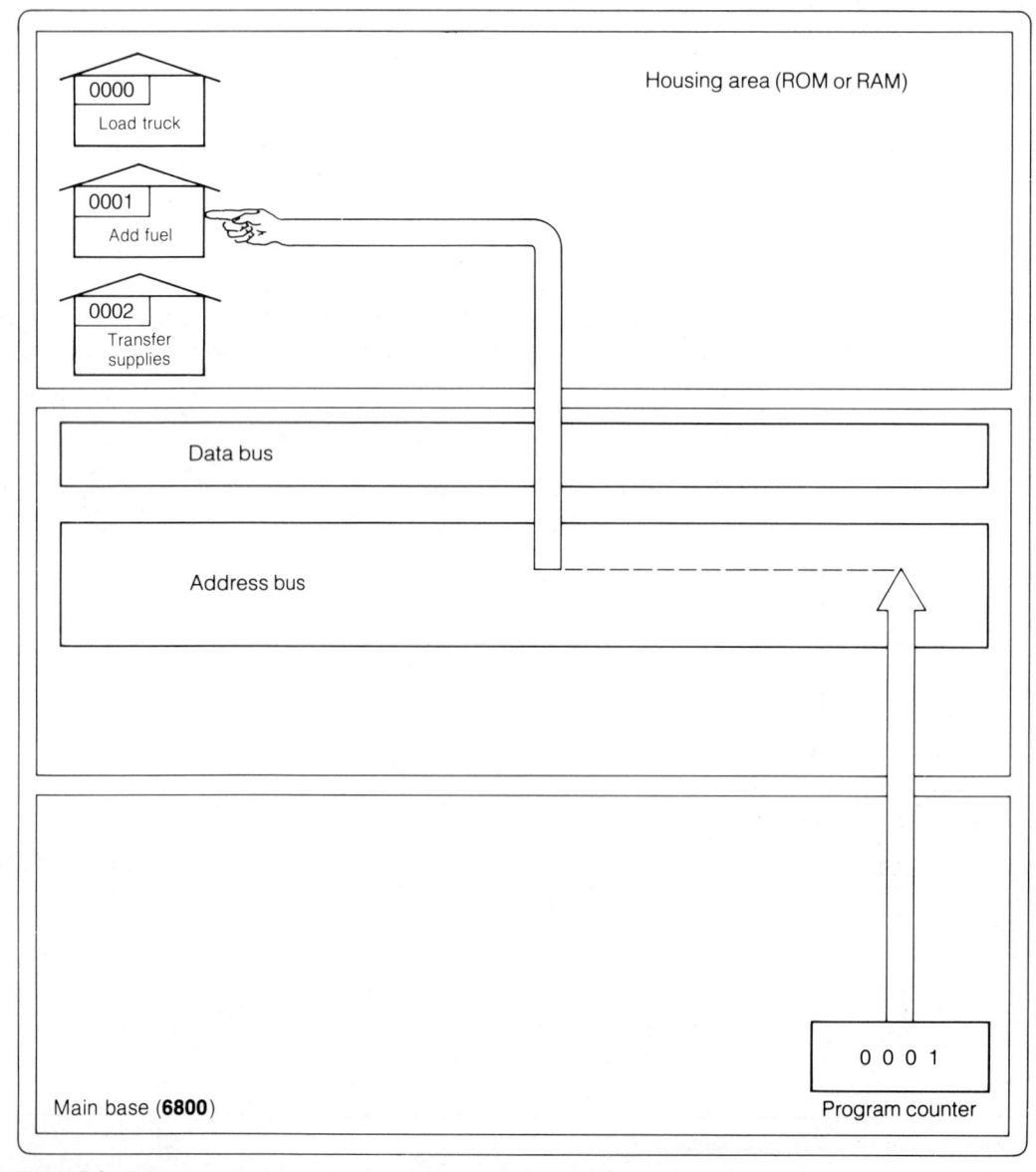

Figure 7.3 Program counter "pointing to" stored-program location $0001 (hex).

In computer language, bringing the operation code and the operand into the microprocessor chip is called a *fetch* operation. Of course, each fetch operation is a data transfer and must obey the where/when data-transfer process.

When fetched into the main base, the verb (op code) is sent to a new register—the *instruction register* (Figure 7.4). A good memory key for the instruction register is the "house of verbs," since that is where each sergeant will stand while shouting out each assigned action.

The object (operand) goes to yet another new register, accumulator A or accumulator B—two of the busiest registers within the microprocessor chip.

Bright idea #7 Place an instruction decoder next to the instruction register.

We already know how necessary it is to decipher the commands of an army sergeant. It is just as important to decipher (decode) each operation code fetched to the instruction register. Since each operation code is an 8-bit word, the instruction decoder will be a 1-of-256 decoder.

Bright idea #8 Add timing and control operations to the base to sequence the fetch and execution of each instruction.

Imagine the timing and control block to be a room full of telephone operators who can communicate instantly with every part of the base. To communicate with external components outside the main base (microprocessor chip), they send data, address, and control signals to the system bus (Figure 7.5). In the 6800, the timing and control block is known as the *controller sequencer* (CON).

Bright idea #9 Include a set of microprograms within the

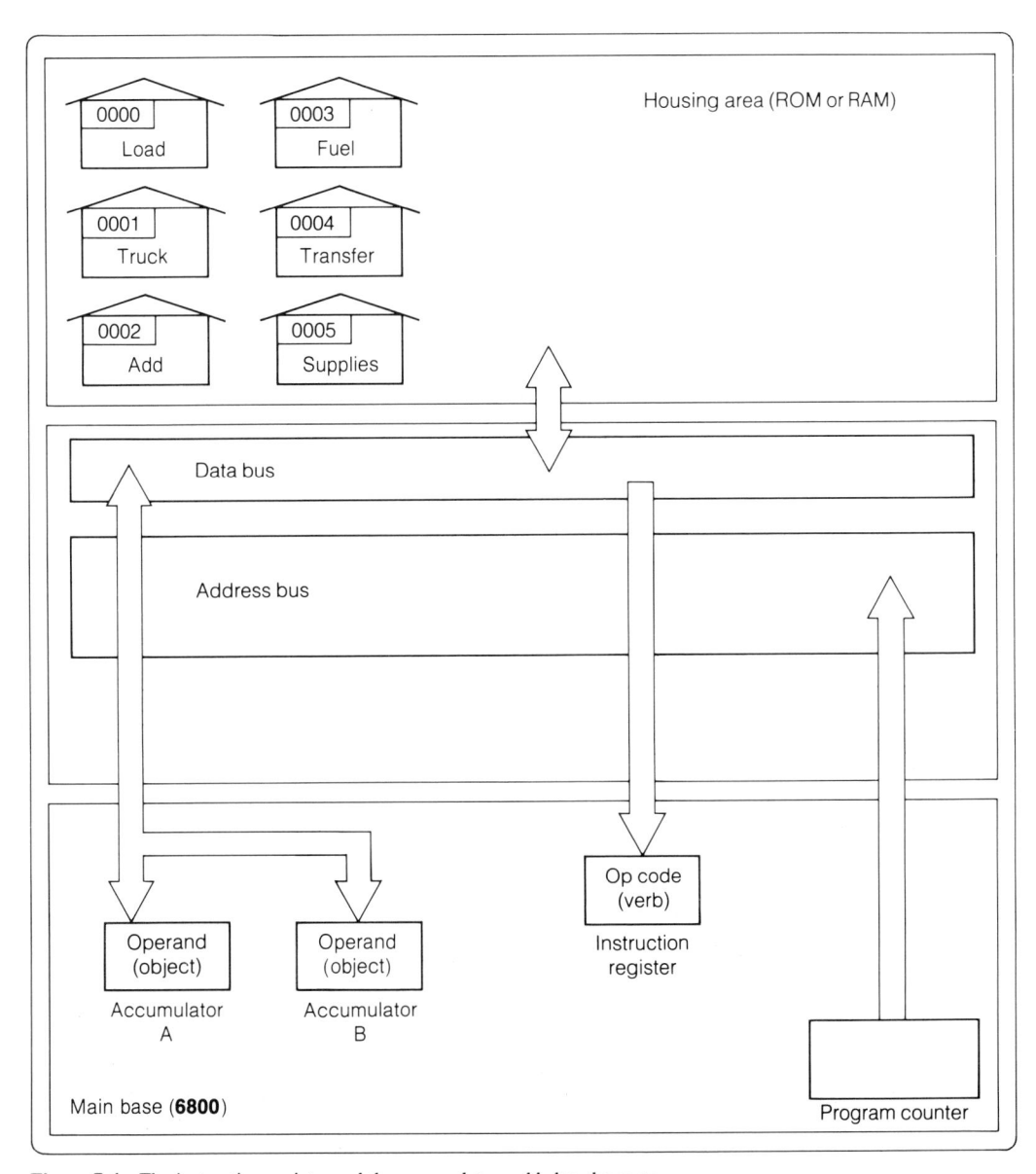

Figure 7.4 The instruction register and the accumulators added to the system.

6800 main base to carry out the detailed processing of each instruction.

Remember the prime rule of computer action: *a computer works by processing a sequential list of instructions*. It follows that the processing of *each instruction* also requires a sequential list of *subinstructions*. These subinstructions, known as *microprograms* (or *microcode*), are permanently stored within the microprocessor chip in a special on-chip array of ROM known as *control storage*. (The sequential list of main instructions pulled from external memory is often called the *macroprogram*.) As soon as a main instruction is fetched, decoded, and identified, it triggers the sequential processing of the proper microprogram. (A built-in set of microprograms is really nothing new. A kitten, for example, has a whole set of built-in microprograms—only they are called *instincts*.)

To understand the concept of a microprogram, imagine a large bookcase in the base headquarters filled with loose-leaf binders—one binder for each operation code (verb). Each binder contains the detailed sequence of microcode subinstructions—page by page—for carrying out each main instruction. As soon as the main-program operation code has been fetched and decoded, the correct microprogram looseleaf binder is identified and selected. As the pages turn, the subinstructions are carried out one by one. With the turn of the last page, the main-program instruction has been completely executed, and the system moves on to fetch, decode, and execute the next main-program macroinstruction.

Bright idea #10   Create a place where instruction execution takes place.

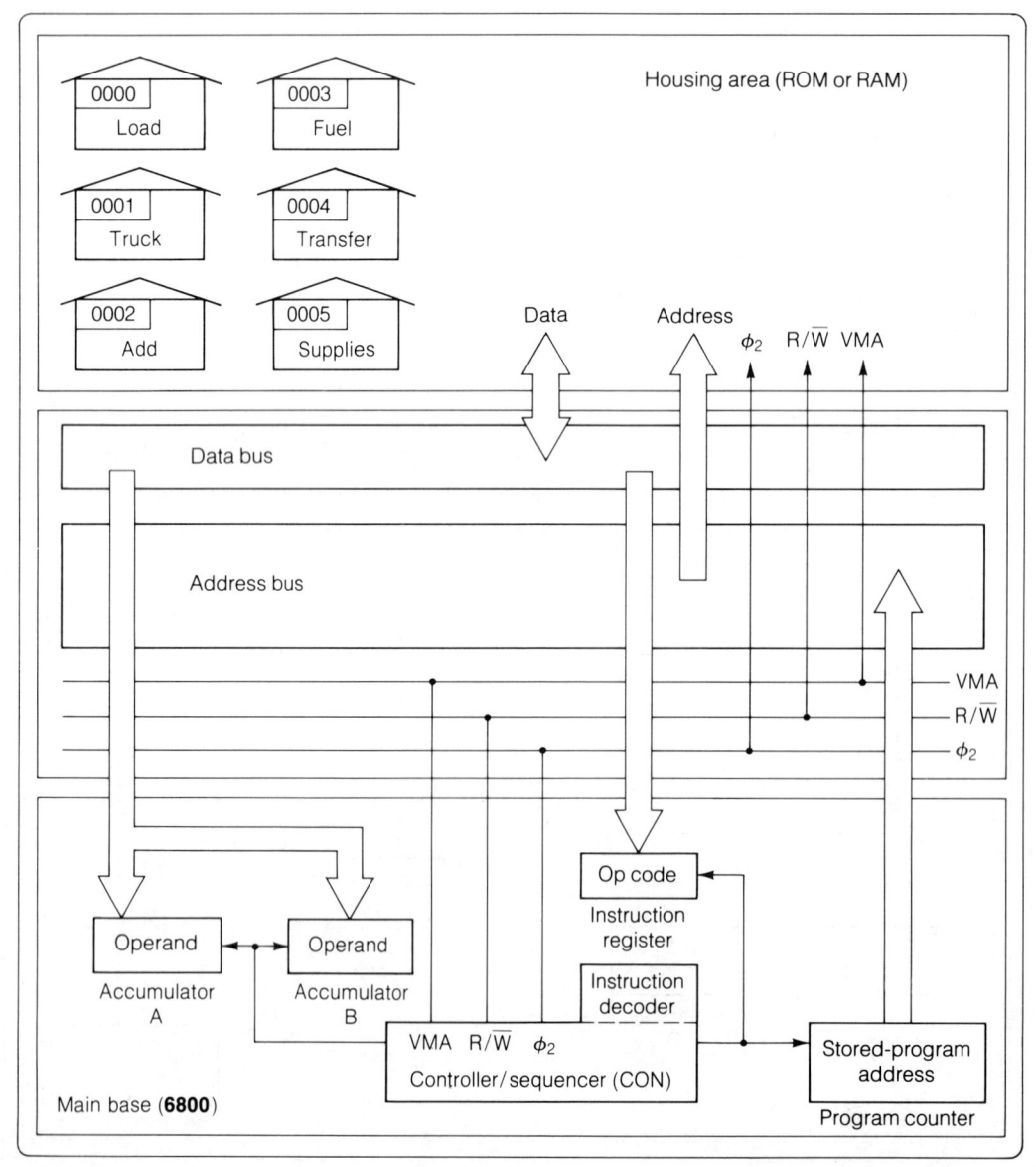

Figure 7.5   Instruction decoder and timing and control blocks added.

Within the army base, this is where the sergeant's command is carried out (the verb acts on the object). Within the 6800 microprocessor, this block is known as the *arithmetic/logic unit,* or simply ALU. During instruction execution, the operand moves from an accumulator to the ALU, where it is acted on by the operation code. As diagrammed in Figure 7.6, the result of the ALU action goes back to an accumulator—revealing why these registers are called *accumulators:* they accumulate the results of processing many instructions.

The Final System

All 10 bright ideas have now been implemented, and Figure 7.7 shows the final system. Like all great innovations, the hardware design is ingenious, yet profoundly simple.

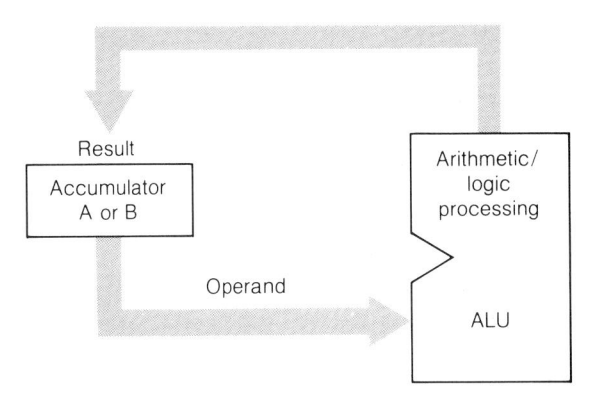

Figure 7.6 Accumulator/ALU processing loop.

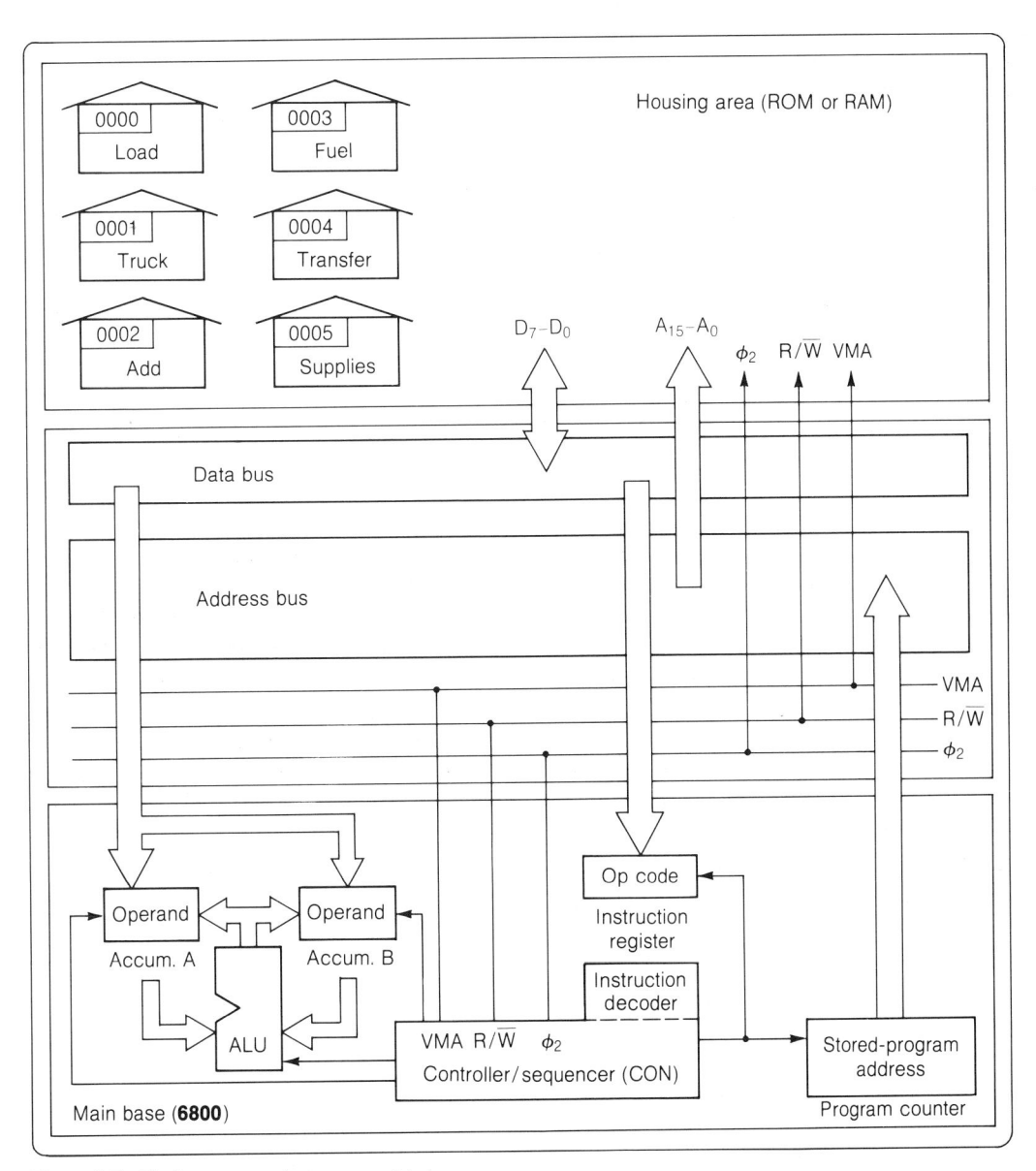

Figure 7.7 Final system, ready to carry out task.

PROCESSING ACTION

Architecture in place, the commanding officer now initiates the task of transporting the supplies. The first step (shown completed in Figure 7.7) is to program the system (place the instructions—or sergeants—in their ROM locations in the proper order). This step is just about the only work the commanding officer must do. But he has to do it right. Almost any mistake in programming will abort the entire process (which lies at the base of the well-known computer adage "garbage in/garbage out").

The commanding officer next sets the program counter to point to the starting location of the program. A where/when data-transfer operation is initiated by timing and control, and the operation code "load" is fetched to the instruction register. The op code is decoded, and the proper looseleaf-binder microprogram identified. Under direction of the "load" microprogram, the program counter is incremented to point to the next memory location. The object "truck" is fetched to an accumulator by way of another where/when data-transfer process.

When both op code and operand have been fetched, the microprogram commands the execution phase, sending the object "truck" to the ALU "loading room." There the supplies are loaded onto the truck, and the result returned to an accumulator. At this point the first instruction has been fully executed and the microprogram looseleaf binder is returned to the shelf.

The execution of the second instruction begins with the PC increment and op-code fetch of the second instruction. There really is no need to review the last two instructions, however, for they are processed in precisely the same way as the first.

In fact, the whole computing process has a definite recurring beat to it, an almost musical rhythm: fetch op code, fetch operand, execute—over and over again (see Figure 7.8).

Of course, there are variations on musical beats, and there are also variations on the basic processing action presented in this chapter. But an analogy can go only so far. An army base is not a computer; it is just similar to a computer. Still, if you have a feeling for basic processing action and generally understand the flow of data between the major registers, you are ready to proceed.

It should not surprise you to find in future chapters that the 6800 contains more internal registers than we have seen so far and that the basic processing action introduced in this chapter can be modified in a number of ways.

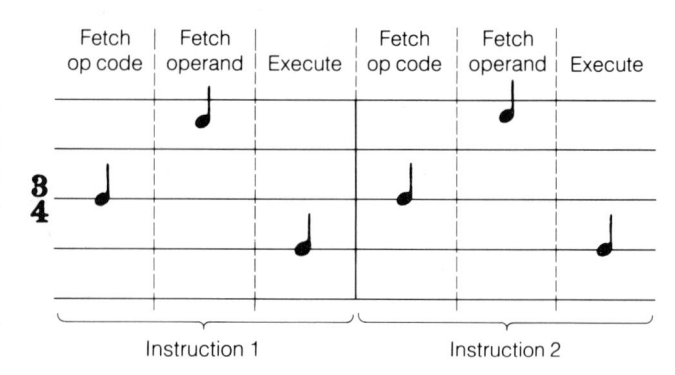

Figure 7.8 Ballad of computer processing—fetch op code, fetch operand, execute.

INTELLIGENT-MACHINE UPDATE

If we interpret life as the ability to respond intelligently to the environment without outside control, then in this chapter we have identified the architecture and processes of computer life. If the basic processes of computer life are so simple, it remains to be seen how computers (as well as people) can perform such complex tasks.

QUESTIONS AND PROBLEMS

1. What kind of information does the program counter hold?
2. When a computer carries out a task by counting, what exactly is it counting?
3. Why is the instruction register called the *house of verbs*?
4. After an operation code has been fetched, what is the very next process that takes place?
5. What is a *micro*program and how does it differ from a *macro*program? How is a microprogram like an *instinct*?
6. What kind of information does an accumulator hold?
7. How do an accumulator and ALU interact during instruction processing?
8. What exactly takes place when a computer is programmed?

part II

Basic Processing Action: The Metabolism of a Computer

While we go about our daily business—working, playing, living—we are scarcely aware of the underlying metabolic activities that continuously go on inside our bodies. We breathe, pump blood, and digest food with little attention to the complex processes involved, for they are governed by the ancient, primordial parts of our mind. A doctor, on the other hand, must care about our metabolic processes, for they mirror our health and well-being.

A computer also has a metabolism—underlying currents of activity, cyclic in nature, that permit the computer to perform its operations. Interested only in results, the computer operator is scarcely aware they exist. To the troubleshooter, though, these underlying cycles and rhythms are the computer's vital signs, revealing the cause of a malfunction in the system. To the designer, they are the fundamental beat with which all parts of the system must synchronize.

The two chapters of Part II, then, cover fundamental processing action, beginning with an introduction to programming. By studying the processing action of a real program, the computer's cycles and waveforms will also be real—with results that can be reproduced in the laboratory.

chapter 8

Introduction to Programming and Program Processing

What does it mean to be alive? What is that mysterious essence separating animate from inanimate objects? For human beings, this question is ageless. For a computer, it can be answered exactly: a computer is "living" when it is processing a sequential list of instructions.

In this chapter we will write a program in the computer's own binary language; we will teach the computer a task by placing a program into its memory; and we will run the program, following through the processing action step by step. Quite simply, in this chapter we will bring the computer to life!

WRITING A PROGRAM

The first step in writing a program is to select a task—something you want the computer to do. Since this will be our very first program, the task should be a simple one. One way to assure simplicity is to select a task that can be learned by a lower-order member of the animal kingdom—such as a mynah bird. A mynah has the often embarrassing ability to repeat—or mimic—the sounds it hears. Because the routine is so simple, the mimic process will be the first task we will teach our computer. When we place a hexadecimal word before its "eyes," it will mimic the word.

The Instruction Set

First, to write a mimic program—indeed, to write anything—we need a vocabulary, a list of instructions that the computer can understand. This list of instructions is known as the computer's *instruction set*. The 6800 instruction set summary appears in Figure 8.1, while a complete instruction set description (reprinted from the *M6800 Programming Reference Manual*) is given in Appendix I. These 72 types of instructions are required to perform typical computer tasks,

ABA	Add Accumulators	CLR	Clear	PUL	Pull Data
ADC	Add with Carry	CLV	Clear Overflow	ROL	Rotate Left
ADD	Add	CMP	Compare	ROR	Rotate Right
AND	Logical And	COM	Complement	RTI	Return from Interrupt
ASL	Arithmetic Shift Left	CPX	Compare Index Register	RTS	Return from Subroutine
ASR	Arithmetic Shift Right	DAA	Decimal Adjust	SBA	Subtract Accumulators
BCC	Branch if Carry Clear	DEC	Decrement	SBC	Subtract with Carry
BCS	Branch if Carry Set	DES	Decrement Stack Pointer	SEC	Set Carry
BEQ	Branch if Equal to Zero	DEX	Decrement Index Register	SEI	Set Interrupt Mask
BGE	Branch if Greater or Equal Zero	EOR	Exclusive OR	SEV	Set Overflow
BGT	Branch if Greater than Zero			STA	Store Accumulator
BHI	Branch if Higher	INC	Increment	STS	Store Stack Register
BIT	Bit Test	INS	Increment Stack Pointer	STX	Store Index Register
BLE	Branch if Less or Equal	INX	Increment Index Register	SUB	Subtract
BLS	Branch if Lower or Same	JMP	Jump	SWI	Software Interrupt
BLT	Branch if Less than Zero	JSR	Jump to Subroutine	TAB	Transfer Accumulators
BMI	Branch if Minus	LDA	Load Accumulator	TAP	Transfer Accumulators to Condition Code Reg.
BNE	Branch if Not Equal to Zero	LDS	Load Stack Pointer	TBA	Transfer Accumulators
BPL	Branch if Plus	LDX	Load Index Register	TPA	Transfer Condition Code Reg. to Accumulator
BRA	Branch Always	LSR	Logical Shift Right	TST	Test
BSR	Branch to Subroutine	NEG	Negate	TSX	Transfer Stack Pointer to Index Register
BVC	Branch if Overflow Clear	NOP	No Operation	TXS	Transfer Index Register to Stack Pointer
BVS	Branch if Overflow Set	ORA	Inclusive OR Accumulator	WAI	Wait for Interrupt
CBA	Compare Accumulators	PSH	Push Data		
CLC	Clear Carry				
CLI	Clear Interrupt Mask				

Courtesy of Motorola, Inc.

Figure 8.1 The 6800 instruction set.

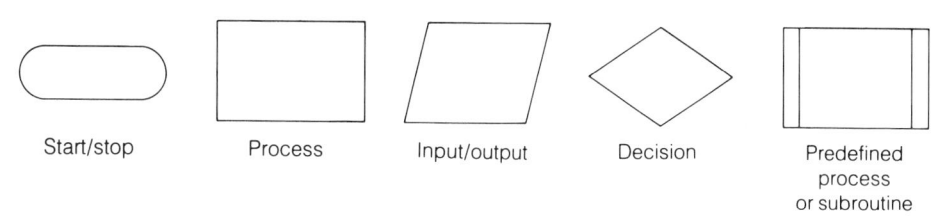

Figure 8.2 Basic flowchart symbols.

and most of them will be recognized—in one form or another—by nearly all microprocessors. (Most of the 72 instruction types will be introduced in Part III.)

To write a mimic program, therefore, we must select the proper instructions from this list of 72, and then place them into the correct sequential order.

The Flowchart

Since a complex program can easily consist of thousands of instructions, we will borrow a practice from the field of writing to help us organize our thoughts. Most novelists summarize or outline the flow of their story before filling in the final details. This practice can be applied to a complex program. It would be very helpful to have some general idea of the program flow before listing the individual instructions. In computer programming, such an outline is known as a *flowchart;* it is a sequential arrangement of blocks—each block representing a portion of the total program.

Although dozens of block categories are used, those shown in Figure 8.2 are the most common ones. The type of operation determines the shape of the block element.

Even though the flowchart is a widely used programming aid, many programmers—particularly those using a structured, high-level language (explained in Chapter 22)—prefer other techniques. However, flowcharts are a useful tool for the beginning machine-language programmer and will be used extensively in this text.

The flowchart for the simple mimic process is easy to develop, since only an input followed by an output operation is involved. As shown in Figure 8.3, the main body of the flowchart therefore involves only parallelograms—the flowchart symbol for I/O operations.

As we can see, the programmer is free to write inside each block any information that will make the program flow easier to understand. The plain everyday language of Figure 8.3a is perfectly acceptable. If you prefer, however, you might choose more technical terms (Figure 8.3b).

WRITING THE SIMPLE MIMIC PROGRAM

The task before us is to select the proper sequence of instructions for carrying out the requirements of each flowchart block. For convenience, the 72 types of instructions have been arranged by Motorola into four major groups (see Appendix II):

1. Accumulator and memory operations
2. Index register and stack pointer instructions
3. Jump and branch instructions
4. Condition code register operations

However, for study purposes, we will divide the 72 instructions into the following smaller and more manageable categories (Appendix III):

1. Data Transfer Group
2. Arithmetic Group
3. Logical Group
4. Branch Group
5. Machine Control Group

Most of the instructions making up each of the five groups will be studied in detail in Part III when the emphasis shifts to software. For now, our task is to simply locate the instruction required to carry out each block in the mimic program flowchart.

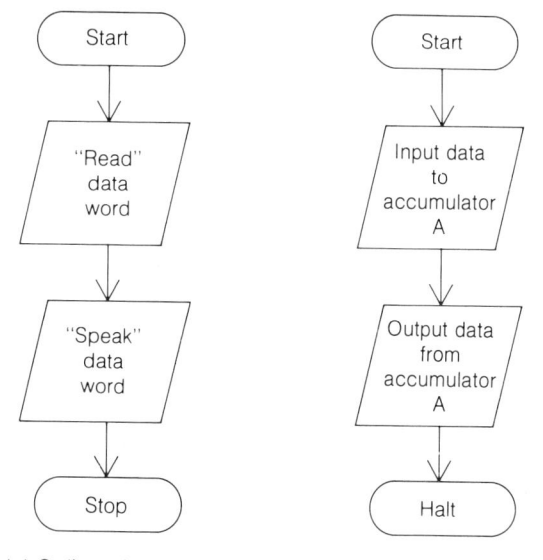

(a) Ordinary language (b) More technical terms

Figure 8.3 Mimic-process flowchart.

Block 1—the Start Block

Can you now carry out the requirements of block 1—the start block—by locating the correct instruction within the correct grouping? The answer is: No instruction at all is required to initiate (start) processor action. Simply free the $\overline{\text{HALT}}$ and TSC (three-state control) pins to the 6800, and processing activity will begin (the $\overline{\text{HALT}}$ and TSC requests are described in the next chapter).

Block 2—the Inport Block

The second block does require an instruction. Let us make use of all available clues to locate the right instruction type among the 72 choices. Since "listen" is an input operation and "ears" are input ports, perhaps you searched the instruction set for an "Inport" type of instruction.

Unfortunately, the 6800 instruction set does not appear to have an inport instruction. We touched on the reason for this earlier: the 6800 is a "memory mapped" processor, one in which I/O ports are treated as memory locations. In other words, no distinction is made in the instruction set (or the addressing space) between I/O port locations and memory locations. To the 6800, *an input port acts as a 1 × 8 ROM chip.*

Therefore, to find the right instruction type to inport data, let's back up and be less specific: *to input data from an input port is the same as transferring data from memory.* Turning to the data transfer group listed below (also see Appendix III), we find the LDA instruction, an instruction that loads a data byte from a memory location *or an input port* to an accumulator:

The 6800 Data Transfer Group

LDA Load Accumulator
LDS Load Stack Pointer
LDX Load Index Register
STA Store Accumulator
STS Store Stack Register
STX Store Index Register
TAB Transfer Accumulators
TAP Transfer Accumulators to Condition Code Register
TBA Transfer Accumulators
TPA Transfer Condition Code Register to Accumulator

Let us take a close look at the LDA instruction, as outlined in the *6800 Programming Reference Manual* (see Figure 8.4).

The verb portion (operation code) usually is easy to follow. "Load," for example, implies a data-transfer operation, commanding the transfer of data from an input port (or memory location) to an accumulator. The source of the data transfer is the input port; the destination is an accumulator. If we wish to transfer to accumulator A, the mnemonic becomes LDAA; if the destination is accumulator B, the mnemonic becomes LDAB. *But how do we determine the source of the data* (there are, after all, 65,536 memory or input port locations to choose from)? The answer, once again, is found in the English language. Below the first instruction from our army base analogy (load truck), we will write the same command, but in a slightly different form:

Verb	Object
1. load	truck
2. load	vehicle in garage 7

Load Accumulator (LDA)

Operation: ACCX ← (M)
Description: Loads the contents of memory into the accumulator.

Addressing Modes	Execution Time (No. of cycles)	Number of bytes of machine code	Coding of First (or only) byte of machine code		
			HEX.	OCT.	DEC.
A IMM	2	2	86	206	134
A DIR	3	2	96	226	150
A EXT	4	3	B6	266	182
A IND	5	2	A6	246	166
B IMM	2	2	C6	306	198
B DIR	3	2	D6	326	214
B EXT	4	3	F6	366	246
B IND	5	2	E6	346	230

Courtesy of Motorola, Inc.

Figure 8.4 The LDA partial instruction summary, highlighting the LDAA EXT addressing mode.

Clearly, if the truck is located within garage 7, both instructions produce the same result. In other words, the instruction does not have to tell *what* the data is—it can specify *where* it is. Therefore, as summarized below, all instructions can be divided into two distinct categories depending on whether the instruction specifies the data or the address of the data.

- *Category 1:* The instruction contains the data (load truck).
- *Category 2:* The instruction contains the address of the data (load vehicle in garage 7).

Now, into which category do you believe our Inport (LDA) instruction falls? Clearly it belongs to the second category, and for a very logical reason: if the instruction contained the data directly, the data would already be in memory and thus there would be no reason for the input operation.

So, we arrive at the following conclusion: *the address of our input port must be part of the LDA instruction.* Here is where things can get a little complicated, for—referring to Figure 8.4—the LDA instruction includes four *addressing modes* (methods of locating the data). Which one of the four is right for us? Since, in this chapter, we are studying basic processing action and not software development, let's leave the full discussion of addressing modes till Chapter 10, and choose the simplest of the four to begin with.

Here, at last, is the instruction that will carry out our input-port operation:

LDAA EXTended

We already know that LDAA refers to a data-transfer operation from memory or an input port into accumulator A. So, once again, it is the operand portion of the instruction (EXTended) that will require further explanation.

Think of the word *extended*—one of the four available addressing modes—as a "pointer"; it "points" to a specific location (a particular input port in our case) where the data can be found. In terms of android anatomy, the word *extended* may specify the "eye" or the "ear." In computer terms, extended represents a full 16-bit address—the address of a particular input port. This address must be supplied in binary form by the programmer. Since the port address is a 16-bit word, up to 65,536 input ports can be uniquely addressed. Of course, any realistic system would contain nowhere near the maximum number of ports; besides, in a memory-mapped system, a considerable chunk of the 65,536 available locations would be reserved for memory.

To process this new type in instruction, another register—the MAR (memory address register)—is included within the 6800 microprocessor, as shown in Figure 8.5. Unlike other register pairs to be introduced, the MAR register pair is

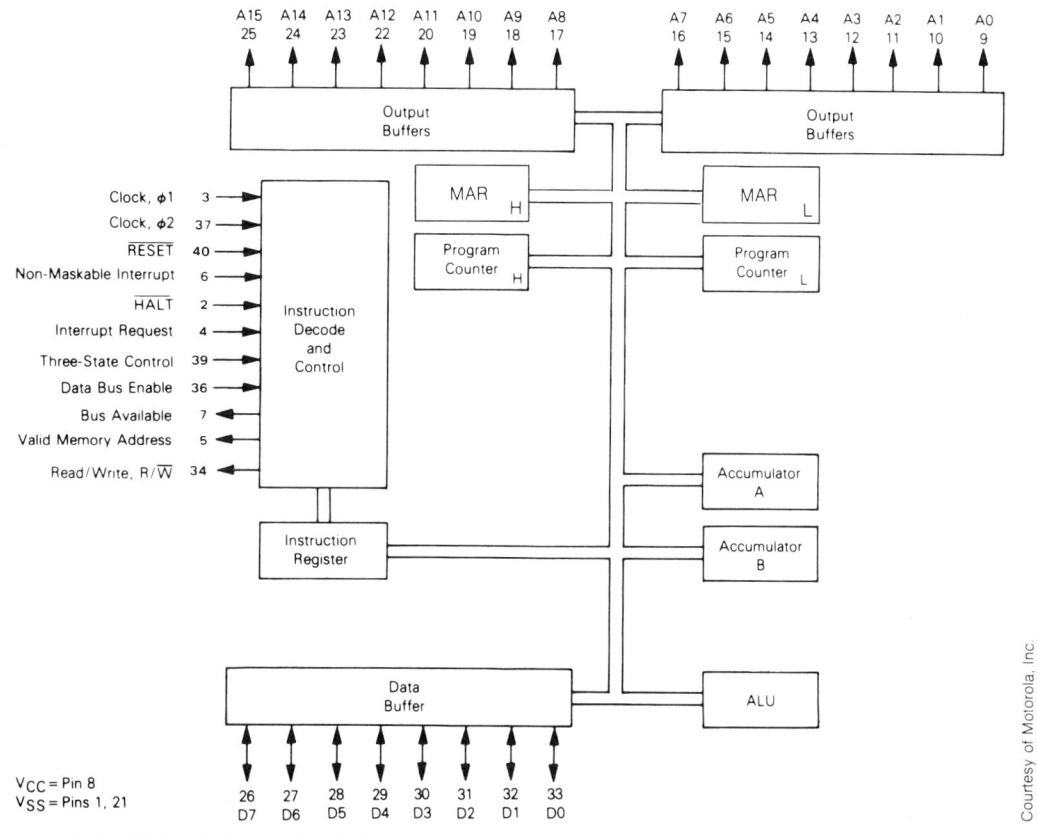

Figure 8.5 6800 partial internal block diagram.

inaccessible to the user (it is invisible). (In fact, quite often it is not even shown on internal block diagrams.)

Because the second category of instructions (those specifying the operand as an address) are more complex than the first category, an extra intermediate step is required during the processing action.

First category
1. fetch op code
2. transfer data

Second category
1a. fetch op code
1b. fetch data address to MAR
2. transfer data

In the case of the LDAA EXTended instruction, this intermediate step is used to fetch the port address to the MAR for temporary storage. This stored address is then used in the final step to select the proper input port for an input of data. Generally speaking, the MAR addresses data during the execution phase; the program counter addresses instruction bytes during the instruction fetch phase.

Looking further into the instruction summary (Figure 8.4), we see that each instruction type is supplied with a plain English statement, spelling out exactly what the instruction will accomplish. For the LDA instruction, it is: "Loads the contents of memory into the accumulator." The symbolism below the "Load Accumulator" title diagrams the instruction's purpose. The term on the right is the source and the term on the left is the destination. The data move in the direction of the arrow from source to destination. The parentheses are generally equivalent to the phrase "contents of." Therefore, this shorthand designation means: The contents of the specified port are moved to accumulator X (the "X" is changed to an A or B when a particular accumulator is specified).

The final part of the instruction summary is a table, listing the actual binary code—the true language of the computer—for each addressing mode. The LDAX EXT instruction is a three-byte instruction, with the first byte carrying the operation code. For the *extended* addressing mode, there is one op code for loading accumulator A ($B6), and another for loading accumulator B ($F6). The second byte holds the high-order address of the data, and the third byte holds the low-order address of the data. It is the programmer's responsibility to fill in the second and third bytes with the exact binary (or hex) address of the selected input port. *This binary address will, in turn, depend on how the port is tied into the address bus.*

Let's be specific and hardwire our input port at location $2000 (the dollar sign indicates that 2000 is a hexadecimal number). This means that when $2000 appears on the address bus, the input port must be enabled. As when addressing a memory chip, we can use either linear, partial decoded, or fully decoded addressing techniques. To illustrate all three techniques, Figure 8.6 shows how our input port is configured for address $2000 operation. Using linear addressing, we can uniquely specify (address) up to 16 input ports; whereas fully decoding the address lines allows us to uniquely specify up to the maximum 65,536 input ports.

Placing $2000 in the second byte of the LDAA instruction, we now complete the binary code for carrying out block 2 and place it beside the flowchart block (Figure 8.7). The binary and hexadecimal formats, of course, are for the computer. For the benefit of people, let us also keep the mnemonic notation.

Block 3—the Outport Block

The third block basically commands the reverse operation. Its similarity to the second block will considerably simplify our job. If we agree that "to speak" is to output data, then perhaps the instruction type "Store" (STA) in the 6800 users manual will carry out the requirements of block 2 (see Figure 8.8a).

If *extended* addressing is used, it is the responsibility of the programmer—as with the LDA EXT instruction—to substitute the binary address of the output port for the word *extended*. To conform to the addressing scheme adopted in Part I, let's assume our output port is hardwired at address $1000. The output instruction then takes on the form of Figure 8.8b.

Block 4—the Stop Block

Stop is really a command to the computer and is not part of the actual mimic process. The machine control group seems like a good place to look for a stop command.

We quickly locate the WAI (WAit for Interrupt) instruction (Figure 8.9), which stops (suspends) processor action. Unlike most instructions, the WAI instruction does not require an operand. The same is true in English—the command *wait* usually stands alone.

As you might suspect from its name, the WAit for Interrupt instruction is part of the interrupt structure of the 6800, and does more than merely stop processor action. In later chapters we will learn more about the WAI instruction, as well as more effective methods of terminating a program.

The Complete Mimic Program

Adding the STA and WAI instructions beside the proper flowchart blocks completes our mimic program (Figure 8.10).

In future chapters we will learn a number of shorthand techniques for writing programs and for translating them from English to binary (from mnemonics to machine language).

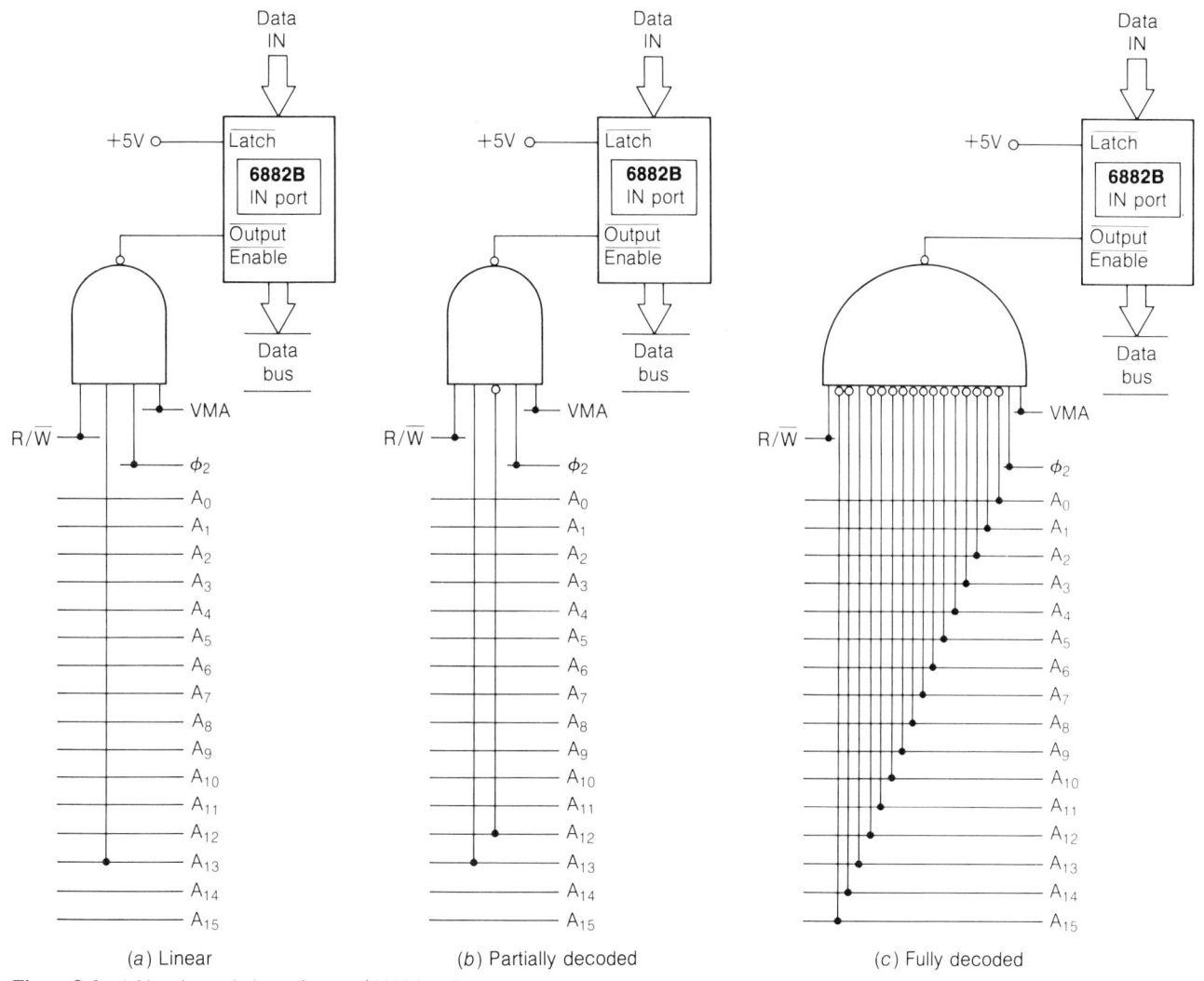

Chapter 8 / Introduction to Programming and Program Processing 89

(a) Linear

(b) Partially decoded

(c) Fully decoded

Figure 8.6 Addressing techniques for port $2000 location.

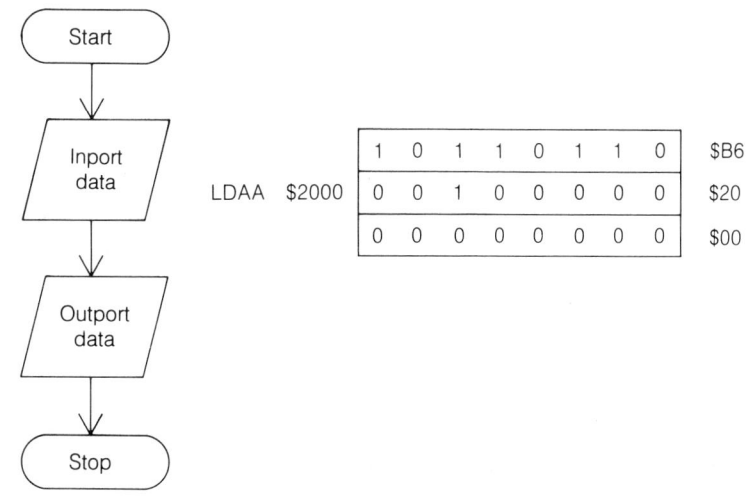

Figure 8.7. Block 2 completed.

Store Accumulator (STA)

Operation: M ← (ACCX)

Description: Stores the contents of ACCX in memory. The contents of ACCX remains unchanged.

Addressing Modes	Execution Time (No. of cycles)	Number of bytes of machine code	HEX.	OCT.	DEC.
A DIR	4	2	97	227	151
A EXT	5	3	B7	267	183
A IND	6	2	A7	247	167
B DIR	4	2	D7	327	215
B EXT	5	3	F7	367	247
B IND	6	2	E7	347	231

Coding of First (or only) byte of machine code

Courtesy of Motorola, Inc.

(*a*) The STA partial instruction summary

Mnemonic	Binary	Hexadecimal
	1 0 1 1 0 1 1 1	$B7
STAA $1000	0 0 0 1 0 0 0 0	$10
	0 0 0 0 0 0 0 0	$00

(*b*) The STAA EXT (output) instruction for port $1000 operation

Figure 8.8 Generating the block 3 instruction.

Wait for Interrupt (WAI)

Description: Suspends execution of the program until a reset is signaled.

Addressing Modes	Execution Time (No. of cycles)	Number of bytes of machine code	HEX.	OCT.	DEC.
INHERENT	9	1	3E	076	062

Coding of First (or only) byte of machine code

Courtesy of Motorola, Inc.

Figure 8.9 The *Wait for Interrupt* partial instruction summary.

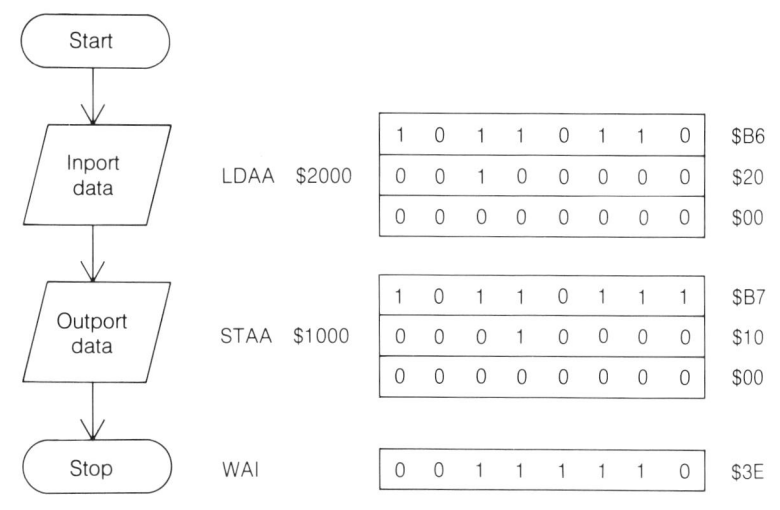

Figure 8.10 The complete mimic program.

LDAA $2000	1 0 1 1 0 1 1 0							$B6
	0 0 1 0 0 0 0 0							$20
	0 0 0 0 0 0 0 0							$00
STAA $1000	1 0 1 1 0 1 1 1							$B7
	0 0 0 1 0 0 0 0							$10
	0 0 0 0 0 0 0 0							$00
WAI	0 0 1 1 1 1 1 0							$3E

TEACHING THE MIMIC TASK

The next step is to "teach" our computer to perform the mimic task. This is the easiest and quickest step of all, for we simply deposit the program into the computer's memory. Programming, as we know, is teaching. Programming is also learning; it just depends on your point of view. As we will see in later chapters, the "deposit" process usually is carried out by a special *monitor* program burned into ROM. To conform to the RAM space used by most 6800-based single-board computers (such as the Heathkit ET-3400A trainer), we will place the mimic program at page $00.

Recall from our historical summary in Chapter 1 that the idea of programming, of placing the instructions as well as the data into memory—the *stored-program concept*—was one of the great forward leaps in computer technology, envisioned early 150 years ago by Babbage. When instructions are stored in the same form as data in the same memory, a computer is known as a *Von Neumann* or *Princeton-class computer*.

PERFORMING THE MIMIC TASK

Our computer has been taught the mimic process (programmed), and we are now ready to cross the threshold between "living" and "nonliving" systems. When we place a data word before the computer's "eyes" and initiate processor action, it will "speak" the word. Not long ago such a process, performed by a mere machine, would have been regarded as sheer magic. (As science fiction author Arthur C. Clarke said, "Any sufficiently advanced technology is indistinguishable from magic.")

The Mimic Process

If life is fleeting for human beings, it is especially so for a computer, for the entire mimic process requires only 8 microseconds or so from start to finish. Let us see exactly what happens during those crucial 8 microseconds by taking an X-ray look inside our intelligent machine (Figure 8.11) and following the processing action step by step. (Remember, not all of the 6800 internal structure is presented here—just those parts necessary to carry out the mimic task.)

Place an arbitrarily chosen data word—such as $BE—before the computer's "eyes," initiate processor action, and the following sequential operations will take place (continued reference to Figure 8.11 should be helpful):

- *Step 1:* The starting address of the program ($0000) is placed into the program counter (this is accomplished by the *monitor* program in ROM—not shown).
- *Step 2:* The program counter points to the first memory location in the program ($0000), and a where/when operation fetches the LDAA $2000 operation code ($B6) to the instruction register.
- *Step 3:* The LDAA $2000 op code is decoded and the proper microprogram selected.
- *Step 4:* The microprogram directs the program counter to increment to $0001, and another where/when data transfer fetches the high-order port address ($20) to the high-order 8 bits of the MAR via the data bus.
- *Step 5:* The program counter increments to $0002, and the low-order port address ($00) is fetched to the low-order 8 bits of the MAR.
- *Step 6:* The fourth and final where/when data-transfer

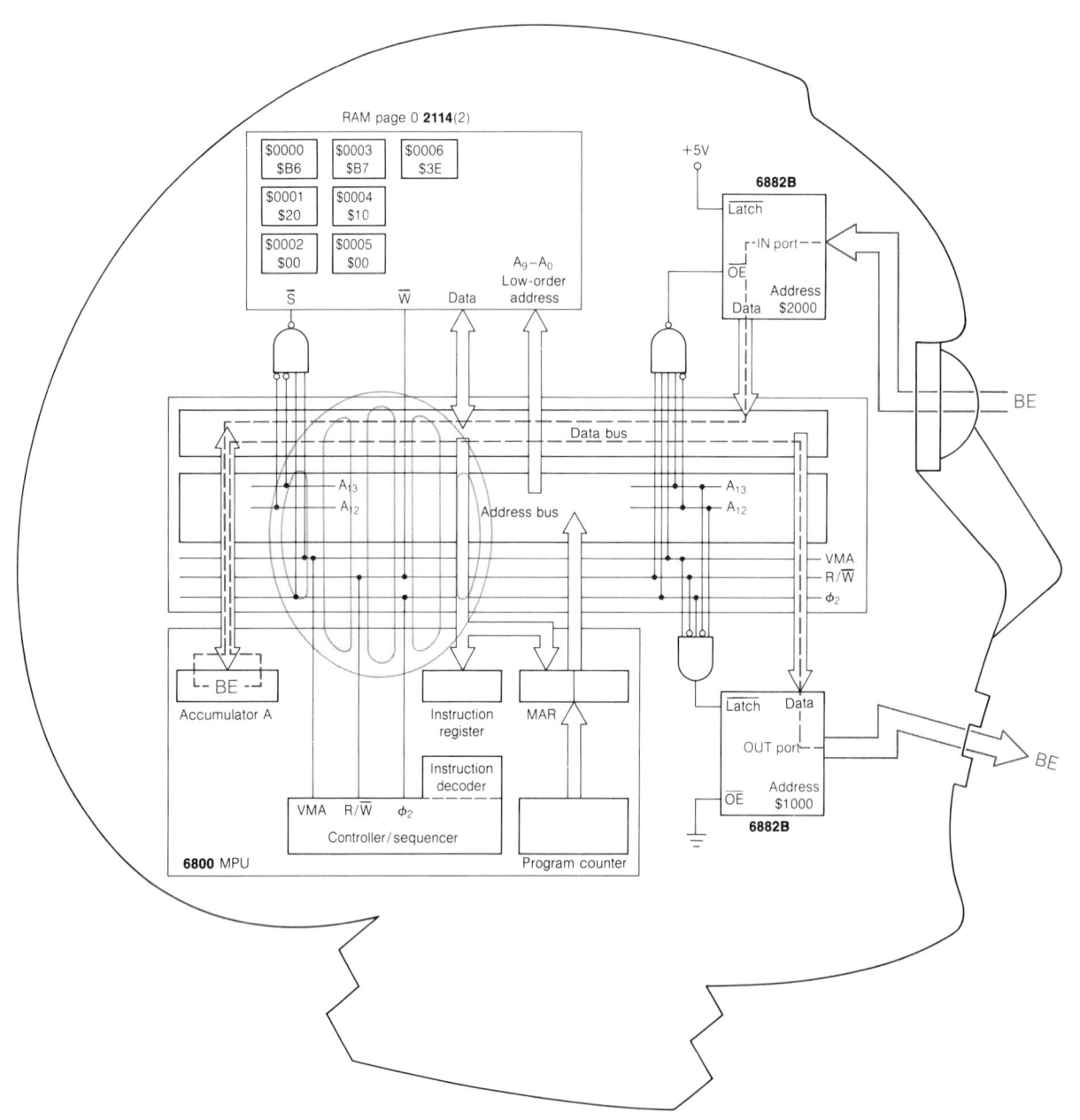

Figure 8.11 A 6800-based mimic machine.

operation for the LDAA $2000 instruction begins with the port address ($2000) in the MAR "pointing to" the "eyes" of the computer, followed by the data word "$BE" INported from the outside world to accumulator A.

- *Step 7:* The first instruction complete, the controller/sequencer increments the program counter to $0003 and fetches the STAA $1000 operation code ($B7) to the instruction register.
- *Step 8:* Under direction of the decoded microprogram, the program counter is incremented to $0004 and $0005 as two consecutive data-transfer operations fetch the OUTport address ($1000) to the MAR.
- *Step 9:* The port address in the MAR ($1000) points to the "voice" of the computer, and the data in accumulator A ($BE) are transferred to the addressed output port and latched in place.
- *Step 10:* The second instruction complete, the operation code for WAIT ($3E) is fetched to the instruction register, decoded, and computer operation is stopped.

One way to exit the halt state and repeat the mimic process is to reset the microprocessor. (The process of initializing the program counter to $0000 after reset must unavoidably remain vague at this time.)

A PROBLEM WITH SYNTAX

Many times the meaning of a commonly used word conflicts with its historical definition, and an ambiguity arises. The word *operand* is a case in point. Historically, *operand* meant *the data operated upon by the op code*. However, with the advent of assembly-language programming (formally introduced in Chapter 13), the word *operand* has come to mean *the operand field of the instruction mnemonic*. The problem, as revealed by the LDAA EXT instruction, is that the operand field of an instruction can be an address. For example, in the instruction LDAA $1000, what is the *operand*? Is it "$1000," the input port's address, or is it the data to be input from the input port? Unfortunately, the answer is, it could be either; it depends on how the writer interprets the word *operand*. As is so often the case, the exact meaning of a word will depend on the context in which it is used.

However, we should be consistent, and we should be up-to-date. Since at the present time all programming (beyond the initial learning stage) is at least written at the assembly-language level (using mnemonics), we will adopt the more modern convention and define the word *operand* to mean *the operand field of the instruction mnemonic*. For example, in the instruction LDAA $1000, "$1000" is the *operand*, while the information transferred from (or inported from) address $1000 will be referred to as the *data* or the *value*.

INTELLIGENT-MACHINE UPDATE

In performing the mimic process, our computer has announced its existence to the world. In the remaining chapters it will develop beyond this infant state by expanding both its anatomy (hardware) and its vocabulary (software). As we will see, our intelligent machine has just begun to grow.

QUESTIONS AND PROBLEMS

1. What technique is used to give an overview of the program before the specific instructions are selected?
2. List the five major flowchart blocks and state the general process to which each corresponds.
3. Write the LDAA EXT instruction (filling in the second and third bytes) for the partially decoded and linear addressing examples shown below:
4. What is the purpose of the *mnemonic* form of each instruction?
5. When the second or third byte of the LDAA EXT instruction is fetched, into what register is it placed?
6. Why does the LDAA EXT instruction require four data transfers?
7. What aspect of computer operation corresponds to "teaching" or "learning"?
8. Based on the linear addressing configuration of Figure 8.6a, how many input ports could be placed in the system? Why will your answer depend on the amount and placement of memory to be added in the future?
9. List the steps involved in processing the STAA EXT instruction.
10. Complete the following: When a port address is fetched, it goes to the _____ via the _____ bus. When it is later used as a pointer, it leaves the _____ via the _____ bus.
11. Using *extended* addressing, write a mimic program that inputs data from port $200F and outputs the data to port $1477 via accumulator B.
12. If the instruction STAB $3010 outports "$E2" from accumulator B, what is the *operand* and what is the *data*?
13. What is the definition of *mnemonic* (consult a dictionary)?

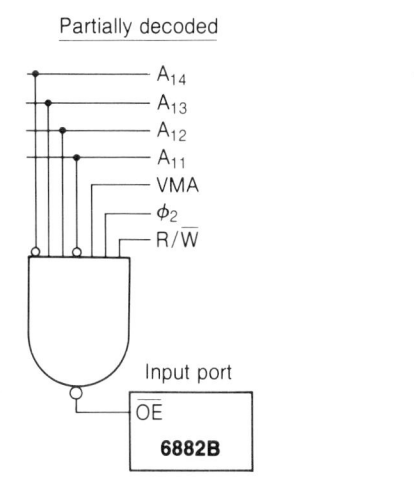

chapter 9

Timing and Processor Cycles

Would a vague and general idea of human anatomy and bodily processes be enough to allow a doctor to diagnose and treat ailments? Would a vague and general idea of computer architecture and processing action be enough to allow a technician or engineer to diagnose and treat computer malfunctions?

The answer to both questions is no—a doctor and a technician must have a detailed knowledge of the systems they are working on. If we have any hope at all of doing design and troubleshooting work, we must increase our knowledge of 6800 processing action.

The one vital area in which we are particularly deficient might be called the computer's *metabolism*—its natural rhythms and timing cycles. Clock signals and processor cycles, therefore, are the major topics of this chapter. As an added bonus, when we are finished with the discussion, we will know the function of nearly all of the 6800's 40 pins (Figure 9.1).

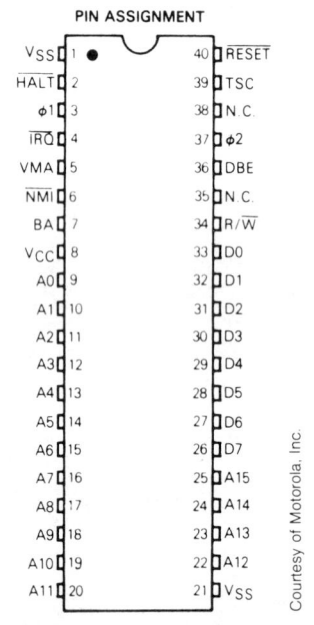

Figure 9.1 The 6800 pin-out.

THE SYSTEM CLOCK

A computer must have a "heartbeat," a precise clock pulse for generating all the necessary timing and sequencing signals required to run the entire system. For 6800-based systems, the MC6875 two-phase clock generator/driver supplies the basic ϕ_1 and ϕ_2 signals, as well as other logic functions useful for system expansion.

The MC6875

The block diagram of Figure 9.2b shows the clock generator's major function: a crystal placed at pins X1 and X2 will generate the ϕ_1 and ϕ_2 clock signals at one-fourth the crystal frequency. The ϕ_1 and ϕ_2 output waveforms, shown below the block diagram, can vary between approximately 500 kHz to 2 MHz, depending on the version of the 6800 (see Figure 9.3). In general terms, the ϕ_1 clock is used for internal 6800 timing, while the ϕ_2 clock is used to synchronize all data transfers between MPU and peripheral chips.

Additional functions provided by the 6875 include:

- A $\overline{Power}$ $\overline{On}$ $\overline{Reset}$ to condition the RESET input.
- A *Memory Clock* output to sequence dynamic memory.
- A *Memory Ready* input, used to stretch the ϕ_1, ϕ_2, and *Memory Clock* outputs when accessing slow memories (stretching the clock signals gives the data from memory more time to travel to the MPU).
- A $\overline{DMA}/\overline{Refresh}$ $\overline{Request}$ to stretch the ϕ_1 and ϕ_2 clock signals in order to inject an additional Memory Clock refresh pulse going to dynamic RAM, or to perform a cycle-stealing DMA operation (explained later). The $\overline{DMA}/\overline{Refresh}$ $\overline{Grant}$ output marks the stretching time reserved for a refreshing or DMA operation.

6800 TIMING CYCLES

Like its human counterpart, a computer is a creature of repetition. One instruction after the other is fetched and exe-

94

Chapter 9 / Timing and Processor Cycles 95

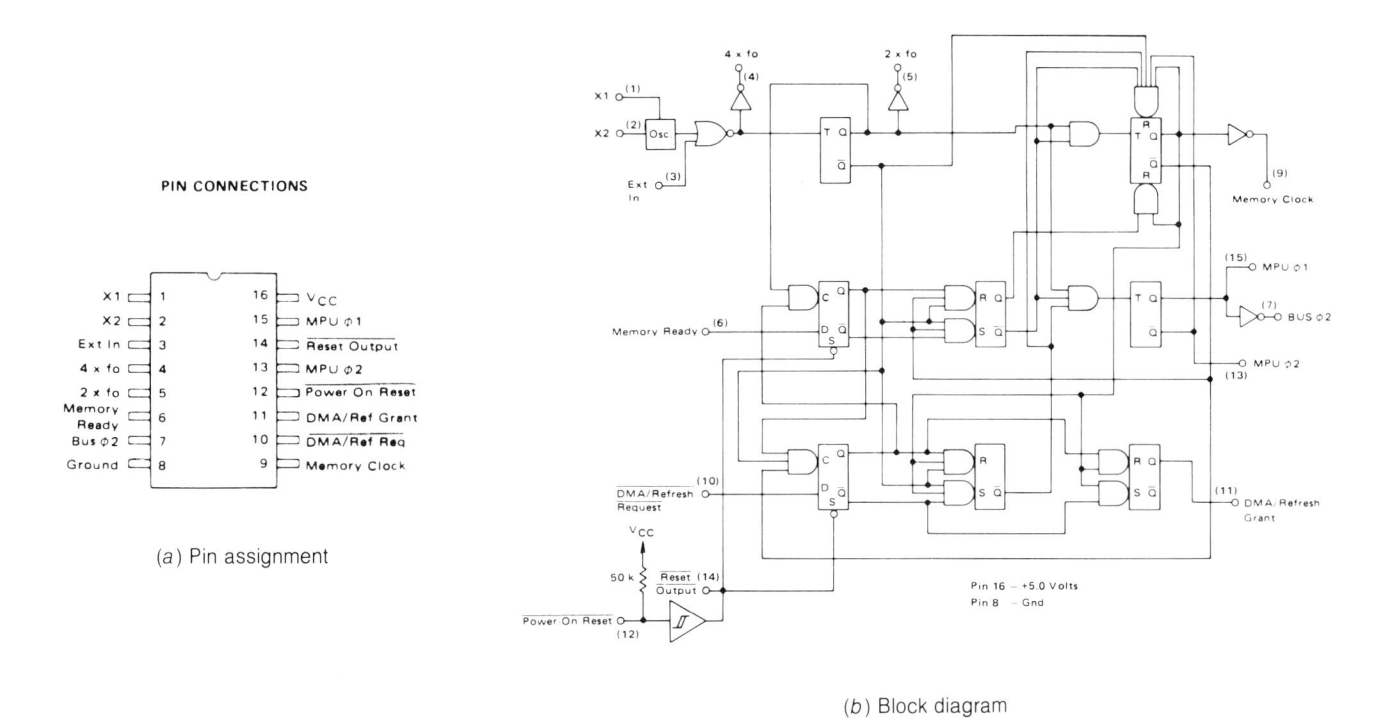

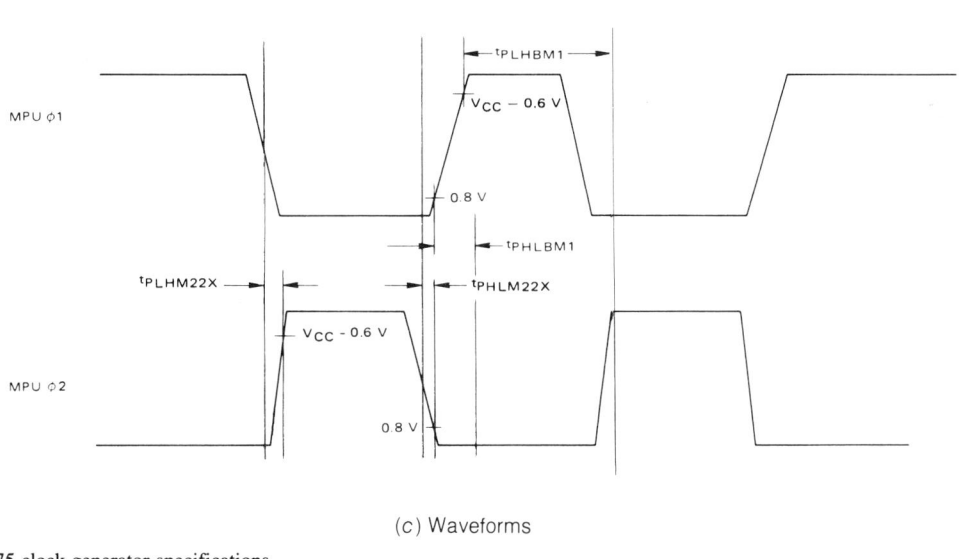

PIN CONNECTIONS

(a) Pin assignment

(b) Block diagram

(c) Waveforms

Figure 9.2 MC6875 clock generator specifications.

	1.0 MHz			1.5 MHz		2 MHz
	0 to 70°C	−40 to +85°C	−55 to +125°C	0 to 70°C	−40 to 85°C	0 to 70°C
Plastic	MC6800P	MC6800CP	—	MC68A00P	MC68A00CP	MC68B00P
Cerdip	MC6800S	MC6800CS	MC6800BQCS	—	—	—
Ceramic	MC6800L	MC6800CL	—	MC68A00L	MC68A00CL	MC68B00L

Courtesy of Motorola, Inc.

Figure 9.3 MC6800 speed, temperature, and package choices.

cuted—just like the recurring theme of a melody. It follows that if we understand in detail the processing of one instruction, we will understand the others.

The longest processing cycle found in the 6800 is the *instruction cycle,* which represents the time required to fetch and execute one complete instruction. Instruction-cycle times can vary widely, depending on the speed of the clock and the complexity of the instruction. A typical 6800 instruction cycle requires approximately 3 microseconds, allowing an average of some 330,000 instructions to be processed every second.

An instruction cycle in turn is made up of 2 to 12 *clock cycles*. The 6800 includes three basic types of clock cycles:

- Read
- Write
- Internal operation

The first two are required every time a data byte is transferred between a peripheral and the 6800 microprocessor. Obviously, these two clock-cycle categories are closely associated with the where/when data transfer operation. The

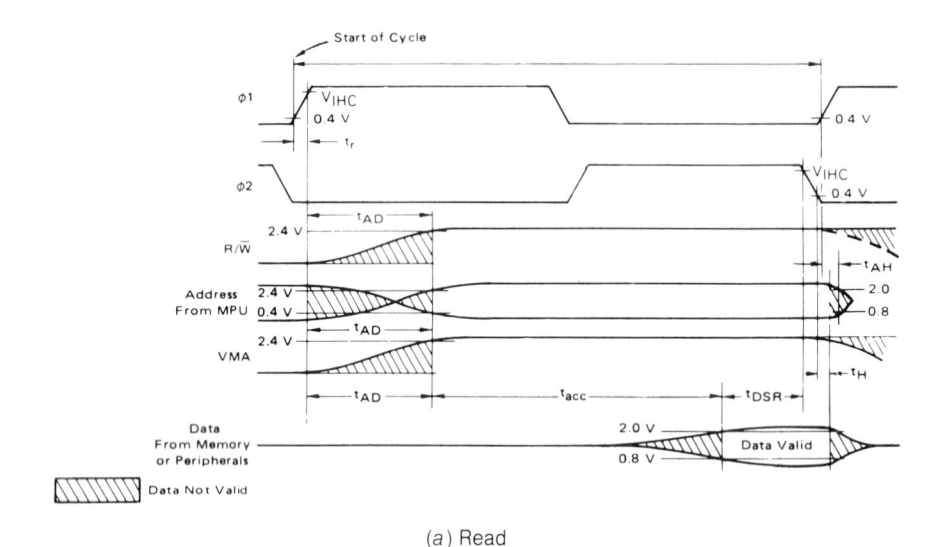

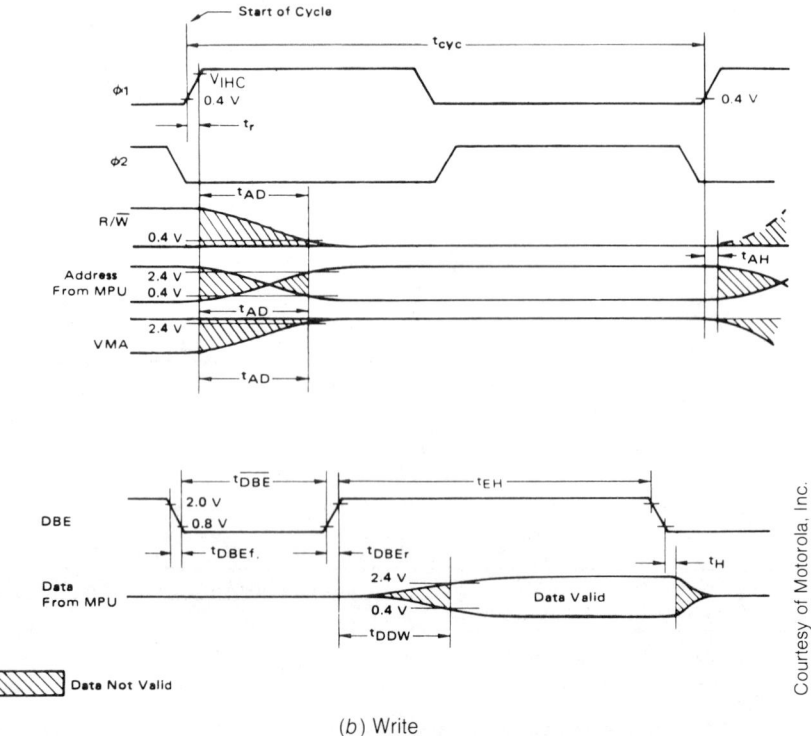

Figure 9.4 The 6800 basic data-transfer waveforms.

third category is reserved for various internal operations. Let's take a close look at the 6800's read and write cycles.

The 6800 Read and Write Waveforms

As expected, the waveforms generated by the 6800 to carry out a read or write data-transfer operation follow the basic where/when pattern, and closely resemble the read and write requirements of the 2114 RAM of Figure 5.7b.

The Read process (Figure 9.4a) begins with the rising ϕ_1 clock. After a brief *address delay* (t_{AD}), caused by a typical 50 pF of bus capacitance, the *where* signals—the address, R/$\overline{W}$ and VMA outputs—are stable on the bus. Following an additional address-stability period, the *when* signal—the ϕ_2 clock—goes active high and data begin to flow from the addressed peripheral. To force the 6800's data bus from its high-impedance state, the ϕ_2 clock usually is connected to DBE (Data Bus Enable), the three-state control signal for the MPU data bus. Valid data read from the peripheral must reach the 6800's data pins within the *peripheral read access time* (t_{acc}), typically 600 ns using the standard 6800 (rather than the higher-speed 68A00 or 68B00). The ϕ_2 clock goes low, terminating the data-transfer process. To be sure the data remain valid, an *address hold time* (t_{AH}) of approximately 40 ns maintains the address, R/$\overline{W}$ and VMA outputs steady before they enter the transition period to the next clock cycle. For the same reason, the data must remain valid for approximately 10 ns after the ϕ_2 clock goes to a zero state (0.4 V or less). When DBE (ϕ_2) goes low, the data pins reenter their high-impedance state.

The Write process waveforms (Figure 9.4b) are nearly identical to the Read process. Since data are sent *from* the MPU, rather than *to* the MPU, the receiving peripheral must have some guarantees about when data are valid. Within a maximum *data delay time* (t_{DDW}) of 225 ns after a rising DBE, the data at the MPU output pins are guaranteed to be valid—and to remain valid at least 10 ns after DBE returns to its low state.

Let's apply what we have learned to a specific case and identify the clock cycles of the familiar STAA EXT instruction.

The STAA EXT Clock-Cycle Sequence

How many clock cycles are contained within the STAA EXT's instruction cycle? The question is not as easy to answer as it may seem because a variety of internal-operation clock cycles are used throughout the 6800 instruction set. However, we know the answer is at least four, because four data-transfer operations are required. Referring to the "Extended Mode Cycle-by-Cycle Operation" chart (Appendix IV) from the *Motorola Microprocessors Data Manual,* we note that the STAA EXT instruction requires five clock cycles. The clock-cycle/waveform diagram of Figure 9.5 will help to make the process clear.

1. The first clock cycle is a *read* cycle involving an operation-code fetch to the instruction register. Of course, all instructions require an op code fetch, and therefore all instruction cycles must consist of at least one clock cycle.

2. Under direction of the STAA EXT instruction's microprogram, the operand's high-order address—located at op code address +1—is fetched to the MAR. Another data transfer to the CPU requires another *read* clock cycle.

3. To bring in the operand's low-order address—located at op code address +2—yet another read clock cycle is processed.

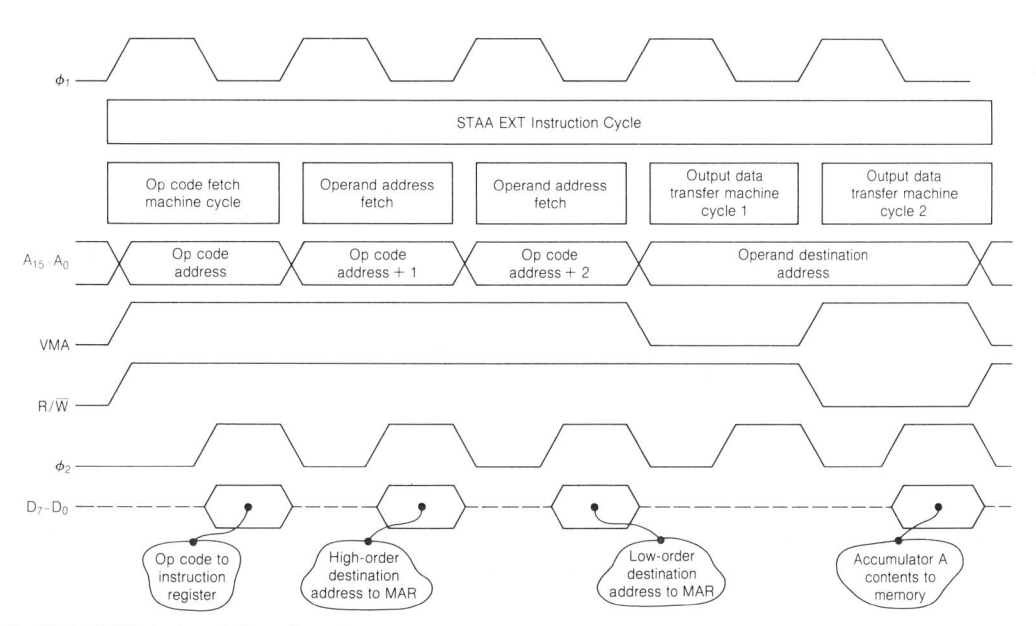

Figure 9.5 The STAA EXT clock-cycle/waveform diagram.

Figure 9.6 The 6800 DMA request pin-out.

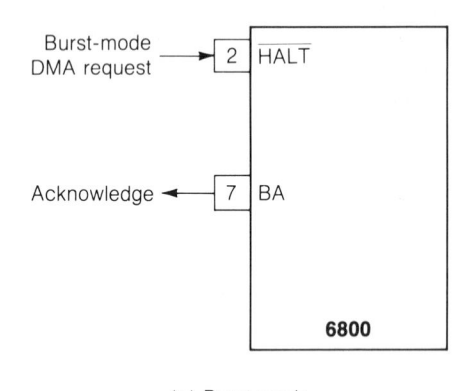

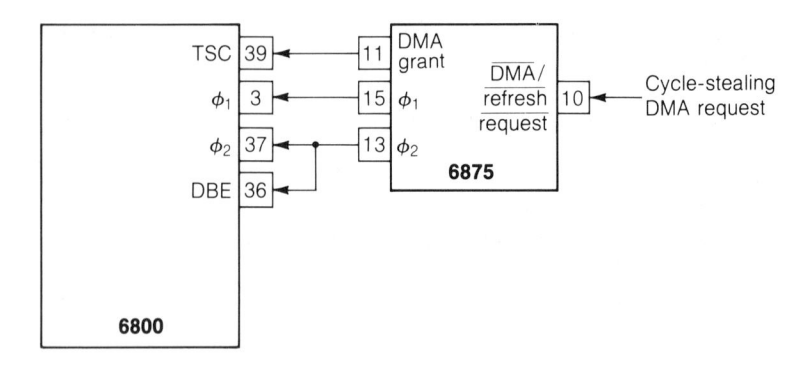

(a) Burst mode

(b) Cycle-stealing mode

4. The fourth clock cycle is an internal-operation cycle, used to ready the operand destination address in the MAR for transmission to the address bus. Note that VMA (valid memory address) is low during this time. Since all memory and port locations include VMA in the decoding circuitry, the data bus will go to the high-impedance tristate condition and the information on the data bus will be irrelevant (as indicated).

5. The fifth and final clock cycle—the execution portion of the STAA EXT instruction cycle—falls into the *write* category, and carries out the transfer of data from accumulator A to selected memory or output port location.

The STAA EXT instruction cycle thus consists of five clock cycles to carry out the four data transfers and one internal operation.

The DMA Request

In the study of computers, *throughput* is the key indicator of computer performance. Throughput is the amount of material processed by a computer system in a given period.

Consider a block transfer of data from one memory area to another. To cycle the data through the accumulator by computer action is relatively slow (instructions must be fetched and address pointers incremented). If the data could be transferred directly between the two storage areas, with the microprocessor totally bypassed, the entire transfer process could be significantly accelerated. To accomplish this direct transfer of data, the 6800 microprocessor must relinquish its control over the bus system—a process known as *direct memory access* (DMA).

The 6800 MPU offers two types of DMA activity: a *burst* mode when a block of data is to be transferred, and a *cycle-stealing* mode, when data are to be transferred a byte at a time.

As shown in Figure 9.6a, the burst mode is initiated by pulling the level-sensitive $\overline{\text{HALT}}$ input low. $\overline{\text{HALT}}$ is synchronized internally and can be requested at any time. When $\overline{\text{HALT}}$ is active low, the processor completes the present instruction, and then enters an "idle" mode, placing the address, data, and R/$\overline{\text{W}}$ lines in the high-impedance state. VMA is forced low to prevent the floating bus from inadvertently activating an external device. The 6800 acknowledges the DMA ($\overline{\text{HALT}}$) state by placing a high on *Bus Available* (BA). When an external *DMA controller* senses a high on BA, it knows it is safe to take over the bus for as long as it likes and perform high-speed data transfers. When $\overline{\text{HALT}}$ is returned high, the 6800 will come out of its idle state, pull BA low, and resume activity. As we shall see in a later chapter, the $\overline{\text{HALT}}$ input is also used for single stepping—a useful troubleshooting technique.

The WAI (Wait for Interrupt) instruction also puts the address, R/$\overline{\text{W}}$, and data bus into the tristate mode (VMA is held low, BA high), and is therefore a *software* DMA request (in addition to its stop and interrupt processing properties).

For cycle-stealing DMA applications, in which an external device may wish to transfer a single byte of information, the 6800 offers the *three-state control* (TSC) input to the 6800. Referring to Figure 9.6b, when a cycle-stealing *DMA request* is made to the 6875 clock generator, transitions of the ϕ_1 and ϕ_2 clocks to the MPU are briefly halted and *DMA grant* goes high, activating TSC. When TSC is active, the address bus and R/$\overline{\text{W}}$ line are floated (as well as the data bus if ϕ_2 is halted low and connected to DBE). A single DMA operation can then take place. When TSC is deactivated (returned low), the address and R/$\overline{\text{W}}$ lines again take over the bus system. Since the MPU contains dynamic registers, the clocks can be stopped for no more than approximately 5 microseconds.

RESET Input

When we study the action of the RESET input, we are also beginning our study of interrupts (Chapter 16), for a RESET acts in many ways like an interrupt.

To prepare for RESET action, place the starting address of the RESET routine into memory locations $FFFE and $FFFF (this is usually done at the factory when the *monitor ROM* is burned). Basically, the level-sensitive, active-low RESET signal—which can come at any time (asynchronously)—causes the contents of $FFFE and $FFFF to be loaded into the program counter to point to the beginning of the RESET routine. For example, if $0000 were placed into memory locations $FFFE and $FFFF, a RESET would vector the processor to $0000—the opposite end of the memory map—to begin processing action.

MPU Flowchart

Figure 9.7 is a simplified diagram of the MPU flowchart. Each pass through the sequence completes one instruction cycle. The 6800 first checks for a DMA request (HALT). If present, it enters the DMA "idle" state, sending BA (Bus Available) high. If no DMA is requested, it next checks for an interrupt request. Finding no interrupts, it fetches the next instruction. If the fetched instruction is a software interrupt (SWI), it jumps to the interrupt process; if not, it executes the instruction. The process is repeated.

The Final System

A complete 6800-based microcomputer system is shown in Figure 9.8. If we assume our STAA $1000 instruction is stored in the PROM module at locations $FF00 through $FF02 and accumulator A is holding $CC, Figure 9.9 shows the generalized STAA EXT waveforms (Figure 9.5) applied to the specific design of Figure 9.8. To review the entire timing/sequencing process, begin at the left side of the STAA $1000 waveforms and follow all signals through the system diagram of Figure 9.8.

GENEALOGY OF THE 6800 FAMILY

The basic 6800 is the root of the 8-bit Motorola family tree. From this single trunk line, three main branches have grown: the general-purpose 8-bit branch, the single-chip branch, and the 16-bit branch. As shown in Figure 9.10, each of the three main branches has further spread out into a number of improved or special-purpose microprocessors. Since some MPUs (e.g., the MC146805) have found applications in both the general-purpose and single-chip branches, they are

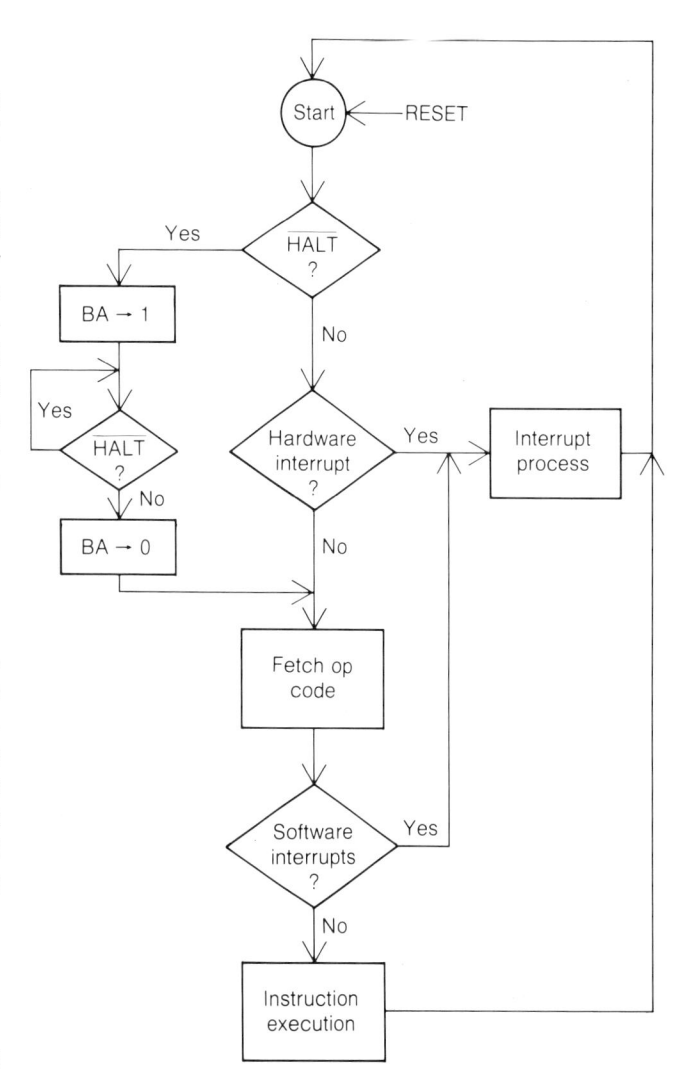

Figure 9.7 Simplified 6800 instruction cycle flowchart.

included in both branches. At the present time, the 16-bit branch is the fastest growing of the three.

In Parts I and II, we have concentrated on the general-purpose 6800, postponing the single-chip branch to Chapter 20, and the 16-bit branch to Chapter 25. Before leaving the subject of the 6800-based 8-bit architecture and processing action, let's take a brief look at the more popular members of the general-purpose branch. These include the MC6802, MC6803, MC6808, MC6809, and MC146805. To ease the pains of upgrading, all are software compatible with the basic 6800 microprocessor.

The MC6802

The 6802—introduced shortly after the 6800—began the trend toward integration: placing more and more functions

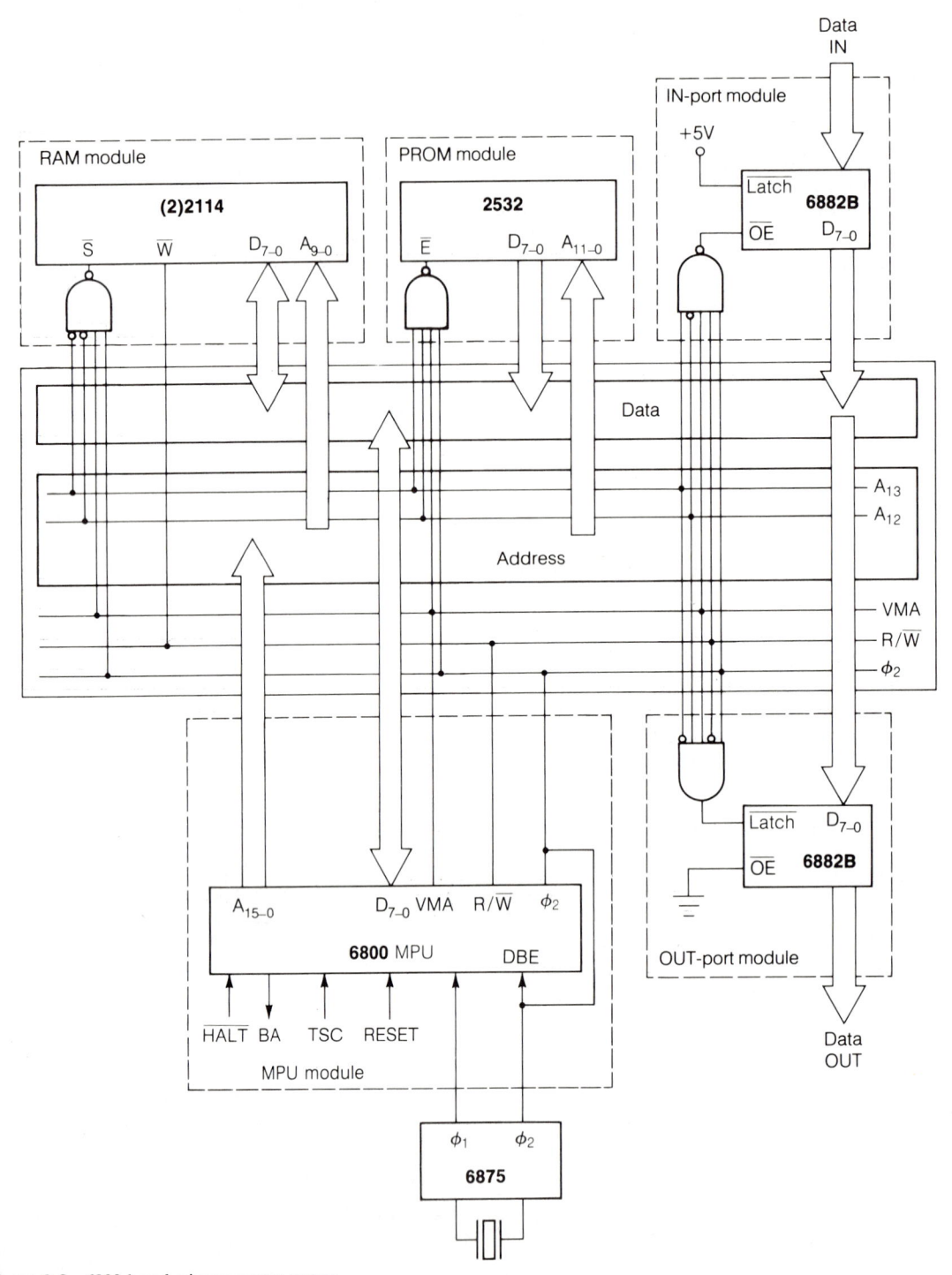

Figure 9.8 6800-based microcomputer system.

on the microprocessor chip. By placing the clock generator and 128 bytes of external RAM on chip, a minimum system can be fashioned from just two chips:

- MC6802 MPU
- MC6846 ROM-I/O timer unit

The 6803 MPU

The 6803 is a hybrid, showing some characteristics of a conventional microprocessor (such as the 6800) and some characteristics of a single-chip microcomputer (such as the

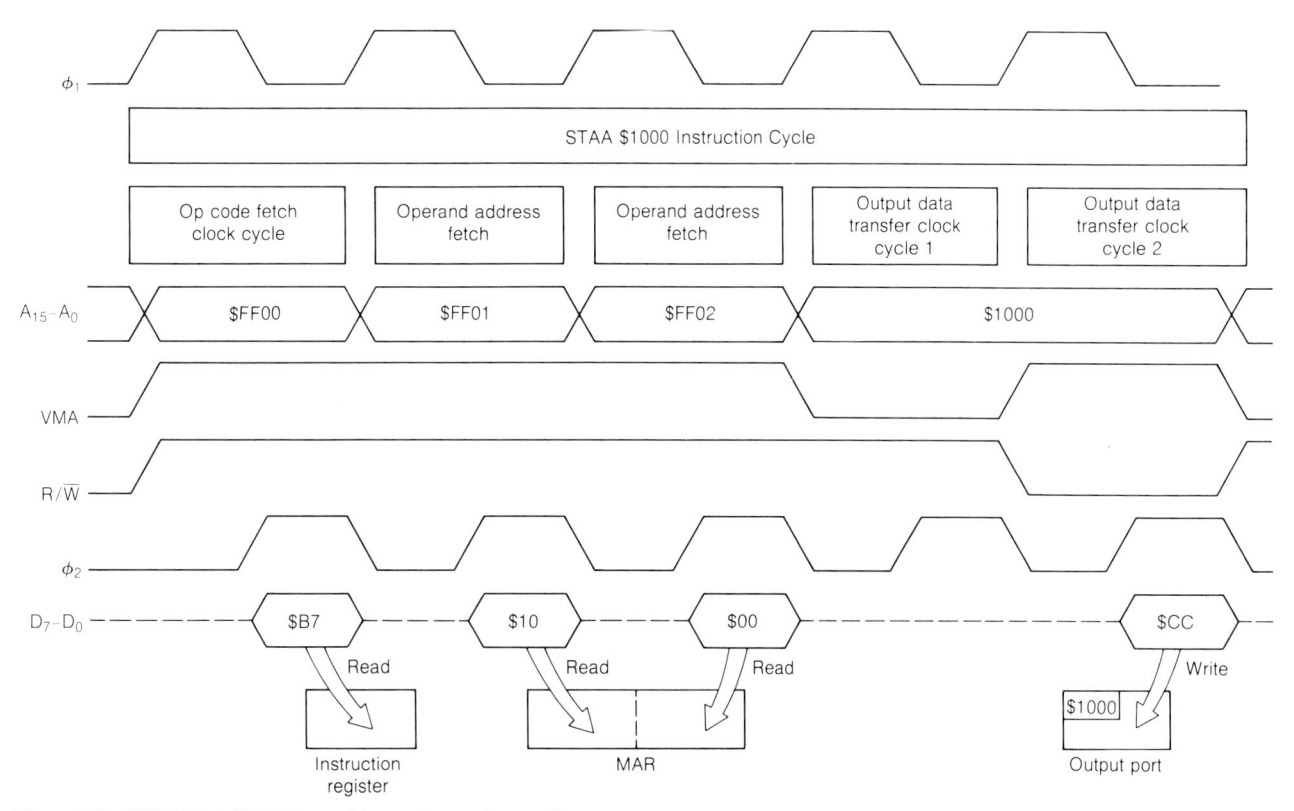

Figure 9.9 6800 STAA $1000 (output) instruction cycle waveforms.

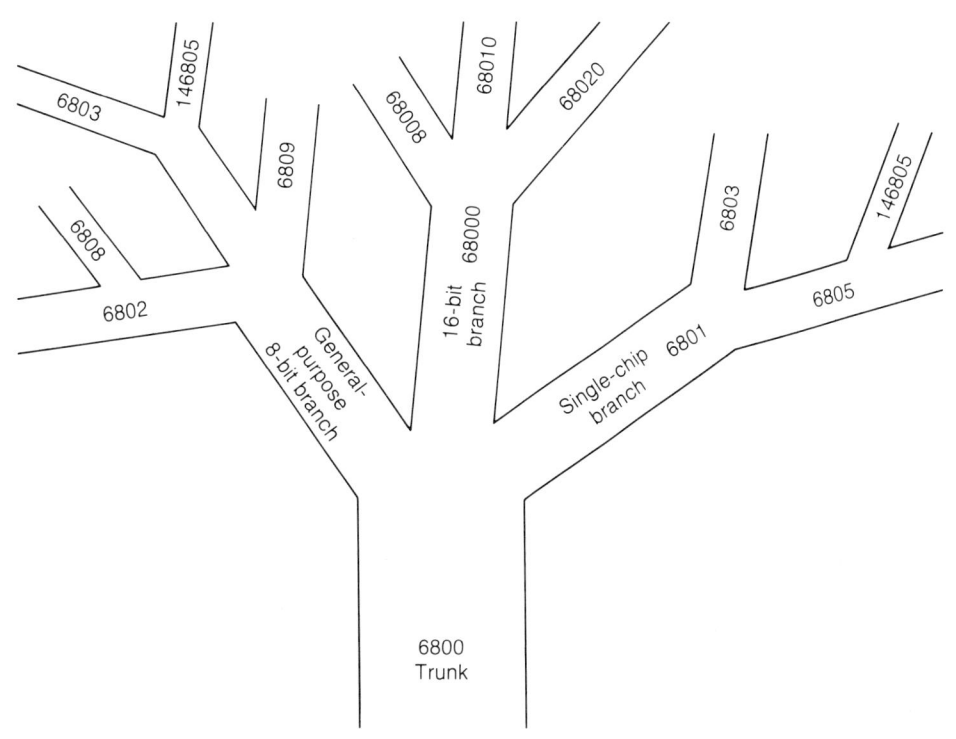

Figure 9.10 The 6800 family tree.

6801). Some of the features borrowed from the single-chip concept include:

- 13 parallel I/O lines
- Internal clock
- Full-duplex Serial Communications Interface (discussed in Chapter 21)
- 16-bit timer with three modes
- 16-bit multiplexed address bus
- 128 bytes on-chip RAM

Add to this an expanded (but 6800-compatible) instruction set and faster execution speed, and you have an MPU of great flexibility.

The MC6808

The low-cost 6808 is basically a 6802, but without the on-chip RAM. Like the 6802, it is fully expandable to 64K of external RAM, ROM, or peripherals (ports).

The MC6809

The most advanced version of the 6800 family unit, the MC6809 is also the highest performer. Although it is an 8-bit processor with an 8-bit bus, it paved the way for 16-bit machines (68000-based) by offering five internal 16-bit registers. Add to this an expanded set of addressing modes, an 8 × 8 hardware multiplier, and improved interrupt structure, and you begin to realize why the 6809 offers up to five times the performance of the 6800.

The 6809 also facilitated programming in a high-level structured language—such as Pascal—by providing efficient handling of compiled code. Add multitask and multiprocessor organization, along with custom peripherals (e.g., the MC6829 Memory Management Unit), and you have a true top-end 8-bit processor.

The MC146805

As the cost and speed barriers are overcome, more and more microprocessors and components will be implemented in CMOS technology. To the major attractions of CMOS—low power drain, high noise immunity, and wide power supply tolerance—the 146805 has added a number of improvements:

- On-chip RAM (112 bytes), timer (programmable), parallel I/O ports (bidirectional), and a clock oscillator (5 MHz)
- Compatible 2K × 8 CMOS ROM (MCM65516), Parallel Interface (MC146823), and RAM/clock (MC146818)
- Bit manipulation and test instructions, along with improved addressing modes, which augment the 6800-based instruction set
- Two low-power standby modes

All purely CMOS processors also offer static design, allowing the system to be clocked at any frequency below the maximum—without loss of information (some "CMOS" microprocessors contain dynamic RAM and cannot be clocked at dc speed).

Although technically a single-chip processor, the 146805E2 is expandable to 8K of external RAM/ROM/ports. It is therefore included in the general-purpose branch as well to provide a solution to those seeking a CMOS general-purpose microprocessor.

8-BIT MICROPROCESSORS FEATURES MATRIX

Device	Tech	Pins	RAM 8X	I/O Lines	Special I/O	Mnem Inst[1]	Ext Addr	Data Size	Clock	Timer
MC6800	NMOS	40	—	—	—	72	64K	8	No	—
MC6802	NMOS	40	128	—	—	72	64K	8	Yes	—
MC6802NS	NMOS	40	128	—	—	72	64K	8	Yes	—
MC6803	HMOS	40	128	13	Serial	82	64K	8	Yes	16-Bit
MC6803NR	HMOS	40	—	13	Serial	82	64K	8	Yes	16-Bit
MC6808	HMOS	40	—	—	—	72	64K	8	Yes	—
MC6809	HMOS	40	—	—	—	59	64K[2]	8	Yes	—
MC6809E	HMOS	40	—	—	—	59	64K[2]	8	No	—
MC146805E2	CMOS	40	112	16	—	61	8K	8	Yes	8-Bit + Prescaler

NOTES:
1. Some Mnemonic Instructions can have many Opcode Instructions. As a result a Microprocessor normally has many more Opcode Instructions than Mnemonic Instructions. For instance the MC6809 has 59 Mnemonic Instructions and 1464 Opcode Instructions.

2. Two megabytes when used with the MC6829 Memory Management Unit.

Figure 9.11 Summary of the Motorola 8-bit general-purpose microprocessor family.

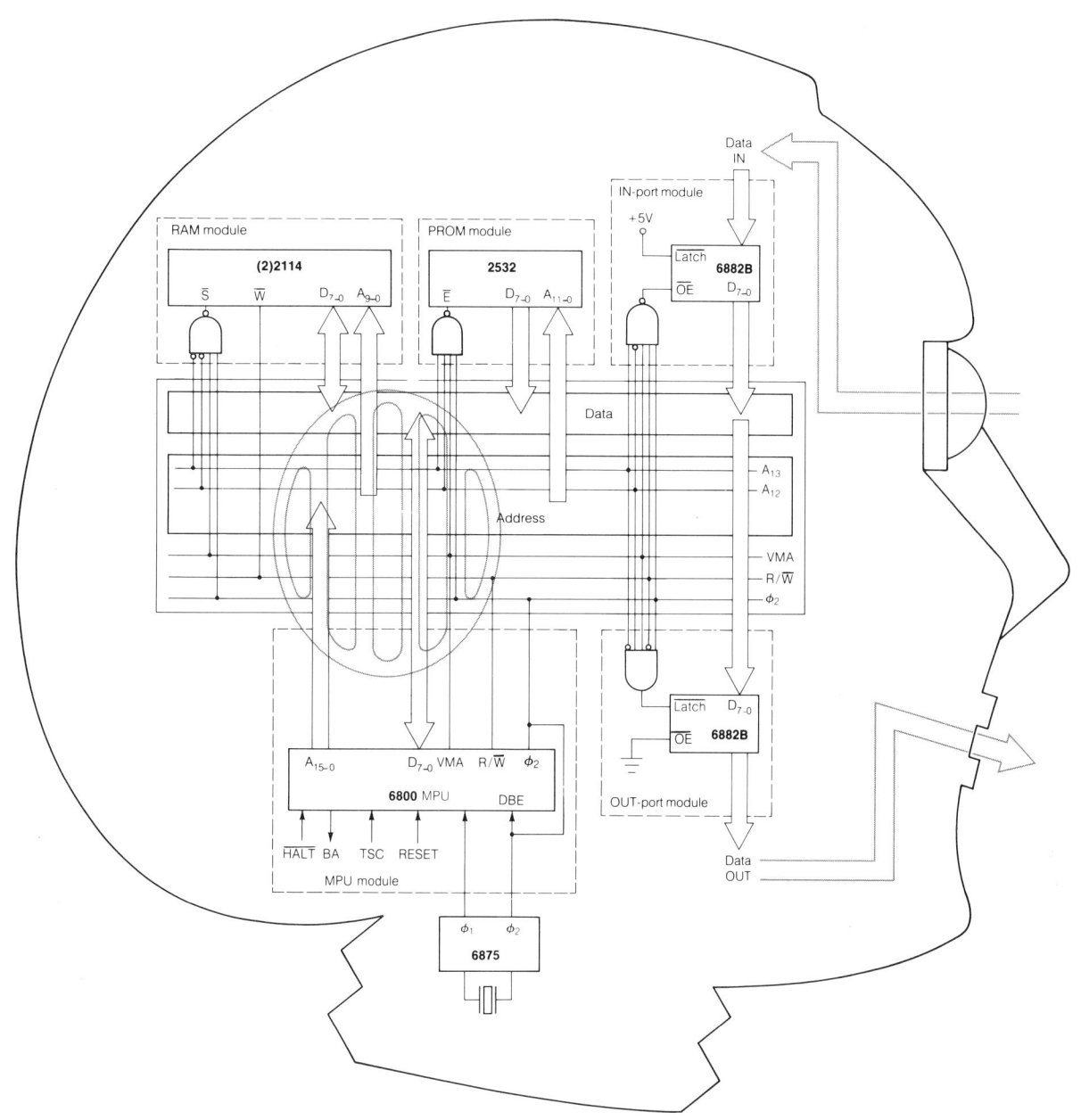

Figure 9.12 Fully functional 6800-based thinking machine.

The Motorola 8-bit general-purpose microprocessor family is summarized in Figure 9.11.

INTELLIGENT-MACHINE UPDATE

Our knowledge of basic computer anatomy—its hardware—is now complete, and we have studied its actions as it spoke its first word. As demonstrated by Figure 9.12, our intelligent machine has developed beyond its infancy.

Fully equipped to learn, our computer can now be sent back to school, where it will expand its vocabulary and be taught many new skills. In other words, starting with the next chapter, the emphasis will shift from hardware and processing action to software and program development.

QUESTIONS AND PROBLEMS

1. If a 2 MHz crystal drives the MC6875 clock generator of Figure 9.2, what are the resulting ϕ_1 and ϕ_2 clock frequencies?
2. Running under a 2 MHz *clock* frequency, how long does a clock cycle last?
3. Name the three types of clock cycles.
4. Under what conditions is a $\overline{\text{HALT}}$ requested? A three-state control (TSC)?
5. What state does the CPU assume when the burst-mode $\overline{\text{HALT}}$ request is honored? When the cycle-stealing TSC request is honored?
6. When does BA (Bus Available) go active high?
7. For the 6800 processor, draw a waveform diagram for the LDAA $2000 instruction similar to Figure 9.9 (the LDAA instruction is stored at PROM locations $FC00 to $FC02).
8. What state does the 6800 assume when DBE (Data Bus Enable) is high? When DBE is low?
9. Why is the ϕ_2 clock usually attached to DBE?
10. If a 6800 is powered by an 8 MHz crystal, how long does it take to process the STAA EXT instruction?
11. Referring to Figure 9.8, why does the decoding circuitry of the 2532 EPROM not include the R/$\overline{\text{W}}$ line?
12. For the STAA $1000 clock-cycle diagram of Figure 9.9, specify the source and destination of each of the four data transfers.
13. If the first instruction of your program is located at $C0A0, what should be placed at locations $FFFE and $FFFF in order to initiate program action via the RESET input?
14. Redraw the waveforms of Figure 9.9 assuming the STAA $4020 instruction is located at $AA00 through $AA02, and accumulator A is holding $D1.
15. What is the difference between the *Memory Ready* and *DMA/Refresh Request* inputs to the 6875?

part III

Software: The Spark of Life

System hardware, whether the cell structure of the human mind or the pieces of a chessboard, has no motion or action about it, no life or direction—it simply exists. But add software—whether programs, neurotransmitters, or chess rules—and the whole scene springs to life. It is software, the sequential flow of actions, that animates the hardware system.

Our intelligent machine now has a working vocabulary of only two words, the familiar LDAX EXT and STAX EXT, and with these two words it can perform only the most simple data-transfer processes—such as the mimic task. Clearly, if our computer is ever going to grow into a skilled and useful intelligent machine, its vocabulary must be enlarged.

A computer's vocabulary is known as its *instruction set*. When a variety of instructions are arranged into a program, the result is known as *software*. In Part III we will be looking at most of the 72 types of instructions that make up the 6800's instruction set. To expand the working vocabulary of our intelligent machine, Part III will introduce many specific examples in the use of the 6800 instructions.

chapter 10

The Data-Transfer Group

Data transfer is a subject we are familiar with, for the functions of seeing, hearing, and speaking—intelligent-machine style—are simply I/O-related data-transfer operations using the familiar LDAX and STAX instructions.

But what about memory-related data-transfer operations ("remembering" and "recalling" information to and from memory)? These data-transfer operations will require a great deal more flexibility than simple I/O-related operations.

Another reason why we need a powerful group of data-transfer instructions is the presence of the stack pointer, index register, and condition code register within the 6800 (Figure 10.1). We have not introduced them before because they were not needed for the simple mimic process. Certainly, we can expect the data-transfer group to move information to and from these three new internal registers.

DATA-TRANSFER VERBS

Below are listed three familiar English instructions, in verb/object format:

Verb	Object
Load	truck
Add	fuel
Transfer	supplies

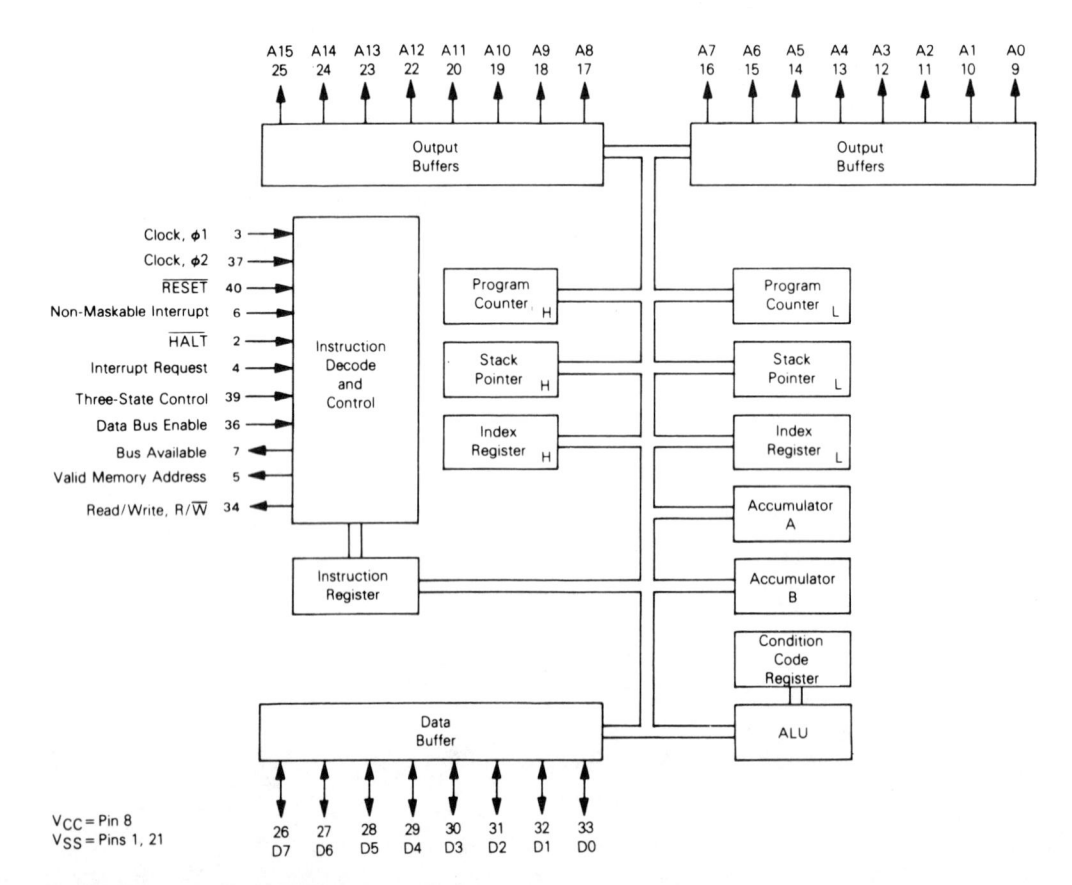

Figure 10.1 6800 MPU functional block diagram.

In each case, is not the verb portion the operative part of the instruction, and does not the verb alone reveal what action the instruction will take? Therefore, referring to Appendix III, let us begin by listing the three verbs that make up the data-transfer group of instructions:

> Load
> Store
> Transfer

In practice, all three verbs refer to the same basic process: the transfer of data from source to destination. However, each verb really means more than this. The verb *Load*, we know from our previous studies, commands the recall process, when data are transferred from memory (or an input port) to an internal register. When we see the verb *Store,* we will know the remembering process is to be carried out, and data transferred from an internal register to a memory location (or an output port). The verb *Transfer* is reserved for data movements within the 6800 microprocessor, and no external memory or I/O port locations are involved at all.

As we can see, the verb content (op code) of each instruction will seldom be difficult to comprehend. It is the object portion (the operand) of each instruction, though, that will give us the greatest difficulty—at least at first.

DATA-TRANSFER ADDRESSING MODES

Before the op code can operate upon the data, it must know the answer to the question, "Where is the data?" Each of the possible techniques for answering this question is an *addressing mode*. Each addressing mode falls into one of the two basic categories we introduced earlier:

- The operand *is* the data (load *truck*).
- The operand is an *address,* telling us *where* the data are located (load *contents of garage 7*).

These same two operand categories are found in the data-transfer group. What complicates the situation is the large variety of addressing techniques within the second category. Furthermore, exactly what is classified as an addressing mode differs slightly from one reference to the next. In addition, some instructions are technically combinations of several addressing modes. However, regardless of the source, there are six *basic* 6800 addressing modes. They are listed below:

1. *Immediate (IMM)*—The instruction contains the data (the operand field of the instruction mnemonic *is* the value that is to be operated on).
2. *Inherent (INH)*—The data are located within the microprocessor in an internal register. Since the internal registers are few in number, the op code alone contains all the address information required (the address is "inherent" in the instruction). For example, a single bit within certain op codes specifies accumulator A or accumulator B.
3. *Direct (DIR)*—The *address* of the value to be operated upon within memory or I/O is contained in the second byte of the instruction (the address is 8 bits wide, allowing only the first page to be selected).
4. *Extended (EXT)*—The *address* of the value to be operated upon is contained in the second and third bytes of the instruction (high order in second byte; low order in third byte). Since the address is 16 bits wide, the full 64K of memory and I/O space can be selected.
5. *Indexed (IND)*—The address of the value to be operated upon is calculated within the CPU by adding the second byte of the instruction to the contents of the index register. The result of the addition (often called the *effective address*) is used to address a memory or I/O location.
6. *Relative (REL)*—A memory address is calculated by adding the contents of the second byte of the instruction to the *present* contents of the program counter. The second byte must be in 2's complement form, giving an addressing range of −126 to +129 (*relative to the present instruction op code*).

Each data-transfer verb (load, store, transfer) will use one or more of the six basic addressing modes. For example, the verb *load* uses four addressing modes (IMM, DIR, EXT, IND), and the verb *transfer* uses one (inherent). *Relative* is the only addressing mode not used by the data-transfer group; it will be introduced in Chapter 13.

As we familiarize ourselves with each of the five modes of addressing used by the data-transfer group, concentrate on two questions: What is the source of the data transfer, and what is the destination? Each data-transfer instruction must in some manner supply this information.

Immediate Addressing Mode

The *immediate* form of addressing is perhaps the easiest to understand, because we have seen it before (load *truck*). If the instruction contains the actual data, it is an *immediate* type of instruction.

A specific example will show how easy it is to work with the *immediate* form of addressing. Referring to the Load Accumulator instruction summary of Figure 10.2*a,* note that the *immediate* addressing mode is used twice, once for loading data immediately to accumulator A and once for loading data to accumulator B.

For the Load Accumulator Immediate type of instruction, can we now answer the two important questions: What is the source of the data transfer, and what is the destination?

Load Accumulator (LDA)

Operation: ACCX ← (M)

Description: Loads the contents of memory into the accumulator. The condition codes are set according to the data.

Addressing Modes	Execution Time (No. of cycles)	Number of bytes of machine code	HEX.	OCT.	DEC.
A IMM	2	2	86	206	134
A DIR	3	2	96	226	150
A EXT	4	3	B6	266	182
A IND	5	2	A6	246	166
B IMM	2	2	C6	306	198
B DIR	3	2	D6	326	214
B EXT	4	3	F6	366	246
B IND	5	2	E6	346	230

(Coding of First (or only) byte of machine code: HEX., OCT., DEC.)

Courtesy of Motorola, Inc.

(a) Instruction summary

Mnemonic	Binary	Hexadecimal
LDAA #$4D	1 0 0 0 0 1 1 0	$86
	0 1 0 0 1 1 0 1	$4D

(b) Example

Figure 10.2 The Load Accumulator instruction type.

The source is memory—it is the second byte of the Load Accumulator Immediate instruction. The destination is either accumulator A or accumulator B—to be determined by the programmer by selecting op code $86 (for accumulator A) or $C6 (for accumulator B).

To test our knowledge of the Load Accumulator Immediate type of instruction, let us write the complete binary (hex) instruction for moving data byte $4D to accumulator A. As shown in Figure 10.2b, just select op code $86, and place the data to be transferred in the second byte of the instruction. Note how we also update the mnemonic to reflect this specific example (the number sign (#) indicates *immediate* addressing).

Incidentally, do you now see the value of the mnemonic notation? Once you know the mnemonic format, a quick glance will tell you exactly what the instruction is to accomplish—a feat not possible with the binary formulation. We will see other advantages of using the mnemonic notation in a later chapter.

To see how the LDAA #$4D instruction is processed, and to review the material of Chapters 8 and 9, Figure 10.3 shows the 6800-based instruction-cycle waveforms, along with a diagram of the data-transfer process.

The four remaining addressing modes are not as simple as the *immediate* form of addressing, for the operand specifies the data by telling *where* they are rather than *what* they are. Let us take a brief look at each of these addressing modes.

Direct Addressing Mode

Turning again to the Load Accumulator type of instruction (Figure 10.2a), we see that it also offers the *direct* addressing mode. That is, the location (address) of the data in memory or an input port is specified *directly* by the second byte of the instruction. Since only a single byte may be used as the address, instructions using the *direct* mode of addressing may only specify addresses from location $00 to $FF—the first page of memory (the *direct* mode of addressing is also called *page zero* addressing).

We are now ready to answer the questions, What is the source of the data transfer, and what is the destination? The source of the data transfer is a memory location within page zero given directly by the second byte of the instruction. The destination is accumulator A or accumulator B.

The clock-cycle diagram of Figure 10.4 shows how the contents of memory location $003D can be moved to accumulator B directly. The absence of the # sign—used in *immediate* addressing to specify data—indicates that the number following the op code ($3D) is an address. A waveform analysis (similar to that shown in Figure 10.3) of the LDAB $3D instruction is left as an exercise.

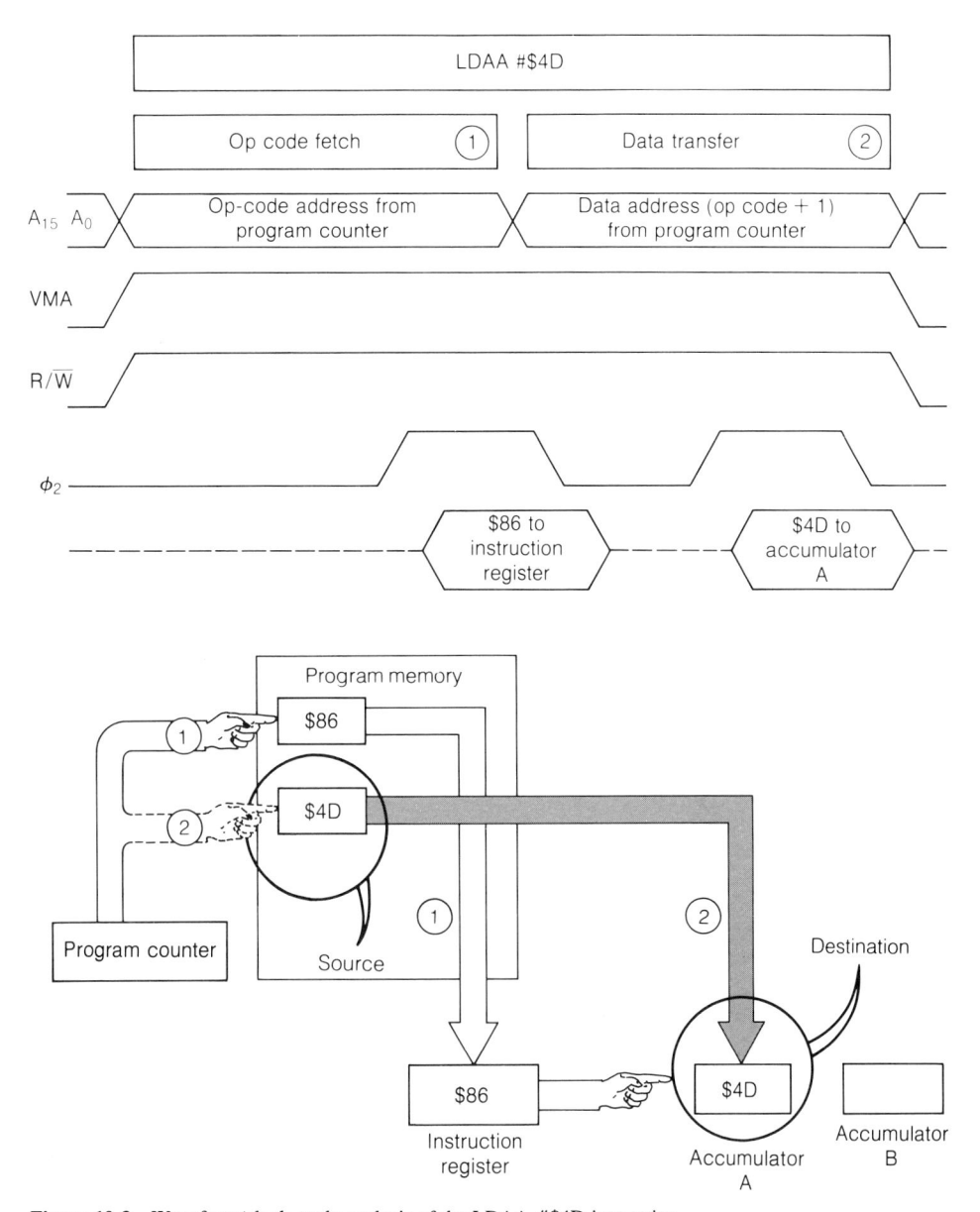

Figure 10.3 Waveform/clock-cycle analysis of the LDAA #$4D instruction.

With the introduction of the *direct* addressing mode, we can at last tie up a long-dangling loose end. During hardware design in Part I, why did we insist on placing ROM (PROM) at the very highest memory location and RAM at the very lowest? We in fact already have answered the first question: we had to place ROM at the highest location to hold the RESET vector at $FFFE and $FFFF. Now, with the introduction of *direct* addressing we have a good reason for placing RAM at page zero. That reason is speed. Since only a single address is required, *direct* addressing involves fewer bytes of program code than *extended* addressing and hence is faster. In most applications, page zero is therefore reserved for scratchpad RAM where high-speed operations are of most importance.

Extended Addressing Mode

Extended addressing—used in our mimic routine—is similar to *direct addressing*: the location of the value to be operated upon is specified *directly* by the instruction. However, two bytes instead of one are used to specify the data, allowing this addressing mode to locate data anywhere from $0000 to $FFFF—over the entire 64K of memory-I/O space.

For the Load Accumulator instruction type, the source of the data transfer is a memory location given directly by bytes 2 and 3, and the destination is accumulator A or accumulator B. The clock-cycle diagram of Figure 10.5 shows how the contents of memory location $4A71 can be moved to accumulator A. (Note that the high-order memory address goes

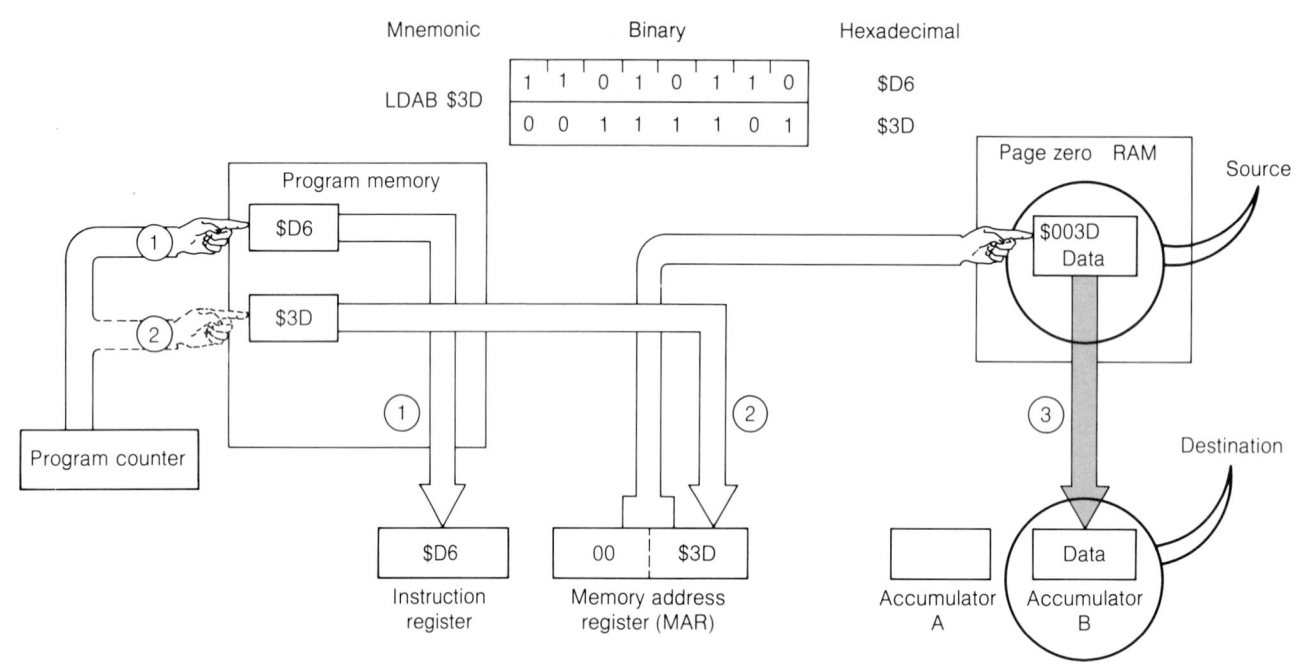

Figure 10.4 The LDAB $3D *direct* addressing instruction and clock-cycle diagram.

in the second byte and the low-order memory address in the third byte.) A waveform analysis is left as an exercise.

Indexed Addressing Mode

An everyday example of *indexed addressing* will help to set the stage for this more involved instruction type. Suppose we would like to determine the address of a particular house, but we don't know the address directly. However, we do know that it is located six house numbers down from the church, and that the address of the church is $3000. In this example, the church is known as the *index,* and the number "6" as the *offset*. To determine the unknown house number, we add the *index* ($3000) to the *offset* (6), and obtain $3006 as the correct address. *Our only restriction is that the offset must be a positive number.* To test your knowledge of *indexed* addressing, can you write the correct instruction to store the contents of accumulator A into memory location $3006 (assume the index register contains $3000)? Selecting the correct op code with the help of Appendix I, compare your answer with Figure 10.6 (note that the symbol "X" is used in the mnemonic to indicate *indexed* addressing).

Indexed addressing is particularly useful when addressing entries in a table. For example, the table below stores the batting averages of 10 players (all, "fortunately," have batting averages of 255 or below, and therefore are accessed by a single byte):

Batting Average Table

Memory location	Batting average
$6000	134
$6001	201
$6002	207
$6003	230
$6004	220
$6005	191
$6006	255
$6007	186
$6008	229
$6009	240
$600A	207

To access the table, first load the index register with the beginning address of the table ($6000). The offset (from 0 to $A) then points to the proper entry. As an exercise, can you determine the instruction that will load accumulator B with the batting average of player number 8? Check your answer with the solution below:

LDAB $8,X $E6, $08

Inherent Addressing

No address locations at all need be supplied when using *inherent* addressing since the source and destination are pre-

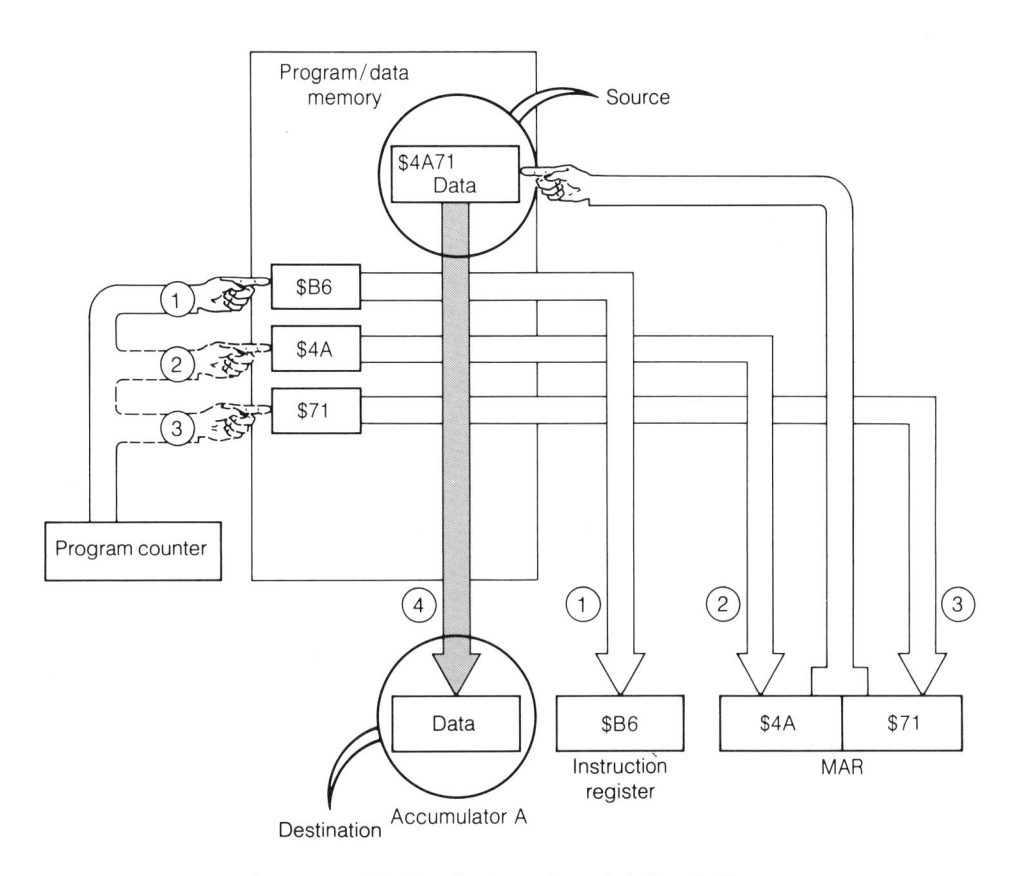

Figure 10.5 The LDAA $4A71 *extended* addressing instruction and clock-cycle diagram.

determined by the op code. The verb *transfer,* from the data-transfer group, uses *inherent* addressing exclusively. For example, the instruction TAB (see Figure 10.7*a*) transfers the contents of accumulator A to accumulator B. The source is accumulator A; the destination is accumulator B. Figure 10.7*b* diagrams the TAB clock-cycle action. Note that during the internal data transfer, the op code of the next instruction is *prefetched*. This overlapping of functions ("killing two birds with one stone") is used by many of the *inherent*-addressing instructions to increase throughput. Advanced 16-bit processors, such as the 68000 and 8086, make extensive use of prefetching to greatly increase processing speed.

INSTRUCTION TYPES

Our study of addressing modes clearly demonstrates why we have been using the term *type of instruction* for each of the 72 basic commands in the instruction set. For example, the LDA instruction *type* of Figure 10.2*a* includes eight op codes—any one of four addressing modes loading data to either of the two accumulators.

To summarize, the 6800 instruction set consists of 72 *types* of instructions, consisting of 197 binary combinations (leaving 59 of the 256 possible codes unassigned).

A DATA-TRANSFER EXAMPLE

We have now completed our study of the three data-transfer verbs (*load, store,* and *transfer*) and have studied the five applicable addressing modes (*immediate, direct, extended, indexed,* and *inherent*). To test our knowledge of the data-transfer instructions and applicable addressing modes, let's write a "checkers" program in which a data byte is commanded to "hop" between various computer locations. The

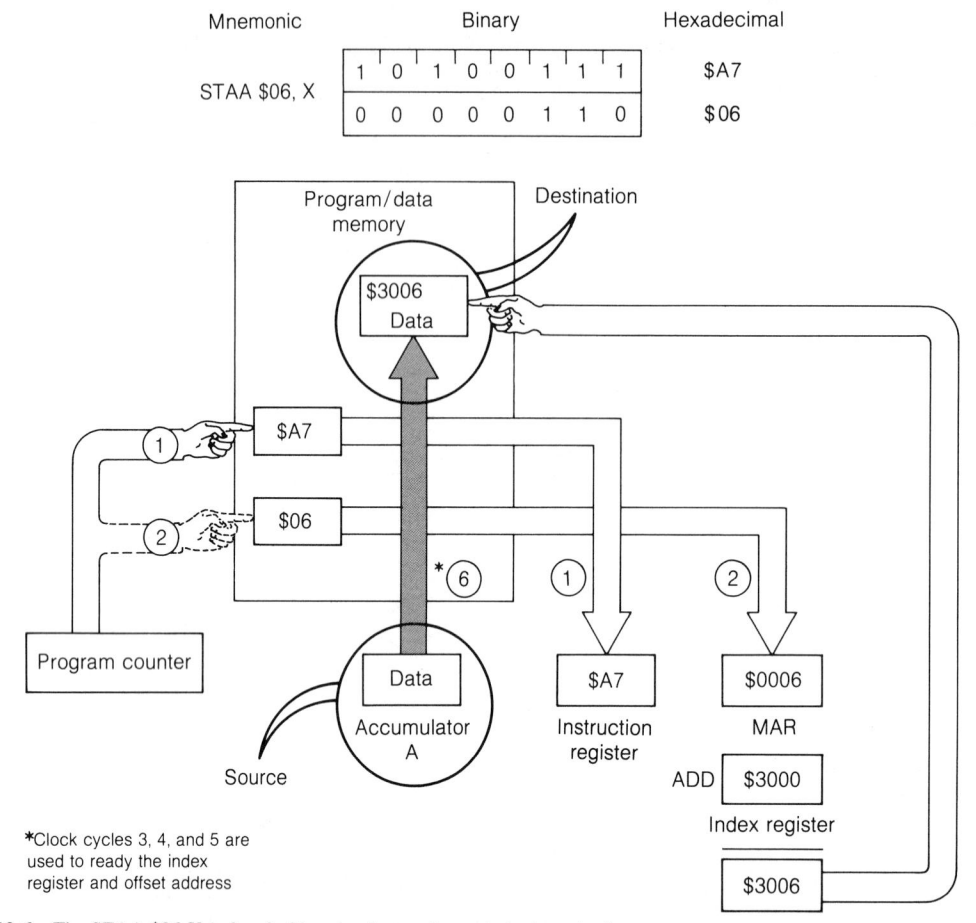

Figure 10.6 The STAA $06,X *indexed* addressing instruction and clock-cycle diagram.

---

task is shown in Figure 10.8. Each leg of the journey is labeled with the desired addressing mode. Let's write the program that will complete the round trip from input port to output port.

- *Leg 1:* We begin with the familiar input-port technique using *extended* addressing. The proper instruction is:

Mnemonic	Machine code
LDAA $2000	$B6, $20, $00

- *Leg 2:* To transfer the data from accumulator A to memory location $002A, we use *direct* (page zero) addressing (because it is faster).

    STAA $2A $97, $2A

- *Leg 3:* Next, for variety, *indexed* addressing is used to transfer the data to accumulator B. First, we load the index register with a convenient value ($0000) using the load index register (*immediate* addressing mode):

    LDX #$0000 $CE, $00, $00

    We then specify an offset of $2A in the instruction:

    LDAB $2A,X $E6, $2A

- *Leg 4:* Leg 4 uses *inherent* addressing to carry out a simple transfer from accumulator B to accumulator A:

    TBA $17

- *Leg 5:* Leg 5 uses *extended* addressing to outport the data to port $1000:

    STAA $1000 $B7, $10, $00

We have looked in detail at most of the instruction types composing the data-transfer group and have reviewed five addressing modes. When the remaining data-transfer instructions—used for a variety of specialized tasks—are added in later chapters (see Appendix III), they can be included in your working vocabulary with a minimum of effort.

Transfer from Accumulator A to Accumulator B (TAB)

Operation: ACCB ← (ACCA)

Addressing Modes	Execution Time (No. of cycles)	Number of bytes of machine code	Coding of First (or only) byte of machine code		
			HEX.	OCT.	DEC.
INHERENT	2	1	16	026	022

Courtesy of Motorola, Inc.

(a) Instruction summary

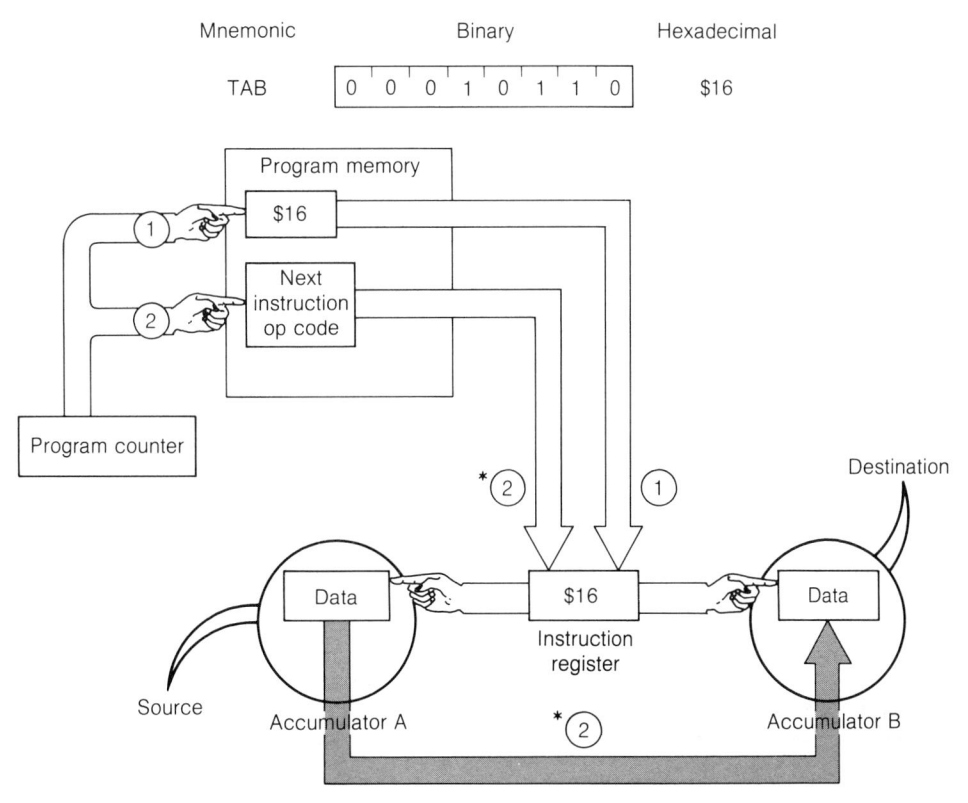

Mnemonic: TAB Binary: 0 0 0 1 0 1 1 0 Hexadecimal: $16

*Data transfer takes place during op code fetch of next instruction

(b) Instruction example and clock-cycle diagram

Figure 10.7 The TAB *inherent*-addressed instruction.

INTELLIGENT-MACHINE UPDATE

In addition to its sensory and speaking abilities, our intelligent machine can now learn, recall, and remember. If it wishes to recite poetry, give a speech, or sing at the "Met," these are essential traits. But what if it wants to become an architect, or an engineer, or a navigator? What is missing is the ability to perform simple arithmetic. The group 2 instructions of the next chapter will expand its vocabulary into this vital area.

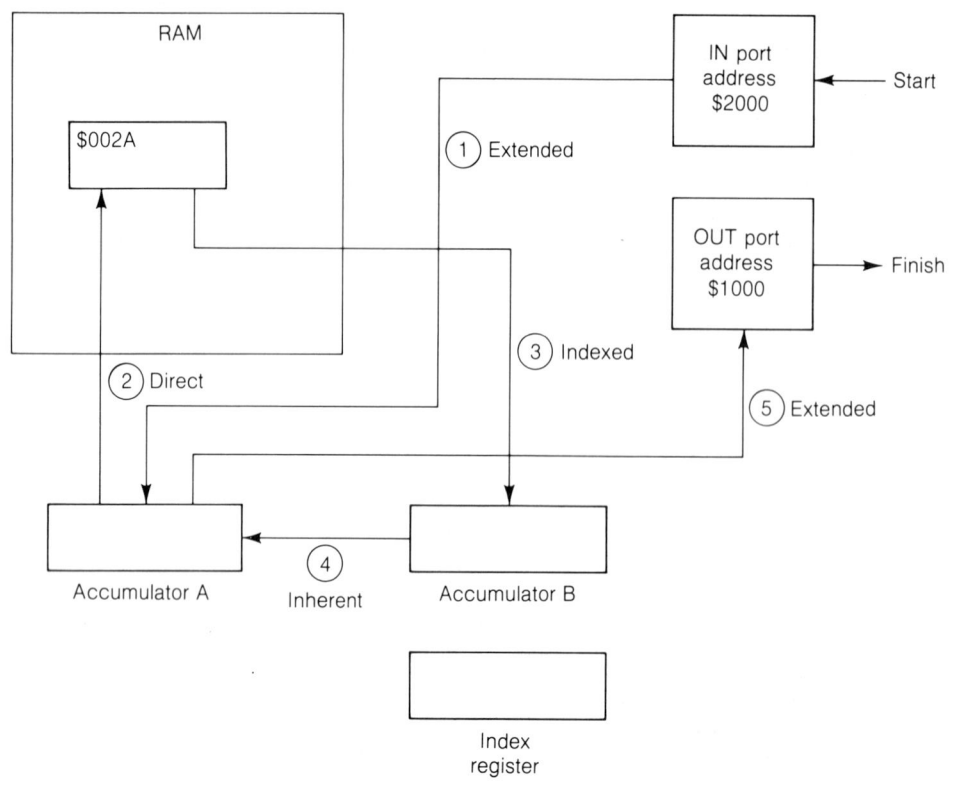

Figure 10.8 Diagram for the "checkers" data-transfer program.

QUESTIONS AND PROBLEMS

1. What is the difference between the data-transfer verbs *load* and *store*?
2. When using the *immediate* mode of addressing, where is the source of the data and where is the destination?
3. Why must all instructions using the *extended* form of addressing be 3 bytes in length?
4. When using the *indexed* form of addressing, how is the memory address found?
5. Write a modified mimic program that inports the data from port $2000 and places it in memory location $0030 (use *direct* addressing whenever possible).
6. What 2-byte instruction transfers a byte of data from accumulator B to memory location $013C?
7. Why do you think the verb *copy* is a valid term to apply to all data-transfer operations?
8. For one or more of the examples of Figures 10.4 through 10.7, draw the instruction-cycle waveforms similar to those shown in Figure 10.3.
9. Why does STA not use *immediate* addressing?
10. Why does *direct* addressing result in faster program processing?
11. How do we know the instruction STAB $30 uses *direct* addressing (rather than *extended*, *immediate*, or *indexed* addressing)?
12. What is the difference between the instructions within each of the following groups?

    (a) LDAA $00,X
        LDAA $0,X
        LDAA 0,X
        LDAA X

    (b) LDAA $0000
        LDAA $0
        LDAA 0

chapter 11

The Arithmetic Group

"What's one and one and one and one and one and one and one and one and one and one?"

"I don't know," said Alice. "I lost count."

"She can't do addition," said the Red Queen. (Lewis Carroll, *Through the Looking Glass*.)

The Red Queen would never have tried to ridicule a computer the way she did Alice, for she picked the one feat at which computers truly excel: high-speed repetitive tasks. This chapter introduces the group 2 arithmetic instructions and generally restricts operations to addition and subtraction of small integers. Chapter 17 refines the arithmetic processes to include many other instructions, data structures, and arithmetic operations.

THE GROUP 2 VERBS

As before, let us begin with a simple listing of the group 2 verbs. Except for the last one, which we will not be involved with for quite some time, they all command well-known actions:

>   Add
>   Subtract
>   Clear
>   Increment
>   Decrement
>   Negate
>   Shift
>   Decimal Adjust

To whittle down the list, let us ignore for now the last two—the Shift and Decimal Adjust verbs—and set aside all instruction types involving a carry or a borrow. These operations will be discussed in later chapters. The remaining mnemonics, mostly involving simple addition and subtraction, will be easy to add to our working vocabulary, for they all make use of the familiar addressing modes introduced in the last chapter:

>   *Immediate*
>   *Inherent*
>   *Direct*
>   *Extended*
>   *Indexed*

That leaves only two possible sources of confusion to clarify. Consider the following simple problem in subtraction. In any subtraction, at least three numbers are involved—the two numbers to be subtracted and the result:

$$\text{SUB} \quad \begin{array}{r} +3 \\ +5 \\ \hline -2 \end{array}$$

The first problem is, *How can we locate three numbers with only one address bus?* The answer is: Assign two of them to an accumulator. That is, one of the two numbers to be subtracted is always stored in accumulator A or accumulator B, and the result of the subtraction is always placed back into an accumulator. Only the third number remains to be located—an easy task for any addressing mode. Figure 11.1 diagrams the basic data flow during arithmetic processing.

The second problem is, How do we deal with negative values? In other words, How do we distinguish positive from

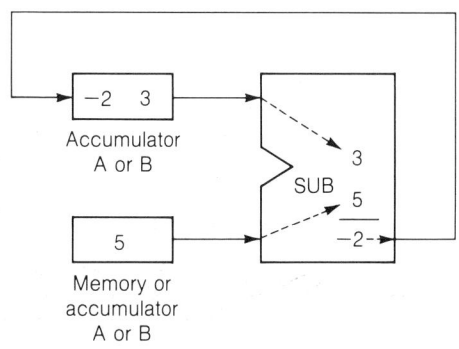

Figure 11.1 Arithmetic-processing flow diagram.

negative numbers? To find the answer, we are going to have to delve into some basic number theory.

POSITIVE AND NEGATIVE NUMBERS

To distinguish positive from negative, our computer takes advantage of a subject that seems to border on sheer magic: *2's complement*. Through the magic of 2's complement, both the addition and the subtraction of positive as well as negative numbers are handled automatically. Just obey a few simple rules.

First, let us define 2's complement. *Two's complement is equal to 1's complement plus 1. (One's complement is the simple inversion of all binary bits.)*

For example, let us take the 2's complement of 7. As shown here, the result certainly does not look like 7, but when using magic, things are not always as they appear:

Before →	00000111	7
Step 1	11111000	1's complement of 7
Step 2	11111000 + 1	ADD 1
After →	11111001	2's complement of 7

Next we will take a look at the rules you must obey in order to make 2's complement arithmetic work.

Signed Numbers

All 2's complement operations must use *signed* numbers. To "sign" a number, place a 0 in the most significant bit position (the leftmost position) if the number is positive and a 1 in the most significant position if the number is negative.

The remaining bits are used to specify the magnitude of the number. They are also governed by rules:

- If the number is positive, the magnitude is entered in true form, as usual.
- If the number is negative, the magnitude is entered in 2's complement form.

It follows that whenever a signed number has a 1 in the most significant bit position, the remaining magnitude bits are always in 2's complement form.

The signed-number convention is demonstrated below using the numbers ±5 and ±7:

Number	Sign bit	Magnitude
+5	0	0000101
−5	1	1111011
+7	0	0000111
−7	1	1111001

When using 8-bit signed numbers, the range of values is from −128 (10000000B) to +127 (01111111B).

Addition and Subtraction of Signed Numbers

To add two signed numbers, simply perform a straightforward binary addition using any of the ADD instructions. If the answer is negative, the result will automatically be in 2's complement form. For example:

```
      +7  0 0000111           -7  1 1111001
ADD   -5  1 1111011    ADD    +5  0 0000101
      +2  0 0000010           -2  1 1111110
```

Note that all negative numbers are entered in 2's complement form, and all negative answers will automatically appear in 2's complement form. (To verify the negative answers, convert the magnitude to true form by reversing the 2's complement process. Or take the 2's complement again. Either method will give the magnitude in true form.)

To subtract two signed numbers (here is where more magic comes in), take the 2's complement of the subtrahend and add! *Subtraction, then, is performed by 2's complement addition.*

Figure 11.2 shows what happens when +7 is subtracted from +2. Since both numbers are positive, they are entered in true form. *Inside the ALU*, the +7 is converted to 2's complement and added to the +2. And (just like pulling a rabbit from a hat) we obtain −5, properly signed with a 1 and with its magnitude in 2's complement form.

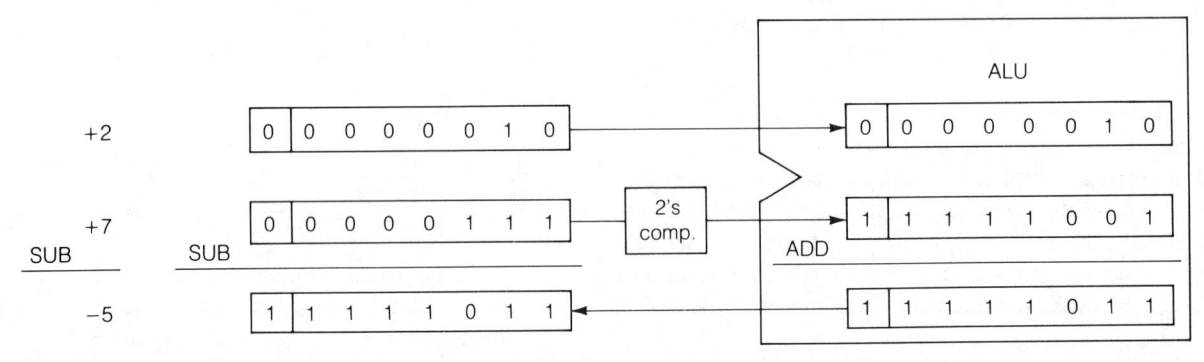

Figure 11.2 Subtracting signed numbers by 2's complement addition.

Of course, for the magic to work, we must make sure the result of the addition or subtraction does not overflow the −128/+127 signed-number bounds (the carry out of the magnitude bits will enter the sign bits, generally causing an erroneous sign change).

To simplify signed-number processing, the 6800 offers the NEG (Negate) instruction (Figure 11.3), which takes the 2's complement of either accumulator or any memory location. Since a computer subtracts by adding the 2's complement, the NEG instruction simply subtracts the number to be negated from 0, which means the 2's complement of the original number is added to 0—giving, of course, the 2's complement.

As an example of the NEG instruction, assume memory location $F087 holds +6. To change the +6 (00000110B) to a −6 (11111010B), simply write:

Mnemonic	Hexadecimal
NEG $F087	$70, $F0, $87

A signed-number problem Once you know the rules, signed numbers are as easy to handle as unsigned numbers. For example, using *immediate* addressing, the program listed below will successively subtract +7, −9, and −5 from accumulator B (the "#" symbol, remember, indicates *immediate* addressing):

Mnemonic	Hexadecimal
SUBB #$07	$C0, $07
SUBB #$F7 ($F7 is 2's complement for −9)	$C0, $F7
SUBB #$FB ($FB is 2's complement for −5)	$C0, $FB

If accumulator B held −6 initially, processing action will proceed as follows: *(Remember: All negative numbers are entered in 2's complement form, and all negative results will automatically appear in 2's complement form.)*

```
  Math operations              Operations within ALU
        −6                              11111010B
 SUB   +7   (00000111)        ADD      11111001B
       ───                              11110011B
       −13

 SUB   −9   (11110111)        ADD      00001001B
       −4                              11111100B
       ───

 SUB   −5   (11111011)        ADD      00000101B
       +1                              00000001B
       ───
```

Sign-Magnitude Entry

Using 2's complement arithmetic, all negative numbers must be entered into the computer already in 2's complement form, and all negative answers are automatically reported in 2's complement form. Since this system is awkward for human beings, we may wish to adopt the *sign-magnitude* convention. Using this convention, all numbers are signed, as before, but all magnitudes (negative as well as positive) are entered in true form. The following chart compares 2's complement with sign magnitude for two arbitrary numbers:

Number	2's complement	Sign magnitude
+6	00000110	00000110
−8	11111000	10001000

Since the computer *must* process all numbers in 2's complement form, we program the computer to automatically convert all sign-magnitude entries to 2's complement form. Also, before answers are outported, all negative numbers

---

Negate (NEG)

Operation: ACCX ← − (ACCX) = 00 − (ACCX)
or: M ← − (M) = 00 − (M)
Description: Replaces the contents of ACCX or M with its two's complement. Note that 80 is left unchanged.

Addressing Modes	Execution Time (No. of cycles)	Number of bytes of machine code	Coding of First (or only) byte of machine code		
			HEX.	OCT.	DEC.
A	2	1	40	100	064
B	2	1	50	120	080
EXT	6	3	70	160	112
IND	7	2	60	140	096

Courtesy of Motorola, Inc.

Figure 11.3 The Negate (NEG) instruction.

are converted to sign-magnitude form. Since a decision is involved (is the number positive or negative?), the conversion program is left as an exercise for Chapter 14.

ARITHMETIC INSTRUCTION EXAMPLES

Five simple arithmetic problems, using a variety of addressing modes, are all the practice we will need to include the basic group 2 instructions in our working vocabulary. Chances are, because we are familiar with both the verbs and the addressing modes, we will be able to select quickly the correct instruction type—including the correct addressing mode—to solve each arithmetic problem.

Problem 1 The contents of accumulator A are to be added to the contents of accumulator B, the result going back to accumulator A. Can you select the correct type of instruction to carry out the addition process (see Appendix I)?

We know the verb is Add and the mode of addressing is *inherent* (the location of all data is implied by the op code). Therefore, the ABA (Add Accumulator B to Accumulator A) instruction is the correct choice (Figure 11.4). Note that accumulator A receives the result (the previous contents of accumulator A are lost).

Problem 2 Write an instruction to add the contents of memory location $0040 to accumulator B. The result will go into accumulator B.

The ADD (Add Without Carry) instruction type of Figure 11.5a will solve the problem. A question: How many of the eight available addressing modes can be used? The answer is three: *B extended*, *B indexed*, and *B direct* (*immediate* addressing, of course, cannot reference any memory location other than the second byte of the instruction). The solutions are given by Figure 11.5b, c, and d. (For the *indexed* mode, assume the index register is holding $0000.)

Add Accumulator B to Accumulator A (ABA)

Operation: ACCA ← (ACCA) + (ACCB)

Description: Adds the contents of ACCB to the contents of ACCA and places the result in ACCA.

Addressing Modes	Execution Time (No. of cycles)	Number of bytes of machine code	Coding of First (or only) byte of machine code		
			HEX.	OCT.	DEC.
Inherent	2	1	1B	033	027

Courtesy of Motorola, Inc.

(a) Instruction summary

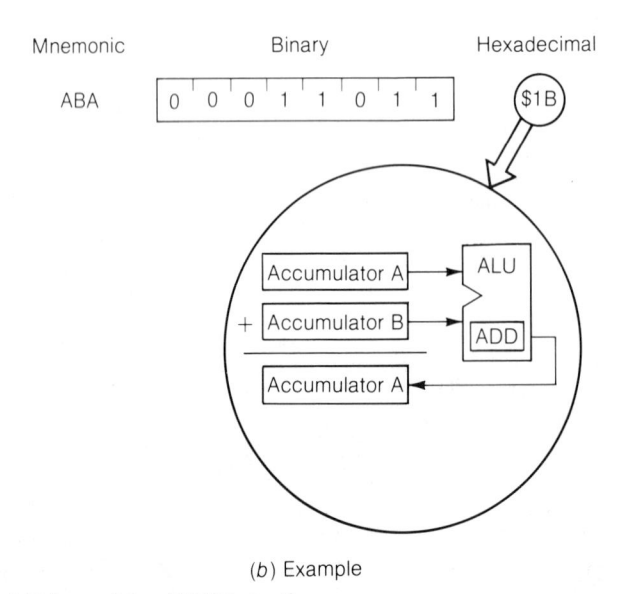

(b) Example

Figure 11.4 The Add Accumulators (ABA) instruction.

Chapter 11 / The Arithmetic Group   119

Add Without Carry (ADD)

Operation: ACCX ← (ACCX) + (M)

Description: Adds the contents of ACCX and the contents of M and places the result in ACCX.

Addressing Modes	Execution Time (No. of cycles)	Number of bytes of machine code	Coding of First (or only) byte of machine code		
			HEX.	OCT.	DEC.
A IMM	2	2	8B	213	139
A DIR	3	2	9B	233	155
A EXT	4	3	BB	273	187
A IND	5	2	AB	253	171
B IMM	2	2	CB	313	203
B DIR	3	2	DB	333	219
B EXT	4	3	FB	373	251
B IND	5	2	EB	353	235

Courtesy of Motorola, Inc.

(a) Instruction summary

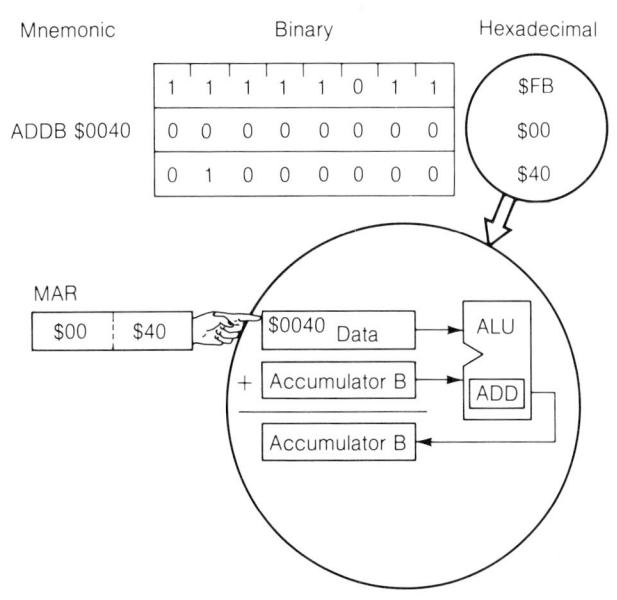

(b) Example using <u>extended</u> addressing

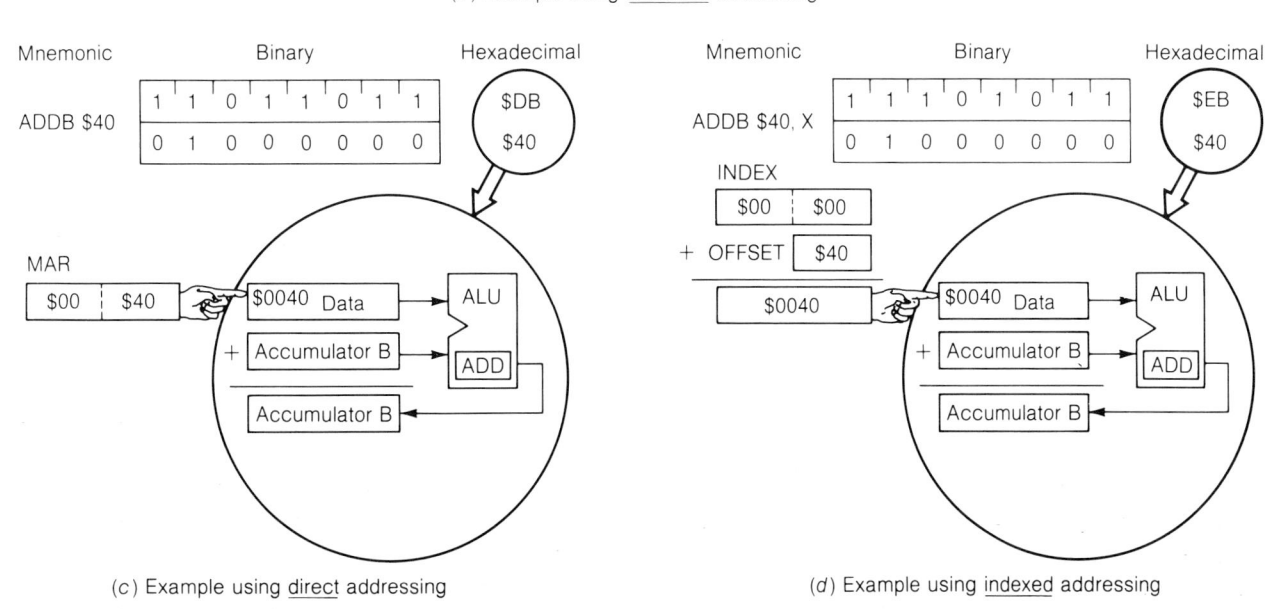

(c) Example using <u>direct</u> addressing

(d) Example using <u>indexed</u> addressing

Figure 11.5   The Add Without Carry (ADD) instruction.

Subtract (SUB)

Operation: ACCX ← (ACCX) − (M)

Description: Subtracts the contents of M from the contents of ACCX and places the result in ACCX.

Addressing Modes	Execution Time (No. of cycles)	Number of bytes of machine code	Coding of First (or only) byte of machine code		
			HEX.	OCT.	DEC.
A IMM	2	2	80	200	128
A DIR	3	2	90	220	144
A EXT	4	3	B0	260	176
A IND	5	2	A0	240	160
B IMM	2	2	C0	300	192
B DIR	3	2	D0	320	208
B EXT	4	3	F0	360	240
B IND	5	2	E0	340	224

Courtesy of Motorola, Inc.

(a) Instruction summary

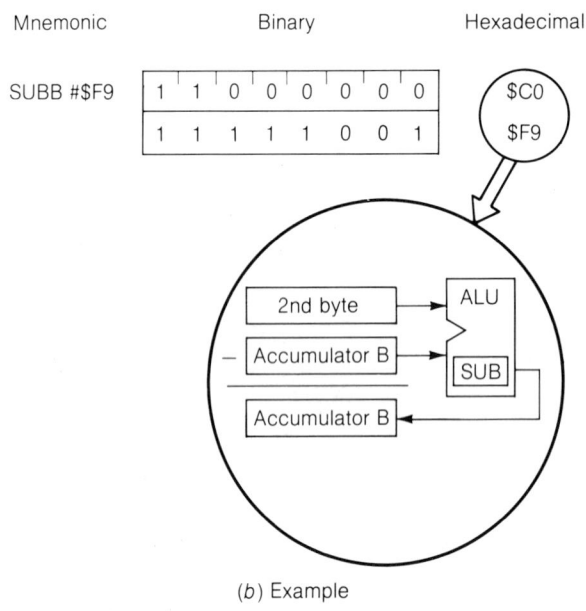

Mnemonic: SUBB #$F9

Binary: 1 1 0 0 0 0 0 0 / 1 1 1 1 1 0 0 1

Hexadecimal: $C0 / $F9

2nd byte → ALU
Accumulator B → SUB
Accumulator B ←

(b) Example

Figure 11.6 The Subtract Immediate instruction.

Problem 3 Suppose we plan to subtract −7 from accumulator B but do not wish to set up an index or preload any memory locations. Then, as listed in Figure 11.a, use the *immediate* form of addressing; it is often the quickest and most direct way to get the job done.

To solve our specific problem, place −7 (*in 2's complement form*) in the second byte of the instruction, update the mnemonic, and problem 3 is complete (Figure 11.6b).

Problem 4 Our next problem involves adding 1 to memory location $0077. Of course we could use the verb Add; but when adding 1, the INC (Increment) instruction (Figure 11.7a) often is preferred because it is more descriptive. Note that even though the data are located in page zero, the INC instruction does not offer the *direct* addressing mode. Therefore, we have the choice of *extended* or *indexed* addressing. With *extended* addressing, Figure 11.7b shows how to increment memory location $0077.

Problem 5 Quite often when performing arithmetic operations it is necessary to clear (set to 0) an accumulator or memory location. The Clear (CLR) instruction type of Figure 11.8 will blank out (set to 0) any accumulator or memory location. For example, if we wish to clear memory location $0199, we simply write:

CLR $0199   ($7F, $01, $99)

Increment (INC)

Operation: ACCX ← (ACCX) + 01
or: M ← (M) + 01
Description: Add one to the contents of ACCX or M.

Addressing Modes	Execution Time (No. of cycles)	Number of bytes of machine code	Coding of First (or only) byte of machine code		
			HEX.	OCT.	DEC.
A	2	1	4C	114	076
B	2	1	5C	134	092
EXT	6	3	7C	174	124
IND	7	2	6C	154	108

Courtesy of Motorola, Inc.

(a) Instruction summary

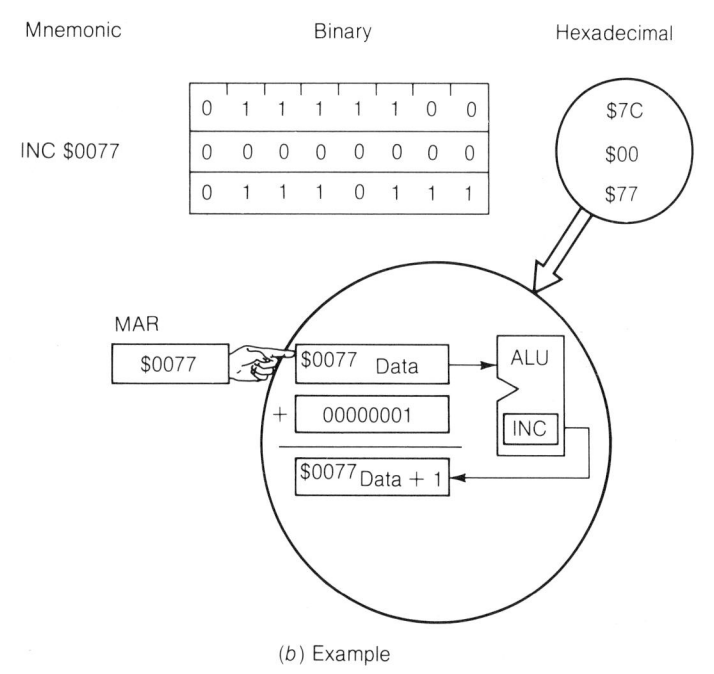

INC $0077

Mnemonic	Binary	Hexadecimal
	0 1 1 1 1 1 0 0	$7C
	0 0 0 0 0 0 0 0	$00
	0 1 1 1 0 1 1 1	$77

(b) Example

Figure 11.7 The Increment (INC) instruction.

Clear (CLR)

Operation: ACCX ← 00
or: M ← 00
Description: The contents of ACCX or M are replaced with zeros.

Addressing Modes	Execution Time (No. of cycles)	Number of bytes of machine code	Coding of First (or only) byte of machine code		
			HEX.	OCT.	DEC.
A	2	1	4F	117	079
B	2	1	5F	137	095
EXT	6	3	7F	177	127
IND	7	2	6F	157	111

Courtesy of Motorola, Inc.

Figure 11.8 The Clear (CLR) instruction type.

AN ARITHMETIC PROGRAM

Including the new arithmetic processes, our intelligent machine now has a working vocabulary of approximately nine basic "verbs" and should be able to perform some useful exercises:

    Load   Increment
    Store   Decrement
    Transfer   Clear
    Add   Negate
    Subtract

To see what our computer can do, let us teach it a simple task: to look at any date on the calendar (except the first) and tell us the previous date. If it looks at the third day of the month, for example, it will say "2." Having already taught our computer the mimic task, we know what the learning procedure will be. (To input data, we'll use port $2000; to output data, port $1000.)

The first step is to produce a flowchart. Figure 11.9a shows how the task is implemented by simply inserting a "SUB 1" block into the middle of the mimic program. The new "SUB 1" block, the only one we are not familiar with, looks simple enough, but actually it is complicated by the number of ways the process can be fulfilled. We will look at several of them.

Perhaps the most obvious choice is to use the Decrement Accumulator A instruction (Figure 11.9b). You may wish to determine for yourself that $4A is the proper hex code. Of course, as shown by Figure 11.9c, we can subtract 1 from accumulator A immediately.

Finally, if we want to adopt a real roundabout method, Figure 11.9d shows us how. Preset the index register to the beginning of any available RAM block (such as $0100) and clear a location in the block (i.e., $012A) using the CLR IND instruction. Then increment that location using the INC IND instruction. Finally, use the SUBA IND (without carry) instruction to subtract 1 from accumulator A.

Three ways to carry out the same task—which one should we choose? Usually the best choice is the simplest, and that is normally the method requiring the least amount of memory. In addition, the shortest program is usually the fastest to run. The first technique—using the Decrement instruction—is therefore the best choice. It requires only 8 stored-program locations and 19 clock cycles—the fewest of any of the three techniques.

EXTENDED VS INDEXED ADDRESSING

If *extended* addressing can access any memory (or port) location, what is the reason for providing an *indexed* mode of addressing? One reason—as with *direct* addressing—is to save memory space. Instructions using *extended* addressing are 3 bytes long, while those using *indexed* addressing take up only 2 bytes. *Indexed* addressing, however, has several drawbacks. First, loading and modifying the index register requires extra memory space. Also, we must make sure all references to memory are within one page of the index. Finally, although each *indexed* addressing instruction takes up fewer memory locations, each requires slightly more processing time (*direct* addressing, on the other hand, requires less memory space *and* processing time).

To compare *extended* with *indexed* addressing, let's write a program that adds together the contents of five memory locations, placing the answer back in memory. As shown by Figure 11.10a, if the bytes of data are scattered throughout the 64K of memory space, *extended* addressing is the most efficient. On the other hand, if all numbers are located within a single page, the index is pointed to the bottom (the lowest address) of the page and all references to memory are made with 2-byte instructions (see Figure 11.10b). The more numbers to be added, the more space is saved by using *indexed* addressing. In Chapter 14, we will see how *indexed* addressing is used within program *loops* to provide *indirect* addressing—another powerful programming tool.

HIGH-LEVEL AND LOW-LEVEL FLOWCHARTING

Referring to Figure 11.9d, we see that the "Subtract 1 from date" flowchart block, unlike the other blocks in the program, represents more than one machine-level instruction. In fact, carrying this idea to the extreme, it is possible for a flowchart to be written in which each block corresponds to many thousands of instructions (see Figure 11.11). Such a flowchart, called a *high-level* or *system* flowchart, is often the first stage of program evolution, when the most general and overall aspects of the program are under development. (Obviously, a system flowchart need not be written with a particular microprocessor in mind.)

At the other end of the spectrum, we find the *low-level* or *instructional* flowchart in which each flowchart block corresponds to very few instructions. A *medium-level* flowchart, often called an *algorithm* flowchart, occupies the middle ground between these two extremes. (An algorithm is a step-by-step problem-solving procedure that can be likened to a recipe in a cookbook. An algorithm also is usually written without a particular microprocessor in mind.)

Clearly, a complex program would first be written at the conceptual (system) level. Then it would be broken down and expanded through the algorithm level to the instruc-

Chapter 11 / The Arithmetic Group   **123**

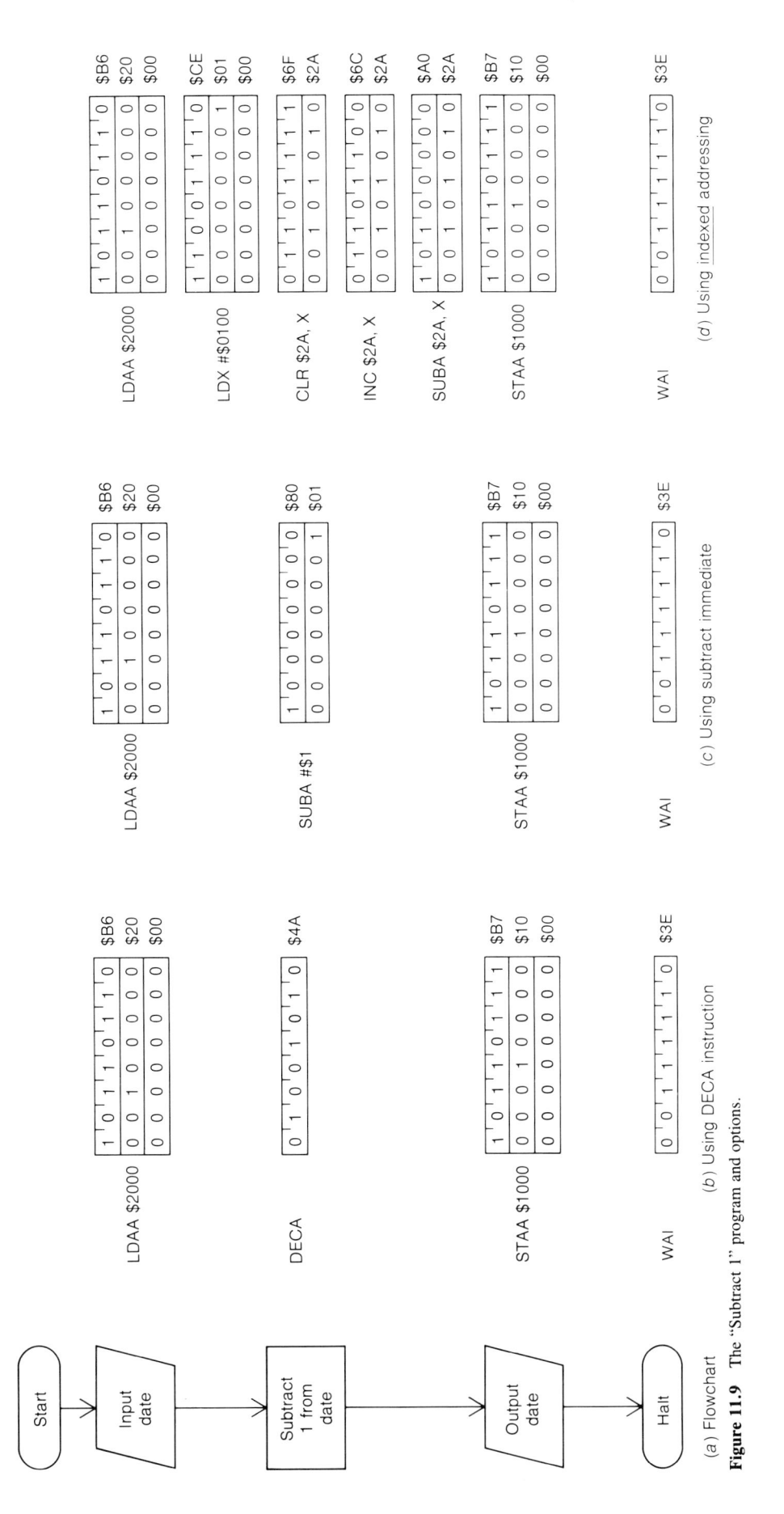

Figure 11.9 The "Subtract 1" program and options.

(a) Flowchart

(b) Using DECA instruction

(c) Using subtract immediate

(d) Using indexed addressing

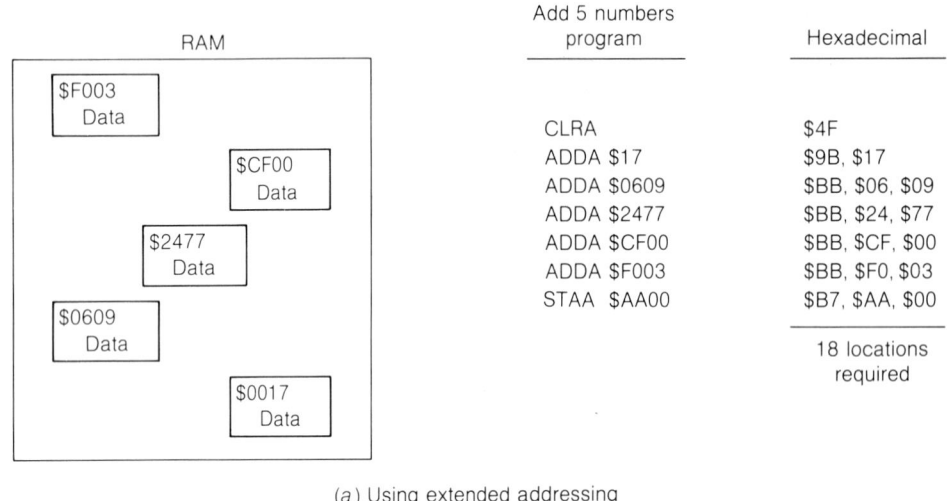

```
                                    Add 5 numbers
              RAM                      program              Hexadecimal

       $F003
       Data
                                    CLRA                  $4F
              $CF00                  ADDA  $17            $9B, $17
              Data                   ADDA  $0609          $BB, $06, $09
       $2477                         ADDA  $2477          $BB, $24, $77
       Data                          ADDA  $CF00          $BB, $CF, $00
  $0609                              ADDA  $F003          $BB, $F0, $03
  Data                               STAA  $AA00          $B7, $AA, $00
              $0017
              Data                                        18 locations
                                                            required
```

(a) Using **extended** addressing

```
       RAM (page $01)

              $01F2
              Data
                                    CLRA                  $4F
              $01AA                  LDX   #$0100         $CE, $01, $00
              Data                   ADDA  $00, X         $AB, $00
   $0147                             ADDA  $13, X         $AB, $13
   Data                              ADDA  $47, X         $AB, $47
              $0113                  ADDA  $AA, X         $AB, $AA
              Data                   ADDA  $F2, X         $AB, $F2
        $0100                        STAA  $44, X         $A7, $44
        Data
                                                         16 locations
                                                            required
```

(b) Using **indexed** addressing

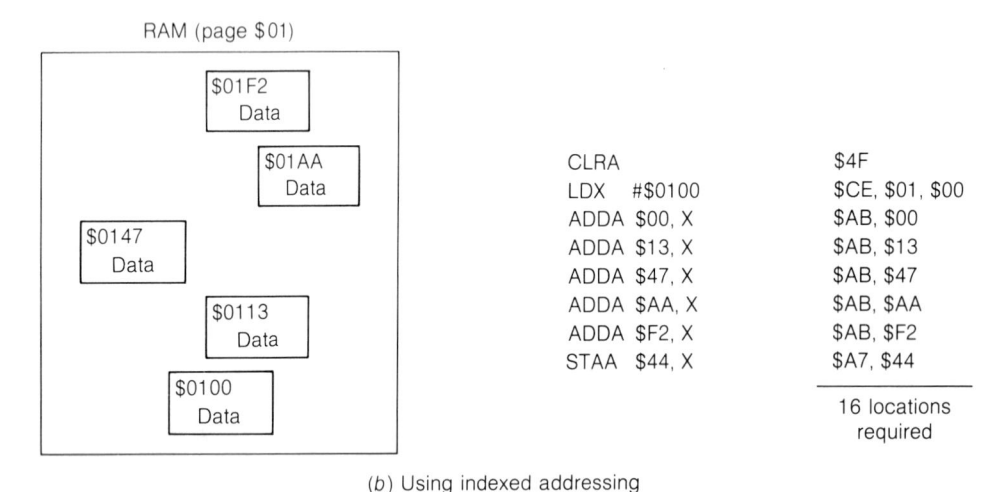

Figure 11.10 Program adding five numbers.

tional-level program. (As discussed in Chapter 22, such a process is part of the concept of *top-down programming*.)

ADDITIONAL STUDY

Although many of the instructions of the arithmetic group will be covered in a later chapter, the student is advised to become generally familiar with those arithmetic instructions not strictly covered in this chapter (see Appendices I and III).

INTELLIGENT-MACHINE UPDATE

As if riding a time machine forward, our android is chasing its human creators through their distant past. With the development of arithmetic abilities, it has at last entered the era of recorded history. From here on, as it moves into the higher-level thought processes, its progress will accelerate.

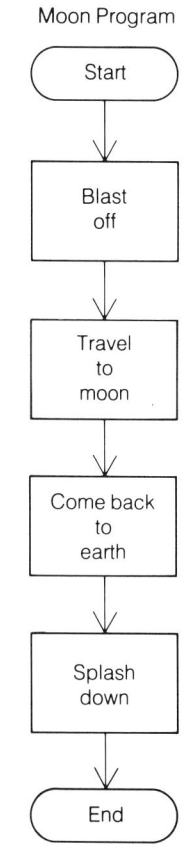

Figure 11.11 Conceptual-level flowchart.

QUESTIONS AND PROBLEMS

1. What role do the accumulators play in the addition process?
2. Using mnemonics, give examples of the ADDB instruction type in each of the four following addressing modes:

   Immediate _____   _____
   Direct   _____   _____
   Extended   _____   _____
   Indexed   _____   _____

3. Write the instruction (in both mnemonic and hexadecimal form) that will add −5 to accumulator B immediately.
4. Convert the following decimal numbers to binary using signed-number rules: −27, +10, −127. Repeat using sign-magnitude rules.
5. Using *immediate* addressing exclusively, write a routine that loads −7 into accumulator A and then subtracts −8 from it. What is the answer, and where will it be found?
6. Using *indexed* addressing, write a program that will add the contents of memory locations $2020 through $2024 and place the result in memory location $2025. Repeat using *extended* addressing.
7. Using the CLR, SUB, and STA instructions, write a three-step routine that will simulate the NEG $01AF instruction.
8. In a system-level flowchart, how many machine-level instructions may correspond to a single flowchart block?

9. Complete a waveform diagram (see Figure 10.3) for each of the following instructions: (a) ADDA $1A, (b) ADDA #$16, (c) SUBB $40,X (index register holds $01A0). Assume that the op code of each instruction is stored at memory location $FC00.
10. Referring to Figure 11.10a, why is the op code for the first ADDA instruction ($9B) different from the rest ($BB)?
11. When writing a program that adds 20 numbers stored in memory, under what circumstances would you make use of each of the following addressing modes: (a) *Direct,* (b) *Extended,* (c) *Indexed*?

chapter 12

The Logical Group

Sherlock Holmes was a master of deduction. Our intelligent machine, on the other hand, is presently incapable of even the simplest logical analysis. The reason is that the data-transfer and arithmetic-group instructions—the only instructions it presently knows—do not contain the elements of deductive logic. These elements are contained within the third major group of instructions—the logical group—and are the subject of this chapter.

THE ELEMENTS OF LOGIC

Consider the following logical situations (based on a famous Sherlock Holmes episode).

> If the moon is full *or* lightning is flashing, *and* the dog did *not* bark, then the suspect is nearby.

This is simple deductive logic—arguing from a premise to a logical conclusion. (If the dog did *not* bark at the moon or the lightning, then the suspect must be nearby, *quieting the dog.*) The key elements of deductive logic may surprise you. They are the simple terms *and, or,* and *not*—all present in our mystery. In fact, according to George Boole, the inventor of symbolic logic, all deductive logic is based on combinations of the terms *and, or,* and *not*. Therefore, to turn our computer into a master sleuth, it appears we should expand its vocabulary to include these terms.

THE LOGICAL-GROUP VERBS

Looking over the eight verbs and 12 instruction types (listed below) that constitute the logical group (also see Appendix III), we find the Boolean terms *and, or,* and *not* (*complement* performs the *not* function), along with a number of miscellaneous operations:

Boolean

Basic verbs	Instructions
AND	AND
OR	ORA
Exclusive OR	EOR
Complement	COM

Miscellaneous Operations

Basic verbs	Instructions
Compare	CMP
	CBA
	CPX
Shift	LSR
Rotate	ROL
	ROR
Test	TST
	BIT

The reason for including the *rotate* and *shift* instruction types in the logical group will be clear shortly. However, the *compare* and *test* instruction types are purely flag oriented, and therefore will be saved for Chapter 14 when flags and decision making are introduced.

Logic designers may be surprised to find that the universal logic gates (NAND and NOR) are not provided directly in the instruction set. The reason is straightforward: one of the major advantages of NAND and NOR gates in hardware design (their lower cost) simply evaporates in software design. In software, the "cost" is time, and all Boolean operations take up the same amount of processing time.

The *exclusive or* function is included in the logical group just for convenience and to save processing time, for as we all know, the *exclusive or* operation can itself be developed from the basic *and, or,* and *not* terms.

Once again, the verb content of the logical instructions will present no problems. This time, understanding the oper-

127

128 Part III / Software: The Spark of Life

Inclusive OR (ORA)
Operation: ACCX ← (ACCX) ⊙ (M)
Description: Perform logical "OR" between the contents of ACCX and the contents of M and places the result in ACCX. (Each bit of ACCX after the operation will be the logical "OR" of the corresponding bits of M and of ACCX before the operation).

Addressing Modes	Execution Time (No. of cycles)	Number of bytes of machine code	HEX.	OCT.	DEC.
A IMM	2	2	8A	212	138
A DIR	3	2	9A	232	154
A EXT	4	3	BA	272	186
A IND	5	2	AA	252	170
B IMM	2	2	CA	312	202
B DIR	3	2	DA	332	218
B EXT	4	3	FA	372	250
B IND	5	2	EA	352	234

Courtesy of Motorola, Inc.

(a)

Logical AND (AND)
Operation: ACCX ← (ACCX) · (M)
Description: Performs logical "AND" between the contents of ACCX and the contents of M and places the result in ACCX. (Each bit of ACCX after the operation will be the logical "AND" of the corresponding bits of M and of ACCX before the operation.)

Addressing Modes	Execution Time (No. of cycles)	Number of bytes of machine code	HEX.	OCT.	DEC.
A IMM	2	2	84	204	132
A DIR	3	2	94	224	148
A EXT	4	3	B4	264	180
A IND	5	2	A4	244	164
B IMM	2	2	C4	304	196
B DIR	3	2	D4	324	212
B EXT	4	3	F4	364	244
B IND	5	2	E4	344	228

Courtesy of Motorola, Inc.

(b)

Exclusive OR (EOR)
Operation: ACCX ← (ACCX) ⊕ (M)
Description: Perform logical "EXCLUSIVE OR" between the contents of ACCX and the contents of M, and place the result in ACCX. (Each bit of ACCX after the operation will be the logical "EXCLUSIVE OR" of the corresponding bit of M and ACCX before the operation.)

Addressing Modes	Execution Time (No. of cycles)	Number of bytes of machine code	HEX.	OCT.	DEC.
A IMM	2	2	88	210	136
A DIR	3	2	98	230	152
A EXT	4	3	B8	270	184
A IND	5	2	A8	250	168
B IMM	2	2	C8	310	200
B DIR	3	2	D8	330	216
B EXT	4	3	F8	370	248
B IND	5	2	E8	350	232

Courtesy of Motorola, Inc.

(c)

Complement (COM)
Operation: ACCX ← ≈ (ACCX) = FF − (ACCX)
or: M ← ≈ (M) = FF − (M)
Description: Replaces the contents of ACCX or M with its one's complement. (Each bit of the contents of ACCX or M is replaced with the complement of that bit.)

Addressing Modes	Execution Time (No. of cycles)	Number of bytes of machine code	HEX.	OCT.	DEC.
A	2	1	43	103	067
B	2	1	53	123	083
EXT	6	3	73	163	115
IND	7	2	63	143	099

Courtesy of Motorola, Inc.

(d)

Figure 12.1 The 6800 Boolean instructions.

and portion of each instruction type is also second nature, for the addressing modes are the same as for the arithmetic group. Furthermore, as shown by Figure 12.1, the Boolean instructions are processed in the same manner as the arithmetic instructions. One of the logical inputs and the result of the Boolean operation reside in accumulator A or accumulator B. The other logical input resides in memory (or an input port) and is located by way of the *immediate, direct, extended*, or *indexed* addressing modes (accumulator A cannot be logically combined with accumulator B, as there are no logical instructions comparable to the *inherent*-addressed ABA).

BOOLEAN OPERATIONS

There is one big difference between the arithmetic and Boolean operations, however, and it shows up when we try to simulate a simple 2-input OR gate on the computer. The question is: How can *two* 8-bit *registers* simulate *one* 2-input OR gate?

The answer is very simple: *Each bit position is ORed together independently of all the others*. When the OR instruction is run, up to eight 2-input OR gates are simulated simultaneously (Figure 12.2a).

If we wish to simulate only one 2-input OR gate rather than the possible eight, we simply select any one of the eight available bit positions and run the OR instruction. All other bit positions are simply "don't care" values (Figure 12.2b).

On the other hand, as shown in Figure 12.2c, if the two variables to be ORed together are in unlike bit positions, they may not be combined as they stand. The variables must first be aligned in the same bit position.

The shift and rotate instructions (Figure 12.3) will solve the problem by allowing the programmer to line up the variables in a like bit position before logical processing.

The various forms of the shift and rotate instructions represent quite a variety of ways to perform the basic "musical chairs" operation (all move left; all move right). For the purpose of lining up variables prior to Boolean operations, almost any of the forms will do. But, when confronted with other programming tasks, one in particular may be tailor-made for the job at hand. So, a brief study and comparison of the shift and rotate family of instructions is in order.

The Shift and Rotate Group

Referring to Figure 12.3, we note that all the shift and rotate operations involve the "C" bit. The C bit is known as the *Carry Flag* and is simply a 1-bit register (flip-flop) that is set to a "1" or cleared to a "0" when certain instructions—such as shift and rotate—are processed.

Returning to Figure 12.3a, the first classification on the list is "Arithmetic Shift." Technically speaking, the arith-

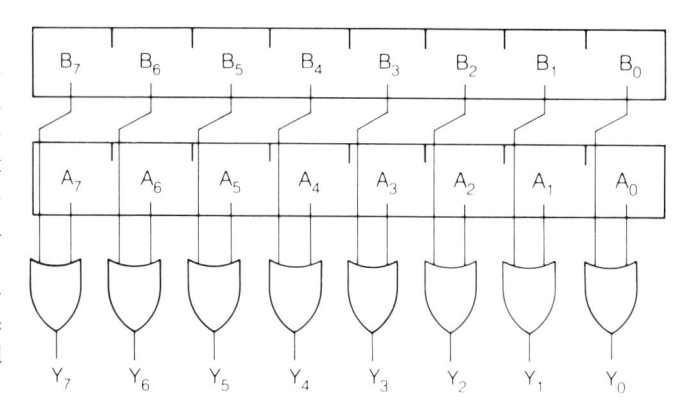

(a) Bit positions ORed together independently eight at a time

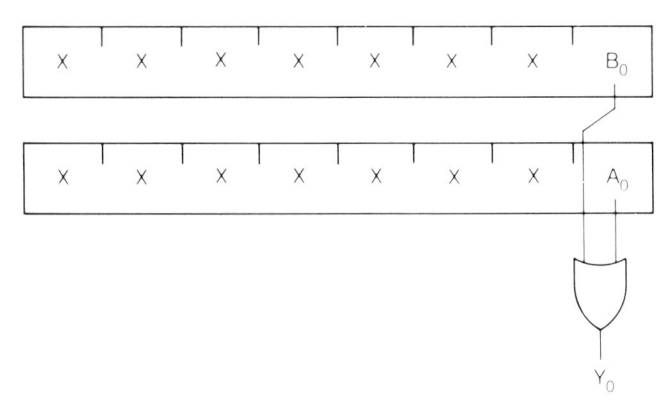

(b) Simulating a single OR gate

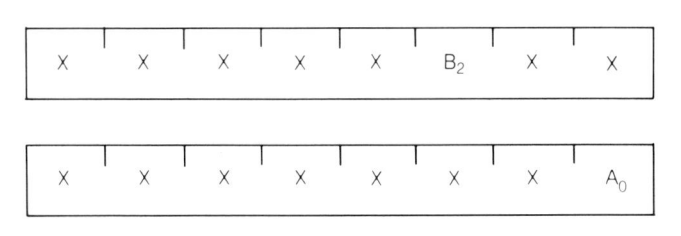

(c) Variables in unlike bit positions, which cannot be logically combined

Figure 12.2 Carrying out logical operations.

metic shift operation should have been introduced in the last chapter, when basic arithmetic operations were covered. However, we held off until all the shift and rotate operations could be introduced and compared at one time.

Basically, the Arithmetic Shift Right (ASR) operation

Arithmetic Shift Left (ASL)

Operation:

Description: Shifts all bits of the ACCX or M one place to the left. Bit 0 is loaded with a zero. The C bit is loaded from the most significant bit of ACCX or M.

Arithmetic Shift Right (ASR)

Operation:

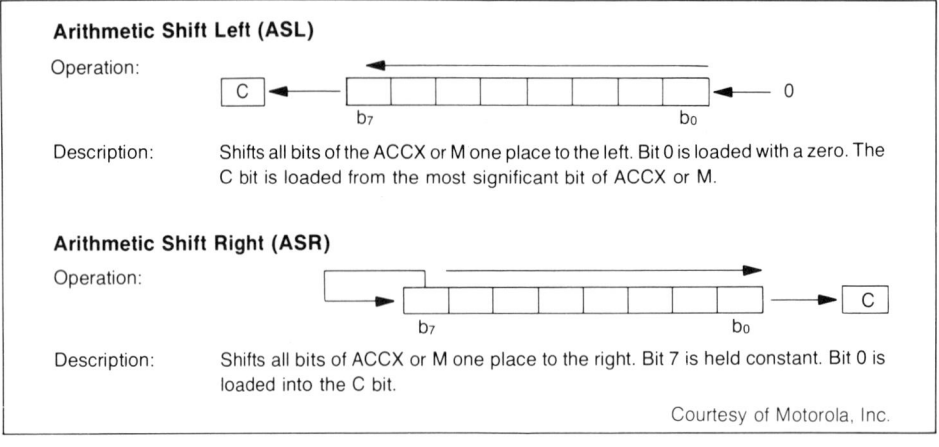

Description: Shifts all bits of ACCX or M one place to the right. Bit 7 is held constant. Bit 0 is loaded into the C bit.

Courtesy of Motorola, Inc.

(a) Arithmetic shift

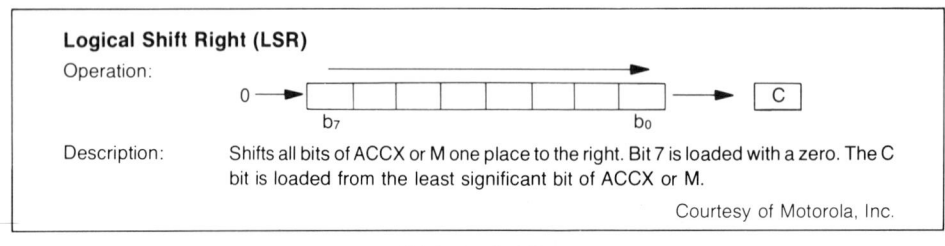

Logical Shift Right (LSR)

Operation:

Description: Shifts all bits of ACCX or M one place to the right. Bit 7 is loaded with a zero. The C bit is loaded from the least significant bit of ACCX or M.

Courtesy of Motorola, Inc.

(b) Logical shift

Rotate Left (ROL)

Operation:

Description: Shifts all bits of ACCX or M one place to the left. Bit 0 is loaded from the C bit. The C bit is loaded from the most significant bit of ACCX or M.

Rotate Right (ROR)

Operation:

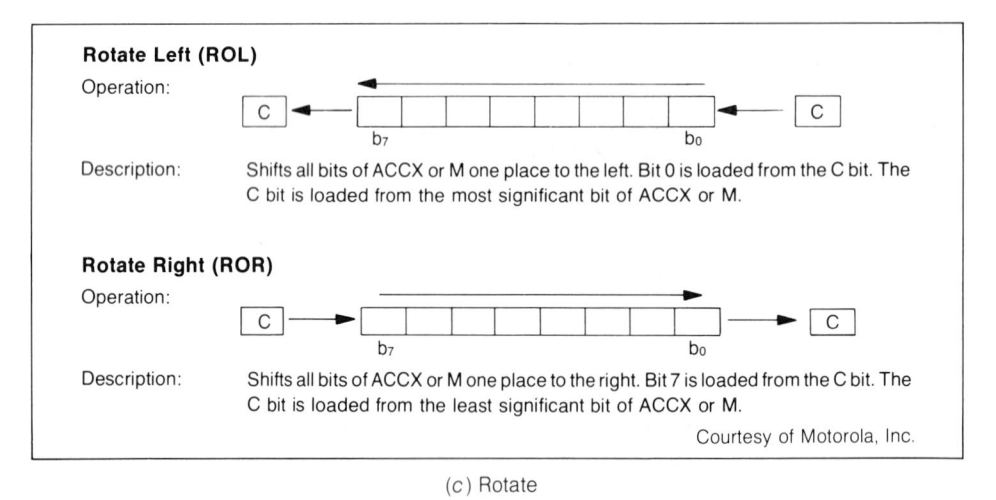

Description: Shifts all bits of ACCX or M one place to the right. Bit 7 is loaded from the C bit. The C bit is loaded from the least significant bit of ACCX or M.

Courtesy of Motorola, Inc.

(c) Rotate

Figure 12.3 The shift and rotate instructions.

divides 2's complement numbers by 2, whereas the Arithmetic Shift Left (ASL) operation multiplies 2's complement numbers by 2. As shown, the shift right operation automatically preserves the sign bit, whereas the shift left operation automatically shifts a zero into the least significant bit. However, the shift left operation does not preserve the sign bit and an erroneous sign change can occur when bit 6 is shifted into the sign bit position. Figure 12.4 tests the arithmetic shift operations with the numbers $+10$ and -20. Verify for yourself that the results are either doubled (ASL) or halved (ASR).

Moving on to the logical shift instructions (Figure 12.3b), the most conspicuous feature is the apparent lack of a Logical Shift Left. That's because the Logical Shift Left operation is identical with the Arithmetic Shift Left operation.

The logical shift operations are used for a variety of Bool-

Before

+10
| 0 | 0 0 0 0 1 0 1 0 |
C   b₇   b₀

−20
| 1 1 1 0 1 1 0 0 |
C

After

+20
| 0 | 0 0 0 1 0 1 0 0 |
C   b₇   b₀

−40
| 1 | 1 1 0 1 1 0 0 0 |
C

(a) Shift left (multiply by 2)

Before

+10
| 0 0 0 0 1 0 1 0 |
              C

−20
| 1 1 1 0 1 1 0 0 |
              C

After

+5
| 0 0 0 0 0 1 0 1 | 0 |
                   C

−10
| 1 1 1 1 0 1 1 0 | 0 |
                   C

(b) Shift right (divide by 2)

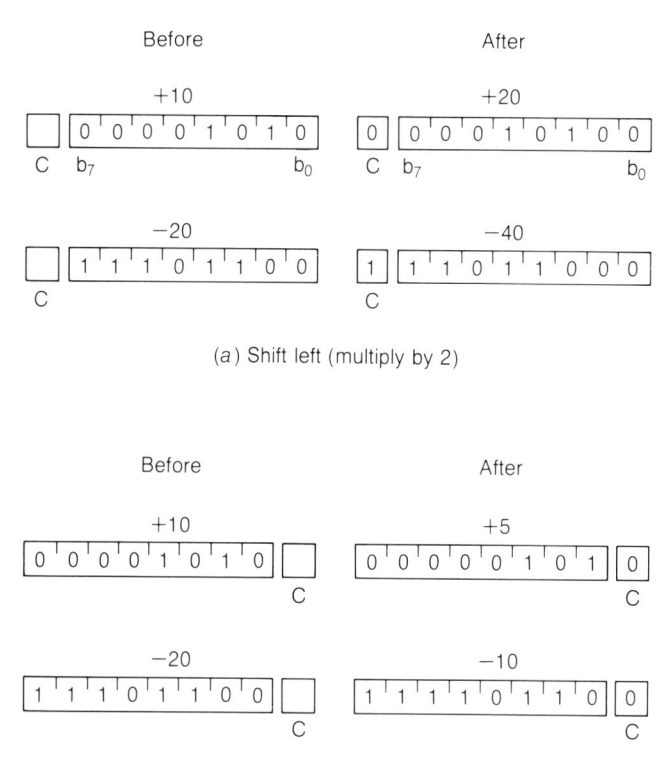

Figure 12.4 The arithmetic shift instruction examples.

ean, bit manipulation, and shift register applications. However, the programmer should be aware that each logical shift operation automatically injects a 0 into the bit pattern and therefore destroys that bit of information.

The rotate instructions (Figure 12.3c), on the other hand, preserve all information by simulating a 9-bit, closed-loop ring counter (the 8 data bits plus the C flag).

With five shift and logical instruction types from which to choose, the challenge to the programmer will be to select the correct shift or rotate instruction to match the application at hand.

Multiple-Input Boolean Operations

To summarize the actions of the Boolean instructions, up to eight 2-input gates can be simulated with a single Boolean instruction. How then would we simulate a multiple-input gate? The answer is: It must be broken down into a sequence of 2-input gates and the Boolean instruction run more than once. Figure 12.5 illustrates the process using a 3-input AND gate.

SOLVING THE MYSTERY

To solve the case of the "dog that did *not* bark," we will build a logic machine to process the clues. The machine will

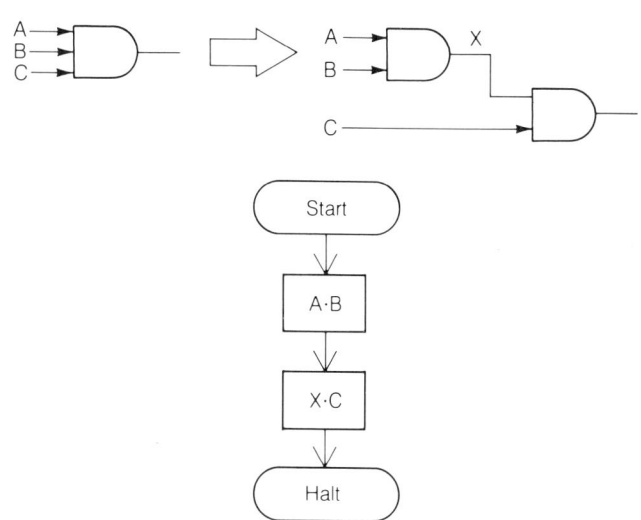

Figure 12.5 Process for simulating gates with more than two inputs using consecutive Boolean instructions.

have three input variables (moon, lightning, and bark) and one output variable (suspect nearby). When these three clues are logically combined, they will indicate whether our suspect is close by.

With our three input variables, there are eight possible combinations of clues. For some of the combinations the output will reveal "suspect nearby" (logic 1); for others it will show "suspect not nearby" (logic 0). When all possible combinations are listed (Figure 12.6), this array of clues becomes the familiar *truth table*. (Verify for yourself the logical conclusion to each clue combination.) The next step is to design a machine to simulate the conclusions of the truth table.

Logic-Machine Design

There are two ways to design a logic machine. Referring to Figure 12.7a, we can use the older combinational-logic method; or, referring to Figure 12.7b, we can make use of a "sequential logic machine" (a computer), simulating the logic by way of software. Let us complete the computer design.

Moon	Lightning	Bark	Suspect nearby
0	0	0	0
0	0	1	0
0	1	0	1
0	1	1	0
1	0	0	1
1	0	1	0
1	1	0	1
1	1	1	0

Figure 12.6 Mystery truth table listing all combinations of clues.

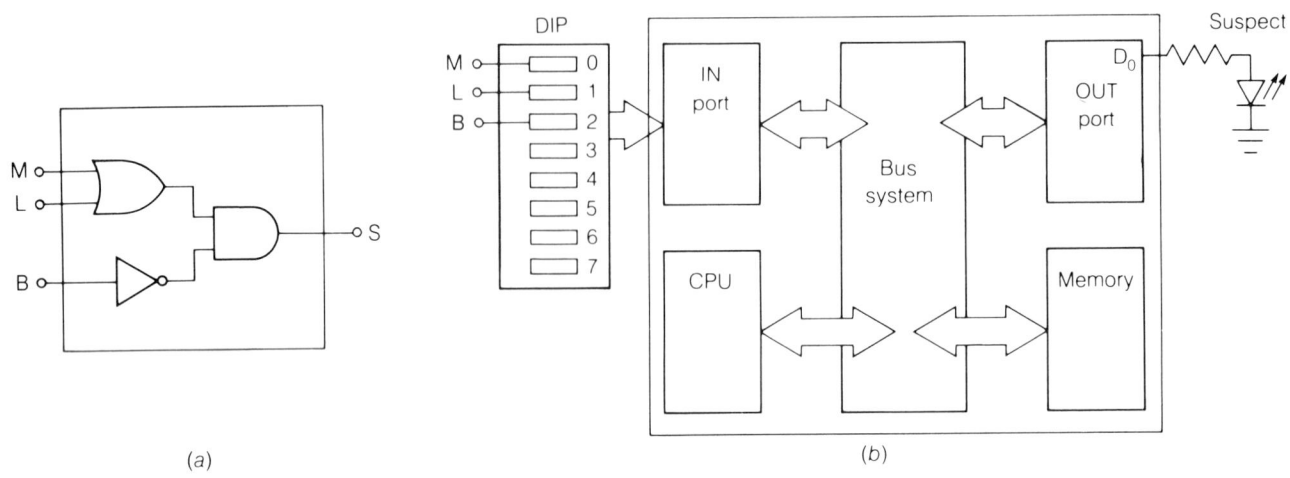

Figure 12.7 Logic-machine design using combinational logic (*a*) and sequential logic (*b*).

Since we are confronted with a typical design problem, we will approach it in a formal manner. First of all, computer design requires a hardware/software balance. In this case, as shown in Figure 12.7*b*, the hardware is very simple: just input the three variables from a DIP switch feeding an input port and view the results on an LED (light-emitting diode) fed by an output port.

Software design, on the other hand, is where most of our time will be spent. As always, software design begins with a high-level flowchart. As shown in Figure 12.8*a*, the process involves four steps.

The instructional-level flowchart and completed program are presented in Figure 12.8*b* for both *extended* and *indexed* mode addressing (to simplify program documentation, only the mnemonic form of each instruction has been listed). Note the shorter length of the *indexed* mode version. To verify each routine, trace the flow of data through the program and see if the correct results are given as required by the truth table of Figure 12.6.

Conventional Logic Design vs Computer Design

Solving the case of the "dog that did not bark" gave us an opportunity to contrast the older, more conventional combinational-logic method (Figure 12.7*a*) with the newer sequential methods of the microprocessor (Figure 12.7*b*). Clearly the older technique—at least in this case—is simpler and less expensive. What, then, is the advantage of using a computer and of writing software? The advantage is basic: when our thinking machine solves the present case and moves on to a new one, requiring a new logical sequence to solve, it is necessary only to change the program in memory—a quick, simple, and inexpensive process. To accomplish the same changeover in hardware would require a time-consuming rewiring of the circuit.

The important point to make is this: computers, like human beings, can easily be adapted to new situations. Simply send them back to "school" to be reprogrammed. Imagine what an advantage this is during the early development stages of an electronic system. Furthermore, as the conventional arrays become larger and larger, the parts count of the computer solution can be many times fewer (remember, software takes the place of hardware). The threshold is reached for a conventional circuit of approximately 20 or more chips. No wonder microprocessors are replacing more and more conventional circuit arrays.

There are two disadvantages to the software technique, however, and they become apparent when *speed* and *reliability* are critical. Using conventional logic, for example, how long does it take to solve the case of the "dog that did not bark"? The answer is: probably no more than 50 nanoseconds—the time it takes the signal to propagate through two levels of gates. Compare that to the software technique, which requires some 13 instruction cycles and 70 clock cycles—more than 50 microseconds, easily some 1000 times longer. And when we compare reliability, combinational-logic circuits cannot get "out of sync" and will automatically recover from glitch-induced errors. Glitches in a microcomputer system, on the other hand, can cause a change in program execution, resulting in a complete system crash. Nevertheless, the computer usually is sufficiently fast and reliable for most applications, and is often the wiser choice.

BIT MANIPULATION

The second important duty performed by the logical group is called *bit manipulation*. An everyday application will reveal what we mean by bit manipulation (also known as *masking*).

A certain large hotel has eight electrical motors located around the building to control air conditioning and heating. To keep all parts of the building under environmental control, it is essential that these eight motors be independently

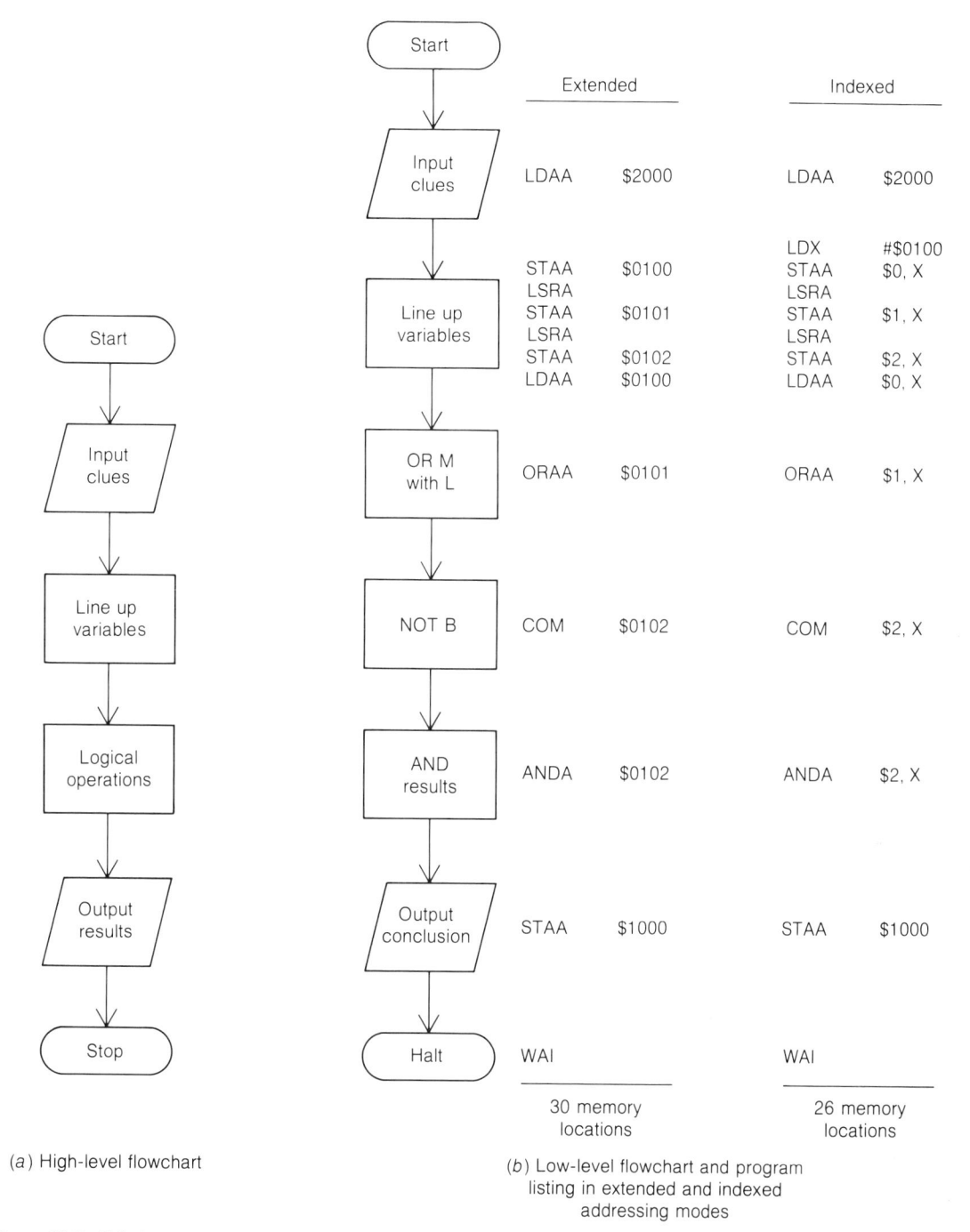

Figure 12.8 Solution to mystery program.

(a) High-level flowchart:

Start → Input clues → Line up variables → Logical operations → Output results → Stop

(b) Low-level flowchart and program listing in extended and indexed addressing modes

Flowchart	Extended		Indexed	
Start				
Input clues	LDAA	$2000	LDAA	$2000
			LDX	#$0100
Line up variables	STAA	$0100	STAA	$0, X
	LSRA		LSRA	
	STAA	$0101	STAA	$1, X
	LSRA		LSRA	
	STAA	$0102	STAA	$2, X
	LDAA	$0100	LDAA	$0, X
OR M with L	ORAA	$0101	ORAA	$1, X
NOT B	COM	$0102	COM	$2, X
AND results	ANDA	$0102	ANDA	$2, X
Output conclusion	STAA	$1000	STAA	$1000
Halt	WAI		WAI	
	30 memory locations		26 memory locations	

controlled. Can a computer be assigned the task, especially one with a single 8-bit output port? (What we really need are eight 1-bit ports.) It does look possible to make use of a single 8-bit port, because, after all, don't the Boolean instructions operate independently on each bit? Let us tie in the eight motors to our single output port and test our theory with an example (Figure 12.9).

Suppose, because of a sudden influx of heat through an open window, we must turn on motor 2 but leave all others unchanged. That is, if some of the other motors are on, leave them on. If they are off, leave them off. The only motor we want to change is motor 2 (Figure 12.9a).

The key to the operation lies in several fundamental Boolean axioms. If we want to force a particular bit position to 1, *OR* that position with a 1. If we want to leave a bit position unchanged, OR that position with a 0.

134 Part III / Software: The Spark of Life

(a) Desired motor control

- D_0 — 0 — } Unchanged
- D_1 — 1 —
- D_2 — 2 — } Turn on
- D_3 — 3 —
- D_4 — 4 —
- D_5 — 5 — } Unchanged
- D_6 — 6 —
- D_7 — 7 —

(b) "Turn on motor 2" program

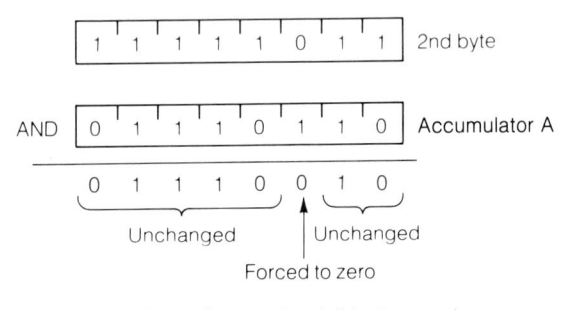

Start → OR $04 with motor states (ORAA #$04) → Output results (STAA $1000) → Halt (WAI)

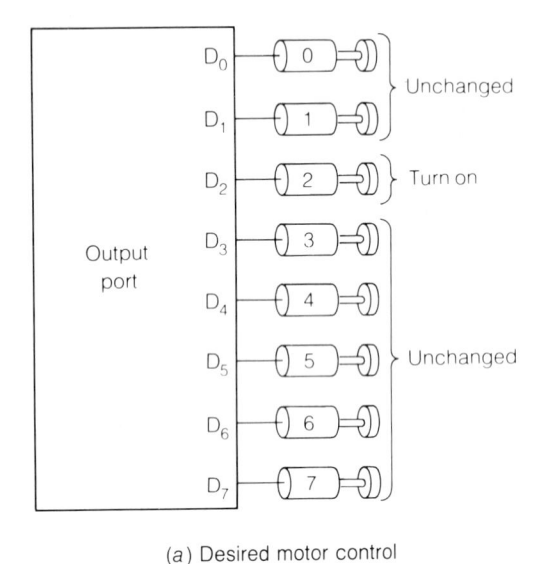

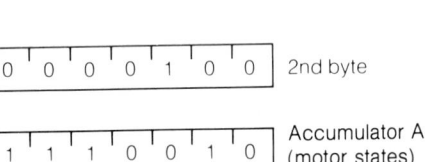

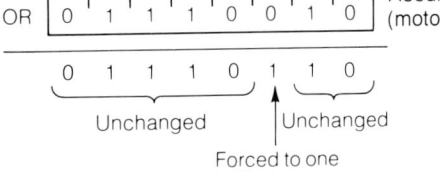

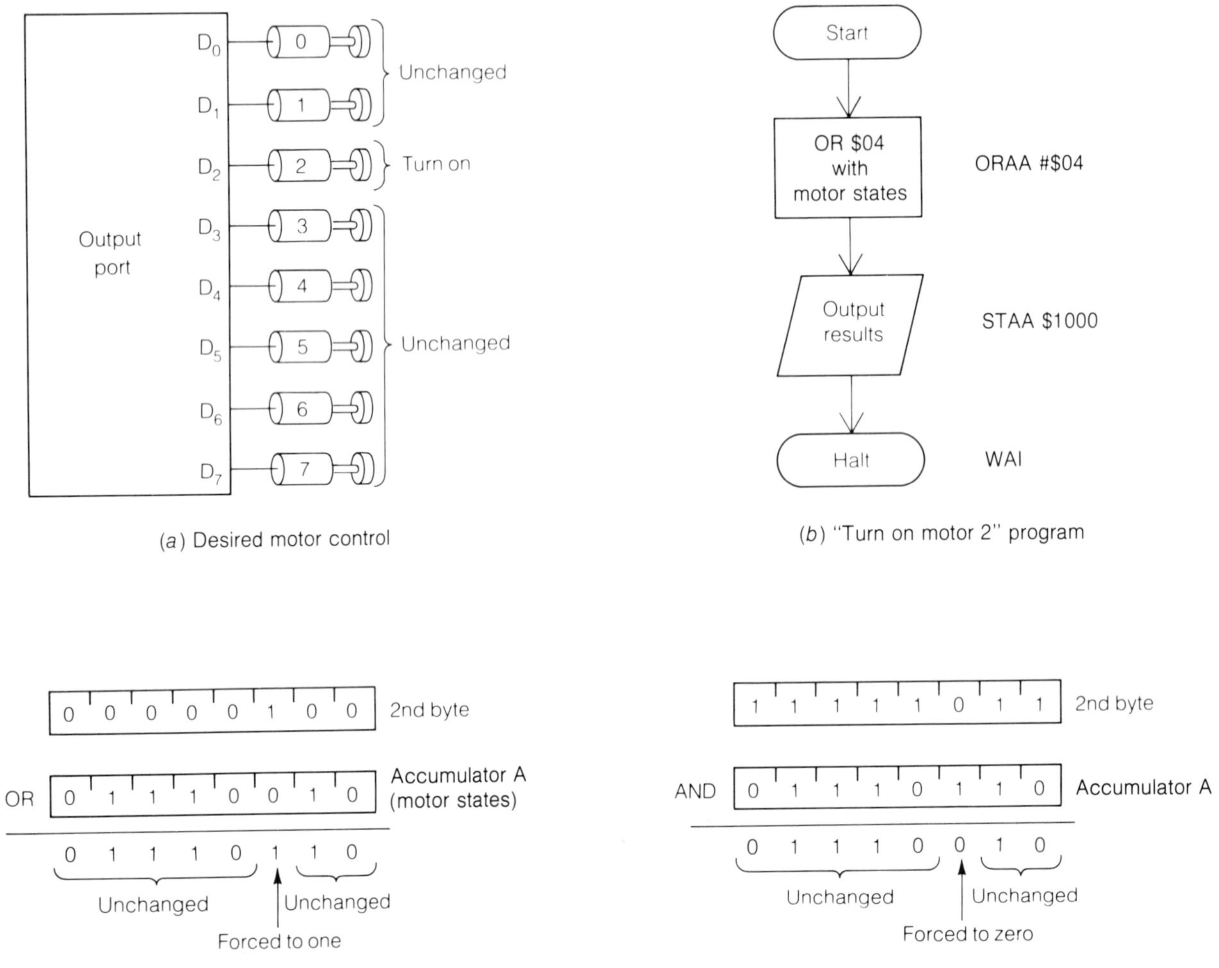

```
    0 0 0 0 0 1 0 0    2nd byte
OR  0 1 1 1 0 0 1 0    Accumulator A (motor states)
    ─────────────
    0 1 1 1 0 1 1 0
    └─Unchanged─┘ │ └Unchanged┘
              Forced to one
```

(c) "Turn on motor 2 only" test example

```
     1 1 1 1 1 0 1 1    2nd byte
AND  0 1 1 1 0 1 1 0    Accumulator A
     ─────────────
     0 1 1 1 0 0 1 0
     └─Unchanged─┘ │ └Unchanged┘
              Forced to zero
```

(d) "Turn off motor 2 only" test example

Figure 12.9 Example of bit manipulation.

$A + 1 = 1$ (force to 1)
$A + 0 = A$ (leave unchanged)

The solution now becomes very easy. If we assume accumulator A is holding the present states of the motors, then, to turn on motor 2 but leave all others unaffected, simply OR *immediate* accumulator A with $04 and outport the result to the bank of motors (Figure 12.9b).

When the routine is tested on an arbitrary profile of motor states, it does give the desired results (Figure 12.9c). Only motor 2 has been changed—in this case, forced to turn on.

Of course, after motor 2 has been turned on for some time and the heat dissipated, it will have to be turned off—again without affecting the other seven motors.

This time we will take full advantage of several axioms involving the AND process. We just AND a 1 to those positions we wish to save and a 0 to those we wish to force to 0.

$A \cdot 1 = A$ (leave unchanged)
$A \cdot 0 = 0$ (force to 0)

As illustrated in Figure 12.9d, if we AND *immediate* the accumulator with $FB and outport the results, the process is reversed: motor 2 is turned off without affecting any of the other seven motors.

Clearly, with an OR/AND sequence (or an AND/OR sequence), the eight motors can be turned on, turned off, or left unchanged in any combination we wish.

Given the ability to manipulate individual bits, we can think of one 8-bit register as equivalent to eight 1-bit registers, or two 4-bit registers, or any combination we wish.

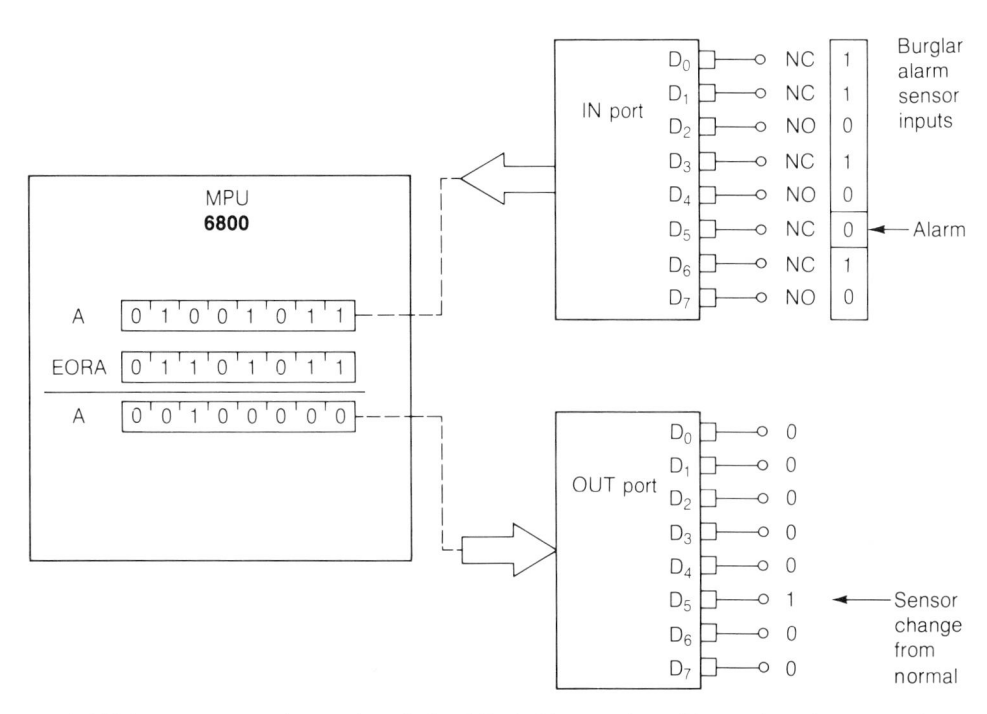

(a) Eight sensor states inported, exclusive ORed with normal condition, and results outported

```
LDAA  $2000
EORA  #$6B
STAA  $1000
```

(b) Determining device change-of-state routine

Figure 12.10 Example of change-of-state bit detection.

BIT CHANGE OF STATE

If the AND and OR processes are useful for changing the state of individual bits, then the Exclusive OR (EOR) instruction is useful for *determining* individual bit changes of state.

Suppose our air-conditioned hotel is also fitted with eight burglar alarm sensors (Figure 12.10a), some normally open (NO) and usually sending a logic 0, while the others are normally closed (NC) and usually sending a logic 1. Therefore, as shown in the diagram, 01101011 represents the normal condition. The routine of Figure 12.10b inputs the sensor states, checks for changes, and outputs a 1 in any bit position where the present sensor state differs from the normal (bit 5 in this case).

OP CODE ORGANIZATION

Now that we have reviewed most of the instructions belonging to the data-transfer, arithmetic, and logical groups, it is time to review the logic behind the op code binary format. As revealed in the figure on the following page (12.11a), it was not selected randomly.

The 8-bit op code is arranged in fields specifying the accumulator, address mode, and operation. For example, if we select register B, *indexed* addressing, and the OR function, we obtain the ORAB IND op code ($EA) as shown in Figure 12.11b.

When bit D_7 of the op code is switched to a 0, all the other op codes outside the data-transfer and arithmetic/logical groups will be selected.

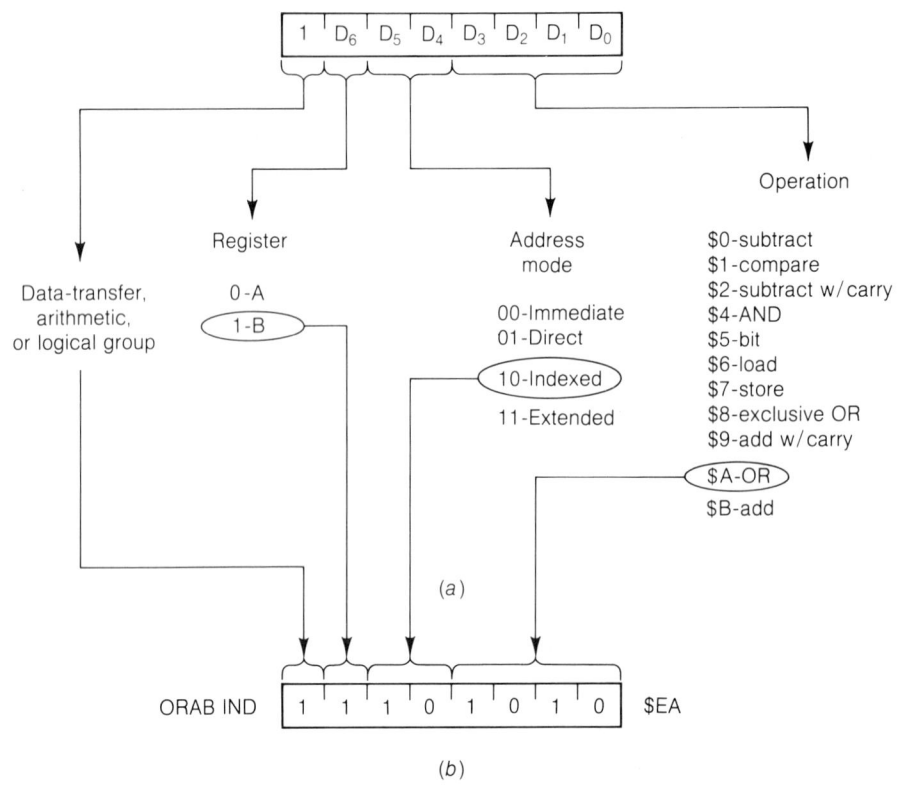

Figure 12.11 6800 op code organization for the data-transfer, arithmetic, and logical groups: format (a) and ORAB IND example (b).

INTELLIGENT-MACHINE UPDATE

The logical group is largely completed, and our intelligent machine can now examine a set of clues and solve a mystery using purely logical techniques. Also it can individually manipulate the digits of each hand by properly sequencing AND or OR instructions. For our intelligent machine, hand and eye and brain are coming together, just as they did for the human species many millions of years ago.

QUESTIONS AND PROBLEMS

1. What 6800 instruction type performs the NOT operation? How is the NOT operation related to the 1's complement process?
2. What role does an accumulator play in the processing of the OR, AND, and Exclusive OR operation?
3. In a logical operation, do the various bit positions have any relationship *to each other*?
4. Why are the rotate and shift instructions included in the logical group?
5. List the two categories of shift instructions and state the difference.
6. Write a program to simulate a 3-input NAND gate. Assume the inputs are bit positions D_0, D_1, and D_2 of input port $2000, and the output is bit position D_0 of the output port $1000.
7. What Boolean operation is used to blank out selected bit positions? To set selected bit positions high?
8. Write a program that will turn on outport bit positions D_0 and D_7, turn off bit positions D_3 and D_4, and leave the remaining bit positions unchanged.
9. Explain how you would simulate six 2-input OR gates on your 6800 system.
10. Explain how you would simulate one 5-input OR gate.
11. When simulating an 8-input AND gate on a 6800 computer, what is the minimum number of times that the AND instruction would have to be used? (*Hint:* The answer is less than 7 but greater than 2.)
12. The four most significant bits (MSBs) of one register are to be combined with the four least significant bits (LSBs) of another register. Making use of logical instructions, how can this be accomplished?
13. What masking instruction placed before the "Out conclusion" block of Figure 12.8b will assure that all unused bit positions (D_1 through D_7) will always be blanked (masked) out?

14. Operating on the bank of motors of Figure 12.9a with the Exclusive OR *immediate* instruction will have what result? Assume an arbitrary array of 1s and 0s for both the motor array and the second byte of the EOR instruction.
15. For the EOR IND instruction, complete the waveform diagram following the format of Figure 10.3. Assume that the op code of the EOR IND instruction is stored at ROM location $FF00, and that the data to be combined with accumulator A are stored at RAM location $00A0 and the index register holds $0090.
16. By changing the order of the input variables, can the program of Figure 12.8b be shortened? If so, how can this be done?
17. Rewrite the mystery program of Figure 12.8b assuming the scratchpad RAM is located at page 0 and therefore accessible by *direct* addressing.
18. Convert each mnemonic instruction of Figure 12.8b into hexadecimal machine code.
19. Based on the op code format of Figure 12.11a, develop the op code for the SUBB EXT instruction and check your answer with Appendix I.
20. Give an example of a "multiply-by-2" Arithmetic Shift Left operation that results in an erroneous sign change.

chapter 13

Loops and Jumps: Introduction to Assembly-Language Programming

We are creatures of repetition. To keep every cell in our bodies continuously awash with a fresh supply of oxygen and nutrients, our hearts may beat well over three billion times. Does it not follow that our memories must hold at least three billion instructions in order to keep our hearts active throughout our life span?

Of course, if that were true, life as we know it would not be possible. Instead, we have a special way of handling routines that repeat themselves over and over again: we place them into a *loop*.

LOOPS AND JUMPS

A loop is a circle. The mimic program developed earlier is presently a straight line (it starts and stops). To turn the process into a repetitive loop, we need a special command that will automatically cause the processor to go back to the LDAA EXT (input) instruction and repeat the mimic process—over and over again. To create a loop, the 6800 instruction set includes the Jump (JMP) and Branch Always (BRA) instructions (Figure 13.1).

Jump (JMP)

Operation: PC ← numerical address

Description: A jump occurs to the instruction stored at the numerical address. The numerical address is obtained according to the rules for EXTended or INDexed addressing.

Addressing Modes	Execution Time (No. of cycles)	Number of bytes of machine code	Coding of First (or only) byte of machine code		
			HEX.	OCT.	DEC.
EXT	3	3	7E	176	126
IND	4	2	6E	156	110

Courtesy of Motorola, Inc.

(a)

Branch Always (BRA)

Operation: PC ← (PC) + 0002 + Rel

Description: Unconditional branch to the address given by the foregoing formula, in which R is the relative address stored as a two's complement number in the second byte of machine code corresponding to the branch instruction.

Addressing Modes	Execution Time (No. of cycles)	Number of bytes of machine code	Coding of First (or only) byte of machine code		
			HEX.	OCT.	DEC.
REL	4	2	20	040	032

Courtesy of Motorola, Inc.

(b)

Figure 13.1 The Jump and Branch Always instructions.

When the JMP or BRA instruction is substituted for the WAI instruction, the program is placed into a repetitive loop (Figure 13.2). Note the flowchart arrow leading from the branch block to the return location.

When the mimic program is placed into a loop, less than 10 memory locations are required—no matter how many times the mimic process is repeated. The saving in memory space is enormous. In addition, we have eliminated the WAI instruction, which really is designed exclusively for interrupt processing.

The JMP and BRA instructions introduce the *branch group*, probably the most powerful and versatile instruction group available to the computer programmer. *The branch group alters normal sequential program flow* (see Appendix III).

Jump vs Branch

Jump and Branch are both *unconditional* branch instructions, which means the branch to a new location *must* take place. The *conditional* branch process of Chapter 14, on the other hand, is dependent on the state of certain processor status flags and *may* or *may not* take place.

Fortunately Jump, the first type of unconditional branch instruction, is rather easy to master. The verb is JMP (jump) and the location to which the program is to jump is determined by *extended* or *indexed addressing*. On completion of this instruction, the program counter is effectively changed to the value specified by the mode of addressing. With the Jump instruction the program can branch to any of the 65,536 memory locations. When the program jumps back to a previous location, it usually forms a loop.

For practice, write the Jump instruction for branching to location $0155 (use both *extended* and *indexed addressing*, and assume the index register holds $0100). Check your answers against the solutions below:

Mnemonic	Hex code
JMP $0155	$7E, $01, $55
JMP $55,X	$6E, $55

The second type of the unconditional branch (Branch Always) uses a new form of addressing: *relative addressing*. Furthermore, a *relative* address can be negative as well as positive. Therefore, before adding the Branch Always instruction to our working vocabulary, a study of *relative addressing* is in order.

Relative Addressing

All of us use *relative addressing* in our everyday lives. For example, we might say the location of the grocery store is five houses down from where we are presently standing. The number "5" is relative to our present location. Using 6800 terminology, the *relative* address is called the *offset*, and the present location is given by the contents of the program counter (PC). To go backward as well as forward from our present location, the *relative* address can be positive as well as negative. Therefore, the *relative* address is given using 2's complement notation. Since the *relative* address is a byte, it can specify branches from +127 to −128.

The BRA Instruction

The BRA (Branch Always) instruction uses *relative addressing* only. The first byte is the op code, and the second byte holds the *relative* address (the offset). It is the programmer's responsibility to calculate the offset and place it in the second byte of the BRA instruction. The process sounds simple enough—just subtract the branch location from your present location.

Unfortunately, it is not that simple. The problem is that most instructions are determined by the location of their op codes, whereas relative branches are determined with respect to program counter contents. *Since the program counter always looks ahead to the next address location, the present contents of the PC at the completion of the 2-byte BRA instruction is actually 2 greater than the location of the BRA op code.* For example, suppose the BRA instruction is located at $AA08 (op code) and $AA09 (offset), and you wish to jump ahead four locations (relative to the BRA op code) to AA0C. What number should you use for the offset? The answer is 2 (not 4), because the present contents of the PC at the time the address calculation is made within the 6800 is $AA0A. To avoid confusion in the calculation of the offset, let's stick to the convention suggested by Motorola.

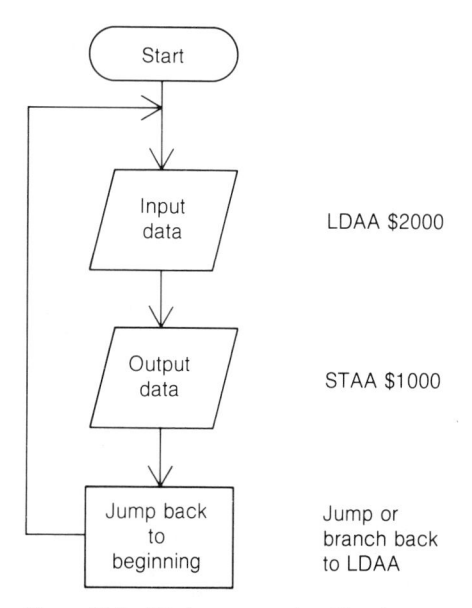

Figure 13.2 Mimic program placed into loop.

Referring to the BRA instruction summary (Figure 13.1b), we find the following formula:

$$PC \leftarrow (PC) + 0002 + Rel$$

where all PC values refer to the op code locations.
Solving for Rel, we obtain:

$$Rel = PC - ((PC) + 0002)$$

Let's try out our formula on our previous example: The BRA instruction op code is located at $AA08 and you wish to jump to location $AA0C. Substituting in our formula:

$$\text{Offset} = \text{target op code} - (\text{present op code} + 0002)$$
$$Rel = \$AA0C - (\$AA08 + 0002) = 2$$

Jumping back The previous example showed how to jump ahead four locations. But suppose we wish to branch *back* four locations (relative to the BRA op code), from $AA08 to $AA04? Substituting in our formula:

$$Rel = \$AA04 - (\$AA08 + 0002)$$
$$= -6 \quad (11111010B \text{ or } \$FA \text{ in 2's complement})$$

The offset is a negative number. In computer work, we specify negative numbers using 2's complement notation.

Let's look at several examples and see if we can calculate the proper offset and write the correct instruction.

- *Example 1:* The BRA op code is located at $0200 and we wish to branch ahead to location $0267. What is the offset?

  $$\text{Offset} = \$0267 - (\$0200 + 2) = \$0065$$

  Therefore, the correct instruction is BRA $65.

- *Example 2:* The BRA op code is located at $0200 and we wish to branch back to location $01E6.

  $$\text{Offset} = \$01E6 - (\$0200 + 2)$$
  $$= \$-1C \quad (\$E4 \text{ in 2's complement})$$

  Adding the offset to the instruction, we obtain BRA $E4.

JUMP INSTRUCTION PROCESSING

The Jump and BRA instructions use the technique of *overlapping* to carry out the process of branching from one stored-program location to another. Let's use the JMP EXT instruction to demonstrate what is involved. As we sequence through the process, we follow the clock-cycle diagram of Figure 13.3, and note how smoothly the computer "passes the baton" from one program sequence to another.

1. The Jump-instruction op code is fetched to the instruction register and decoded.

2. The Jump microprogram updates the program counter and directs the transfer of instruction bytes 2 and 3 to the MAR.

3. When the three clock cycles of the Jump instruction are completed, the processor initiates the op-code fetch sequence for the next instruction. However, rather than releasing the PC contents onto the address bus, the MAR contents are fed to the address bus.

4. Simultaneously, the MAR is incremented to look ahead to the next machine cycle and is loaded into the program counter.

Based on these four steps, the actual jump takes place when the contents of the MAR, rather than the contents of the program counter, are fed to the address bus. This action takes place during the first clock cycle *following* the Jump instruction (the Jump instruction therefore overlaps into the next instruction).

Any of the programs from previous chapters can be placed into a loop, thereby eliminating the need to reset the computer after each program run (see Figure 13.4).

ASSEMBLY-LANGUAGE PROGRAMMING

Looking over the routine of Figure 13.4, we have apparently developed the natural habit of listing just the instruction mnemonics rather than the pure binary or hexadecimal machine-language formulation. Clearly binary or hexadecimal numbers just do not convey the same meaning as shorthand English statements. For this reason the list of mnemonics often is developed before the actual binary machine-language program; it is called *assembly-language programming*. Such a mnemonic-based program is easy to write, interpret, and correct.

An assembly-language program, called a *source listing*, is arranged in four columns, called *fields* (see Figure 13.5).

Code Field

By its very name the *code field* is closely related to the operation code of each instruction, and is basically the list of mnemonic verbs. ORG, which stands for *origin*, serves merely to identify the very beginning of the program. Origin is known as a *pseudo-instruction*, since it is not actually part of the program but serves to supply information necessary for final program development.

Operand Field

As expected, the *operand field* is the list of instruction operands—in mnemonic form. As always, the sign "$" preced-

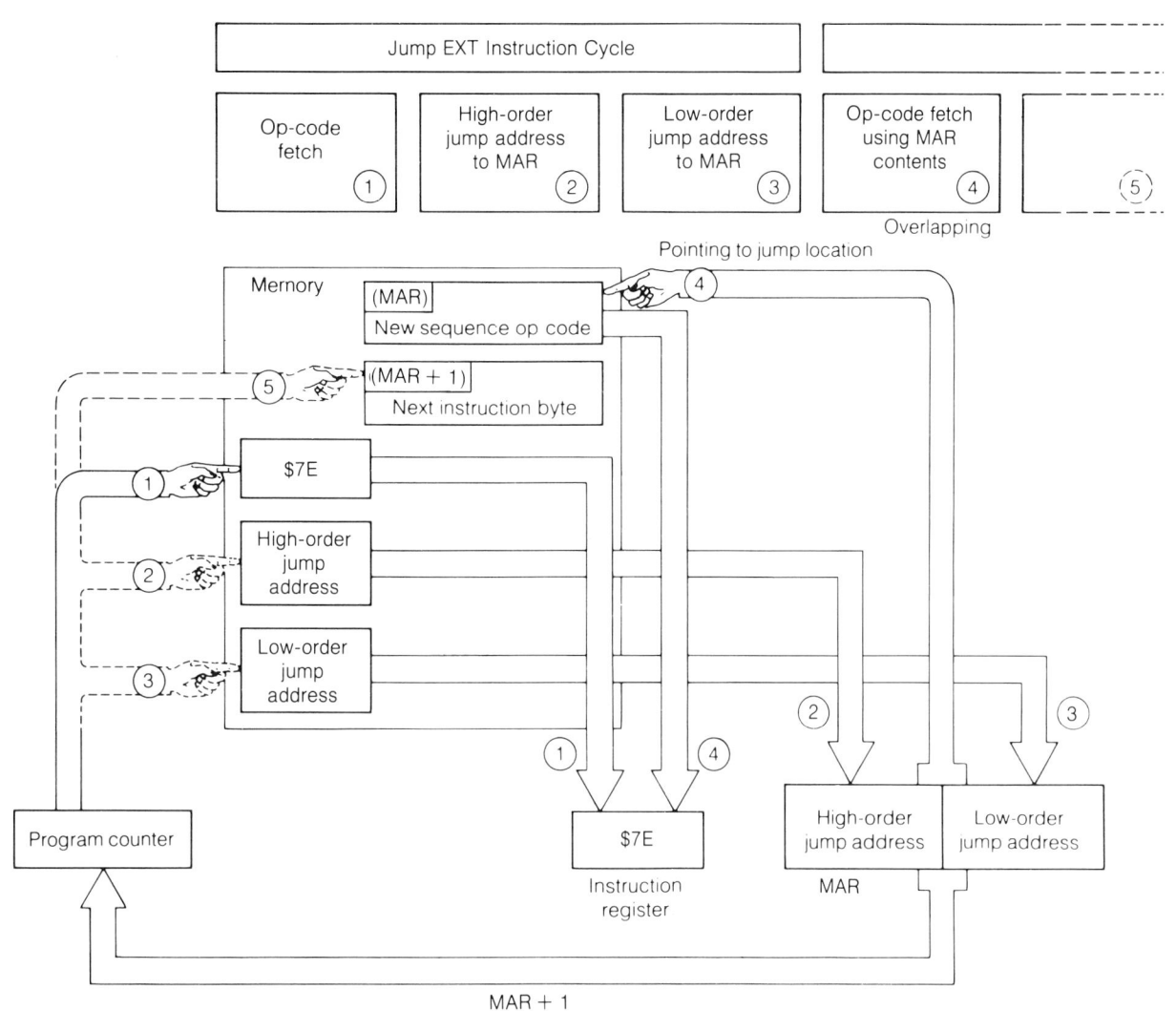

Figure 13.3 Jump EXT instruction timing and clock-cycle diagram.

ing all numbers indicates a hexadecimal number (octal numbers are identified with an "O" or "Q," binary numbers with a "B," and decimal numbers with either a "D" or the absence of any letter designation).

The last entry in the operand column represents one of the most important features of assembly-language programming. What kind of an operand is "start"? *Start is a symbolic representation of an address* (in this case $0000). But why use a symbol—why not just use the numerical address directly? After we introduce the label field in the source listing, the reason will be clear.

Label Field

The *label field* is where the memory addresses would normally be. Surprisingly, it is mostly blank. In fact, *start* is the only entry. The label concept arose because some very practical questions were asked during the early development stages of programming. Perhaps the most obvious question is: Why should I list all memory addresses if most are merely sequential? And does it not follow from this that the only time I need worry about addresses is at the very beginning of the program and whenever a program branch is involved? In answer to these and other questions, assembly-language programming developed the *symbolic address*.

Start in our program is a symbolic address and stands for the location to which the program branches when the jump instruction is executed. *Start,* in other words, provides the address link when the program branches to an out-of-sequence location. No other labels are required because all other addresses are sequential!

The use of the symbolic address, rather than the hexadecimal address, greatly simplifies and speeds up the initial program development, when concepts, rather than details, are important.

Figure 13.4

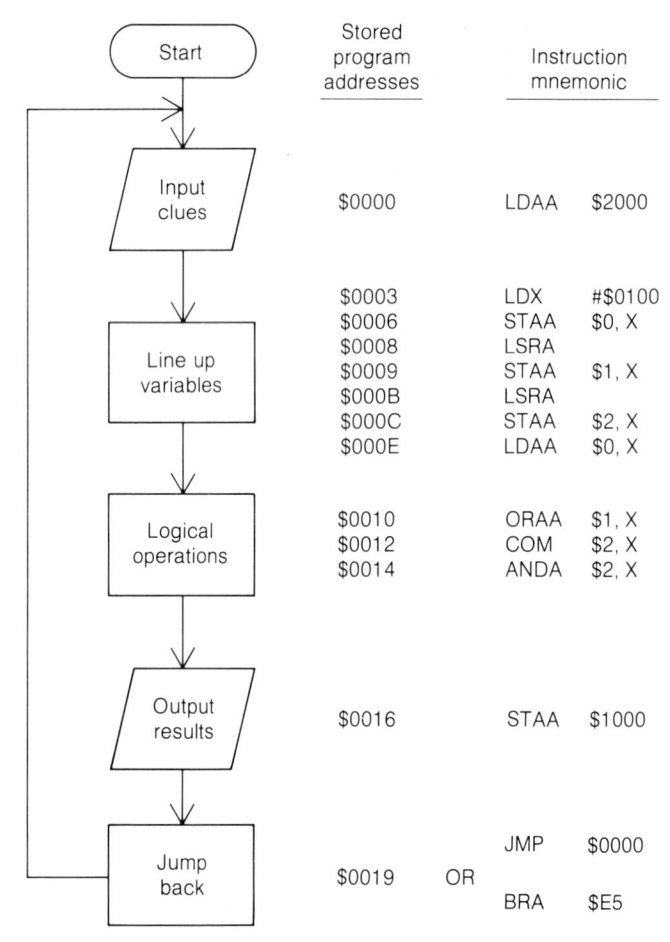

	Stored program addresses		Instruction mnemonic	
Input clues	$0000		LDAA	$2000
Line up variables	$0003		LDX	#$0100
	$0006		STAA	$0, X
	$0008		LSRA	
	$0009		STAA	$1, X
	$000B		LSRA	
	$000C		STAA	$2, X
	$000E		LDAA	$0, X
Logical operations	$0010		ORAA	$1, X
	$0012		COM	$2, X
	$0014		ANDA	$2, X
Output results	$0016		STAA	$1000
Jump back	$0019	OR	JMP	$0000
			BRA	$E5

Figure 13.4 Mystery program placed into loop.

Comment Field

The last field is the *comment field*. And here there are no hard and fast rules: any comment helping to document the program and to aid others in understanding its content is proper.

PROGRAM ASSEMBLY

Once the assembly-language program is written, most of the work is done. But certainly the program is not ready to enter into the computer. It must be assembled into the proper hexadecimal or binary sequence of numbers, known as the *object program*. Of course, all symbolic addresses must be fully identified.

For very complex programs, the assembly process is accomplished by a computer under the direction of a program called an *assembler*. For simple programs, or when an assembler is not available, all programs are hand assembled.

Machine Assembler

When a machine assembler is available, the art of assembly-language programming takes on new dimensions. For example, there are nearly a dozen different ways in which to specify an operand, and even arithmetic computations may be included. Furthermore, a machine assembler is programmed to recognize a great number of pseudo-instructions, including *macros*. (A macro is a single-line pseudo-instruction that stands for a group of instructions previously defined.)

The assembly process is usually performed in two passes over the source program (a two-pass assembler). The first pass expands macros, substitutes *relative* addresses for symbols, and writes the program into a temporary storage space (a file in a floppy). During the second pass all symbolic op codes and operands are assigned numeric values and an object program is generated.

As an example of the machine-assembly process, Figure 13.6 shows our mystery program of the previous chapter

Chapter 13 / Loops and Jumps: Introduction to Assembly-Language Programming **143**

Source Listing

Label	Code	Operand	Comments
	ORG	$0000	Starting location of routine
START:	LDAA	$2000	Input clues to accumulator A
	LDX	#$0100	Load index register
	STAA	$0, X	Place "MOON" into $0100
	LSRA		Rotate clues right
	STAA	$1, X	Place "LIGHTNING" into $0101
	LSRA		Rotate clues right
	STAA	$2, X	Place "BARK" into $0102
	LDAA	$0, X	Return "MOON" to accumulator A
	ORAA	$1, X	OR "MOON" with "LIGHTNING"
	COM	$2, X	Complement "BARK"
	ANDA	$2, X	AND "BARK" with "M" or "L"
	STAA	$1000	Give result
	BRA	START	Place into loop

Figure 13.5 Mystery routine programmed in assembly language.

```
                                       6800/6801/6802 ASSEMBLER VER.3.3      1

 1                       ; This is our first machine-assembler printout
 2
 3                ;Label      Code    Operand     Comments
 4
 5 0000                       ORG     $0      ; Starting location
 6 0000 B6 20 00   START:     LDAA    $2000   ; Input clues to accum A
 7 0003 CE 01 00              LDX     #$0100  ; Load IR with RAM location
 8 0006 A7 00                 STAA    $0,X    ; Place "MOON" into $0100
 9 0008 44                    LSRA            ; Rotate clues right
10 0009 A7 01                 STAA    $1,X    ; Place "LIGHTNING" in $0101
11 000B 44                    LSRA            ; Rotate clues right
12 000C A7 02                 STAA    $2,X    ; Place "BARK" into $0102
13 000E A6 00                 LDAA    $0,X    ; Return "MOON" to accum A
14 0010 AA 01                 ORAA    $1,X    ; OR "MOON" with "LIGHTNING"
15 0012 63 02                 COM     $2,X    ; Complement "BARK"
16 0014 A4 02                 ANDA    $2,X    ; AND "BARK" with "M" or "L"
17 0016 B7 10 00              STAA    $1000   ; Give result
18 0019 20 E5 0000            BRA     START   ; Place into loop
19 001B                       END

ERRORS = 0000


MEMORY M 0000    STACK  S 0000    START    0000
```
Figure 13.6 Machine-assembled printout of mystery program (list file).

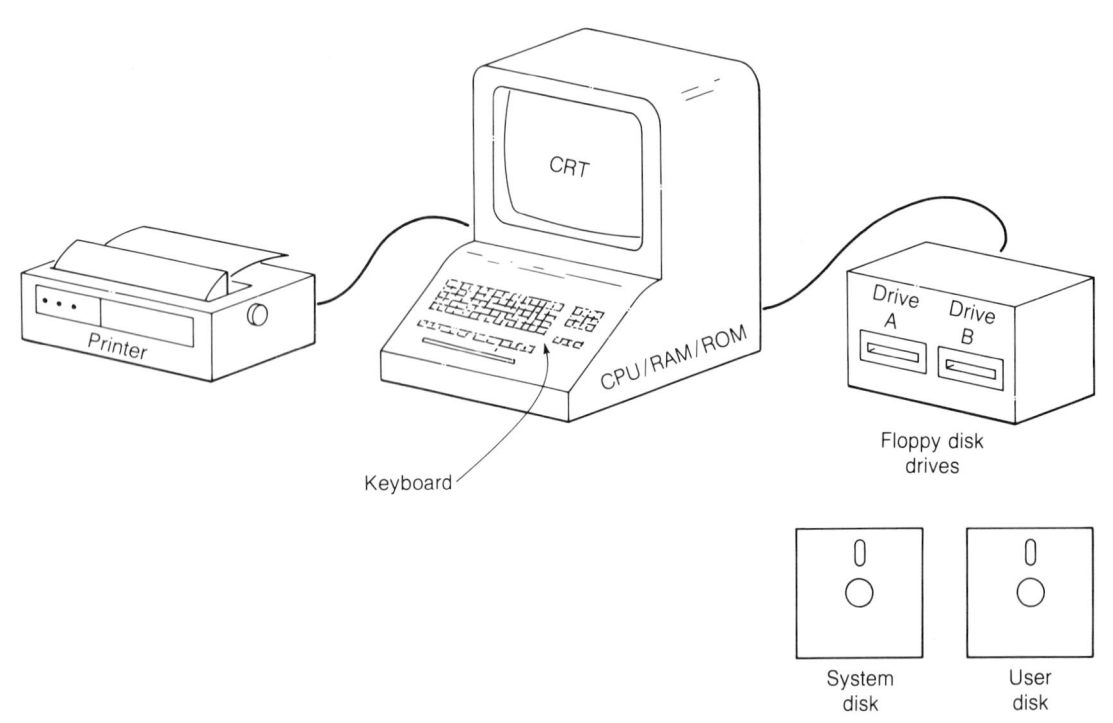

Figure 13.7 A machine-assembly system.

coded by a machine assembler. Let's see how this assembled program was generated.

The hardware required for machine assembly is shown in Figure 13.7, and consists of a computer (with internal RAM and ROM), a video monitor, two disk drives, a printer, and system and user floppy disks. The software is stored as files (a program with a name) on the system disk, and includes an operating system, word processor, and assembler.

A typical machine-assembly process begins by "booting up" (transferring) the operating system from the system disk to the computer's internal RAM (the "boot" routine is stored in ROM within the computer). Running under the operating system, the user commands the word processor file to be transferred into internal RAM and executed. Using the facilities of the word processor, the user types in the source program in assembly language. When the user is satisfied with the program as written (it may later require corrections and modifications), the program is transferred to the user floppy disk and becomes a file. A typical file name might be B:MYSTERY.SRC (B: is the disk drive identification number).

Using an operating system command (such as ASM68 B:MYSTERY.SRC), the 6800 macroassembler is evoked and the program is automatically assembled. The completed assembly process generates two new files on the user disk: an object file (MYSTERY.OBJ) and a list file (MYS-TERY.LST).

The object file (Figure 13.8a) is the binary machine-language code represented by ASCII characters, and is ready to run on a 6800-based system. As seen, many of the ASCII characters are interpreted by the printer as graphics elements. The object file obviously is of little use to the programmer for the purpose of documentation or program debugging. However, if we convert the binary object file to

(a) Interpretation of binary code by printer

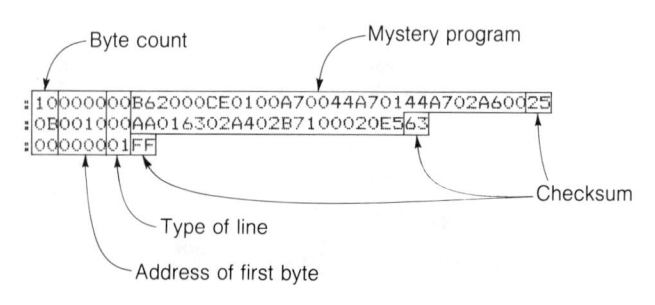

(b) MYSTERY.HEX—binary code converted to hexadecimal

Figure 13.8 Mystery program object file.

```
                        6800/6801/6802 ASSEMBLER VER.3.3      1
         1              ; This is our first machine-assembler printout
         2
         3                ;Label     Code    Operand    Comments
         4
         5  0000                     ORG     $0        ; Starting location
         6  0000 B6 20 00   START:   LDAA    $2000     ; Input clues to accum A
         7  0003 CE 10 00            LDX     #$1000    ; Load IR with RAM location
    Q    8  0006 87 00 00            STA     $0,X      ; Place "MOON" into $0100
   ( 0)
    F    9  0009 44                  LSRA    $0,X      ; Rotate clues right
   ( 8)
        10  000A A7 01               STAA    $1,X      ; Place "LIGHTNING" in $0101
        11  000C 44                  LSRA              ; Rotate clues right
        12  000D A7 02               STAA    $2,X      ; Place "BARK" into $0102
        13  000F A6 00               LDAA    $0,X      ; Return "MOON" to accum A
    Q   14  0011 8A 00 00            ORA     $1,X      ; OR "MOON" with "LIGHTNING"
   ( 9)
        15  0014 63 02               COM     $2,X      ; Complement "BARK"
    F   16  0016 94 02               ANDA    $2 X      ; AND "BARK" with "M" or "L"
   ( 14)
        17  0018 B7 10 00            STAA    $1000     ; Give result
    U   18  001B 20 E3 0000          BRA     LOOP      ; Place into loop
   ( 16)
        19  001D                     END

    ERRORS = 0005
    ( 18)

MEMORY M 0000    STACK  S 0000    START    0000
```

Figure 13.9 List file showing five errors.

hexadecimal (accomplished by an operating-system utility program), we can at least determine what is contained in MYSTERY.OBJ. Examining the result (MYSTERY.HEX of Figure 13.8b), we see that the object file contains information in addition to the mystery program code. Each line starts with a count of the number of bytes of program data in that line (i.e., there are $10 or 16D bytes of program code in the first line). Next is placed the address of the first byte of program code ($0000), followed by the type of line ("00" is a code line; "01" is a termination line). At the end of each line a checksum byte is used to verify that the conversion to hexadecimal was made without error.

The list file (MYSTERY.LST) of Figure 13.6 is, however, of great use to the programmer during the development process. The list program is a listing of hexadecimal machine code placed side by side with the source program. Note that all addresses—including the branch address—have been filled in automatically. As an added bonus most assemblers will notify the operator if certain types of syntax errors were made in the source listing. Since none was found in the program of Figure 13.6, it prints "no errors" at the bottom of the sheet.

If syntax errors are found, they are identified in the source listing (the assembler, of course, cannot check for errors in programming logic). For example, the program of Figure 13.9—as indicated—contains five errors. To help identify the type and location of an error, a variety of error codes are printed on the same line as the statement in error: "Q" indicates an op code/operand combination that is not valid, "F" indicates a general programmer-generated error, and "U" indicates an undefined symbol (symbolic name in argument field which has never appeared in label field). Identifying the five errors is left as an exercise.

Entire books are written on assembly-language programming techniques, and many systems are on the market. If you have access to a machine assembler, it would be wise to consult the manufacturer's literature and to read through a separate textbook on assembly-language programming.

Because of the increased availability of machine assemblers, we will introduce a number of advanced features in the chapters to follow.

Hand Assembly

When a machine assembler is not available, most manufacturers provide an "assembly-language reference card" to aid the process of hand assembly. The mnemonics are conveniently arranged in instruction groups and all possible addressing combinations provided. Most of the information contained in the 6800 reference card appears in Appendix II.

INTELLIGENT-MACHINE UPDATE

When placed into a loop, our intelligent machine seems much more alive. No longer does it function in bursts from reset to halt, but now processes continuously. Is it the presence of loops that gives us continuous life? It seems like a reasonable theory.

The many program loops working to keep our bodies functioning were developed millions of years ago, and they certainly are not the higher-level thought processes that give our species the almost unique ability to reason. Is it the ability to reason and to make decisions that will allow us at last to part company with our intelligent machine?

Not at all, for as we will see in the next chapter, even the ability to reason affords the human being no real sanctuary from our rapidly developing machine.

QUESTIONS AND PROBLEMS

1. Bytes 2 and 3 of the Jump instruction contain what information?
2. If a Jump instruction is stored at memory location $2040 (through $2042), what range of numbers placed into bytes 2 and 3 will place the processor into a loop? For the BRA instruction (byte 2)?
3. What role does the MAR play in the branch process?
4. How many of the 64K memory locations can the JMP instruction branch to? Can we jump forward as well as backward?
5. Repeat question 4 for the BRA instruction.
6. The memory location to which the processor jumps should always contain what kind of information?
7. If the BRA instruction op code is stored at location 01A0, what is its branching range?
8. What is the advantage of using the BRA instruction over the JMP instruction?
9. Assuming an origin (ORG) of $00A6, write the loop mimic program of Figure 13.2 using each of the three available jump instructions: JMP EXT, JMP IND, and BRA. (Assume the index register holds $00A6.)
10. List several advantages of assembly-language programming over machine-language programming.
11. List and briefly describe each of the four fields of assembly-language programming.
12. What are *source, object,* and *list* programs?
13. What are *symbolic* addresses, and why were they developed?
14. Why are symbolic addresses placed in the label field?
15. What is an *assembler*? What is a *two-pass* assembler?
16. When programming in assembly language, is it necessary for the programmer to know the exact memory locations where the program will be stored?
17. Locate and correct the five syntax errors of Figure 13.9.
18. What operand will cause the BRA instruction to jump to itself?
19. Using information from the *Hexadecimal Values of Machine Codes* table in Appendix II, disassemble (convert from hex to mnemonics) the following program (be sure to use the ORG statement and labels):

Address	Code
$0000	$D6
$0001	$00
$0002	$17
$0003	$8B
$0004	$02
$0005	$97
$0006	$9C
$0007	$7E
$0008	$00
$0009	$00

20. If the BRA op code is located at $0200 and we wish to jump ahead to $02C7, why would an assembler error result?
21. What is a *cross assembler*? (Research will be required.)

chapter 14

Reasoning: The Conditional Jump

Leonardo da Vinci could reason. A caveman could reason. And you and I can reason. But can a computer reason? Many people say no. A computer, they argue, can only do what it is told to do—what it is programmed to do. But the catch is: that is also true of us. We reason because we are programmed to reason from birth, and so can a computer be programmed to reason.

THE ELEMENTS OF REASONING

First of all, let us reduce the elements of reasoning to more concrete terms; reasoning, after all, is a very abstract concept.

> To *reason* is to *decide*.
> To *decide* is to *choose*.

So reasoning is decision making, and it is choosing—something we do every day. We *choose* to stop at the intersection if the light is red; otherwise we ignore the signal and go on through. We *choose* to go to the beach if the sun is shining; otherwise we stay at home.

These two examples of decision making have several features in common. First, each involves a branch concept—the sort of action you take when coming to a fork in the road. When you arrive at the branch point, you must make a decision—a choice. You can go straight ahead, or you can branch away. And what determines if a branch should be made or ignored? In the first case the traffic signal determines our course of action, and in the second case it is the sun. When these *signs* are consulted, the correct decisions are made.

Based on these simple ideas, the process of decision making can be flowcharted as a two-step process (Figure 14.1):

1. The signs are set. For example, the sun comes out.
2. A branch is made—or ignored. It all depends on the sun. (Note the flowchart symbol for branching and how it resembles a fork in the road. There is only one way in, but two ways out.)

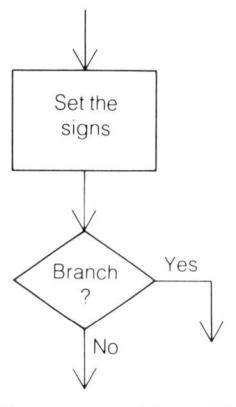

Figure 14.1 The two-step decision-making process.

And that is how we make a decision—such as going to the beach. *A computer makes a decision in exactly the same way.* In a computer, however, the *signs* are called *flags,* and the branch can still be called a *branch* or it can be called a *jump*—either term will do. To teach our computer to make decisions we will have to locate the right instructions to carry out each of the two flowchart blocks in the decision-making process.

The Flag-Setting Block

For us, almost anything can be a *flag* or sign, including a flag itself. The 6800 microprocessor, on the other hand, uses six flags—electronic flags—each one a single flip-flop:

> Carry (C) flag
> Overflow (V) flag
> Zero (Z) flag
> Negative (N) flag
> Interrupt (I) flag
> Half Carry (H) flag

147

148 Part III / Software: The Spark of Life

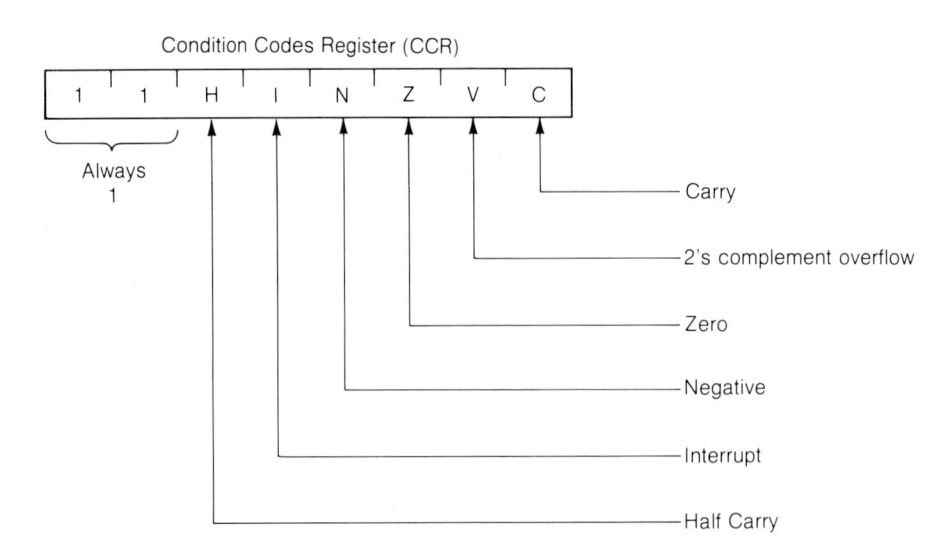

```
         Condition Codes Register (CCR)
        ┌──┬──┬──┬──┬──┬──┬──┬──┐
        │ 1│ 1│ H│ I│ N│ Z│ V│ C│
        └──┴──┴──┴──┴──┴──┴──┴──┘
         └─┬─┘  │  │  │  │  │  │
         Always│  │  │  │  │  └── Carry
           1   │  │  │  │  └───── 2's complement overflow
               │  │  │  └──────── Zero
               │  │  └─────────── Negative
               │  └────────────── Interrupt
               └───────────────── Half Carry
```

Figure 14.2 The contents of the condition codes register.

As shown in Figure 14.2, these six flags are grouped together in a special register called the *condition codes register* (CCR). To simplify the decision-making process at first, we will ignore for now all flags involving signed number processing, interrupts, and BCD arithmetic. The use of these flags will be covered in Chapters 16 (Interrupts) and 17 (Mathematical Refinement). The two flags that remain, the Zero and Carry flags, are by far the most commonly used and will be covered in this chapter.

Like the sun, which is either shining or not shining (in a two-valued system), each flag is also two-valued, and can be set to a 1 or reset to a 0. *It is the purpose of the flag-setting instructions to translate the state of the system on which decisions are based (sun out?) into flag values.* Most of the flag-setting instructions come from the arithmetic or logical group. It works like this: when an arithmetic or logical instruction is run, the flags are set or reset, *depending on the numerical outcome of the operation.* (In most cases, an accumulator holds the result of an arithmetic or logical operation.) It follows that the set-flags block of our two-step decision-making process is usually an arithmetic or logical instruction.

Besides the arithmetic/logical flag-setting instructions, which indirectly set the flags based on the outcome of an operation, the 6800 instruction set also includes the Condition Codes Register instruction group (Figure 14.3), which gives the programmer direct control over the six flags.

A flag-setting example   As an example of a flag-setting instruction, let us see how the simple ABA (Add Accumu-

		IMPLIED			BOOLEAN OPERATION	COND. CODE REG.					
						5	4	3	2	1	0
OPERATIONS	MNEMONIC	OP	~	#		H	I	N	Z	V	C
Clear Carry	CLC	0C	2	1	0 → C	•	•	•	•	•	R
Clear Interrupt Mask	CLI	0E	2	1	0 → I	•	R	•	•	•	•
Clear Overflow	CLV	0A	2	1	0 → V	•	•	•	•	R	•
Set Carry	SEC	0D	2	1	1 → C	•	•	•	•	•	S
Set Interrupt Mask	SEI	0F	2	1	1 → I	•	S	•	•	•	•
Set Overflow	SEV	0B	2	1	1 → V	•	•	•	•	S	•
Acmltr A → CCR	TAP	06	2	1	A → CCR			─(1)─			
CCR → Acmltr A	TPA	07	2	1	CCR → A	•	•	•	•	•	•

R = Reset
S = Set
• = Not affected

① (ALL) Set according to the contents of Accumulator A.

Courtesy of Motorola, Inc.

Figure 14.3 The Condition Codes Register instructions.

> **Add Accumulator B to Accumulator A (ABA)**
>
> Operation: ACCA ← (ACCA) + (ACCB)
>
> Description: Adds the contents of ACCB to the contents of ACCA and places the result in ACCA.
>
> Condition Codes:
> H: Set if there was a carry from bit 3; cleared otherwise.
> I: Not affected.
> N: Set if most significant bit of the result is set; cleared otherwise.
> Z: Set if all bits of the result are cleared; cleared otherwise.
> V: Set if there was two's complement overflow as a result of the operation; cleared otherwise.
> C: Set if there was a carry from the most significant bit of the result; cleared otherwise.
>
> Boolean Formulae for Condition Codes:
> $H = A_3 \cdot B_3 + B_3 \cdot \overline{R}_3 + \overline{R}_3 \cdot A_3$
> $N = R_7$
> $Z = \overline{R}_7 \cdot \overline{R}_6 \cdot \overline{R}_5 \cdot \overline{R}_4 \cdot \overline{R}_3 \cdot \overline{R}_2 \cdot \overline{R}_1 \cdot \overline{R}_0$
> $V = A_7 \cdot B_7 \cdot \overline{R}_7 + \overline{A}_7 \cdot \overline{B}_7 \cdot R_7$
> $C = A_7 \cdot B_7 + B_7 \cdot \overline{R}_7 + \overline{R}_7 \cdot A_7$
>
> | Addressing Modes | Execution Time (No. of cycles) | Number of bytes of machine code | Coding of First (or only) byte of machine code |||
> |---|---|---|---|---|---|
> | | | | HEX. | OCT. | DEC. |
> | Inherent | 2 | 1 | 1B | 033 | 027 |
>
> Courtesy of Motorola, Inc.

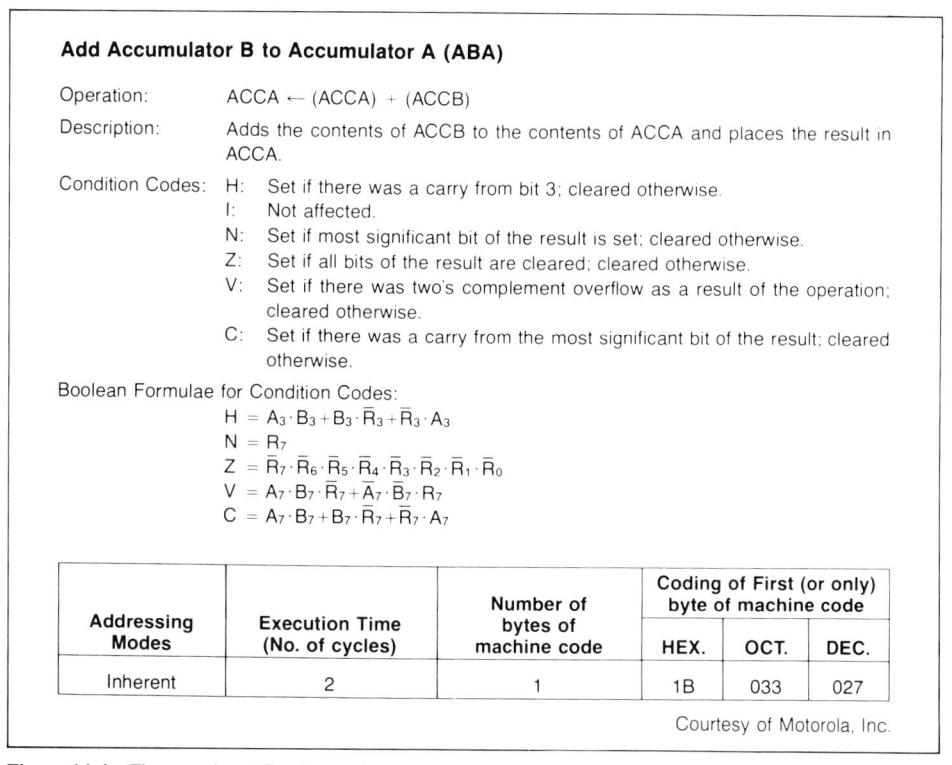

Figure 14.4 The complete ABA instruction summary, including condition codes information.

lator B to Accumulator A) instruction affects the Carry and Zero flags (see Figure 14.4). As shown, we have included flag information in our instruction summary for the first time. Note that both the Z and C flags are affected by the ABA instruction.

When the ABA instruction is processed, the Z and C flags will tell you something about the result:

- If the result of the ABA process produces a zero sum in accumulator A, the Z flag goes high. Otherwise, if the result is nonzero, the Z flag goes low.

- If the result of the ABA process produces a carry from the most significant bit in accumulator A, the C flag goes high. Otherwise, the C flag goes low.

Those who desire a mathematically precise version of the flag-setting process will note the *Boolean Formulae for Condition Codes* given in the ABA instruction summary ("R" means "Result of operation"). Let's analyze the formulas for the Z and C flags and see what we can learn.

The Boolean formula for the Z flag ($Z = \overline{R}_7 \cdot \overline{R}_6 \cdot \overline{R}_5 \cdot \overline{R}_4 \cdot \overline{R}_3 \cdot \overline{R}_2 \cdot \overline{R}_1 \cdot \overline{R}_0$) is clear: only when all zeros result from the ABA operation will the Z flag be set (go high).

The Boolean condition for the Carry flag ($C = A_7 \cdot B_7 + B_7 \cdot \overline{R}_7 + \overline{R}_7 \cdot A_7$), however, is not so obvious. Referring to Figure 14.5, there are three ORed conditions that will set the Carry flag. The first condition ($A_7 \cdot B_7$) is no problem. When both A_7 *and* B_7 are one, both numbers are greater than or equal to 128, giving a result greater than 255 and a carry overflow.

The second condition ($B_7 \cdot \overline{R}_7$) requires the following line of reasoning: the only way that both a 0 can appear in the $\overline{R}_7$ position and a 1 in the B_7 position is for a single 1 to be added to the 1 in the B_7 position. This single 1 can result either from a 1 in position A_7 (thus overlapping the first condition) or from a carry out of bit position $\overline{R}_6$. Either way, when a single 1 is added to the 1 in position B_7, a zero and a carry will always result. The third condition ($\overline{R}_7 \cdot A_7$) is symmetric with the second and follows the same line of reasoning.

The Boolean formulas for condition codes give the exact mathematical conditions under which flags will be set, and can be quite complex. However, using plain English rather than mathematics, the Carry flag conditions can be summed up in a single sentence: *If the result of the addition is greater than 255, the Carry flag will be set.*

Therefore, although the complexities of the Boolean formulas make for interesting mathematical analysis, there generally are much simpler ways of stating the same thing. Consequently, the Boolean formulas will seldom be consulted when writing decision-making programs.

To summarize the ABA flag-setting process, Figure 14.6 shows the results of adding 64 (base 10) and 192 (base 10).

150 Part III / Software: The Spark of Life

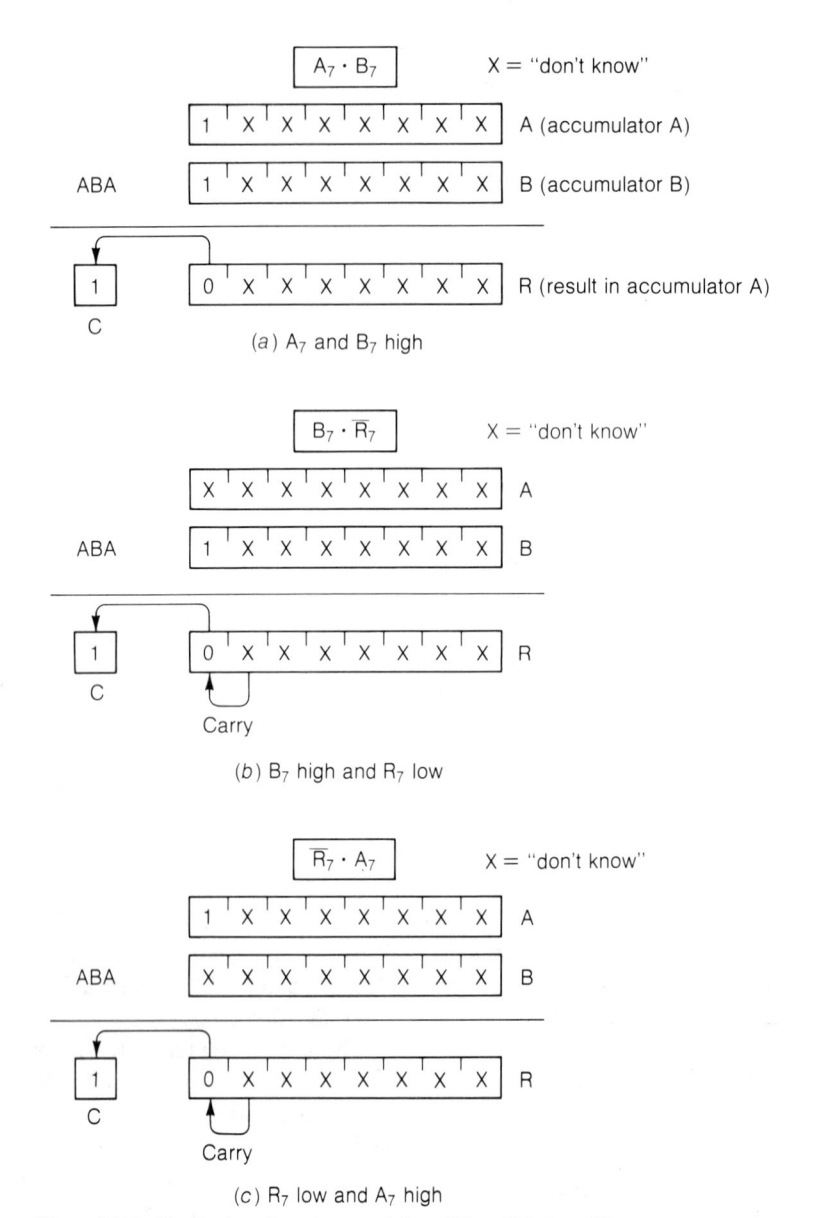

Figure 14.5 The Boolean formulas, consisting of three ORed conditions, for setting the Carry flag using the ABA instruction.

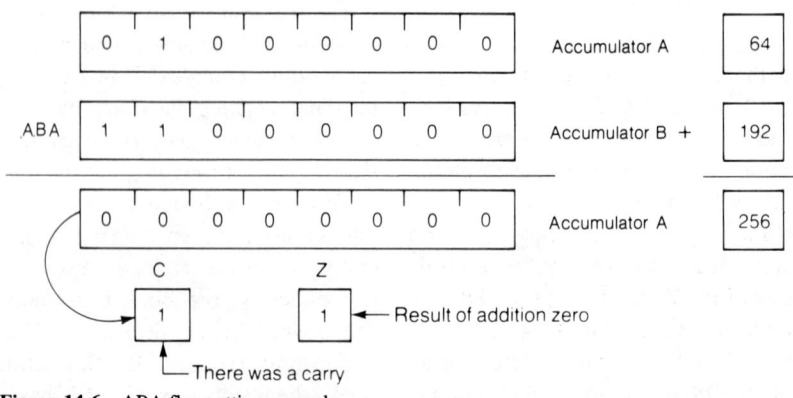

(a) A_7 and B_7 high

(b) B_7 high and R_7 low

(c) R_7 low and A_7 high

Figure 14.6 ABA flag-setting example.

The Branch Block

Once the flags are set or reset by one or more arithmetic/logic instructions, it is the job of the branch block to see that the correct path is taken. To jump or not to jump—that is the question. *The flags will provide the answer.*

Obviously, the branch block is processed by a jump-type instruction. But it certainly cannot be the unconditional jump that we learned about in the last chapter. The unconditional jump says you must jump (you must go to the beach, even if the sun is hidden).

The 14 *conditional branch* instructions—grouped below as 7 complementary pairs—are the answer:

Operations	Mnemonic	Boolean condition for branch
Branch if Carry Clear	BCC	C = 0
Branch if Carry Set	BCS	C = 1
Branch if Equal	BEQ	Z = 1
Branch if Not Equal	BNE	Z = 0
Branch if Higher	BHI	C + Z = 0
Branch if Lower or Same	BLS	C + Z = 1
Branch if Plus	BPL	N = 0
Branch if Minus	BMI	N = 1
Branch if Overflow Clear	BVC	V = 0
Branch if Overflow Set	BVS	V = 1
Branch if >= Zero	BGE	N + V = 0
Branch if < Zero	BLT	N + V = 1
Branch if > Zero	BGT	Z + (N + V) = 0
Branch if <= Zero	BLE	Z + (N + V) = 1

The conditional branch is one of the most powerful programming tools available, and will allow the computer to reason, to make a choice—to jump or not to jump. You will be pleased to learn that the conditional branch instructions use *relative addressing*, the same as the BRA instruction of the last chapter.

Again, to simplify the conditional branch process at first, let's ignore for now all conditional branching instructions involving signed numbers. The six remaining conditional branch instructions of Figure 14.7 will be easier to master for they use only the Carry and Zero flags.

The key word in the conditional branch mnemonics is "if"—the same word that performs decision making in a high-level language such as BASIC or Pascal. (High-level language programming will be covered in Chapter 22.) The basic format is:

Jump to specified location IF condition is true

If the condition is not true, ignore the jump and continue on to the next instruction.

Description	Mnemonic	Boolean condition
Branch if Carry Clear	BCC	C = 0
Branch if Carry Set	BCS	C = 1
Branch if Equal	BEQ	Z = 1
Branch if Not Equal	BNE	Z = 0
Branch if Higher	BHI	C + Z = 0
Branch if Lower or Same	BLS	C + Z = 1

Figure 14.7 The six conditional branching instructions based on unsigned numbers.

Summary of the Two-Step Decision-Making Process

And that is how decisions are made. For people or for machines, it is the same two-step process: set flags based on the state of the system, and jump *if* the flag condition is true. As shown in Figure 14.8, the set-flags operation usually is performed with a math or logical operation, while the branch process is accomplished with one of the conditional branch instructions.

Therefore, when writing programs involving decision making, each decision will require the programmer to:

1. Select the correct flag-setting instruction.
2. Select the correct conditional branch instruction.

Nearly every program developed in the remainder of this book will involve one or more of these two-step decision-making processes.

A DECISION-MAKING EXAMPLE

To put the two-step decision-making process to work, let us write a modified mimic program to mimic only the year in

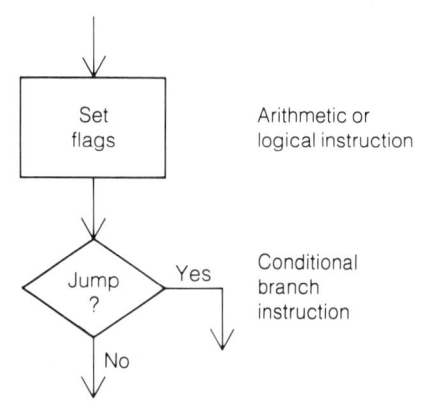

Figure 14.8 The two-step decision-making process for a computer.

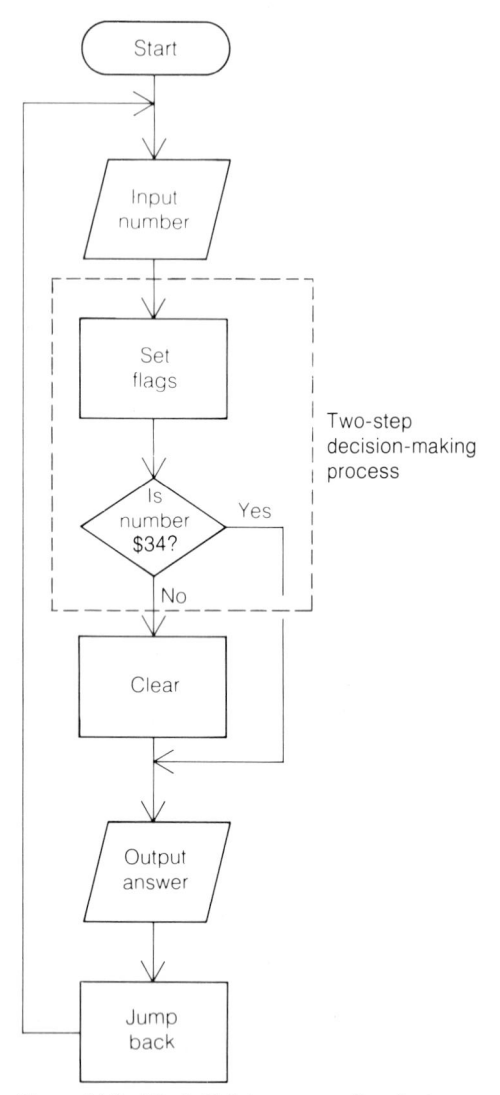

Figure 14.9 Mimic-birthday program flowchart.

The Flag-Setting Block

Passing by the familiar input block, we move to the set-flags block, where the decision-making process begins. How are we going to set the flags to determine if the inported number is equal to $34? Here is where we learn that programming is an art as well as a science. Like playing the game of chess, we must rely largely on *heuristics* to solve the problem. (Heuristics is a method of education in which the student proceeds along empirical lines, using rules of thumb, to find answers.) One fact looks promising: when two numbers are exclusive ORed, the result is zero only when they are equal. And only when the result is zero will the Z flag go high. Therefore, the set-flags block will use the Exclusive OR (EORA) instruction to search for a match. When a match is found, the Z flag will go high. *In other words, the set-flags block has translated a unique physical condition (number equal to $34) into a unique flag condition (Z flag high).*

The set-flags block completed, we move on to the second part of decision making, the conditional branch.

The Conditional Branch Block

The question is, Which of the six selected conditional branch instructions of Figure 14.7 is the proper choice? The answer is easy when we examine the clues generated by the flag-setting instruction (EORA): *When the numbers are equal, the result of the Exclusive OR operation will be zero, and the Z flag will go high.* Therefore, we are looking for the branch instruction that will correspond to any of the following conditions:

1. Branch *if* contents of accumulator Equal to contents of memory.
2. Branch *if* result of Exclusive OR operation zero.
3. Branch *if* Z flag high.

All three statements are really saying the same thing (branch if the two numbers are equal); and we find all three in the BEQ (Branch if Equal) instruction summary of Figure 14.10. If the two numbers are equal, then when they are exclusive ORed the result will be zero—and the Z flag will go high.

Just to make sure we selected the proper conditional branch instruction, let's go through the decision-making process using the Exclusive OR *immediate* flag-setting instruction. If the inported number is indeed $34, the Exclusive OR operation gives a result of zero (the two numbers are equal), and the Z flag goes to one. Since we Branch if Equal (branch if result of Exclusive OR operation is zero and Z flag goes high), we jump around the clear block and outport the number $34 unchanged. On the other hand, if the inported number is not $34, the Exclusive OR operation gives a nonzero result, the Z flag is reset to zero, and we do not jump, but pass through the clear block and outport a zero. (Because

which you were born and blank out all other years. We know a decision is involved, for the computer must decide if the inported number is the correct year, then pass on the one correct number and zero out all others. To make the problem specific, let us assume you were born in "52" (1952).

The first step, as always, is a flowchart. Do you see how the strategy of Figure 14.9 will solve the problem? If the incoming number is 52 (34 in hexadecimal), simply jump around the clear block; otherwise, the number must pass through the clear block and be blanked out.

The next task is to select the proper instructions to carry out each flowchart block. As we develop the assembly-language program, we will allow a software error (bug) to find its way into the routine. If you haven't found the bug when we are finished, we will show how programming in assembly language allows for quick and easy program corrections.

Branch if Equal (BEQ)

Operation: PC ← (PC) + 0002 + Rel if (Z)=1

Description: Tests the state of the Z bit and causes a branch if the Z bit is set.
See BRA instruction for further details of the execution of the branch.

Condition Codes: Not affected.

Addressing Modes	Execution Time (No. of cycles)	Number of bytes of machine code	Coding of First (or only) byte of machine code		
			HEX.	OCT.	DEC.
REL	4	2	27	047	039

Courtesy of Motorola, Inc.

Figure 14.10 The Branch if Equal (BEQ) conditional branch instruction.

the Z flag goes to a one only when the result of the operation is zero, the Z flag is often tricky to work with and may require some practice.)

Just complete the remaining blocks with well-known instructions, and the "birthday" program is complete (Figure 14.11a).

But will the program work? No, it will not, for, as promised, there is a software error in the routine (an error, incidentally, in logic rather than syntax, and therefore would be overlooked by a machine assembler). The problem is this: When we set the flags using the Exclusive OR instruction, we also destroy the inported information when a match is found. Therefore, as written, the program always outports a zero. One solution, shown in Figure 14.11b, is to save the inported number in accumulator B and then set the flags according to accumulator A. (An alternative method, using the compare instruction, is saved for an exercise.)

When the program is written in assembly language, note how easy it is to make corrections. We simply add or delete instructions at will, paying no attention to the increased program length—the addresses and labels will not be set until the final assembly process.

A list file (MIMIC.LST) of our mimic-birthday program is shown in Figure 14.12. Access to a machine assembler here is greatly appreciated since the tricky *relative* address calculations are done by the assembler rather than by hand. In other words, all we have to do is "label" the source and destination of the jumps and the machine will do the rest. (You may wish to verify for yourself that $01 and $F2 are the correct *relative* addresses.)

MACHINE-ASSEMBLY UPDATE—I

It is convenient here to present our first "machine-assembly update," in which we introduce the more commonly used features of a machine assembler that greatly improve program efficiency, readability, and error correction. *Many of the features will be useful even if the program is to be hand assembled.*

A good rule for writing source programs is: the more humanlike, the better. Therefore, as shown in Figure 14.12, we are allowed to write the date (52) in the more convenient decimal form. The assembler—which only can work on binary/hexadecimal—will perform the necessary translation from decimal to hexadecimal *automatically*. As with the *relative* address calculation, letting the machine do the work saves time and reduces the chances of error.

THE TEST AND BIT TEST INSTRUCTIONS

A welcome addition to any instruction set are instructions designed to save time. The Test (TST) and Bit Test (BIT) flag-setting instructions of Figure 14.13 are such examples. They provide a means of checking the state of an accumulator or memory location without affecting their contents. Of course, we could accomplish the same thing with a combination of data transfer, arithmetic, and Boolean masking instructions, but the TST and BIT instructions are easier and more direct.

If we save negative number processing for Chapter 17, then the TST instruction is simply used to determine if an accumulator or memory location is zero or nonzero. The process is easy: zero is subtracted from a specified accumulator or memory location, and the Z flag is set or reset based on the result of the operation. Obviously, the original contents of the test location remain unchanged.

As an example of the TST instruction, the program of Figure 14.14 tests each memory location in page 1 and outports the number of locations that are cleared (holding all zeros). (Note the simulated halt at the end of the program.)

154 Part III / Software: The Spark of Life

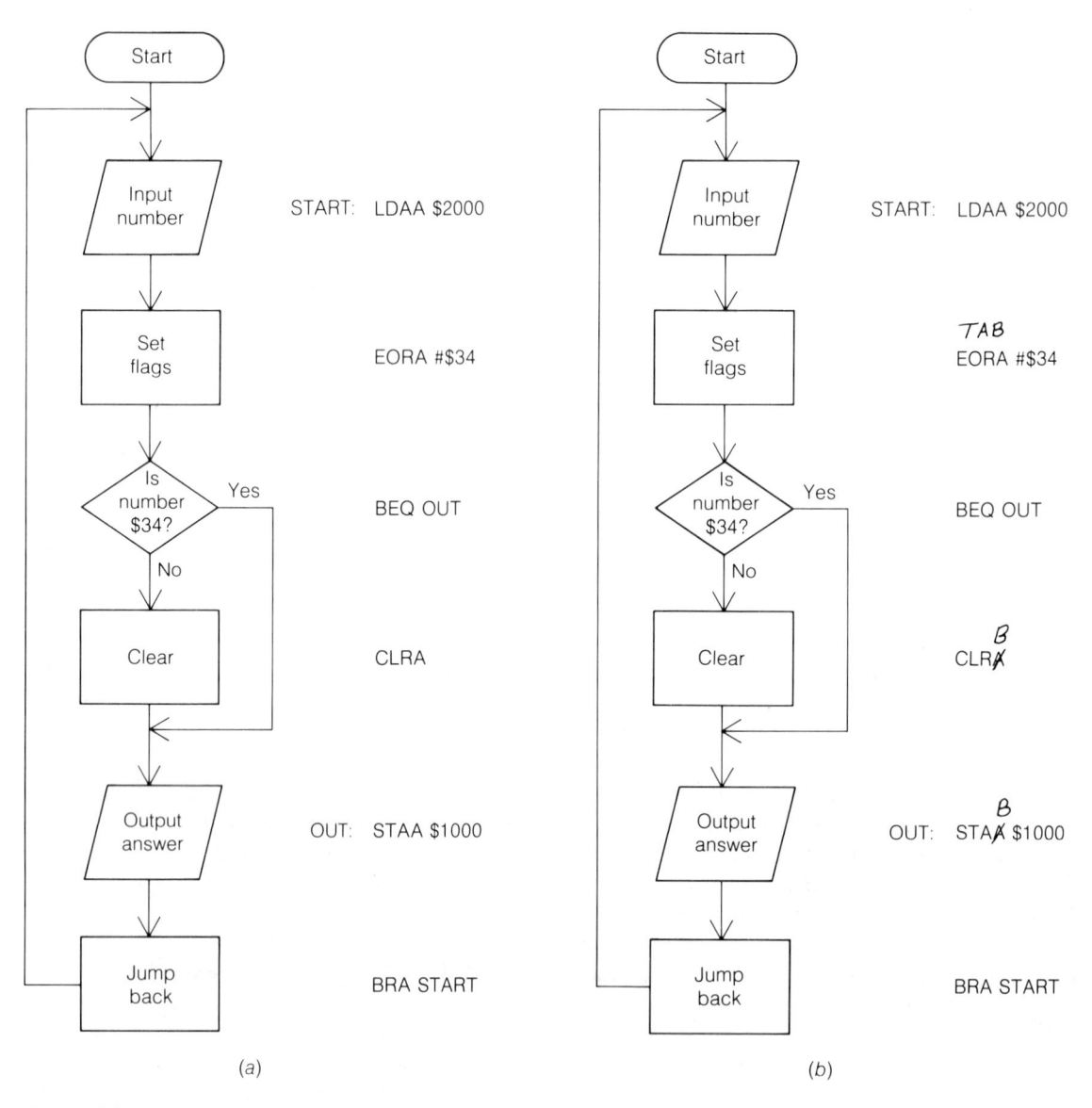

Flowchart (a):
- Start
- Input number — START: LDAA $2000
- Set flags — EORA #$34
- Is number $34? — BEQ OUT
- No → Clear — CLRA
- Yes → (skip to Output)
- Output answer — OUT: STAA $1000
- Jump back — BRA START

Flowchart (b):
- Start
- Input number — START: LDAA $2000
- Set flags — TAB / EORA #$34
- Is number $34? — BEQ OUT
- No → Clear — CLRB
- Yes → (skip to Output)
- Output answer — OUT: STAB $1000
- Jump back — BRA START

(a)   (b)

Figure 14.11 Mimic-birthday program with "bug" (a) and with "bug" removed (b).

```
                              6800/6801/6802 ASSEMBLER VER.3.3        1

  1                    ; This program only mimics numbers equal to 52
  2                    ; This program also demonstrates the automatic
  3                    ; conversion from decimal (52) to hexadecimal
  4                    ; ($34) during assembly.
  5
  6 0000                       ORG     $0
  7 0000 B6 20 00  START:      LDAA    $2000  ; Input test date
  8 0003 16                    TAB            ; Store in accum B
  9 0004 88 34                 EORA    #52    ; Test number in accum A
 10 0006 27 01 0009            BEQ     OUT    ; Jump if = $34
 11 0008 5F                    CLRB           ; Clear accum B
 12 0009 F7 10 00  OUT:        STAB    $1000  ; Output answer
 13 000C 20 F2 0000            BRA     START  ; Loop back
 14 000E                       END

    ERRORS = 0000


        MEMORY M 0000    OUT      0009   STACK  S 0000    START     0000
```

Figure 14.12 Mimic-birthday program list file.

Test (TST)

Operation: (ACCX) − 00
(M) − 00

Description: Sets condition codes N and Z according to the contents of ACCX or M.

Addressing Modes	Execution Time (No. of cycles)	Number of bytes of machine code	Coding of First (or only) byte of machine code		
			HEX.	OCT.	DEC.
A	2	1	4D	115	077
B	2	1	5D	135	093
EXT	6	3	7D	175	125
IND	7	2	6D	155	109

Courtesy of Motorola, Inc.

(*a*)

Bit Test (BIT)

Operation: (ACCX) · (M)

Description: Performs the logical "AND" comparison of the contents of ACCX and the contents of M and modifies condition codes accordingly. Neither the contents of ACCX or M operands are affected. (Each bit of the result of the "AND" would be the logical "AND" of the corresponding bits of M and ACCX.)

Addressing Modes	Execution Time (No. of cycles)	Number of bytes of machine code	Coding of First (or only) byte of machine code		
			HEX.	OCT.	DEC.
A IMM	2	2	85	205	133
A DIR	3	2	95	225	149
A EXT	4	3	B5	265	181
A IND	5	2	A5	245	165
B IMM	2	2	C5	305	197
B DIR	3	2	D5	325	213
B EXT	4	3	F5	365	245
B IND	5	2	E5	345	229

Courtesy of Motorola, Inc.

(*b*)

Figure 14.13 The Test (TST) and Bit Test (BIT) flag-setting instructions.

The BIT instruction is more specific, for it is designed to test individual bits within an accumulator or memory location. The BIT instruction is similar to the AND instruction in that both perform the logical AND (mask) function between an accumulator and memory location. However, the BIT instruction prevents the result of the AND process from going to an accumulator. Like the TST instruction—if we ignore for now negative number operations—it sets the Z flag only.

As an example of the BIT instruction, let's count the number of memory locations in page 1 having a "1" in bit position 5. The only modification to Figure 14.14 is to preload accumulator B with the mask data (00100000), and substitute the BITB $0,X instruction for the TST $0,X instruction. Rewriting the program is left as an exercise.

GREATER-THAN/LESS-THAN DECISIONS

Suppose we assign our computer the task of mimicking certain numbers, as before, but this time, rather than passing on only the number $34, it is to mimic all (unsigned) numbers *less than* $34 and blank out all (unsigned) numbers $34 *or greater*. Can our computer handle this task as easily as it did the first assignment?

Yes, but only after we introduce the *compare* instruction—an instruction type specifically designed to handle *greater-than/less-than/equal-to* decision making. As usual, it comes in various forms and addressing modes. The compare instructions of Figure 14.15 are the most commonly

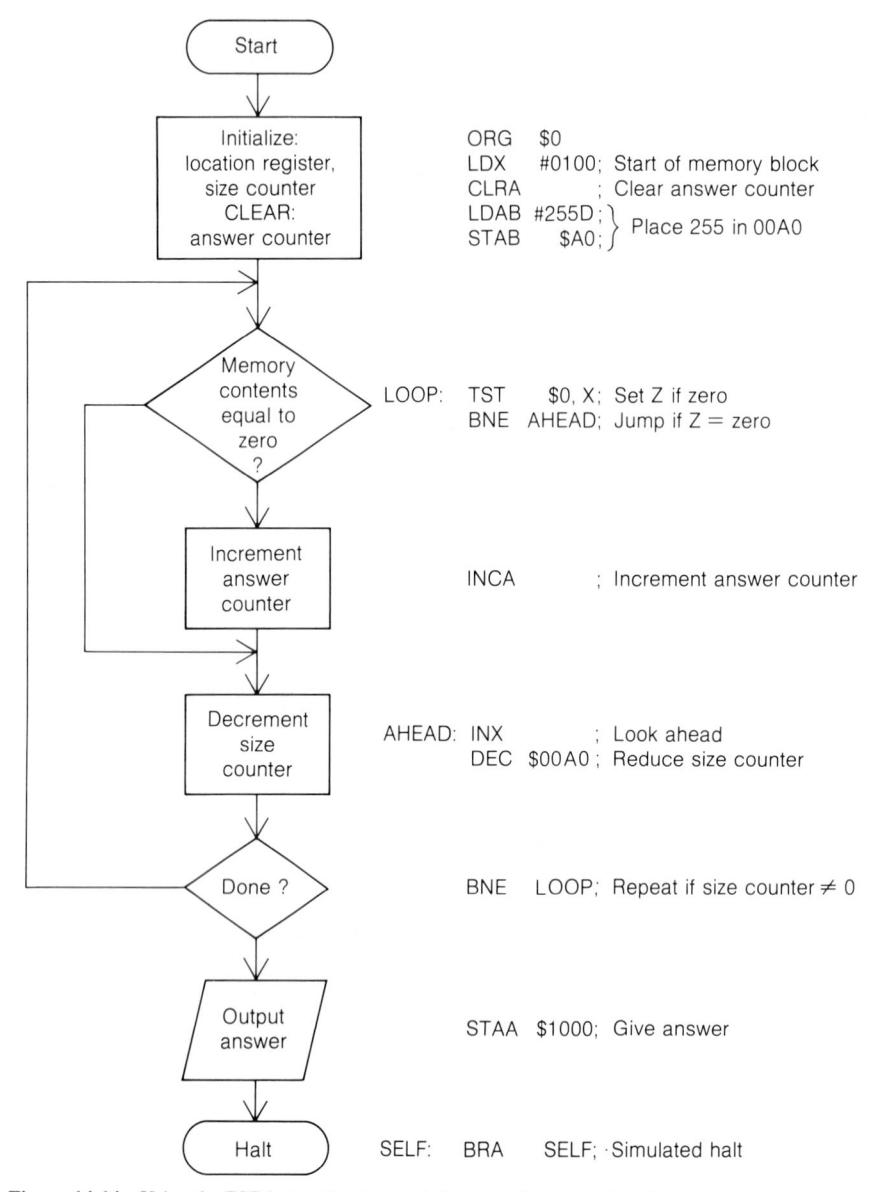

```
                    Start
                      │
                      ▼
             ┌─────────────────┐    ORG   $0
             │   Initialize:   │    LDX   #0100; Start of memory block
             │location register│    CLRA        ; Clear answer counter
             │  size counter   │    LDAB  #255D;⎫
             │     CLEAR:      │    STAB  $A0; ⎬ Place 255 in 00A0
             │ answer counter  │                ⎭
             └─────────────────┘
                      │
                      ▼
              ╱╲
             ╱  ╲
            ╱ Mem╲
           ╱ory   ╲
          ╱contents╲        LOOP:  TST   $0, X; Set Z if zero
          ╲equal to╱               BNE   AHEAD; Jump if Z = zero
           ╲zero  ╱
            ╲  ? ╱
             ╲  ╱
              ╲╱
               │
               ▼
           ┌─────────┐
           │Increment│
           │ answer  │        INCA         ; Increment answer counter
           │ counter │
           └─────────┘
                │
                ▼
           ┌─────────┐
           │Decrement│        AHEAD: INX        ; Look ahead
           │  size   │        DEC  $00A0; Reduce size counter
           │ counter │
           └─────────┘
                │
                ▼
              ╱╲
             ╱  ╲
            ╱Done╲             BNE   LOOP; Repeat if size counter ≠ 0
            ╲  ? ╱
             ╲  ╱
              ╲╱
                │
                ▼
           ┌─────────┐
           │ Output  │         STAA  $1000; Give answer
           │ answer  │
           └─────────┘
                │
                ▼
             ( Halt )          SELF: BRA  SELF; Simulated halt
```

Figure 14.14 Using the TST instruction to search for cleared memory locations.

used. A complete listing of the compare instructions is found in Appendix I.

Using the *compare immediate* addressing mode as an example, accumulator A or accumulator B is compared to the second byte of the instruction and placed into one of three categories, depending on whether it is less than, equal to, or greater than the second byte of the instruction. (Actually, the compare process is nothing more than a subtraction. In this case, the second byte of the compare immediate instruction is subtracted from an accumulator and the flags are set according to the result.)

The Carry flag handles the greater-than/less-than requirements of the instruction, for if the second byte is bigger than the accumulator, a borrow is required, which sets the Carry flag. If the second byte is equal to or less than the accumulator, no borrow is required and the Carry flag is cleared. Only when the two numbers are exactly equal will the result be zero and the Z flag set. As shown here, a particular combination of the Carry and Zero flags uniquely identifies the three categories:

Data less than accumulator	*Data equal to accumulator*	*Data greater than accumulator*
C = 0	C = 0	C = 1
Z = 0	Z = 1	Z = 0

Compare Accumulators (CBA)

Operation: (ACCA) − (ACCB)

Description: Compares the contents of ACCA and the contents of ACCB and sets the condition codes, which may be used for arithmetic and logical conditional branches. Both operands are unaffected.

Addressing Modes	Execution Time (No. of cycles)	Number of bytes of machine code	Coding of First (or only) byte of machine code		
			HEX.	OCT.	DEC.
INHERENT	2	1	11	021	017

Courtesy of Motorola, Inc.

(*a*)

Compare (CMP)

Operation: (ACCX) − (M)

Description: Compares the contents of ACCX and the contents of M and determines the condition codes, which may be used subsequently for controlling conditional branching. Both operands are unaffected.

Addressing Modes	Execution Time (No. of cycles)	Number of bytes of machine code	Coding of First (or only) byte of machine code		
			HEX.	OCT.	DEC.
A IMM	2	2	81	201	129
A DIR	3	2	91	221	145
A EXT	4	3	B1	261	177
A IND	5	2	A1	241	161
B IMM	2	2	C1	301	193
B DIR	3	2	D1	321	209
B EXT	4	3	F1	361	241
B IND	5	2	E1	341	225

Courtesy of Motorola, Inc.

(*b*)

Figure 14.15 The compare instructions CBA and CMP.

There is, however, one important difference between the *compare* and *subtract* processes. The compare process inhibits the answer from being placed in the accumulator, and is often called an *invisible subtraction*. In other words, the original number in the accumulator is not changed as a result of the compare process—only the flags are affected. Obviously, the compare instruction is exclusively a flag-setting instruction and is always used for greater-than/less-than/equal-to decision making. It has no other purpose.

The complete solution to our problem is given in Figure 14.16. Trace through the program and convince yourself that all input numbers less than \$34 will be mimicked and all numbers \$34 or greater will be blanked out. As noted, the Z flag has no role in the decision-making process because the Carry flag alone uniquely determines the numbers to be mimicked.

THE CONDITIONAL BRANCH CLUES

Look again at the BEQ (Branch if Equal) instruction of Figure 14.10. As previously noted, there are three clues you can use for determining if this is the proper instruction to complete the decision-making process:

1. Branch if Equal.
2. Branch if *result* of flag-setting operation is zero.
3. Branch if Z flag high.

Now we know where the first clue (Branch if Equal) comes from. *It assumes that the flag-setting instruction is Compare*. In other words, branch if the compare instruction determines that the two numbers are equal. Since Compare is quite often used as the flag-setting instruction, this method

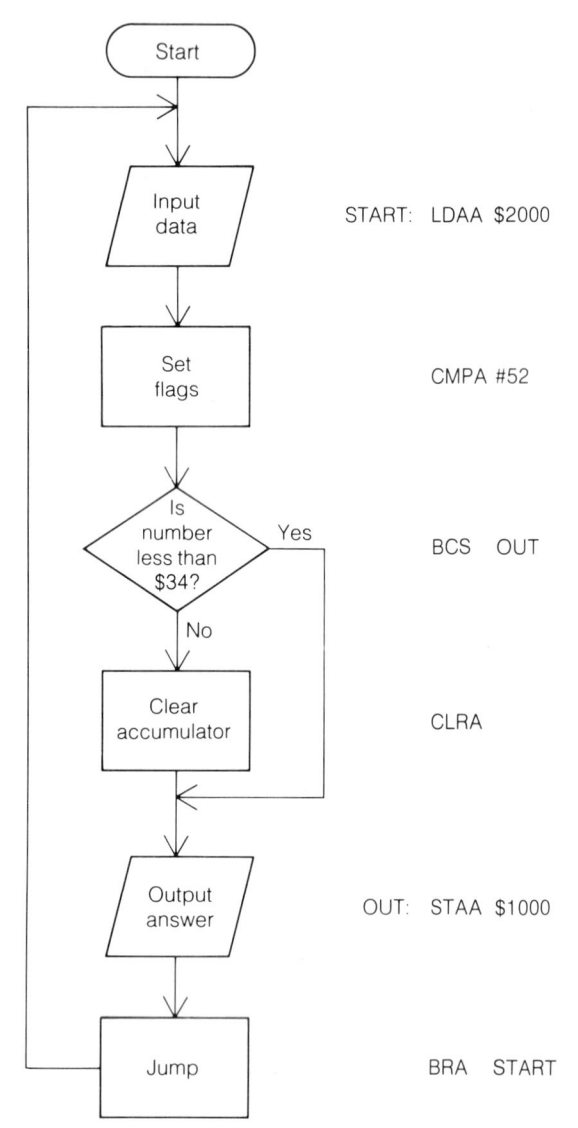

```
                    Start
                      │
                      ▼
                 ┌─────────┐
                 │  Input  │            START:  LDAA  $2000
                 │  data   │
                 └─────────┘
                      │
                      ▼
                 ┌─────────┐
                 │   Set   │            CMPA  #52
                 │  flags  │
                 └─────────┘
                      │
                      ▼
                    ╱  Is  ╲    Yes
                  ╱ number  ╲─────►     BCS   OUT
                  ╲less than╱
                   ╲ $34? ╱
                      │ No
                      ▼
                 ┌─────────┐
                 │  Clear  │            CLRA
                 │accumul. │
                 └─────────┘
                      │
                      ▼
                 ┌─────────┐
                 │ Output  │            OUT:  STAA  $1000
                 │ answer  │
                 └─────────┘
                      │
                      ▼
                 ┌─────────┐
                 │  Jump   │            BRA   START
                 └─────────┘
```

Figure 14.16 Program for mimicking numbers less than $34.

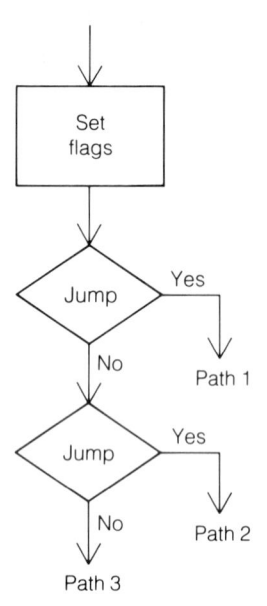

```
                      │
                      ▼
                 ┌─────────┐
                 │   Set   │
                 │  flags  │
                 └─────────┘
                      │
                      ▼
                    ╱Jump╲   Yes
                    ╲    ╱───────► Path 1
                      │ No
                      ▼
                    ╱Jump╲   Yes
                    ╲    ╱───────► Path 2
                      │ No
                      ▼
                   Path 3
```

Figure 14.17 Three-pronged decision-making flowchart.

of labeling the conditional branch instructions is reasonable and will often simplify the selection process. However, if Compare is not the flag-setting instruction, it may be best to ignore this "high-level" clue (i.e., written in English) and go right to the flag clue (Branch if Z flag high).

MULTIPRONGED FORKS IN THE ROAD

Decisions often involve more than a simple choice between two alternatives. Suppose we have three options to choose from—a three-pronged fork in the road. Can our computer pick out the correct path from the three choices? Figure 14.17 shows how it is done: just make two 2-valued decisions in a row. There is one way in, but three ways out.

By extending this process to any number of flag-setting instructions, we see that the decision-making ability of a computer is not at all hampered by an increased number of choices.

THE DELAY LOOP

To a computer, 1 second is a very long period of time, for it can easily process 200,000 instructions in a single second. Yet, to human beings, a second is a very brief period of time. Because of this discrepancy, there often is a need to delay the processing action at various points in the program. This slowdown is made possible by the *time-delay loop*, a routine making use of the conditional branch instruction. Here is how it works:

1. A number is loaded into an accumulator or memory location.
2. The computer decrements the number and, using the BNE (Branch if Not Equal) instruction, checks to see if it is zero.
3. If it is not zero, the computer jumps back to the decrement instruction for another pass. If it is zero, the computer continues to the next instruction.

Clearly, the number of cycles the computer loops through is directly proportional to the size of the number loaded into the register, which in turn is approximately proportional to the magnitude of the delay time span. Figure 14.18 shows the delay-loop flowchart and program.

imately $\frac{1}{3}$ second can be developed. Obviously this nesting process can be continued indefinitely, producing delay times as long as you wish.

PROGRAM TIMING

A crystal-controlled digital system offers yet another advantage over a purely analog system: all times and events can be specified exactly. For example, we can determine precisely how long it takes to run through the "mimic-birthday" program of Figure 14.20—all we have to do is count clock cycles. (The number of clock cycles required to process each instruction is included with each instruction summary in Appendix I.) Figure 14.20 shows the results of counting the states for our "birthday" program, when processed on a 6800

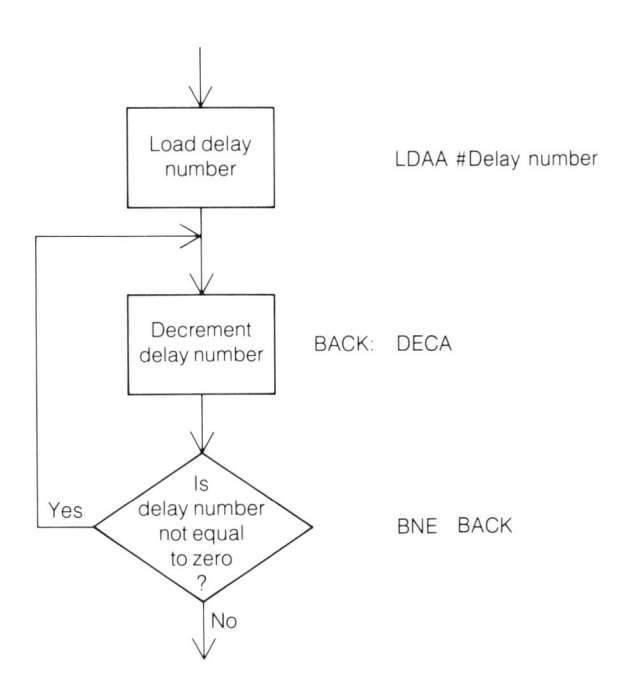

Figure 14.18 Delay-loop flowchart and program.

NESTING

Although the computer can be forced to circle the delay loop up to 256 times, this still gives a delay of barely one millisecond. Many applications may require delays of many seconds, or minutes, or hours, or even days. To produce these longer delay times, two or more delay loops can be *nested* (one delay loop placed inside another). Figure 14.19 shows how this process is done for a double-nested loop.

Delay numbers corresponding to the inner loop and the outer loop are loaded into two memory locations (memory locations are chosen because more than likely at least one accumulator would be required for other program action). Let us assume that the inner delay-loop number is 10 (base 10) and is loaded into memory location $A0, and the outer delay-loop number is 15 (base 10) and is loaded into location $A1.

When the processor decrements the inner-loop memory location ($A0) down to zero and drops out of the inner delay loop, it enters the outer loop. After decrementing the outer-loop memory location ($A1) by 1, it jumps back and reloads 10 into memory location $A0. Therefore, each time the processor passes around the outer loop, it is forced to spin around the inner loop 10 more times. Since the processor circles the outer loop 15 times before decrementing memory location $A1 down to zero and dropping out of the double-nested delay loop entirely, the inner loop is circled 150 times during one pass through the entire delay routine.

Using a double-nested delay loop, delay times of approx-

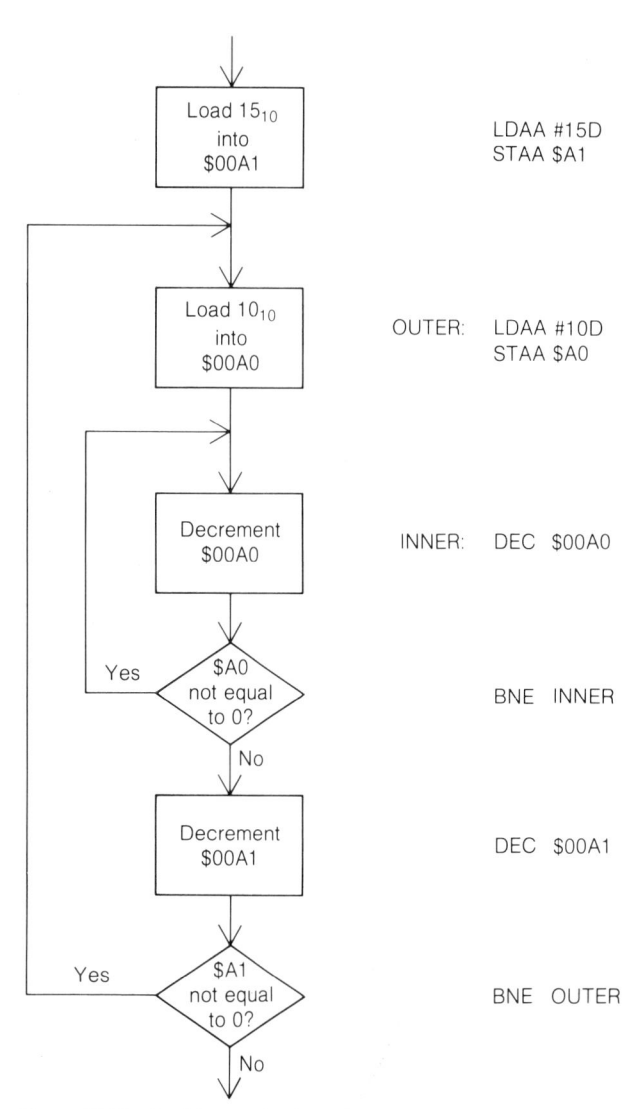

Figure 14.19 Double-nested delay loop.

160 Part III / Software: The Spark of Life

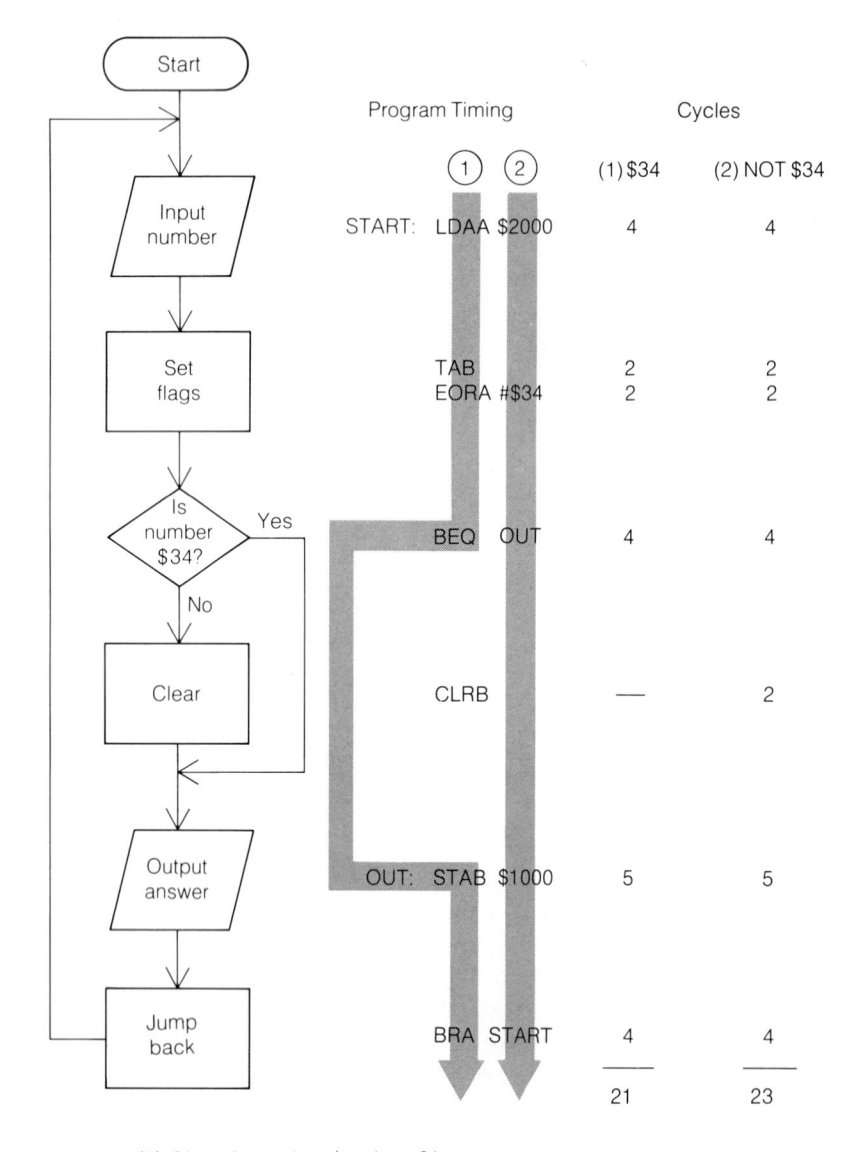

	Program Timing		Cycles	
	(1) (2)		(1) $34	(2) NOT $34
START:	LDAA $2000		4	4
	TAB		2	2
	EORA #$34		2	2
	BEQ OUT		4	4
	CLRB		—	2
OUT:	STAB $1000		5	5
	BRA START		4	4
			21	23

(1) 21 cycles × 1 μs/cycle = 21 μs
(2) 23 cycles × 1 μs/cycle = 23 μs

Figure 14.20 Mimic-birthday program timing.

system running at 1 MHz. As we see, the total processing time depends on which path is taken through the decision-making process.

As a second example of program timing, let's write a program to provide a delay of 1 second. Of course, with a digital machine, we will not be able to delay *exactly* 1 second, but let's get as close as we can. To shorten the program and at the same time provide a high degree of accuracy, we will resort to a couple of tricks.

Referring to Figure 14.21, the first trick is to use the 16-bit index register to hold the delay number. Able to count down from 65,536 (256 × 256), the register will simulate a double-nested loop (which uses two 8-bit registers). The second trick is to include two-cycle NOP (NO OPeration) instructions both inside and outside the loop to fine-tune the delay time. Of course, to save memory locations, the fewer NOPs the better.

First of all, for a 1 MHz clock, convince yourself that the formula of Figure 14.22a relates the overall delay time to the delay number and number of NOPs.

After considerable trial-and-error juggling, we find that a delay number of 55,555, with five NOPs inside the loop and four NOPs outside the loop, will generate a delay of 1.000001 seconds (see Figure 14.22b).

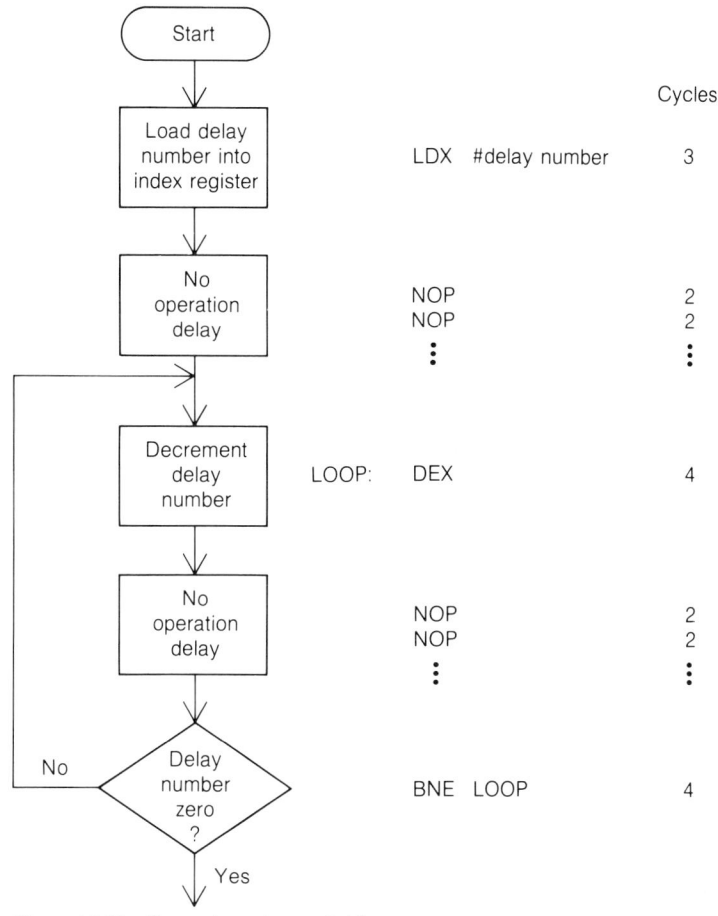

```
                Start
                  │
                  ▼
         ┌─────────────────┐                                    Cycles
         │ Load delay      │
         │ number into     │         LDX  #delay number           3
         │ index register  │
         └─────────────────┘
                  │
                  ▼
         ┌─────────────────┐
         │ No              │         NOP                          2
         │ operation       │         NOP                          2
         │ delay           │          ⋮                           ⋮
         └─────────────────┘
                  │
       ┌──────────▼──────────┐
       │  ┌─────────────────┐│
       │  │ Decrement       ││
       │  │ delay           ││ LOOP:  DEX                         4
       │  │ number          ││
       │  └─────────────────┘│
       │           │         │
       │           ▼         │
       │  ┌─────────────────┐│
       │  │ No              ││        NOP                         2
       │  │ operation       ││        NOP                         2
       │  │ delay           ││         ⋮                          ⋮
       │  └─────────────────┘│
       │           │         │
       │           ▼         │
       │       ◇ Delay ◇     │
       │  No  ◇ number ◇     │
       └─────◇  zero   ◇     │        BNE  LOOP                   4
              ◇   ?   ◇
                  │ Yes
                  ▼
```

Figure 14.21 Generating a 1-second delay.

LOOPS AND INDEXED ADDRESSING

In previous chapters we learned that *indexed addressing*—which requires only a single byte (the offset) to address any memory location—can often shorten a program. Now, with the introduction of conditional loops in this chapter, we will find that *indexed addressing* and loops can team up to provide another powerful program-shortening tool. The key lies with the ability to manipulate the index register with the instructions from the data-transfer and arithmetic groups listed below:

CPX   Compare index register
DEX   Decrement index register
INX   Increment index register
LDX   Load index register
STX   Store index register

As shown in Figure 14.23, our "add 5 numbers" program of Figure 11.10 has been drastically shortened. In fact, the size of the program is nearly independent of the number of integers to be added. When the offset remains constant (usually zero) and the index changes, this type of addressing is

$$\text{Delay time} = 1\,\mu s \left[N_0(8 + N_1 \times 2) + N_2 \times 2 + 3 \right]$$

N_0 = delay number
N_1 = NOPs inside loop
N_2 = NOPs outside loop

(*a*) General formula

$$1.000001 \text{ seconds} = 1\,\mu s \left[55{,}555(8 + 5 \times 2) + 4 \times 2 + 3 \right]$$

(*b*) Generating a 1-second delay

Figure 14.22 Calculating delay times.

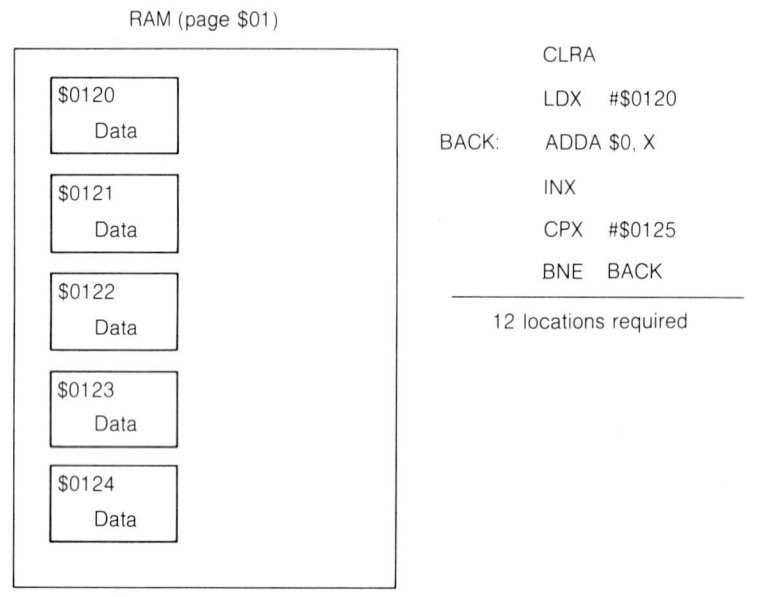

```
                    RAM (page $01)
                                              CLRA
        ┌─────────────────────┐               LDX    #$0120
        │  ┌──────┐           │       BACK:   ADDA   $0, X
        │  │$0120 │           │               INX
        │  │ Data │           │               CPX    #$0125
        │  └──────┘           │               BNE    BACK
        │  ┌──────┐           │       ─────────────────────
        │  │$0121 │           │          12 locations required
        │  │ Data │           │
        │  └──────┘           │
        │  ┌──────┐           │
        │  │$0122 │           │
        │  │ Data │           │
        │  └──────┘           │
        │  ┌──────┐           │
        │  │$0123 │           │
        │  │ Data │           │
        │  └──────┘           │
        │  ┌──────┐           │
        │  │$0124 │           │
        │  │ Data │           │
        │  └──────┘           │
        └─────────────────────┘
```

Figure 14.23 Combining loops and *indexed* addressing to dramatically shorten repetitive routines.

generally known as *indirect addressing*. In the next section, we will put loops, *indirect addressing,* and delays into action and generate a sequence of notes (a song!).

COMPUTER MUSIC

As a final application of decision making, Figure 14.24*a* is a program listing for generating a simple one-note-at-a-time melody.

Basically a melody is nothing more than a sequence of notes, each with its own frequency, duration, and (optional) rest parameters. These parameters are stored in sequential memory locations and are pulled from memory as the melody progresses. An analysis of the program is left as an exercise.

Figure 14.24*b* is a listing of the frequency and duration parameters required to play the old English folk song "Greensleeves."

MACHINE-ASSEMBLY UPDATE—II

Our next machine-assembly update introduces the EQU (equate) command. Referring to Figure 14.25, we note the following assembler directive:

DELAY1 : EQU 15

When DELAY1 is equated to 15, it means we can use the more descriptive English-like "DELAY1" anywhere in the program instead of the number 15. As shown, we even can perform mathematical calculations within the program (note that $0A is properly generated from the *expression* DELAY1–5). Since DELAY1 is a label, just like INNER and OUTER, it is fully identified in the *symbol table* at the bottom of the listing.

INTELLIGENT-MACHINE UPDATE

In one brief chapter, our intelligent machine has passed through the age of reason. No longer is it a mere puppet to its human creators, for now it can make decisions on its own. Does our computer now have free will? Can it learn by experience and be capable of high-level thought processes? It is simply too early to say.

QUESTIONS AND PROBLEMS

1. When human beings make decisions, we consult "signs" (e.g., sun or traffic light). In a computer, what are analogous to signs?
2. What are the two general steps in the decision-making process?
3. Most of the flag-setting instructions are from what two groups?
4. At the present time, accumulator A is holding 200_{10}. Trace the states of the Z and C flags through the program below:

    ADDA #55
    INCA
    TAB

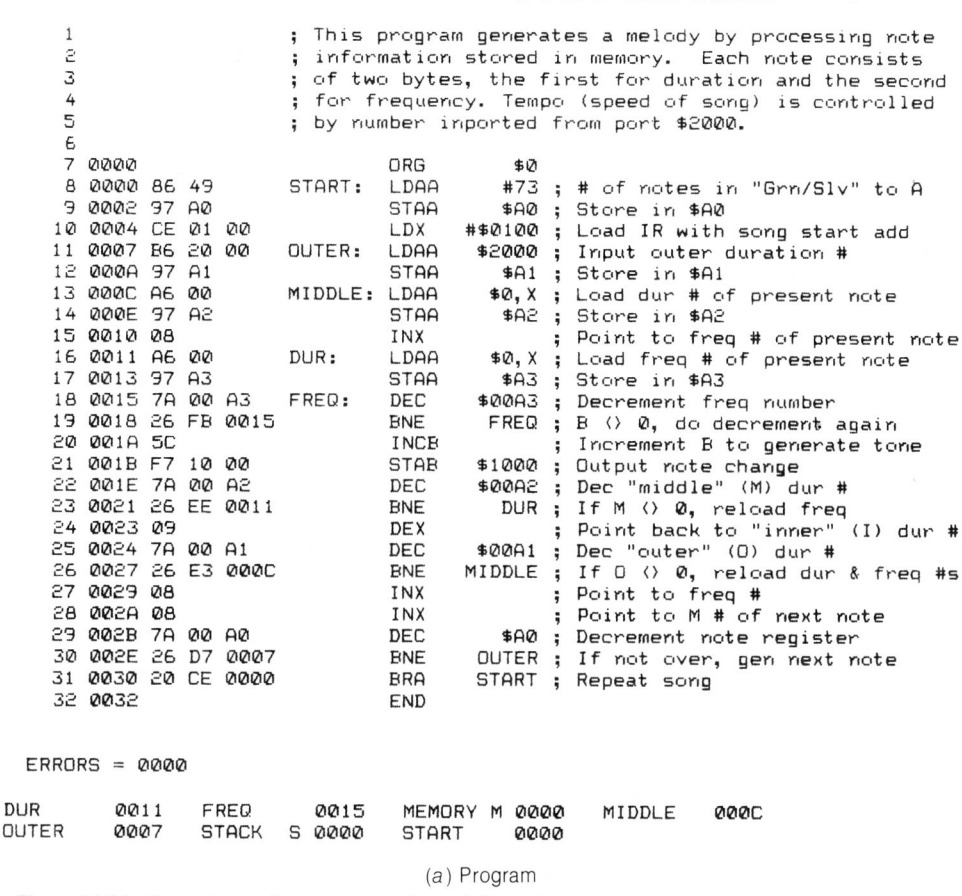

```
                        6800/6801/6802 ASSEMBLER VER.3.3    1

 1              ; This program generates a melody by processing note
 2              ; information stored in memory. Each note consists
 3              ; of two bytes, the first for duration and the second
 4              ; for frequency. Tempo (speed of song) is controlled
 5              ; by number inported from port $2000.
 6
 7 0000                    ORG     $0
 8 0000 86 49      START:  LDAA    #73     ; # of notes in "Grn/Slv" to A
 9 0002 97 A0              STAA    $A0     ; Store in $A0
10 0004 CE 01 00            LDX    #$0100  ; Load IR with song start add
11 0007 B6 20 00   OUTER:  LDAA    $2000   ; Input outer duration #
12 000A 97 A1              STAA    $A1     ; Store in $A1
13 000C A6 00      MIDDLE: LDAA    $0,X    ; Load dur # of present note
14 000E 97 A2              STAA    $A2     ; Store in $A2
15 0010 08                 INX             ; Point to freq # of present note
16 0011 A6 00      DUR:    LDAA    $0,X    ; Load freq # of present note
17 0013 97 A3              STAA    $A3     ; Store in $A3
18 0015 7A 00 A3   FREQ:   DEC     $00A3   ; Decrement freq number
19 0018 26 FB 0015         BNE     FREQ    ; B <> 0, do decrement again
20 001A 5C                 INCB            ; Increment B to generate tone
21 001B F7 10 00           STAB    $1000   ; Output note change
22 001E 7A 00 A2           DEC     $00A2   ; Dec "middle" (M) dur #
23 0021 26 EE 0011         BNE     DUR     ; If M <> 0, reload freq
24 0023 09                 DEX             ; Point back to "inner" (I) dur #
25 0024 7A 00 A1           DEC     $00A1   ; Dec "outer" (O) dur #
26 0027 26 E3 000C         BNE     MIDDLE  ; If O <> 0, reload dur & freq #s
27 0029 08                 INX             ; Point to freq #
28 002A 08                 INX             ; Point to M # of next note
29 002B 7A 00 A0           DEC     $A0     ; Decrement note register
30 002E 26 D7 0007         BNE     OUTER   ; If not over, gen next note
31 0030 20 CE 0000         BRA     START   ; Repeat song
32 0032                    END

ERRORS = 0000

DUR    0011   FREQ     0015    MEMORY M 0000   MIDDLE   000C
OUTER  0007   STACK  S 0000    START    0000
```

(a) Program

Figure 14.24 Computer music—program and note information.

5. Why do you think the Carry flag is not affected by the INC (Increment) or DEC (decrement) instructions?
6. Write a program that will scan through 10 consecutive memory locations looking for the number $FF and printing its location when found. (*Note*: No more than one location holds $FF.)
7. Modify the above program to print (outport) the number of times $FF is found.
8. The Boolean instructions (AND, OR, EOR, and COM) have what effect on each of the flags?
9. Using the BIT instruction to set flags, write a program that will mimic only odd numbers (blanking out even numbers).
10. How does a computer use decision making to choose the right path among three possible choices?
11. Write a "bandpass" program that passes (mimics) only numbers between 32 and 64 (base 10).
12. By nesting delay loops 10 deep, what is the maximum delay period that can be produced? (*Hint*: The result will show why you should not attempt to verify your answer in the laboratory.)
13. Rewrite the mimic program of Figure 14.12 using the Compare *immediate* instruction.
14. Hand assemble (convert to hexadecimal) the program of Figure 14.14, paying particular attention to the simulated halt (SELF: BRA SELF).
15. Write a program that will search a list of numbers for a particular *sequence* of two numbers (a *string*), outporting the location of the first number. (Assume the string exists once and only once.)
16. Rewrite Figure 14.16 to mimic numbers *greater* than $34. (Why are both the Z and C flags involved?)
17. When a branch instruction makes use of the N (negative) and V (overflow) flags, branching is based on what type of numbers?
18. Write a program that produces as close as possible the musical note A (880 Hz).
19. Write a program that produces a square-wave tone

164   Part III / Software: The Spark of Life

Note	Data	Note	Data	Note	Data	Note	Data
A	05 6B	and	05 6B	ny	18 6B	sleeves	11 3B
las	0B 5A	I	0B 5A	Green	19 3B	was	08 3F
my	06 50	have	06 50	sleeves	19 3B	my	0E 47
love	15 47	loved	15 47	—	08 3F	heart	0D 50
—	08 3F	—	08 3F	was	0E 47	of	05 5E
you	0E 47	you	0E 47	all	0D 50	gold	0D 79
do	0D 50	oh	0D 50	my	05 5E	—	05 6B
me	05 5E	so	05 5E	joy	0D 79	and	0A 5E
wrong	0D 79	long	0D 79	—	05 6B	who	0B 5A
—	05 6B	—	05 6B	—	0A 5E	but	0A 5E
to	0A 5E	de	0A 5E	Green	0B 5A	my	09 6B
cast	0B 5A	light	0B 5A	—	05 6B	la	09 71
me	05 6B	—	0A 5E	sleeves	0E 6B	—	04 7F
off	0D 6B	ing	09 6B	—	04 79	dy	09 71
—	04 79	in	09 71	was	09 6B	Green	20 6B
dis	09 6B	—	04 7F	my	0A 5E	sleeves	48 6B
cour	0A 5E	your	09 71	de	04 79		
teous	04 79	com	09 6B	light	13 90		
ly	07 90	pa	05 6B	Green	19 3B		

(b) Note information

Figure 14.24   Computer music—program and note information (*continued*)

```
                        6800/6801/6802 ASSEMBLER VER.3.3        1

  1                     ; This machine assembly update--based on a double-
  2                     ; nested delay loop--introduces the EQU directive
  3                     ; and expressions
  4
  5 000F        DELAY1: EQU     15          ; DELAY1 = 15
  6
  7 0000                ORG     $0
  8 0000 C6 0F          LDAB    #DELAY1     ; Load outer delay number
  9 0002 86 0A  OUTER:  LDAA    #DELAY1-5   ; Load inner delay number
 10 0004 4A     INNER:  DECA                ; Decrement inner number
 11 0005 26 FD 0004     BNE     INNER       ; Loop if inner <> 0
 12 0007 5A             DECB                ; Decrement outer number
 13 0008 26 F8 0002     BNE     OUTER       ; Loop if outer <> 0
 14 000A                END


ERRORS = 0000

DELAY1    000F    INNER    0004    MEMORY M 0000    OUTER    0002
STACK  S  0000
```

Figure 14.25 Machine-assembly update—using the EQU directive to create an expression.

whose pitch (frequency) is approximately proportional (inversely) to an inported number.

20. Write a reaction-time program that turns on an LED and then outports in milliseconds the time required to react and throw an input-port switch.
21. By modifying Figure 14.14 according to the suggestions in the text, write a program that outports the number of locations in page 1 RAM having a 1 in bit position D5.
22. What delay numbers placed into the program of Figure 14.19 will result in the longest possible delay? (*Hint:* The answer is not all $FFs.)
23. Assume your ideal weight is 150 lb. Write a program that outports a 1 if the inported number (weight) is less than 150, a 2 if exactly equal to 150, and a 3 if over 150.
24. Write a "copy" program that moves the block of data at locations $0150 through $016F to locations $01A0 through $01BF.
25. Explain the difference between the following instructions: (a) TSTA, (b) CMPA #$0, (c) ANDA #$FF, (d) BITA #$FF, (e) SUBA #$0.
26. Using the CLR, LDX, STX, and ADD instructions and making use of *indexed addressing* techniques, write an "add 5 numbers" program in which the data are spaced $10 (16) locations apart.
27. Referring to Figure 14.11*b*, why won't the following correction work? (*Hint:* What does the TBA instruction do to the flags?)

```
START:   LDAA $2000
         TAB              ; Save number
         EORA #$34
         TBA              ; Restore number
         BEQ OUT
         CLRA
OUT:     STAA $1000
         BRA  START
```

28. Flowchart the music program of Figure 14.24*a*.
29. Write a conversion program that inports all signed numbers between −128 and +127, converting them to sign-magnitude form (see Chapter 11). Also, write a routine to reverse the process.
30. What is the difference between *indexed, relative,* and *indirect addressing*?
31. For the music program of Figure 14.24*a*, why should the frequency delay number times the duration delay number be a constant for all notes of equal duration (i.e., quarter note, half note, etc.)?
32. Modify the music program of Figure 14.24*a* by adding a short rest between each note.
33. In general terms, how would you add volume control for each note to the music program of Figure 14.24*a*?
34. Based on the format of Figure 14.24*b*, derive the note information for a song of your choice. Summarize how you derived your note information.
35. Why is the Boolean condition C + Z = 0 (followed

by the BHI instruction) equivalent to C = 0 AND Z = 0?

36. There are two common ways to determine when to end a loop: *loop counting* and *event detection*. Using a flowchart and assembly-language programming, give an example of each.

37. Write a program that uses the Compare Index Register (CPX) instruction to terminate a loop.

38. Write a program to implement the game of *Sumo Wrestling*. Output 1s to LEDs 3 and 4 (representing the two wrestlers). When the LEDs go off after a certain amount of time, the player able to throw the corresponding switch first (DIP bit D_0 for player A and bit D_7 for player B) wins, and the two LEDs move over one position in the proper direction and reappear. The process continues until one "wrestler" is pushed off the "mat."

39. Modify the *Sumo Wrestling* program of question 38 so that the period of time in which the players wait for the LEDs to go off is semirandom. (*Hint*: Reaction time is semirandom.)

chapter 15

Subroutines, Calls, and Stacks

A minstrel performing a medley of popular songs must learn long passages of words and music. Our intelligent machine, with its ability to remember and recall information, seems to possess all the required skills. Unfortunately, its concert debut is unsuccessful, for part way into the first ballad it runs out of memory. What our computer requires is a method of storing long program sequences in limited amounts of memory—a feat that seems impossible at first glance. How do we pour 5 quarts of water into a 4-quart container? The answer is: parts of the 4-quart container are used more than once.

This chapter introduces subroutines, a powerful new technique for shortening programs. When our study is complete, we will discover an important side benefit: our programs will be easier to write.

SUBROUTINES

A technique from the world of music will show us how to make more effective use of our computer's limited memory capacity.

A typical musical composition may consist of four verses. Following each verse is the *chorus, a routine that remains unchanged.* If this musical score is placed into the computer's memory, three memory locations, each storing the chorus, will have precisely the same sequence of instructions. And that results in wasted memory space—lots of it.

A solution is found in many popular musical scores. To save space, *the chorus of the song is written once but used many times.* When performing the song, we simply jump back and forth between the chorus and the three verses as required. This is precisely the technique we will use to reduce our computer's memory requirements. That is how we will pour 5 quarts of water into a 4-quart container.

In computer terminology, the chorus is known as a *subroutine,* and the three verses of the ballad make up the *main program.* As shown in Figure 15.1, the chorus subroutine is stored in only one place in memory and is accessed by the Jump instruction. And just that simply our major goal has been achieved: we have saved memory space—in this case an amount of memory equal to approximately three chorus routines.

Unfortunately, it is not that simple. There is no problem with jumping *to* the chorus subroutine whenever it is needed; a simple unconditional jump will suffice. The problem is, how do you get *back* to the proper verse when the chorus is over? It could be verse 2 or verse 3 or verse 4.

We could solve the problem through the *conditional branch* process and some clever flag setting. But these methods are unwieldy at best, and fortunately are not required at all.

THE JSR AND BSR INSTRUCTIONS

To process subroutines, computer designers have given us the JSR (Jump to Subroutine) and BSR (Branch to Subroutine) instructions (see Figure 15.2). They look complicated, but they handle subroutines like magic. Known collectively as a *subroutine CALL,* the Jump or Branch to Subroutine process is basically a jump, but with an extra twist thrown in. That extra twist involves some new terms that we should explain:

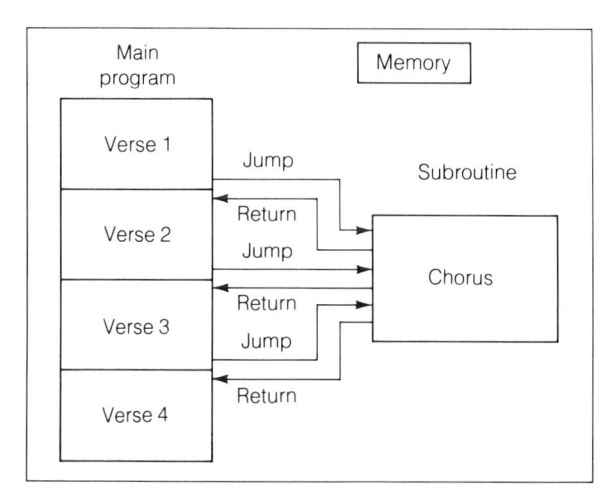

Figure 15.1 The repetitive chorus as a subroutine.

Branch to Subroutine (BSR)

Operation: PC ← (PC) + 0002
↓ (PCL)
SP ← (SP) − 0001
↓ (PCH)
SP ← (SP) − 0001
PC ← (PC) + Rel

Description: The program counter is incremented by 2. The less significant byte of the contents of the program counter is pushed into the stack. The stack pointer is then decremented (by 1). The more significant byte of the contents of the program counter is then pushed into the stack. The stack pointer is again decremented (by 1). A branch then occurs to the location specified by the program.

See BRA instruction for details of the execution of the branch.

Condition Codes: Not affected.

Addressing Modes	Execution Time (No. of cycles)	Number of bytes of machine code	Coding of First (or only) byte of machine code		
			HEX.	OCT.	DEC.
REL	8	2	8D	215	141

Courtesy of Motorola, Inc.

(*a*)

Jump to Subroutine (JSR)

Operation:
Either: PC ← (PC) + 0003 (for EXTended addressing)
or: PC ← (PC) + 0002 (for INDexed addressing)
Then: ↓ (PCL)
SP ← (SP) − 0001
↓ (PCH)
SP ← (SP) − 0001
PC ← numerical address

Description: The program counter is incremented by 3 or by 2, depending on the addressing mode, and is then pushed onto the stack, eight bits at a time. The stack pointer points to the next empty location in the stack. A jump occurs to the instruction stored at the numerical address. The numerical address is obtained according to the rules for EXTended or INDexed addressing.

Condition Codes: Not affected.

Addressing Modes	Execution Time (No. of cycles)	Number of bytes of machine code	Coding of First (or only) byte of machine code		
			HEX.	OCT.	DEC.
EXT	9	3	BD	275	189
IND	8	2	AD	255	173

Courtesy of Motorola, Inc.

(*b*)

Figure 15.2 The CALL subroutine instructions BSR and JSR.

- The *stack* is a special block of memory. Theoretically, it could be any available block of memory. However, a given computer will often require a specific stack location.
- The *stack pointer* is a 16-bit register that points to a location in the stack in much the same way the program counter points to a stored program location in ROM (or RAM). The stack pointer can be loaded from or stored into memory (LDS, STS); incremented or decremented (INS, DES); or transferred to or from the index register (TSX, TXS). (See Appendix I.)

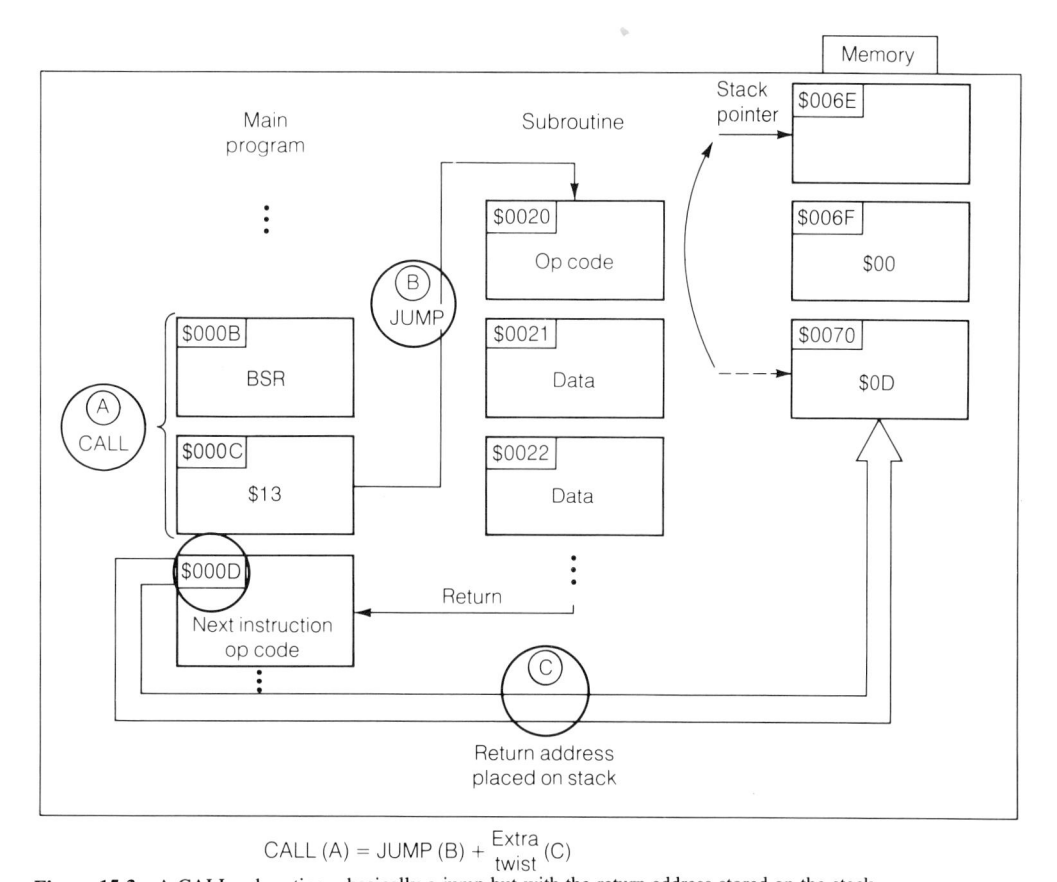

Figure 15.3 A CALL subroutine—basically a jump but with the return address stored on the stack.

$$\text{CALL (A)} = \text{JUMP (B)} + \frac{\text{Extra}}{\text{twist}} \text{(C)}$$

CALL vs Jump

Now that we have been introduced to the stack and the stack pointer, what is that extra twist separating a CALL from a single jump? It is this: the return location—the place in the main program where we would like to return after the subroutine is complete—is stored in the stack. And what location would we like to return to? The answer is: *the very next location following the CALL*. The process is much like marking a road map with our present position before retiring for the night (CALLing our sleep routine). When we arise the next morning, a quick glance at the map will tell us where we are on the main route and allow us to pick up precisely where we left off.

Figure 15.3 illustrates the main ideas. Since both the main program and the subroutine are stored within page 0, the more efficient Branch to Subroutine (BSR) instruction can be used. Selecting arbitrary memory locations from page 0, we find three memory areas involved in the CALL process: the main program, the subroutine, and the stack. These three areas can be placed anywhere in memory as long as they don't overlap or interfere with the operation of the computer.

To get a better idea of what is involved, let us go through the eight clock cycles of the BSR instruction (Figure 15.4). Remember what to look for: a jump with an extra twist (i.e., the return address will be placed on the stack).

The first two clock cycles are the Jump part of the BSR instruction, and are basically the same as the two clock cycles of a BRA instruction. Clock cycle 3 involves an internal operation.

Clock cycles 4 and 5 give us that extra twist. The main-program return address ($000D) is pushed on the stack during these two clock cycles. ("Push" is the technical term for placing data onto the stack.) The process is particularly easy, for the return address—the address of the next instruction following the BSR instruction—just happens to be the present contents of the program counter at the completion of the BSR $13 fetch operation. (Remember, early in each instruction fetch operation the contents of the program counter are latched, thus freeing the program counter to look ahead to the next instruction byte to fetch.) Clock cycles 6, 7, and 8 are used for internal operations. Subroutine processing begins when clock cycle 1' fetches the op code from the first subroutine location.

The RETURN

Once the JSR or BSR instruction has been executed, the computer continues along, processing the subroutine. But when it arrives at the end of the subroutine, how does it use the return address in the stack to get back to the main pro-

170 Part III / Software: The Spark of Life

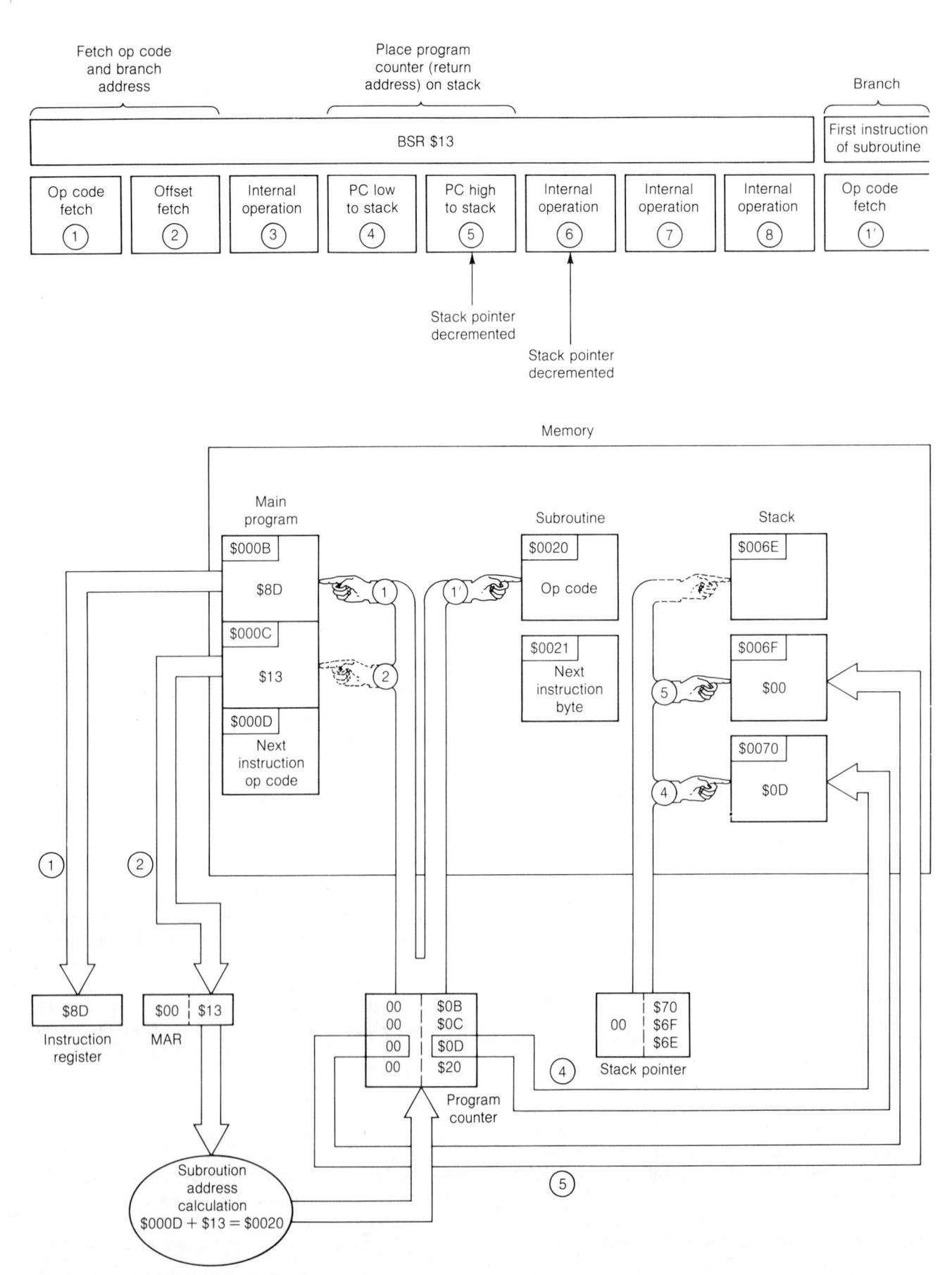

Figure 15.4 The BSR instruction clock-cycle sequencing.

Return from Subroutine (RTS)

Operation: SP ← (SP) + 0001
            ↑ PCH
            SP ← (SP) + 0001
            ↑ PCL

Description: The stack pointer is incremented (by 1). The contents of the byte of memory, at the address now contained in the stack pointer, are loaded into the 8 bits of highest significance in the program counter. The stack pointer is again incremented (by 1). The contents of the byte of memory, at the address now contained in the stack pointer, are loaded into the 8 bits of lowest significance in the program counter.

Condition Codes: Not affected.

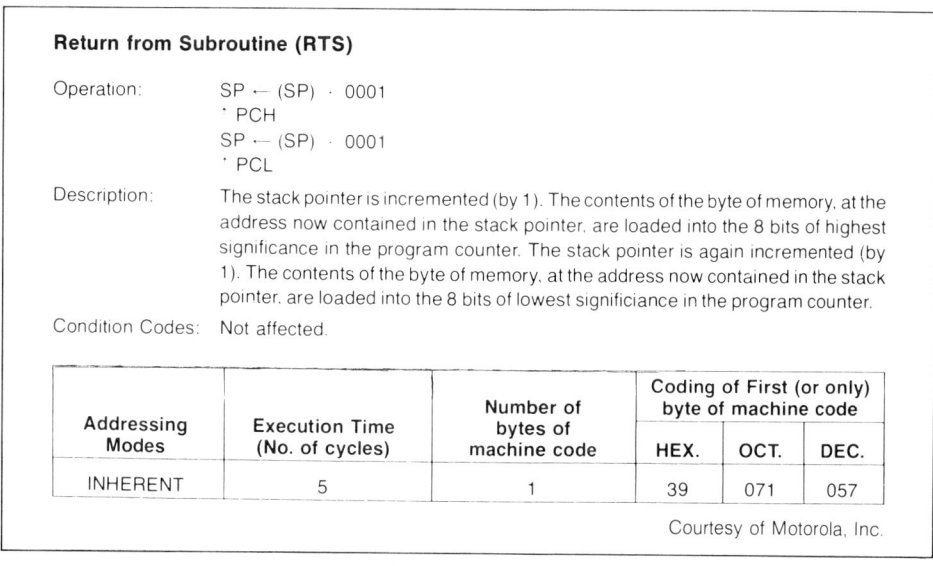

Addressing Modes	Execution Time (No. of cycles)	Number of bytes of machine code	HEX.	OCT.	DEC.
INHERENT	5	1	39	071	057

Coding of First (or only) byte of machine code

Courtesy of Motorola, Inc.

Figure 15.5 The Return from Subroutine (RTS) instruction summary.

gram? Another instruction—the Return from Subroutine (RTS) instruction of Figure 15.5—will enable it to complete the round trip back to the main program.

The RTS instruction simply reverses the CALL process, and (using the stack pointer as a guide) pulls the RETURN information off the two top positions of the stack and places them back onto the program counter. ("Pull" is the technical term for removing data from the stack.) Like the BSR instruction, the RTS instruction is basically a jump—except the return address comes from the stack rather than the MAR. During the RETURN process the stack pointer is incremented twice to again point to the original stack location.

When the Return from Subroutine instruction is added to the end of the subroutine (Figure 15.6), our musical program is complete and ready to run. Clearly, the JSR/BSR and RTS instructions always appear together as a pair. Figure 15.7 reviews the entire CALL/RETURN sequence.

Stack Rules

During the CALL/RETURN operation, automatic increment and decrement processes make sure the stack pointer obeys the following important rule: *The stack pointer always points to the top of the stack* (or, to be more exact, the next available location).

Another rule obeyed by the stack goes by the name of FILO (or LIFO). All data bytes are added to or removed from the stack on a *first in/last out* (FILO) or a *last in/first out* (LIFO) basis. The process is similar to stacking dishes: the last dish added to the stack must be the first one removed.

A SUBROUTINE EXAMPLE

To put what we have learned so far to work, we show Figure 15.8a, our familiar mimic program with a DELAY subrou-

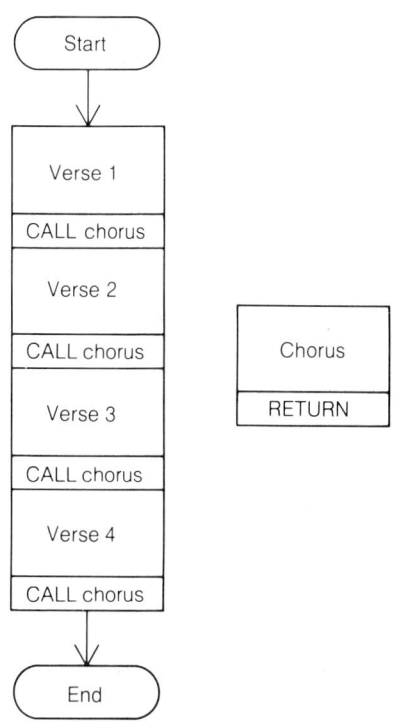

Figure 15.6 Complete musical program using chorus subroutine.

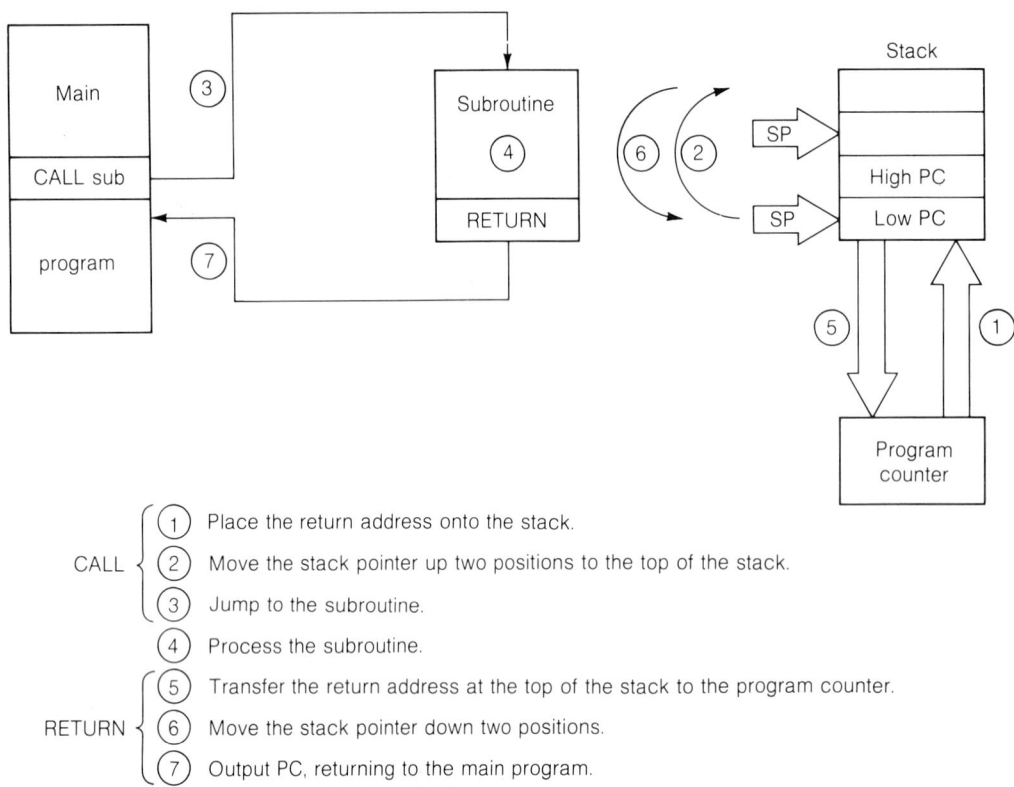

```
            ┌─────────┐                    ┌──────────┐
            │  Main   │────③──────────────▶│Subroutine│         Stack
            │─────────│                    │    ④     │        ┌────────┐
            │CALL sub │                    │──────────│   ⑥ ② SP▶│        │
            │─────────│                    │  RETURN  │        ├────────┤
            │ program │◀───────⑦───────────│          │      SP▶│High PC │
            └─────────┘                    └──────────┘        ├────────┤
                                                               │ Low PC │
                                                               └────────┘
                                                                  ⑤  ①
                                                               ┌────────┐
                                                               │Program │
                                                               │counter │
                                                               └────────┘
```

         ⎧ ① Place the return address onto the stack.
  CALL ⎨ ② Move the stack pointer up two positions to the top of the stack.
         ⎩ ③ Jump to the subroutine.
           ④ Process the subroutine.
         ⎧ ⑤ Transfer the return address at the top of the stack to the program counter.
 RETURN ⎨ ⑥ Move the stack pointer down two positions.
         ⎩ ⑦ Output PC, returning to the main program.

Figure 15.7 The seven steps of the CALL/RETURN process.

tine inserted between the input and output. Note that simple labels link the subroutine with the main program. Figure 15.8b shows how the ORG pseudo-instruction (or *directive*) specifies both the main program and the subroutine locations for machine assembly.

NESTING SUBROUTINES

Referring to Figure 15.6, we see that CALLing the chorus portion of our four-verse ballad has saved a great deal of stored-program space. Unfortunately, there still is insufficient memory space to store a second ballad. Is there a way we can make even more efficient use of our limited memory? There is, and the good news is that it still involves the CALL process.

Zoom in on the chorus subroutine of our musical score (Figure 15.9) and note that a particular phrase is repeated three times. This is more wasted memory space of the same kind we saw before.

Therefore, the solution is the same as before (Figure 15.10). Turn the subroutine phrase into a sub-subroutine, and CALL it whenever needed. In doing so we have placed a subroutine within another subroutine. Or, to use a more familiar term, we have *nested* subroutines.

In fact, it is nesting that demonstrates the real power of the CALL process. First of all, this nesting process can go on indefinitely. (Within a sub-subroutine it is possible to have repetitive data blocks made into a sub-sub-subroutine and called several times during the sub-subroutine.) When subroutines are deeply nested, the real beauty of the CALL process is revealed, for as we go into and out of our routines and subroutines, the return addresses are automatically sorted on the stack, leaving almost nothing for the programmer to worry about. As we go deeper and deeper into the nested subroutines, the stack grows, and as we come out of them, it shrinks (see Figure 15.11).

THE PUSH AND PULL INSTRUCTIONS

One problem with subroutines is the possible internal accumulator/flag tug-of-war set up between routines and subroutines. At the point a CALL is made from the main program, suppose both accumulators and the condition codes register (flags) are holding crucial main-program information that cannot be lost. The problem is that more than likely the subroutine also makes use of these same internal registers and flags. When the action returns to the main program, the

Chapter 15 / Subroutines, Calls, and Stacks

(a) Delay written as a subroutine CALL

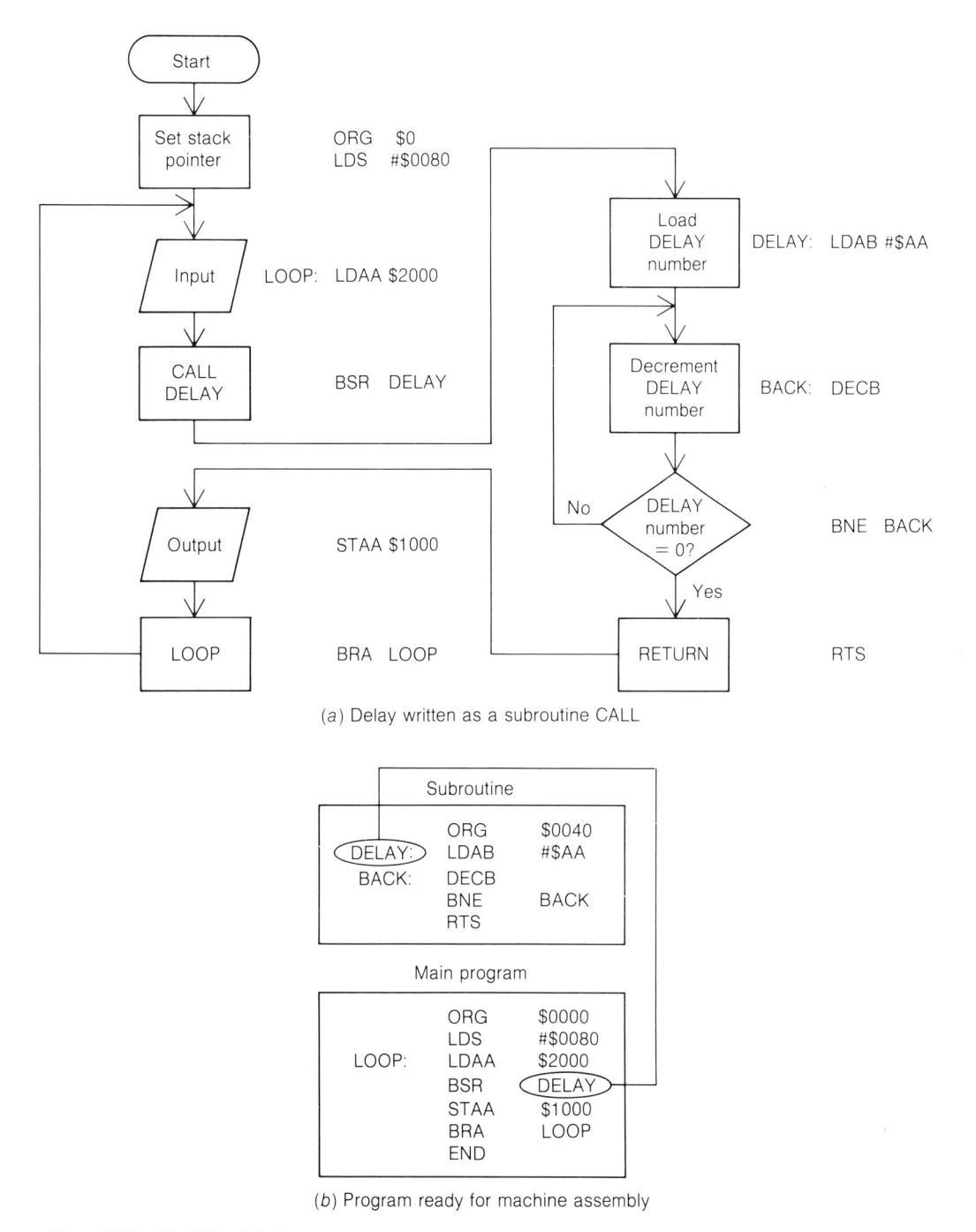

```
              Subroutine
              ORG      $0040
    DELAY:    LDAB     #$AA
    BACK:     DECB
              BNE      BACK
              RTS

              Main program
              ORG      $0000
              LDS      #$0080
    LOOP:     LDAA     $2000
              BSR      DELAY
              STAA     $1000
              BRA      LOOP
              END
```

(b) Program ready for machine assembly

Figure 15.8 The Delay-Mimic program.

original accumulator and flag information will be lost. In other words, both the main program and the subroutine are competing for the same registers and flags.

The solution lies with the stack. Consider the stack to be a safe, whose purpose is to store away for safekeeping all crucial main-program information before a jump to the subroutine. When the subroutine is completed, the main-program information is taken from the "safe" and used to restore the original main-program conditions.

To store and retrieve accumulator and flag information,

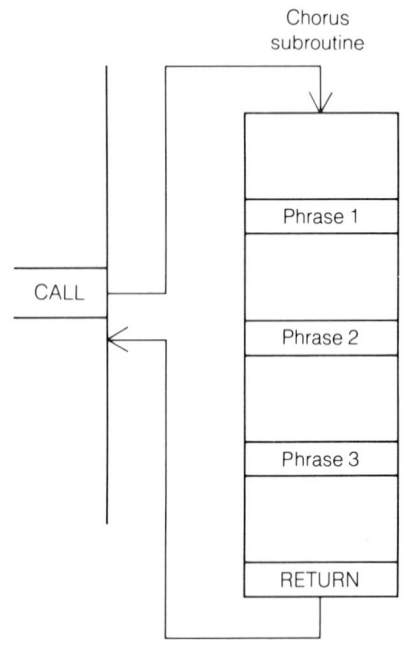

Figure 15.9 Chorus subroutine showing phrase repeated three times.

Figure 15.10 Subroutine nesting.

the PSH, PUL, TAP, and TPA instructions have been provided (Figure 15.12). You *push* accumulator and flag information onto the stack and you *pull* it off, one byte at a time.

Accumulator information is pushed onto and pulled from the stack directly by the PSH and PUL instructions. However, to push and pull flag information, you must first transfer the information to accumulator A. Therefore, the following sequence will push both accumulators and flag information onto the stack:

> PSHA (Push Accumulator A onto Stack)
> PSHB (Push Accumulator B onto Stack)
> TPA (Transfer Flags to Accumulator A)
> PSHA (Push Flags onto Stack)

Once accumulator and flag information is safely stored on the stack, these registers are completely free to be used by the subroutine. Of course, to keep the stack pointer aimed at the top of the stack (the next available location), each 1-byte information push will automatically decrement the stack pointer by 1. The pull instructions will reverse the process and restore the accumulator and flag information so the main program can continue where it left off. During each PULL the stack pointer is incremented once. Therefore, as shown in Figure 15.13, a typical CALL process will involve from one to four PUSH/PULL/TRANSFER pairs. Following the FILO rule, the accumulator and flag data are PULLed off the stack in reverse order to being PUSHed onto the stack. Figure 15.14 illustrates the clock-cycle action of a typical PUSH process. Note the op code prefetch during clock cycle 2.

WHEN TO CALL

The CALL process should be used whenever memory space is saved. (The CALL process itself does introduce a tiny loss of speed.) To put it another way, the more times subroutines are called, the larger they are; and the greater the depth of nesting, the greater the need.

Another factor to consider is software development cost. Using CALLs, all or part of a main program can be written in block form. That is, the program can consist of software blocks (modules) arranged and linked together by the proper sequence of CALLs. In addition, the software blocks can be divided among several programmers, and in fact may already be available in a software library. This idea—related to the concept of top-down modular design—represents the software counterpart of using LSI blocks to create the computer hardware system. Using software blocks, programs are usually easier to write and to interpret.

For example, let's select the familiar mystery program of Chapter 12 and apply the lessons of top-down modular design. Figure 15.15 shows the result. The main program is nothing

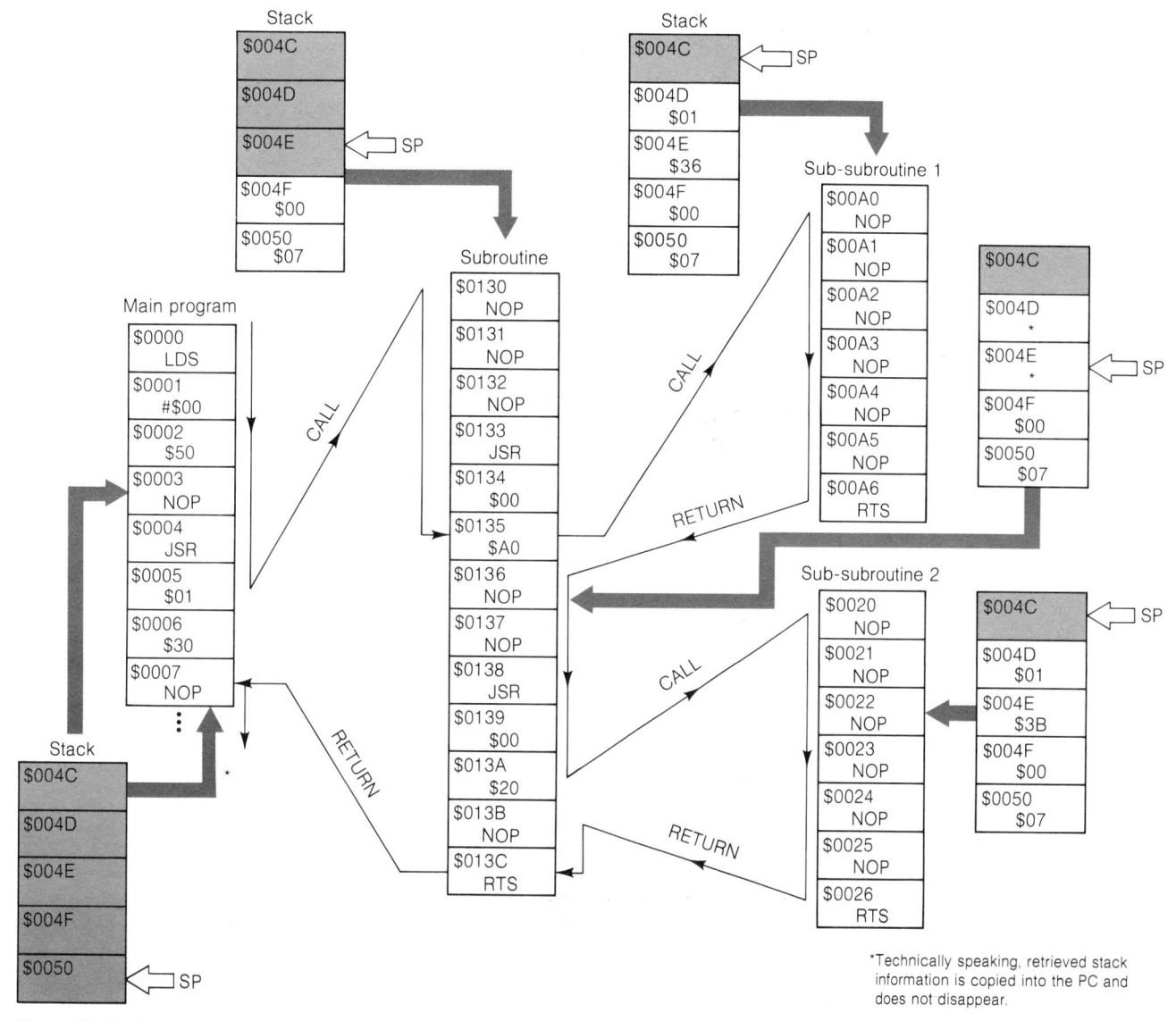

Figure 15.11 Stack contents when nesting subroutines.

but calls! *But it is easy to read*—like the table of contents of a book—because the program is summarized in general terms without the low-level programming details clouding its overall intent. We will return to the subject of top-down *modular* design in Chapter 22 and see how program modules (called *procedures*) are implemented in high-level structured languages.

PARAMETER PASSING

The top-down modular design concepts of the last section are especially vital when large, complex, "real-world" programs are to be written. If the program requires one man-year to write, and the product must be released to market in 4 months, clearly the problem must be broken up into "bite-size" modules and parceled out among several programmers. *For efficiency, each module should be independent of the others.* That is, when a module is written or modified, the new or modified program code should not ripple back, scattering bugs (software errors) throughout the entire program. However, it is also clear that quite often data will have to be transmitted back and forth between modules. Furthermore, each time a module is "CALLed," the transmitted data may be different. How can the various modules maintain independence and still communicate with each other? The answer is, they pass *parameters*.

A *parameter* is a piece of data generated by one module and used by another. To maintain independence as the parameters cross the border from one module to another, the parameters are usually placed in new memory locations—accessible only by the receiving module. In other words—

Push Data onto Stack (PSH)

Operation: ↓ (ACCX)
SP ← (SP) − 0001

Description: The contents of ACCX is stored in the stack at the address contained in the stack pointer. The stack pointer is then decremented.

Condition Codes: Not affected.

Addressing Modes	Execution Time (No. of cycles)	Number of bytes of machine code	Coding of First (or only) byte of machine code		
			HEX.	OCT.	DEC.
A	4	1	36	066	054
B	4	1	37	067	055

Courtesy of Motorola, Inc.

(a)

Pull Data from Stack (PUL)

Operation: SP ← (SP) + 0001
↑ ACCX

Description: The stack pointer is incremented. The ACCX is then loaded from the stack, from the address which is contained in the stack pointer.

Condition Codes: Not affected.

Addressing Modes	Execution Time (No. of cycles)	Number of bytes of machine code	Coding of First (or only) byte of machine code		
			HEX.	OCT.	DEC.
A	4	1	32	062	050
B	4	1	33	063	051

Courtesy of Motorola, Inc.

(b)

Transfer from Accumulator A to Processor Condition Codes Register (TAP)

Operation: CC ← (ACCA)

Description: Transfers the contents of bit positions 0 thru 5 of accumulator A to the corresponding bit positions of the processor condition codes register. The contents of accumulator A remain unchanged.

Condition Codes: Set or reset according to the contents of the respective bits 0 thru 5 of accumulator A.

Addressing Modes	Execution Time (No. of cycles)	Number of bytes of machine code	Coding of First (or only) byte of machine code		
			HEX.	OCT.	DEC.
INHERENT	2	1	06	006	006

Courtesy of Motorola, Inc.

(c)

Transfer from Processor Condition Codes Register to Accumulator A (TPA)

Operation: ACCA ← (CC)

Description: Transfers the contents of the processor condition codes register to corresponding bit positions 0 thru 5 of accumulator A. Bit positions 6 and 7 of accumulator A are set (i.e. go to the "1" state). The processor condition codes register remains unchanged.

Condition Codes: Not affected.

Addressing Modes	Execution Time (No. of cycles)	Number of bytes of machine code	Coding of First (or only) byte of machine code		
			HEX.	OCT.	DEC.
INHERENT	2	1	07	007	007

Courtesy of Motorola, Inc.

(d)

Figure 15.12 The PSH, PUL, TAP, and TPA stack storage instructions.

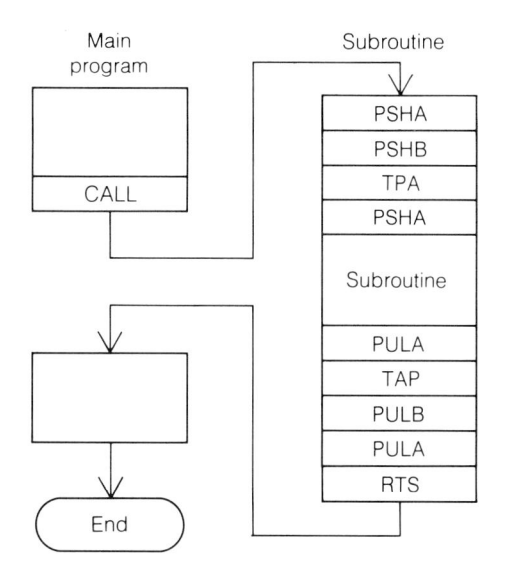

Figure 15.13 PUSH/PULL/TRANSFER sequencing to store and retrieve accumulator and flag data.

to use high-level language terminology—the parameters are *local* to each module, rather than *global* to the entire program. (When all modules have access to a global parameter, it is all too easy for one module to "destroy" data needed by another.) The stack is often used as the parameter-passing vehicle. When the stack is turned over to parameter passing, the STS (Store Stack Pointer) and LDS (Load Stack Pointer) instructions can be used to "remember" the original position of the stack pointer.

In the next section, we will see how parameter passing is used in assembly-language programming, and in Chapter 22 we will see how parameters are passed between *procedures*.

MACHINE-ASSEMBLY UPDATE

Our next machine-assembly update is a natural for this chapter because it introduces MACROs, a concept similar to subroutine CALLs.

A MACRO is a single-line assembly-language statement which stands for a group of assembly-language instructions. Based on this definition, a MACRO and a subroutine CALL seem identical. Of course they are not, and here is the difference: A MACRO "calls" a sequence of assembly-language instructions *during assembly;* a subroutine CALL calls a group of machine-language instructions *during execution*.

Both MACROs and CALLs lend themselves to the block-structured, modular design concepts of the last section. So—which is best? The answer is, there is a tradeoff involved, and most programs will involve a combination of both MACROs and CALLs. To get a better idea of how MACROs are used, let's examine the structure of a MACRO using our simple "Delay-Mimic" program.

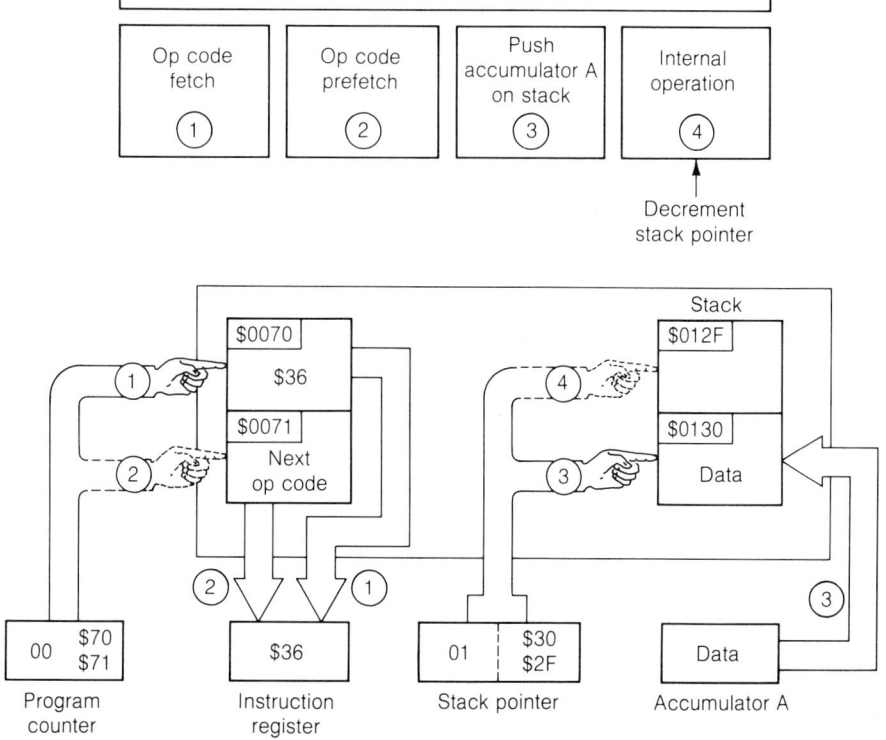

Figure 15.14 PSHA clock-cycle diagram.

178 Part III / Software: The Spark of Life

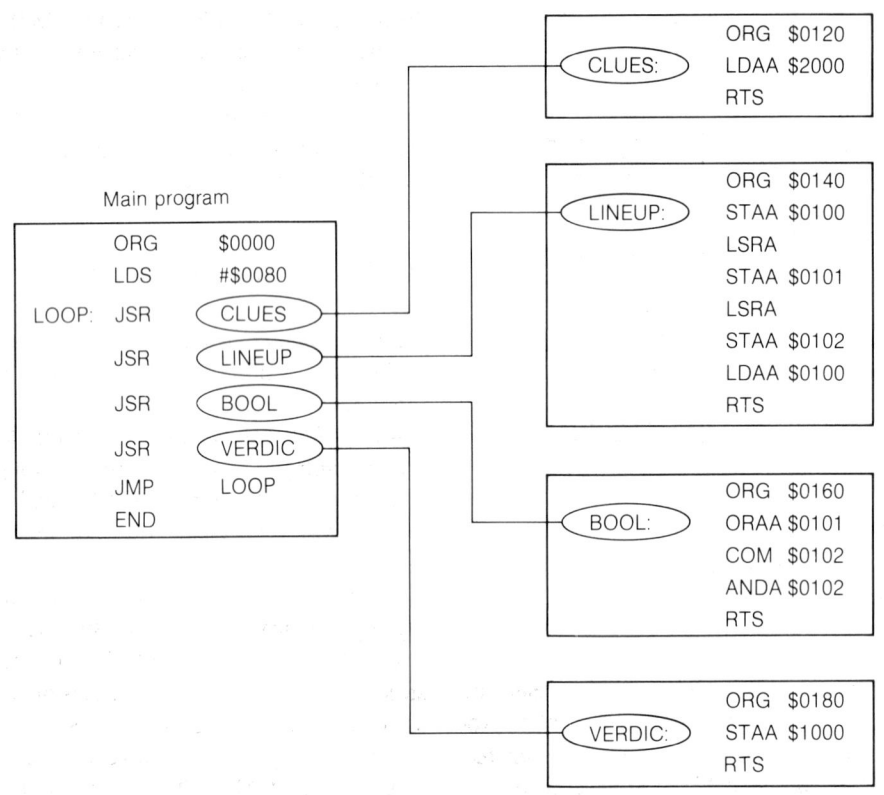

```
                Main program
              ┌─────────────────────┐
              │  ORG      $0000     │                        ┌─ CLUES:  ORG    $0120
              │  LDS      #$0080    │                        │          LDAA   $2000
              │  LOOP: JSR  CLUES ──┼────────────────────────┘          RTS
              │        JSR  LINEUP ─┼──────────┐
              │        JSR  BOOL ───┼────┐     │             ┌─ LINEUP: ORG    $0140
              │        JSR  VERDIC ─┼──┐ │     └─────────────┘          STAA   $0100
              │        JMP  LOOP    │  │ │                              LSRA
              │        END          │  │ │                              STAA   $0101
              └─────────────────────┘  │ │                              LSRA
                                       │ │                              STAA   $0102
                                       │ │                              LDAA   $0100
                                       │ │                              RTS
                                       │ │
                                       │ └───────────────── BOOL:  ORG    $0160
                                       │                           ORAA   $0101
                                       │                           COM    $0102
                                       │                           ANDA   $0102
                                       │                           RTS
                                       │
                                       └─────────────────── VERDIC: ORG    $0180
                                                                    STAA   $1000
                                                                    RTS
```

Figure 15.15 Using subroutines for modular design.

```
DELAY   MACRO
        LDAB    #$AA        ; Load delay number
LOOP:   DECB                ; Decrement delay number
        BNE     LOOP        ; Branch if not 0
        ENDM

        ORG     $0          ; Start of main program
START:  LDAA    $4000       ; Input number
        DELAY               ; Call MACRO
        STAA    $2000       ; Output number
        BRA     START       ; Place into loop
        END
```

The three instructions making up the MACRO are bracketed by the reserved words MACRO and ENDM (End Macro). The MACRO name ("DELAY") is written before the word MACRO in the label column. As shown, the MACRO is "called" by writing its name in the main program.

Now let's look at the list program of Figure 15.16 and see how the assembler processed the MACRO. When the assembler arrived at the MACRO name "DELAY" in the main program, it *substituted* the three instructions making up the body of the MACRO for the MACRO name, just as if the three instructions were written in the original program (note the three "+" signs). *Observe that no subroutine CALLs were generated!* Subroutine CALLs would appear in the program only if they were written into the body of the MACRO or the main program to begin with.

A MACRO is a program module, and program modules should be independent. Therefore, it should come as no surprise to learn that MACROs communicate by way of parameters. Our Delay-Mimic routine is a natural for passing a parameter, because it may be used many times during a program—each time generating a different delay. Therefore, each time the MACRO is called, we might send it a different delay number. The process is shown below:

```
DELAY   MACRO   #XX         ; Declare MACRO with
                              parameter
        LDAB    ##XX        ; Load delay number with
                              parameter
LOOP:   DECB                ; Decrement delay number
        BNE     LOOP        ; Branch if not 0
        ENDM                ; End of MACRO

        ORG     $0          ; Start of main program
START:  LDAA    $4000       ; Input number
        DELAY   $AA         ; Call MACRO; send
                              delay parameter
        STAA    $2000       ; Output number
        BRA     START       ; Place into loop
        END
```

```
                6800/6801/6802 ASSEMBLER VER.3.3      1

 1              ; In this program, the three instructions comprising a
 2              ; simple delay loop are written as the MACRO DELAY
 3
 4              DELAY   MACRO           ; Declare MACRO DELAY
 5                      LDAB    #$AA    ; Load delay number
 6              LOOP:   DECB            ; Decrement delay number
 7                      BNE     LOOP    ; Branch if <> 0
 8                      ENDM            ; End of MACRO
 9
10 0000                 ORG     $0      ; Start of main prog
11 0000 B6 20 00  START: LDAA   $2000   ; Input number
12 0003                 DELAY           ; Call MACRO DELAY
12 0003 C6 AA   +       LDAB    #$AA    ; Load delay number
12 0005 5A      +LOOP:  DECB            ; Decrement delay number
12 0006 26 FD 0005+     BNE     LOOP    ; Branch if <> 0
13 0008 B7 10 00        STAA    $1000   ; Output number
14 000B 20 F3 0000      BRA     START   ; Place into loop
15 000D                 END

ERRORS = 0000

LOOP    0005    MEMORY M 0000   STACK S 0000   START    0000
```

Figure 15.16 The Delay-Mimic program with the DELAY routine written as a MACRO.

Looking at the assembled printout (Figure 15.17), we see that the parameter (called the *actual parameter*) follows the MACRO name. The actual parameter is sent to the MACRO by way of the *formal parameter* (#XX). The actual parameter ($AA) is then substituted for the formal parameter wherever it appears in the body of the MACRO (i.e., LDAB ##XX). (The formal parameter contains two Xs because the actual parameter contains two characters.)

To summarize, parameters allow MACROs to be written and modified independently of other MACROs and to operate upon different sets of data. Still, we haven't answered our original question: Which is better, MACROs or subroutine CALLs? A difficult question, for our Delay-Mimic program can be written either way:

Using Subroutine CALLs

```
          ORG     $0100
DELAY:    LDAB    #AA
LOOP:     DECB
          BNE     LOOP
          RTS

          ORG     $0
          LDS     #$0080
START:    LDAA    $4000
          JSR     DELAY
          STAA    $2000
          BRA     START
          END
```

Using MACROs

```
DELAY     MACRO   #XX
          LDAB    ##XX
LOOP:     DECB
          BNE     LOOP
          ENDM

          ORG     $0
START:    LDAA    $4000
          DELAY   $AA
          STAA    $2000
          BRA     START
          END
```

Although the two programs look similar, they do not assemble the same. Let's look at the advantages and disadvantages of each. The MACRO version (Figure 15.17) executes faster and uses less memory than the subroutine version (Figure 15.18) because there are no subroutine CALLs in the final assembled object program. (A subroutine CALL uses up time in storing and retrieving data from the stack and in making the jump.) However, if the DELAY routine were needed many times, then code would be generated each time. Clearly, in this case, subroutine CALLs—although slightly slower—would use far less memory space. Therefore, it follows that *the ideal use of MACROs is in conjunction with subroutines*. MACROs can be used to simplify

```
                          6800/6801/6802 ASSEMBLER VER.3.3      1

  1              ; In this demonstration program, delay parameter
  2              ; $AA is sent to MACRO DELAY.  This "generalized"
  3              ; MACRO--able to process any delay number--is more
  4              ; flexible
  5
  6              DELAY   MACRO    #XX    ; Declare MACRO with parameter
  7                      LDAB     ##XX   ; Load delay No with parameter
  8              LOOP:   DECB            ; Decrement delay No
  9                      BNE      LOOP   ; Branch if () 0
 10                      ENDM            ; End MACRO
 11
 12 0000                 ORG      $0     ; Start of program
 13 0000 B6 20 00  START: LDAA    $2000  ; Input number
 14 0003          DELAY  $AA            ; Call MACRO--send delay para
 14 0003 C6 AA      +    LDAB    ##$AA   ; Load delay No with parameter
 14 0005 5A        +LOOP: DECB          ; Decrement delay No
 14 0006 26 FD 0005+    BNE      LOOP   ; Branch if () 0
 15 0008 B7 10 00       STAA     $1000  ; Output number
 16 000B 20 F3 0000     BRA      START  ; Place into loop
 17 000D                END


ERRORS = 0000

LOOP      0005    MEMORY M 0000   STACK  S 0000    START     0000
```

Figure 15.17 Sending a delay parameter ($AA) to MACRO DELAY.

the coding of programs, with no loss in execution speed, while subroutine CALLs can be used to save memory space. Both MACROs (via formal and actual parameters) and CALLs (via the stack) will support parameter passing.

Figure 15.19a is a final version of our Delay-Mimic source program, one that includes all we have learned in this section (to require the use of a PUSH/PULL pair, we have constrained the program to use only accumulator A). Analysis of the machine-assembled printout of Figure 15.19b is left for the Questions and Problems section.

The modular-oriented programs developed in this chapter have been relatively simple. In contrast, imagine a large, complex program containing numerous MACROs, each appearing numerous times, and sending different actual parameters to the MACRO body. Further, imagine numerous nested subroutine CALLs within each MACRO body. It is clear that many of the techniques used in assembly-language programming that seem cumbersome in small programs (MACROs and parameter passing, for example) are critical when the program assumes real-world dimensions. Without a doubt, assembly-language programming is a skilled art.

```
                          6800/6801/6802 ASSEMBLER VER.3.3      1

  1              ; This time the three instruction delay loop
  2              ; is written as a subroutine CALL
  3
  4 0100                 ORG      $0100  ; Subroutine start address
  5 0100 C6 AA   DELAY:  LDAB     #$AA   ; Subroutine is labeled DELAY
  6 0102 5A      LOOP:   DECB
  7 0103 26 FD 0102     BNE       LOOP
  8 0105 39              RTS             ; Return to main prog
  9
 10 0000                 ORG      $0     ; Main prog start address
 11 0000 8E 00 80        LDS      #$0080 ; Initialize stack pointer
 12 0003 B6 20 00  START: LDAA    $2000
 13 0006 BD 01 00       JSR       DELAY  ; CALL subroutine DELAY
 14 0009 B7 10 00       STAA      $1000
 15 000C 20 F5 0003     BRA       START
 16 000E                END


ERRORS = 0000

DELAY     0100    LOOP     0102    MEMORY M 0000   STACK  S 0000
START     0003
```

Figure 15.18 The Delay-Mimic program with the DELAY routine written as a subroutine CALL.

```
        ; In a complex program, both subroutine CALLs and
        ; MACROs would be used--each in its best way

        DELAY:   MACRO    #XX    ; Declare MACRO & formal para
                 PSHA            ; Place input number on stack
                 LDAA     ##XX   ; Load accum A with passed para
                 JSR      LOOP   ; CALL delay loop
                 PULA            ; Pull input No from stack
                 ENDM            ; End of MACRO DELAY

                 ORG      $0100  ; Specify subroutine location
        LOOP:    DECA            ; Decrement delay number
                 BNE      LOOP   ; Loop if <> 0
                 RTS             ; Return from subroutine

                 ORG      $0     ; Start of main prog
        START:   LDAA     $2000  ; Input number
                 DELAY    $AA    ; CALL MACRO DELAY--send para
                 STAA     $1000  ; Output number
                 BRA      START  ; Place into loop
                 END
```
(a) Source program

```
                         6800/6801/6802 ASSEMBLER VER.3.3      1

 1                   ; In a complex program, both subroutine CALLs and
 2                   ; MACROs would be used--each in its best way
 3
 4                   DELAY:   MACRO    #XX    ; Declare MACRO & formal para
 5                            PSHA            ; Place input number on stack
 6                            LDAA     ##XX   ; Load accum A with passed para
 7                            JSR      LOOP   ; CALL delay loop
 8                            PULA            ; Pull input No from stack
 9                            ENDM            ; End of MACRO DELAY
10
11 0100                       ORG      $0100  ; Specify subroutine location
12 0100 4A         LOOP:      DECA            ; Decrement delay number
13 0101 26 FD 0100            BNE      LOOP   ; Loop if <> 0
14 0103 39                    RTS             ; Return from subroutine
15
16 0000                       ORG      $0     ; Start of main prog
17 0000 B6 20 00   START:     LDAA     $2000  ; Input number
18 0003                       DELAY    $AA    ; CALL MACRO DELAY--send para
18 0003 36          +         PSHA            ; Place input number on stack
18 0004 86 AA       +         LDAA     #$AA   ; Load accum A with passed para
18 0006 BD 01 00    +         JSR      LOOP   ; CALL delay loop
18 0009 32          +         PULA            ; Pull input No from stack
19 000A B7 10 00              STAA     $1000  ; Output number
20 000D 20 F1 0000            BRA      START  ; Place into loop
21 000F                       END

ERRORS = 0000
LOOP   0100    MEMORY M 0000   STACK  S 0000   START   0000
```
(b) Machine assembled printout of list file

Figure 15.19 The Delay-Mimic program using a subroutine CALL within a MACRO.

INTELLIGENT-MACHINE UPDATE

Through the use of nested subroutines, our intelligent machine finally is able to squeeze the entire ballad into its available memory space and to successfully complete its concert debut. Our intelligent machine will remember the lesson it learned: the clever use of software can save hardware. In later chapters, it will find the reverse also to be true: the clever use of hardware can save software.

QUESTIONS AND PROBLEMS

1. A CALL (JSR/BSR) is basically a *jump,* but with an extra twist thrown in. What is that extra twist?

2. Does the stack grow toward smaller locations or toward larger locations?

3. When a JSR or BSR instruction is processed, what information is placed onto the stack?

```
ORG    $0000
LDS    #$0080
LDX    #$FF00
LDAA   $4000
JSR    $50, X
  ⋮
```

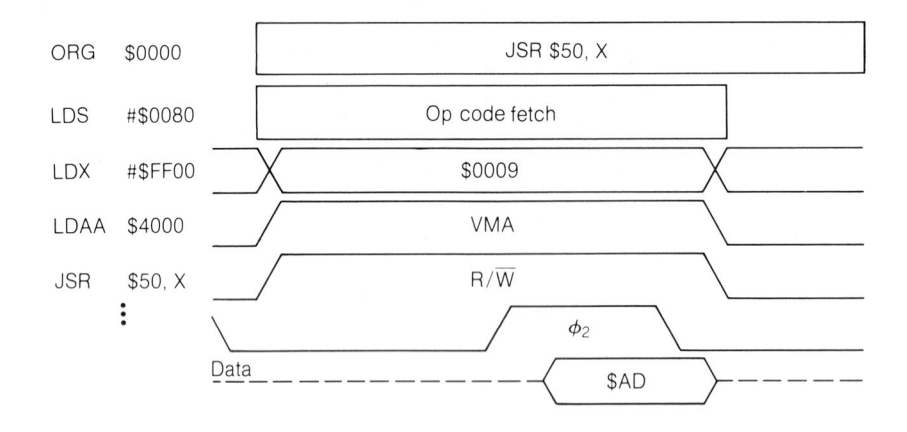

Figure 15.20 Program and diagram for problem 13.

4. Why are nine machine cycles required to process the JSR EXT instruction?
5. The stack pointer always points to what part of the stack?
6. The stack pointer is presently holding $7A03 when the BSR instruction is processed. At what stack locations is the return address placed?
7. What does the term *FILO* stand for, and how does it relate to the use of the stack?
8. When using CALLs, does the programmer have to specify any return addresses? Why?
9. Under what conditions are PUSH/PULL pairs used during subroutine processing?
10. A program may be constructed from software blocks linked together by a series of CALL instructions. Why is such a "modular" program easy to write and to interpret?
11. What is the difference between a *return* and a *jump*?
12. Write a clock-cycle diagram for the PULB process (similar to Figure 15.14).
13. For the program shown in Figure 15.20, complete the 6800 timing diagram (also shown in the figure) for the JSR IND instruction.
14. Hand-assemble the Delay-Mimic source program of Figure 15.8b.
15. For the program given, show the contents of the stack and the position of the stack pointer at each of the points shown in Figure 15.21.

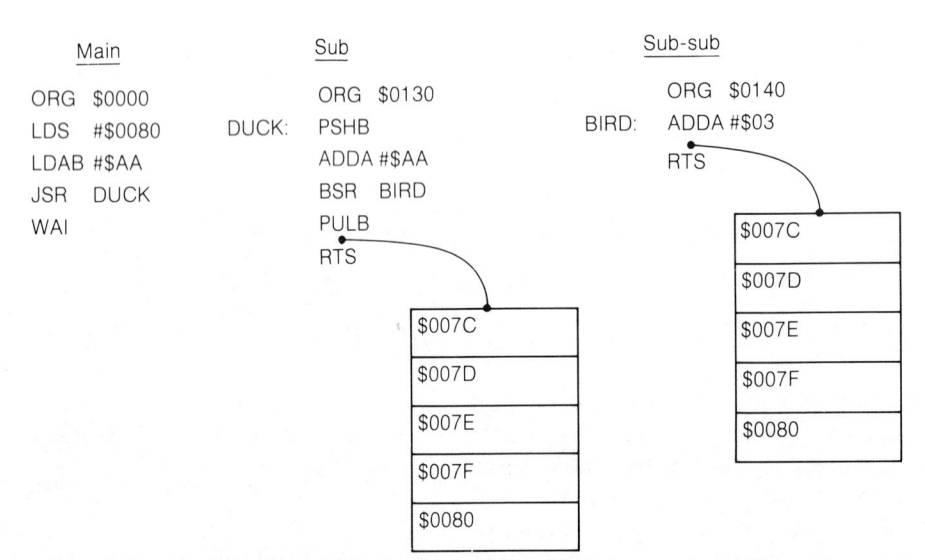

```
        Main                    Sub                    Sub-sub

    ORG   $0000             ORG  $0130             ORG  $0140
    LDS   #$0080    DUCK:   PSHB           BIRD:   ADDA #$03
    LDAB  #$AA              ADDA #$AA              RTS
    JSR   DUCK              BSR  BIRD
    WAI                     PULB
                            RTS
```

| $007C |
| $007D |
| $007E |
| $007F |
| $0080 |

| $007C |
| $007D |
| $007E |
| $007F |
| $0080 |

Figure 15.21 Program for problem 15.

16. Why is the following program guaranteed to overflow the stack?

    START: BSR   START

17. Rewrite the mystery program of Figure 12.8 (use addressing mode of your choice) using the following MACROs: CLUES, LINEUP, BOOL, and VERDICT.
18. Why is the MACRO version of our Delay-Mimic program (Figure 15.16) faster than the subroutine version (Figure 15.18)?
19. What is accomplished by the STS $00,X instruction?
20. Why is accumulator and flag information PULLed from the stack in reverse order to being PUSHed onto the stack?
21. Why is it advantageous for program modules to be written and modified independently of each other?
22. Referring to Figure 15.8, show the contents of the stack and the position of the stack pointer while in the delay loop.
23. If a subroutine CALL is to be nested 4 deep (a main program and 3 nested subroutines), and accumulator B and the flags are to be saved on the stack each time, how much memory must be reserved for the stack?
24. What is a *parameter*?
25. To increase the delay time of our Delay-Mimic routine of Figure 15.8, CALL another delay loop from *within* the present subroutine loop.
26. When a subroutine is to be CALLed many times, why is it more efficient to place any required PUSH/PULL pairs in the subroutine rather than the main program?
27. Referring to the index register instructions of Appendix II, how would you PUSH/PULL the index register contents?
28. Program *patching* is the addition or deletion of a group of instructions without going through the process of re-assembly. In general terms, how would a patch be implemented?

chapter 16

Interrupts

Able to call subroutines, and thereby make efficient use of its available memory, our intelligent machine can generate long and complex programs. But what does it do when the power suddenly fails?

Able to learn and recall duties, it can be programmed to be an obedient butler. But what does it do when the phone rings?

In each of these cases our intelligent machine is helpless, and for a very basic reason: it has no means at all for reacting to the unexpected. Power failures and phone calls are all natural but unexpected events, and it is essential for computers as well as human beings to be able to handle them.

In computer terminology, the unexpected is known as an *interrupt* and these interrupts are the subject of this chapter.

AN EVERYDAY EXAMPLE

A phone call is a good place to begin our study of interrupts, for all the major elements of interrupt processing are found there.

First of all, a question: Are those unexpected events that will trigger an interrupt really a complete surprise? Not at all, for we know the power can fail and phones can ring. The point is, we do not know precisely when, or even if, unexpected events will occur. Nevertheless, we had better prepare ourselves with contingency plans, just in case they are needed. For a computer, each contingency plan is known as an *interrupt-service routine* (or *interrupt-handling routine*), and usually is placed in the computer's permanent memory.

The next step is to enable the interrupt system so it will function when needed. For us, that simply means remaining within earshot of the phone.

Contingency program in place and interrupt system enabled, we go about our normal duties. Suddenly, unexpectedly, the phone rings. In essence, an interrupt is requested. We respond by finishing our immediate task and branching to the contingency plan (which causes the phone to be answered).

When finished with the phone call, we return to the original main program and take up where we left off.

The major elements of interrupt processing contained in our telephone example are condensed into the following four steps (assume the interrupt-service routine is already deposited in memory):

1. Enable the interrupt system.
2. Request an interrupt.
3. Call and perform the interrupt-service routine.
4. Return to the main program.

Further condensing these four steps into a single sentence, we arrive at:

AN INTERRUPT IS AN UNEXPECTED
SUBROUTINE CALL.

Because an interrupt involves a subroutine CALL, many of the steps will be familiar. But, because an interrupt is unexpected, many of the steps will be new. Our next task is to apply these four basic elements of interrupt processing to a 6800 system, paying particular attention to what is new.

6800 INTERRUPT PROCESSING

The need for interrupts generally falls into three categories:

1. Input/output data transfers from peripheral devices
2. Input signals to be used for timing purposes
3. Emergency situations

Focusing on the third category, if the unexpected is considered to be an emergency (panic) situation, then naturally a "panic button" is required. On the 6800 there are two panic buttons: $\overline{\text{IRQ}}$ (Interrupt Request) and $\overline{\text{NMI}}$ (Nonmaskable Interrupt). (See Figure 16.1.)

Concentrating on the $\overline{\text{IRQ}}$ input first, we find that interrupt

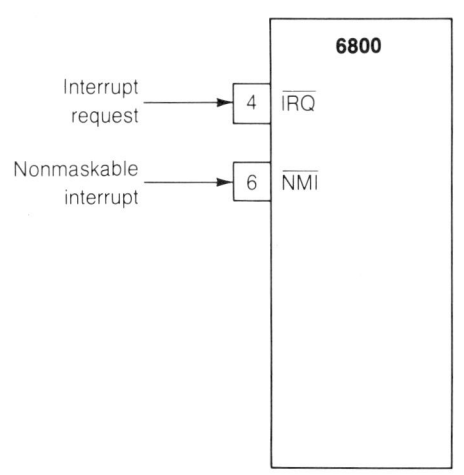

Figure 16.1 6800 interrupt request inputs.

processing on a 6800 system follows the same four-step sequence as our earlier telephone example.

Step 1—Enable the interrupt system After 6800 reset, the $\overline{\text{IRQ}}$ interrupt is automatically disabled (interrupt mask bit set to 1). In general, masking is used to prevent unwanted interrupts. For example, the processor may be involved in a critical timing loop or I/O operation, and an interrupt would add an unwanted time increment to the processor's programmed operations.

To give the programmer control over interrupt operations, the 6800 provides the Clear Interrupt Mask (CLI) and Set Interrupt Mask (SEI) instructions (Figure 16.2), which set or reset bit D4 of the condition codes register. Before the $\overline{\text{IRQ}}$ interrupt can be accepted, the interrupt mask bit must be cleared with a CLI instruction.

In practice, the programmer would bracket those portions of the program in which an interrupt is allowed with the CLI/SEI pair. In those cases where the entire program can be safely interrupted, the CLI instruction would be placed early in the main program.

Step 2—Request an interrupt With reference to Figure 16.1, an interrupt is requested by pulling the level-sensitive input $\overline{\text{IRQ}}$ low. This can be done asynchronously (at any time). At the end of the present instruction, a special interrupt sequence is initiated. (To maintain the integrity of the

---

Clear Interrupt Mask (CLI)

Operation: I bit ← 0

Description: Clears the interrupt mask bit in the processor condition codes register. This enables the microprocessor to service an interrupt from a peripheral device if signalled by a high state of the "Interrupt Request" control input.

Addressing Modes	Execution Time (No. of cycles)	Number of bytes of machine code	HEX.	OCT.	DEC.
INHERENT	2	1	0E	016	014

Coding of First (or only) byte of machine code

Courtesy of Motorola, Inc.

(a)

Set Interrupt Mask (SEI)

Operation: I bit ← 1

Description: Sets the interrupt mask bit in the processor condition codes register. The microprocessor is inhibited from servicing an interrupt from a peripheral device, and will continue with execution of the instructions of the program, until the interrupt mask bit has been cleared.

Addressing Modes	Execution Time (No. of cycles)	Number of bytes of machine code	HEX.	OCT.	DEC.
INHERENT	2	1	0F	017	015

Coding of First (or only) byte of machine code

Courtesy of Motorola, Inc.

(b)

Figure 16.2 The interrupt flag instructions—CLI and SEI.

main program, the instruction in progress is allowed to complete.)

Step 3—Call and perform the interrupt-service routine As with all CALLs, the interrupt sequence begins with storing the vital internal registers on the stack. Since an interrupt is unexpected, there is no way to determine which internal registers are holding vital data—so all are pushed onto the stack (the program counter, the accumulators, the index register, and the condition codes register). The interrupt system is automatically disabled (interrupt mask bit set), and will remain disabled until the RTI (Return from Interrupt) or CLI (Clear Interrupt) instruction is processed. This arrangement prevents an external device (perhaps the same external device) from interrupting the processor out of the present interrupt routine.

From here on, the action is similar to the RESET process introduced in Chapter 9. Using two data-transfer clock-cycle operations, the address information (interrupt vector) stored at locations $FFF8 and $FFF9 are transferred (jammed) into the program counter. (During a RESET operation, remember, the reset vector at locations $FFFE and $FFFF is jammed into the program counter.) The interrupt vector fetched from $FFF8 and $FFF9 is the starting location of the interrupt-service routine (ISR). ISR processing begins when the first service-routine op code is fetched from the vector location.

Step 4—Return to the main program Since the $\overline{IRQ}$ process performs the same functions as a CALL, we return to the main program by placing the RTI (Return from Interrupt) instruction at the end of the interrupt-service routine. Unlike the RTS (Return from Subroutine) instruction, the RTI instruction automatically restores the condition codes register, accumulators B and A, and the index register, as well as the program counter (see Figure 16.3). (The RTS instruction, remember, restores only the program counter, so *pushes* and *pulls* must be included to protect the contents of the additional registers.) *The interrupt mask bit will be reset (and the interrupt system reenabled) when the previous condition codes contents are pulled from the stack and placed back into the condition codes register* (assuming, of course, the Interrupt bit is still zero). The sequence of events during an $\overline{IRQ}$ is summarized in Figure 16.4.

Nonmaskable Interrupt ($\overline{NMI}$) Instruction

$\overline{NMI}$ is a true "panic button," for the input cannot be masked out. Processing is activated by the negative-going edge of the $\overline{NMI}$ input (pin 6), and is independent of the state of the interrupt mask bit. $\overline{NMI}$ is therefore ideal for emergency situations (such as power failure) when action must be taken immediately, without hesitation.

Except for the edge-sensitive input, immunity to the interrupt mask bit, and location of the interrupt vector ($FFFC and $FFFD), processing action is similar to that of $\overline{IRQ}$.

The Software Interrupt (SWI) Instruction

Since interrupts are generally reserved for unexpected events, a software-initiated interrupt may not seem logical. However, it can be used during system design and development to simulate a hardware interrupt. For example, to determine

---

Return from Interrupt (RTI)

Operation:
SP ← (SP) + 0001 , ↑CC
SP ← (SP) + 0001 , ↑ACCB
SP ← (SP) + 0001 , ↑ACCA
SP ← (SP) + 0001 , ↑IXH
SP ← (SP) + 0001 , ↑IXL
SP ← (SP) + 0001 , ↑PCH
SP ← (SP) + 0001 , ↑PCL

Description: The condition codes, accumulators B and A, the index register, and the program counter, will be restored to a state pulled from the stack. Note that the interrupt mask bit will be reset if and only if the corresponding bit stored in the stack is zero.

Condition Codes: Restored to the states pulled from the stack.

Addressing Modes	Execution Time (No. of cycles)	Number of bytes of machine code	HEX.	OCT.	DEC.
INHERENT	10	1	3B	073	059

Coding of First (or only) byte of machine code

Courtesy of Motorola, Inc.

Figure 16.3 The Return from Interrupt (RTI) instruction.

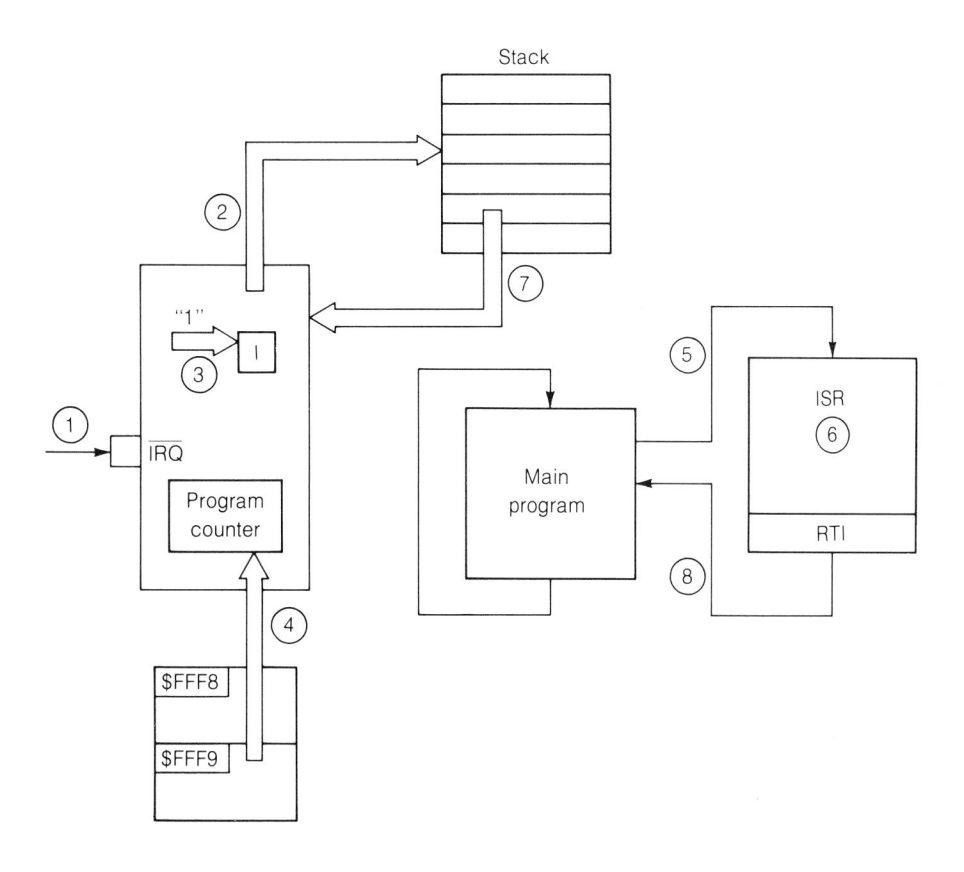

Figure 16.4 The interrupt request ($\overline{IRQ}$) sequence.

① Request interrupt.
② Save internal registers on stack.
③ Interrupt mask bit is set (I = 1).
④ Interrupt vector fetched.
⑤ Jump to interrupt-service routine.
⑥ Execute interrupt-service routine.
⑦ Internal registers restored.
⑧ Resume main program execution.

the consequences of an interrupt at a particular location during program execution, simply place the SWI instruction (Figure 16.5) at that location. The SWI instruction is also used to perform the single-step and breakpoint functions on the ET-3400A trainer. When the SWI instruction is processed, the vital registers and program counter are pushed onto the stack, the interrupt mask bit is set (goes to 1), and the interrupt-service-routine vector is pulled from memory locations $FFFA and $FFFB and jammed into the program counter. RTI at the end of the ISR restores the system to its previous state.

The Wait for Interrupt (WAI) Instruction

Although an interrupt is a very useful and attractive device, we pay a penalty in speed when it is used too often. It requires approximately 10 clock cycles to carry out the interrupt process, and another 10 clock cycles to restore the system to its original condition.

To reduce this time penalty, the instruction set includes the WAI (Wait for Interrupt) instruction that we used earlier simply to halt processor action (see Figure 16.6). When the system arrives at the point where an interrupt must be

Software Interrupt (SWI)

Description: The program counter is incremented (by 1). The program counter, index register, and accumulator A and B, are pushed into the stack. The condition codes register is then pushed into the stack, with condition codes H, I, N, Z, V, C going respectively into bit positions 5 thru 0, and the top two bits (in bit positions 7 and 6) are set (to the 1 state). The stack pointer is decremented (by 1) after each byte of data is stored in the stack.

The interrupt mask bit is then set. The program counter is then loaded with the address stored in the software interrupt pointer at memory locations (n-5) and (n-4), where n is the address corresponding to a high state on all lines of the address bus.

Addressing Modes	Execution Time (No. of cycles)	Number of bytes of machine code	Coding of First (or only) byte of machine code		
			HEX.	OCT.	DEC.
INHERENT	12	1	3F	077	063

Courtesy of Motorola, Inc.

Figure 16.5 The Software Interrupt (SWI) instruction.

processed, it executes the WAI instruction, and gets a head start on the interrupt process by performing the time-consuming process of storing the vital registers onto the stack. The processor then waits in an internal loop until an interrupt is sensed on the $\overline{IRQ}$ or $\overline{NMI}$ input lines. During the wait, the address, R/$\overline{W}$, and data buses are floated, VMA goes low, and BA goes high to indicate that the bus is available for DMA activity. When an $\overline{IRQ}$ or $\overline{NMI}$ is initiated within the WAI state, the processor skips the stack push operations and proceeds to memory to load the interrupt vector into the program counter.

The Interrupt Vector Map

The interrupt vector map of Figure 16.7 summarizes the 6800 interrupt structure. Including RESET (which is inter-

Wait for Interrupt (WAI)

Description: The program counter is incremented (by 1). The program counter, index register, and accumulators A and B, are pushed into the stack. The condition codes register is then pushed into the stack, with condition codes H, I, N, Z, V, C going respectively into bit positions 5 thru 0, and the top two bits (in bit positions 7 and 6) are set (to the 1 state). The stack pointer is decremented (by 1) after each byte of data is stored in the stack.

Execution of the program is then suspended until an interrupt from a peripheral device is signalled, by the interrupt request control input going to a low state.

When an interrupt is signalled on the interrupt request line, and provided the I bit is clear, execution proceeds as follows. The interrupt mask bit is set. The program counter is then loaded with the address stored in the internal interrupt pointer at memory locations (n-7) and (n-6), where n is the address corresponding to a high state on all lines of the address bus.

Addressing Modes	Execution Time (No. of cycles)	Number of bytes of machine code	Coding of First (or only) byte of machine code		
			HEX.	OCT.	DEC.
INHERENT	9	1	3E	076	062

Courtesy of Motorola, Inc.

Figure 16.6 The Wait for Interrupt (WAI) instruction.

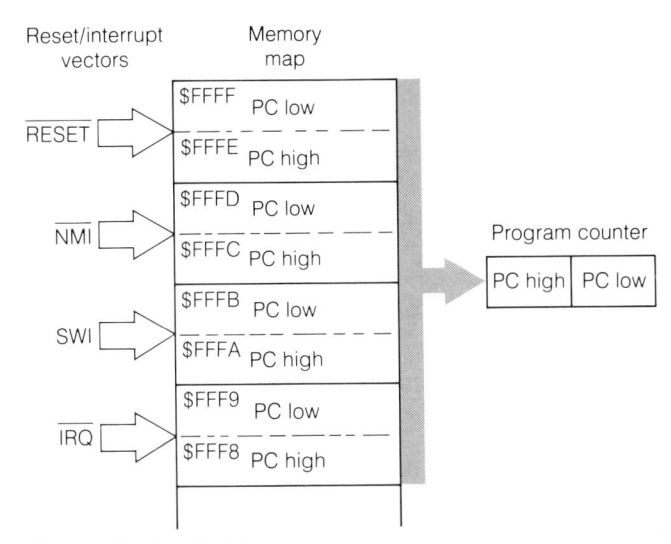

Figure 16.7 The 6800 interrupt and reset vectors.

ruptlike in its action), the 6800 processor includes four modes of interrupt. All are basically similar, causing an interrupt vector (starting location of corresponding service routine) to be pulled from memory at the locations shown and jammed into the program counter.

A SIMPLE INTERRUPT TEST PROGRAM

For a simple test of the vectored interrupt process, let's make the familiar mimic program an interrupt-service routine (ISR); each time an interrupt is requested, the contents of inport $2000 are transferred to outport $1000. The software design is given by Figure 16.8. When the program is executed, the following steps take place:

1. The stack pointer is set to RAM location $0070 by the LDS #$0070 instruction.
2. The IRQ interrupt input is enabled by the CLI instruction.
3. Using BRA, the processor loops to itself, awaiting an interrupt (we could have made use of WAI).
4. IRQ is pulled low and an interrupt is requested.
5. After completion of the present BRA instruction sequence, the processor stores the vital register/flag information on the stack, disables the interrupt system by setting the I flag (remember, the original I = 0 flag state is now safely stored in the stack), pulls the $0100 IRQ vector (placed into memory prior to execution) from locations $FFF8 and $FFF9, and jams it into the program counter.
6. Control is transferred to the ISR at location $0100 and the mimic process is performed.
7. The RTI instruction restores the system to its preinterrupt state (the interrupt system is reenabled when the I = 0 flag bit stored on the stack is returned to the CCR).

ADDITIONAL INTERRUPT CONSIDERATIONS

When peripherals are serviced by way of hardware interrupts, the I/O processes are entirely asynchronous and no longer under complete control of the processor. A number of considerations therefore arise when devices are interfaced by way of interrupts.

Priority and Multiple Interrupts

A telephone is only one type of interrupting device found in everyday life. In general, your home or office will have many such interrupting devices: a doorbell, an auto horn, the bark of a dog, or a fire alarm. In addition, these multiple inputs are often given priority according to importance. That is, if more than one interrupt is requested simultaneously, the one with the highest priority would be recognized (i.e., the fire alarm).

Considering the many peripheral devices available, it is more than likely that any computer system will also interface with many peripheral devices on a priority basis.

When multiple devices communicate with the CPU via interrupts, the basic purpose of the interrupt system is to jam into the program counter the starting service-routine address of the highest-priority device requesting service.

As illustrated by Figure 16.9, three general methods are available for making sure the right service-routine address gets placed into the program counter. These are the scanned, vectored, and daisy-chain techniques described below.

Scanned In the *scanned* interrupt system, the multiple external devices are ORed to a single interrupt line. When one or more devices request an interrupt, the computer must scan (poll) the devices to determine which one is requesting service. Priority is automatically provided by the order in which the devices are scanned. Any number of peripherals can be serviced using this technique. The circuit of Figure 16.9a shows one possible scanned configuration. When an interrupt is requested, the interrupt-service routine inports the status word. Using masking or rotate instructions, the highest-priority interrupting device can easily be determined and the proper service-routine address generated. The scanned technique is usually a *single-level* interrupt system, since only a single interrupt vector is in use.

Vectored A *vectored* interrupt system is one in which the highest-priority device requesting service causes a direct branch (vector) to the proper service routine. The microcomputer does not need to poll the devices to determine which one caused the interrupt. With each device tied to a separate interrupt line, the number of devices serviced is limited to the available vectored interrupt levels.

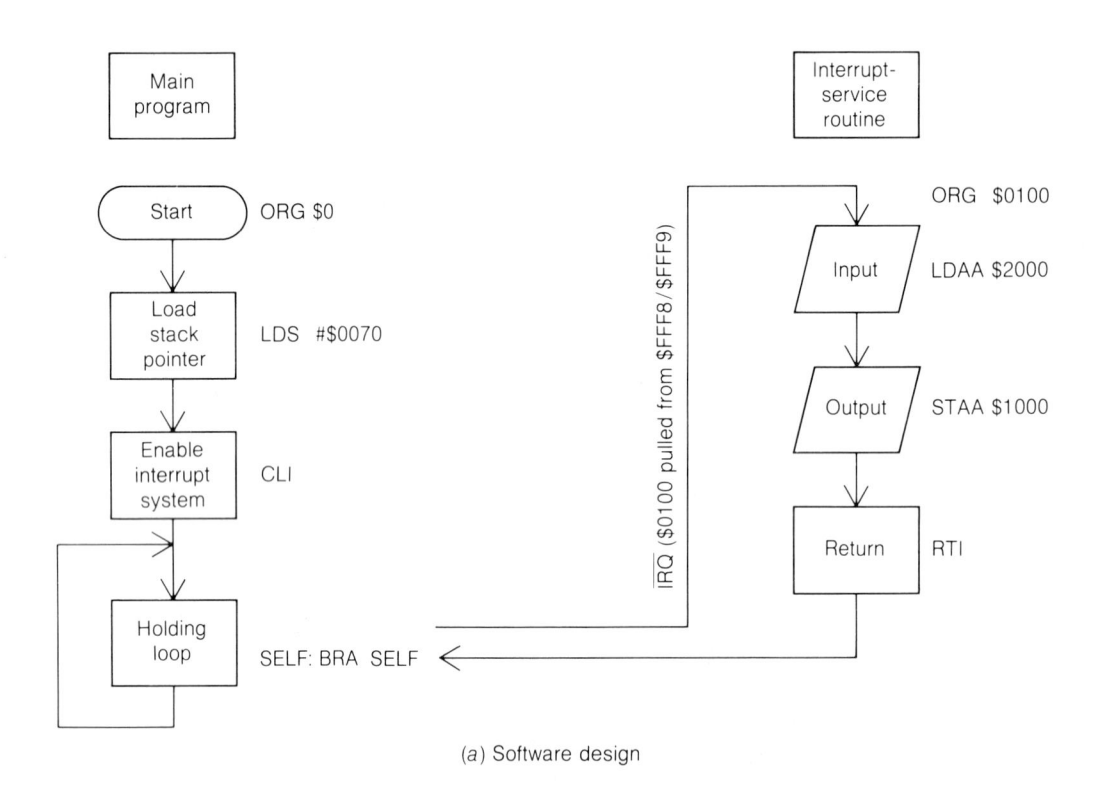

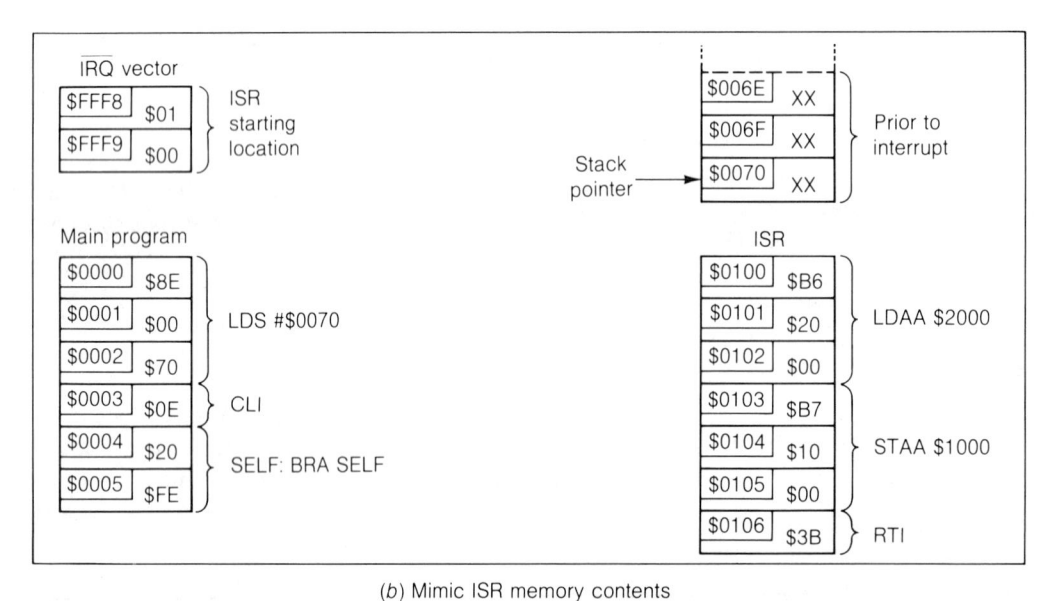

Figure 16.8 Interrupt test system using mimic interrupt-service routine (ISR).

(a) Software design

(b) Mimic ISR memory contents

The 6800 is inherently a vectored interrupt system, with its two interrupt request inports ($\overline{IRQ}$ and $\overline{NMI}$) fetching interrupt vectors directly from memory.

To increase the number of prioritized vectored interrupts from 2 to 9, we can include the additional hardware of Figure 16.10. Follow the sequence below and see how the additional interrupt vectors are generated:

1. One or more interrupt inputs to the 74148 priority encoder are pulled active low, causing the $\overline{IRQ}$ input to go active low.

2. The 6800 enters the $\overline{IRQ}$ interrupt sequence, first pushing the vital registers onto the stack.

3. $FFF8 appears on the address bus, the ROM is selected

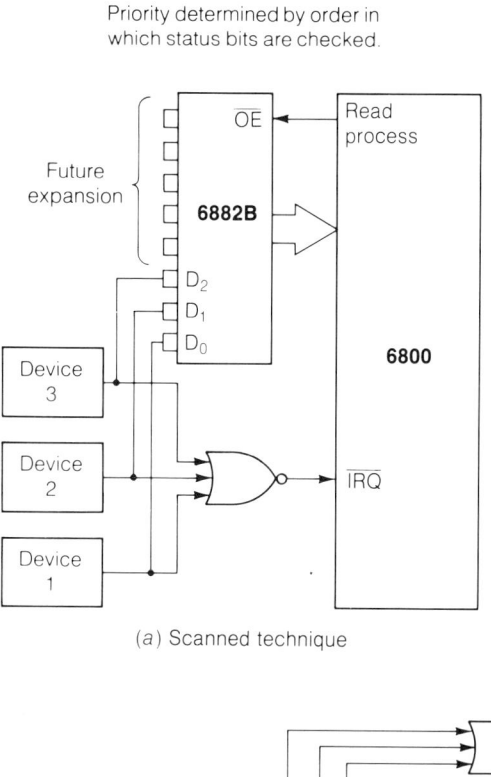

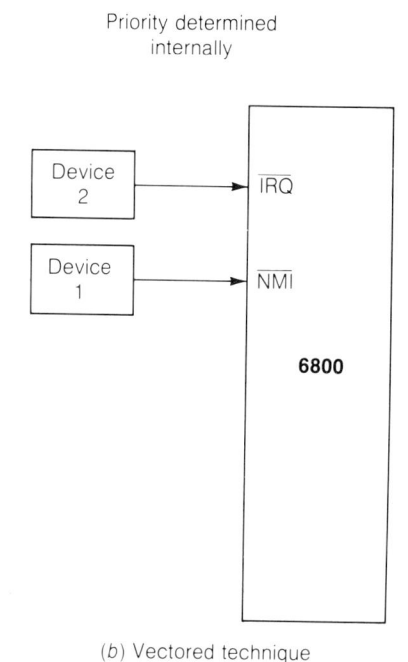

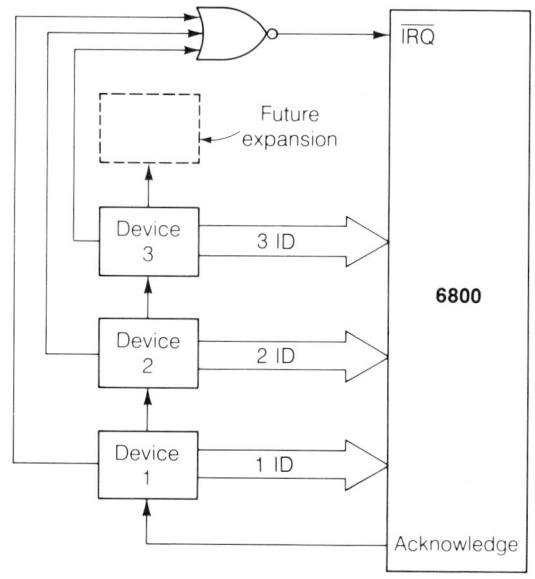

Figure 16.9 The three basic interrupt techniques for multiple-priority interrupt systems.

by the address decoder, and the high-order interrupt vector flows to the high-order program counter.

4. $FFF9 appears on the address bus and the priority encoder buffer is selected. The highest-priority low-order vector (determined by the 3-bit code injected by the 74148) is jammed into the program counter.

5. The processor vectors to the proper ISR and tends to the needs of the interrupting device. (To avoid crowding, a jump to the corresponding ISR would probably be placed at each vector location.)

Daisy chain In a single-level *daisy-chain* interrupt system, a device is identified through an acknowledge signal hardware propagated through the peripheral devices. The daisy-chain (or *serial-priority*) technique is intermediate in speed between the scanned and vectored interrupt methods.

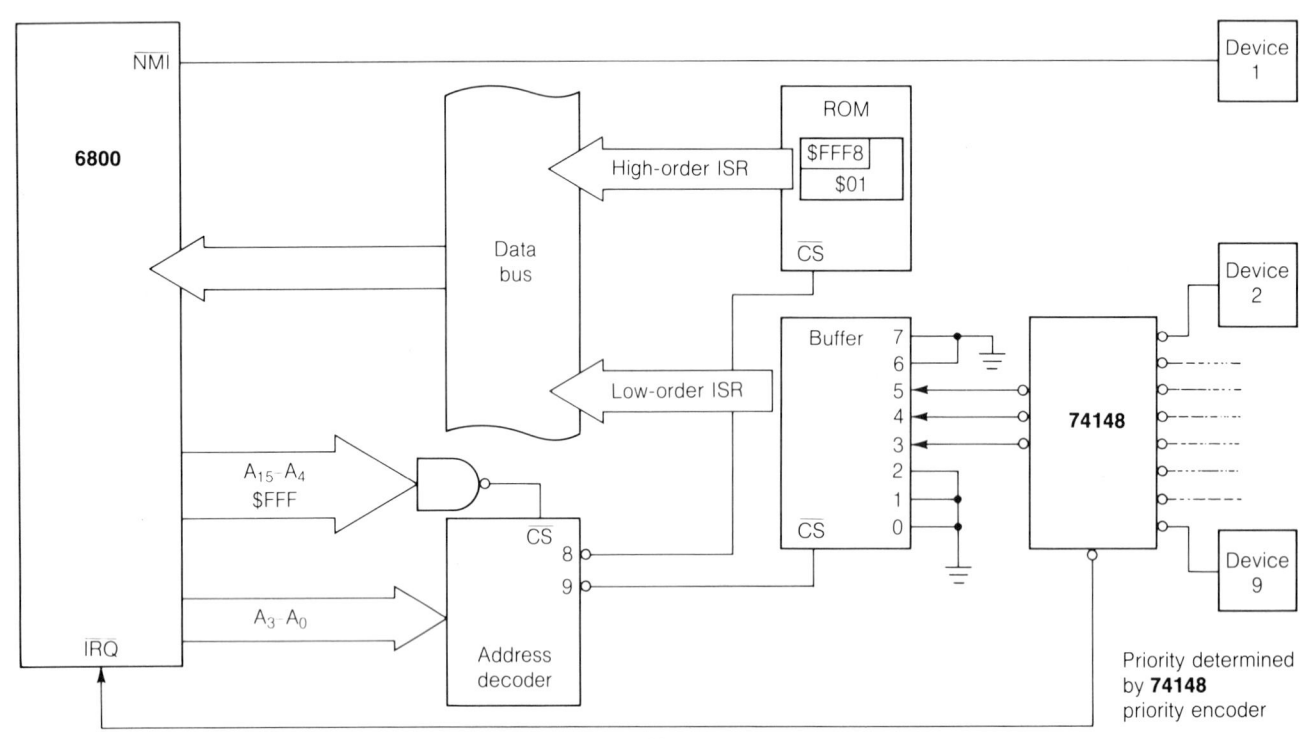

Figure 16.10 Using an 8-to-3 encoder to increase the number of vectored interrupts.

As illustrated in Figure 16.9c, an interrupt request by one or more peripherals will drive the processor into a service routine. This service routine generates an interrupt-acknowledge signal that is hardware propagated (and therefore at high speed) through the peripheral devices. When the first interrupting device is found, the propagating acknowledge signal is halted, and the device places its identification number (address) onto the data bus. This ID number is read by the microprocessor and is used to generate the address of the interrupt-service routine. Priority is automatically established by the order of the peripherals.

Nested Interrupts

When the processor is in one interrupt-service routine, can another interrupt pull the processor from this service routine into another, perhaps of higher priority? Generally, the answer is no. In fact, as we have seen, when any interrupt is recognized, the entire interrupt system is disabled (except, of course, for $\overline{NMI}$) just to prevent such an occurrence. Stack overflow is the problem. Each time the processor is pulled from an interrupt-service routine by another vectored interrupt (or the same vectored interrupt), 7 additional bytes are added to the stack. Eventually, if this were allowed to continue, the stack would overflow.

Nevertheless, interrupts can be nested if the proper debouncing and stack-overflow provisions are met. To nest interrupts we must place the enable-interrupt instruction near the beginning of each interrupt-service routine.

However, when using nested subroutines and interrupts, we should be alert to a possible danger. If, for example, we are within a multiply subroutine when interrupted, and the same multiply subroutine is "reentered" within the interrupt subroutine (the interrupt service routine called the same multiply subroutine), much of the original multiplication data stands to be destroyed. The solution is to use a *reentrant* multiply subroutine.

A subroutine is said to be reentrant if it can be interrupted at any time and called again within the interrupt-service routine without affecting the interrupted calculation. To make a subroutine reentrant, simply arrange to have all registers and memory locations holding vital data pushed onto the stack when an interrupt occurs. The interrupt-service routine can then safely reuse the multiply subroutine. After the interrupt service routine, the original partial results can be pulled from the stack and the original multiplication continued.

Masking Interrupts

When interrupts are nested, it is logical that only interrupts of higher priority be allowed to pull the processor from its present ISR. Figure 16.11 shows how the scanned circuit of Figure 16.9a is modified to include masking. A 3-bit mask (perhaps corresponding to the present ISR) is written to the

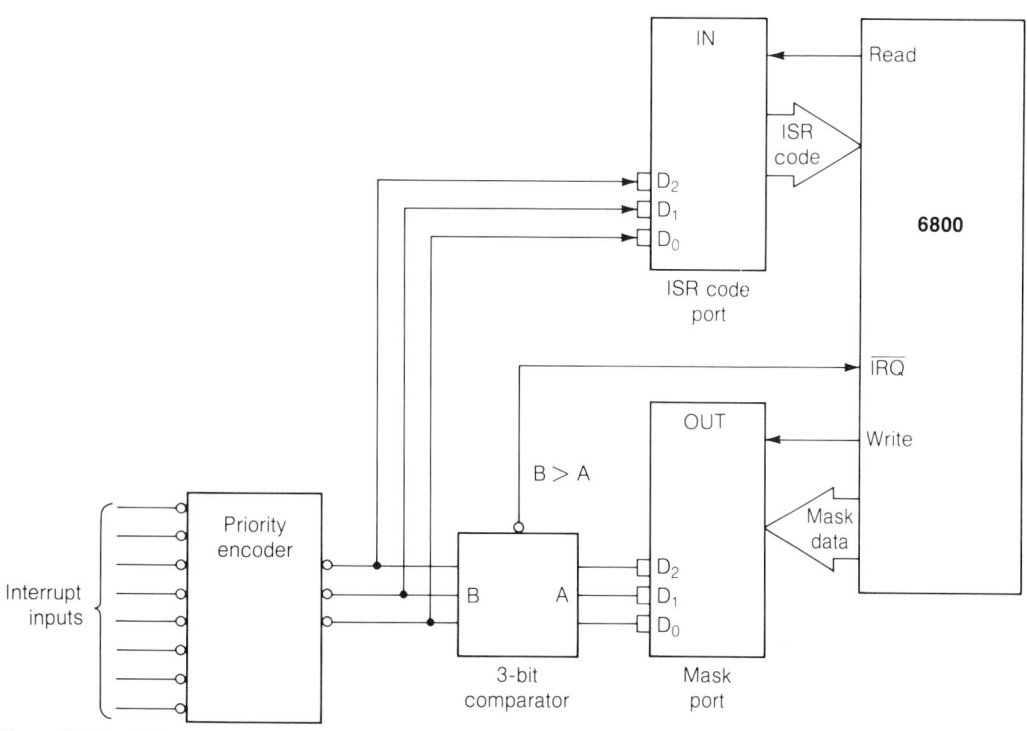

Figure 16.11 Adding priority encoding and masking to the basic scanned technique.

mask register (an output port). Only if the 3-bit code from the priority encoder is greater than the mask data will an interrupt be generated.

In Chapter 23, we will see how the 6828 *Priority Interrupt Controller* implements multiple/vectored/prioritized/maskable interrupts with far less hardware than any of the schemes presented in this chapter.

Debouncing

The 6800-based system of Figure 16.12 is designed to count up by one each time a pushbutton switch is activated. To work properly, we must CALL the interrupt-service routine once and only once for each pressing of the pushbutton switch.

Using this design, we run into trouble, for all mechanical switches bounce (they bounce when you make contact, and they bounce when you break contact). Because of switch bouncing, a single activation of the pushbutton switch will initiate multiple counts.

To solve the problem of mechanical switch bouncing, we have at our disposal both software and hardware techniques.

Hardware debouncing For level-activated interrupt inputs ($\overline{IRQ}$), the circuit of Figure 16.13a will solve the problem. The acknowledge signal, generated and outported by the

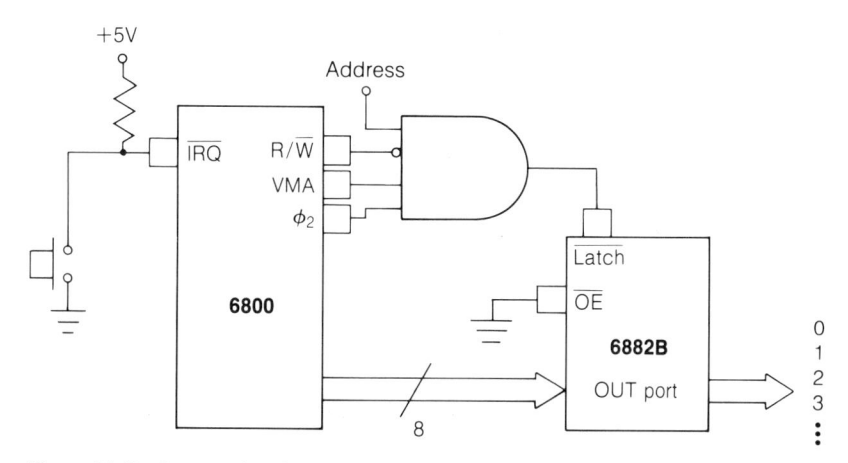

Figure 16.12 Interrupt-based count system.

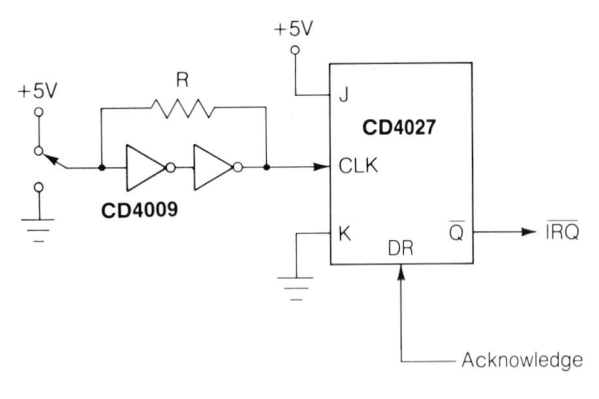

(a) Flip-flop debouncing

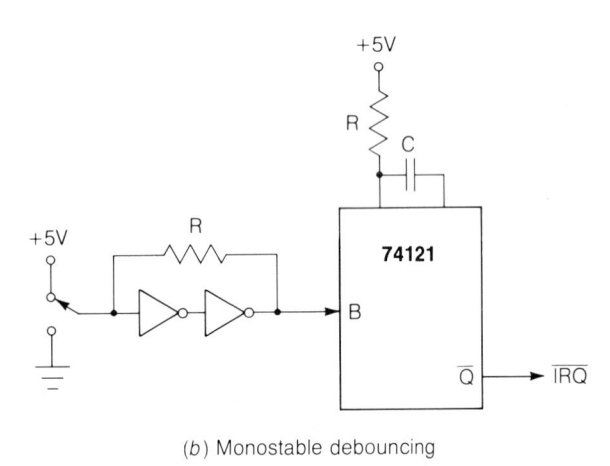

(b) Monostable debouncing

Figure 16.13 Hardware debouncing of level-active interrupt requests.

interrupt-service routine, will reset the flip-flop and make sure the interrupt request is inactive when action returns to the main program. The positive feedback inverter circuit will prevent multiple set commands to the flip-flop for each switch activation ("machine-gunning"). As an added feature, if the processor is currently involved in an interrupt-service routine, the interrupt request will be stored until action returns to the main program.

If an interrupt-acknowledge signal is not readily available, the one-shot of Figure 16-13b also will debounce the level-active lines. The monostable time must be long enough to assure that an interrupt will be requested (the worst case is when the request occurs at the beginning of a 9-clock-cycle instruction), yet short enough to assure that the interrupt input line will be high when action returns to the main program.

For edge-triggered interrupt inputs ($\overline{NMI}$), only the positive feedback portion of the debounce circuit (the inverters) would be required.

Software debouncing The simplest way to software debounce an interrupt line is to add a delay loop to the interrupt-service routine. After vectoring to the ISR, we simply wait for the switch to stop bouncing before returning. Other possibilities include inporting the $\overline{IRQ}$ input to check for level stability before entering or exiting the ISR.

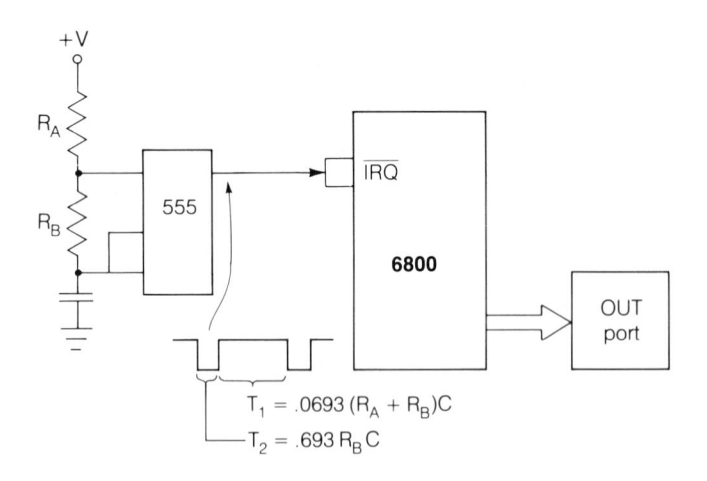

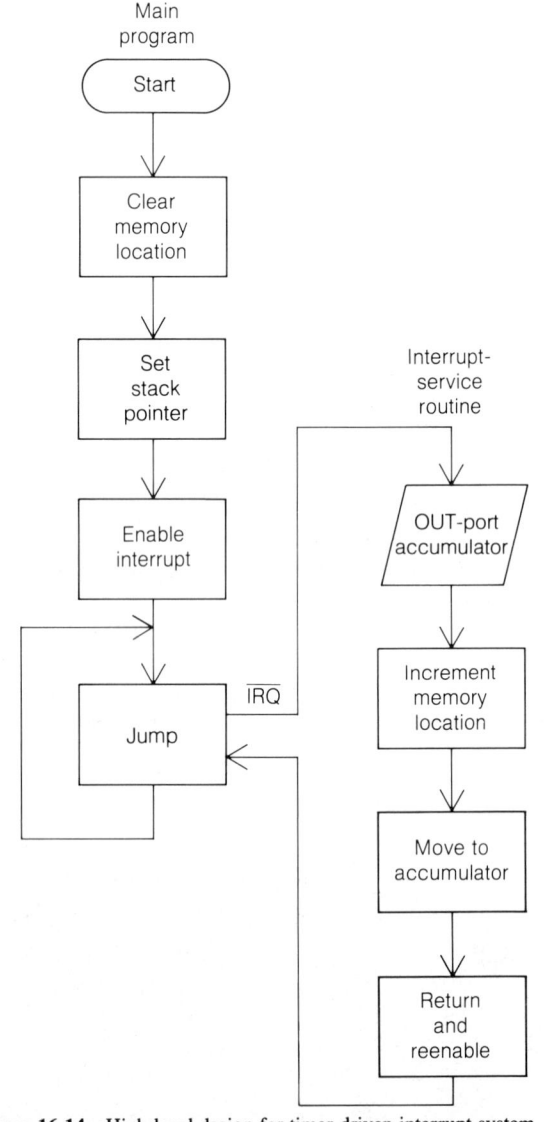

Figure 16.14 High-level design for timer-driven interrupt system.

For the 555 timer circuit:
$T_1 = .0693(R_A + R_B)C$
$T_2 = .693 R_B C$

```
                              6800/6801/6802 ASSEMBLER VER.3.3      1

     1                  ; This program defines the interrupt vector, and shows
     2                  ; how an interrupt service routine (ISR) is handled
     3                  ; just like a subroutine CALL (RTI replaces RTS)
     4                  ;
     5                  ; Interrupt Service Routine (ISR)
     6                  ;
     7  0100                    ORG     $0100   ; Starting address of ISR
     8  0100 7C 00 30           INC     $0030   ; Increment $0030
     9  0103 96 30              LDAA    $0030   ; Load contents of $0030
    10  0105 B7 10 00           STAA    $1000   ; Output incremented No.
    11  0108 3B                 RTI             ; Return from ISR
    12                  ;
    13                  ; Main program
    14                  ;
    15  0000                    ORG     $0      ; Starting address of main prog
    16  0000 7F 00 30           CLR     $0030   ; Clear $0030
    17  0003 8E 00 80           LDS     #$0080  ; Set stack pointer
    18  0006 0E                 CLI             ; Enable interrupt
    19  0007 20 FE 0007 SELF:   BRA     SELF    ; Loop and wait for inter
    20                  ;
    21                  ; Define the IRQ vector
    22                  ;
    23  FFF8                    ORG     $FFF8   ; Location of IRQ vector
    24  FFF8 01 00              DW      $0100   ; Define IRQ vector
    25  FFFA                    END

ERRORS = 0000


MEMORY  M 0000    SELF    0007    STACK   S 0000
```

Figure 16.15 Machine-assembled list file of interrupt demonstration program.

A 6800 INTERRUPT DESIGN EXAMPLE

The counter circuit of Figure 16.14 is designed to count from 0 to 255 at the rate of 1 Hz. It uses a timer-initiated interrupt and hardware debouncing. As a review exercise, follow through one complete cycle until all facets of interrupt processing included in the system are clear. The values of R_A and R_B of the 555 timer must be carefully chosen to produce a pulse that lies within the active-low "window." If the pulse is too narrow, the interrupt may not be accepted. If the pulse is too wide, more than one count may take place for each 555 cycle. (If the edge-sensitive $\overline{NMI}$ input were used, the pulse width would not be a factor.)

MACHINE-ASSEMBLY UPDATE

Our next machine-assembly update is primarily a reminder: an interrupt-service routine (ISR) is handled just like a subroutine. The only difference is that the interrupt vectors must be loaded into the proper memory locations ($FFF8 through $FFFF). To accomplish this we make use of the DW (Define Word) directive. (DW is also known as *FDB*.) The DW directive simply loads the directive's operand into the location specified by the ORG command. Suppose we choose an arbitrary location in page 0 for the $\overline{IRQ}$ vector; here is how the loading is done:

ORG $FFF8   ; $\overline{IRQ}$ vector location
DW $0100   ; $\overline{IRQ}$ vector

To demonstrate interrupt-based programs, Figure 16.15 shows how our timer-driven problem of Figure 16.14 is written and machine assembled. As directed, locations $FFF8 and $FFF9 are assigned the $\overline{IRQ}$ vector $0100.

HEATHKIT ET-3400A INTERRUPT PROCESSING

When we look at interrupt processing on the ET-3400A single-board microcomputer, we find two facts in apparent contradiction. First of all, as shown in Figure 16.7, all three interrupts vector to page $FF. But pages $FC through $FF are reserved for the monitor ROM (the program that runs the keyboard). How can we ever hope to get to our service routines, which must be placed in RAM at page 0 or 1?

The answer is related to a well-known Olympic event— the *hop, step,* and *jump*. That is, we hop, step, jump to the interrupt-service routine. Using the $\overline{IRQ}$ interrupt as an example, and referring to Figure 16.16, here is how it works:

① *The hop*—When the $\overline{IRQ}$ vectored interrupt is initiated, we "hop" to locations $FFF8 and $FFF9.

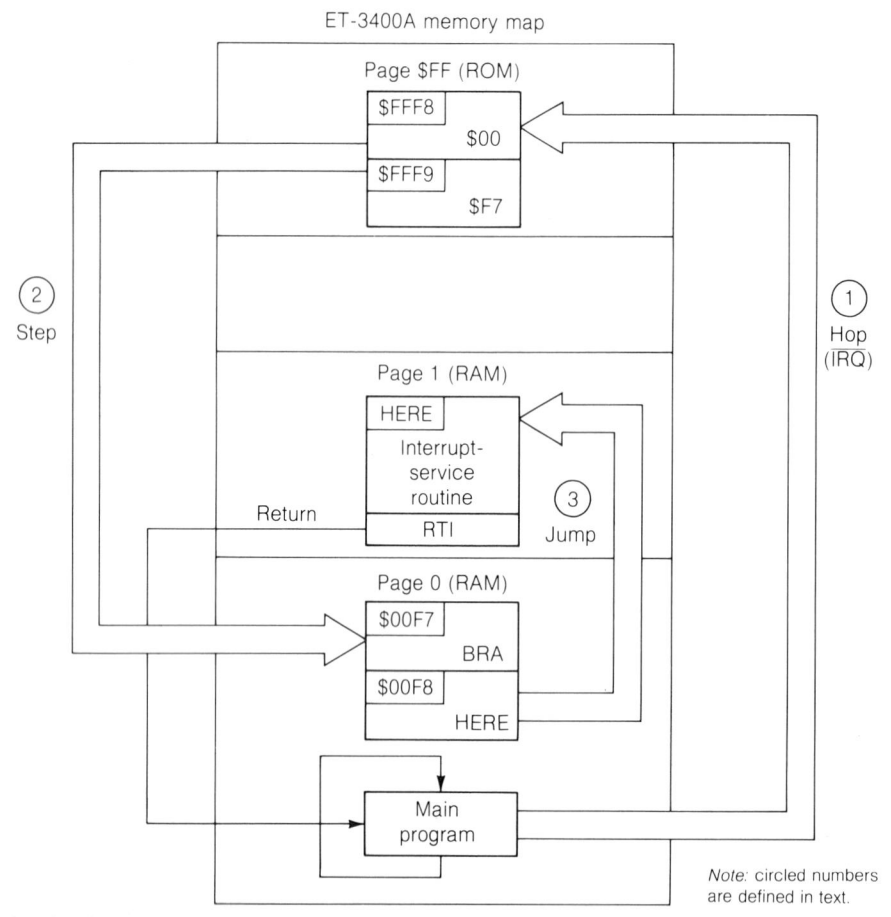

Figure 16.16 "Hop, step, jump" interrupt processing on the ET-3400A.

② *The step*—At that location in the monitor ROM, we find the interrupt vector $00F7 telling us to "step" to word location $F7 in page 0. (The $00F7 vector to page 0 was burned into the monitor ROM at the factory.)

③ *The jump*—At reserved location $00F7 in RAM, we find a "jump" instruction (placed there by the programmer prior to execution) to finally carry us to the interrupt-service routine. (The final jump is required because the interrupt vectors for $\overline{IRQ}$, $\overline{NMI}$, and SWI are too close together to make room for all the interrupt-handling routines.)

INTELLIGENT-MACHINE UPDATE

Now able to react to the unexpected, our intelligent machine has fully matured. Its anatomy (hardware) and vocabulary (software) have fully developed, and it seems to possess all the tools required to enter the real world. Still, to this purely digital machine, the outside world is an alien and unfamiliar environment. Before our machine can leave the "nest," it must learn to interact with the world about it.

QUESTIONS AND PROBLEMS

1. On a 6800-based computer, how is an *interrupt* initiated?
2. What is a *vectored* interrupt, and why is it especially fast?
3. What is special about the $\overline{NMI}$ interrupt?
4. Which of the following conditions is especially suited for interrupts: (a) 10 tasks, each of which requires equal processing time, or (b) 10 tasks, two of which occur infrequently and irregularly? Why?
5. If an $\overline{IRQ}$-initiated interrupt-service routine begins at location $A076, what should be placed in locations $FFF8 and $FFF9?
6. Using a single interrupt input, how can 10 interrupting devices be serviced?
7. Can interrupts be nested? Why is the CLI instruction required when nesting interrupts?
8. Referring to Figure 16.10, draw a memory map showing all nine vector storage locations.
9. Explain one hardware-debouncing technique and one software-debouncing technique.

10. Why is the daisy-chain method of multiple-interrupt processing faster than the scanned technique, but generally slower than the vectored technique?
11. Under what conditions might you disable the interrupt system?
12. For the scanned circuit of Figure 16.9a, how would you determine which peripheral requested service?
13. By adding a latching output port and AND gate inputs to Figure 16.9a, design into the scanned interrupt technique the ability to individually mask out the interrupt inputs.
14. How is the interrupt system affected when the 6800 is RESET?
15. By what automatic process does the 6800 make sure the interrupt system is not enabled until the processing action returns to the main program (unless nesting is desired)?
16. With reference to Figure 16.8, what are the stack contents and what is the position of the stack pointer when the processor is within the ISR?
17. Compare the similarities and differences of the four interrupt modes of Figure 16.7.
18. Why is it logical that a multiple-prioritized interrupt system also include masking?
19. Why is it unnecessary to debounce the $\overline{IRQ}$ input for the ISR of Figure 16.8?
20. Assuming the $\overline{IRQ}$ input for the program of Figure 16.8 is not debounced, modify the ISR so the number of "bounces" for each switch activation can be determined.

part IV

Applications and Interfacing: Living in a Real World

The final stage of human development, based on the imaginative prose of the futurists, is pure thought—a formless world of light and energy, completely self-contained and isolated from its surroundings.

The human species, of course, has not yet reached this final stage of development, and neither have the computers we create. In other words, we do not build computers so they may merely contemplate their existence. Indeed, our actions are as basic as they can be: we build computers to be slaves!

Consequently, a computer must interact and communicate with its environment, and it must perform useful tasks—all at our command. This we will teach our computer to do in Part IV of this book.

chapter 17

Mathematical Refinement

A digital computer helped guide the Apollo 11 spacecraft to the moon. If our intelligent machine, in its present state of development, attempted to repeat the flight of Apollo 11, the mission would be quickly aborted, and for a number of good reasons.

How can our intelligent machine undertake trips of 240,000 miles when it can handle numbers no larger than 255? Even more basic, how does it determine distance at all when it cannot multiply velocity times time? Even descending to the surface of the moon is presently out of the question, for the acceleration is negative when landing, and our computer cannot efficiently process negative numbers. In other words, it cannot tell up from down. And, finally, what do the passengers do when the landing altimeter flashes 1CFA? We are used to readouts in the decimal number system, so we could not quickly determine the descent distance to the surface of the moon.

Before our intelligent machine can guide us to the moon, we must solve these and other arithmetic problems—the subject of this chapter.

MULTIPLE-PRECISION NUMBERS

Using the decimal number system, we require only six digits to specify the distance to the moon. Convert that same number to binary, however, and an incredible 18 digits are required:

$$\text{Decimal} \qquad \text{Binary}$$
$$240{,}000_{10} = \underbrace{00000011}_{\text{Zeros added to complete byte}}\ 10101001\ 10000000_2$$

Such numbers are known as *triple-precision numbers* because 3 bytes of data are required to describe them. *Double-precision* numbers require 2 bytes of data; numbers of 2 or more bytes are generalized as *multiple-precision* numbers.

Triple-precision numbers are easy enough to store—just use three memory locations. The real question is: Can they be operated on by the instructions of the arithmetic group? That is, can we add and subtract triple-precision numbers? The real problem lies in the generation of carries and borrows from one byte to the next. This really turns out to be no problem at all, for the arithmetic group already includes a set of special add and subtract instructions specifically designed to handle carries and borrows (Figure 17.1).

To see how these instructions process multiple-precision numbers, we will set up a simple exercise. We have traveled 54,000 miles into space, and our on-board computer indicates we have another 186,000 miles to go to reach the moon. We will instruct our computer to add the two numbers together and see if they total 240,000. First, all numbers must be converted to hexadecimal or binary. Hexadecimal is usually chosen because it is more convenient.

Decimal	Hexadecimal
186,000	02 D6 90
+ 54,000	+ D2 F0
240,000	03 A9 80

In preparation for the addition, all numbers are stored in memory. The exact memory locations chosen are not important, for the index pointer can quickly be "aimed" anywhere in memory.

The addition begins as if we were doing it on paper, with the least significant bytes added first using the simple ADD (Add Without Carry) instruction. Since a carry is generated from the answer, the simple ADD instruction cannot be used to calculate the total of the middle bytes (it would ignore the carry).

The Add with Carry (ADC) instruction (Figure 17.1a), however, does include the carry and will give us the right answer. Of course, the final addition of the most significant bytes must also use the ADC instruction to account for a possible carry from the middle bytes. Figure 17.2 summarizes the triple-precision addition operation. (Multiple-precision subtraction is left as an exercise.)

MULTIPLICATION

How can the Apollo 11 spacecraft determine its distance from the earth? In the emptiness of space there is no way to

Add with Carry (ADC)

Operation: ACCX ← (ACCX) + (M) + (C)

Description: Adds the contents of the C bit to the sum of the contents of ACCX and M, and places the result in ACCX.

Addressing Modes	Execution Time (No. of cycles)	Number of bytes of machine code	Coding of First (or only) byte of machine code		
			HEX.	OCT.	DEC.
A IMM	2	2	89	211	137
A DIR	3	2	99	231	153
A EXT	4	3	B9	271	185
A IND	5	2	A9	251	169
B IMM	2	2	C9	311	201
B DIR	3	2	D9	331	217
B EXT	4	3	F9	371	249
B IND	5	2	E9	351	233

Courtesy of Motorola, Inc.

(*a*)

Subtract with Carry (SBC)

Operation: ACCX ← (ACCX) − (M) − (C)

Description: Subtracts the contents of M and C from the contents of ACCX and places the result in ACCX.

Addressing Modes	Execution Time (No. of cycles)	Number of bytes of machine code	Coding of First (or only) byte of machine code		
			HEX.	OCT.	DEC.
A IMM	2	2	82	202	130
A DIR	3	2	92	222	146
A EXT	4	3	B2	262	178
A IND	5	2	A2	242	162
B IMM	2	2	C2	302	194
B DIR	3	2	D2	322	210
B EXT	4	3	F2	362	242
B IND	5	2	E2	342	226

Courtesy of Motorola, Inc.

(*b*)

Figure 17.1 Multiple-precision add and subtract instructions—ADC and SBC.

directly measure distance traveled or velocity attained. The only motion that can be sensed directly is acceleration. But acceleration is really enough—providing you have the ability to multiply, for velocity is equal to acceleration times time, and distance in turn is equal to velocity times time. After the two multiplication processes, you have the distance. (Actually, since acceleration and velocity would in general be variables, a double *integration* would be required. However, it is not necessary to introduce such a complication here. The concept of integration will be discussed in Chapter 24.)

Unfortunately, the instruction set of the 6800 does not contain a multiply instruction, but it does not have to, for multiplication really is successive addition—and addition is something our computer can do very well. The multiplication process involves a *test/shift/add* algorithm. The simple 6 times 5 binary multiplication problem of Figure 17.3 will reveal the steps involved.

The process is initialized by clearing the *cumulative total register* (a name assigned to any register or memory location). First we test the lowest multiplier position. Since it is 1, we add the multiplicand to the cumulative total register to form our first partial product (110). Then we rotate the multiplicand left to prepare for the next cycle.

The process is repeated for the next highest multiplier-bit position. Since this position is 0, we delete the addition step. The multiplicand is again rotated left one position and the final multiplier bit tested. The 1 tells the program to add the twice-rotated multiplicand to the cumulative total register to form the final product (11110). With all multiplier-bit positions tested, the contents of the cumulative total register are reported as the answer. For numbers as large as the

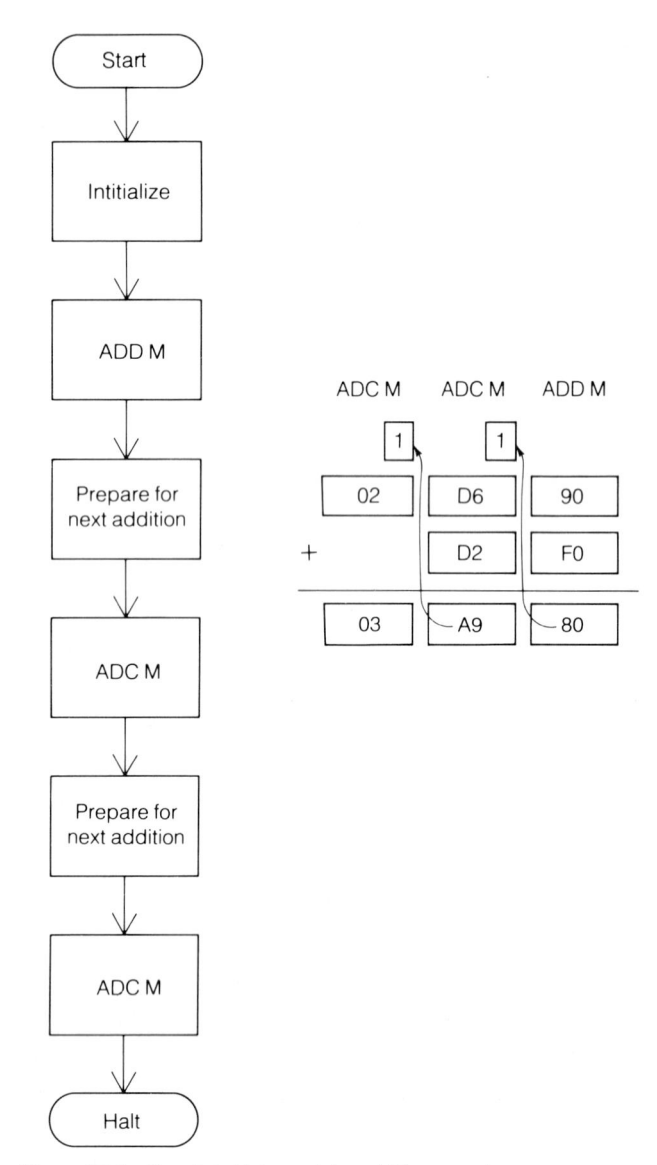

Figure 17.2 Complete triple-precision addition operation.

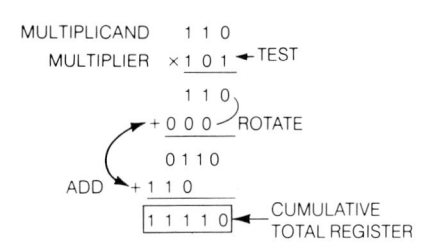

Figure 17.3 Binary multiplication routine.

distance to the moon, the successive additions and rotations would be triple precision.

Using arbitrary memory locations to hold the multiplier, multiplicand, and number of multiplier bits, Figure 17.4 shows the assembly-language program and flowchart for the multiplication process.

For multiplications involving 8-bit numbers and 16-bit results, it is more convenient to rotate the partial products right, rather than the multiplicand left. The technique is left as an exercise.

DIVISION

Binary division is basically the reverse of the multiplication process. As with multiplication, division proceeds along the same lines as it does on paper. A high-level flowchart and example problem are presented in Figure 17.5.

Since most later-generation microprocessors (e.g., the 6809 and 68000) include multiply and divide instructions in their instruction set, and since they can be coupled with powerful LSI math processor chips, the need to write basic mathematical algorithms is rapidly disappearing.

PROCESSING NEGATIVE NUMBERS

In Chapter 11 we introduced signed numbers in order to perform the subtraction operation. In Chapters 13 and 14 signed numbers were required to specify the *relative* addresses used in the branch instructions. However, these actions are a long way from the full-scale signed-number processing capability offered by the 6800. For one thing we have yet to use the Negative (N) and Overflow (V) flags, and the eight *signed-number* conditional branch instructions that we skipped in earlier chapters:

- BMI (Branch if Minus) $N = 1$
- BPL (Branch if Plus) $N = 0$
- BVC (Branch if Overflow Clear) $V = 0$
- BVS (Branch if Overflow Set) $V = 1$
- BLT (Branch if Less than Zero) $N \oplus V = 1$
- BGE (Branch if Greater than or Equal to Zero) $N \oplus V = 0$
- BLE (Branch if Less than or Equal to Zero) $Z + (N \oplus V) = 1$
- BGT (Branch if Greater than Zero) $Z + (N \oplus V) = 0$

The N and V Flags

First, let's see how the N and V flags are affected by signed-number processing.

The N (Negative) flag is the essence of simplicity. If the result of an arithmetic or logical operation produces a negative result, the N flag is set; if the result is positive, the N flag is reset. In other words, the N flag corresponds to the state of bit R7. ("R," remember, stands for "Result of Operation.")

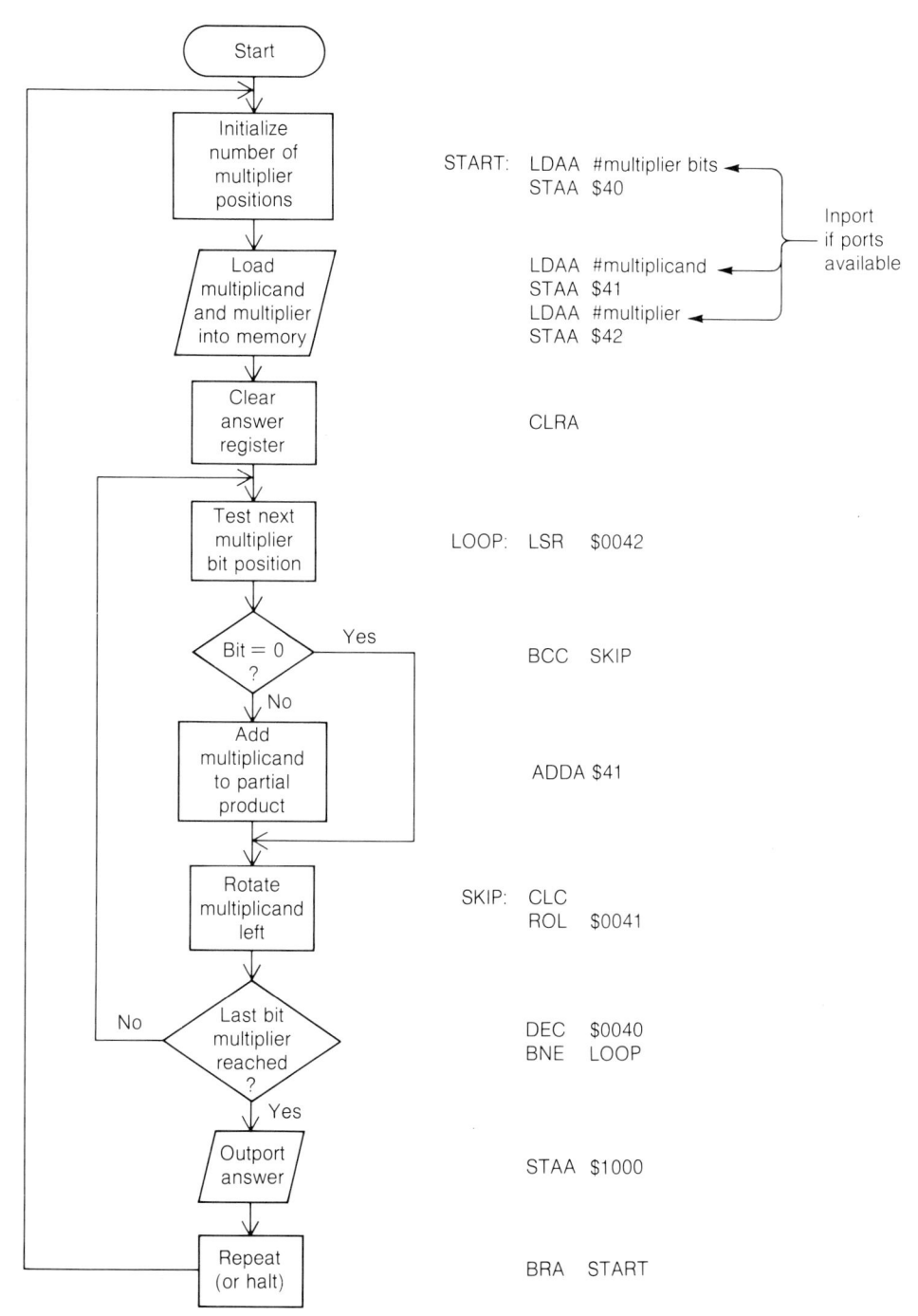

```
                                    START:  LDAA  #multiplier bits
                                            STAA  $40

                                            LDAA  #multiplicand
                                            STAA  $41
                                            LDAA  #multiplier
                                            STAA  $42

                                            CLRA

                                    LOOP:   LSR   $0042

                                            BCC   SKIP

                                            ADDA  $41

                                    SKIP:   CLC
                                            ROL   $0041

                                            DEC   $0040
                                            BNE   LOOP

                                            STAA  $1000

                                            BRA   START
```

Figure 17.4 Binary multiplication flowchart and program.

The V flag (also known as *2's complement overflow indicator*) responds to results that exceed the +127 to −128 8-bit signed-number range (i.e., the sign bit is affected). If the result is within the range, the V flag is reset; if outside the range (overflow or underflow), it is set.

The two problems of Figure 17.6 review the signed-number flag-setting process for the four flags (N, C, V, and Z) that are tested by the conditional branch instructions.

The Signed-Number Conditional Branch Instructions

Let's briefly review each of the four pairs of signed-number conditional branch instructions. To make the process clear, let's be application oriented.

BMI (Branch if Minus) and BPL (Branch if Plus) If the decision (Which fork in the road should I take?) is based on

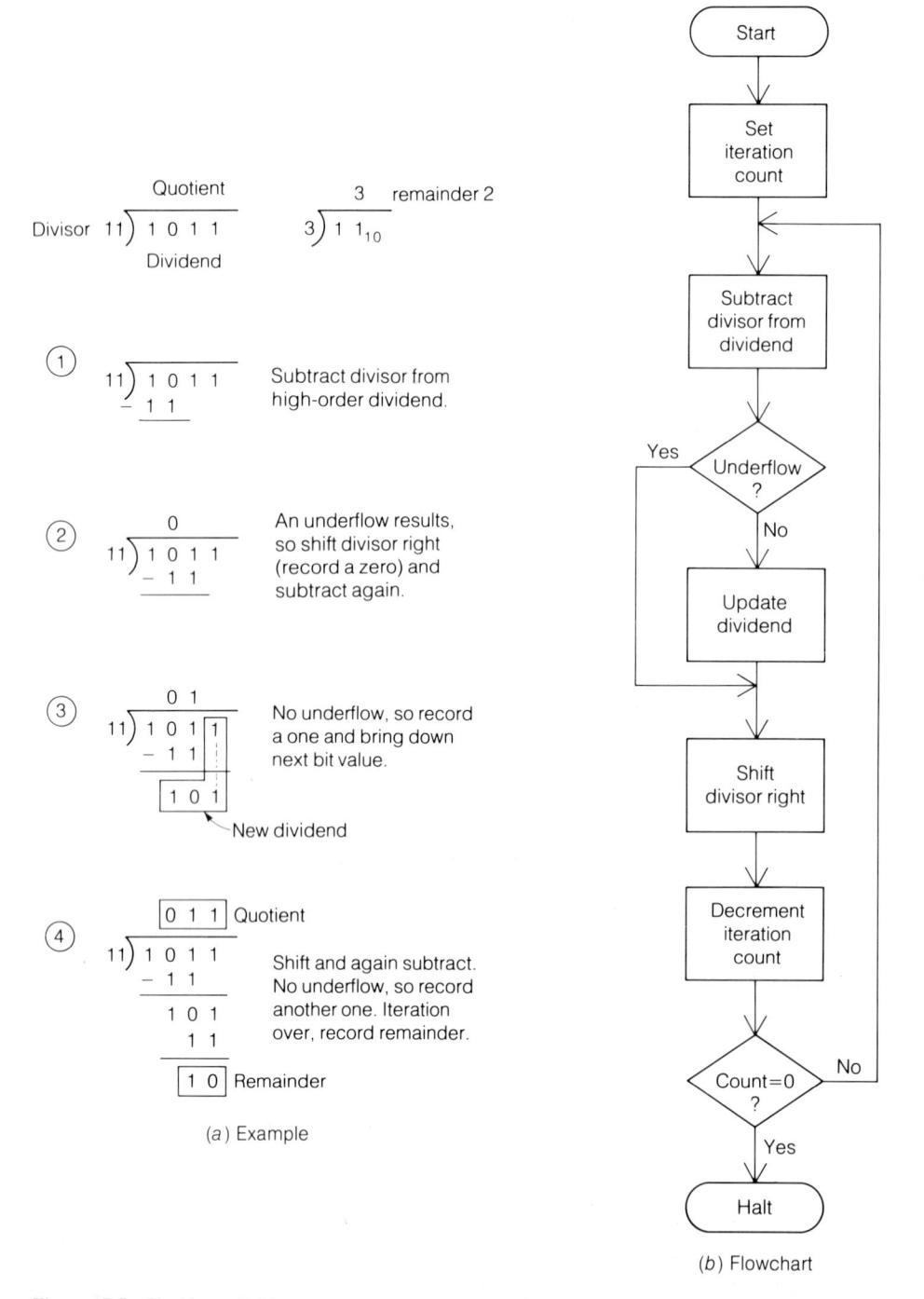

Figure 17.5 The binary division process.

(a) Example

(b) Flowchart

a straightforward plus or minus result, then the branch block of our two-step decision-making process will be either the BMI or BPL conditional branch instruction. The "Mimic only negative numbers" program of Figure 17.7 is a simple case in point.

BVC (Branch if Overflow Clear) and BVS (Branch if Overflow Set) If the results of an arithmetic operation overflow the 8-bit +127 to −128 range, an error will result. This error can be detected by sampling the V flag. Figure 17.8 shows a possible application. In this example, each inported number is added to accumulator A. However, before the addition is finalized, it is tested. If no overflow is detected, the addition is allowed; if the result would overflow, it is inhibited.

The CLV (Clear Overflow) and SEV (Set Overflow)

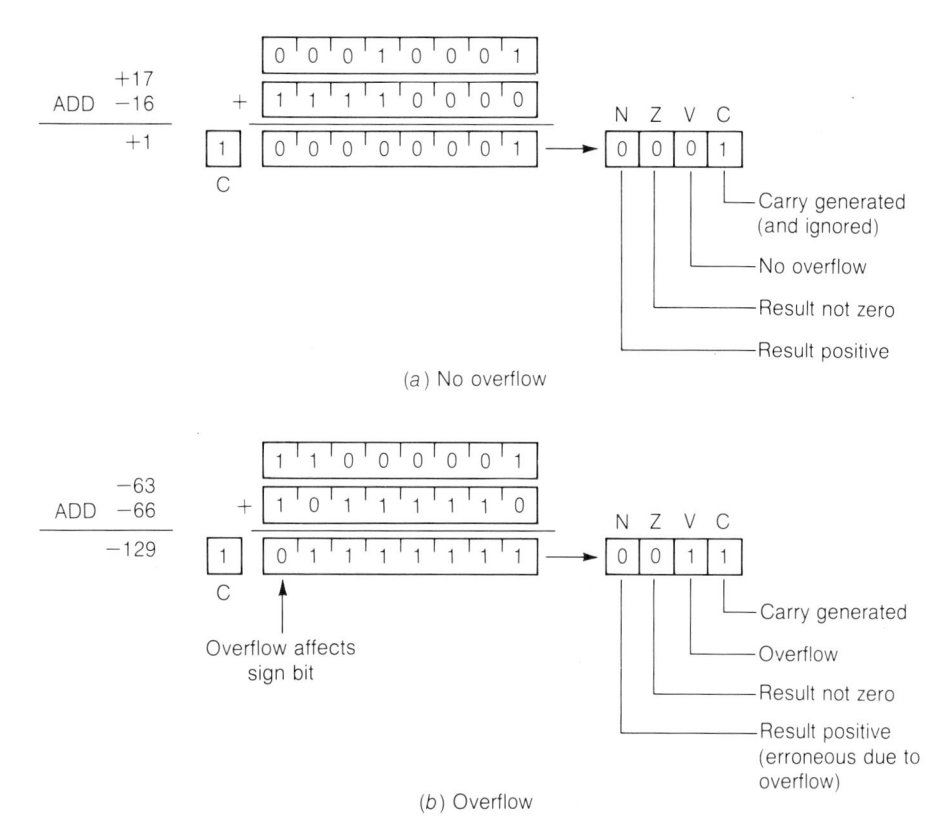

Figure 17.6 Signed-number flag-setting examples.

instructions provide the programmer with direct control of the V flag.

BLT (Branch if Less than Zero) and BGE (Branch if Greater than or Equal to Zero) The BLT and BGE signed-number conditional branch instructions normally follow a compare or subtract flag-setting instruction. That is, decisions are based on the size relationship between two numbers. To see how it works, let's select at random the BGE instruction.

In most cases it boils down to this: When BGE follows a COMPARE, *branch if the signed number in the accumulator is greater than or equal to the signed number in memory.* (See the BGE instruction description in Appendix I.)

For our application example, the mimic program of Figure 17.9 "mimics" all numbers greater than or equal to −10 ($F6 in 2's complement).

BLE (Branch if Less than or Equal to Zero) and BGT (Branch if Greater than Zero) Again, assuming that COMPARE or SUBTRACT sets the flags, the branching conditions reduce to:

- BLE (Branch if *the signed number in the accumulator is less than or equal to the signed number in memory.*)

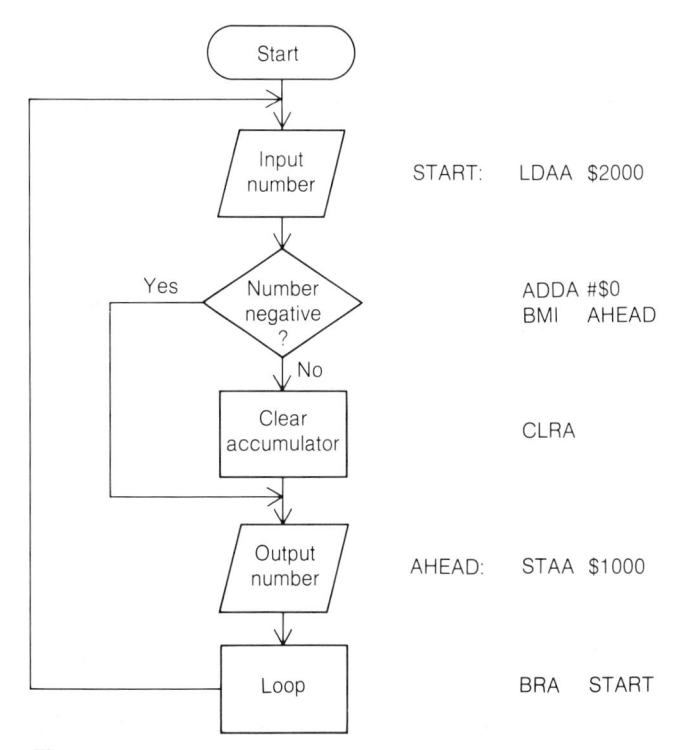

```
START:   LDAA  $2000

         ADDA  #$0
         BMI   AHEAD

         CLRA

AHEAD:   STAA  $1000

         BRA   START
```

Figure 17.7 "Mimic only negative numbers" application example of BMI instruction.

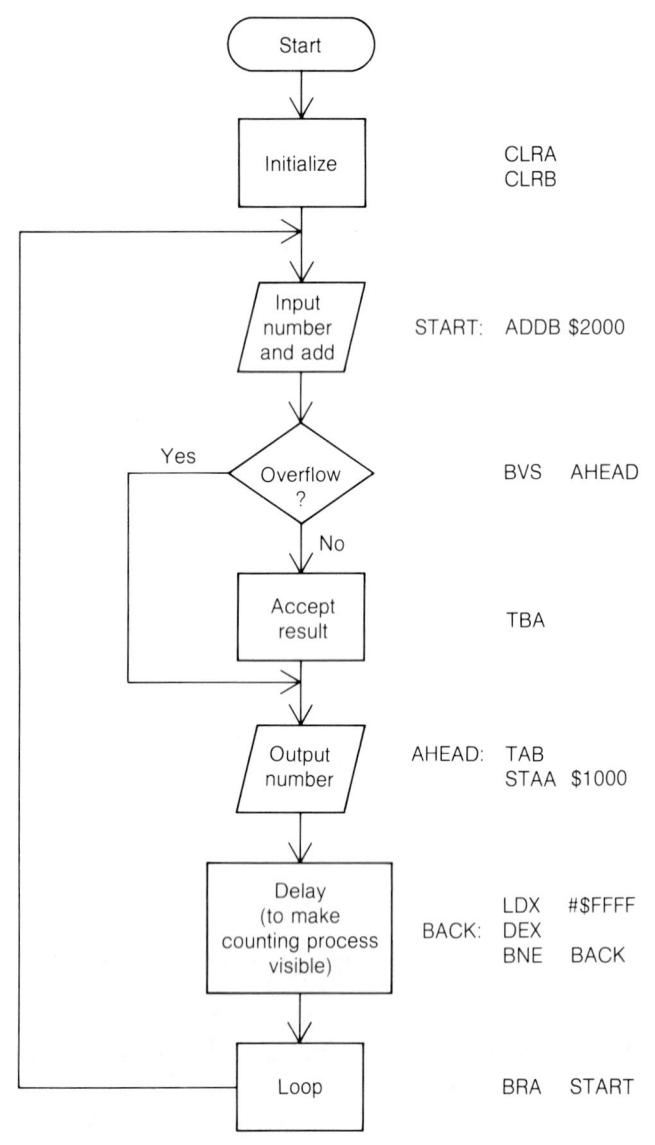

```
                                                        Start
      Start                                               │
        │                                                 ▼
        ▼                                              ┌────────┐
   ┌─────────┐        CLRA                             │ Input  │       START:   LDAA   $2000
   │Initialize│       CLRB                             │number  │
   └─────────┘                                         └────────┘
        │                                                 │
        ▼                                    Yes      ╱─────────╲                CMPA   #$F6
   ┌─────────┐                              ◄────────◄  Number   ◄               BGE    AHEAD
   │ Input   │       START:  ADDB  $2000              ╲ ≥ −10?  ╱
   │number   │                                          ╲   *  ╱
   │and add  │                                           ╲─────╱
   └─────────┘                                             │ No
        │                                                  ▼
   Yes  ╱───────╲                                      ┌────────┐
  ◄────◄Overflow ◄   BVS   AHEAD                       │ Blank  │         CLRA
       ╲   ?   ╱                                       │  out   │
        ╲─────╱                                        └────────┘
          │ No                                             │
          ▼                                                ▼
     ┌─────────┐      TBA                             ┌────────┐
     │ Accept  │                                      │ Output │        AHEAD:  STAA   $1000
     │ result  │                                      │number  │
     └─────────┘                                      └────────┘
          │                                                │
          ▼                                                ▼
     ┌─────────┐      AHEAD:  TAB                     ┌────────┐
     │ Output  │              STAA  $1000             │  Loop  │         BRA    START
     │ number  │                                      └────────┘
     └─────────┘
          │                                    *−9 is greater than −10.
          ▼
     ┌─────────┐                            **Figure 17.9**  "Mimic greater than or equal to −10" application example
     │ Delay   │      LDX    #$FFFF                    of BGE instruction.
     │(to make │ BACK: DEX
     │counting │      BNE    BACK
     │process  │
     │visible) │
     └─────────┘
          │
          ▼
     ┌─────────┐      BRA   START
     │  Loop   │
     └─────────┘
```

Figure 17.8 "Inhibit addition if overflow" application example of BVS instruction.

- BGT (Branch if *the signed number in the accumulator is greater than the signed number in memory.*)

Application examples are left as an exercise.

Boolean Formulations

Recall from Chapter 14 that to select the correct signed-number conditional branch instruction solely on the basis of its Boolean formulation was a difficult task indeed. Nevertheless, the process proved to be an interesting exercise in Boolean logic, so let's do it one more time.

Selecting at random the BLT (Branch if Less than Zero) instruction, here is the logic behind the Boolean formulation (Branch if N $\oplus$ V = 1):

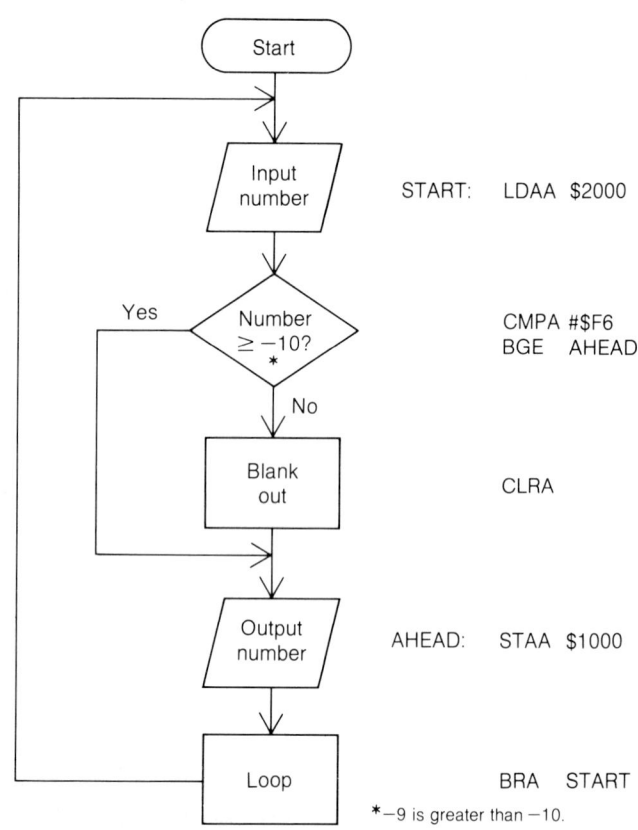

If a larger number is subtracted from (compared to) a smaller number, then *the answer is less than zero*. If the answer is less than zero, it is negative and the N flag will be set. However, this is only true if no overflow occurs. Therefore, one condition for branching is:

$$\text{Branch if (N)} = 1 \quad \text{and} \quad (V) = 0$$

However, if the resulting negative number lies outside the −128 bounds (i.e. −100 minus +100 = −200), then the V flag will be set and the overflow will toggle the R7 bit to a zero. Therefore, another condition for branching is:

$$\text{Branch if (N)} = 0 \quad \text{and} \quad (V) = 1$$

Both of these conditions can be condensed into the single Boolean condition:

$$\text{Branch if (N)} \oplus (V) = 1$$

BCD ADDITION

The next mathematical refinement, strangely enough, is due to an accident of nature, when our distant ancestors evolved 10 fingers and relegated us to the decimal number system.

Decimal Adjust ACCA (DAA)

Operation: Adds hexadecimal numbers 00, 06, 60, or 66 to ACCA, and may also set the carry bit, as indicated in the following table:

State of C-bit before DAA (Col. 1)	Upper Half-byte (bits 4-7) (Col. 2)	Initial Half-carry H-bit (Col.3)	Lower to ACCA (bits 0-3) (Col. 4)	Number Added after by DAA (Col. 5)	State of C-bit after DAA (Col. 6)
0	0-9	0	0-9	00	0
0	0-8	0	A-F	06	0
0	0-9	1	0-3	06	0
0	A-F	0	0-9	60	1
0	9-F	0	A-F	66	1
0	A-F	1	0-3	66	1
1	0-2	0	0-9	60	1
1	0-2	0	A-F	66	1
1	0-3	1	0-3	66	1

Courtesy of Motorola, Inc.

```
           59  (BCD)
      ADD  78  (BCD)
           D1
         + 66      ← DAA
          ───
          137 (BCD)
```

Figure 17.10 The Decimal Adjust ACCA instruction that adjusts binary addition answers back to BCD.

In a sense, however, computers were "born" with 2 fingers, for they prefer the binary number system. As we all know, computer and human being got together, compromised, and developed *binary coded decimal* (BCD).

The storage of BCD numbers is no problem—but the addition is. If we attempt to add in the normal manner, using any of the ADD instructions, we will not arrive at the correct answer.

The solution is to *adjust* the incorrect result back to BCD by using the Decimal Adjust ACCA (DAA) instruction. Carefully following the example of Figure 17.10, the DAA process involves adding +6 to both the high-order and low-order nibbles of the result of the addition process. After the DAA process, the number is back in BCD form.

Remember, the DAA instruction does not convert binary numbers to BCD numbers; it adjusts the result of adding two numbers already in BCD format. Furthermore, the DAA instruction is designed to adjust the result of an ADD operation only. Just remember, when working with BCD numbers, to follow every ADD instruction with the DAA instruction. (Advanced processors include a number of additional BCD instructions.)

FRACTIONS

Weighted number systems (decimal, binary, hexadecimal) handle fractions through a very old and clever invention—the decimal point. Numbers greater than 1 are to the left of the decimal point, and numbers less than 1 are to the right. In binary, each position to the left is weighted by increasing powers of 2, and each position to the right is weighted by negative increasing powers of 2.

$$\leftarrow 2^3\ 2^2\ 2^1\ 2^0 \bullet 2^{-1}\ 2^{-2}\ 2^{-3}\ 2^{-4} \rightarrow$$

(Decimal point ↓)

The following examples demonstrate that signed numbers with fractions are added and subtracted using the same procedures as whole numbers. (Generally, we are free to place the decimal point between any two bit positions.)

Example 1:

```
                    Sign
                    bits
        - 5.25    1 1010.110
   ADD  + 7.50    0 0111.100
        + 2.25    0 0010.010
```

Example 2:

```
        - 4.875
   SUB  + 6.250
        ───────
        - 11.125
```

```
                    Sign
                    bits
        - 4.875    1 1011.001
   ADD  - 6.250    1 1001.110
        ───────    ─────────
        - 11.125   1 0100.111
```

FLOATING-POINT NUMBERS

Computers are useful in areas ranging from microbiology to astronomy. Consequently, number magnitudes vary from very large to very small, and even multiple-precision techniques are impractical. To handle numbers that vary widely in magnitude, computers have adopted the *floating point*, a technique related to scientific notation.

The floating-point format of Figure 17.11a—an ANSI (American National Standards Institute) FORTRAN standard—is typical of those used throughout the computer industry. The 32-bit format is divided into two parts: a fraction (often called the *mantissa*) and an exponent. The fraction requires 25 bits and is in sign-magnitude form. The exponent uses the remaining 7 bits and is in (excess 64) 2's complement form.

Starting from bit 0 (see Figure 17.11a), the format is as follows:

1. Bit 0 is the sign bit for the fraction. A "1" is negative; a "0" is positive.
2. Bits 1 through 7 specify the exponent in 2's complement. However, the sign bit is inverted (excess 64 notation). A "1" indicates a positive exponent, a "0" a negative exponent. *The exponent is a power of 16.*
3. Bits 8 through 31 specify the magnitude of the fraction. The decimal point is assumed to be to the left of the most significant bit.

The ANSI FORTRAN floating-point format handles numbers from $.1 \times 16^{-64}$ to $.FFFF \times 16^{+64}$ (approximately 10^{-79} to 10^{+76}). The examples of Figure 17.11b should make the coding process clear.

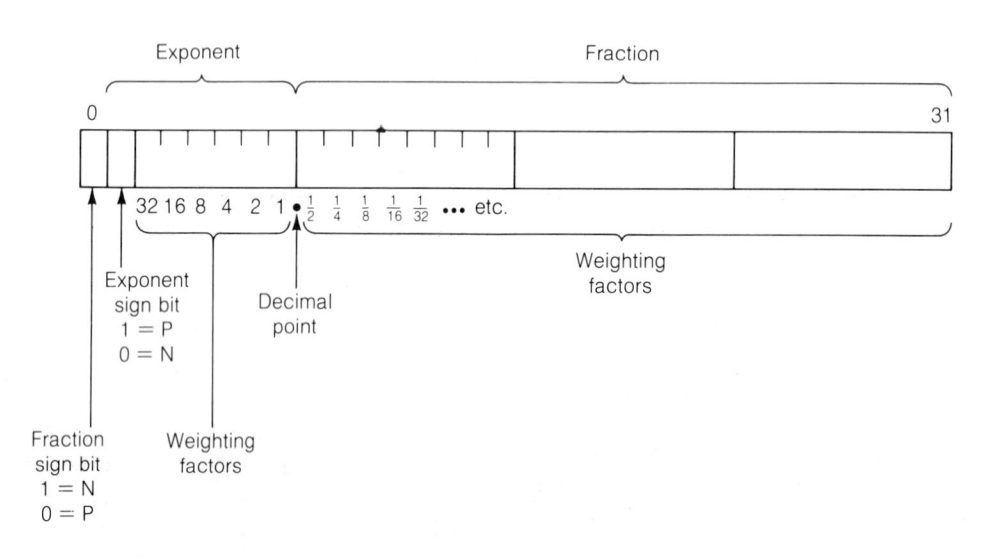

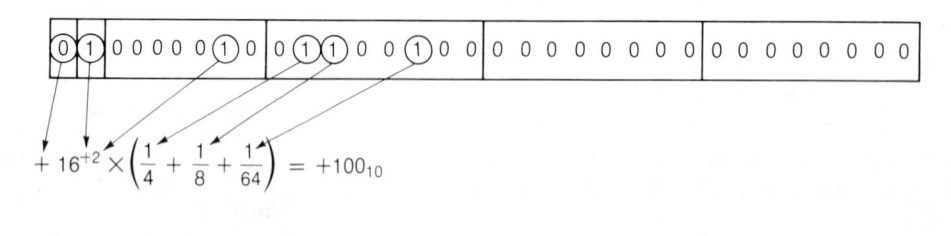

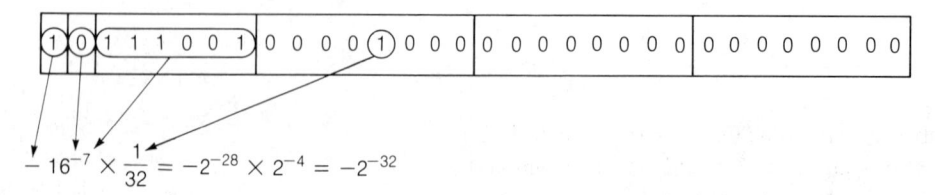

$$+ 16^{+2} \times \left(\frac{1}{4} + \frac{1}{8} + \frac{1}{64}\right) = +100_{10}$$

$$- 16^{-7} \times \frac{1}{32} = -2^{-28} \times 2^{-4} = -2^{-32}$$

(b) Examples

Figure 17.11 The ANSI FORTRAN floating-point standard.

Although multiplication and division of floating-point numbers are simplified by the property of adding and subtracting exponents, addition and subtraction are quite involved.

LSI MATHEMATICAL PROCESSORS

Many real-time process-control and signal-processing operations require number crunching beyond the capability of even the fastest microprocessors. However, specialized LSI arithmetic-processing chips, designed from the ground up to handle fixed or floating-point mathematical operations, are giving microcomputers a second chance at complex control and signal-processing applications.

In addition to basic addition, subtraction, multiplication, and division, these chips perform many complex operations such as square roots and logarithmic and trigonometric operations.

Compared to microcomputers, the processing speed is quite remarkable and can easily represent a hundredfold improvement in throughput. Sixteen-bit fixed-point addition can be polished off in a mere 8 µs (2 MHz clock), and a 16 × 16-bit multiplication can be performed in as little as 100 ns. Using GaAs technology, an 8 × 8-bit multiplication has been performed in an incredible 5 ns!

A typical programmable math chip may have 30 to 40 arithmetic instructions. The host CPU will write an instruction into the device, followed by the data. The math chip, a microprocessor in its own right, carries out the command by performing a sequential operation directed by a microprogram within its built-in ROM. When the operation is over, an "end of execution" pulse signals the CPU to read out the answer.

DATA STRUCTURES

A data structure is simply a way of classifying data. Technically speaking, simple integers (1, 2, etc.) and real numbers (+1.25, −7.9, etc.) are data structures. However, the term usually is reserved for *organized collections of data*. By grouping or associating a number of data elements together, we may form the following data structures:

- *Table*—a collection of data in which each item is uniquely identified by a label or by its relative position to other items
- *List*—an ordered set of items
- *Array*—a collection of data in multidimensional matrix form
- *Vector*—an ordered set containing a fixed number of items, all of the same type
- *Tree*—data arranged in a pyramid structure, such as a family tree

Because data structures are so common, the computer programmer must be able to handle them efficiently. Searching, sorting, and table lookup are three examples of typical mathematical operations performed on various data structures.

Searching

Suppose a series of consecutive memory locations are storing the batting averages of a major-league baseball team:

Address	Average
0100	234
0101	167
0102	253
0103	200
0104	247
0105	207

We may wish to search this table for the value of the highest batting average. Using two decision-making blocks, the flowchart of Figure 17.12 shows how it is done. The first value (234) is moved to an accumulator and compared with the second value (167). Since the first value is larger than the second, it remains in the accumulator. Next we compare the accumulator value with the next number in line (253). Since the next number is greater than the accumulator value, it replaces the accumulator value. The process continues through all six numbers, and the largest number found is outported.

Sorting

Suppose we wish to arrange (sort) the batting averages of the preceding section in ascending order from lowest to highest.

| Before-sort process || After-sort process ||
Address	Average	Address	Average
$0100	234	$0100	167
$0101	167	$0101	200
$0102	253	$0102	207
$0103	200	$0103	234
$0104	247	$0104	247
$0105	207	$0105	253

A familiar sorting technique is called *bubble sort*, because the smaller values tend to "bubble up" toward one end of the list. The process requires a number of passes through the list of numbers. During each pass, each two adjacent numbers are compared, and if they are out of order they are interchanged. After the first pass, the largest value is at the

Table Lookup

Suppose we wish to design a temperature transducer around the inexpensive thermistor (resistance is a function of temperature). The problem is that the thermistor is not a linear device but obeys the curve of Figure 17.13a. If the thermistor controls the current into a simple inverting amplifier (current to voltage transducer of Figure 17.13b), the resulting inverted scaled voltage (to be sent to the analog-to-digital or A/D converter) also obeys this nonlinear curve. How are we going to convert the voltage inputs to corresponding temperature values?

One method always is open to us: we can derive an equation relating temperature and resistance, and program the computer to solve the equation for each inported voltage. However, we have an alternative—to use the inported voltage as an address to "point to" a location in a sequence of memory locations (a table). If we are using a 16-level A/D system, the table would resemble that shown in Figure 17.13c. (The voltage input becomes the lowest-order nibble of the index register.)

Since no calculations are required, the table method is simpler to implement, but becomes unwieldy as the need for accuracy and the number of table entries increase (note the inaccuracy of the table at low temperatures).

STRINGS

More complex operations are required when the data are in the form of *strings,* or sequences of data bytes regarded as a single entity. For example, each name in a list of names is a string, since each letter in each name must be converted to ASCII and stored in an individual memory location. Searching for a specific name means searching for a given *sequence* of letters (a string).

As we will see in Chapters 23 and 25, many microprocessors (for example, Zilog Z80 and Motorola 68000) include instructions specifically designed to streamline the processing of data structures and strings.

MACHINE-ASSEMBLY UPDATE

Our next machine-assembly update brings us back to modular programming. In particular, we emphasize the desirability (indeed, necessity) of dividing up a large program into smaller "bite size" modules—*independent of each other.*

True independence means that each module should be separately assembled, debugged, and tested before they are combined into one main program. But how can we assemble a module when we don't know precisely at what absolute addresses it will be stored in memory? And how can we combine all these separately assembled object modules into one large program (we can't use MACROs, for they are

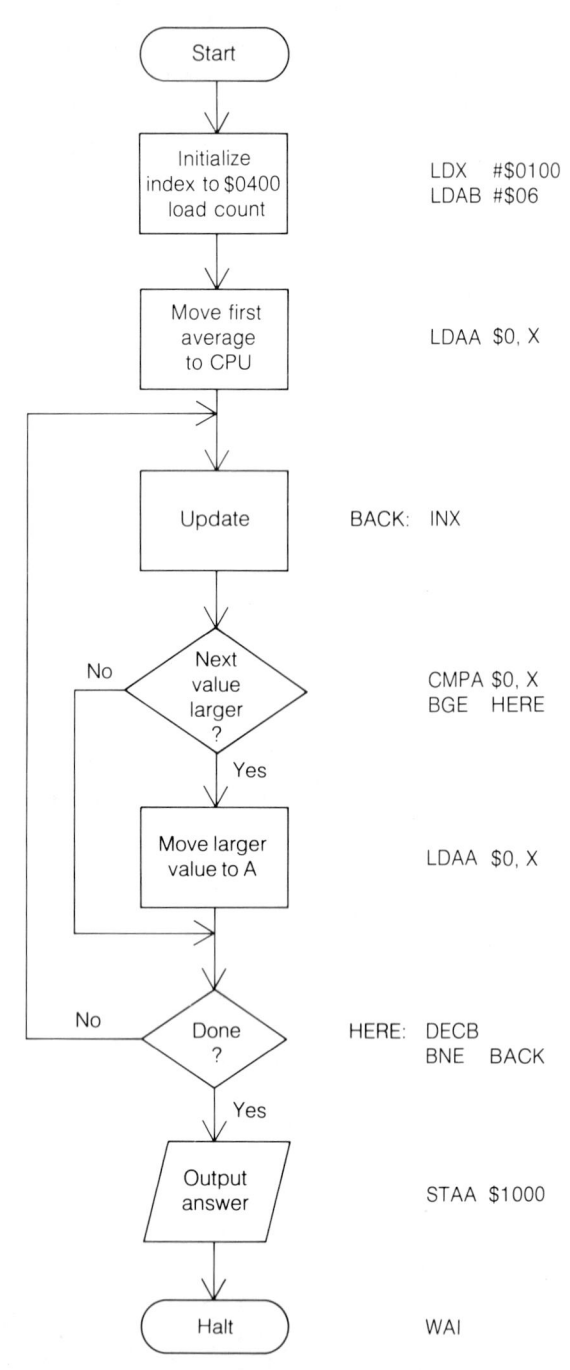

Figure 17.12 Searching a table for the largest value.

```
                    LDX   #$0100
                    LDAB  #$06

                    LDAA  $0, X

              BACK: INX

                    CMPA  $0, X
                    BGE   HERE

                    LDAA  $0, X

              HERE: DECB
                    BNE   BACK

                    STAA  $1000

                    WAI
```

end of the list. Each successive pass places the next largest value in the next position. After $n - 1$ passes (n = length of list), the numbers are sorted.

Translating the bubble sort algorithm to an assembly-language program is left as an exercise.

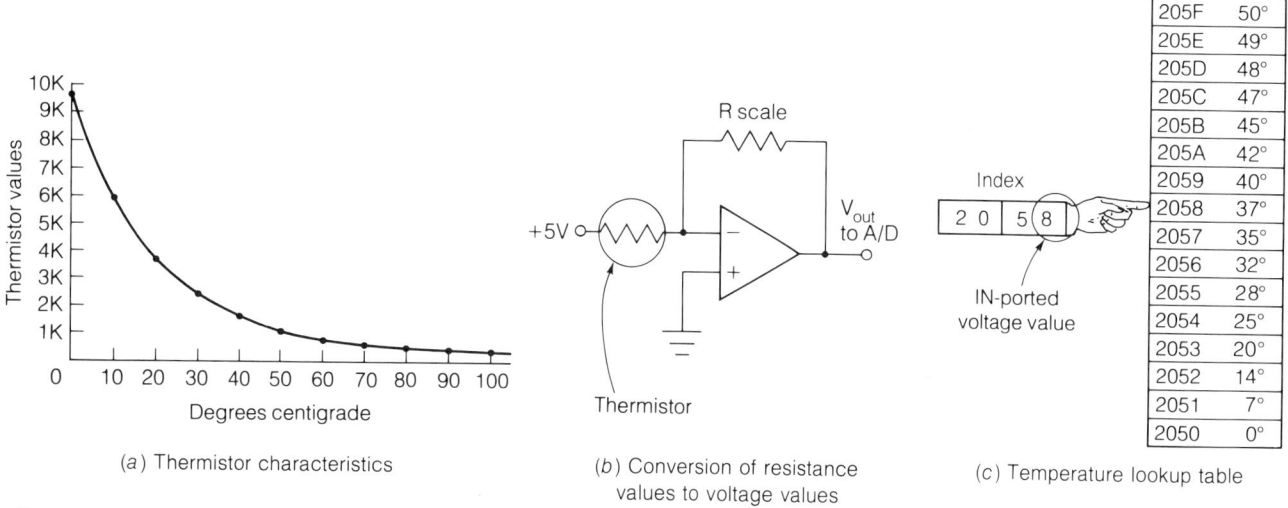

Figure 17.13 Performing a calculation by table lookup.

(a) Thermistor characteristics

(b) Conversion of resistance values to voltage values

(c) Temperature lookup table

eliminated *during* assembly)? The answer is, by using two new utility programs: LINK and LOCATE.

As usual, for clarity, let's direct the discussion toward a specific example. We have just been assigned the task of writing the "Mimic only 52 with Delay" (MIMDEL for short) program, which combines two routines we are already quite familiar with (the MIMIC routine and the DELAY routine).

Following good modular concepts, we break up the program into two blocks (modules)—one called MIMIC and the other called DELAY—and assign each to a separate programmer. The results of their activity (each is well aware of the LINK and LOCATE utilities) are shown in Figure 17.14. Note that each programmer has preceded the modules with the CSEG (Code SEGment) directive. The CSEG directive (also known as *PSCT*) is the key to modular programming, for it commands the assembler to generate *relocatable* code—code which is "floating" and not tied down to absolute memory locations. (As shown, the ORG directive is not given since each module is *temporarily* assumed to start at $0.)

The next step is to LINK together the two separately compiled (and presently independent) object modules into a single object module, just as if the entire program had been written and compiled as a single block. The LINK command is given as follows:

LINK B:MIMIC.OBJ, B:DELAY.OBJ
TO B:MIMDEL.LNK MAP

The linker will blend together MIMIC.OBJ and DELAY.OBJ, placing the MIMIC module first and the DELAY module second (the order in which they were listed), with the first instruction of DELAY.OBJ following the last instruction of MIMIC.OBJ. The optional attribute "MAP" directs the linker to generate the MIMDEL.MAP file of Figure 17.15*a*. MIMDEL.MAP lists both the linked input modules and the name and length of the output module.

The linker output file (B:MIMDEL.LNK) is still object code in relocatable format. To establish absolute addresses, we evoke the LOCATE command:

LOCATE B:MIMDEL.LNK CODE ($0020) MAP

We now have a single program module called MIMDEL (no extension), with $0020 as its starting location—and ready to run! The attribute MAP generates the memory map of Figure 17.15*b*, which shows that 18 bytes (decimal) of code were generated to run from locations $0020 to $0031. Since no stack or data locations were specified in the LOCATE directive, those shown are default values.

Breaking up a large programming task into smaller modules, writing and compiling relocatable code, testing each module independently, linking together the modules to form one main program, and locating the program at absolute addresses are elements of the general industrywide technique for generating large complex programs. In Chapter 22, we will renew the process using high-level languages.

INTELLIGENT-MACHINE UPDATE

Number crunching (processing numbers at high speed) is an area in which computers quickly surpassed their human creators. Even ENIAC, the world's first electronic computer, could process numbers far faster than human beings. When mathematical refinements are included, along with ultrafast processing speeds, the number-crunching ability of the computer is truly superhuman. Our intelligent machine makes good use of its high-speed mathematical abilities to compensate for the lack of the sophisticated analog- and parallel-processing abilities of the human mind.

```
                        6800/6801/6802 ASSEMBLER VER.3.3        1

   1                   ; Using the CSEG (or PSCT) directive to produce
   2                   ; MIMIC.LST in relocatable code
   3                   ;
   4                           CSEG
   5  0000 B6 20 00            LDAA    $2000
   6  0003 81 34               CMPA    #52
   7  0005 27 01 0008          BEQ     AHEAD
   8  0007 4F                  CLRA
   9  0008 B7 10 00    AHEAD:  STAA    $1000
  10  000B                     END

ERRORS = 0000

AHEAD   C 0008    MEMORY M 0000    STACK   S 0000
```

(a) MIMIC.LST

```
                        6800/6801/6802 ASSEMBLER VER.3.3        1

   1                   ; Using the CSEG (or PSCT) directive to produce
   2                   ; DELAY.LST in relocatable code
   3                   ;
   4                           CSEG
   5  0000 C6 A0               LDAB    #$A0
   6  0002 5A        BACK:     DECB
   7  0003 26 FD 0002          BNE     BACK
   8  0005 20 FE 0005 SELF:    BRA     SELF
   9  0007                     END

ERRORS = 0000

BACK   C 0002    MEMORY M 0000    SELF   C 0005    STACK   S 0000
```

(b) DELAY.LST

Figure 17.14 Relocatable list programs.

```
LINK MAP OF MODULE MIMDEL
WRITTEN TO FILE B:MIMDEL.LNK
                                    MEMORY MAP OF MODULE MIMDEL
SEGMENT INFORMATION:                READ FROM FILE B:MIMDEL.LNK
START   STOP  LENGTH REL NAME       WRITTEN TO FILE B:MIMDEL

              $12    B   CODE       START   STOP  LENGTH REL NAME

INPUT MODULES INCLUDED:             $0020  $0031    $12   B  CODE
   B:MIMIC.OBJ(MODULE)               $0032  $003D    $C   B  STACK
   B:DELAY.OBJ(MODULE)               $003E  $F6BF  $F6BF  B  MEMORY
```

(a) Module MIMDEL link map   (b) Module MIMDEL memory map
    (generated by LINK process)   (generated by LOCATE process)

Figure 17.15 Machine-assembler link and memory maps.

QUESTIONS AND PROBLEMS

1. In a 6800-based system, how large can an unsigned triple-precision number be?
2. What is the difference between the ADD instruction and the ADC instruction?
3. Write the assembly-language division program corresponding to the flowchart of Figure 17.5.
4. Using the Subtract with Borrow instructions, write a program to subtract 54,000 (base 10) from 186,000 (base 10). All numbers are in memory.
5. What range of values (positive to negative) can a double-precision signed number take on?
6. Based on the ANSI FORTRAN format of Figure 17.11a, convert the following numbers to floating-point standard: (a) 200, (b) -2^{-4}.
7. If BCD numbers 97 and 44 are added together, explain how the DAA instruction adjusts the answer back to BCD.
8. What are several advantages of table lookup over direct calculations? Disadvantages?
9. An arithmetic operation results in a number whose magnitude appears in 2's complement form. What is the state of the sign flag?
10. Rewrite the multiplication program of Figure 17.4 by rotating the partial products right rather than the multiplicand left.
11. Using a table, write a program that converts binary numbers 0000 ($0) to 1111 ($F) to BCD.
12. Explain how table lookup can be used to convert Celsius (centigrade) to Fahrenheit. The formula is:

$$F = 9/5C + 32$$

13. Write a modified MIMIC program which mimics only numbers greater than -10. (Figure 17.9 mimics only numbers greater than *or equal to* -10.)
14. When -103 is added to -64, why does the operation give an erroneous sign change?
15. What instruction will toggle (correct) the sign bit but leave the magnitude unchanged?
16. What flag states are generated by the compare instruction within the program of Figure 17.9 when the following numbers are inported: (a) -15, (b) -10, (c) -5, (d) 0, (e) $+5$. Which of these cases will result in a branch?
17. What is *relocatable* code?
18. Program modules can be "linked" before assembly by using MACROs, or after assembly by using the LINK command. What is the advantage of the second method?
19. What is a program *library*? (Research will be required.)
20. What is the difference between an integer and a real number?
21. Referring to the section in this chapter that describes the bubble sort technique, write an assembly-language program that sorts the six batting averages from lowest to highest.

chapter 18

Basic I/O and Interfacing Techniques

When we leave our familiar home base and travel throughout the world, we are confronted with a wide variety of cultures and customs. When the computer leaves its comfortable and precise digital environment and enters the real world, it too is confronted with an incredible variety of peripheral components, each with its own interfacing and I/O requirements. The purpose of this chapter is to introduce the basic I/O and interfacing concepts and terminology used throughout Part IV.

SYNCHRONOUS VS ASYNCHRONOUS

When interfacing components to a computer system, perhaps the most basic question we can ask is: Is the transfer of information *synchronous* or *asynchronous*?

First of all, let us paint the difference between synchronous and asynchronous in broad strokes:

- Synchronous is predictable transfer of data.
- Asynchronous is unpredictable transfer of data.

In a synchronous data transfer or I/O operation, all transfer events are tied to a common system clock and are usually under the direction and control of the CPU. Up to now, all of our I/O and interfacing designs have been strictly synchronous. For example, transfers of information between CPU and primary memory are normally synchronous. By choosing a RAM chip with the required access time and factoring in the effects of propagation delay, we are assured that the transfer of data between CPU and RAM will take place *predictably,* within a specified period of time (the RAM is always ready for communication).

If the data transfer or I/O process is unpredictable (asynchronous), however, the information transferred is not tied to a common system clock but can come at any time and at irregular rates and intervals. In addition, asynchronous data transfers often are initiated by external devices. For asynchronous I/O operations, therefore, special techniques will have to be developed to assure proper timing and identification of data. Most of these new techniques will be introduced during our discussion of I/O and interfacing techniques (this chapter) and data communications (Chapter 21).

The choice between synchronous and asynchronous transfer of information often depends on the type of peripheral device to be added to the system. If the device is a fast RAM with well-known timing characteristics and specifications, we choose synchronous transfer of data because it is high speed. If, on the other hand, the device is mechanical, such as a printer or a Winchester disk system, then the data words may be transferred at irregular rates and intervals, and asynchronous techniques may have to be employed.

REQUIREMENTS OF ASYNCHRONOUS TRANSMISSION

During asynchronous data transfers, we must find some means of regulating the flow of information between source and destination. The most general technique, known as *handshaking,* consists of a separate set of synchronizing signals used to coordinate the data transfers. These handshaking signals can be completely separate from the data and use separate signal pathways, or can be included *along with the data* (time multiplexed on the same line). The second method—designed to reduce the number of interconnecting lines—is a data-communication technique and will be covered in Chapter 21. In this chapter, all handshaking signals will be in parallel with the data.

HANDSHAKING

Handshaking refers to a set of back-and-forth "hand" signals coordinating the flow of data between computer and peripheral. The terminology is appropriate because handshaking signals occur in a given sequence and often consist of a request followed by an acknowledge. *That is, each event is*

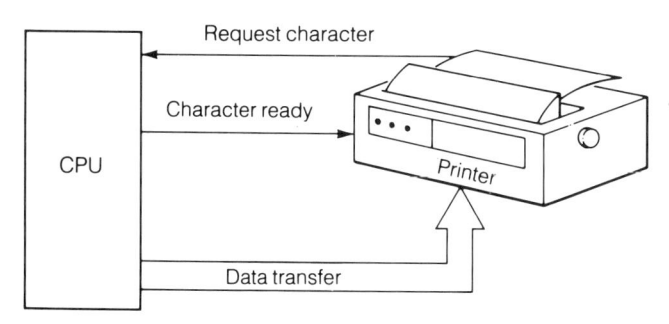

Figure 18.1 Printing characters by handshaking.

initiated (request) *as a result of a signal indicating completion of a previous operation* (acknowledge).

A printer is a common peripheral often requiring handshaking signals, for such a mechanical device can in no way keep up with the maximum rate at which a computer can spew out characters. Handshaking between computer and printer may consist of a request/ready sequence (Figure 18.1):

- The computer waits for the printer to request the next character.
- Eventually the printer says: "Send the next character."
- The CPU responds and, when the character is ready, replies: "Character ready."
- The character is read in and printed. The next character is requested by the printer and the process is repeated.

Using the popular *Centronics* handshaking standard as a specific example, handshaking consists of the three signals shown in Figure 18.2a. The three-step handshaking "conversation" for transferring a single byte of data to the printer follows that of Figure 18.2b.

① The printer says, "I'm done, send me the next character," by sending an $\overline{ACKNLG}$ (acknowledge) pulse and pulling BUSY low.

② The MPU reacts to the printer's request by placing the next character at the output pins to the printer. When the data character is stable, the MPU says, "Here is the data,"

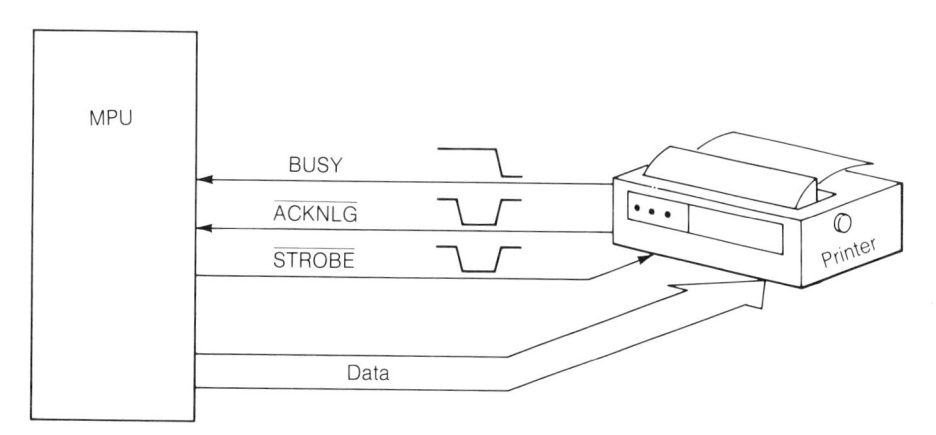

(a) MPU/printer interconnections

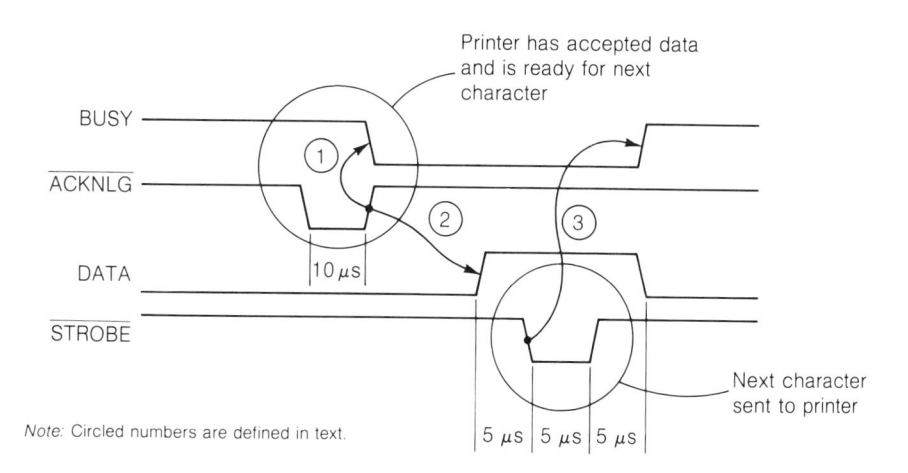

(b) Handshaking sequence

Figure 18.2 The Centronics printer interface standard.

by issuing the $\overline{\text{STROBE}}$ pulse. The $\overline{\text{STROBE}}$ pulse automatically causes the printer to set BUSY high. ("Thanks, I received the character.")

③ The printer performs the function indicated by the data, and when done, again issues $\overline{\text{ACKNLG}}$ and BUSY ("I'm ready for the next character")—and the three-step sequence is repeated.

Why did the printer send both $\overline{\text{ACKNLG}}$ *and* BUSY when requesting the next character? The signals seem to be redundant, since both are conveying the same information ("I'm ready for the next character"). The answer is flexibility. As we will see in the following sections, the $\overline{\text{ACKNLG}}$/BUSY combination offers the designer a variety of handshaking schemes.

PROGRAMMED I/O VS INTERRUPT I/O

A handshaking signal to the CPU—such as the Centronics standard BUSY signal of the last section—can be accepted in one of two ways: it can be inported or it can initiate an interrupt.

The first technique is known as *programmed I/O* (or *polling*), since the sampling of the request signal takes place under main-program control. Usually the computer is placed into a wait loop, where it continuously *polls* the request-handshaking signal via an input port. Only when the request signal (or external flag) is detected does it exit the loop and send the next character to the printer (Figure 18.3). As shown, the BUSY handshaking signal is designed for polled operation because it is level active; that is, it stays active until recognized.

Since the request signal is initiated by the printer and can occur at any time and at irregular intervals, handshaking is an asynchronous technique (although the *exact* time of data transfer may be under CPU control and synchronous with the system clock). Using an ordinary input port to poll the status of the printer, programmed I/O minimizes the use of hardware at the expense of software.

The Centronics $\overline{\text{ACKNLG}}$ pulse is too short to be of use in a polling environment (unless latched), and therefore is more appropriate for interrupt I/O. Furthermore, it offers both negative-going and positive-going edges, giving the designer additional flexibility. Of course, even with interrupt I/O, the 10 μs-wide $\overline{\text{ACKNLG}}$ signal must be latched by MPU peripheral circuitry (otherwise, should the interrupt be masked out, it may come and go without being noticed).

When more than one I/O device interfaces the system, the program polls the devices in order, looking for a request signal. For example, the three output devices of Figure 18.4a are sequentially polled by inporting the status flags and checking each bit in turn. When a bit is found to be active, it is used to generate the address of the service routine. The devices are ranked in priority according to the order in which they are polled. Many software priority schemes are possible.

Figure 18.4b shows another programmed I/O method for identifying the highest-priority device requesting service. Any zero in the inported code (assuming active-low outputs of the priority encoder) will cause the program to branch to the service routine identified by the code. The addition of hardware (the priority encoder) has lessened the software overhead (sequential polling of status bits is not necessary) and speeded up the process. In addition, priority determination is automatic.

Although simple to implement, the polling technique has several drawbacks. First of all, polling—the continuous checking of status bits—can take up all of the computer's time (all peripheral devices must be checked, even when servicing is not required). Second, the response time can be slow, for the sequential polling process as well as the software time used to generate the address of the service routine can consume a great deal of time.

Interrupt I/O, the second major I/O technique, is designed to largely overcome these two drawbacks of programmed I/O. In interrupt I/O, the request-handshaking signal becomes an interrupt request. When interrupted, the computer branches (vectors) directly to the interrupt-service routine and sends the next character to the printer.

As discussed in Chapter 16, interrupt I/O can service the needs of multiple-prioritized I/O devices by way of the scanned, priority, or daisy-chain techniques (see Figure 16.9). Under interrupt I/O control, the computer services the peripherals only when necessary and is free to process other information during its spare time. In general, using interrupt I/O improves the response time. However, the need for PUSH/PULL register storage on the stack introduces an often significant delay.

DMA I/O

Direct memory access (DMA), first introduced in Chapter 9, is a different form of I/O process. A DMA request ($\overline{\text{HALT}}$) allows a peripheral device to gain access to memory without going through the microprocessor at all. By eliminating the processor "middleman," memory transfers are greatly accelerated. To see why, consider the following simple routine, used to inport and transfer data from a peripheral device to system RAM:

```
BACK:   LDAA  $4000
        STAA  X
        INX
        DECB
        BNE   BACK
```

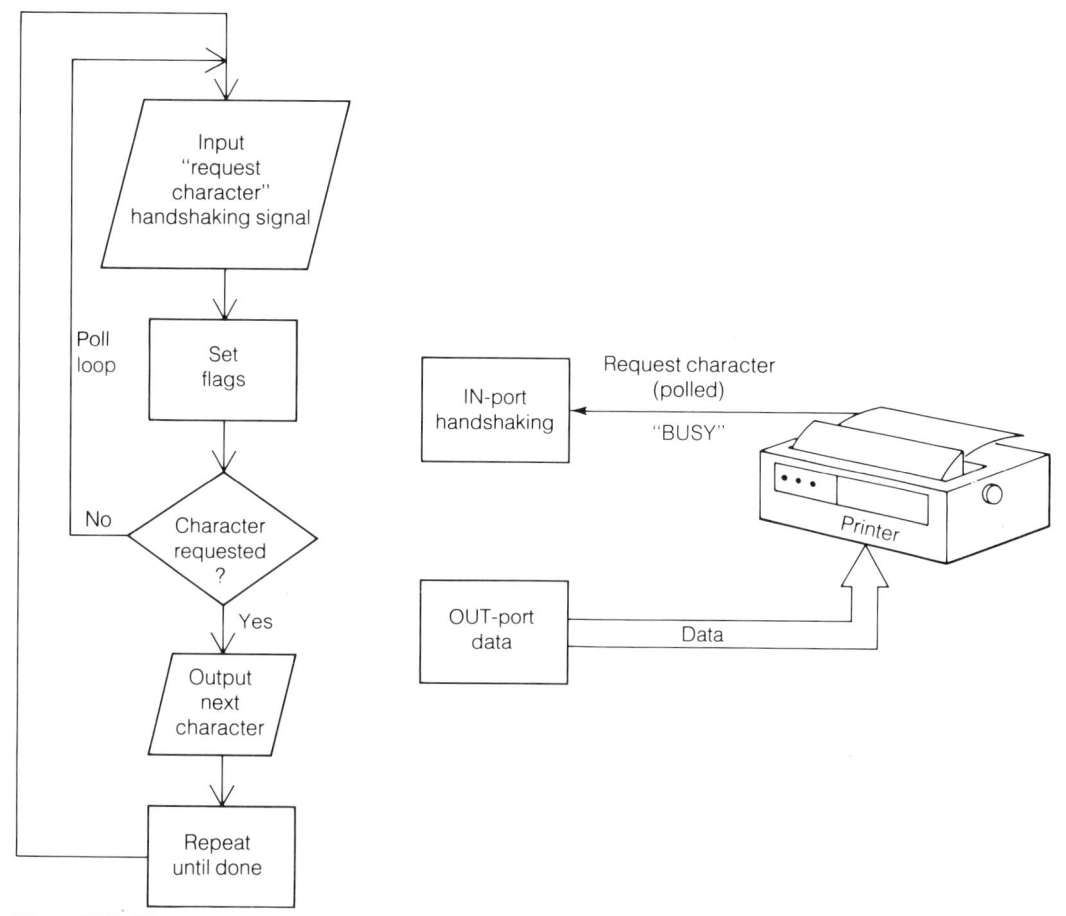

Figure 18.3 The programmed I/O technique.

Driven by a 1 MHz clock, one transfer loop uses up approximately 18 μs, which translates to a data-transfer rate of slightly more than 50,000 bytes/s. Under DMA control, on the other hand, the processor's address, data, and control lines are floated (tristated) and the CPU is completely out of the picture. The DMA device issues its own sequential addresses and can oversee the transfer of data as quickly as the access times of the peripheral device and RAM allow. If we assume a 500 ns transfer time, the data-transfer rate jumps to nearly 2 megabytes/s—some 40 times faster!

A simplified DMA system is shown in Figure 18.5 in which high-speed block transfers between floppy disk and RAM are under DMA control. The sequence is as follows: Prior to the DMA operation, the starting address, number of words to be transferred, and direction of travel are loaded into the DMA controller. The disk requests a DMA operation. The DMA controller acquires control of the system bus by way of the $\overline{\text{HALT}}$ signal to the CPU. After receiving an acknowledge (BA), the DMA controller initiates a block-transfer operation, generating in sequence the where/when waveforms required for direct read or write operations between peripheral and memory. When the specified number of data bytes has been transferred, the DMA controller informs the CPU that the DMA operation is complete, thereby handing control back to the processor. Many DMA controllers are programmable, single-chip devices.

DIGITAL-TO-ANALOG CONVERSION

The real world is largely an *analog* world in which the various parameters—temperature, pressure, mass—can assume a continuous range of values. In order for a digital computer to "speak" to this analog world, a translator is required—a digital-to-analog converter (DAC). The simplest digital-to-analog configuration is the ladder network of Figure 18.6a. Using the superposition principle, it can be demonstrated that the contribution of each input is weighted in an 8-4-2-1 manner from bit D_3 to bit D_0. The high-impedance voltage amplifier scales and buffers the output.

An alternative configuration that also provides weighted inputs, buffering, and amplification is the current-summing

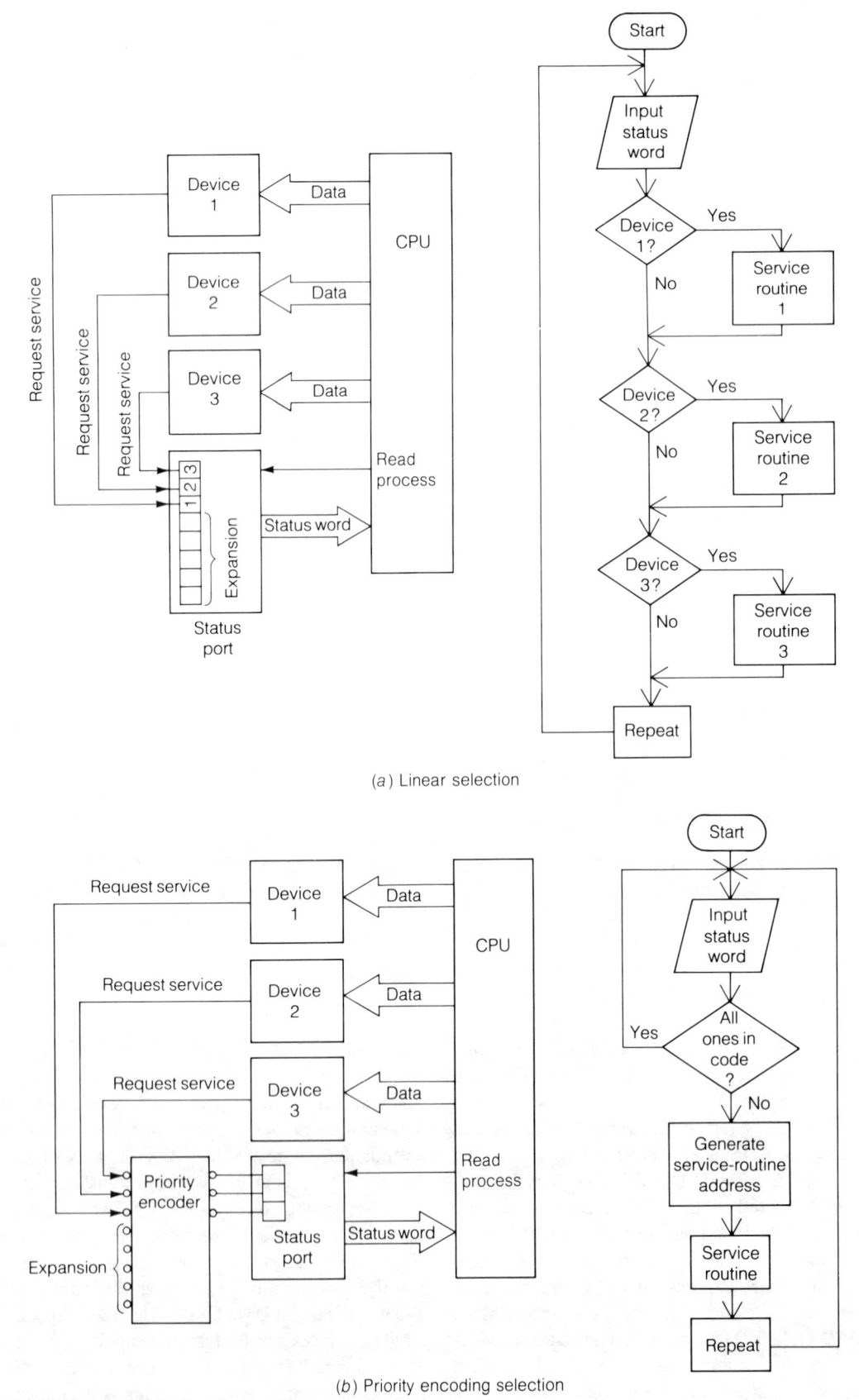

Figure 18.4 Multiple-device programmed I/O techniques.

(a) Linear selection

(b) Priority encoding selection

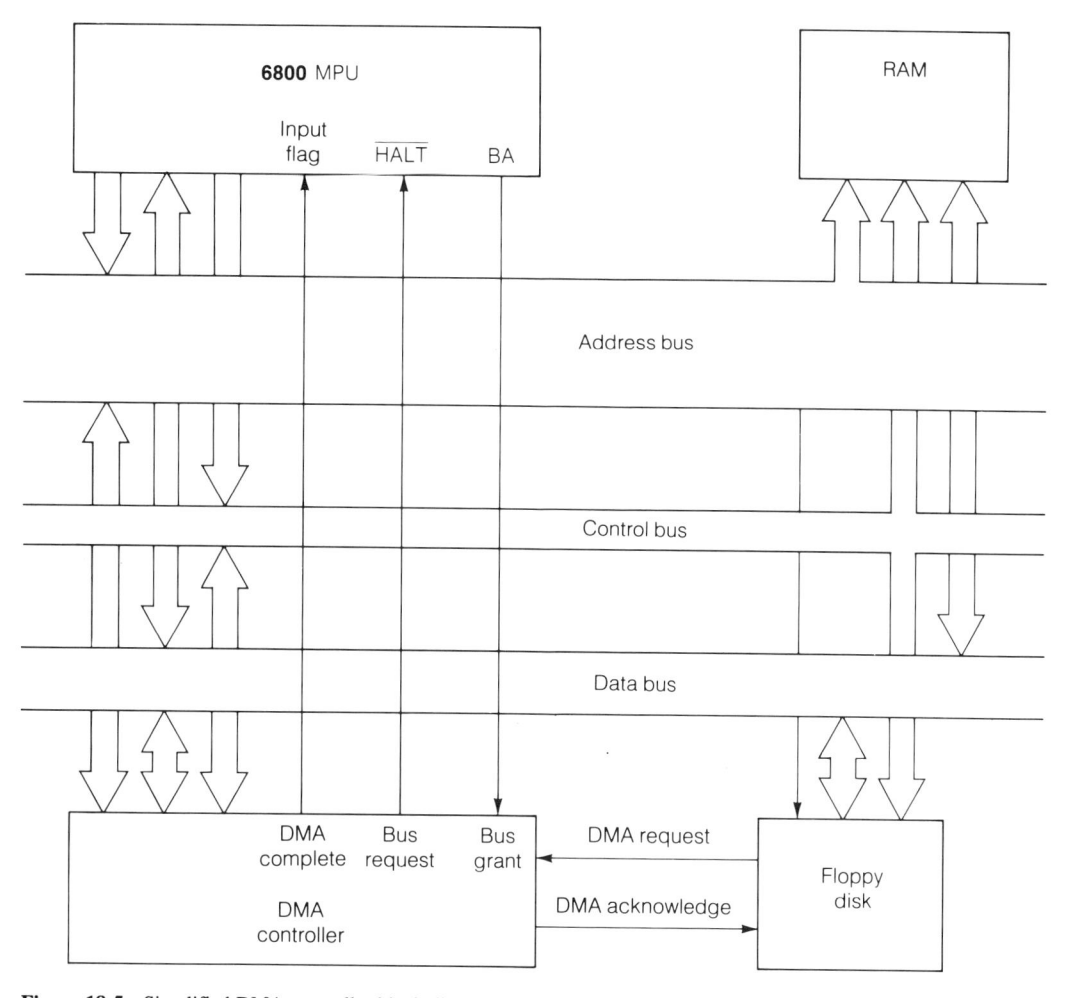

Figure 18.5 Simplified DMA-controller block diagram.

method of Figure 18.6b. Here current is weighted in an 8-4-2-1 pattern by selecting proper resistor values. The feedback resistor (R_f) provides the overall scaling factor.

For the ultimate in convenience, the designer can select from the many single-chip (monolithic) DACs on the market. Shown in Figure 18.7a is the AD558 8-bit digital-to-analog converter. By means of the voltage-switching technique, it offers a settling time (input to stable output) of 1 μs.

Interfacing the AD558 to the 6800 (Figure 18.7b) is a simple process. When a digital word is written to the AD558, its analog equivalent is available at the output line 1 μs later.

External jumpers from V_{out} (pin 16) to a selected feedback resistor (pins 13, 14, and 15) provide a choice of voltage gain values.

Many DACs—such as Motorola's MC6890—output a *current* proportional to a digital input. An external current-to-voltage transducer (Figure 18.8) changes the current to the desired voltage range.

ANALOG-TO-DIGITAL CONVERSION

It is easier to convert from digital to analog (D/A) than from analog to digital (A/D)—that is, it is easier for a computer to "speak" to us than to "listen" to us. Analog-to-digital conversion is a *sampled* data process: the incoming analog signal is sampled at regular intervals and each voltage converted to a parallel digital word (Figure 18.9).

There are four well-known techniques for A/D conversion:

- Counter

- Successive approximation

- Ramp method

- Flash technique

(The simple counter technique is saved for an exercise.)

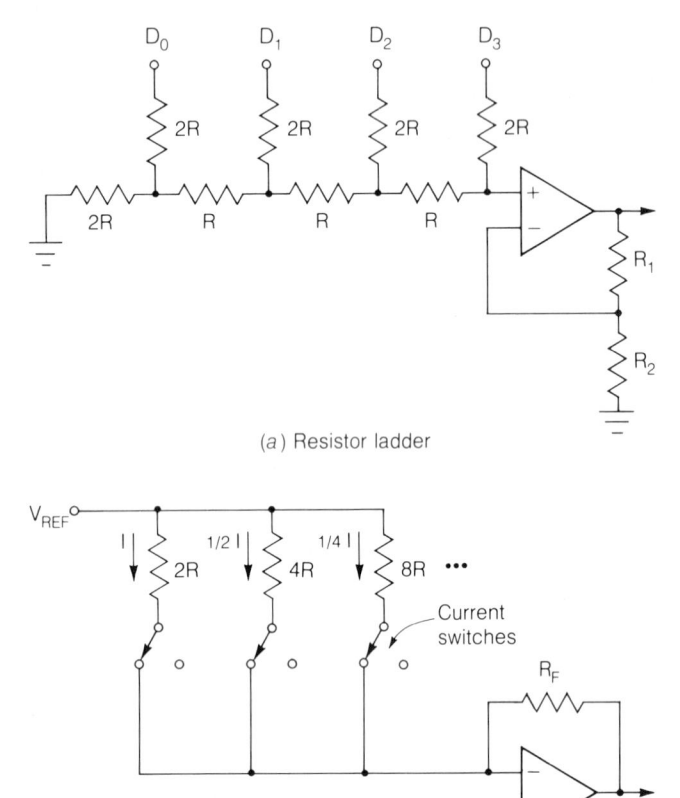

Figure 18.6 Digital-to-analog techniques.

(a) Resistor ladder

(b) Current summing

Successive-Approximation A/D Conversion

Successive approximation is the most popular method of A/D conversion. To see how successive approximation works, consider the following puzzle: Buried treasure is located in one of four quadrants on an island. By asking just two questions, can you determine the proper quadrant? Here is how it is done:

- *First question:* Is the treasure located in the north half or the south half of the island? *Answer:* It is located in the north half.
- *Second question:* Is the treasure located in the upper or lower part of the northern half of the island? *Answer:* It is located in the lower part.

We have homed in on the correct spot by successively cutting in half the space where the treasure can lie (Figure 18.10a). To see how a computer uses this technique to home in on the correct analog input voltage, let us follow through a single sampling event (for example, when the analog input voltage is 10.4 volts).

Referring to Figure 18.10b, note how each successive-approximation iteration sets the next bit position, starting with the most significant bit (MSB). (For greater accuracy, we have extended the process to four iterations.)

Successive approximation is a trial-and-error process. The routine begins by placing a logic 1 in the most significant position. This test voltage is compared to the input voltage. If the input voltage is greater, the 1 is kept. If the input voltage is less, the 1 is masked out. A logic 1 is then placed in the next most significant position and another comparison test is made with the input voltage to determine if this logic 1 should be kept. The process continues through an "elimination pyramid," with each iteration determining the next most significant bit, until the correct slot is found among the 16 possibilities. The process is as simple as finding buried treasure; we home in on the input voltage by successively cutting in half the space where the answer lies.

Clearly we could continue the process any number of additional steps, driving our test voltage closer and closer to the true analog input voltage and thus reducing the error.

Successive-approximation analog-to-digital conversion is popular because it arrives at the answer very quickly. For example, with just four iterations of the test routine, we have placed the actual voltage within a 1-volt slot out of a possible 16-volt range, giving the answer to within $6\frac{1}{4}\%$ of full-scale voltage. Each additional iteration cuts the error in half. After eight successive subdivisions, we know the answer to within 0.4%.

Only two pieces of hardware are required to build the converter system: a digital-to-analog converter to send out the test voltages and a comparator to determine if the test voltage is greater than or less than the input voltage (Figure 18.11a).

It is the job of the software to send out the proper sequence of test voltages, based on the comparator output at each test point. Figure 18.11b is a high-level flowchart of the successive-approximation routine. The program is left as an exercise.

The Ramp Technique

The *ramp technique* for A/D conversion, also known as the *integration* or *slope method*, is often used in digital voltmeters. It is slower than successive approximation, but more accurate. Referring to Figure 18.12, we measure the time it takes a capacitor to charge under the unknown analog input voltage. Then we discharge the capacitor under a known reference voltage. The ratio between our known and unknown voltages is equal to the ratio of the two time measurements. If implemented by a microcomputer, it is the job of the software to switch between the unknown and reference volt-

Figure 18.7 The AD558 single-chip DAC.

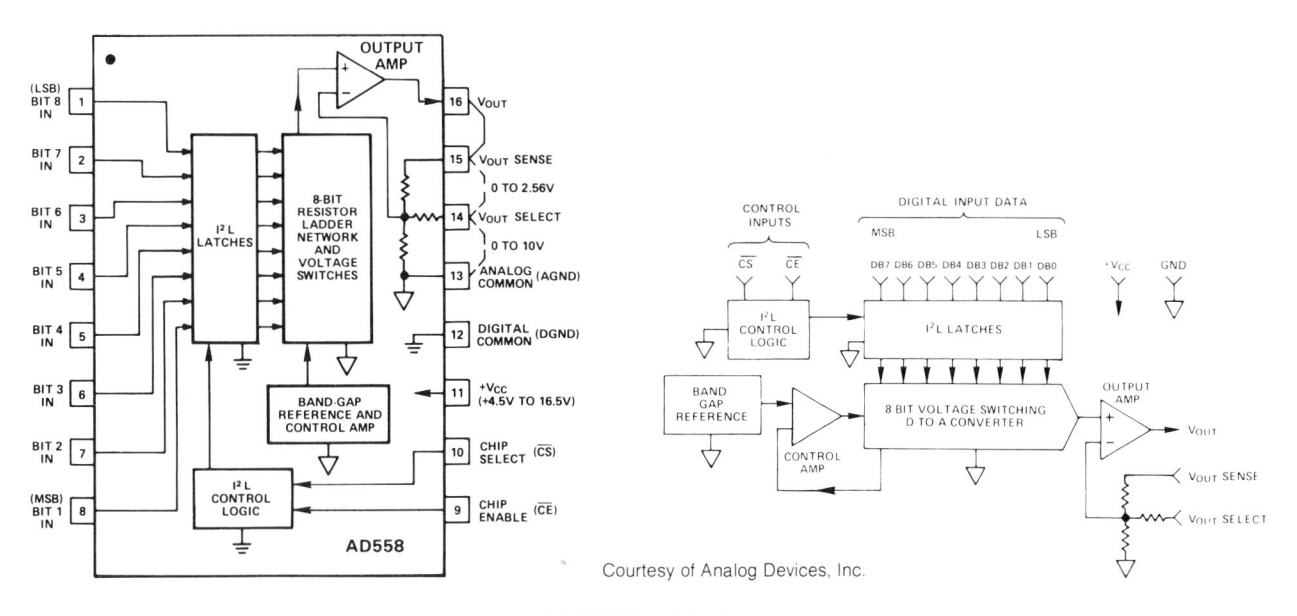

(a) AD558 architecture

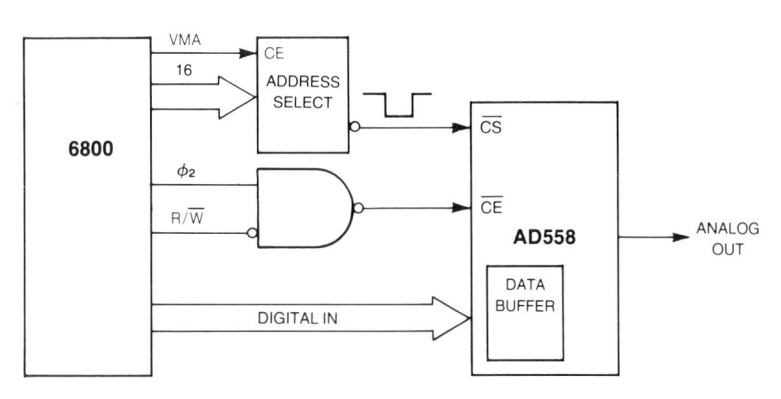

(b) Interfacing the AD558 to the 6800

ages and to measure the times involved and compute the unknown voltage.

Flash Converters

For superfast conversion rates, the iteration process of the successive-approximation method and the capacitive charging time of the ramp method are too slow, and we must switch to pure hardware techniques. Figure 18.13 depicts the simultaneous method (also known as the *flash* technique). Conversion speed is a function only of the propagation delay of the circuitry. For example, TRW's TDC1029J 6-bit flash converter provides 100 million samples per second, while an experimental 6-bit Josephson A/D flash converter has achieved a conversion rate of 2 billion samples per second!

A/D Parameters

When selecting the correct A/D converter to meet your needs, the following criteria should be considered:

- *Range*—the input voltage span over which the converter will work

- *Linearity*—the degree to which all voltage steps are the same size

- *Resolution*—the number of states into which the signal can be divided (equal to the value of the LSB)

- *Absolute accuracy*—the difference between measured and ideal full-scale output

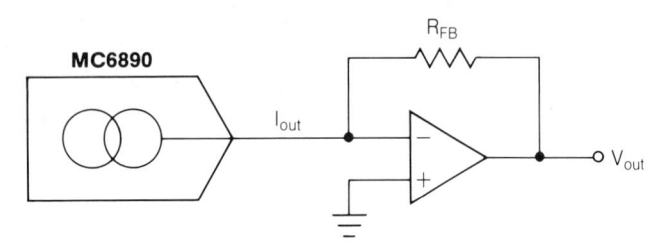

Figure 18.8 The MC6890 DAC, showing external current-to-voltage transducer.

Single-Chip A/D Converters

As with DACs, A/D converters are also available in single-chip form, using all the standard technologies (bipolar, MOS, CMOS, TTL).

The AD574, shown in Figure 18.14a, is a typical state-of-the-art, precision, successive-approximation, 12-bit A/D converter, performing a complete conversion in 25 μs—corresponding to a 40 kHz sample rate.

The complete A/D process involves two steps:

- Analog-to-digital *conversion*
- A microprocessor *read* of the converted digital word

The timing for both the *conversion* and *read* actions is displayed in Figure 18.14b. Basically, to initiate conversion, $\overline{CS}$ and R/$\overline{C}$ are both pulled low; status (STS) goes high to indicate conversion under progress. When the conversion process is complete—after 10 to 40 μs—STS goes low, signaling *end of conversion*. By driving $\overline{CS}$ low and R/$\overline{C}$ high, the output pins will come out of their floating state and allow the data to be read in by the microprocessor.

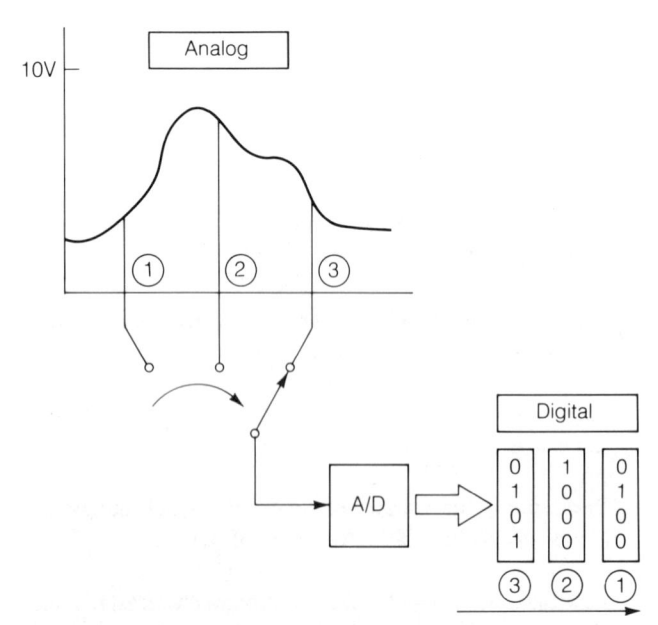

Figure 18.9 A sampled-data system.

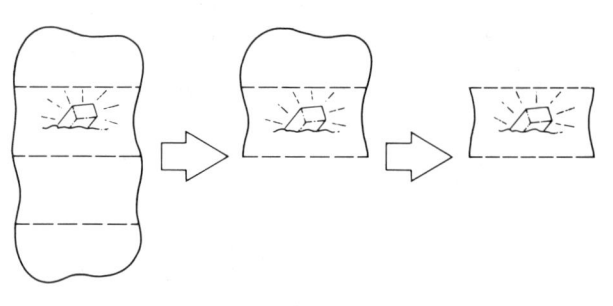

(a) Locating treasure

(b) Computer technique

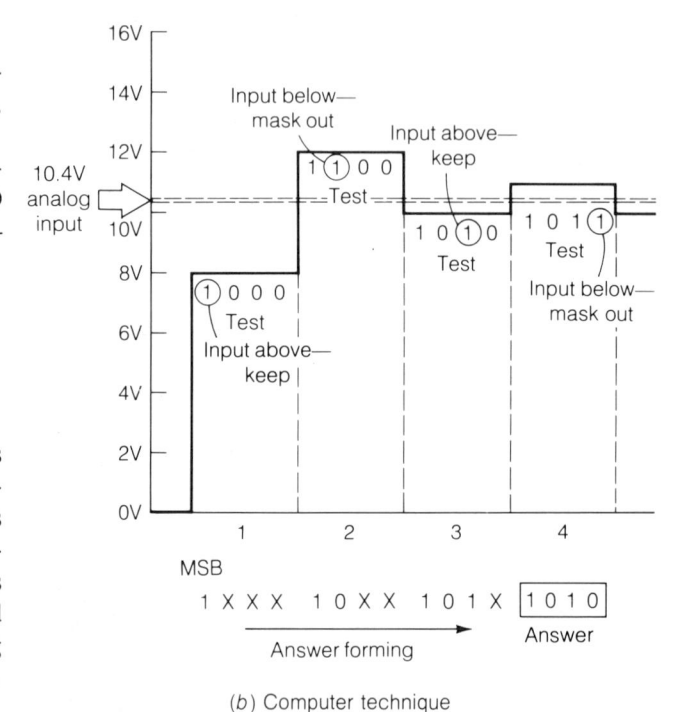

Figure 18.10 Successive-approximation A/D conversion.

KEYBOARD INPUT

For many applications, a keyboard is the most convenient method for entering information into the computer system. The two most common keyboard configurations are hexadecimal and ASCII. A hexadecimal keypad includes 16 input keys (0 through F) and several control keys. An ASCII keyboard closely resembles a typewriter keyboard and includes approximately 60 keys (the shift key doubles the number of possible inputs).

The keypad is organized into rows and columns, with each row and column fed by a conducting line. Pressing a key causes a contact between the corresponding row and column, thereby identifying the active key by coincident selection. Because of this technique, a large number of keys can be serviced with only a small number of interfacing lines.

The *scanning* method is the most popular technique for inputting information from a keyboard, and can be imple-

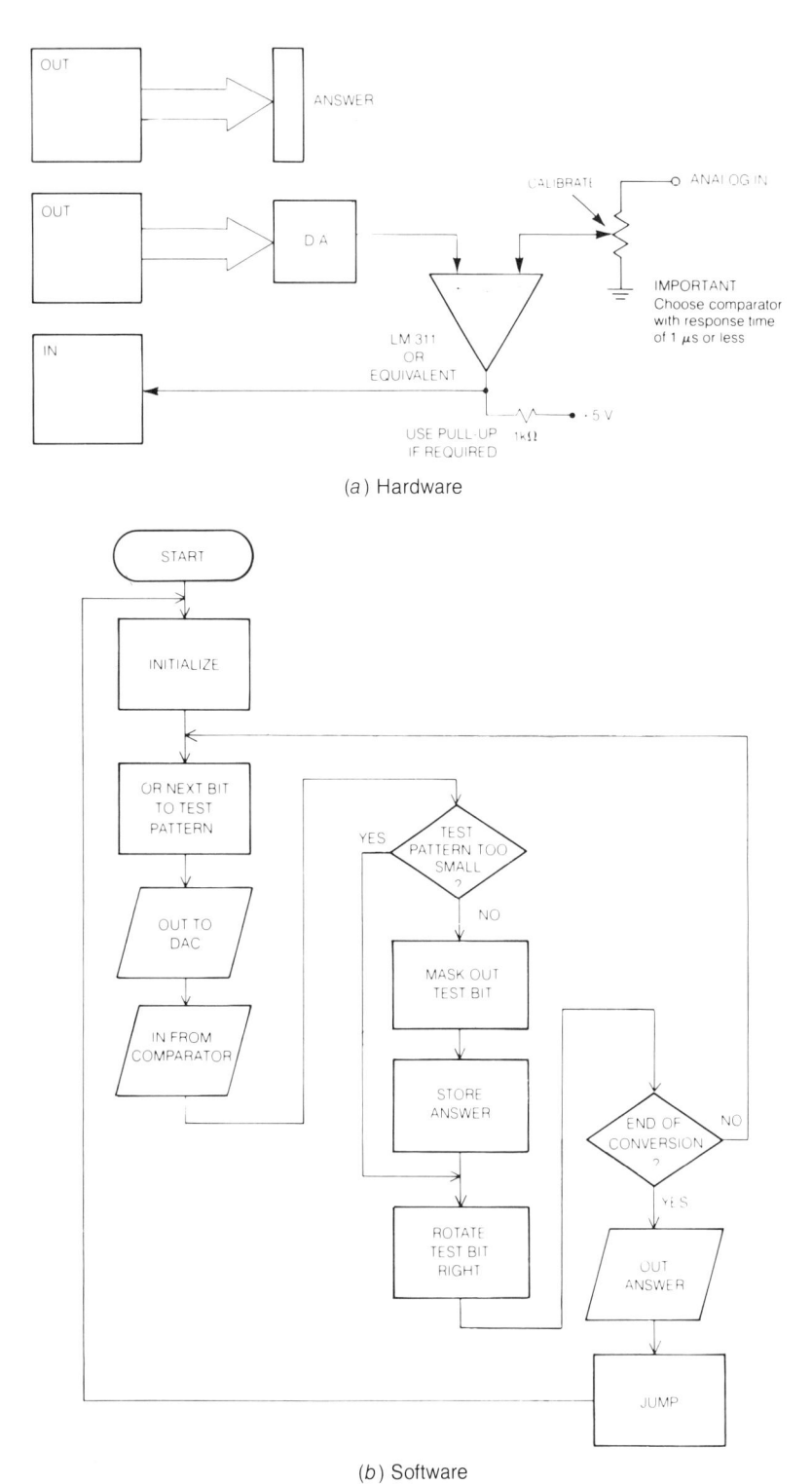

Figure 18.11 Successive-approximation A/D technique.

mented by using either the hardware or the software method. With the software method, the rows and columns can be interfaced to the computer in a variety of ways.

Figure 18.15 shows one novel approach, in which each column is assigned a unique input-port address. During a series of input-port instruction cycles, each column is activated in turn by way of the address bus. The row data are inported and checked for a zero (indicating a key in that column was activated). The computer uses the row-column information to generate the proper hex-code word or initiate the proper command. Debouncing is also accomplished under software control, perhaps by including a delay loop in the keyboard program.

The software method of Figure 18.15 uses a minimum of hardware but requires the constant attention of the CPU. For complex systems, we cannot afford to tie up the computer's time with simple keyboard scanning.

Using interrupt I/O to solve the problem, the computer is interrupted whenever any key is pressed. Within the interrupt-service routine, the CPU scans the keyboard looking for the pressed key.

TOUCH-SCREEN DISPLAYS

A favorite "user-friendly" I/O device is the *touch-screen display*. Using familiar lightpen techniques, as well as various exotic techniques such as infrared light beams, surface-wave acoustics, and conductive membranes, we can determine the position of an object (finger, lightpen, pencil) in front of the CRT screen.

The lightpen—the oldest and most common screen-position device—is basically a pulse-detection device. As the electron beam scans past the pen, the pulse is detected and an interrupt is issued. Since the electron-beam position is always "known," the lightpen position can easily be determined within the ISR by reading row and column registers.

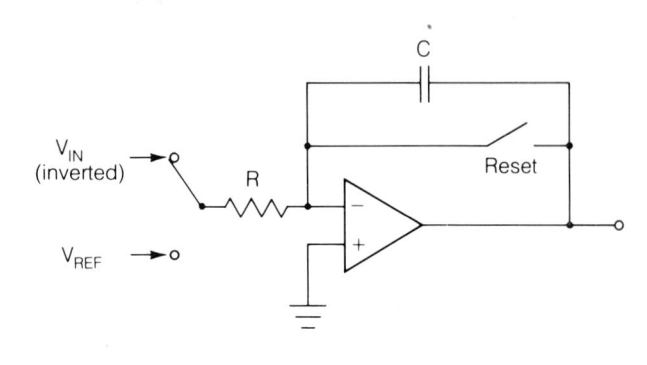

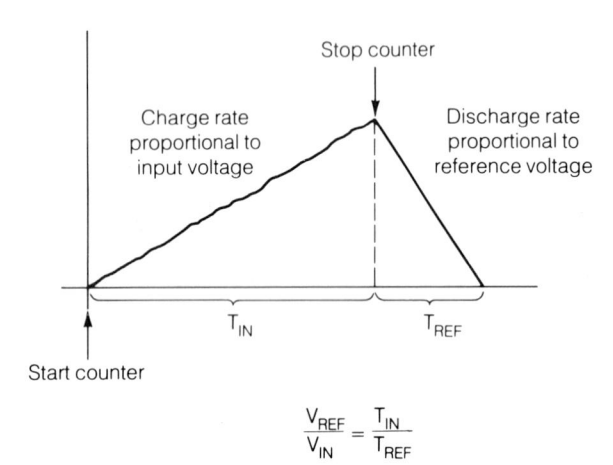

$$\frac{V_{REF}}{V_{IN}} = \frac{T_{IN}}{T_{REF}}$$

Figure 18.12 The dual-slope method of A/D conversion.

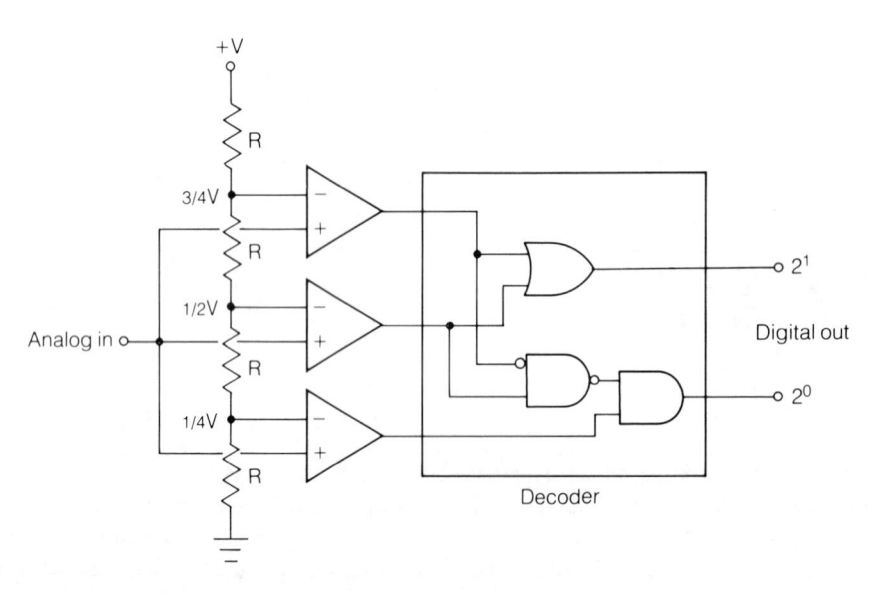

Figure 18.13 Two-bit simultaneous (flash) A/D converter.

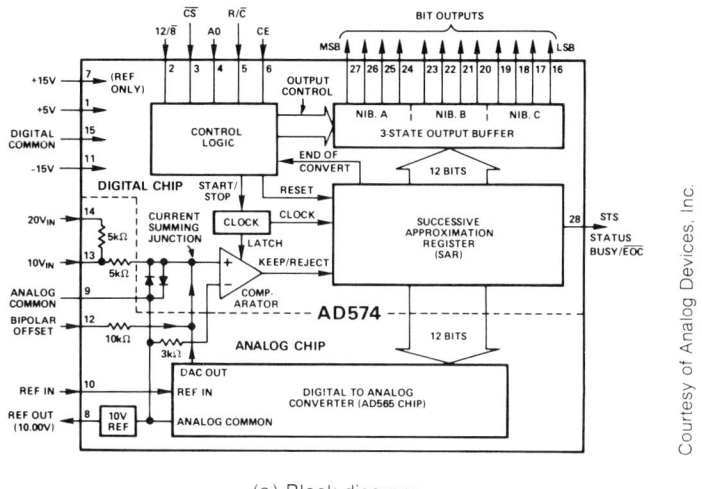

(a) Block diagram

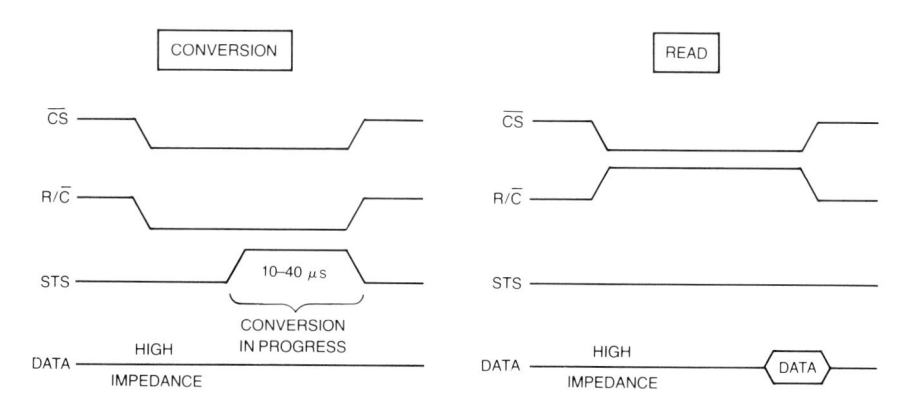

(b) Conversion and read timing

Figure 18.14 The AD574 analog-to-digital converter.

THE MOUSE

The latest in computer ergonomics (the science of adapting working conditions to suit the workers) is called the *mouse*. Developed in the early sixties, the mouse is a handheld input device that slides along the desk, translating hand motion to cursor movement on the video screen. When the cursor is at the proper position on the screen, a simple press of a button located on the mouse will initiate the selected action. The mouse is slated to become a popular and widely used input device because of two key features:

1. It allows quick and accurate cursor location without the necessity to shift eyes from the screen.
2. It frees the user from issuing potentially confusing command sequences from the keyboard.

DISPLAY MULTIPLEXING

The concept of scanning (multiplexing) also reduces the hardware requirement of multiple character displays. As shown in Figure 18.16, the technique is similar to keyboard scanning.

Seven-segment information is sent to all displays simultaneously. However, only one of the seven-segment displays—the one to be illuminated—is grounded by port 2. By grounding the segments in sequence, and sending synchronized BCD information to the display array, we drive the system. (Display flicker is reduced to acceptable levels as the scanning rate is increased.)

Keyboard/display interface chips (such as Intel's 8279) provide automatic keyboard scanning and display refreshing, and operate in the interrupt I/O mode.

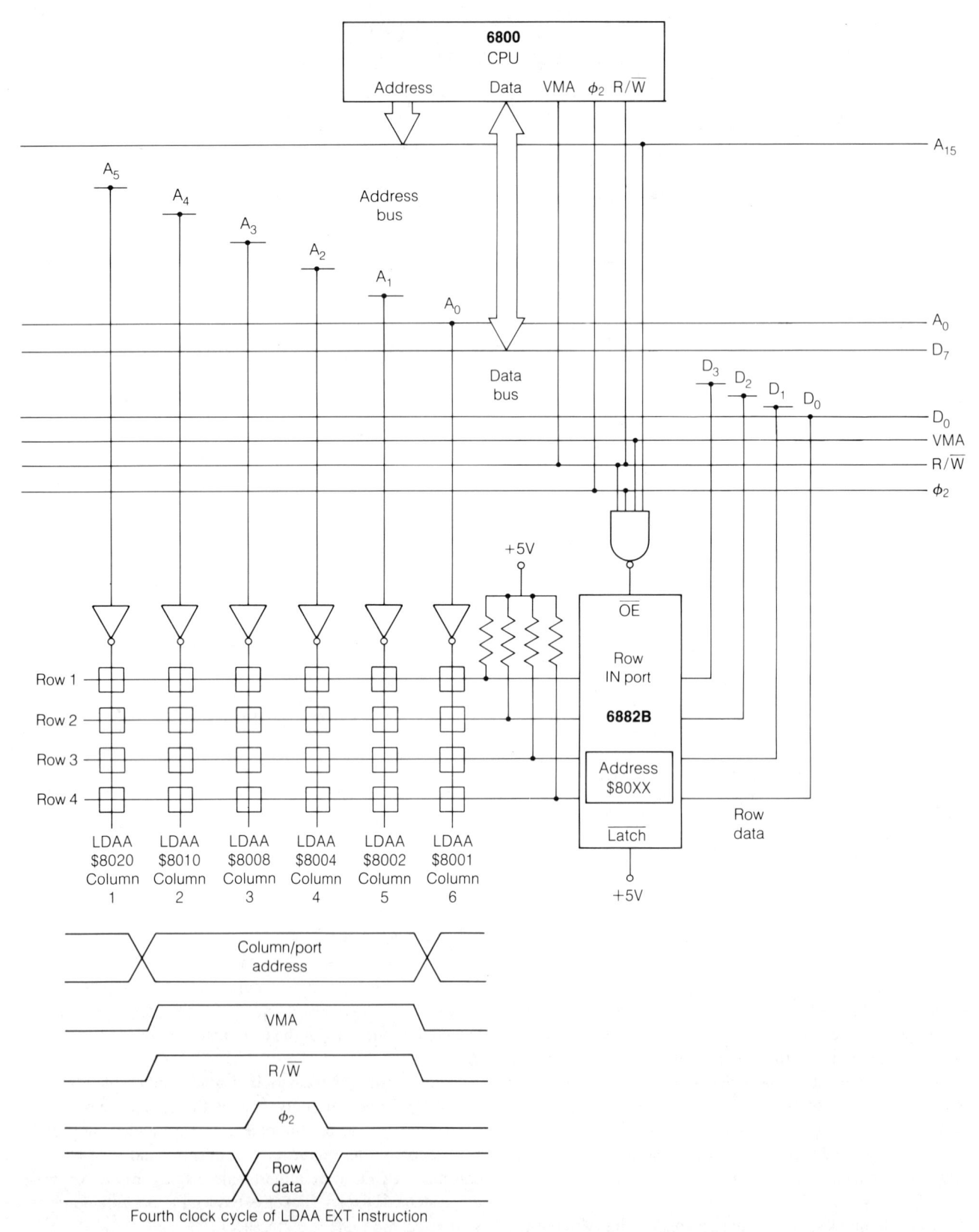

226 Part IV / Applications and Interfacing: Living in a Real World

Figure 18.15 Software-controlled keyboard scanning by assigning each column a unique input-port address.

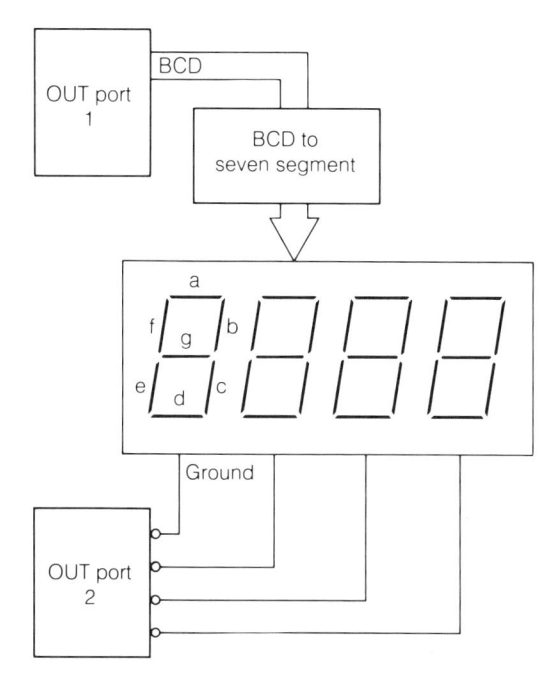

Figure 18.16 Seven-segment display multiplexing.

MONITOR PROGRAMS

Single-board computers that use scanned keyboards and multiplexed seven-segment displays always include a ROM with a built-in program called a *monitor*. It is the monitor program (the program the computer automatically runs when RESET) that the computer "wakes up" into.

A monitor program performs two fundamental tasks: (1) basic housekeeping duties such as keyboard and display interfacing, and (2) the acceptance and execution of simple commands issued by way of the keyboard. Typical commands accepted by the JBUG monitor program of the MEK6800D2 single-board computer, or by the monitor program of the ET-3400A trainer, include:

- Display and modify internal registers and memory locations
- Enter, examine, and execute programs
- Perform single stepping
- Set breakpoints (As detailed in Chapter 22, a *breakpoint* stops computer action at a specific point.)

When more advanced computers (such as Apple II, IBM PC) entered the scene, the simple monitor program grew into a full-fledged *operating system*, able to both carry out the more complex housekeeping operations required for floppy disk drives, video monitors, and printers, as well as accept very high level commands issued by the operator via the keyboard. We will continue our discussion of operating systems in Chapter 22.

VIDEO DISPLAY

A video monitor is the most popular method for displaying large numbers of ASCII characters. A video monitor is similar in operation to an ordinary television set.

Basic Television Operation

A video monitor "paints" an image onto a monitor screen by sweeping an electron beam rapidly across the face of the screen. The on-off pattern of the electron beam produces the ASCII characters.

Starting at the upper-left corner of the screen (Figure 18.7), the beam sweeps horizontally from left to right, laying down one line of the image for each pass. When the beam reaches the right side of the screen, it is blanked out and quickly returned to the left side. The beam is deflected downward a small amount for each pass, so the second line is traced out slightly below the first. The scanning continues back and forth until the bottom of the screen is reached. The beam then returns to the upper-left corner and the process is repeated.

For displaying ASCII characters, the screen is subdivided into a number of character spaces. The simplest format allows for 16 lines of 32 rows, for a total of 512 characters. Again using the simplest format, each character space is in turn divided into a 5 × 7 matrix. As the electron beam scans through the dot matrix, each dot is either illuminated or left blank. From the many dot-matrix patterns possible, all ASCII characters can be generated. Typically, two horizontal dot positions and three vertical positions are left blank to provide spacing between the characters. Figure 18.18 shows a dot-matrix pattern holding the letter R.

Generating the Characters

Let us assumbe a 512 × 8 RAM is presently holding the 512 characters to be displayed on the CRT screen. We must

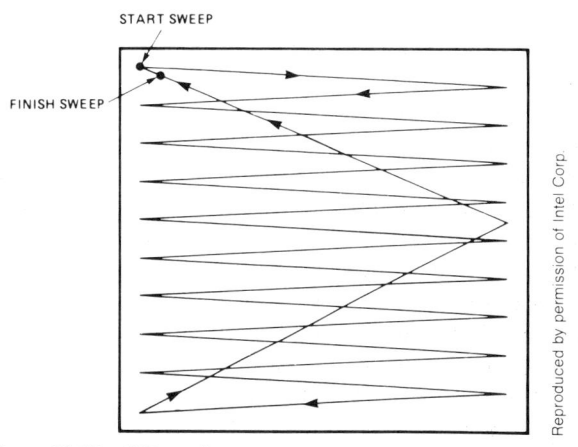

Figure 18.17 CRT monitor raster.

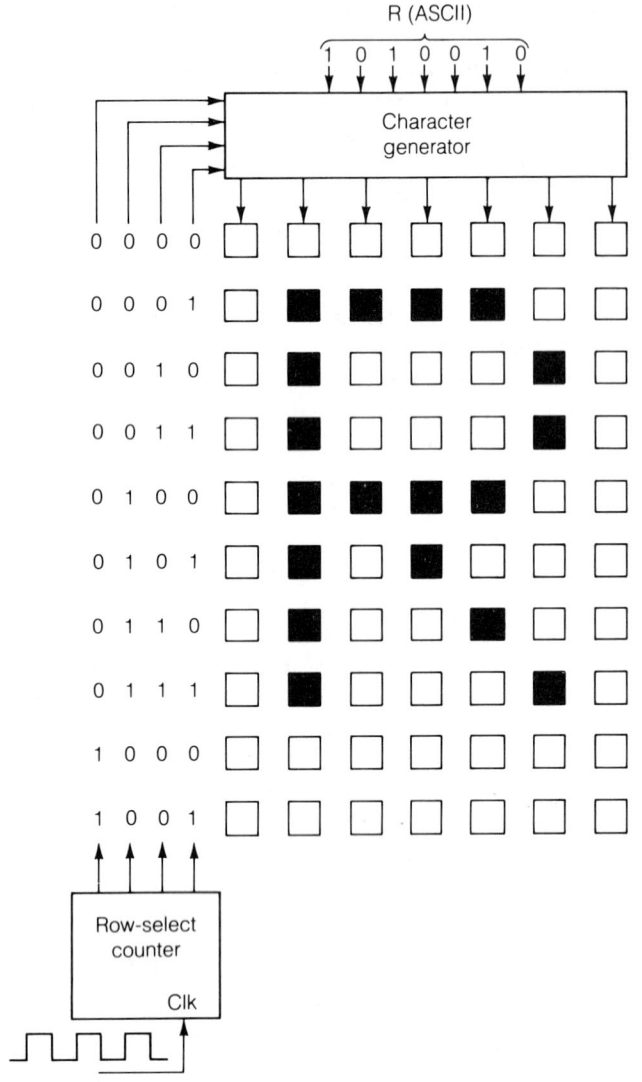

Figure 18.18 Generation of dot-matrix pattern for the letter R.

are scanned on the CRT, like RAM locations are also scanned (addressed) simultaneously and in synchronization.

Figure 18.19 is a simplified block diagram of the display system. It works as follows: At the present time, let us assume the line and character counters are arbitrarily addressing the second line, sixth character (holding an R). The ASCII code for R appears at the output lines of the RAM and is fed into the character generator. Also, we assume the row-select counter feeding the character generator is set to the second row (the top of the letter). Therefore, 0111100 appears at the output of the character generator (refer back to Figure 18.18) and enters the parallel-to-serial shift register. The seven dots in the top row of the letter R are clocked out in serial, combined with necessary video information, and fed to the CRT. After seven clock pulses of the master clock, the top of the letter R is traced onto the CRT screen.

The divide-by-7 counter overflows and clocks the character counter to address the next RAM location in the same row. The process is repeated seven more master clock cycles, and the top of the next character is traced onto the screen. Assuming the next character is an E, Figure 18.20*a* shows the result.

After the top row of all 32 characters has been traced out on the CRT, a divide-by-32 counter clocks the character generator's row-select counter, and the next row of each letter is selected. After all 10 rows are traced out, the 2 characters fully appear (Figure 18.20*b*).

When the tenth row of the last character is traced out, a pulse increments the RAM line counter, and it addresses the next line of characters stored in RAM. The entire process is then repeated. As always, a number of video LSI controller chips are available to ease the design task.

GRAPHICS

When the character-generation concepts of the last section are expanded and coupled with VLSI technology, we move from simple character generation to *graphics*—the ability to display any figure on the CRT screen (limited only by resolution).

Especially promising are the new text processors (such as Intel's 82730 *text coprocessor*). By modifying a table of pointers (linked list) to update the display (rather than moving data from one location to another), speed is greatly enhanced. In addition, by including a huge library of characters on chip (15,000) and allowing characters to be redefined "on the fly" (by software), a flexible, high-resolution graphics system can be implemented.

However, at present, most graphics systems are based on the concept of *bit mapping* rather than character generation. Interestingly, bit-mapping technology is not new; such graphics display systems are relatively late bloomers because they consume vast amounts of high-speed primary memory—a commodity only recently available in large quantities at low prices.

devise a method of transferring the RAM information into a dot-matrix pattern generated by the serial tracing of an electronic beam.

This seemingly difficult task is actually made quite simple once we accept one crucial fact: since the electron beam is controlled by digital circuitry (counters), we know at all times precisely at which of the 35,000 dots the electron beam is pointing. Furthermore, the display circuitry contains only one circuit we have not seen before: the *character generator*.

The character generator is really a preprogrammed ROM, with the address inputs divided into four row-select and seven ASCII-code inputs. As shown in Figure 18.18, when an ASCII code is entered (for example, the code for R), the proper dot matrix is generated as the rows are sequenced.

The first step in understanding the total operation of the system is to visualize each RAM location as corresponding to a like position on the CRT screen. As the character spaces

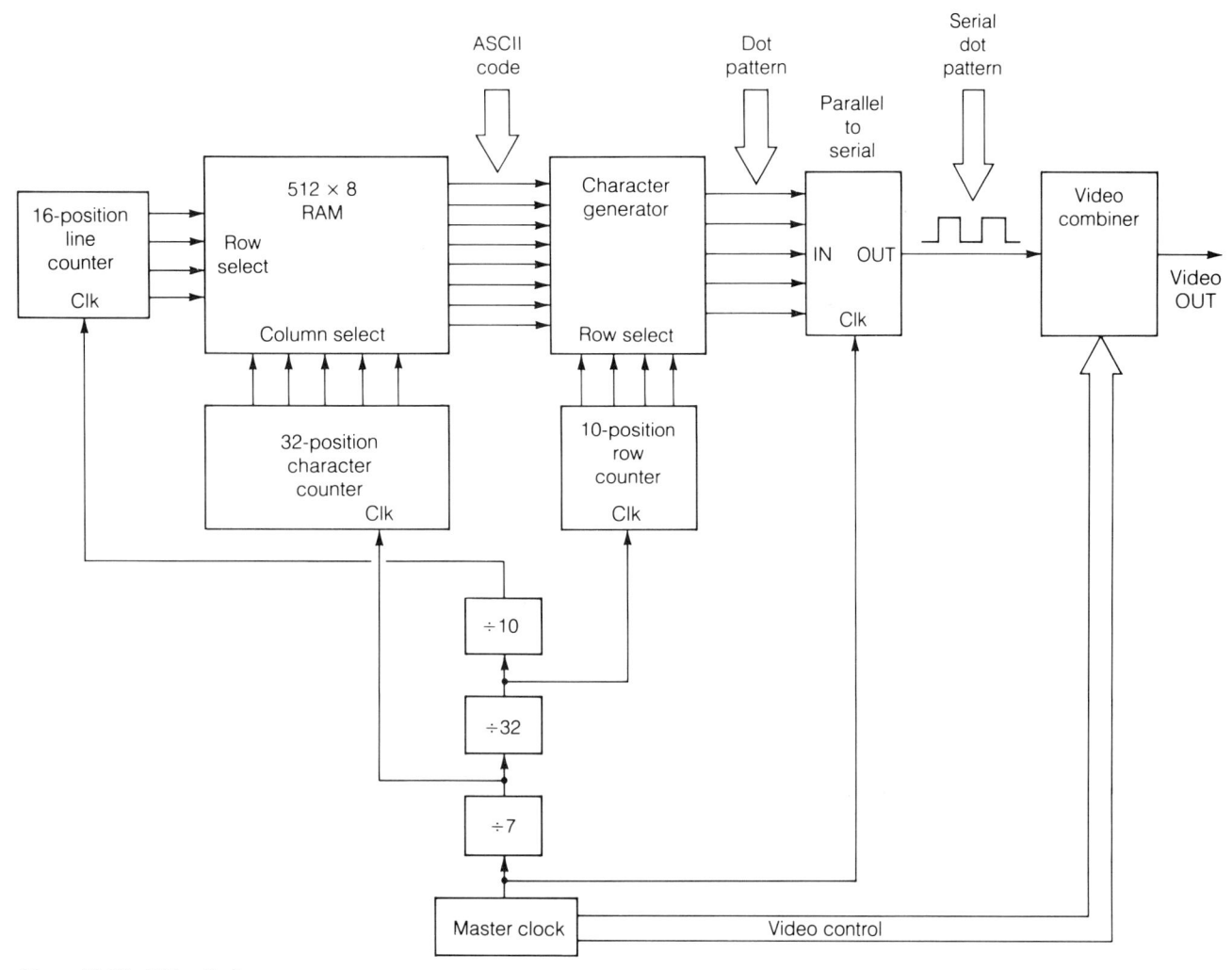

Figure 18.19 Video display system.

Bit Mapping

To understand bit mapping, imagine a CRT screen divided into 320 by 200 dots (see Figure 18-21). Each dot, which can be illuminated by the electron beam, is called a *picture element* (or *pixel*). Further imagine each dot to correspond to a single bit in a 64K × 1 RAM array called a *bit plane* (320 × 200 = 64,000). If a 1 is stored in a particular bit location, the corresponding pixel is turned on (white); if a 0 is stored, the corresponding pixel is blank (black). It is the responsibility of the video refresh circuitry to translate the pattern of 1s and 0s in the bit plane to whites and blacks on the CRT screen. To avoid tying up software for such a routine operation, video refreshing is now performed by a sophisticated *video interface chip,* or VIC. (This is how the Commodore VIC computer got its name.)

For flexibility, video interface chips and boards are available to drive two types of video displays: *raster scan* and *vector.* Raster scan is the technique used by television (see Figure 18.17), whereas the vector technique is found on oscilloscopes. Each technique has its advantages. The raster scan (the most popular) updates the screen at a constant rate (usually 30 or 60 Hz) and therefore avoids flicker. However, a straight line is seldom perfectly straight, for it must be drawn in increments from one fixed pixel to the next in staircase fashion. The vector method, which is able to move the electron beam to anywhere on the screen at any time, draws perfectly straight lines, but is subject to flicker if too many lines are on the screen at one time. Perhaps the most important difference between the two display technologies is that color-based graphics are accomplished more readily with raster scan.

High-Resolution Displays

Our 320 × 200 pixel graphics display, although more versatile than a character-generation system, is still rather crude by state-of-the-art standards. It is medium resolution at best and offers only one color or shade of gray (on or off). Clearly, to provide various colors and intensities, each pixel must be represented by more than 1 bit. Four bits per pixel, for example, gives us 16 combinations of color and intensity.

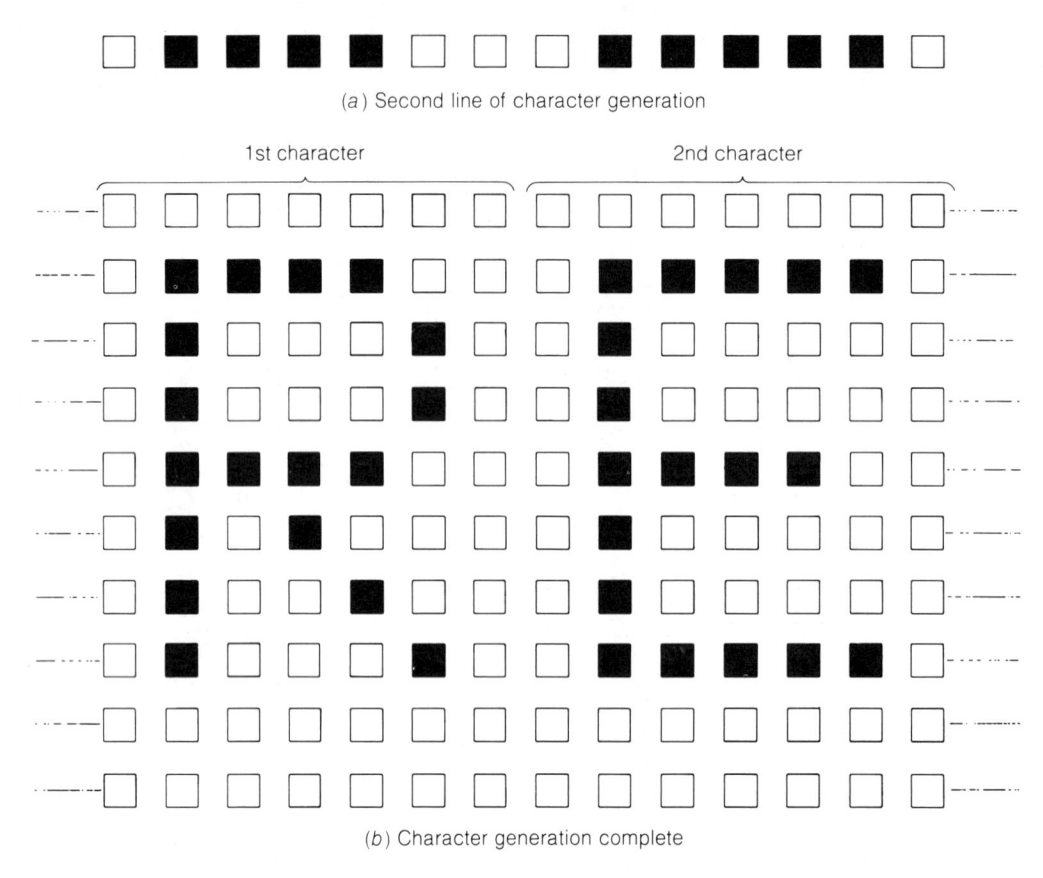

Figure 18.20 Generation of two ASCII characters.

And, to improve resolution, let's go to a 364 × 720 pixel screen (the size of Apple's 68000-based *Lisa* computer). To support such a system requires over 1 megabit of high-speed RAM (364 × 720 × 4 = 1,048,320). Moving further up the scale brings us to state-of-the-art 2048 × 2048 pixel resolution, with 16-megabit requirements—and we begin to see why graphics is so dependent on low-cost, large-scale primary memory. (With character generation, each 7 × 10 pixel character space requires only a single byte, accounting for its greatly reduced memory requirements when compared to bit mapping.)

Figure 18.22 shows us how to visualize the bit-mapped RAM for our high-resolution system. Each like position in the four bit planes is accessed (addressed) as a unit. The 4

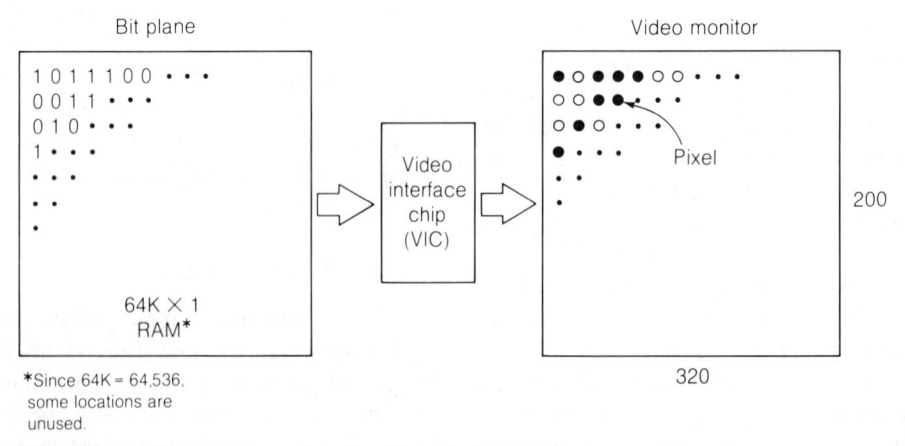

Figure 18.21 Correspondence of memory bit positions in the bit plane to like pixel positions on the video monitor.

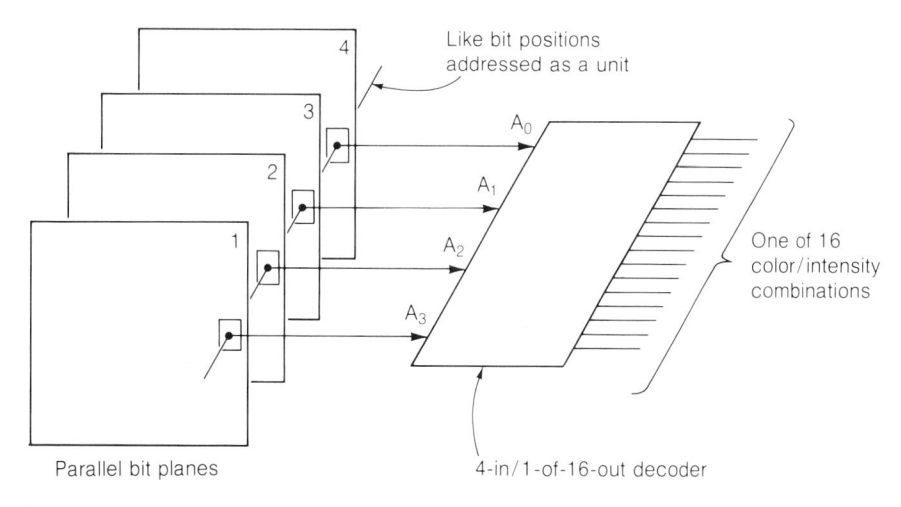

Figure 18.22 Four-bit-plane graphics storage system.

bits (one from each plane) are then used to set the color/intensity combination of the selected pixel.

If we wish to have 256 color/intensity combinations, clearly we can expand the number of bit planes to 8. However, even though primary memory is relatively inexpensive, it is not free. So, for such a system, a compromise is in order. We can still select from among 256 color/intensity combinations; but to save bit planes, we select only 16 at any one time. The hardware of Figure 18.23 shows how the compromise is implemented. We preload the 16 8-bit registers with the selected 16 color/intensity combinations from our "palette" of 256 selections. For each pixel, our four-bit-plane RAM array selects one of the 16 registers, which in turn sends the 8-bit (one-of-256) color/intensity information to the video interface system.

Clearly we can expand the size of our 16 8-bit registers to give us a larger selection (16-bit registers will allow us to select from 65,536 combinations of intensity and color). It is even possible to mix graphics with character generation by assigning one or more bit planes to text and the rest to graphics.

Software

Once the bit-mapped RAM array and video interface chips are in place, graphics generation is all software. The question is, What information is written to the bit-plane array to

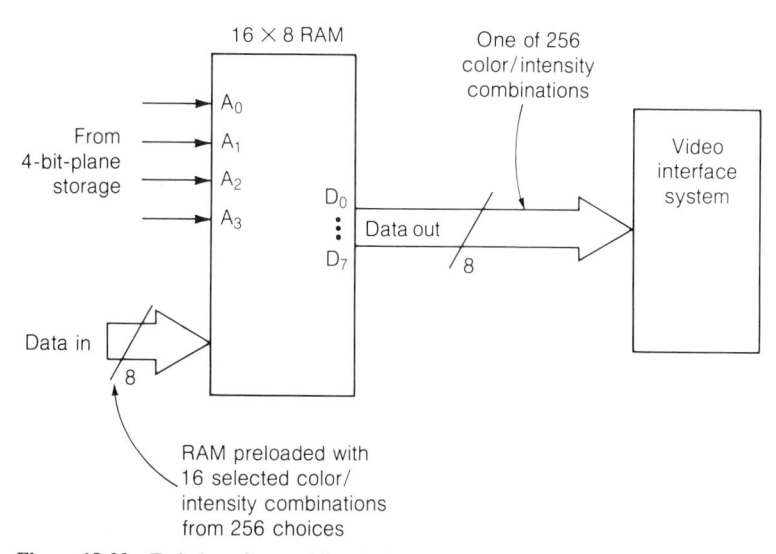

Figure 18.23 Technique for providing 256 color/intensity combinations—but only 16 at a time.

produce the desired graphics display? Since the answer is quite complex—even for a geometric figure as simple as a straight line—we must take full advantage of block-structured, modular design principles. Recall from our *machine-assembly updates,* that whenever we write a basic routine that we expect to use many times, we make it a subroutine (using CALLs and MACROs) and call it whenever needed—passing any necessary parameters. In high-level-language programming, these subroutines are called *procedures*.

Putting block-structured techniques into action for our straight-line problem, we begin by writing low-level software "primitives" to control individual pixels. To draw a straight line, we must identify each pixel and write information to its corresponding bit-map position (most graphics systems generate figures by combinations of straight-line segments).

The next level of software might generate a line by specifying only its end points, calling and sending parameters to the necessary low-level primitives as needed. As shown below, such a line routine can be written in Pascal, a high-level language to be discussed in Chapter 22.

```
PROCEDURE LINE (x1,y1,x2,y2,value : integer);
VAR x,y,dx,dy,slope : real;
BEGIN
  If x1 <> x2 THEN
    Begin
      dy := y2 - y1;
      dx := x2 - x1;
      slope := dy/dx;
      FOR x := x1 to x2 DO
        BEGIN
          WRITETOPIXEL (x,ROUND(y),value);
          y := y + slope;
        END
    END
  ELSE
    IF y1 = y2 THEN
      WRITETOPIXEL (x1,y1)
      ELSE ERROR:
END;
```

Procedure *Linedraw* then becomes a subroutine to be called from a still higher level of software. Turtle graphics, a software system that provides a vehicle to create simple line and figure graphics, is a perfect case in point.

Turtle graphics Turtle graphics is a collection of midlevel movement commands (procedures) based on the polar and Cartesian coordinate systems. Using these commands, the "turtle" lays down a track, like a spider spinning a web. For example, to draw a simple line requires the following four procedures:

```
MOVETO(140,95);
PENCOLOR(white);
TURNTO(30);
MOVE(10);
```

When these four procedures are sequenced in a program, the turtle performs the following actions:

1. When procedure MOVETO is called and center-of-screen parameters (140,95) are sent, the turtle will move to the center of the screen.
2. Procedure PENCOLOR is called and parameter *white* turns on the turtle (makes its track visible when it moves).
3. Procedure TURNTO receives parameter 30 and the turtle "faces" 30 degrees.
4. Parameter 10 is sent to procedure MOVE, and the turtle moves across the screen from its present position 10 units, laying down a visible track.

By including such midlevel turtle-graphics language procedures in a Pascal program, we can create graphics that fall into the realm of simple art. For example, the program below (using Apple Pascal) will create the "fireworks" display of Figure 18.24.

```
PROGRAM FIREWORKS;
USES TURTLEGRAPHICS, APPLESTUFF;
VAR A,B,N : INTEGER;

BEGIN
  INITTURTLE;
  REPEAT
    A := RANDOM MOD 278;
    B := RANDOM MOD 195;
    MOVETO(A,B) ;
    PENCOLOR(WHITE);
    FOR N := 1 TO 30 DO
      BEGIN
        MOVE(100);
        TURN(12);
        MOVETO(A,B);
      END;
    PENCOLOR(NONE);
  UNTIL KEYPRESS;
END.
```

Even with turtle graphics we are far from state of the art. To generate 3-D and surfaces, we are into *computer-aided design* (CAD), where 16-bit computers and high-level graphics languages are found. Add solid figures, and we are into advanced computer art, where only 32-bit mainframe computers have the required power. Clearly, the field of computer graphics has many surprises in store for us as hardware and software technology advances.

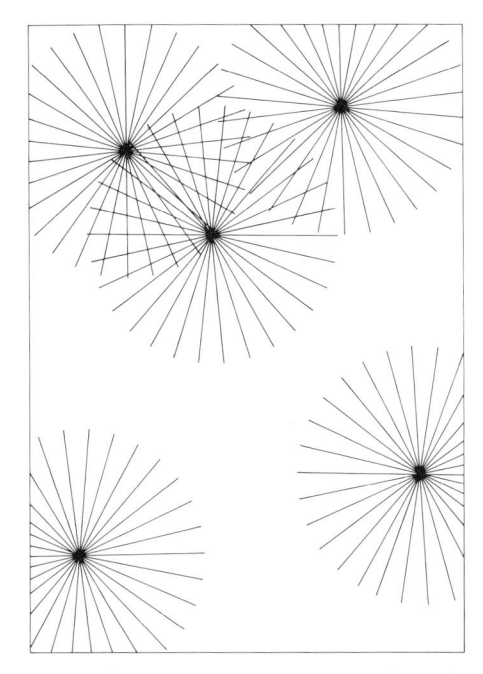

Figure 18.24 The "fireworks" display using turtle graphics.

DATA ACQUISITION

Over the years, computers have become more "sociable," leaving the purely mathematical world of data processing and number crunching to enter the real world, where most of the data to be collected and analyzed consist of physical parameters of an analog nature (pressure, acceleration, temperature). To exist in this multisensor analog world, the computer clothed itself in a *data-acquisition system* (DAS). A typical system (Figure 18.25) consists of sensors and transducers sending analog data to an analog-acquisition signal processor. The analog processor samples (multiplexes) the analog inputs, holds the signal steady, amplifies the signal if necessary, and feeds each analog voltage to a high-speed A/D converter. Acquisition is complete when a microcomputer accepts, categorizes, and stores the digital information.

If data are measured, acquired, and stored automatically, the DAS is known as a *data logger.* Data loggers are often CMOS, battery-operated systems, suitable for remote, unattended data-gathering applications.

The data-acquisition system is also available in highly integrated form. Figure 18.26 shows a two-package hybrid DAS specifically designed for microprocessor interfacing. The first package is the analog section and holds the programmable 16 single-ended (or 8 differential) analog multiplexer, buffer, and sample-and-hold amplifier. The microprocessor selects the 1-of-16 analog inputs by way of the input channel select (AE, A2, A1, and A0). The second section is a conventional 12-bit analog-to-digital converter.

MACHINE-ASSEMBLY UPDATE

Our final machine-assembly update is important because it refines the *linkage* process—the key to modular programming. Linkage, remember, is the combining of two or more independently assembled, relocatable program modules.

As a case in point, refer back to Figure 17.14. Instead of ending the program with a simulated halt (SELF: BRA SELF), suppose we wish to place the program into a loop. Proceeding as we have in the past, we place the label *START* in the

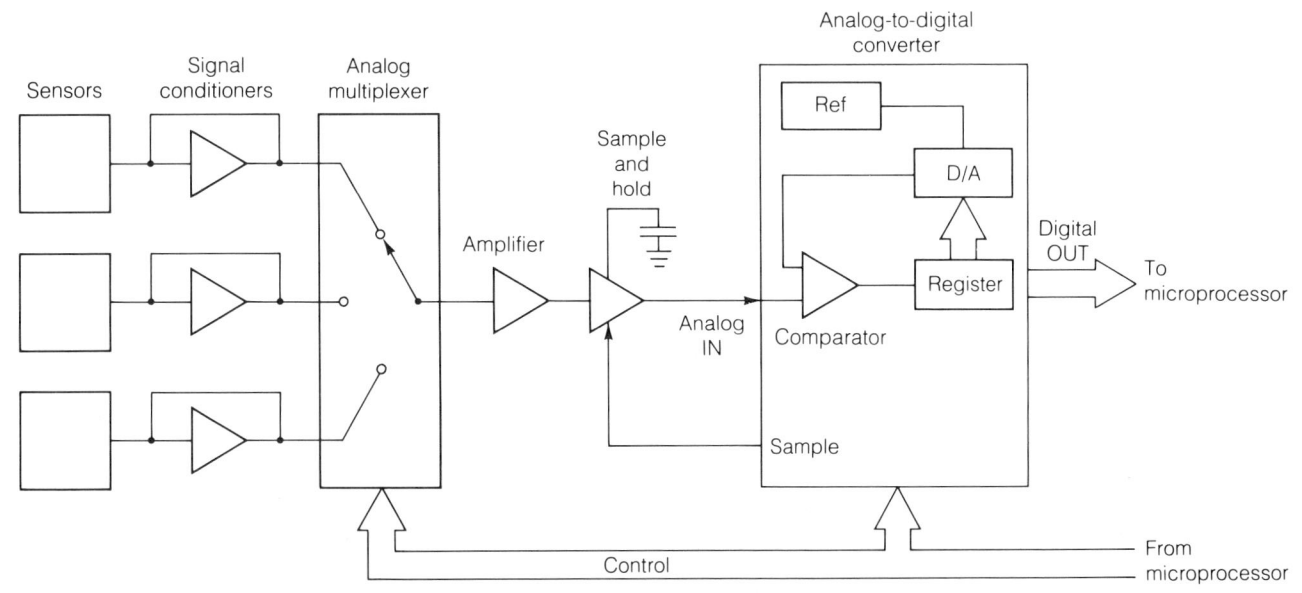

Figure 18.25 Block-level data-acquisition system.

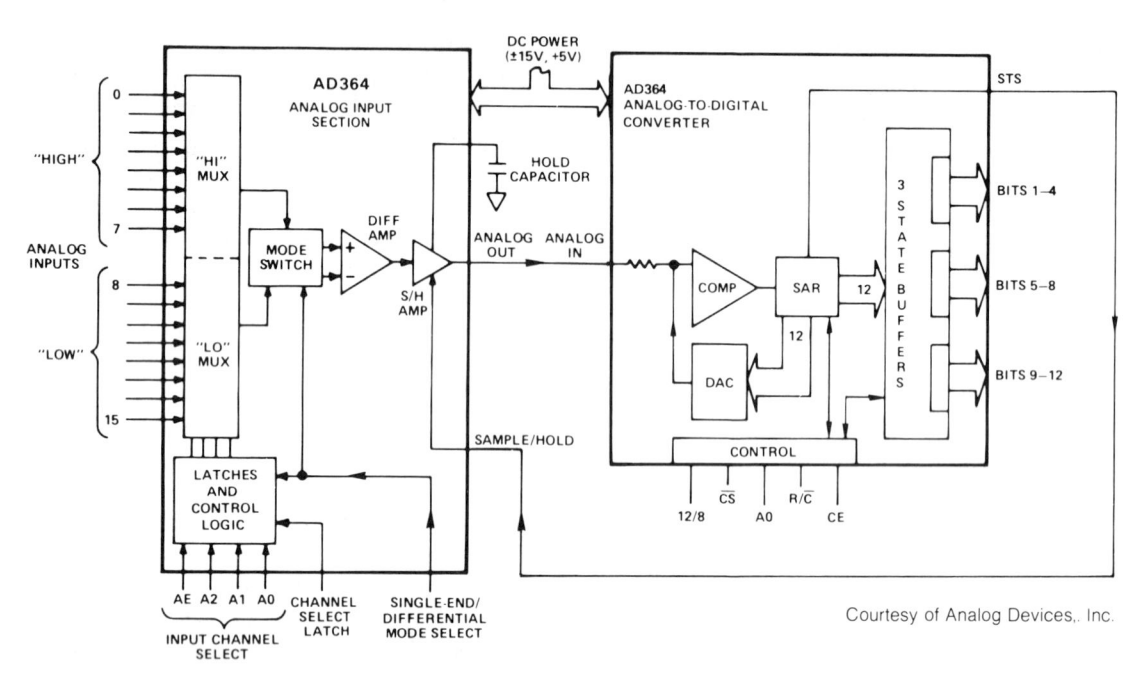

Figure 18.26 The AD364 data-acquisition system.

label field at the beginning of module MIMIC, and in the operand field of module DELAY after BRA. Clearly this time we have a problem. How will the assembler handle labels that cross module boundaries (known as *global* symbols)? Any symbol not defined in some manner within the program module will be tagged as an error.

The solution rests with two new directives: PUBLIC and EXTRN. For each label that appears in two or more modules we must ask the following question: Is the label *defined* (declared) in the present module and *used* elsewhere, or is it *used* in the present module and *defined* elsewhere? Referring to Figure 18.27, we find that:

- Label START is *defined* in module MIMIC (i.e., it appears in the label field), so we make it accessible to external programs by listing it after the PUBLIC directive (also known as *XDEF*).
- Label START is *used* by module DELAY (i.e., it appears in the operand field), so we use the EXTRN (external) directive (also known as *XREF*) to tell the assembler and linker that label START is *defined* in another module.

Note the switch to the JMP op code, since BRA cannot be used with global symbols. Also note the "E" after the assembled jump address to indicate the address is based on an external label and will be fully established during the LINK and LOCATE processes.

With the PUBLIC and EXTRN directives included in our "bag of tricks," we can safely use labels that cross module boundaries, and add still more power to the concept of modular programming.

INTELLIGENT-MACHINE UPDATE

Once completely a digital device, unable to function in an analog world, our intelligent machine has clothed itself in layers of I/O and interfacing circuitry and is now at home in the real world. It is becoming a truly social, well-behaved machine, and it will soon be easy to forget that at its core lies a purely digital system.

QUESTIONS AND PROBLEMS

1. What are some of the characteristics that make human conversation normally an asynchronous information-transfer process?
2. Why is handshaking not required when reading data from primary memory?
3. What is the major advantage of interrupt I/O over programmed I/O?
4. When interfacing multiple devices, why is interrupt I/O generally faster than programmed I/O?
5. Why is DMA I/O an especially fast I/O process?
6. Design a 2-bit DAC, using the weighted-current technique.
7. Complete the successive-approximation A/D program of Figure 18.11*b*.
8. What is the accuracy of a 12-bit A/D system?
9. Why must ultrahigh-speed A/D converters use the simultaneous (flash) method?
10. What is the major advantage of the scanned method of keyboard entry?

```
                        6800/6801/6802 ASSEMBLER VER.3.3        1

        1                       ; MIMIC.LST in relocatable code.
        2                       ; Label START is declared PUBLIC (XDEF)
        3                       ; and may be used by module DELAY.
        4
        5                               CSEG
        6                               PUBLIC    START
        7 0000 B6 20 00    START:      LDAA      $2000
        8 0003 81 34                   CMPA      #52
        9 0005 27 01 0008              BEQ       AHEAD
       10 0007 4F                      CLRA
       11 0008 B7 10 00    AHEAD:      STAA      $1000
       12 000B                         END


ERRORS = 0000

AHEAD  C 0008    MEMORY M 0000    STACK  S 0000    START  C 0000
```

(a) Program listing all labels <u>defined</u> in the present module
but used elsewhere after the PUBLIC directive

```
                        6800/6801/6802 ASSEMBLER VER.3.3        1

        1                       ; DELAY.LST in relocatable code.
        2                       ; Label START has been defined
        3                       ; EXTERNALLY (XREF) in module MIMIC
        4
        5                               CSEG
        6                               EXTRN     START
        7 0000 C6 A0                   LDAB      #$A0
        8 0002 5A         BACK:        DECB
        9 0003 26 FD 0002              BNE       BACK
       10 0005 7E 00 00 E              JMP       START
       11 0008                         END


ERRORS = 0000

BACK   C 0002    MEMORY M 0000    STACK  S 0000    START  E 0000
```

(b) Program listing all labels <u>used</u> in the present module but
defined elsewhere after the EXTRN directive

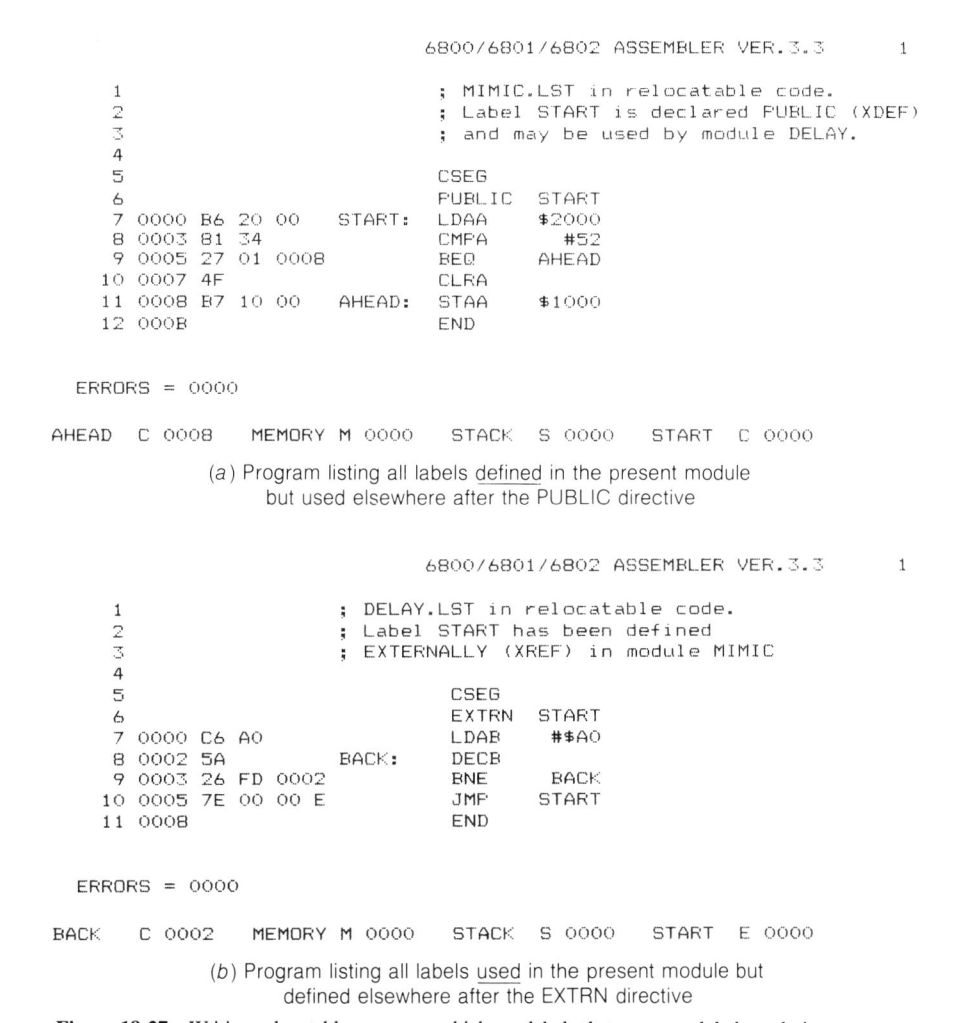

Figure 18.27 Writing relocatable programs which use labels that cross module boundaries (global symbols).

11. Flowchart a method of driving the scanned keyboard circuit of Figure 18.15.
12. Flowchart a method of driving the multiplexed display of Figure 18.16.
13. What is the minimum number of input-port locations that must be reserved for the keyboard system of Figure 18.15?
14. What is a *pixel*?
15. How much bit-mapped RAM would be required to support an 8000 × 8000 pixel display, each having a full 256 color/intensity variation?
16. To prove that high-level programming languages are "English-like," analyze the Pascal program that generated the fireworks display of Figure 18.24 and summarize how it was done (don't worry if you haven't had Pascal).
17. What is a *character generator*?
18. What are the three major components of a data-acquisition system?
19. Write a lowpass filter program that will exclude (out-port 0) all voltage waveforms changing at a rate of 1 V/ms or faster.
20. Although not covered directly in this text, how would you use a transistor to buffer the output lines of MOS or CMOS components to drive a high-current LED?
21. Based on the hardware of Figure 18.15, write a simple keyboard/display monitor routine to perform the examine/examine-next function (display contents of successive memory locations). (Select 16 keys for the hex inputs, leaving one of the remaining 8 for the examine/examine-next function. *Hint:* Allow for loading of the index register from the keyboard in order to increment from one memory location to the next.)

22. Based on the hardware of Figure 18.11a, write an A/D program based on the counter method. (Output a staircase to the DAC until the analog input and staircase level are equal. If calibrated properly, the number of steps taken equals the answer.)
23. Why does a bit-mapped graphics video display require so much more memory than a purely character-generation system?
24. Is the $R/\overline{W}$ signal to the NAND gate of Figure 18.7b absolutely necessary?
25. More realism could be obtained for the fireworks display of Figure 18.24 by erasing "old" bursts as "new" ones are produced. In general terms, how might you modify the fireworks program listed in the text to include this feature?
26. Following up question 25 above, even more realism would result from tracing the path of the rocket to the burst point. Again in general terms, how might this be accomplished?
27. Under what conditions would you use the PUBLIC (XDEF) and EXTNL (XREF) directives in a program module?
28. Using the 6800-based computer system developed in Part I, simulate a simple single-pole (one brake frequency), low-pass filter using digital filtering techniques. (Research will be required.)

chapter 19

Programmable Peripheral Chips

All animals that share this planet—as well as human beings—are a blend of hardware and software characteristics. The high-order animals are rich in software properties; they are adaptable and can be "programmed" to meet new situations. The lower-order animals, on the other hand, have few software properties; their actions are "hardwired" and purely instinctive. When facing the challenges of the real world, each property has its advantages as well as its drawbacks.

Animals with a high degree of programmability (software-oriented) can modify their behavior, and—given the flexibility of learning—have a reduced need for specialized anatomy. However, the process of learning new tasks is often slow and agonizing, and once learned, the tasks are often performed slowly, inefficiently, and unreliably.

Animals that rely on hardware have developed highly specialized anatomy and instincts to best fit their particular niche in the environment; they have advantages in speed, efficiency, and reliability—*provided the task they are doing is one for which they are inherently suited*. (All the specialized "tools" they have acquired over the generations can turn against them should the environment change too suddenly.)

Today, computers are in a similar situation: they are a blend of software and hardware. To design a system based primarily on software is to design a system that is flexible and adaptable—but one that requires a vast amount of programmer time, and in the end, one that may be too slow for the task at hand. Switch to a purely hardware system and we have a high-speed, reliable machine with no need for expensive software development—but one that is not easily modified, and exhibits no (artificial) intelligence. *Clearly the ideal computer system is a compromise.*

The *programmable peripheral chip*—the subject of this chapter—is designed with such a compromise in mind. Intended to link up with microprocessors—which are inherently software oriented—the programmable peripheral chip is primarily a hardware device. But, as we have seen, a purely hardware device lacks flexibility; designers do not have the time or room to order and stock the numerous specialized circuits required for every computer application.

So they made this chip programmable *to fit a range of related applications*.

Once nature discovered the benefits of a hardware/software blend, the animal kingdom flourished, each member exhibiting the ideal blend of dedicated-anatomy (hardware) and adaptability (software) to prosper in its local environment. The computer world, now armed with the programmable peripheral chip, is once again merely following suit.

BASICS OF PROGRAMMABLE PERIPHERAL CHIPS

A programmable peripheral chip is a multimode integrated circuit, programmed by the user to match specific needs. In other words, a programmable peripheral chip is really many chips in one, and the user decides what configuration the chip will assume.

There are two general categories of programmable peripheral chips: those that are hardware programmable, and—more important—those that are software programmable.

Hardware-Programmable Chips

The popular 6882B octal buffer/latch (the "eyes" and "ears" of our intelligent machine) is an example of a chip that can be hardware programmed. The 6882B has a split personality, which is what makes it programmable. It can become either an input port or an output port, depending on the use of the Output Enable (OE) and Latch lines. By placing two 6882Bs side by side, one facing out and the other facing in, we have a true hardware-programmable I/O port module (Figure 19.1). To program the module for input operations, tie "mode" high; for output operations, tie "mode" low.

There is also a big disadvantage to hardware programming. Once the chip is wired for one operation (say input-port operation), external circuitry changes are required to convert to an output-port operation (the mode line must be grounded).

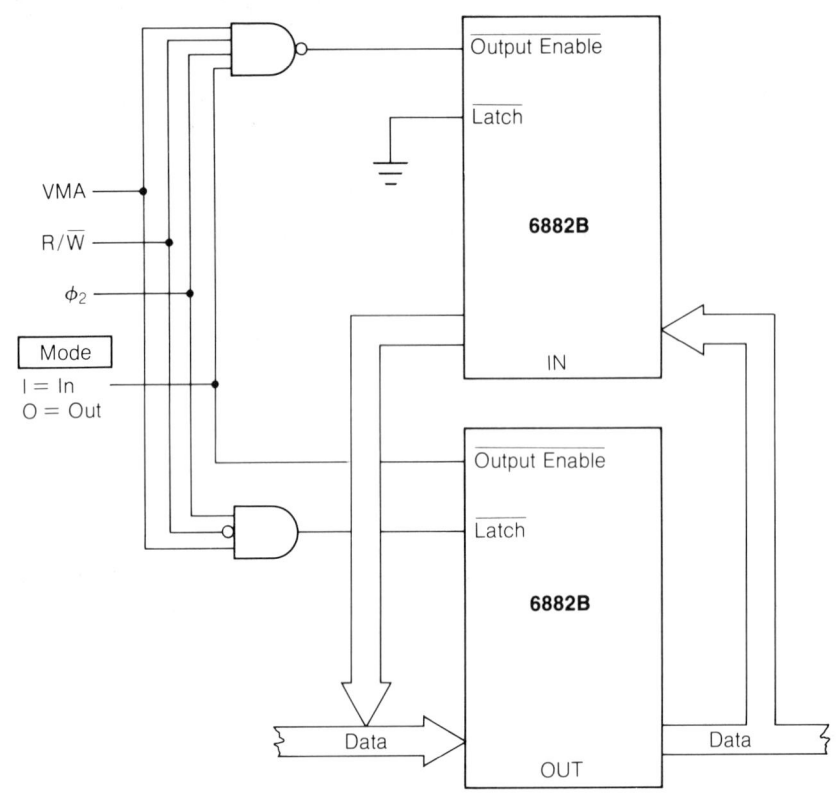

Figure 19.1 Hardware-programmed I/O module.

Software-Programmable Chips

The solution to this problem in hardware programming revolutionized the computer industry. Instead of *hardwiring* the "mode" line for either input or output operation, why not set this line with another latched output port? That way, the computer, *by way of program action,* will set the I/O module for either input or output operation. No hardware changes are required at all—the changes are made through software, *by the computer*.

Place both types of ports inside one chip, provide a means for addressing each, and you have the birth of a true programmable peripheral chip, one that is software programmable (Figure 19.2a).

To configure this new chip for input operations, simply write a logic 1 to the mode-control port (or as it is now called, the *mode-control register*) by following the where/when sequence of Figure 19.2b. The control/data (C/$\overline{\text{D}}$) input line is used to distinguish between control registers and data registers and will tie in to the address bus. If at a later time you would like to convert to output operation, write a logic 0 to the mode-control register.

You may even wish to include within the chip a special input-port register that will allow the computer to read in the mode status at any time. (Is the device presently configured for input operation or for output operation?) Such a register is called a *status* register.

Although this simple programmable peripheral I/O chip we have developed does not really exist in integrated form, look for all programmable peripheral chips presently on the market to include the three types of internal registers shown in Figure 19.3: a data register to hold true data, a control register to set the mode of operation, and a status register to determine the internal state of the chip. Also, look for a method of addressing each register type, and expect the chip to operate in either the programmed I/O or interrupt I/O mode.

So powerful is the concept of software programmability that a veritable flood of programmable peripheral chips has flowed onto the market, and there is no end in sight:

- MC6821 Peripheral Interface Adapter
- MC6828 Priority Interrupt Controller
- MC6850 Asynchronous Communications Interface Adapter
- MC6839 Floating-Point ROM
- MC6840 Programmable Timer
- MC6843 Floppy-Disk Controller
- MC6852 Synchronous Serial Data Adapter
- MC6854 Advanced Data Link Controller

In this chapter we will take a close look at the first two on the list, while the third item—the 6850—will be covered in detail in Chapter 21. Keep in mind that, since all programmable peripheral chips have a great deal in common,

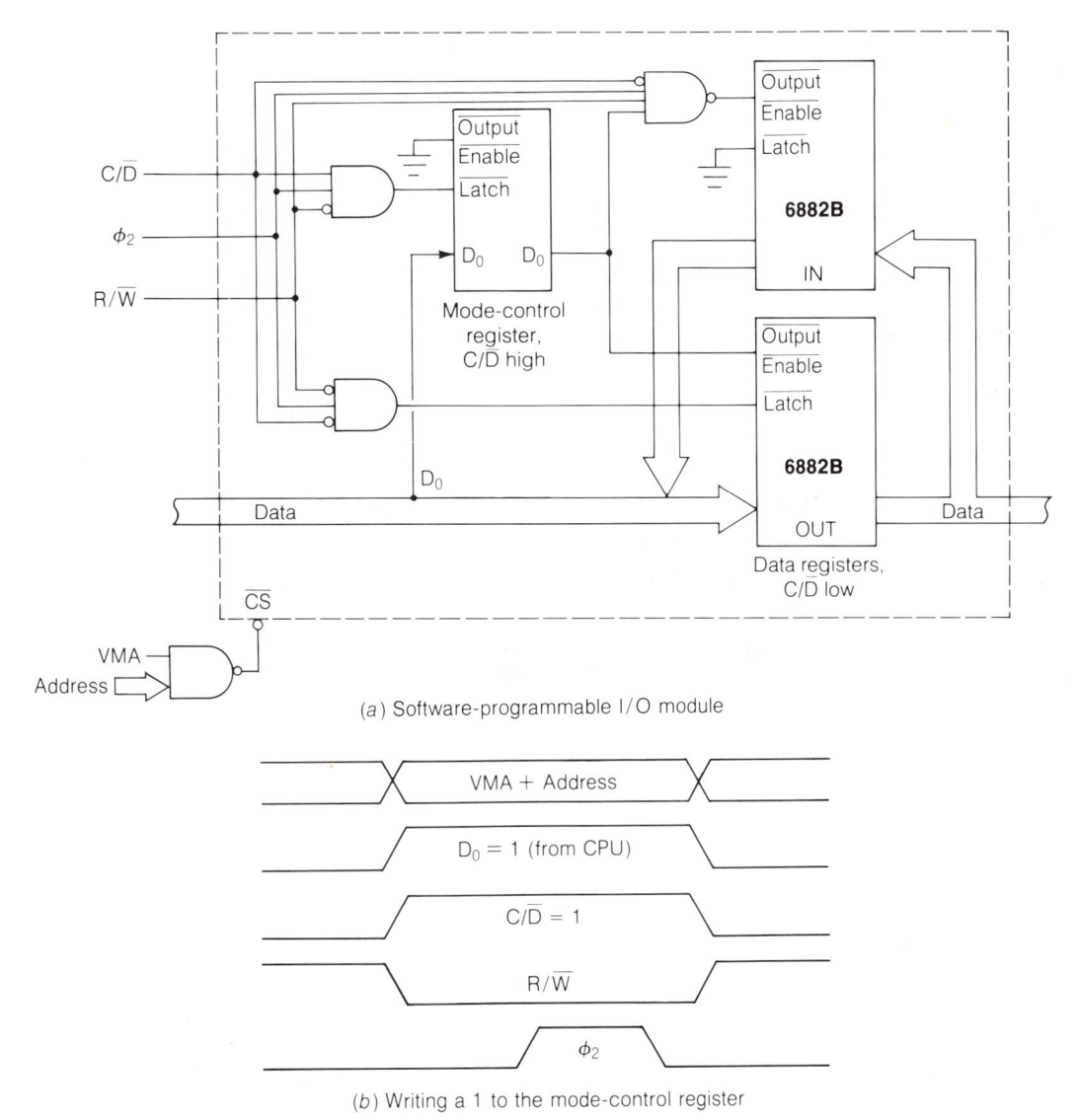

Figure 19.2 The programmable peripheral chip.

(a) Software-programmable I/O module

(b) Writing a 1 to the mode-control register

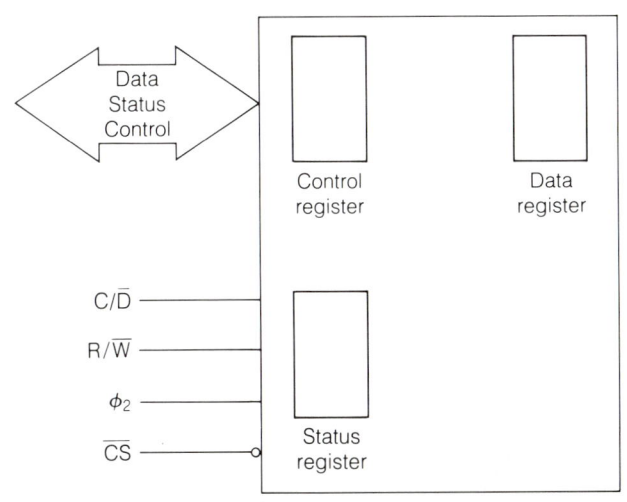

Figure 19.3 Typical programmable, peripheral-chip, internal-register types and bus interfacing.

mastery of several representative examples will help you to understand the theory and use of all programmable peripheral chips.

THE 6821 PERIPHERAL INTERFACE ADAPTER

The 6821 Peripheral Interface Adapter, or PIA, is perhaps the most common type of programmable peripheral chip in use today, and consequently has been selected for detailed study.

The 6821 is a two-port general-purpose I/O device, designed to interface a variety of peripheral equipment to the system bus—and to do it with greater ease than ever before. Being programmable, its functional configuration is selected by software, thereby greatly reducing the need for additional interfacing hardware.

Looking inside the 6821 (Figure 19.4), we find the three expected types of registers—data, control, and status—arranged in two groups, A and B. Each group is nearly identical, consisting of a peripheral interface (PI), output register (OR), control register (CR), data direction register (DDR), and interrupt status control register (interrupt status is actually determined by reading bits 6 and 7 of the control register). The control registers (CRA and CRB) are what make the 6821 programmable. By writing various control words to the control registers, the 6821 can be custom configured for a specific application—in fact, too many applications to cover at one time—so, once again, the best approach is to learn by example.

Interfacing the 6821 to a Printer

Here is our design assignment: to output parallel data to a printer at the maximum possible rate, but still allow the computer ample time to process other data. We conclude immediately that *our system must be of asynchronous design using handshaking signals in the interrupt I/O mode*. The 6821 looks like the answer: it provides data and handshaking ports, and offers the option of interrupt I/O.

The Centronics parallel interface sequence we studied earlier will serve as the model (Figure 19.5). This time, because the handshaking input to the 6821 is latching, we will use the $\overline{\text{ACKNLG}}$ (Acknowledge) pulse, rather than the level-active BUSY signal. Basically, by way of review, the $\overline{\text{ACKNLG}}$ pulse from the printer says, "Send me more data"; the $\overline{\text{STROBE}}$ pulse from the CPU responds, "Okay, here it is."

The design consists of the following four phases:

1. Interfacing the 6821 to the computer bus
2. Programming the mode of operation
3. Interfacing the 6821 to the printer
4. Writing and testing the output routine

Phase 1—Interfacing the 6821 to the computer bus As illustrated in Figure 19.6, interfacing the 6821A to a 6800-based system bus is very straightforward and should present little difficulty. (After all, one purpose of the programmable

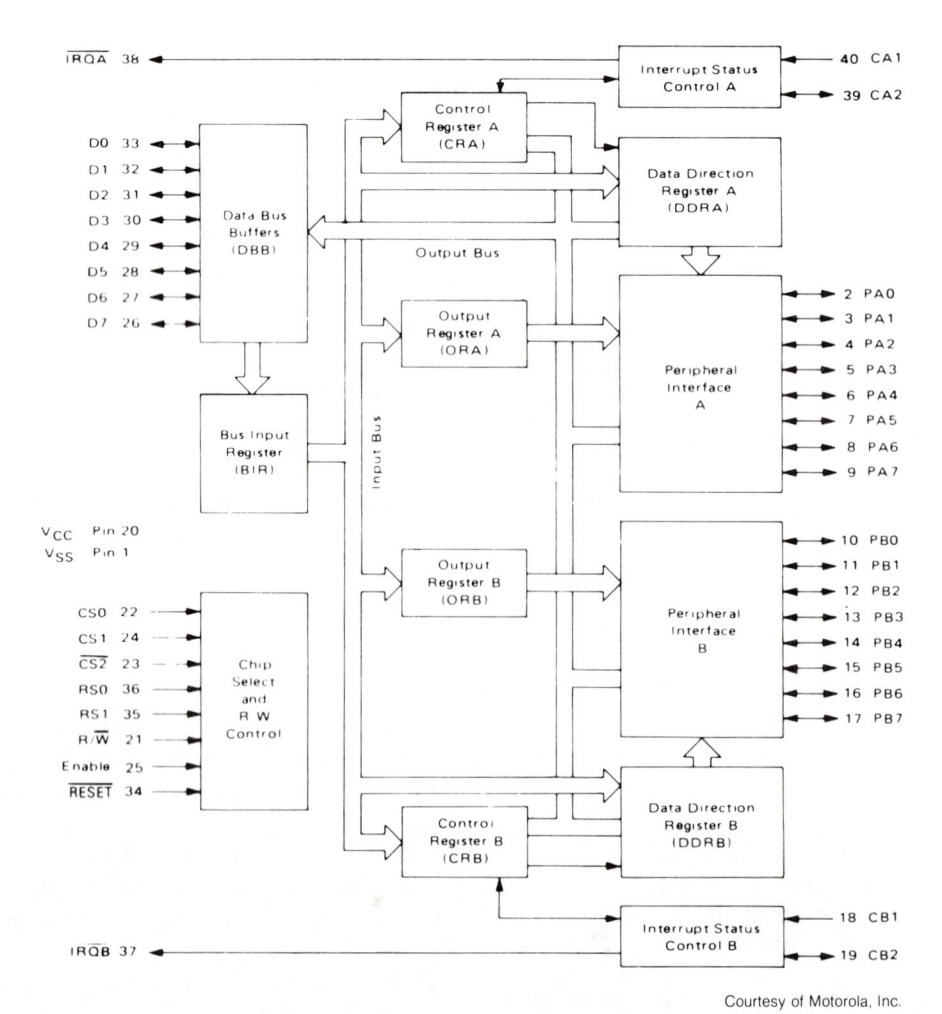

Courtesy of Motorola, Inc.

Figure 19.4 MC6821 Peripheral Interface Adapter (PIA) block diagram.

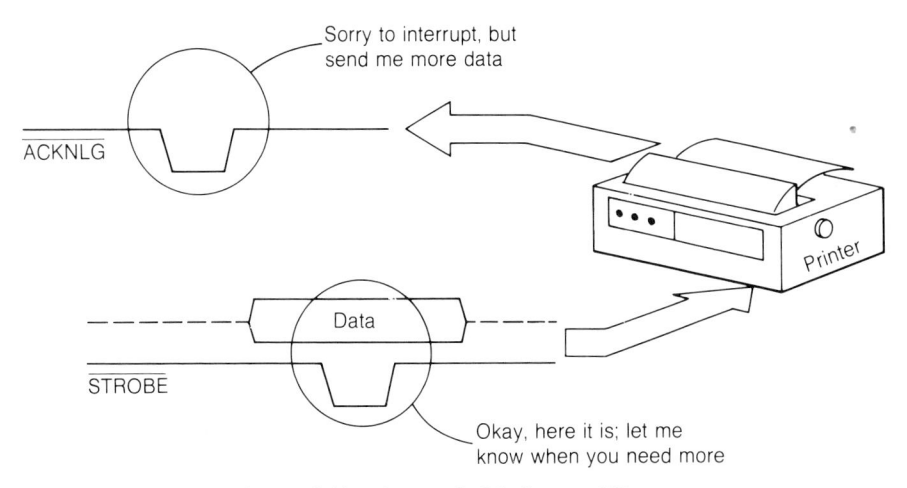

Figure 19.5 The Centronics parallel interface standard for interrupt I/O.

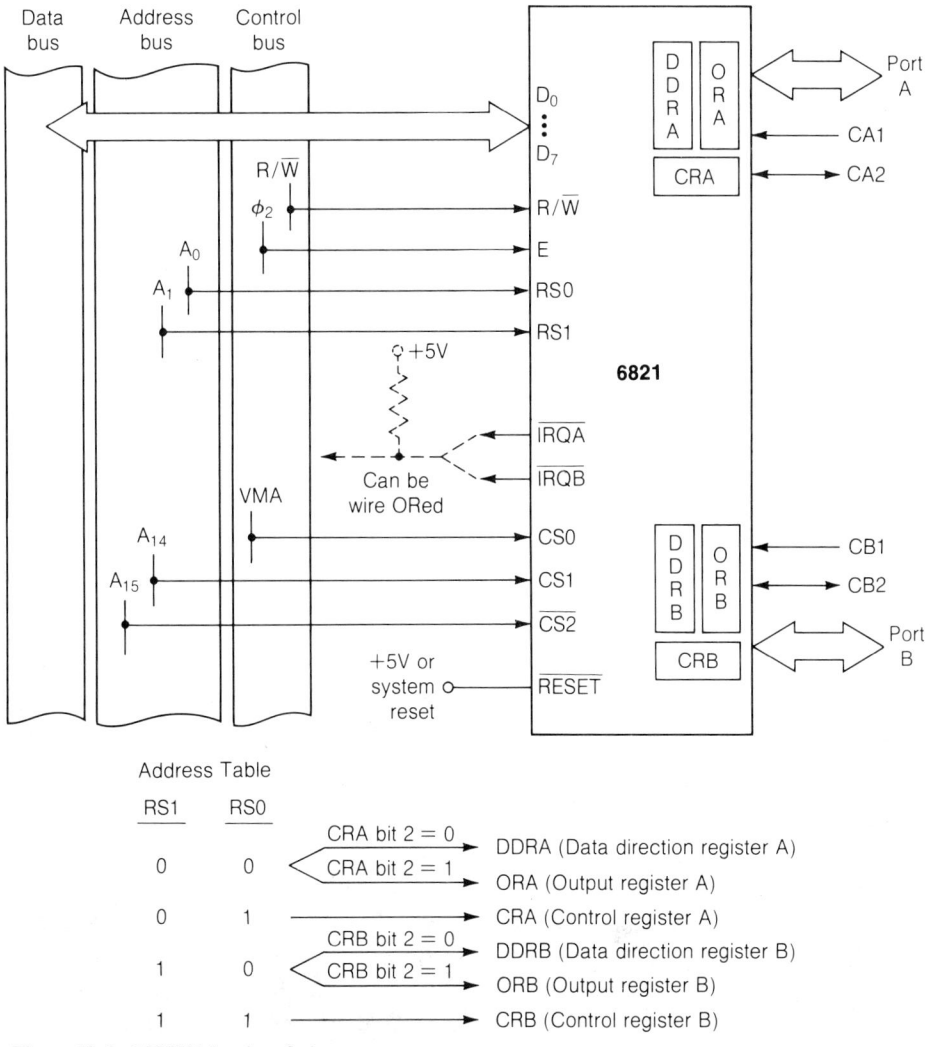

Figure 19.6 MC6821 bus interfacing.

Address Table

RS1	RS0		
0	0	CRA bit 2 = 0 → DDRA (Data direction register A)
0	0	CRA bit 2 = 1 → ORA (Output register A)
0	1	→ CRA (Control register A)
1	0	CRB bit 2 = 0 → DDRB (Data direction register B)
1	0	CRB bit 2 = 1 → ORB (Output register B)
1	1	→ CRB (Control register B)

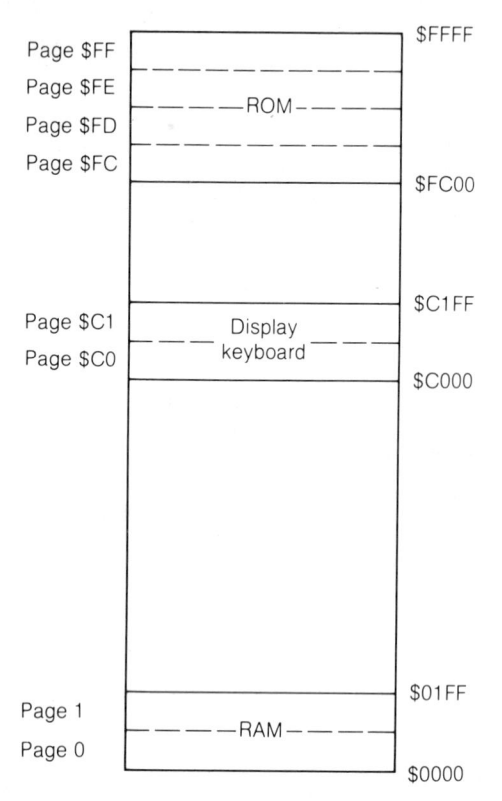

Figure 19.7 The Heathkit ET-3400A trainer memory map, showing areas available for expansion.

peripheral chip is to simplify the hardware interface.) Since our system is small, we will combine the techniques of linear and decoded addressing to place our 6821 at a convenient location. As usual, our only concern is that the two memory-mapped port locations of the 6821 do not overlap any existing ROM, RAM, and I/O ports. Just for practice, let's consider the memory map of the Heathkit trainer (Figure 19.7), and see where we can fit in our 6821 PIA.

First of all, the lower 32K looks less cluttered, so let's connect A_{15} to the active-low CS2. Then, to make sure we stay away from RAM's territory, let's connect A_{14} to active-high CS1. The foldback range of addresses is shown below:

```
A15 ─────────── A0
0100 0000 0000 0000     $4000
0111 1111 1111 1111     $7FFF
```

With our 6821 now properly positioned in the memory map, we move inside the 6821 to distinguish between the six control/data registers. The address table of Figure 19.6 shows us how. Note that if the RS0 input equals 1, the control registers can be accessed. If the RS0 input equals 0, either the data direction registers (DDR) or the peripheral data registers (PDR) can be accessed—*which one will depend on the value of bit 2 in the corresponding control register.*

Therefore, before reading or writing data to either a DDR or a PDR, make sure to enter the appropriate bit value to bit 2 of the control register first.

Phase 2—Programming the mode of operation To match the 6821 to our needs, we must answer a simple question: What 8-bit control words will we write to the control registers in order to set up the system for asynchronous, interrupt I/O transmission of parallel data using handshaking? The answer is found in the control-word format of Figure 19.8. Since the control-word format is identical for both group A and group B, it appears that either can be used. *However, as we will see shortly, group B is more suited for output operations.*

Starting from bit position 0, the proper control word to be written into CRB is assembled as follows (see Figure 19.9):

- Bit 0 enables or disables the interrupt request line (CB1) to the 6821. Interrupt I/O operation requires that this bit be a 1.

- Bit 1 determines the active transition direction (low-to-high or high-to-low) for the interrupt request on line CB1. Since $\overline{ACKNLG}$ is a short pulse containing both negative-going and positive-going edges, either direction will do. However, to save a fraction of a second, we choose negative-going (it occurs slightly earlier).

- Bit 2 steers the data to either the data direction register or the output register. Anticipating the need to program the DDR after setting the mode of operation, we select a 0 (data direction register selected).

- Bits 3, 4, and 5 determine the function of the single line CB2. Since CB2 will be used as the $\overline{STROBE}$ handshaking line to the printer, we place a "1" in bit position 5 to establish this line as an output.

  Choosing the values of bits 3 and 4 will require some careful reading of the material of Figure 19.8. Looking over the section regarding CB2 as an output, we learn that the 6821 contains provisions for *automatic* handshaking control. We will test the process later to make sure we are right, but for now when we compare the "Write strobe with E restore" mode description, with the Centronics interface standard (Figure 19.5) it looks like we have a match. Bit b4 = 0 and bit b3 = 1 should program the 6821 for output with handshaking. (Incidentally, by selecting the b4 = 1 option, the proper handshaking signals can be generated and detected by direct program action, rather than automatically.)

- Bit 6 is an interrupt flag bit, used when CB2 has been programmed as an input. It is purely a status bit, used for programmed I/O, and cannot be written to, so it does

Chapter 19 / Programmable Peripheral Chips

Determine Active CA1 (CB1) Transition for Setting Interrupt Flag IRQA(B)1 — (bit 7)
b1 = 0: IRQA(B)1 set by high-to-low transition on CA1 (CB1)
b1 = 1: IRQA(B)1 set by low-to-high transition on CA1 (CB1).

CA1 (CB1) Interrupt Request Enable/Disable
b0 = 0: Disables IRQA(B) MPU Interrupt by CA1 (CB1) active transition.[1]
b0 = 1: Enable IRQA(B) MPU Interrupt by CA1 (CB1) active transition.
1. IRQA(B) will occur on next (MPU generated) positive transition of b0 if CA1 (CB1) active transition occurred while interrupt was disabled.

IRQA(B) 1 Interrupt Flag (bit 7)
Goes high on active transition of CA1 (CB1); Automatically cleared by MPU Read of Output Register A(B). May also be cleared by hardware Reset.

Control Register

b7	b6	b5	b4	b3	b2	b1	b0
IRQA(B)1 Flag	IRQA(B)2 Flag	CA2 (CB2) Control			DDR Access	CA1 (CB1) Control	

IRQA(B)2 Interrupt Flag (bit 6)
When CA2 (CB2) is an input, IRQA(B) goes high on active transition CA2 (CB2); Automatically cleared by MPU Read of Output Register A(B). May also be cleared by hardware Reset.
CA2 (CB2) Established as Output (b5 = 1): IRQA(B) 2 = 0, not affected by CA2 (CB2) transitions.

Determines Whether Data Direction Register Or Output Register is Addressed
b2 = 0: Data Direction Register selected.
b2 = 1: Output Register selected.

CA2 (CB2) Established as Output by b5 = 1
(Note that operation of CA2 and CB2 output functions are not identical)

b5	b4	b3	
			CA2
1	0	b3 = 0:	**Read Strobe with CA1 Restore** CA2 goes low on first high-to-low E transition following an MPU read of Output Register A; returned high by next active CA1 transition, as specified by bit 1.
		b3 = 1:	**Read Strobe with E Restore** CA2 goes low on first high-to-low E transition following an MPU read of Output Register A; returned high by next high-to-low E transition during a deselect.
			CB2
		b3 = 0:	**Write Strobe with CB1 Restore** CB2 goes low on first low-to-high E transition following an MPU write into Output Register B; returned high by the next active CB1 transition as specified by bit 1. CRB-b7 must first be cleared by a read of data.
		b3 = 1:	**Write Strobe with E Restore** CB2 goes low on first low-to-high E transition following an MPU write into Output Register B; returned high by the next low-to-high E transition following an E pulse which occurred while the part was deselected.

b5	b4	b3	
1	1		**Set/Reset CA2 (CB2)** CA2 (CB2) goes low as MPU writes b3 = 0 into Control Register. CA2 (CB2) goes high as MPU writes b3 = 1 into Control Register.

CA2 (CB2) Established as Input by b5 = 0

b5	b4	b3	
0			**CA2 (CB2) Interrupt Request Enable/Disable** b3 = 0: Disables IRQA(A) MPU Interrupt by CA2 (CB2) active transition.* b3 = 1: Enables IRQA(B) MPU Interrupt by CA2 (CB2) active transition. *IRQA(B) will occur on next (MPU generated) positive transition of b3 if CA2 (CB2) active transition occurred while interrupt was disabled.
			Determines Active CA2 (CB2) Transition for Setting Interrupt Flag IRQA(B)2 — (Bit b6) b4 = 0: IRQA(B)2 set by high-to-low transition on CA2 (CB2). b4 = 1: IRQA(B)2 set by low-to-high transition on CA2 (CB2).

Courtesy of Motorola, Inc.

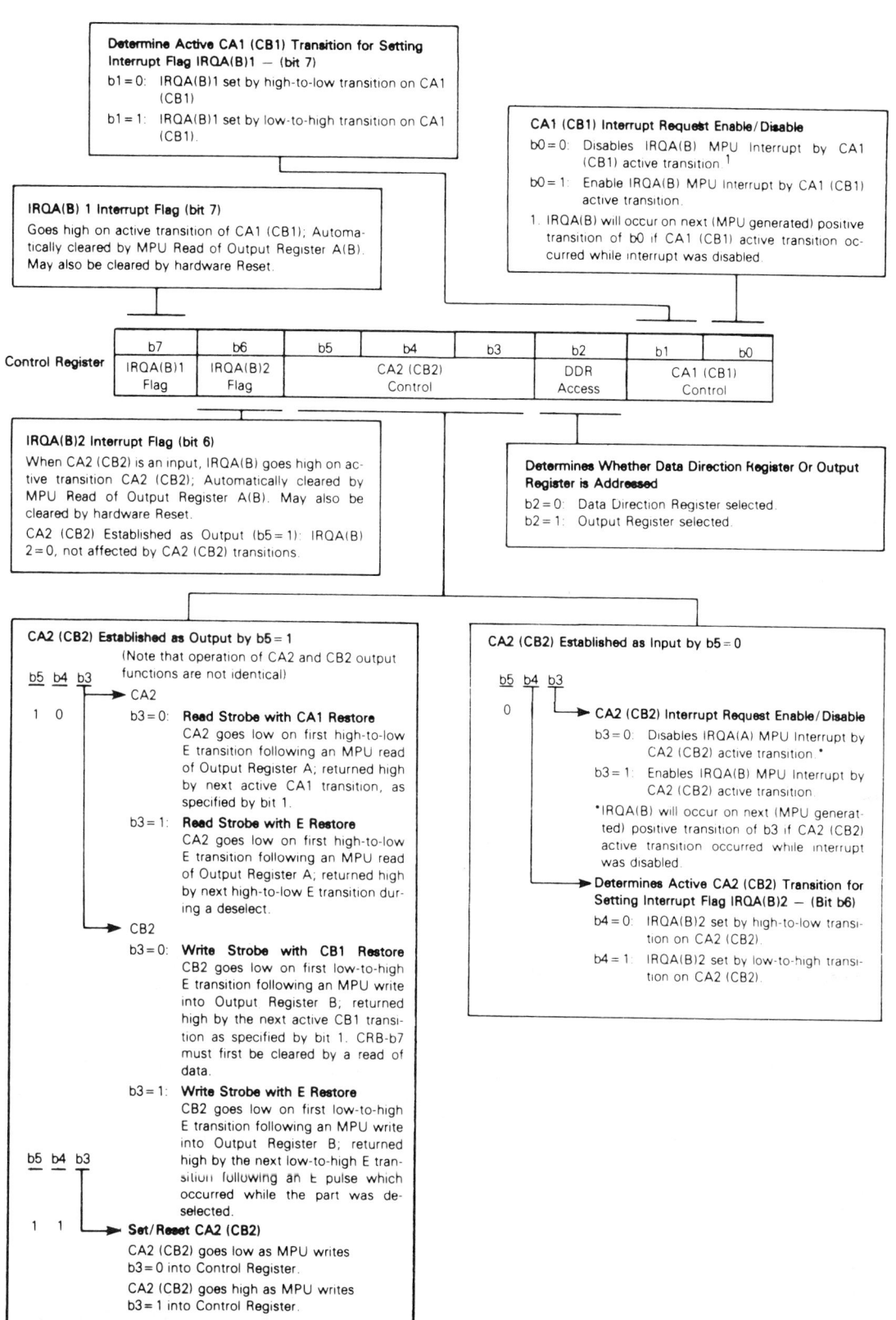

Figure 19.8 The 6821 PIA control-word format.

Control Register B

7	6	5	4	3	2	1	0
IRQB1 flag	IRQB2 flag	CB2 control			DDR access	CB1 control	
0	0	1	0	1	0	0	1

- Bit 0, 1: Enable negative-going interrupt on CB1
- Bit 2: 1 — Output register selected. 0 — Data direction register selected.
- Bits 3, 4, 5: Write strobe with E restore.
- Bit 6: Cannot be written to. Automatically set to 0 when CB2 programmed as output (b5 = 1).
- Bit 7: Cannot be written to. Set by active transition of CB1. Cleared by MPU read of output register B.

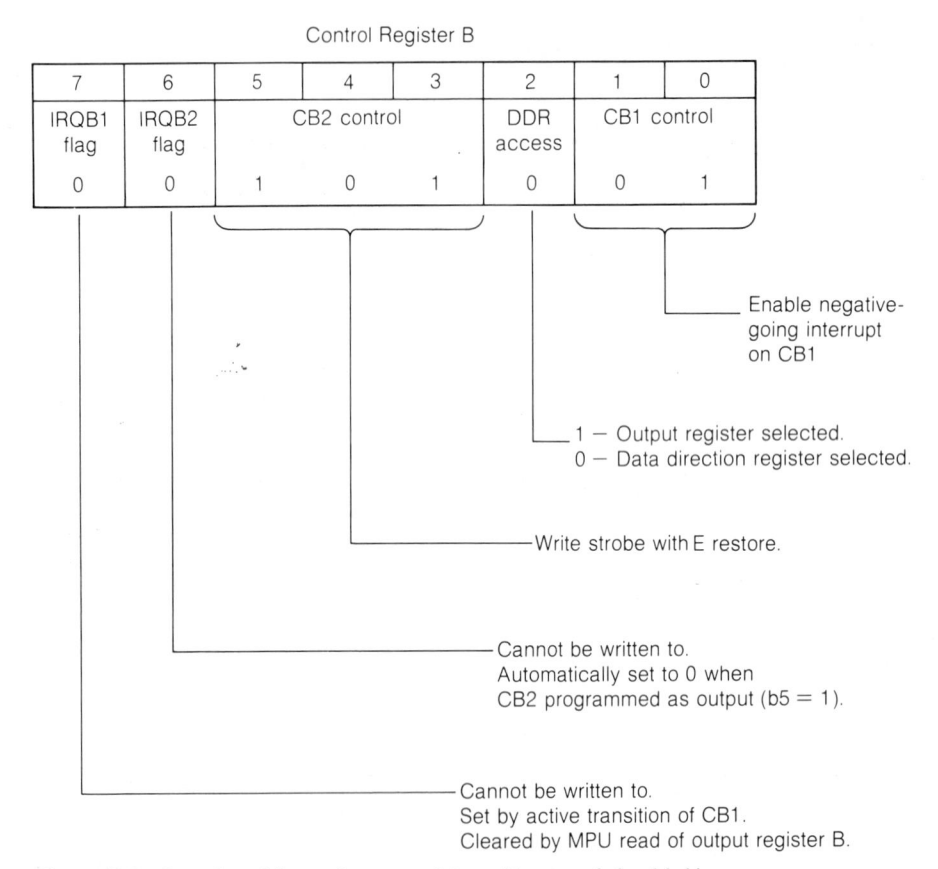

Figure 19.9 Control-word format for output of data with automatic handshaking.

not matter what we place in bit position 6. Besides, when CB2 is established as an output, bit 6 is automatically set to 0.

- Bit 7 is the second interrupt flag, and goes high upon active transition of CB1. It also is purely a status bit, and cannot be written to. Bit 7 is cleared by an MPU read of output register B. We will arbitrarily place a 0 in bit position 7.

Establishing all eight lines of port B as an output port is also part of phase 2 (programming the mode of operation), and is accomplished by writing $FF to data direction register B (DDRB). To address DDRB, place a 0 in bit 2 of CRB, and follow the addressing requirements of Figure 19.6.

To summarize phase 2 of our design, Figure 19.10 shows the complete routine for programming the 6821 for output-mode interrupt I/O operation.

First we load the control word of Figure 19.9 into control register B, following the addressing scheme of Figure 19.6. After all eight lines of port B are configured for output operations, we use a simple masking sequence to set bit 2 of control register B high, so subsequent data written into the 6821 by the MPU will flow to output register B (ORB) and on to the printer.

Phase 3—Interfacing the 6821 to the printer By interfacing the two handshaking signals to the printer and sending the interrupt output to the CPU, phase 3 of our design is quickly completed (see Figure 19.11).

Phase 4—Writing and testing the output routine Before we write the output routine and test our system, let's review the output handshaking scheme programmed into the 6821.

Let's pick up the action when the printer has just finished printing one character and issues the $\overline{\text{ACKNLG}}$ pulse to inform the 6821 it is ready for the next character. The sequence unfolds as follows (refer to Figures 19.11 and 19.12):

① The negative-going edge of the $\overline{\text{ACKNLG}}$ pulse is received by the 6821 on CB1. The IRQB1 flag (bit 7 of CRB) is set high; the $\overline{\text{IRQB}}$ output pin automatically goes low and requests an $\overline{\text{IRQ}}$ interrupt from the 6800.

② Within the interrupt-service routine (ISR), the computer writes the next data word into output register B (address $4002). IRQB1 is then cleared by a read of output register B (so the level-sensitive interrupt line will be inactive when action returns to the main program).

is considerably reduced—and so is the workload of the programmer. As shown in the test program of Figure 19.13, the output program is a very straightforward interrupt output routine (the strobed-output handshaking sequence is invisible to the CPU).

In a real situation, means must be provided for determining when the correct number of bytes had been transferred to the printer. Under these conditions, it might be best to turn to the polled mode of operation, in which the "request character" (Acknowledge) signal from the printer can be detected by a status-read of control register B (bit 7) to determine the state of input CB1. Also, in a real situation, $\overline{BUSY}$ probably would be used in conjunction with $\overline{ACKNLG}$ to indicate the state of readiness of the printer.

Multiple I/O Operations

With its 16 individually programmed I/O lines and its multiple modes of operation, the 6821 can interface with multiple devices in a variety of ways. For example, if all four control lines are configured for interrupt operation, both interrupt output lines can be wire-ORed to the 6800. Within the ISR, the MPU checks the four interrupt status bits (according to priority) to see who is requesting service. Since all interrupt requests are latched, the request is not lost, even if the interrupt flag in the 6800 were set (interrupt disabled) at the time of request.

THE STANDARD MICROCOMPUTER SYSTEM

With the 6821 parallel interface (PIA) in place, we can now introduce the *standard microcomputer system* (Figure 19.14). Consisting of four chips—MPU, RAM, ROM, and PIA—it is neither the simplest nor the most complex system possible, but has the flexibility and power to solve many application problems. In Chapter 21 we will add the 6850 UART *serial* communication block to our standard microcomputer system, giving it still greater power and flexibility.

THE MC6828 PRIORITY INTERRUPT CONTROLLER

Closely behind the PIA in importance and widespread use is the 6828 Priority Interrupt Controller (PIC), designed to speed up the process of handling multiple, maskable, prioritized interrupts.

The 6828 places a great deal of *software on silicon,* as it replaces any polling software required to locate the highest priority interrupt and generate the corresponding vector. But before we delve into the intricacies of the 6828, let's have the basic two-step vectored interrupt process well in mind:

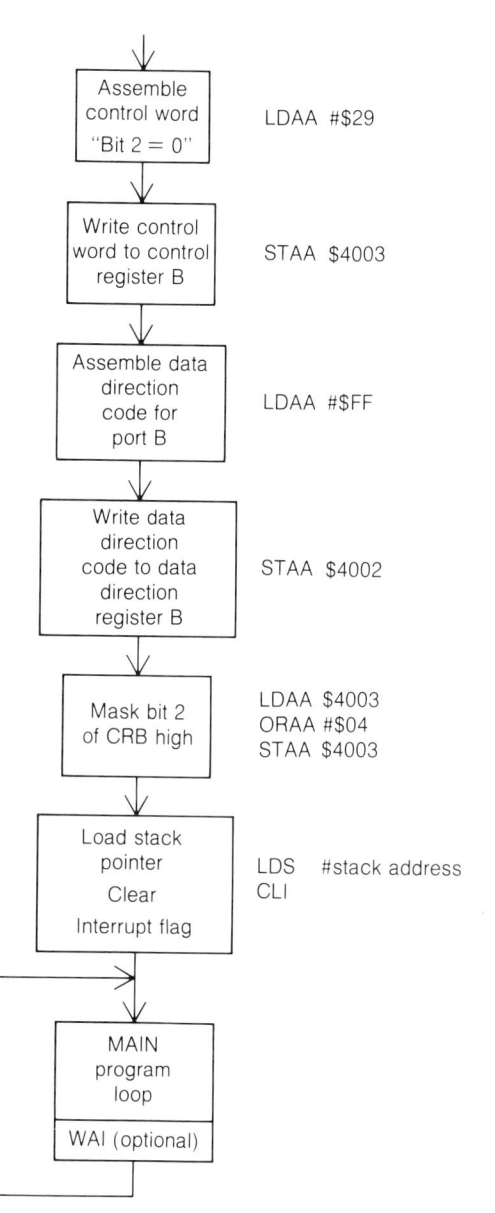

Figure 19.10 Initializing the 6821 for automatic-handshaking, interrupt-I/O operation.

Step	Instruction
Assemble control word "Bit 2 = 0"	LDAA #$29
Write control word to control register B	STAA $4003
Assemble data direction code for port B	LDAA #$FF
Write data direction code to data direction register B	STAA $4002
Mask bit 2 of CRB high	LDAA $4003 / ORAA #$04 / STAA $4003
Load stack pointer / Clear Interrupt flag	LDS #stack address / CLI
MAIN program loop	WAI (optional)

③ $\overline{STROBE}$ (CB2) automatically goes low on the next E transition following the data write to output register B (ORB).

④ $\overline{STROBE}$ is automatically returned high on the next low-to-high E transition.

⑤ The printer carries out the operation commanded by the character.

⑥ When the printer is ready for the next word, it sends the $\overline{ACKNLG}$ signal, and action returns to step 1.

What makes the strobed-output process so useful is that most of the housekeeping tasks required to feed data to the printer are handled by the 6821. The workload on the CPU

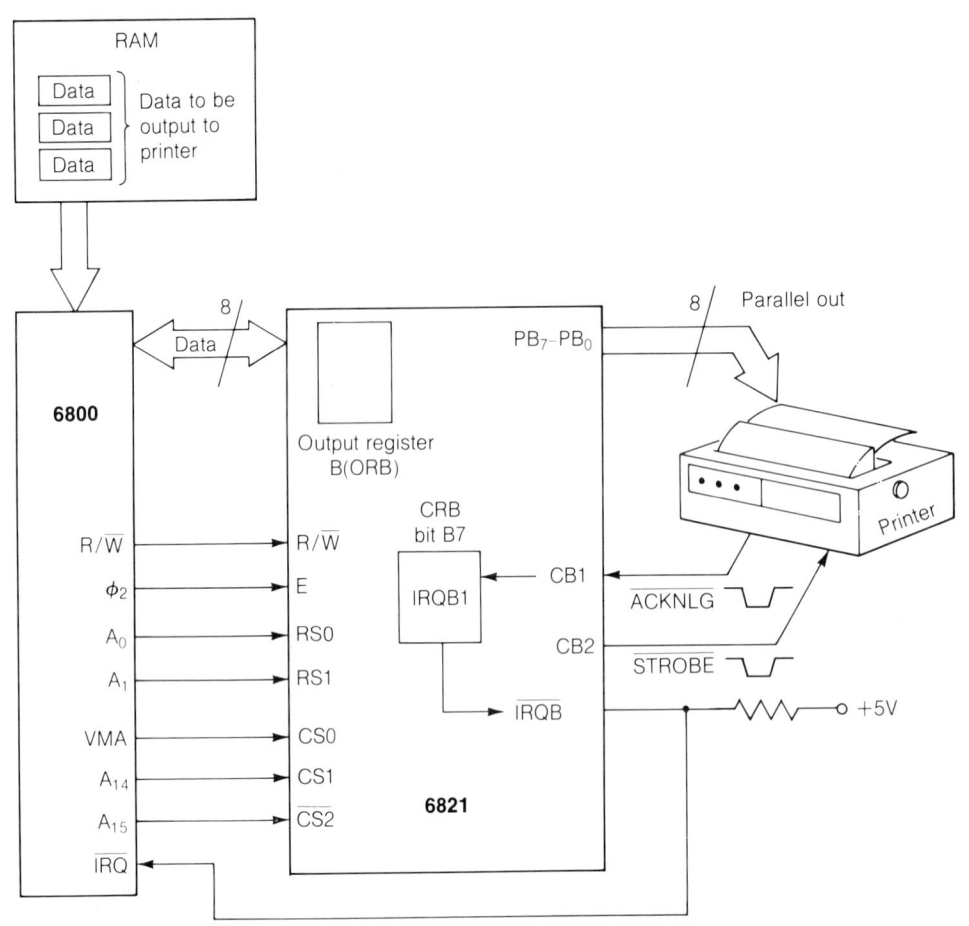

Figure 19.11 Strobed-output-mode hardware design (interrupt-I/O mode).

1. An interrupt is requested by pulling $\overline{\text{IRQ}}$ low.
2. The contents of $FFF8 and $FFF9 (the starting address of the interrupt routine) are pulled from ROM and jammed into the program counter.

There are eight interrupt requests to the 6828 (Figure 19.15), so there must be eight starting locations stored in

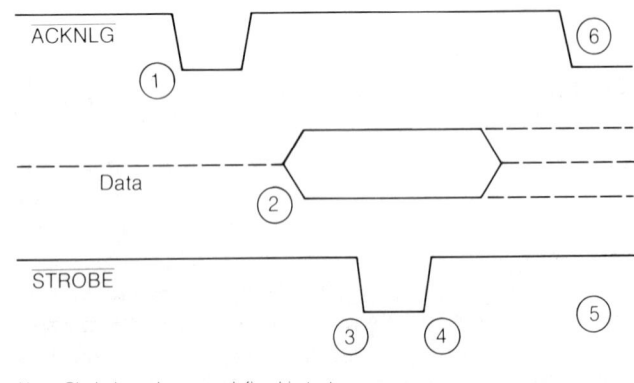

Note: Circled numbers are defined in text.

Figure 19.12 The strobed-output handshaking sequence.

ROM. Let's put the design problem in terms of a challenge: How can we pull eight different vectors from eight different ROM locations when the processor presently accesses only ROM locations $FFF8 and $FFF9 in response to the $\overline{\text{IRQ}}$ interrupt?

The answer is, The 6828 *modifies* the vector ROM addresses as the interrupt request is processed. Looking to Figure 19.16, we see in general terms how it is done. When an interrupt is initiated by pulling one or more of the eight inputs ($\overline{\text{IN0}}$–$\overline{\text{IN7}}$) active low, $\overline{\text{INT}}$ goes low and an $\overline{\text{IRQ}}$ interrupt request is sent to the 6800. The 6828 responds as usual by sending out consecutive ROM vector addresses $FFF8 and $FFF9. *Within the PIC, address lines A_1, A_2, A_3, and A_4 are trapped, and replaced with address information corresponding to the highest priority interrupt requested.* (If two or more interrupts are requested at the same time, the vector corresponding to the highest interrupt number is automatically generated.) The new modified address is sent on to the ROM to fetch the vector. As shown, each interrupting device is assigned a unique ROM location that contains the corresponding starting address of the ISR. For example, if $\overline{\text{IN4}}$ is pulled low, $FFF8 and $FFF9 will be trapped and replaced by $FFF0 and $FFF1. In cases where the added delay time

Chapter 19 / Programmable Peripheral Chips **247**

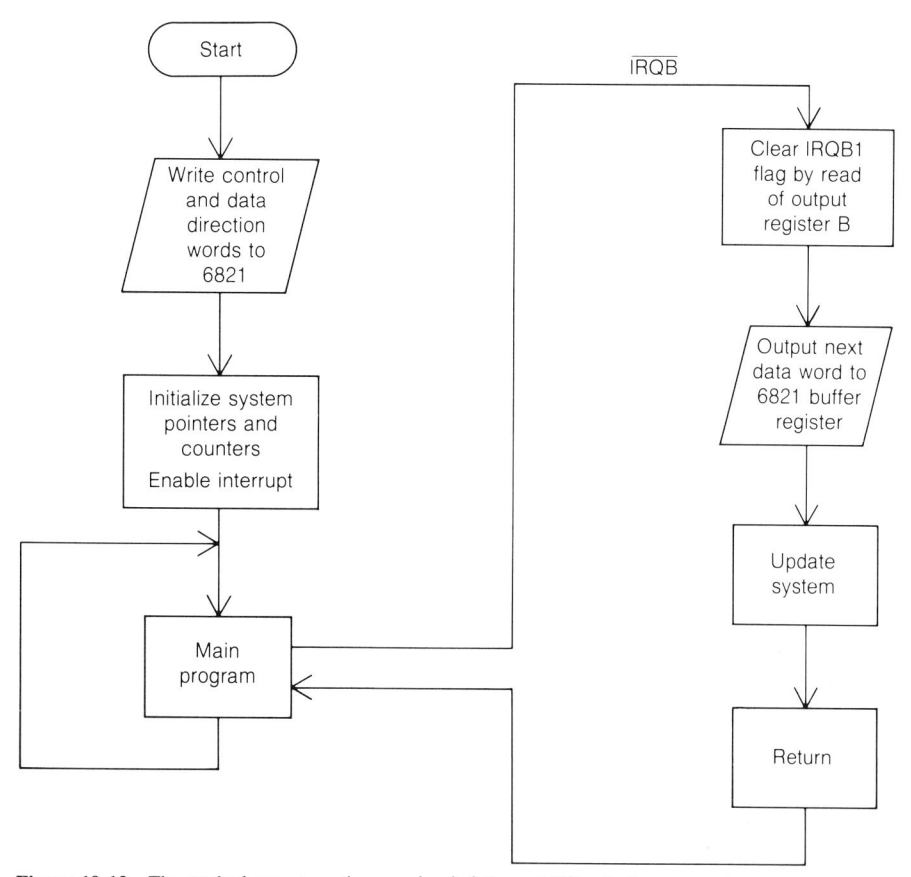

Figure 19.13 The strobed-output routine—a simple interrupt-I/O output sequence to a port.

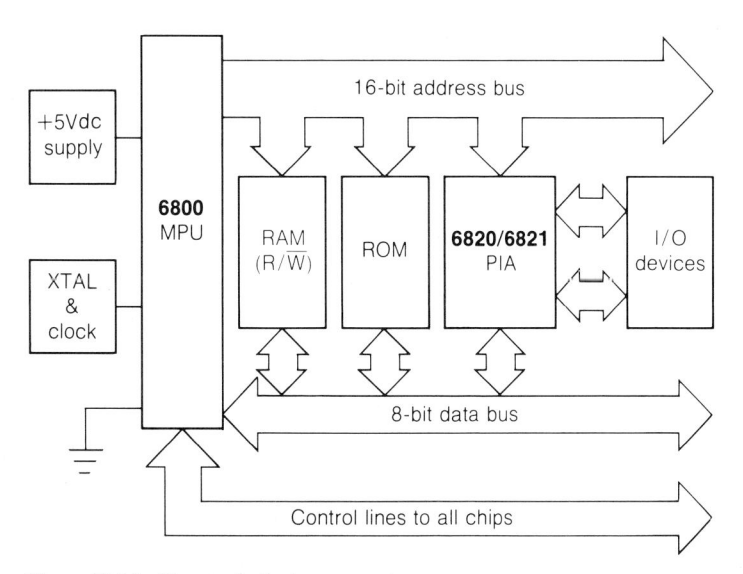

Figure 19.14 The standard microcomputer system.

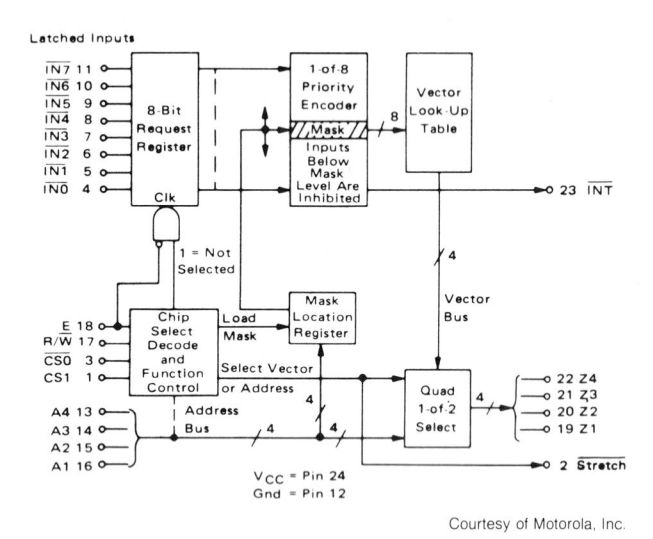

Figure 19.15 The 6828 Priority Interrupt Controller internal block diagram.

required to modify the address is unacceptable, a stretch input is used to momentarily slow the processor's clock (see Figure 19.15). To provide interrupt-request latching, all interrupt inputs are loaded into an internal 8-bit D latch on each falling edge of E (ϕ_2).

When the PIC is not selected (not in the interrupt mode), address lines A_1, A_2, A_3, and A_4 pass through the 6821 unmodified.

As we have seen, all vector address modifications and priority determination are done by hardware. Where, then, is the programmability of the 6828? It comes in when we introduce masking. Examining the internal block diagram of the 6828 (Figure 19.15), we find the *mask location register*. Into this register we will write a number from 0 to 7. Only those interrupt requests of greater priority (higher number) will be allowed to pass.

Priority Interrupt Example

Through the more detailed diagram of Figure 19.17, let's demonstrate the use of the 6828 through a specific example. To our 6800-based home computer we would like to add a sprinkler control and fire alarm (a computer is chosen because we desire intelligent control). Clearly, in this case, the fire alarm has priority. Since at the present time the $\overline{NMI}$ input is used as a power-failure detector, we must use the $\overline{IRQ}$ input for both requests. For high speed and convenient future expansion, we select the 6828 PIC.

Our design is a simple three-step process:

1. *Interface the 6828 to the 6800 bus.* By fully decoding address lines A_5 through A_{15}, we make sure that the 6828 is selected only for addresses $FFF8 or $FFF9. ($A_1$ through A_4 are decoded internally, and A_0 goes directly to the ROM in order to sequentially address the 2 bytes associated with each 16-bit interrupt vector.) For these two addresses, address translation takes place according to the table of Figure 19.18. *For all other addresses, the 6828 is deselected and address lines A_1 through A_4 pass through the 6828 unaffected.*

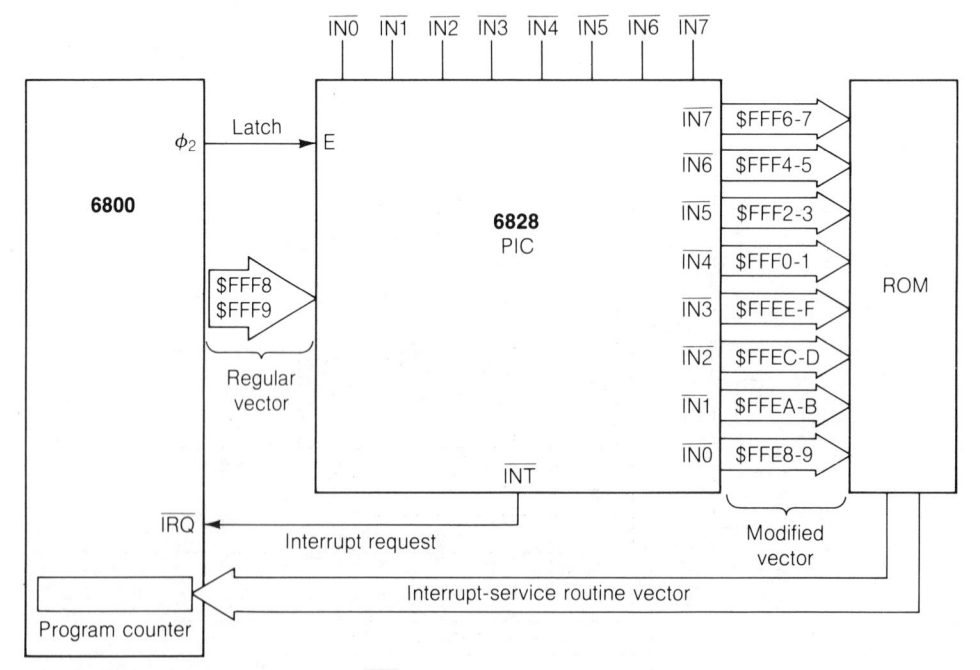

Figure 19.16 Modifying the incoming $\overline{IRQ}$ vector to give one of eight interrupt vectors corresponding to the highest priority requested.

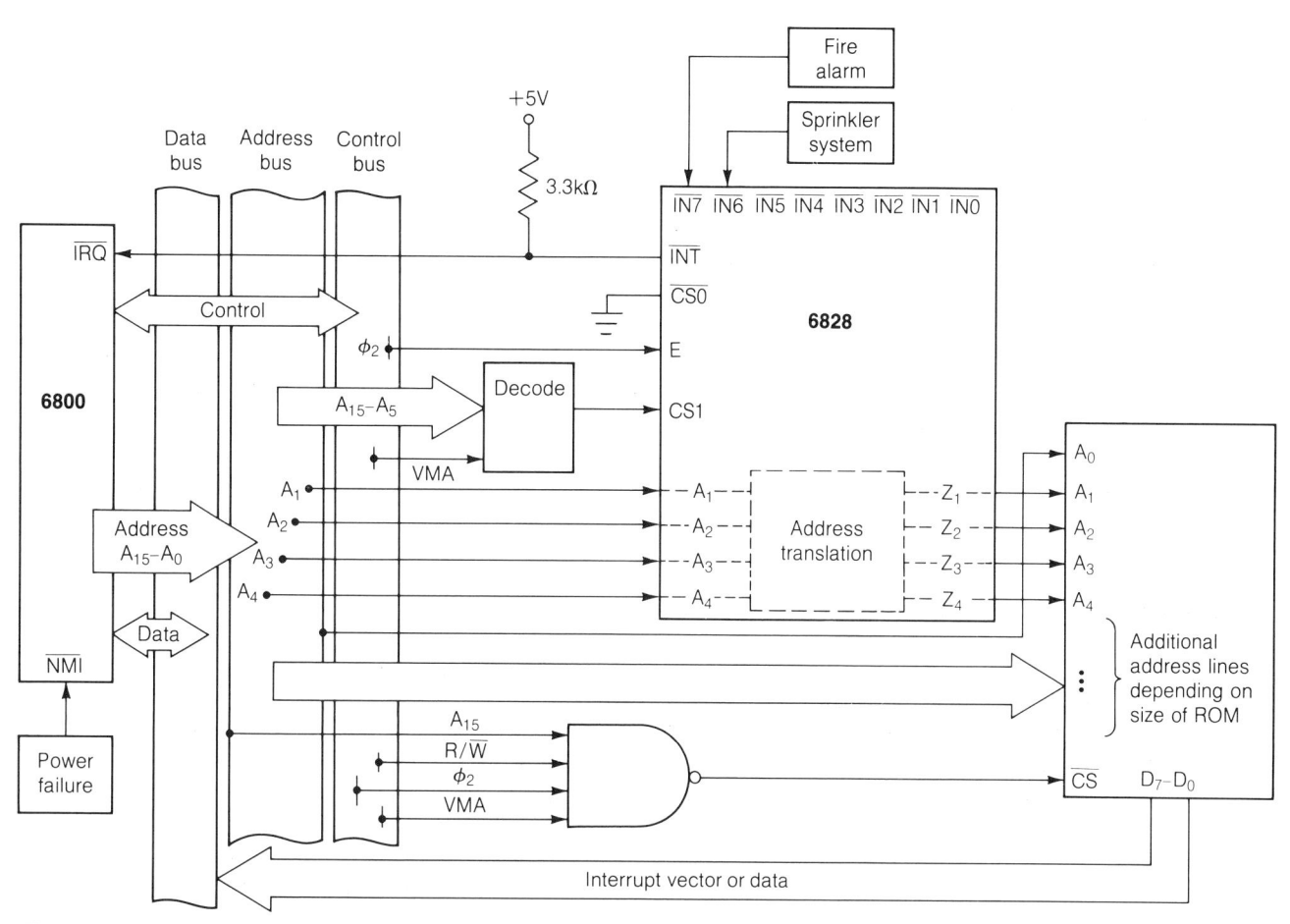

Figure 19.17 Interfacing the 6828 to the 6800 bus.

2. *Load the mask register.* Since we are not using six of the interrupt inputs, let's mask them out just to be safe. To mask out all interrupt inputs below $\overline{\text{IN6}}$, we must place 0110 (6) into the mask location register (see Figure 19.15). The process is the essence of simplicity. We simply *write* to location:

1111111111110110X

The mask register contents will automatically be loaded with 0110, *regardless of the data on the data bus.* Therefore, the initialization software is probably as simple as you will find:

STAA   111111111110110XB

(To avoid activating the ROM during loading of the mask

Active Input		Output When Selected				Equivalent to Bits 1-4 of B0, B1..., B15 Hex Address	Address ROM Bytes Contain Address of:
		Z4	Z3	Z2	Z1		
Highest	$\overline{\text{IN7}}$	1	0	1	1	F F F 6 or 7	Priority 7 Routine
	$\overline{\text{IN6}}$	1	0	1	0	F F F 4 or 5	Priority 6 Routine
	$\overline{\text{IN5}}$	1	0	0	1	F F F 2 or 3	Priority 5 Routine
	$\overline{\text{IN4}}$	1	0	0	0	F F F 0 or 1	Priority 4 Routine
	$\overline{\text{IN3}}$	0	1	1	1	F F E E or F	Priority 3 Routine
	$\overline{\text{IN2}}$	0	1	1	0	F F E C or D	Priority 2 Routine
	$\overline{\text{IN1}}$	0	1	0	1	F F E A or B	Priority 1 Routine
Lowest	$\overline{\text{IN0}}$	0	1	0	0	F F E 8 or 9	Priority 0 Routine
	None	1	1	0	0	F F F 8 or 9	Default Routine*

Courtesy of Motorola, Inc.

Figure 19.18 Truth table for $FFF8/$FFF9 address modification by 6828 PIC.

register, note that R/$\overline{W}$ is fed to the ROM decoding circuitry.)

3. *Test the system*. Running the applications program, the processor accesses the ROM in the normal manner, waiting for an interrupt; A_1 through A_4 pass through the 6828 and address the ROM as if the 6828 were not there.

An interrupt is requested. Let's assume that both $\overline{IN7}$ (the fire alarm) and $\overline{IN6}$ (the sprinkler request) are both active low when clocked into the latch register. The highest priority interrupt ($\overline{IN7}$) is automatically selected by internal hardware, checked against the mask register, and passed on. $\overline{INT}$ goes low, and an $\overline{IRQ}$ interrupt is requested. When the 6800 releases consecutive addresses $FFF8 and $FFF9 to the address bus, the 6828 is selected. The interrupt addresses are translated to $FFF6 and $FFF7 within the 6828 and sent on to the ROM. The interrupt vector stored at $FFF6 and $FFF7 is jammed into the program counter via two consecutive fetch operations, and action jumps to the interrupt-service routine (remember, A_0 distinguishes between the high-order and low-order interrupt vector bytes). After the ISR is complete, an RTI returns the system to the original state.

To provide additional interrupt inputs, 6828s can be cascaded by tying the $\overline{INT}$ outputs of up to eight 6828s to each $\overline{INX}$ input of a "master" 6828. Each activated 6828 provides a translated interrupt vector, and the vectors are combined to locate the correct ISR.

A FINAL WORD

Although we have configured specific programmable chips for specific operations, we have learned a number of lessons common to nearly all programmable peripheral chips:

- Look for one or more control/mode registers to configure the system for a specific task.
- Expect a programmable peripheral chip to offer both interrupt and polled operation.
- Expect a wide variety of ways to distinguish between the various data/control/status registers.
- Expect the software to be simplified when switching over to programmable peripheral chips. (Programmable peripheral chips add hardware to eliminate software.)
- Expect a system to include many types of programmable peripheral chips.

INTELLIGENT-MACHINE UPDATE

When using programmable peripheral chips, computers are displaying a high-order trait that human beings cannot match: computers can change their configuration to match their environment. Human beings—creatures who adapt very slowly—must instead change their environment to match their needs. Computers, on the other hand, unhampered by biological shackles, can expand into areas where human beings cannot go. The intelligent machine of tomorrow, it seems, may be as different from us as we are from the dinosaurs—creatures that could not adapt to a changing environment.

QUESTIONS AND PROBLEMS

1. What is the major advantage of software programming over hardware programming?
2. What are the three types of registers normally found in programmable peripheral chips?
3. Within the 6821, what is the purpose of each of the following: (a) control register (CR), (b) data direction register (DDR), (c) output register (OR).
4. Why is the $\overline{ACKNLG}$ handshaking signal of the Centronics interface standard especially tailored for interrupt I/O?
5. What does $\overline{STROBE}$ "tell" the printer?
6. How does the 6821 address six internal registers with only two input low-level address lines (RS0 and RS1)?
7. For a 6800-based system, why is ROM usually placed at the highest memory locations, and RAM at the lowest?
8. Based on the 6821 control-word format of Figure 19.8, write a program that toggles CB2 high and low 10 times by *direct program action*.
9. When the PIA is RESET, why do you think all ports are initialized to input?
10. Referring to Figure 19.11, the IRQB1 (bit B7) flag is set by CB1 action. How is the flag reset?
11. Flowchart an interrupt I/O program to output data to the printer using two 6882B port chips, rather than a 6821. (Compare your flowchart to the ISR of Figure 19.13.)
12. List the components of a standard microcomputer system.

13. Referring to Figure 19.17, why is A_0 the only address line not decoded (remember, A_1 through A_4 are decoded internally)?
14. What instruction will mask out all interrupts below $\overline{IN3}$ to the 6828?
15. When an interrupt is requested by the sprinkler system of Figure 19.17, list the steps that take place from interrupt request to final return to main program from ISR.
16. For the 6821 PIA, write a program that will configure port A as five input lines (PA0 through PA4) and three output lines (PA5 through PA7). The program will toggle the output lines, read the input lines, and store the contents in memory location $01A0.
17. Fill in the memory map of Figure 19.7 for the add-on PIA of Figure 19.6. Using the addressing scheme developed in Part I, would our two 6882B ports overlap the address space of our newly added 6821?
18. Using 8205s and the addressing scheme of your choice, add our 6821 PIA to Figure 9.8.
19. Name several features common to all programmable peripheral chips.
20. What is important about each of the following 6828 features: (a) multiple interrupt inputs, (b) priority determination, (c) maskable interrupts, (d) latched interrupt inputs, (e) cascaded units.
21. Using the PIA hardware design of Figure 19.6, write a mimic program in which the 6821's port A is an input port and port B is an output port.

chapter 20

Controllers

Like all warm-blooded animals, we are able to hold our body temperature to within 1 or 2 degrees of normal, even when the ambient environment fluctuates widely over many tens of degrees. Of course, this amazing ability is no accident of nature, for temperature control is just one of the many precision *cybernetic* control systems operating in the human body. In this chapter we will examine the computer as a cybernetic control system, and we will introduce the single-chip microcomputer, a device specifically designed for control applications.

CYBERNETICS

Cybernetics is the science of communication and control. Although cybernetics encompasses many disciplines, most cybernetic systems have one element in common: a circular motion or closed loop in which an action institutes a reaction—which in turn *feeds back* and alters the original action.

It is *feedback*, then, that is the central feature of cybernetic control systems. As illustrated in Figure 20.1, however, there are two ways in which the reaction can be fed back:

- Positively, by aiding the original action
- Negatively, by opposing the original action

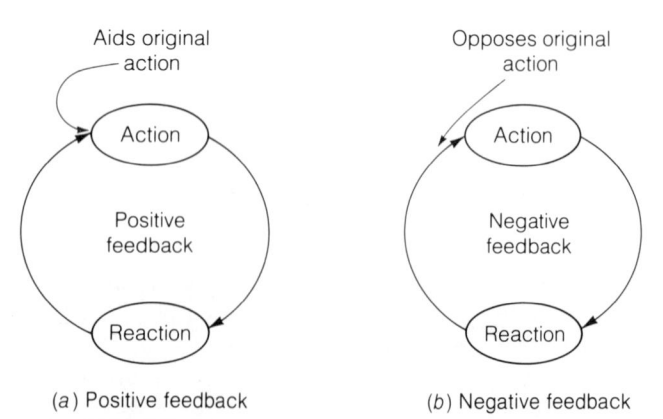

Figure 20.1 Closed-loop cybernetic feedback system.

Positive feedback usually leads to runaway or explosive situations, such as snowballing. (The faster a snowball rolls downhill, the more snow it gathers. But the more snow it gathers, the faster it travels. The effect quickly builds and soon we have a full-scale avalanche.) Since positive feedback leads to unstable situations, it is of little use in control systems.

Negative feedback, on the other hand, does lead to stability and control, and is at the heart of all control systems.

To begin with, how does negative feedback so accurately maintain our body temperature near 98.6°F? As expected, the process is a cybernetic, closed-loop, negative-feedback control system. Step outside on a cold winter day, and that action quickly leads to a slight lowering of the body temperature. This lowered temperature is sensed, and the body reacts by increasing its metabolism—which in turn drives the temperature back to normal. When we step back inside the warm house, another closed-loop, negative-feedback sequence is set in motion. Our increased metabolism causes our body temperature to rise slightly. This increased temperature is sensed, which leads to a lowering of the metabolism and increased perspiration—which pulls the body temperature back to normal again. Negative feedback, then, is the magic process allowing our body temperature to remain stable amid large fluctuations in air temperature (see Figure 20.2).

When we put the concept of control into the simplest possible terms, *a negative-feedback control system compares where you are with where you want to be and sends out an error signal whose purpose is to drive where you are to where you want to be*. To bring the design needs more in focus, we diagram the process in block form (Figure 20.3). The error output can be a two-valued signal (high or low), can equal the difference between the inputs, or can be related to the inputs in a more complex manner.

Damping

When negative feedback drives the actual state of a system toward the desired state, often a degree of built-in inertia allows the actual state to swing past the desired state, even

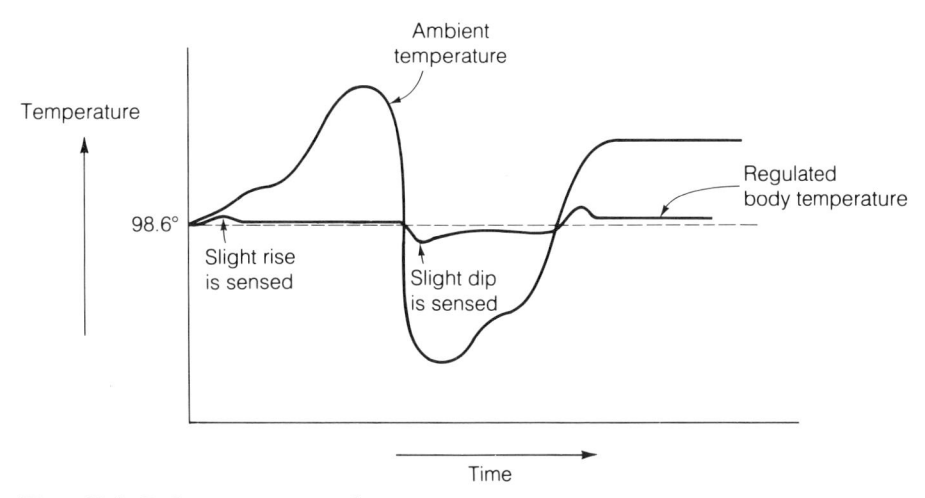

Figure 20.2 Body-temperature control.

when the feedback driving force is turned off when the states are equal.

For example, the flight-control system of a rocket is a negative-feedback control system. If the actual pitch of the rocket is different from the desired pitch (sent by guidance), steering thrust will be applied to rotate the rocket toward the desired state. If the thrust is maintained until the actual and desired states are just equal, the inertia of the rocket will carry it beyond the desired pitch in the other direction. Again, opposite thrust is applied to bring it back, and again inertia causes it to swing past the desired point. The result is an oscillating motion. If the oscillating swings become too large, the system can go completely out of control.

To cure the problem, we must *damp* the system. When the system is properly damped, the actual state will settle into the desired state, with little or no overswing. Damping can be achieved in a number of ways. For example, the feedback can be turned off *before* the actual state reaches the desired state, thereby allowing the system to "coast" to the desired point by way of friction.

Perhaps the most popular damping technique is *derivitive feedback*. Often used in robotic systems (to be discussed shortly), we subtract rate (derivitive) information from the basic error signal to generate the *damped error signal*. That is, if the system is moving rapidly toward the desired state, decrease the net error signal to avoid overswing; if not moving at all, transmit the full error signal to the "steering" device; and if moving in the opposite direction, away from the desired point, enhance the basic error signal with negative rate information.

Clearly, many of the steps in the closed-loop process (compare, outport and inport, damping) can be handled by a computer. To see how it is done, we will design a simple computerized cybernetic temperature-control system.

A COMPUTERIZED TEMPERATURE-CONTROL SYSTEM

Here is our assignment: Design a computerized control system to maintain a gallon of water to within two degrees of a selected temperature.

The hardware design, given in Figure 20.4, consists of a resistive heater and thermoelectric heat pump, both fed by digital-to-analog converters. (A thermoelectric heat pump is a solid-state device that pumps heat from one side of the device to the other when driven by suitable electric current.) Also included is a temperature transducer feeding an A/D converter. To simplify the software, the A/D converter is a monolithic chip (such as the AD574 of Figure 18.14). The signal conditioner buffers and scales the output of the temperature probe, so the expected voltage range of the transducer corresponds to the acceptable voltage range of the A/D converter. The output port displays the actual temperature so that the performance of the system can be monitored.

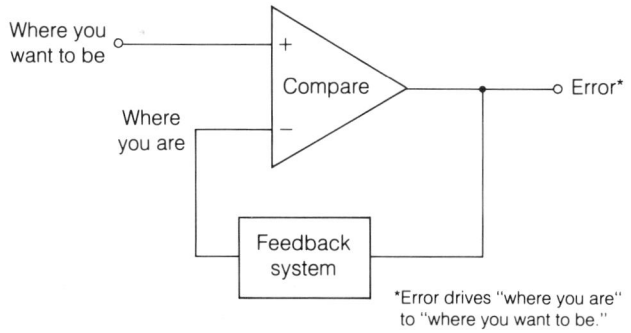

Figure 20.3 Negative-feedback, closed-loop system.

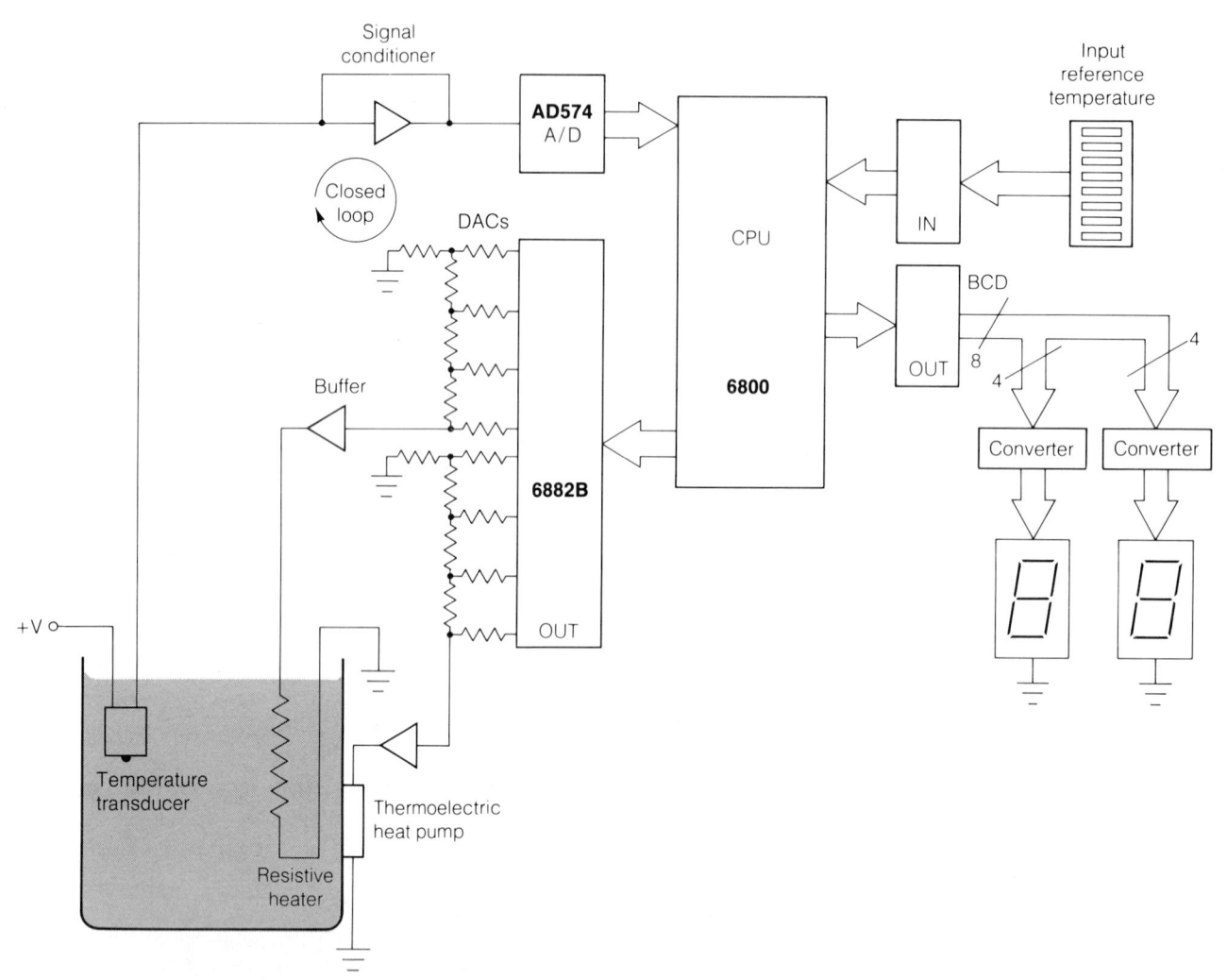

Figure 20.4 6800-based, temperature-control system.

The high-level flowchart of Figure 20.5 reflects the closed-loop concept:

- Block ① inputs the reference temperature (the goal) from the DIP switch.
- Block ② inputs the actual temperature (the present temperature of the water) from the A/D converter.
- Block ③ converts the actual temperature to BCD and sends the result to the displays. (With only two seven-segment displays, multiplexing is not necessary.)
- Block ④ subtracts the input present temperature from the desired temperature reference to produce the basic signed-number error signal (+ if water is too cold; − if too hot).
- Block ⑤ generates the (signed number) damping term by subtracting the present actual temperature from the previous actual temperature (the greater the result, the greater the rate of change).
- Block ⑥ subtracts the damping term from the basic error signal to generate the (signed number) damped error signal to be sent to the "steering" system.
- Block ⑦ determines if the damped error signal is positive or negative (check the sign bit).
- Block ⑧ is processed if the damped error signal is positive. Since a positive signal generally indicates that the water is too cold, the heating device will be activated. (It is possible for the rate term to overwhelm the error term, indicating the water is too hot but cooling off very rapidly—in fact so rapidly that, paradoxically, the heating element is activated to "head off" a possible overswing.)
- Block ⑨ converts the negative damped error term to true form prior to transmission to the steering system.
- Block ⑩ powers the cooling device at a rate proportional to the magnitude of the damped error signal.
- Block ⑪ adds a delay in order to give the system time to

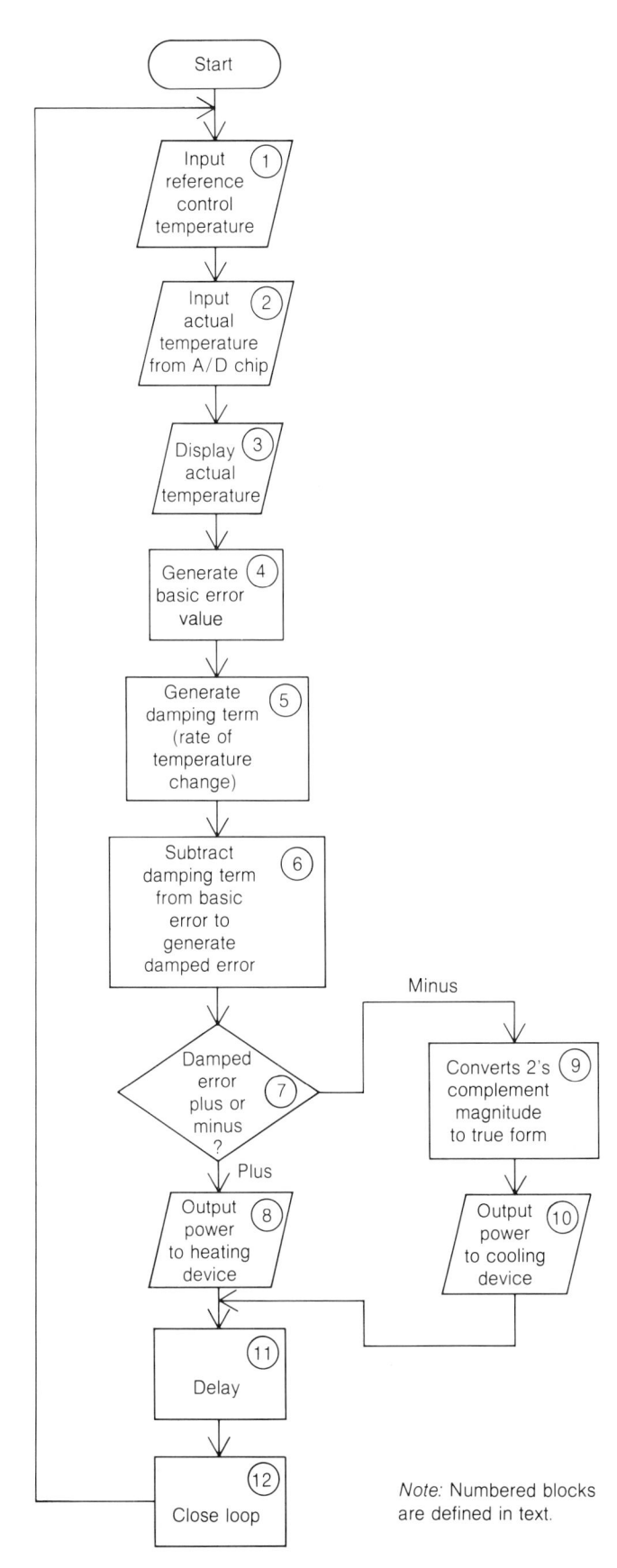

Figure 20.5 Closed loop, temperature-control routine, including damping.

change so reasonable rate information can be generated by block ⑤.
- Block ⑫ closes the feedback loop.

When our temperature-control system is activated, it should closely simulate temperature control in the human body (refer to Figure 20.2). Of course, if outside temperature varies too quickly or over too wide a range, the regulation system will be unable to maintain control. (Final hardware/software development is left as an exercise.)

Our temperature-control system is an example of a *real-time process*. A real-time process is one in which the input parameters reflect the present state of the system, and the results of processing are required immediately for the control process. Most industrial *process-control* systems (manufacturing steps controlled by a computer) are real-time systems.

SINGLE-CHIP MICROCONTROLLERS: INTELLIGENT MACHINES ON A CHIP

Our temperature-regulating system of the last section is an example of a low-end control process. That is, the design is relatively simple and only small amounts of program ROM, data RAM, and I/O ports are required. Clearly, in this case, the high flexibility and capacity of a general-purpose microprocessor are not needed. Suppose all required memory and ports could be placed on a single microprocessor chip. Suppose we included other features as needed, such as a timer and serial communications port. And suppose the instruction set could be tailored for high-speed control applications. We would then have a true *computer on a chip*—a single IC, ideally suited for control applications and unmatched for reliability, low cost, and ease of use.

As we know, such single-chip microcontrollers do exist and are offered by a number of manufacturers. The Motorola family of single-chip microprocessors is known as the *MC6801 family unit*. The table of Figure 20.6 will give us some idea of the scope, depth, and variety of the single-chip family. Let's concentrate on the 6801 and follow up with a brief spotlight on several of the other single-chip choices.

The 6801 Branch

The MC6801 is the flagship of the Motorola single-chip family. The overall architecture and major characteristics of the 6801 are summarized in Figure 20.7.

The recipe for making a 6801 single-chip microcontroller is simple: Take a single chip of silicon and integrate every required component on it. That includes the clock and timer, the ROM (enough to handle dedicated control applications), the RAM (enough to perform scratchpad calculations), and I/O ports (enough to interface with a variety of peripheral devices).

SINGLE-CHIP MICROCOMPUTER FAMILIES FEATURES MATRIX

		141000 Family			MC3870	M6805 Family				
		MC141000	MC141200	MC141099		MC6805P2	MC6805P4	MC6805U2	MC6805R2	MC6805T2
Processor	Bits	4 Bits			8 Bits	8 Bits				
	Instruction Set	TMS1000			F8	Control Optimization of MC6800				
	Registers	7 Special Registers			7 Registers	2 General Purpose and 3 Special Registers				
	Addressing Modes	5 Addressing Modes			5 Addr Modes	10 Addressing Modes				
	Basic Inst Types	43 Basic Inst Types			54 Basic Inst	59 Basic Instruction Types				
	Total Instructions	43 Total Instructions			76 Total Inst	207 Total Instructions				
	μs/Avg Inst	10 μs/Instruction (600 kHz)			4.7 μs/Inst	4.9 to 5.4 μs per Average Instruction (1 MHz)				
	Subroutines	1 Subroutine Level			1 Level	13 Subroutine Levels				
Technology		CMOS			NMOS	HMOS				
Memory	Mask ROM	1K ROM	1K ROM	No ROM	2K ROM	1K ROM	1K ROM	2K ROM	2K ROM	2.5K ROM
	EPROM	–	–	–	–	–	–	–	–	–
	RAM Bytes	32 RAM	32 RAM	32 RAM	64 RAM	64 RAM	112 RAM	64 RAM	64 RAM	64 RAM
Package Size		28 Pins	40 Pins	48 Pins	40 Pins	28 Pins	28 Pins	40 Pins	40 Pins	28 Pins
Input/Output Pins	Inputs	4 Inputs	4 Inputs	4 Inputs	–	–	–	8 Inputs	2 to 5 In	–
	Outputs	19 Outputs	24 Outputs	21 Outputs	–	–	–	–	–	–
	Mask Bidir	–	–	–	32 I/O	–	–	–	–	–
	Prog Bidir	–	–	–	–	20 I/O	20 I/O	24 I/O	24 I/O	19 I/O
	Spec. Func	–	–	–	–	–	–	–	1 to 4 Analog	2 Special
Expansion Bus		–	–	To ROM, PLA	–	–	–	–	–	–
Special Function I/O	Display Decoder	7 Segment PLA			–	–	–	–	–	–
	High Current Drive	20 mA, All Outputs			–	10 mA Drive on 8 Pins				
	Analog Inputs	–	–	–	–	–	–	–	8-Bit A/D	–
	Serial I/O	–	–	–	–	Shift Register I/O with Bit Manipulation Instructions			
	Freq Synth	–	–	–	–	–	–	–	–	Freq Synth
Standby RAM		–	–	–	–	Stby. RAM	–	–	–	–
Timer	Prescale Bits	No Timer			÷200 Prescale	7 Prescaler Bits				
	Counter Bits				8-Bit Counter	8-Bit Counter				
	Timer Functions				1 Function	1 Timer Function at a Time				
Interrupts	Timer Interrupt	No Interrupts			Timer IRQ or 1 Ext IRQ	Timer Interrupt				
	External IRQ					1 Ext IRQ	1 Ext IRQ	2 Ext IRQs		1 Ext IRQ
	Serial I/O IRQ									
Development Support	ICs	ROM-Less Version			–	EPROM and ROM-Less Versions				
	Dev System	EXORciser*			EXORciser*	EXORciser*				
	Emulation	User System Emulator			USE	User System Emulator				
	Assembler	Assembler			Assembler	Macro Assembler				
	HL Language	–			–					

Figure 20.6 The Motorola single-chip family.

Of course, we can't place a full 64K of RAM-I/O on a single chip (as yet), but we can give the 6801 enough capacity to handle dedicated control tasks—and it will do them more efficiently and at lower cost than a general-purpose microprocessor system.

An important feature of all single-chip microcomputers is *flexibility,* the ability to be configured in a variety of modes to match the needs of the designer. The MC6801 provides three fundamental operating modes (see Figure 20.8):

- Single chip
- Expanded nonmultiplexed
- Expanded multiplexed

The single-chip mode is for stand-alone applications, and it provides the maximum 29 I/O lines. The expanded nonmultiplexed configuration uses port 4 to address an additional 256 external memory locations; in the expanded multiplexed mode, port 3 is multiplexed with address information and combined with port 4 to provide 16 bits of addressing, thereby allowing a full 64K of external memory to be added to the system.

Programming the mode of operation is done by placing the proper logic levels into pins P_{20}, P_{21}, and P_{22} at the time of RESET.

In addition to the basic 72 instruction types of the 6800, the 6801 has 11 new instructions, giving increased arithmetic-processing power, including an 8-bit multiply.

Additional features include a serial communications interface through three pins of port 2 (transmit, receive, and baud rate) and an internal 16-bit timer.

MC6805 Family (continued)						M6801 Family				
MC68705P3	MC68705U3	MC68705R3	MC146805G2	MC146805F2	MC146805E2	MC6801	MC68701	MC6803		
8 Bits						8 Bits			Bits	Processor
Control Optimization of MC6800						Super Set of MC6800			Instruction Set	
2 General Purpose and 3 Special Registers						2 General, 4 Special Reg			Registers	
10 Addressing Modes						7 Addressing Modes			Addressing Modes	
59 Basic Instruction Types			61 Basic Inst Types			75 Basic Inst Types			Basic Inst Types	
207 Total Instructions			209 Total Instructions			219 Total Instructions			Total Instructions	
4.9 to 5.4 μs per Average Instruction (1 MHz)			3.9 to 4.0 μs/Avg Inst (1 MHz)			3.7 μs/Avg Inst (1 MHz)			μs Avg Inst	
13 Subroutine Levels			29 Levels	13 Levels	29 Levels	Indefinite Levels			Subroutines	
HMOS			CMOS			HMOS				Technology
–	–	–	2K ROM	1K ROM	No ROM	2K ROM	–	No ROM	Mask ROM	Memory
1.8K EPROM	3.8K EPROM	3.8K EPROM	–	–	–	–	2K EPROM	–	EPROM	
112 RAM	112 RAM	112 RAM	112 RAM	64 RAM	112 RAM	128 RAM	128 RAM	128 RAM	RAM Bytes	
28 Pins	40 Pins	40 Pins	40 Pins	28 Pins	40 Pins	40 Pins	40 Pins	40 Pins		Package Size
–	8 Inputs	2 to 5 In	–	4 Inputs	–	–	–	–	Inputs	Input Output Pins
–	–	–	–	–	–	–	–	–	Outputs	
–	–	–	–	–	–	–	–	–	Mask Bidir	
20 I/O	24 I/O	24 I/O	32 I/O	16 I/O	16 I/O	24 to 31 I/O			Prog Bidir	
–	–	1 to 4 Analog	–	–	–	0 to 7 Special Funct Pins			Spec Func	
–	–	–	–	–	8K Addr	64K Addressability				Expansion Bus
–	–	–	–	–	–	–	–	–	Display Decoder	Special Function I/O
–	10 mA Drive on 8 Pins		10 mA, 4 Pins	–	–	–	–	–	High Current Drive	
–	–	8-Bit A/D	–	–	–	–	–	–	Analog Inputs	
Shift Register I/O with Bit Manipulation Instructions						8-Bit UART + Bit Rate Gen			Serial I/O	
–	–	–	–	–	–	–	–	–	Freq Synth	
–	–	–	–	–	–	–	–	–		Standby RAM Pin
7 Prescaler Bits						–	–	–	Prescale Bits	Timer
8-Bit Counter						16-Bit Timer			Counter Bits	
1 Timer Function at a Time						3 Simultaneous Timer Functions			Timer Functions	
Timer Interrupt						3 Timer Interrupts			Timer Interrupt	Interrupts
1 Ext IRQ	2 Ext IRQs			1 Ext IRQ		2 Ext Interrupts			External IRQ	
–	–	–	–	–	–	2 Serial I/O IRQs			Serial I/O IRQ	
EPROM and ROM-Less Versions						EPROM and ROM-Less Versions			ICs	Development Support
EXORciser*						EXORciser*			Dev System	
User System Emulator						User System Emulator			Emulation	
Macro Assembler						Macro Assembler			Assembler	
–						Fortran, Basic, MPL			HL Language	

Courtesy of Motorola, Inc.

Figure 20.6 (*continued*)

A 6803 version, which deletes the internal 2K × 8 ROM and operates only in modes 2 and 3, and a 68701 version, which substitutes an EPROM for the ROM, round out the 6801 single-chip group.

The 6805 Family

One way to lower hardware costs is to pay only for what you need. True low-end dedicated applications generally do not require the 6801's expansion capability to 64K. Therefore, the 6805 family offers the perfect low-cost solution when the number of on-board RAM/ROM and I/O ports offered by the factory is sufficient.

Except for the lack of expansion memory, the 6805 family is similar to the more powerful and versatile 6801, offering a variety of on-board RAM/ROM and I/O port size options, as well as a scaled-down timer and interrupt structure.

The MC146805E2

For battery-powered applications, the MC146805E2 CMOS single-chip MPU is the proven answer. Breaking tradition with the other 6805 members, it does offer a modest 8K of expansion memory. Low power consumption, however, is its most important feature. In its power-down STOP mode (processing activity halted), it draws a mere 200 μA of current (maximum).

SINGLE-CHIP TEMPERATURE CONTROL

Since the 6801 single-chip family is specifically designed for control applications, we should be able to redesign our water-temperature-control system around a single-chip microcontroller and produce a more efficient, low-cost design.

258 Part IV / Applications and Interfacing: Living in a Real World

(a) Pin-out

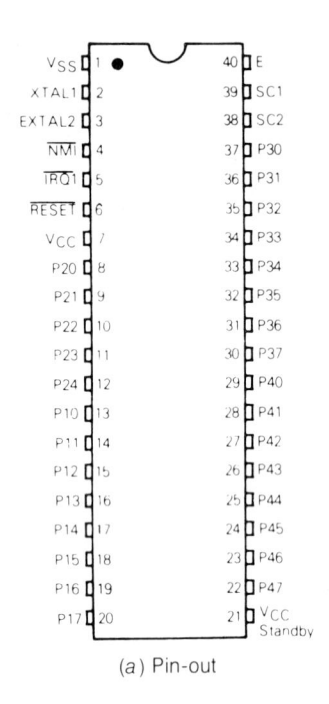

- Enhanced MC6800 Instruction Set
- 8 × 8 Multiply Instruction
- Serial Communications Interface (SCI)
- Upward Source and Object Code Compatibility with the M6800
- 16-Bit Three-Function Programmable Timer
- Single-Chip or Expanded Operation to 64K Byte Address Space
- Bus Compatibility with the M6800 Family
- 2048 Bytes of ROM (MC6801)
- 128 Bytes of RAM (MC6801 and MC6803)
- 64 Bytes of RAM Retainable During Powerdown (MC6801 and MC6803)
- 29 Parallel I/O and Two Handshake Control Lines
- Internal Clock Generator with Divide-by-Four Output
- Interrupt Capability

(b) Major features

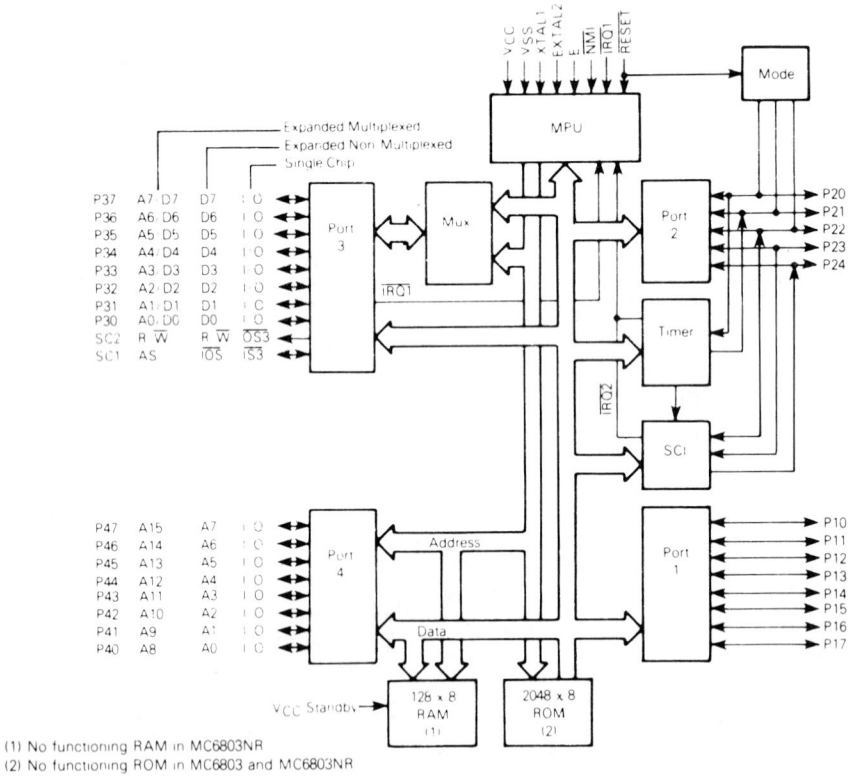

(1) No functioning RAM in MC6803NR
(2) No functioning ROM in MC6803 and MC6803NR

(c) Block diagram

Courtesy of Motorola, Inc.

Figure 20.7 The Motorola 6801 single-chip microcomputer.

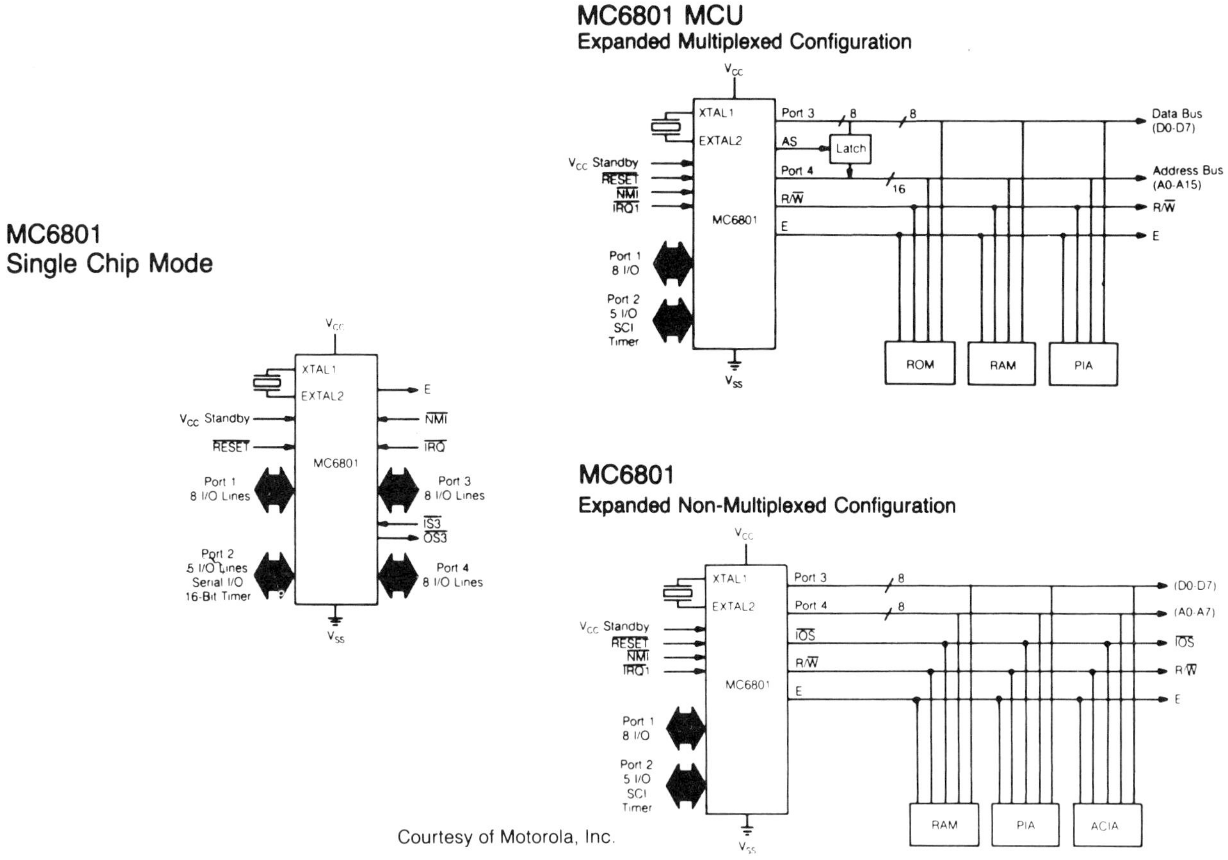

Figure 20.8 The three basic modes of operation of the 6801.

With the many chips to choose from, however, which member of the 6801 family is best suited for our needs? The simplicity of our control system gives it away: the basic, low-cost 6805 looks like our best choice. Since our system is of low speed and relatively simple hardware/software design, the 1K of on-board ROM, 64 bytes of on-board RAM, and 20 I/O lines will be adequate. In addition, the high degree of code efficiency (most instructions will be 1 or 2 bytes long) will assure high-speed operation. However, to make the design problem more challenging, let's assume the system is battery-operated. (Of course, if that's the case, we are not talking about controlling large bodies of water exposed to severe temperatures.)

With no hesitation, we select the 146805 CMOS version of the 6805 family. Under full-speed operating power it still draws a mere 35 mW of power (compared to 400 mW for a conventional 6805 HMOS version). Even more appealing are two power-saving standby modes which we will work into our design to further conserve battery life. Anticipating the need for a large number of I/O lines, we select the 40-pin MC146805G2 (see Figure 20.9).

TEMPERATURE CONTROL USING THE MC146805G2

Figure 20.10 shows our temperature-control system built around the special-purpose 146805 rather than the general-purpose 6800. The design is greatly simplified and improved.

- All memory and I/O lines are on-board, requiring no external ROM/RAM or I/O ports.

- Each port—like the 6821—is equipped with a data direction register. Our design takes advantage of the ability to individually program all 32 I/O lines by adding a scanned keyboard and display.

- After some experimentation, we determine that the temperature control and display/keyboard refresh routine need only be cycled through once each 10 ms. Since the entire program requires less than 1 ms to run, we use the WAIT instruction to place the 146805 in the power-down mode after each run. While in WAIT (some 90% of the time), the 146805 consumes less than 25% of its normal operating power. To exit the WAIT state every 10 ms, we

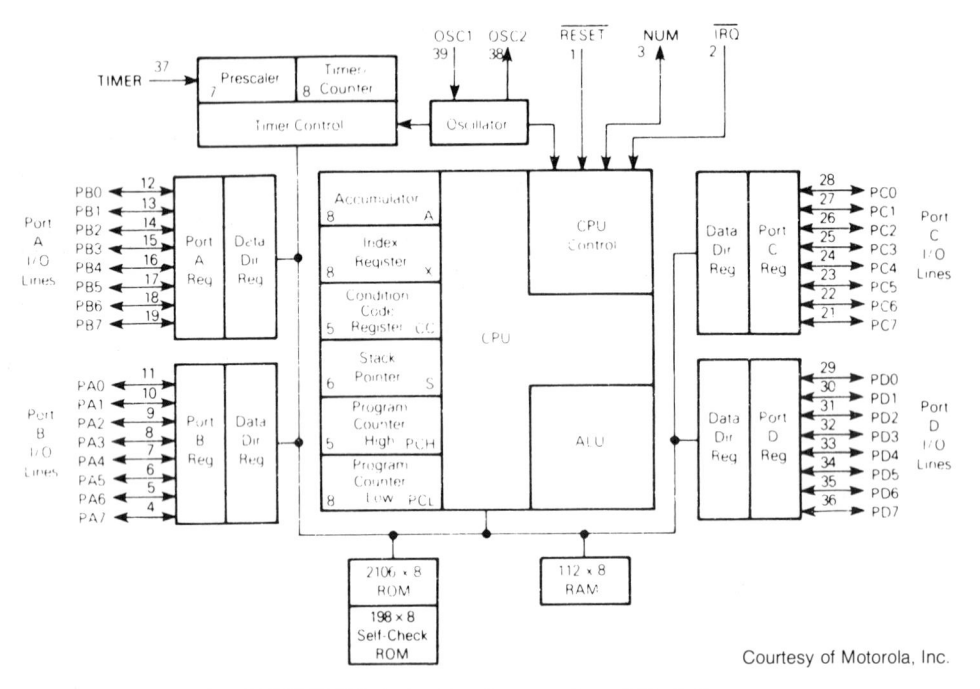

Figure 20.9 The MC146805G2 CMOS single-chip microcomputer unit block diagram.

make use of a timer-initiated interrupt to allow a periodic exit from the WAIT state.

By placing nearly all system components on chip, the 146805 has greatly lowered the cost of our temperature-control system. In the future, as the need arises, we can expect additional specialized single-chip microcomputers to become members of the 146805 family.

STEPPER MOTOR

A *stepper motor* is a precision motor device that allows the rotor to be accurately incremented in precise steps (typically varying from 3.75° to 90°) *without the use of feedback.* When we remove the *acknowledge* aspect of the feedback signal, however, an important assumption must be made: When the computer issues a command to the stepper motor (for example, rotate 5°), we must assume the command will be carried out precisely.

The technique that allows the rotor to be turned by a predetermined amount (in this case, 90°) is shown in Figure 20.11. Two well-known properties of magnetic fields are involved: (1) like poles repel and unlike poles attract; and (2) a magnetic pole can be created by sending a current through a coil of wire (reverse the current and the pole direction reverses). There are two center-tapped stator coils and therefore four windings (labeled W_1, W_2, W_3, and W_4). The purpose of the center tap is to allow the direction of current to change in each of the two coils by proper grounding of the winding outputs (thereby allowing each of the windings to be driven by a current-sinking transistor). A motor employing this winding scheme is known as a *four-phase stepper motor.* (Stepping in increments smaller than 90° is entirely a function of the number of rotor and stator poles designed into the motor. In a realizable four-phase system, the number of windings remains constant, with each winding activating many stator poles.)

From Figure 20.11 we can also see how the rotor can be turned in precise 90° increments. By grounding W_1 and W_4, we have created side-by-side south poles that hold the rotor in place as shown by magnetic attraction. If the grounds on W_1 and W_4 were rotated clockwise to W_2 and W_4, it is clear that the rotor also would rotate clockwise 90°, following the new south-pole orientation. When this rotating pair of grounds is diagrammed (Figure 20.12), we note a simple rotate pattern—a pattern easily produced by a 6800 system. We simply copy the bit pattern into both nibbles of the accumulator and use the Rotate Left (for clockwise rotation) and Rotate Right (for counterclockwise rotation) instructions.

Using the 6821 peripheral interface adapter to drive the motor, Figure 20.13 summarizes our final hardware/soft-

(a) Hardware

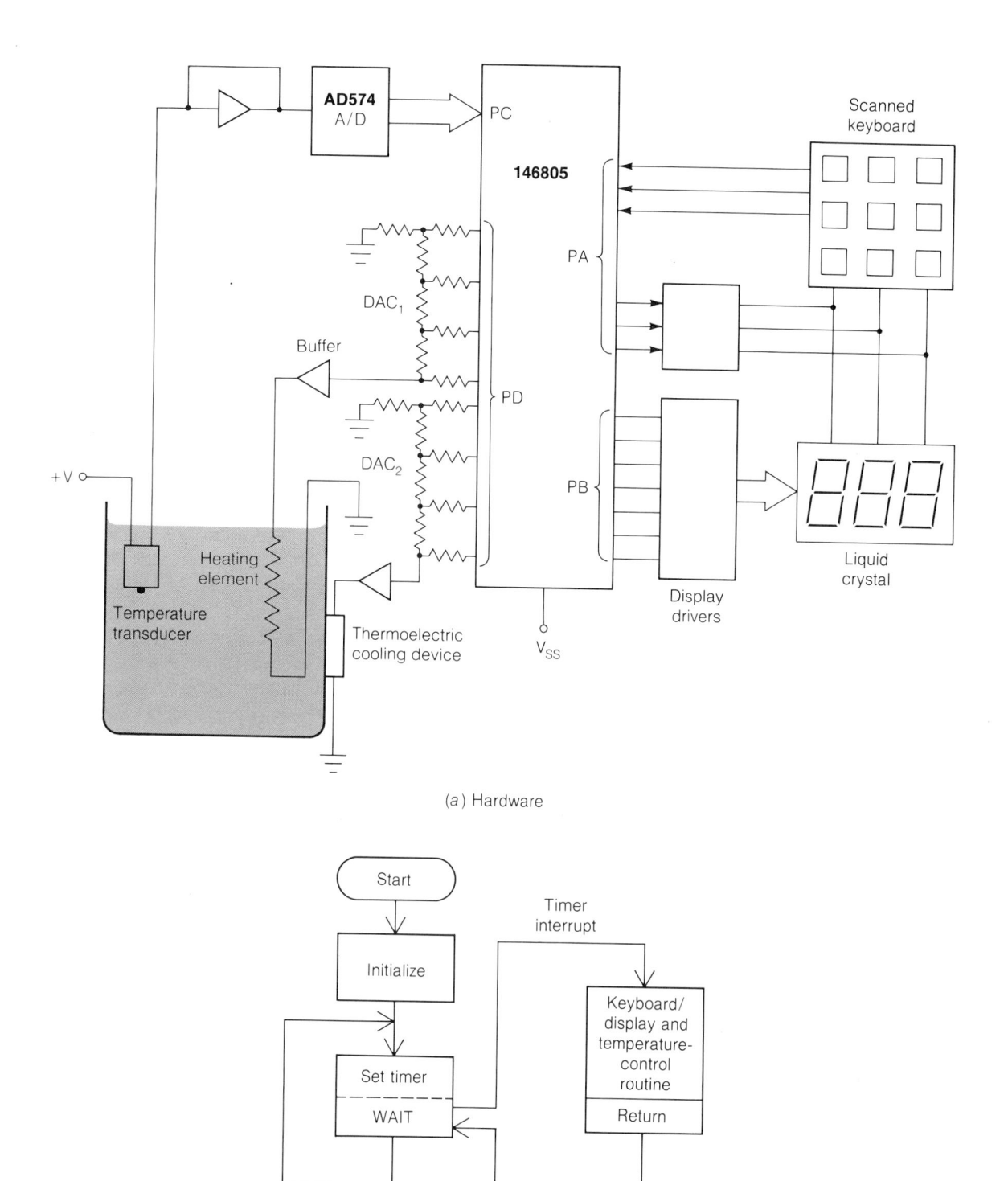

(b) Software

Figure 20.10 Temperature-control system built around the 146805.

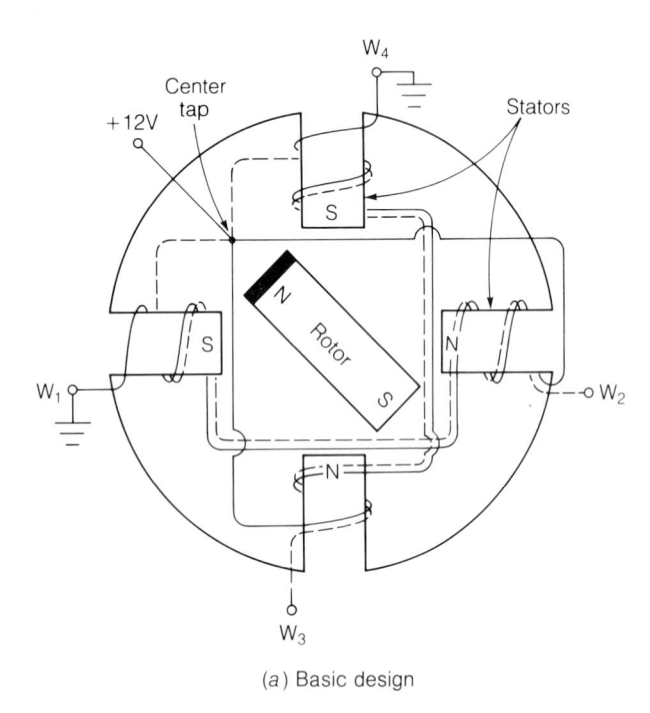

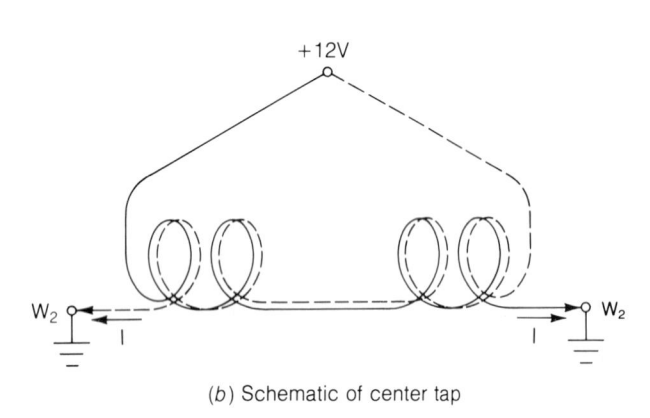

Figure 20.11 Stepper motor.
(a) Basic design
(b) Schematic of center tap

ware stepper-motor design. (The diodes are for back EMF protection.) Motor direction is determined by an inported flag bit, and motor speed depends on size of inported number transferred to the delay loop. If signed-number convention is used, the most significant bit (MSB) will control the direction, while the remaining 7 bits—in 2's complement notation for negative signs—will control the speed of rotation. A stepper motor will be used in Chapter 24 to implement a microcomputer application.

ROBOTICS

A *robot* is a specialized controller that simulates one or more simple human functions. As simulation improves, the robot may someday evolve into an *android*, a machine that closely resembles a human.

A Robotic System

The simplest kind of robotic system is shown in Figure 20.14. It is a basic cybernetic system consisting of a sensor and a movable arm, all under program control. Sensors are the "eyes" of the robot, servomechanisms are the "muscles" of the robot, and the stored program is the "brains" of the robot. Let's take a look at each of these areas.

Sensors Robots can be fitted with devices (sensors) that simulate the five human senses: sight, hearing, touch, smell, and taste. They even can be endowed with *extrasensory perception* (ESP) by sensing such stimuli as magnetic fields, which humans cannot detect.

Robots "hear" through microphones. When speech recognition is added (Chapter 21), they can be given high-level commands verbally.

Robots "feel" by way of strain gauges. By using a piezoelectric crystal within a resonant LC circuit, for example, pressure can be converted to frequency. Placed in the "fingers" of a robot, these tiny flat crystals can provide the feedback necessary to close the cybernetic loop when the robot lifts an object.

Robots "taste" and "smell" through the science of chemistry. For example, the presence of ammonia in the atmosphere will cause clouding of an HCl solution. An LED/phototransistor combination can easily detect the change from transparency to opaqueness.

The "eyes" of the robot It is the "eyes" of the robot that are receiving the greatest attention. The simplest eyes of a robot are two phototransistors and a pair of prism glasses. These can do little more than determine light direction. As shown in Figure 20.15, when light enters from directly ahead, it is almost totally reflected by the sharp angle of attack on the rear surface; when light enters from the right, it is refracted into light sensor A; when light enters from the left, sensor B is activated. Through a simple cybernetic control program, the robot can be programmed to turn to face the light source. Add a filter, and the robot will be sensitive to only a single color.

W$_1$	W$_3$	W$_2$	W$_4$
0	0	1	1
0	1	1	0
1	1	0	0
1	0	0	1

Clockwise ← → Counterclockwise

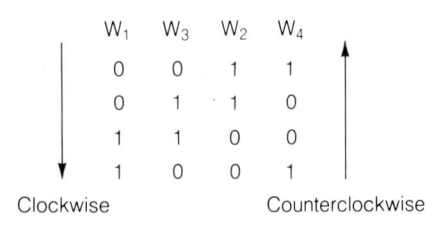

Figure 20.12 Shift-register pattern of four-phase, stepper-motor rotation.

(a) Hardware

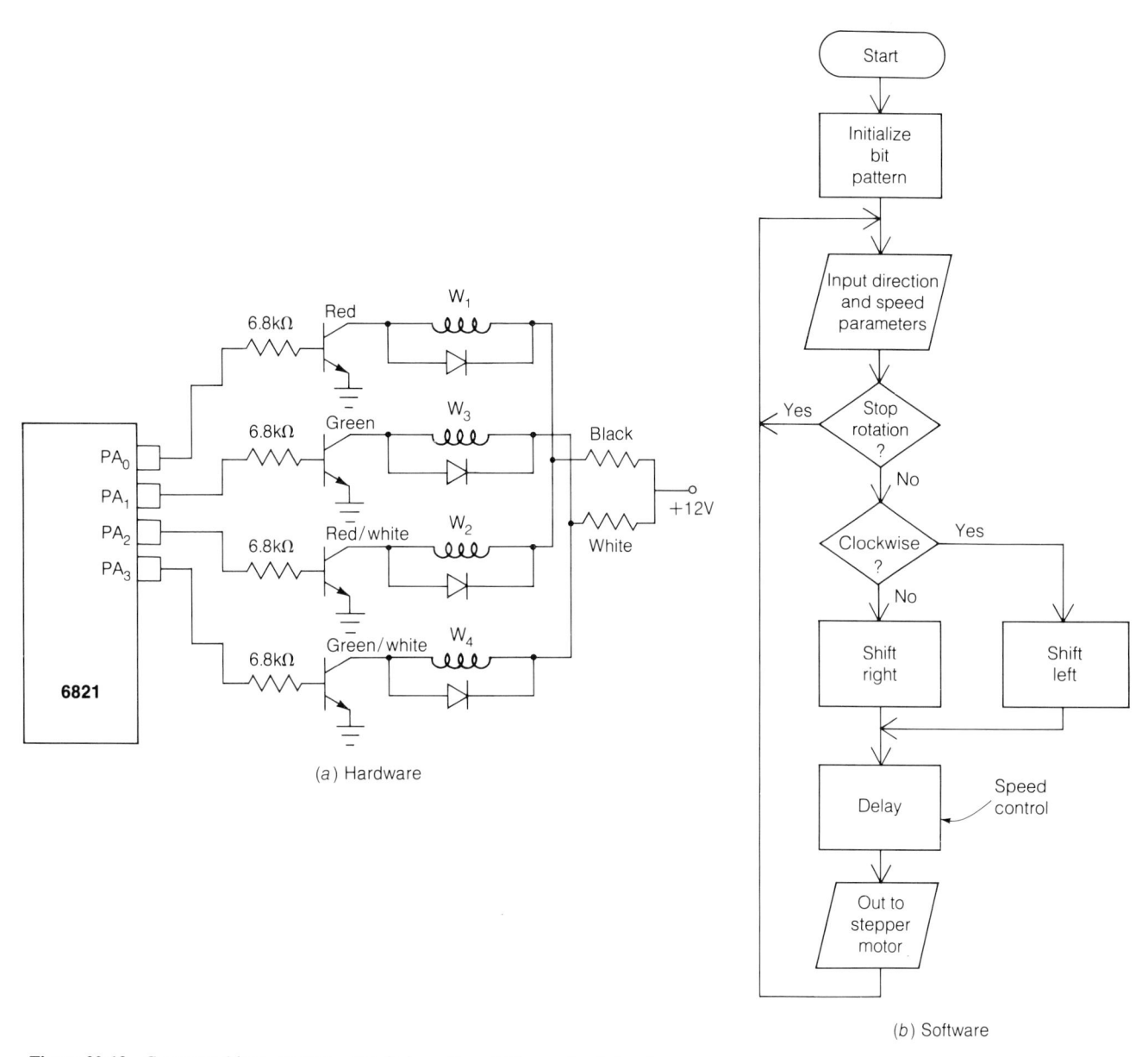

(b) Software

Figure 20.13 Computer-driven, stepper-motor design with variable speed and direction.

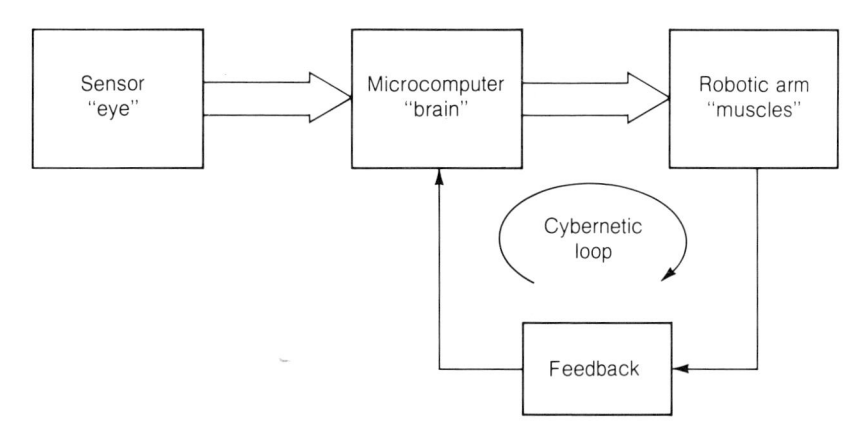

Figure 20.14 Basic robotic system block diagram—a specialized cybernetic control system.

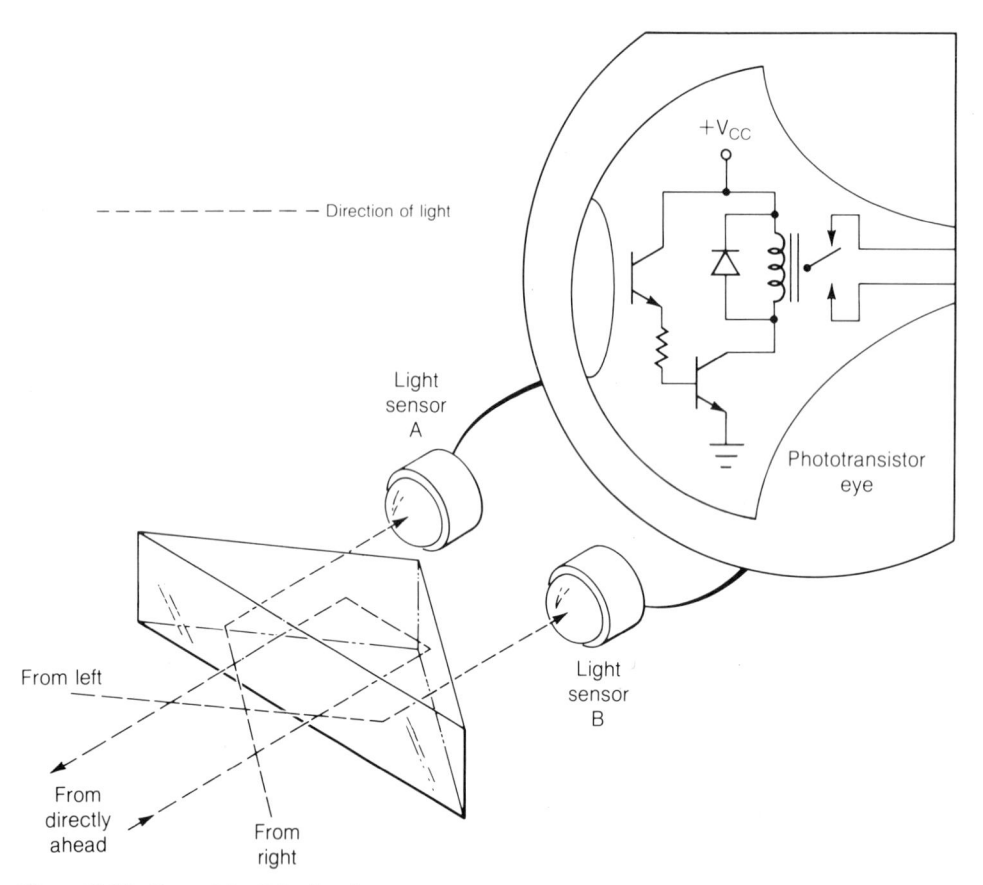

Figure 20.15 Determining light direction.

At the other end of the scale are advanced imaging systems. A typical system uses a solid-state, charge-coupled-device camera that recognizes objects by a technique known as "training by showing" (comparing an object with images of known objects shown earlier). More advanced systems offer "bin-picking" capability, in which a robot can recognize parts that are randomly positioned atop one another. As with graphics, vision technology is constrained by the need to handle vast amounts of data quickly. Even to begin to simulate human sight, a vision system must process a 100 × 100 pixel image in under 100 ms—still only a designer's dream.

The muscles of a robot At the present time, most industrial robots are equipped with a single "arm." To simulate human movement requires several degrees of freedom. The polar coordinate system of Figure 20.16 is a popular method of achieving three degrees of freedom (plus gripper action). For simple movements, each degree of freedom is controlled by a stepper motor (nonservo). For accurate positioning and high speed, the arm movements must be servo-controlled (using feedback). A servomechanism is a cybernetic control system designed for mechanical activation (a "muscle").

The basic system of Figure 20.17 reveals several details of operation. The potentiometer is a specialized position sensor known as a *transducer*: it converts input (position) to output (voltage) in a linear relationship.

For large-scale systems, the arm must be damped to avoid oscillations and to allow rapid but smooth arm motion. Using the same technique as our water control system, we damp the robotic arm by subtracting rate (derivative) information from the basic error signal (see Figure 20.18a). The mathematics of the system is summarized by Figure 20.18b. By adjusting the damping coefficient (K), and gain characteristics (A) of a system with a given moment of inertia (I), we can achieve the ideal critically damped motion. Of course in a realizable system, all the required mathematics would be implemented in software, rather than hardware.

The brains of a robot In the last 2,400 years, ever since Hippocrates located the seat of the intellect inside the skull, we have made only modest inroads into understanding the human brain—that electrochemical intelligent machine that far outclasses today's computers.

Nevertheless, we can simulate some actions of the human mind, and endow our robot with a very crude form of intel-

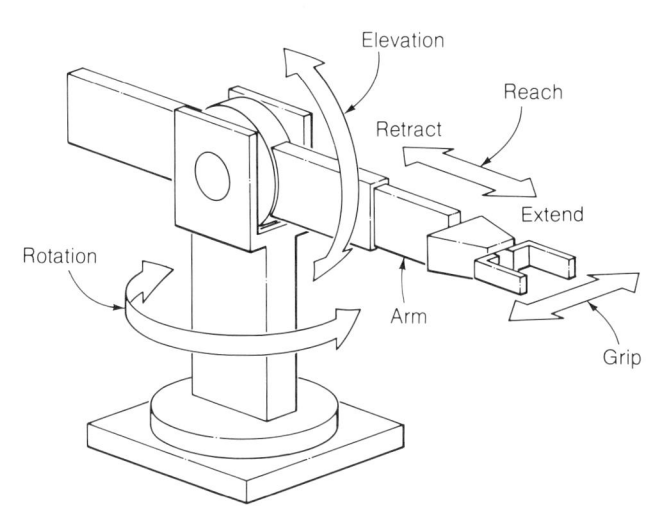

Figure 20.16 Three degrees of freedom (plus grip) based on the polar coordinate system.

ognize immediately the principles of top-down modular design! The chain of command in top-down design is represented by levels of software, with the higher levels calling the lower-level subroutines when needed.

Moving back to the world of human beings for an example, let's see how top-down design principles are involved in a simple roboticslike task: shifting the gears of a car. First of all, when learning to drive, we developed a special-purpose midlevel language, consisting of the following procedures:

```
CLUTCHDOWN
CLUTCHUP
ACCELERATORUP
ACCELERATORDOWN
MOVEGEARLEVER
```

At a lower software level, each of these procedures calls simple movement "primitives" into action. We then form a higher-level command structure by combining the midlevel procedures. For example, the higher-level procedure "SHIFTGEAR" is performed by calling the proper combination of midlevel procedures:

```
PROCEDURE:  SHIFTGEAR
         *  ACCELERATORUP
         *  DOWNCLUTCH
         *  MOVEGEARLEVER
         *  UPCLUTCH
         *  ACCELERATORDOWN
END
```

After some practice, we no longer think of the individual midlevel commands (they become automatic) and merely issue the high-level command "SHIFTGEAR" whenever we desire to change gears. Eventually, after more practice, we move to a still higher level of software by placing procedure SHIFTGEAR into program GETUPSPEED:

The Chain-of-Command Concept

Human actions follow a hierarchical goal-directed behavior: a pyramid structure, with a high-level goal at the top (say, ride bicycle), triggering a number of subgoals (such as, move pedals), until the original goal is translated into the numerous "primitive" actions (such as, tense ankle muscles) required to carry out the original high-level goal. Such a hierarchical "chain of command" is the basis of controlling any complex structure, such as a government or a military organization. *A hierarchical control system limits the complexity of any action (module) to manageable limits regardless of the complexity of the overall system.*

How can this hierarchical goal-directed behavior—exhibited by humans—be implemented on a computer? We rec-

ligence. Let's look at several areas in which there is a degree of similarity between computer brain and human brain. In general, the brains of a robot are the software routines stored in program memory.

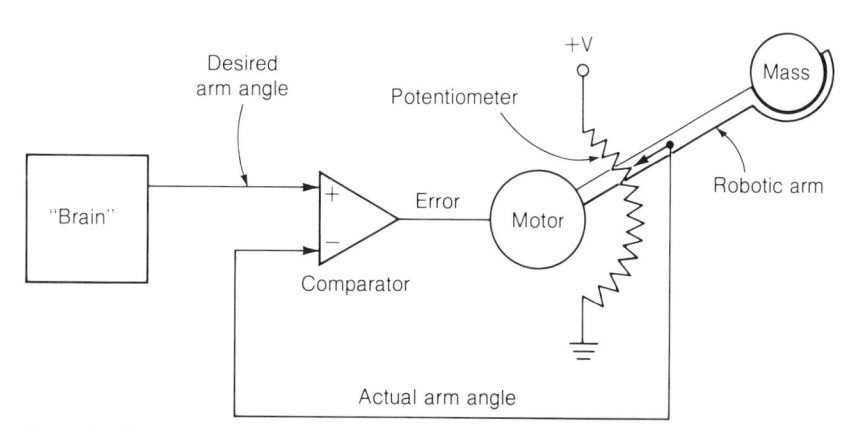

Figure 20.17 The servomechanism as a robotic arm.

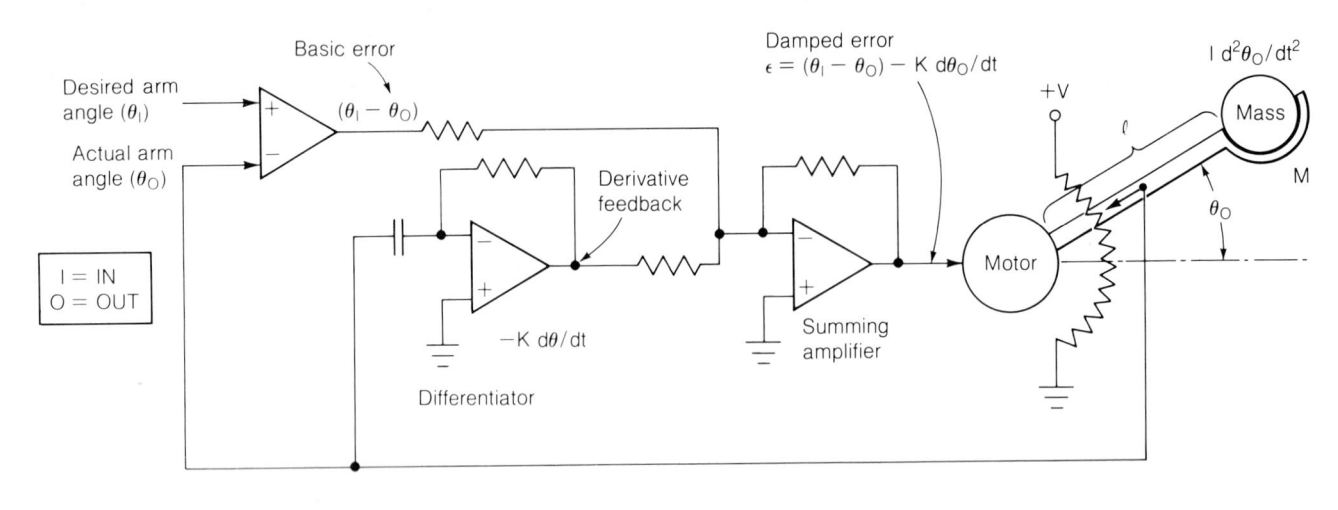

266 Part IV / Applications and Interfacing: Living in a Real World

(a) Damping circuitry added to basic servomechanism

M = mass of weight
l = length of arm
θ_I = input (desired) arm angle
θ_O = output (actual) arm angle
A = motor gain characteristics
K = damping coefficient
I = moment of inertia ($I = Ml^2$ for massless arm)
$d\theta_O/dt$ = rate of change (speed) of arm angle (angular velocity)
$d^2\theta_O/dt^2$ = angular acceleration
ϵ = damped error signal sent to motor

Input torque		Resulting motion
$A\epsilon$	=	$I\, d^2\theta_O/dt^2$
$A[(\theta_I - \theta_O) - K\, d\theta_O/dt]$	=	$I\, d^2\theta_O/dt^2$

or

$$I\, d^2\theta_O/dt^2 + AK\, d\theta_O/dt - A(\theta_I - \theta_O) = 0$$

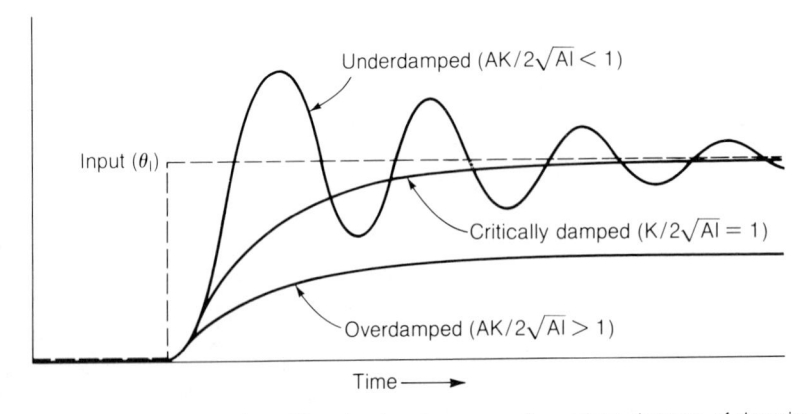

Underdamped ($AK/2\sqrt{AI} < 1$)
Critically damped ($K/2\sqrt{AI} = 1$)
Overdamped ($AK/2\sqrt{AI} > 1$)

(b) Equation of motion and resulting step-input response for various degrees of damping

Figure 20.18 The robotic arm as a servomechanism.

```
PROGRAM:  GETUPSPEED
          FOR gears = 1 to 4 DO
             SHIFTGEAR(gears)
          END
```

Very high level program GETUPSPEED calls the next level (SHIFTGEAR) four times, each time sending an updated gearshift parameter (1, 2, 3, and 4). Clearly this process can be continued indefinitely, until we reach the point where the next higher level is dependent on the application at hand. *Writing a program using top-down design, then, consists of combining these highest-level-possible modules (procedures) into a solution of the problem.* Each English-like high level procedure could correspond to hundreds of thousands of machine-language instructions.

Writing robotics software follows the same top-down principles. First we define a set of midlevel commands (procedures), specifically designed for robot actions. For example, listed below are a few of the commands from the programming language VAL. They are essentially a set of elemental-move commands, passing parameters to lower-level subroutines:

```
MOVE(parameters)
GRASP(parameters)
OPEN(parameters)
CLOSE(parameters)
```

As always, these elemental robot-oriented movement commands can be combined to implement a task:

```
PROCEDURE: PICKUP
    FOR N = 1 to 10
        MOVE(N)
        GRASP(N)
    END
```

The robot will raise its arm while closing its gripper in 10 short movements (perhaps reaching for the gearshift!). Of course, procedure PICKUP can now be included in still higher-level routines. When a useful task is written at any level, it can be included in a library of procedures and "linked" to the main program whenever needed. (Note the similarity of our robotics routines to the turtle graphics programs of Chapter 18.)

By including IF-THEN conditional branching and WHILE-DO looping in our high-level programs, the robot can select from one of several different program pathways and continue or break off repetitive tasks depending on sensed conditions. Using EE-PROMs, it can also modify its behavior in response to external conditions, thereby exhibiting a crude form of learning. (Incidentally, program GETUPSPEED and procedure PICKUP are written in *pseudocode,* an informal English-like language, similar to a high-level programming language, that allows the program logic to be initially expressed without obeying all the coding rules of a formal computer language.)

Parallel Processing

Another important human characteristic is the ability to process information in parallel at many hierarchical levels. When we touch a hot surface, the reflex action must take place quickly and independently, without passing up through higher thought levels. The same is true of a robot. Low-level data—such as servo feedback information—requires very little processing, but must be done quickly. Analysis of high-level verbal commands using speech recognition, on the other hand, is at a higher level and requires considerably more processing—but at a slower rate.

When a full range of sensory feedback at all possible levels is considered, even structured programming, with its layers of subroutines, cannot handle the simultaneous actions required. Image processing, in particular, is dependent on a highly parallel organization (such as the human vision system). One solution is to offload parallel tasks to special-purpose peripheral chips (replacing slower-speed software with higher-speed hardware). A *servo-controller* chip, for example, could handle the low-level feedback processing at high speed, while receiving midlevel commands as necessary, and offering midlevel status information when needed. Communication between processing modules is done through a common memory, known as the *mail box.*

Even more exciting are the new fifth generation computers—computers that will break out of the serial-processing constraints of von Neumann machines. Instead of a sequential list of instructions operating upon a separately located data bank, these new parallel machines operate simultaneously on "chunks" of data and instructions (called *packets*).

To match the hardware of these new parallel machines—promising to be 100 times faster than a von Neumann machine—new "declarative" languages such as LISP have been created. Based on formal deductive logic and set theory, they allow a complex task to be subdivided into many simpler tasks *that can be executed in parallel.* (The subtasks created using Pascal, on the other hand, are designed to be executed in series.)

Still we are a long way from true artificial intelligence. To think like a human, a robot must plan and it must problem solve; it must understand language (not just recognize speech); and finally, it must be able to compose music or write a novel, and *know that it has done so.*

INTELLIGENT-MACHINE UPDATE

The science of cybernetics is often associated with robots and androids—for good reason. The human body requires literally thousands of cybernetic feedback systems in order to regulate the multitude of physical and chemical actions going on continuously. Without feedback systems we would be unable to maintain control—of our environment as well as ourselves.

When parallel processing and declarative languages are combined with cybernetics, our intelligent machine will take control of the physical world. Precisely how much control it takes away from us remains to be seen.

QUESTIONS AND PROBLEMS

1. Give several everyday examples of positive feedback and how it leads to instability.
2. Why is a control system said to be a *closed-loop system*?
3. In a feedback system, what is the *error* signal equal to?
4. What is the usual result if a negative-feedback system is not damped? Give at least one technique for damping a closed-loop system.
5. What are the major features of the 6801 single-chip microcomputer that make it ideal for control applications?
6. What features of the 6801 instruction set make it highly code efficient?
7. How does the 146805 differ from the 6805, and how does this difference relate to product development?
8. When a 6801 system is expanded with additional memory, how are the high-level address lines produced?
9. What is a real-time process?
10. Why is feedback not necessary when driving a stepper motor?
11. Write an assembly-language program for the closed-loop routine of Figure 20.5.
12. Write an assembly-language program for the stepper-motor routine of Figure 20.13.
13. By starting with an elemental command set (of procedures) for running a lap, construct a high-level routine (using pseudocode) for running a mile (four laps).
14. What are the three major blocks of a robotic system?
15. By referring to Figure 20.6, make a list of the special functions available in the 6801 single-chip family.
16. What does the term *critically damped* mean?
17. What is the major advantage of using the 146805 CMOS microprocessor?
18. Why is parallel processing so crucial for sophisticated robotic action?
19. LISP and Pascal both solve a problem by breaking it up into modules. What, therefore, is the difference between LISP and Pascal?
20. What is *pseudocode*?
21. Rather than generating derivative feedback electronically as shown in Figure 20.18a, could we achieve the same effect mechanically by adding a "shock absorber" to the robotic arm? What is the advantage of the electronic method?

chapter 21

Data Communication

With the invention of the drum, our early ancestors discovered a great deal about communication at a distance. Information could best be sent asynchronously in serial form, coded in pulses, and modulated by a hollow log. Today, communication at a distance also often involves the techniques of conversion, coding, modulation, and asynchronous transmission.

Today's communication systems, however, must do a great deal more, for microcomputers are increasingly being linked together in distributed processing networks, or accessed from remote terminals over telephone lines, or called on to transmit data at ultrahigh rates.

Because data communication implies information transfer at a distance, there is a strong need to reduce the number of interconnecting lines. Therefore, unlike the parallel interfacing techniques discussed in Chapter 18, serial format is most often used for data transmission, and address/control/sync information is time multiplexed with the data (rather than sent on separate lines). For human beings, the ear is a serial, one-word-at-a-time data-communication system, while the eye is massively parallel. Although "a picture is worth a thousand words," over long distances it often is more convenient to transmit the spoken word.

SYNCHRONOUS VS ASYNCHRONOUS

As with the simple I/O and interfacing considerations of Chapter 18, the most basic question we can ask about data communication is: Is it synchronous or asynchronous?

- To communicate asynchronously is to transmit data words one at a time at irregular intervals and rates. The arrival of the data is *unpredictable*.
- To communicate synchronously, both receiver and transmitter are driven at the same clock rate and phase, and data flow occurs precisely in step with this common clock. The arrival of the data is *predictable*.

Asynchronous transmission, known as *start/stop* transmission, is the less sophisticated of the two. Generally used with human-machine interfaces (where the transmission is irregular), asynchronous transmission is reserved for data-transfer rates below 10,000 b/s. In asynchronous transmission systems, the clocks of receiver and transmitter are unmatched and may differ slightly in frequency and phase. Since data characters come at irregular rates (any time), the necessary timing and synchronization information is derived *from each character transmitted*. To assure proper reception of data, each serial byte of a TTY (teletype) bit stream is bracketed by synchronizing information called *start* and *stop* bits (Figure 21.1).

In the idle condition, when information is not being transmitted, the serial line is high (marking time). To signal the start of transmission, the transmitter precedes each byte with a logic 0 start bit. The negative-going (leading) edge of this start bit is used by the receiver to synchronize *each character*. By the time the last bit is read in, the receive clock will be slightly out of phase (skewed) from the transmitted bits—but not enough to prevent proper capture of the byte. The stop bits at the end of each character allow a short "breathing space" when characters are being transmitted at the maximum rate. (If spaces exist between characters, the stop bits are indistinguishable from the idle state.) The start and stop bits represent a timing overhead that can take up to 20% of the total transmission time.

When high data-transfer rates are required, above approximately 20,000 b/s, the more complex synchronous method is adopted. Synchronous transmission, usually reserved for

Reproduced by permission of Intel Corp.

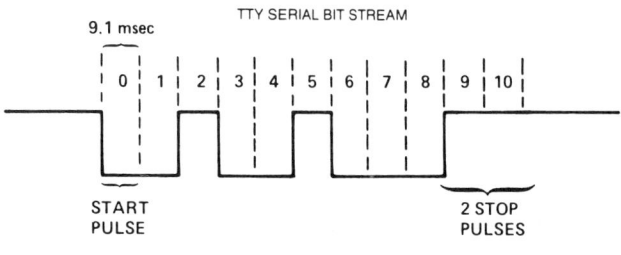

Figure 21.1 TTY asynchronous serial-transmission format.

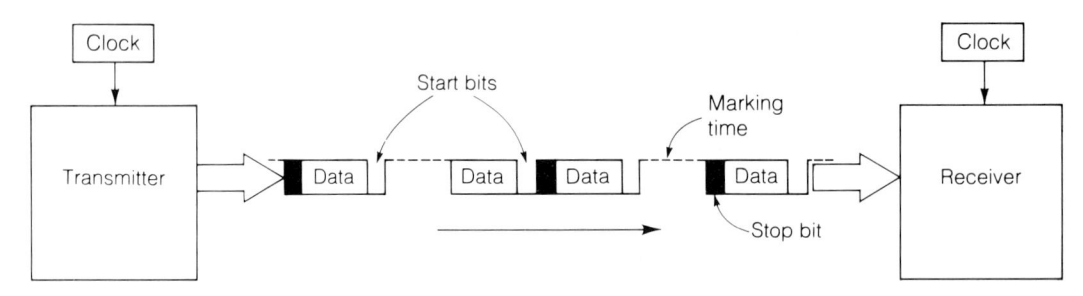

Figure 21.2 Asynchronous/synchronous comparison.

(a) Asynchronous system—data flow at irregular rates and intervals, requiring each data word to be synchronized by the receiver

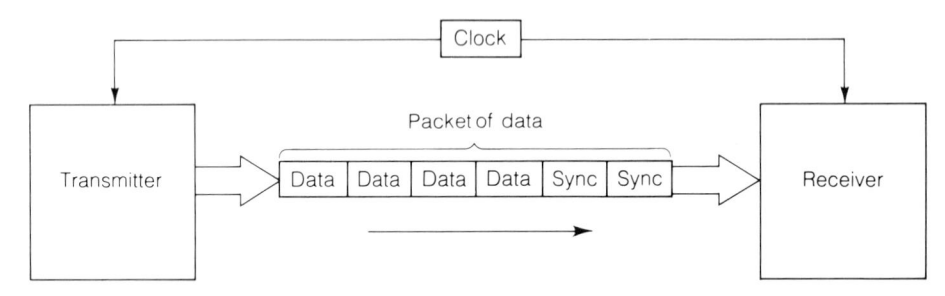

(b) Synchronous system—data flow at regular rates; once receiver and transmitter are synchronized by the initial sync words, data (or additional sync characters) flow continuously

machine-machine communication, sends information in *packets* rather than individually. In synchronous transmission we assume the transmitter and receiver are being driven at the same clock rate. Receiver and transmitter are matched initially by the transmission of a special sync pattern consisting of one or more synchronization characters. Once synchronization is achieved, the receiver is locked onto the data and little or no additional timing information is required. With synchronous systems the timing pulse overhead is only about 1%. Figure 21.2 compares synchronous with asynchronous data transmission.

SIMPLEX/DUPLEX TRANSMISSION

Physically, communication between the CPU and peripheral can take place in one of the three basic modes shown in Figure 21.3. As diagrammed, *simplex* transmission is unidirectional (one direction only), *half-duplex* is bidirectional (one direction at a time), and *full duplex* is simultaneous bidirectional (both directions at the same time). Which of these three modes of communication is chosen depends on a number of factors, many of which are covered in this chapter.

TRANSMISSION CODES

Providing that each character is first converted into an alphanumeric code, a computer can, in a sense, speak in English. When using an alphanumeric code, each letter or symbol is converted into a unique sequence of binary bits.

In response to the need for standardization, the American National Standards Institute has published an American Standard Code for Information Interchange (known as the *ASCII code*). ASCII, now widely used in the computer industry, uses 7 bits in its code to provide 128 combinations for coding letters, numbers, and symbols (see Figure 21.4). When sent in serial form, ASCII adds an extra parity bit. Extended Binary-Coded Decimal Interchange Code (EBCDIC), a 9-bit code giving 256 combinations, is the standard language of IBM equipment.

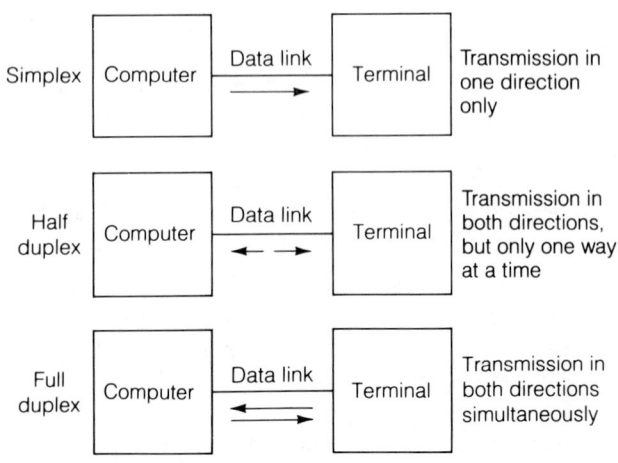

Figure 21.3 Simplex, half-duplex, and full-duplex communications.

Bits	b₄	b₃	b₂	b₁	b₇ b₆ b₅ COLUMN ROW	0 0 0 0	0 0 0 1	0 0 1 2	0 1 1 3	1 0 0 4	1 0 1 5	1 1 0 6	1 1 1 7
	0	0	0	0	0	NUL	DLE	SP	0	@	P	`	p
	0	0	0	1	1	SOH	DC1	!	1	A	Q	a	q
	0	0	1	0	2	STX	DC2	"	2	B	R	b	r
	0	0	1	1	3	ETX	DC3	#	3	C	S	c	s
	0	1	0	0	4	EOT	DC4	$	4	D	T	d	t
	0	1	0	1	5	ENQ	NAK	%	5	E	U	e	u
	0	1	1	0	6	ACK	SYN	&	6	F	V	f	v
	0	1	1	1	7	BEL	ETB	'	7	G	W	g	w
	1	0	0	0	8	BS	CAN	(	8	H	X	h	x
	1	0	0	1	9	HT	EM	)	9	I	Y	i	y
	1	0	1	0	A	LF	SUB	*	:	J	Z	j	z
	1	0	1	1	B	VT	ESC	+	;	K	[	k	{
	1	1	0	0	C	FF	FS	,	<	L	\	l	|
	1	1	0	1	D	CR	GS	-	=	M	]	m	}
	1	1	1	0	E	SO	RS	.	>	N	^	n	~
	1	1	1	1	F	SI	US	/	?	O	_	o	DEL

Hex | Machine commands | Numbers and symbols | Uppercase | Lowercase

Figure 21.4 American Standard Code for Information Interchange (ASCII).

BUS AND COMMUNICATION STANDARDS

Imagine a world of intercommunication without standards—without uniform guidelines for transferring information from point to point. For each new product, the designer would create a unique interface from scratch. For every 100 systems there would be 100 new cables and 100 new documentation packages.

Often, however, a scheme proposed by one manufacturer proves to be successful and is adopted by other manufacturers—a standard is born. Instead of hundreds of bus schemes, there is a mere handful, each designed to satisfy the needs of a particular area of data communication. Shown in Figure 21.5 are six popular existing and proposed communication bus standards. In general, they are categorized according to distance and rate of transmission, as well as parallel or serial.

Serial Standards

RS-232C The Electronic Industries Association (EIA) No. RS-232C serial communication standard was one of the first standards developed, and in fact predates integrated circuits. Therefore, the logic levels are not defined in terms of the standard +5-volt IC levels. Instead, the RS-232C standard defines a space or logic 0 as a voltage level from +3 to +15, and a mark or logic 1 as a voltage level from −3 to −15. (To allow for noise and voltage losses of up to 2 volts, the transmitter specifications are from +5 to +15 and −5 to −15.)

The RS-232C standard further specifies a 25-pin connector (see Figure 21.6), with all pins except data used for supervisory or control purposes. Data Set Ready and Data Terminal Ready are start-up signals sent by the transmitter

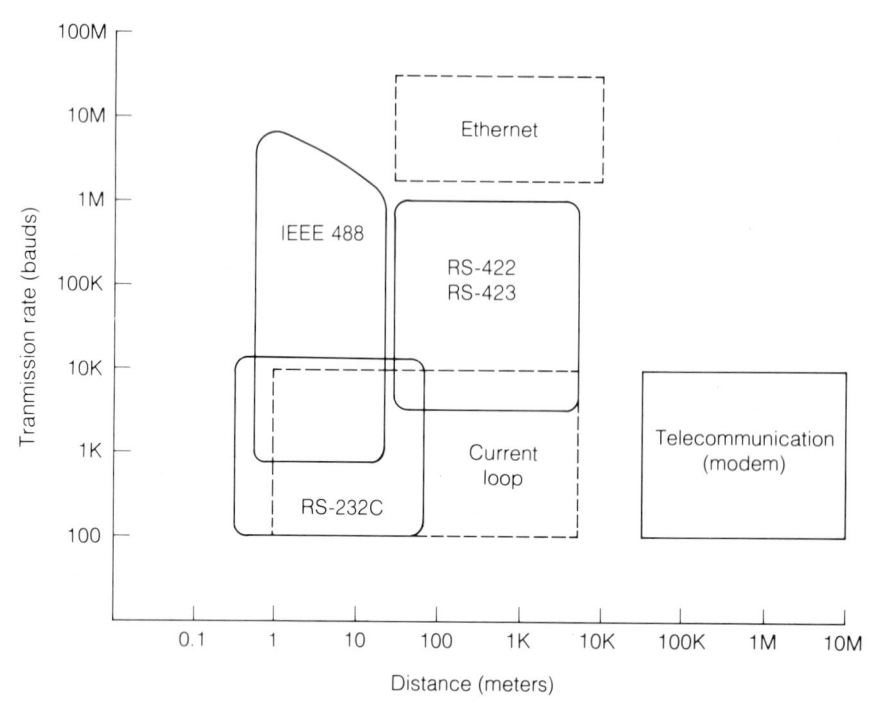

Figure 21.5 Microcomputer parallel and serial communication standards.

and receiver to indicate a readiness state to each other. Request to Send and Clear to Send are used for handshaking. Many of the available pins are seldom used.

Unfortunately, the high-impedance, single-ended termination restricted the line length to about 50 feet and the data transmission rate to 20 kilobauds. For distances of up to several miles, the signal can be amplified by line drivers and a terminal can be connected to the computer over twisted-pair wires.

Since RS-232C terminals are wholly incompatible with +5-volt microcomputer systems, special interfacing circuitry is required. Figure 21.7 shows the use of an MC1489 and MC1488 driver/receiver pair to effect communication to an old-style CRT terminal. With this system, the standard transmission rate is 110 bauds.

By using differential signals and low-Z drivers, the RS-422 and RS-423 standards extend the transmission rate to 10 megabauds and the transmission distance to more than 5,000 feet. Widespread acceptance of RS-232C has decreased the popularity of the more advanced RS-422 and -423 standards.

20/60 mA current loop Teletypewriters, introduced in the early 1960s, are responsible for the popularity of the current loops. A current loop is a closed circular path connecting transmitter with teletype (Figure 21.8a). The return path is often replaced with a common ground. A logic 1 is represented by a flow of 20 mA (or 60 mA), and a logic 0 is represented by no flow of current.

By using current rather than voltage as the logic standard, the voltage drops and noise that normally would occur on a long transmission line are suppressed. The standard transmission rate for TTY is also 110 bauds. Often systems requiring current loops can also make use of the standard RS-232C connector format. Although the current loop is

Figure 21.6 RS-232C line assignments.

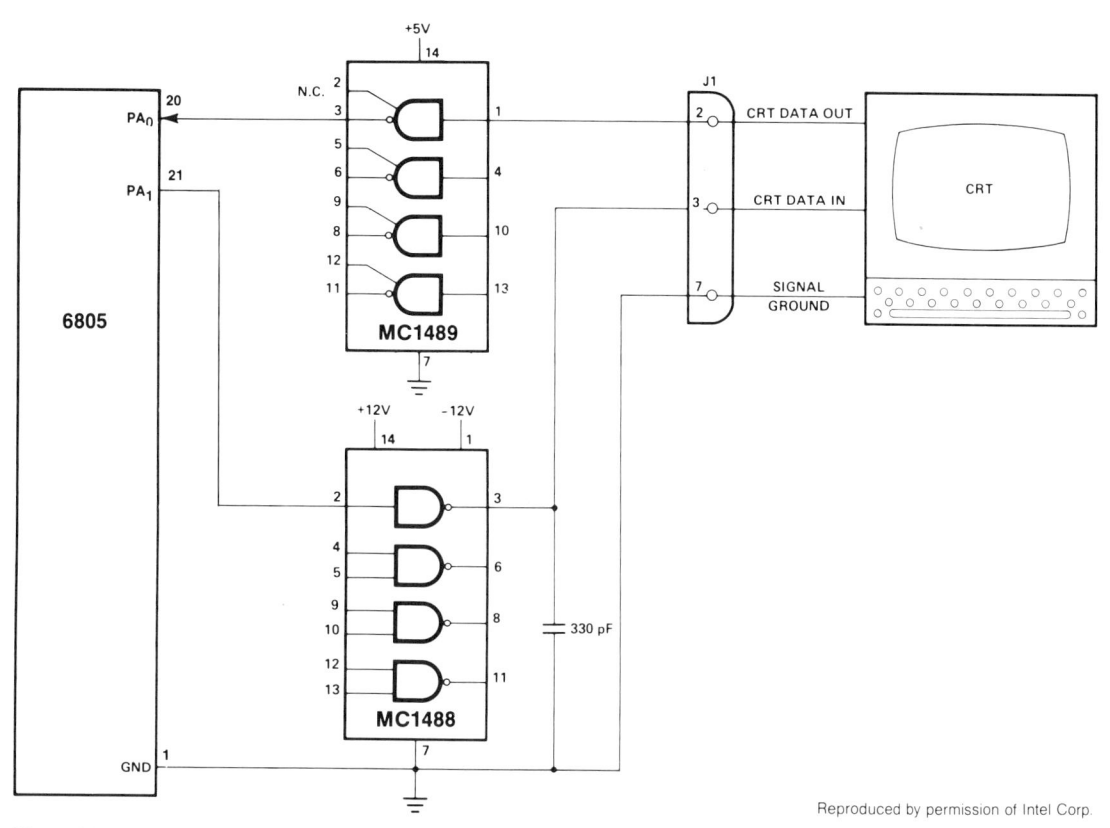

Figure 21.7 RS-232C interface.

still a common form of data transmission, its use is decreasing.

To interface a TTY to the 6805, the transistor is often used as the current source. The send/receive current loop is created as shown in Figure 21.8b.

Parallel Standards—IEEE 488

The IEEE 488 (also known as the *general purpose interface bus*—or GPIB) is a parallel communication standard developed by Hewlett-Packard in the early 1970s and is specifically designed to tie together programmable peripherals and instrumentation systems under control of a microcomputer. Although data transfer is parallel, there still is a strong need to keep the number of interconnecting lines to a minimum. The GPIB accomplishes this by multiplexing the data, address, and control information on the same set of eight lines.

The 24 lines composing the GPIB bus consist of three types of signals: eight data/address/control bus lines, three handshake lines, and five bus-interface management lines (see Figure 21.9). The remaining lines are used for grounding and shielding.

With one controller, up to eight devices can be interconnected using the format of Figure 21.10. Each device can be any combination of talker (transmitter), listener (receiver), and controller. The maximum cable length is 20 meters, with no more than 2 meters per device. (New GPIB "extenders" increase the maximum cable length to 1000 meters.)

With the help of the five bus-management lines, data are transferred at up to 1 Mbyte/s using any of the three basic I/O techniques: programmed I/O, interrupt I/O, and DMA I/O. For example, if device D is to transmit (talk) onto the bus (Figure 21.10), the controller (computer) first must program D as a "talker." This is accomplished by transmitting a special command byte to device D while ATN is low. (Bits D_0 through D_4 are D's address; bits D_5 and D_6 program D as a "talker.") When ATN is high, device D can transmit data onto the bus using a handshake sequence (programmed I/O).

To cause device B to listen, the sequence is similar. Device B is addressed and programmed as a "listener" by a special command word sent by the controller (ATN low). When ATN goes high, data are sent to device B by way of handshake signals.

The IEEE 488 system has been successful because it interfaces equally well with most instrumentation systems and most microprocessors.

Figure 21.8 Communication by current loop.

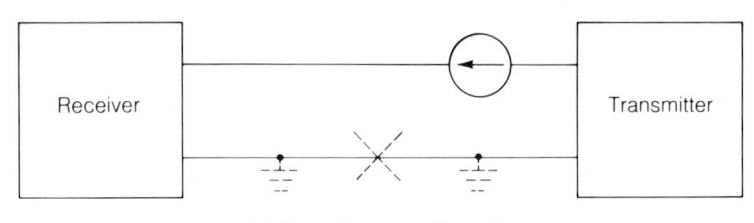

(a) Current-loop configuration

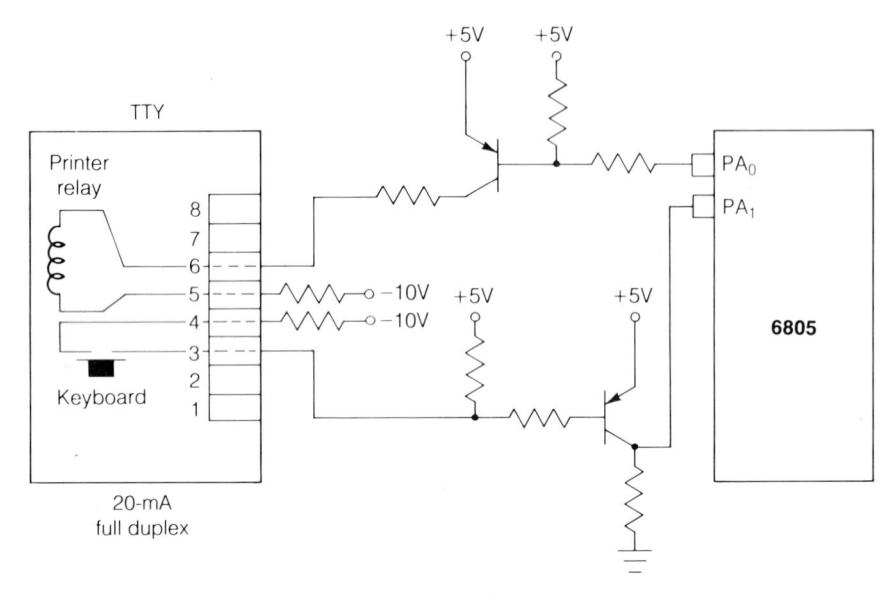

(b) 6805 20 mA current-loop/TTY communication

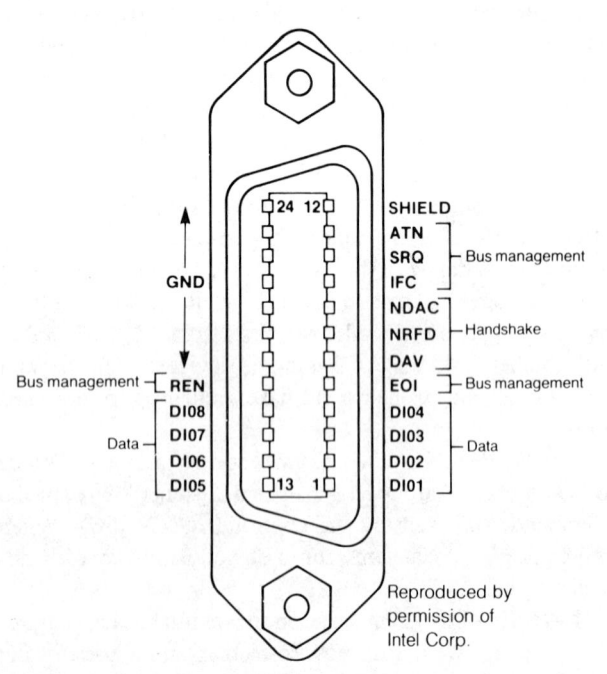

Figure 21.9 GPIB connector and signal categories.

Reproduced by permission of Intel Corp.

THE 6850 ASYNCHRONOUS COMMUNICATIONS INTERFACE ADAPTER (ACIA)

As an application of several of the data-communication topics introduced so far, Figure 21.11 illustrates one of the simplest and most common forms of data communication: simplex, asynchronous, 110-baud, point-to-point (two-station), serial transmission of data to a printer. We assume the printer is close enough to the CPU to warrant direct RS-232C or current-loop interconnections. Timing and identification of data are done asynchronously, by way of the start-and-stop bit format of Figure 21.1. Because of the slow rate of transmission, handshaking is not required. (We assume the receiver can accept and "digest" the data at 110 bauds. If it cannot, information will be lost.)

The universal asynchronous receiver/transmitter (UART) is the most common device for implementing such a system. Although the UART can be programmed to operate in many modes, we will concentrate on one-way (simplex), asynchronous, 110-baud data flow to a printer (150 and 300 are also popular baud rates).

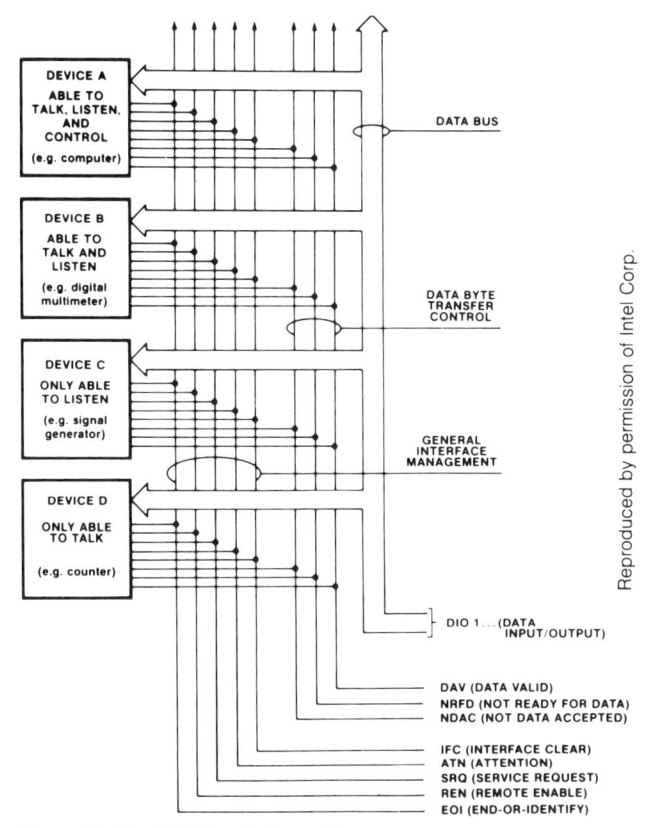

Figure 21.10 GPIB interfacing and bus structure.

The internal block diagram of the 6850 is given in Figure 21.12. Within the various blocks are found parallel and serial buffers, and control and status registers. Also shown are software-serviced 1-bit I/O ports (Clear to Send, Data Carrier Detect, and Request to Send), which are provided for controlling various external hardware (e.g., modems) in certain applications. For simplicity, these 1-bit I/O ports will not be required in our transmission system.

Adding a simplified version of the 6850 block diagram to our asynchronous CPU-to-printer communication system, we arrive at the design of Figure 21.13. The addressing scheme adopted places our 6850 at foldback locations $8000 through $BFFF, just above the space reserved for our 6821 PIA of Chapter 19.

The next step is to configure the UART by writing the correct word to the control register.

Control-Word Format

The 6850 is software programmed for asynchronous transmission by assembling the proper control word based on the format of Figure 21.14, and writing the information into the internal control register.

Actually, we must write to the control register twice during initialization: once to reset the 6850 and again to configure the system. The software RESET is required because internal reset logic detects the power-on line transition and holds the chip in a RESET state to prevent erroneous output signals prior to initialization. To release the system from this RESET "lock" state, we write 1s to control register bits CR0 and CR1. After master reset, we are free to initialize the 6850 via its control register.

To match our requirements for asynchronous transmission, the command word takes on the configuration of Figure 21.15. Beginning with the least significant bits, let's review each control bit selection:

- *CR0/CR1*—These bits program the number of clock input cycles required (1, 16, or 64) to transmit or receive a single serial bit. The 16 and 64 modes enable the receiver to check for false starts and to synchronize the incoming data to its internal clock. In our selected divide-by-16 mode, for example, eight consecutive "lows" must be

As our system develops, contrast the *serial*, RS-232, 6850-based communication system of this section with the *parallel*, Centronics standard, 6821-based printer interface of Chapter 18.

BASIC DESCRIPTION

The 6850 Asynchronous Communications Interface Adapter (or UART) is basically a parallel-to-serial/serial-to-parallel converter that operates in the asynchronous mode only. (A USART, or universal synchronous/asynchronous receiver/transmitter, operates in both synchronous and asynchronous modes.)

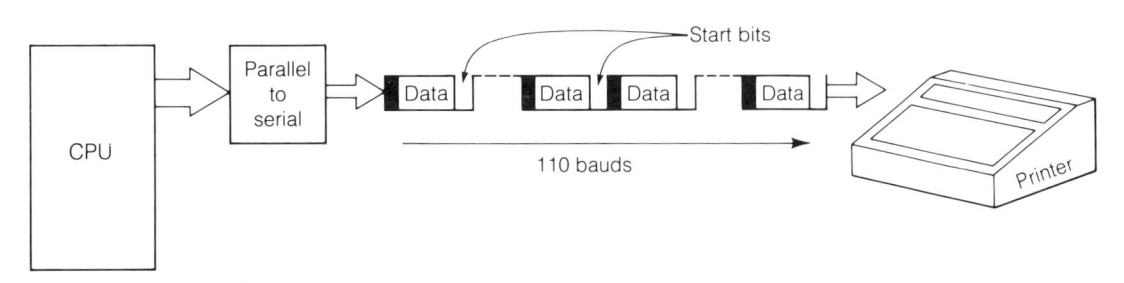

Figure 21.11 Simplex, asynchronous, serial data flow to a printer.

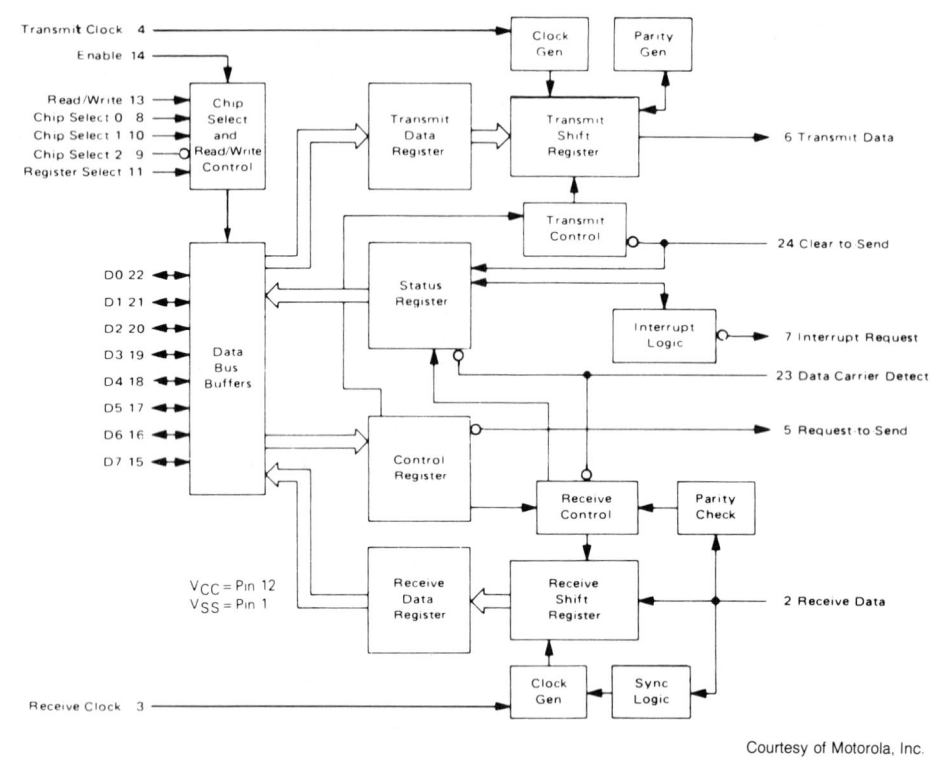

276 Part IV / Applications and Interfacing: Living in a Real World

Figure 21.12 The MC6850 Asynchronous Communications Interface Adapter (ACIA) internal block diagram.

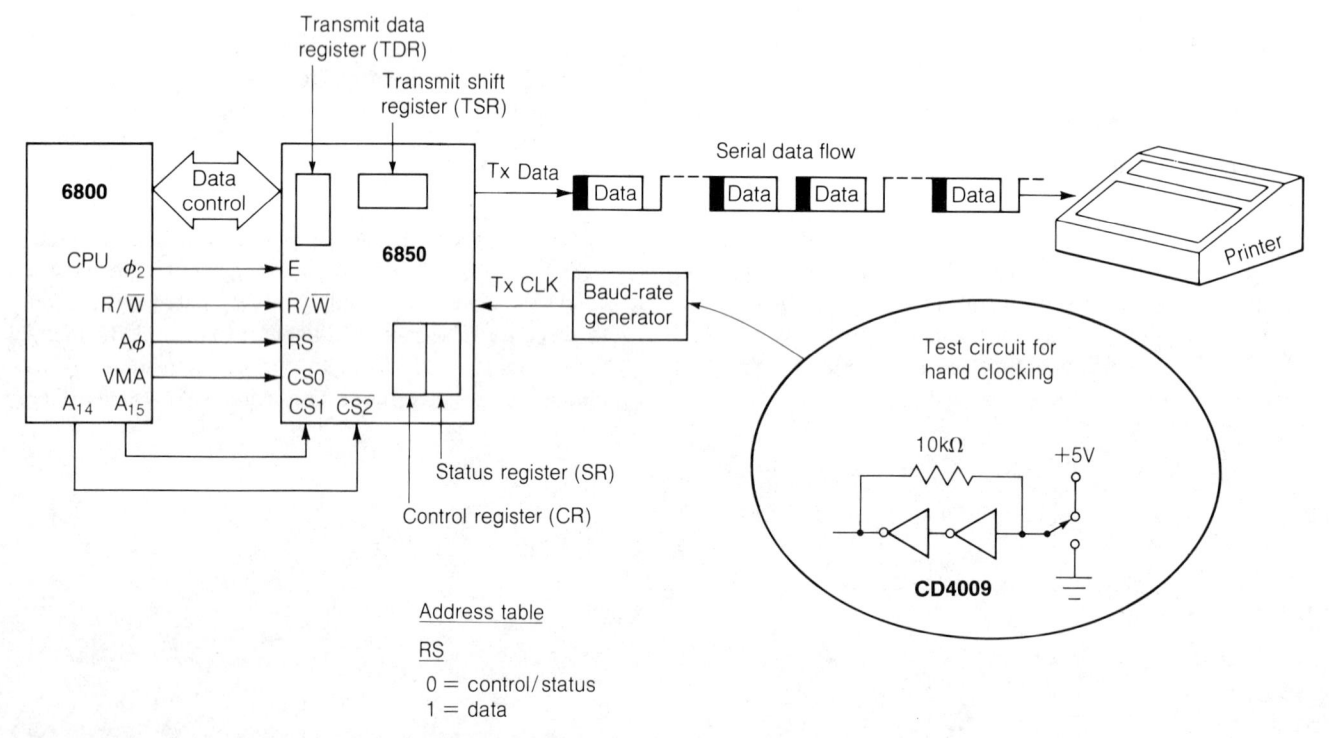

Figure 21.13 UART-based, serial, asynchronous transmission system.

CR7	CR6	CR5	CR4	CR3	CR2	CR1	CR0

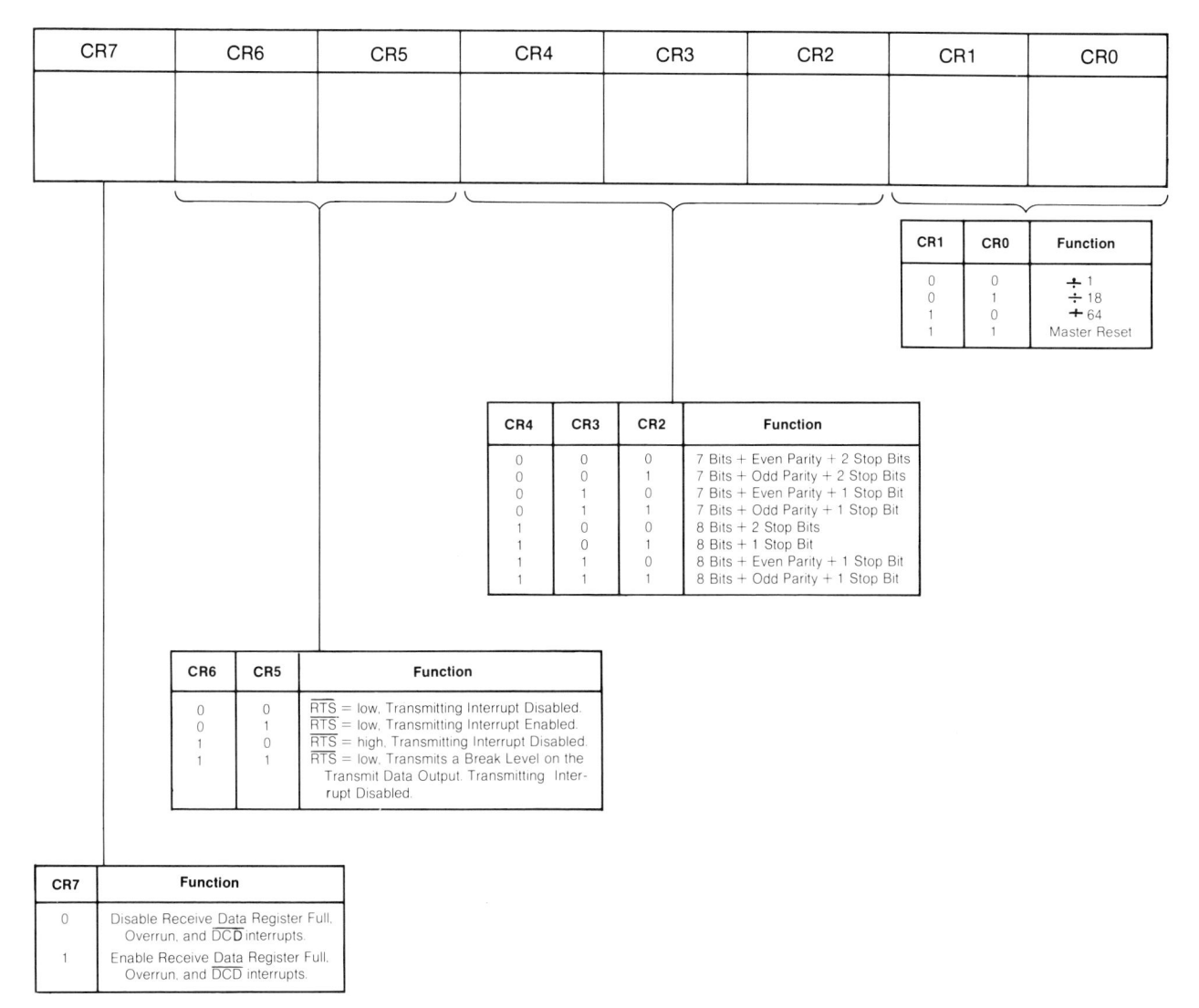

CR1	CR0	Function
0	0	÷ 1
0	1	÷ 16
1	0	÷ 64
1	1	Master Reset

CR4	CR3	CR2	Function
0	0	0	7 Bits + Even Parity + 2 Stop Bits
0	0	1	7 Bits + Odd Parity + 2 Stop Bits
0	1	0	7 Bits + Even Parity + 1 Stop Bit
0	1	1	7 Bits + Odd Parity + 1 Stop Bit
1	0	0	8 Bits + 2 Stop Bits
1	0	1	8 Bits + 1 Stop Bit
1	1	0	8 Bits + Even Parity + 1 Stop Bit
1	1	1	8 Bits + Odd Parity + 1 Stop Bit

CR6	CR5	Function
0	0	$\overline{RTS}$ = low, Transmitting Interrupt Disabled.
0	1	$\overline{RTS}$ = low, Transmitting Interrupt Enabled.
1	0	$\overline{RTS}$ = high, Transmitting Interrupt Disabled.
1	1	$\overline{RTS}$ = low, Transmits a Break Level on the Transmit Data Output. Transmitting Interrupt Disabled.

CR7	Function
0	Disable Receive Data Register Full, Overrun, and $\overline{DCD}$ interrupts.
1	Enable Receive Data Register Full, Overrun, and $\overline{DCD}$ interrupts.

Figure 21.14 6850 control-word format.

CR7	CR6	CR5	CR4	CR3	CR2	CR1	CR0
0	0	1	0	0	0	0	1

Disable receive interrupt | Enable transmit interrupt | 7 bits, even parity, 2 stop bits | Serial bit transmitted every 16 transmit clock pulses

Figure 21.15 6850 control-word format for interrupt-I/O mode.

detected by the receiver before a valid start bit is assumed. The data bits are then strobed in—one every 16 clock inputs—at approximately the center of each bit period.

- *CR2/CR3/CR4*—The word select bits are used to select word length, parity, and the number of stop bits. Since we are sending ASCII characters to our printer, we will choose 7 bits, even parity (arbitrarily), and 2 stop bits (slow printer).
- *CR5/CR6*—Here is where we must decide on interrupt I/O or programmed I/O operation. That is, will the 6850 interrupt the MPU when ready for the next ASCII character, or will the MPU poll the 6850's status register? Arbitrarily choosing interrupt I/O, we enable the transmit interrupt.
- *CR7*—When high, this bit enables a special set of automatic interrupts: Overrun, Receive Data Register Full, and active transition on the Data Carrier Detect signal line. Since these are used only in the receiving mode, we will disable them for now.

Status-Read Format

If we adopt the polled (programmed I/O) mode of operation, it will be necessary to determine when various data registers are empty and to check error flags. By reading this information from the 6850 status register of Figure 21.16, we can implement the polled mode of operation.

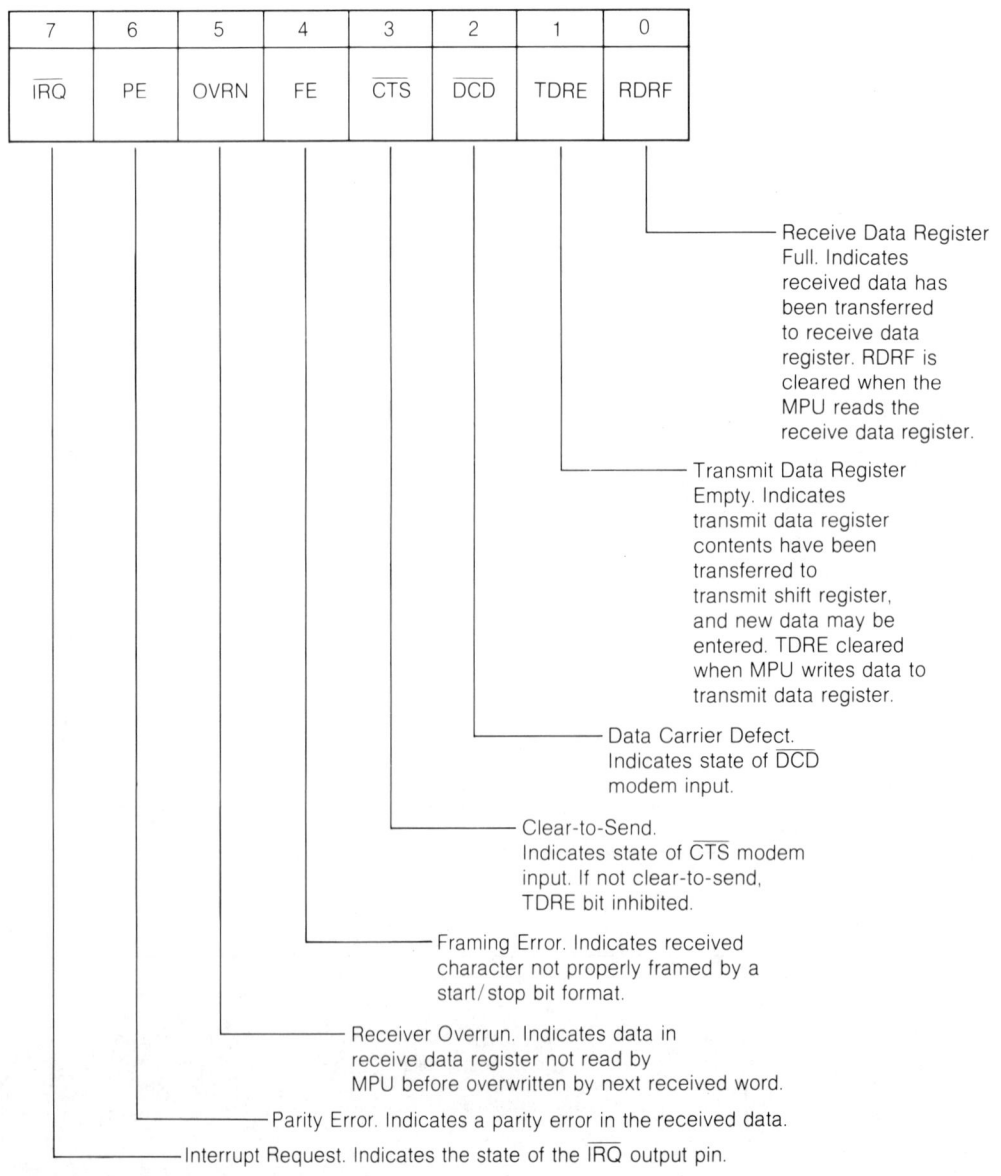

7	6	5	4	3	2	1	0
$\overline{IRQ}$	PE	OVRN	FE	$\overline{CTS}$	$\overline{DCD}$	TDRE	RDRF

- Receive Data Register Full. Indicates received data has been transferred to receive data register. RDRF is cleared when the MPU reads the receive data register.
- Transmit Data Register Empty. Indicates transmit data register contents have been transferred to transmit shift register, and new data may be entered. TDRE cleared when MPU writes data to transmit data register.
- Data Carrier Defect. Indicates state of $\overline{DCD}$ modem input.
- Clear-to-Send. Indicates state of $\overline{CTS}$ modem input. If not clear-to-send, TDRE bit inhibited.
- Framing Error. Indicates received character not properly framed by a start/stop bit format.
- Receiver Overrun. Indicates data in receive data register not read by MPU before overwritten by next received word.
- Parity Error. Indicates a parity error in the received data.
- Interrupt Request. Indicates the state of the $\overline{IRQ}$ output pin.

Figure 21.16 6850 status register, used for programmed I/O operations.

(a) Interrupt I/O technique

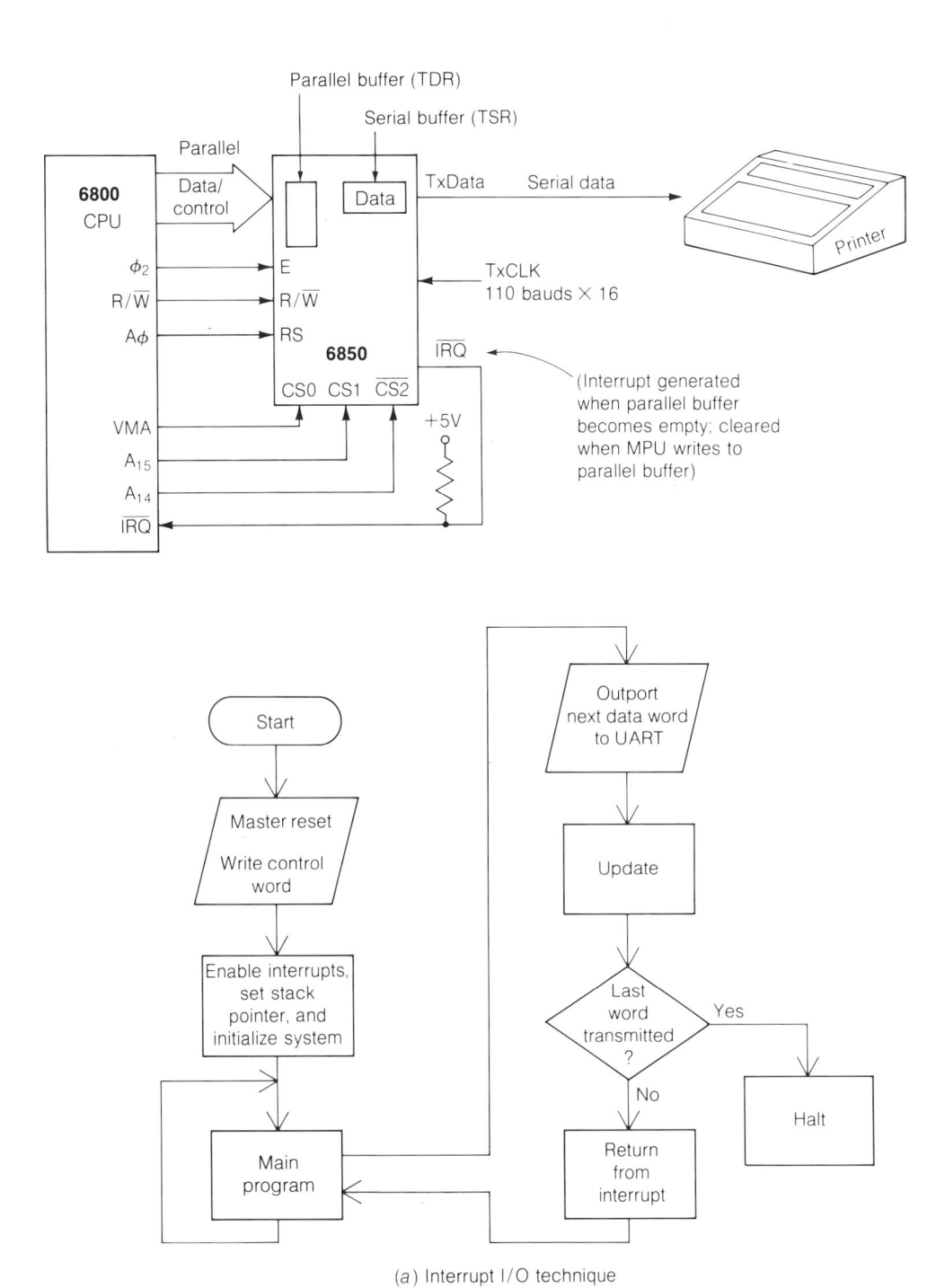

Figure 21.17 UART-based asynchronous transmission to printer.

Completed Hardware/Software Design

Our final system design is revealed in Figure 21.17a (interrupt I/O) and 21.17b (programmed I/O).

Briefly, the operation of the system is as follows: Under polled or interrupt control, the CPU writes the next word to be transmitted into the *parallel* buffer (transmit data register) using the where/when waveforms of Figure 21.18. Whenever the *serial* transmit buffer (transmit shift register) becomes empty, this next data word is immediately (and automatically) transferred from the parallel buffer to the serial buffer. The start, stop, and parity bits are automatically added and the bits are "walked out" of the TxData pin in serial format at the rate controlled by the TxClk (transmit clock) input (start bit followed by least significant bit).

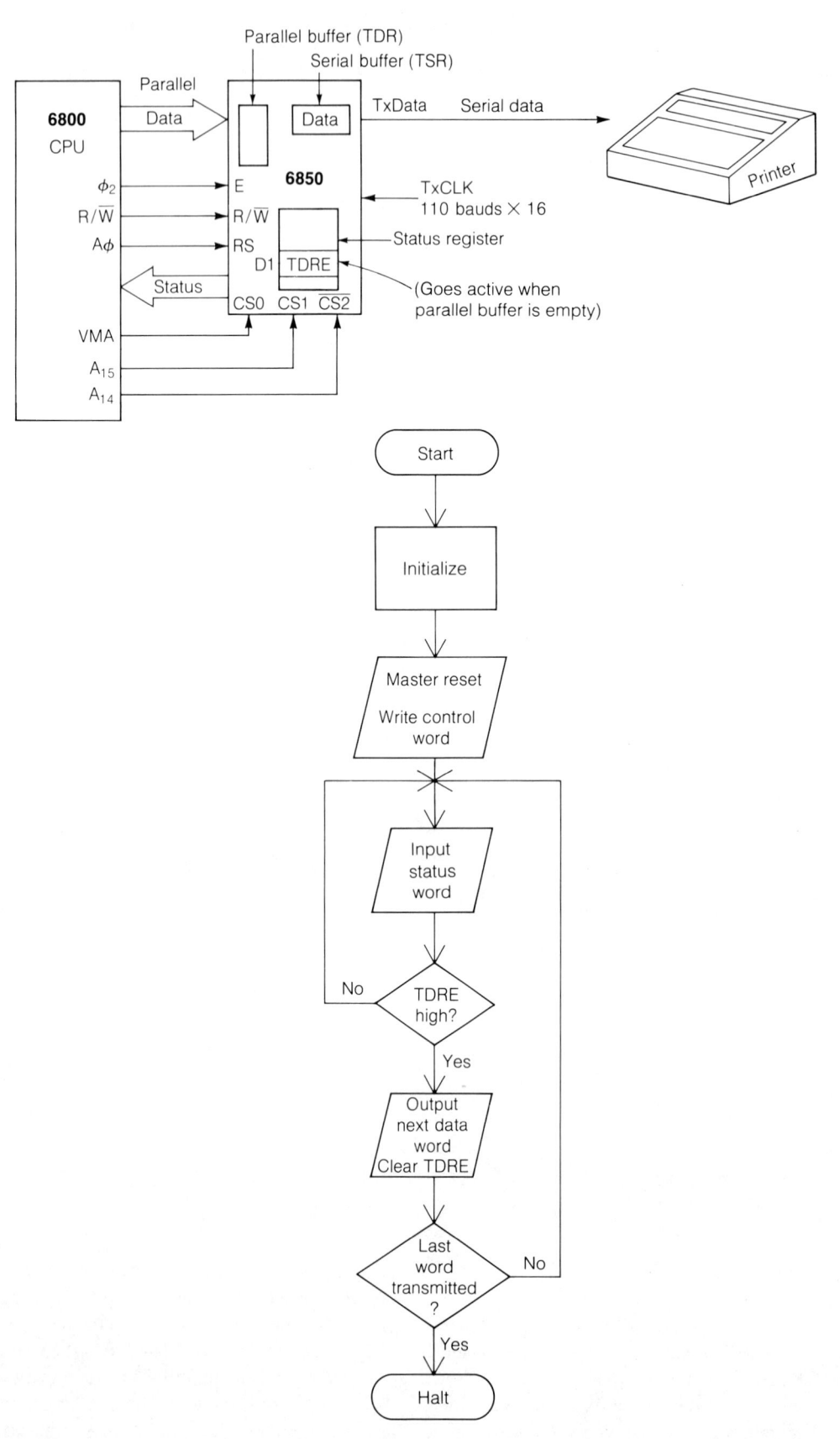

280   Part IV / Applications and Interfacing: Living in a Real World

(b) Programmed I/O technique

Figure 21.17 (continued)

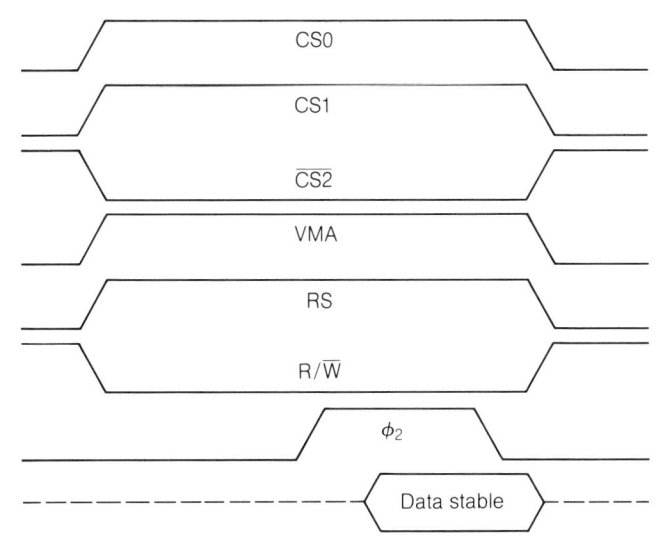

Figure 21.18 6800 waveforms for writing next data word to parallel buffer.

As soon as the parallel buffer is again empty, an interrupt is automatically generated by the $\overline{\text{IRQ}}$ (interrupt request) pin, and the CPU writes the next word into the parallel buffer (automatically deactivating the $\overline{\text{IRQ}}$ line). For the polled operation of Figure 21.17b, the CPU continuously reads the state of the TDRE (Transmit Data Register Empty) status flag, looking for the "parallel register empty" condition (TDRE = 1). When the next data word is written to the parallel buffer, the TDRE status bit is automatically cleared.

On the receiving end, a "print character" operation begins when each start bit is detected and mechanical operation is initiated. When all data, start, stop, and parity bits have been received (number of bits times 9.09 ms/bit), a character is struck. The stop bits give the printing mechanism time to prepare for the next start bit. (Chances are the printer will contain a buffer in order to store information during such time-consuming activities as a carriage return.)

On many serial communication systems, the receiving end is also a 6850 UART, programmed for serial reception of data (Figure 21.19). As before, each transmitted word is synchronized by the high-to-low transition of each start bit. To assure a valid start bit, the receive UART automatically rechecks the state of the input line approximately $\frac{1}{2}$-bit period after the high-to-low transition. If the input is still low, a valid start bit—rather than a glitch—is assumed, and the bits are clocked into the RxData (receive data) pin at a rate controlled by the RxCLK (receive clock) input pin. When a full word is strobed into the serial buffer, it is stripped of its parity, start, and stop bits and transferred to the parallel buffer. The receiving device is immediately notified of the "parallel buffer full" condition by way of the $\overline{\text{IRQ}}$ interrupt pin or a polling of the RDRF status flag. A read operation removes the word from the receive parallel buffer, automatically resetting the RDRF flag and $\overline{\text{IRQ}}$ interrupt line.

Software-accessible status flags within the status register of the receive UART (see Figure 21.16) are set to detect parity, overrun (printer does not read in a character before the next one becomes available), or framing (valid stop bit not detected) errors. (Without the 6850, errors would have to be detected by software processing of the data.)

Once again we find the workload on the CPU considerably reduced by the use of a programmable peripheral chip. To the CPU the transmit and receive operations are nothing more than interrupt or programmed I/O operations to and from a parallel register. All other aspects of asynchronous serial transmission are handled automatically by the 6850.

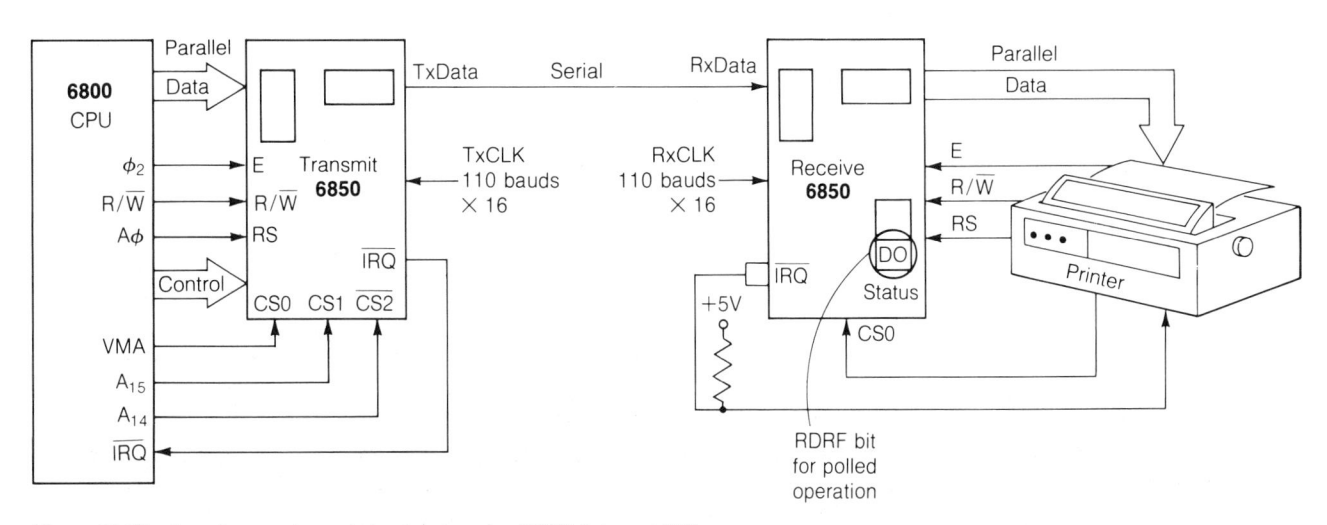

Figure 21.19 Asynchronous transmission using receive UART (interrupt I/O).

COMMUNICATION PROTOCOLS

The printer of our previous example is known as a "dumb" terminal because it merely displays data just as it receives it. A dumb terminal cannot check for errors, cannot be combined with other terminals on the same line and addressed, cannot ask for retransmission of data should an error occur, and cannot operate synchronously.

"Smart" terminals, on the other hand, contain internal processing capability (intelligence) and can perform all of these functions and more. Therefore, smart terminals (also known as *intelligent* terminals) require *communication protocols*.

A communication protocol is a set of rules governing information flow in a "smart" data-communication system. Basically, a communication protocol defines the special control/address/error-checking words to be injected into the serial data stream. (With only a single serial line of communication, all data, address, and control information must of course be multiplexed on the same line.) As shown in the following list, communication protocols are divided into two basic groups: the more advanced *bit-oriented protocols* (BOP) and the earlier *byte-control-oriented protocols* (BCP).

- Bit-oriented protocols:
  SDLC—Synchronous Data-Link Control
  ADCCP—Advanced Data-Communication Control Procedures
  HDLC—High-Level Data-Link Control
  BDLC—Burroughs Data-Link Control
- Byte-control-oriented protocols:
  DDCMP—Digital Data-Communication Message Protocol
  BISYNC—BInary SYNchronous Communication

In general terms, a bit-oriented protocol is one in which the content and format of the data between the opening and closing flag words may take on any form and be from any source. That is, there are no restrictions on the data codes or character length, and no special control characters are required.

When using byte-control-oriented protocols, on the other hand, the data words are generally 8 bits in length and special control and sync words are required. There are many other subtle differences between BOP and BCP, as we will see when we look at an example of each.

SDLC Protocol (BOP)

The Synchronous Data-Link Control (SDLC) bit-oriented protocol is an IBM communication-link protocol designed for a master/slave-system configuration with one primary station communicating with up to 256 secondary stations. There are few restrictions on the kind of primary/secondary stations allowed, and they can vary from standard terminals to satellites. For added flexibility, communication can occur in either half or full duplex.

A single communication element between master and slave stations, called a *frame,* is used for both data control and data transfer. Long-term transmission consists of a sequence of frames, with each frame consisting of six fields. As demonstrated by Figure 21.20*a,* a frame format is similar to the magnetic recording formats used by floppy-disk and Winchester storage devices (see Chapter 6).

- The opening flag field identifies the start of a frame and always consists of a 01111110 sequence. (To prevent this unique flag word from appearing anywhere in the text, a binary 0 bit is automatically inserted after five contiguous 1s are detected. The inserted 0s are automatically deleted in the received bit stream.)
- The 8- or 16-bit address field is used to designate the secondary station for which the frame is intended.
- The control field contains such information as the frame sequence number and handshaking bits to control send/receive timing.
- The information field contains the data to be transmitted and can vary in length. The data can be configured in any code structure—binary, BCD, ASCII, and so on.
- The error field contains the well-known cyclic-redundancy-check characters that are also used in magnetic-storage protocols.
- A closing flag indicates the end of a frame. (When a frame is immediately followed by another frame, the ending flag of the first frame is also the starting flag of the next frame.)

BISYNC (BCP)

Probably the most common character-oriented protocol is IBM's Binary Synchronous Communication (BISYNC) protocol, intended for half-duplex (start/stop) operations. The BISYNC format is shown in Figure 21.20*b.*

The two 8-bit sync words indicate start of transmission. The header field starts with the address of the receiving station, followed by a block identification number. The control block identifies the text field as carrying data information or control information. The acknowledgment section allows the receiver to acknowledge (echo) previously received data. (The need for continuous acknowledgment limits BISYNC to half-duplex operation.) The text field contains data or control information. During idle periods, when no data are sent, sync characters are automatically inserted in the data stream. The last field—the BCC (Block Check Character) field—is used for CRC error checking.

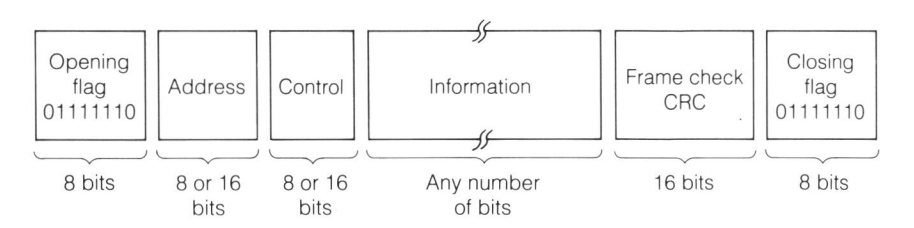

Figure 21.20 Two popular serial communication protocols.

(a) Synchronous Data-link Control (SDLC) frame

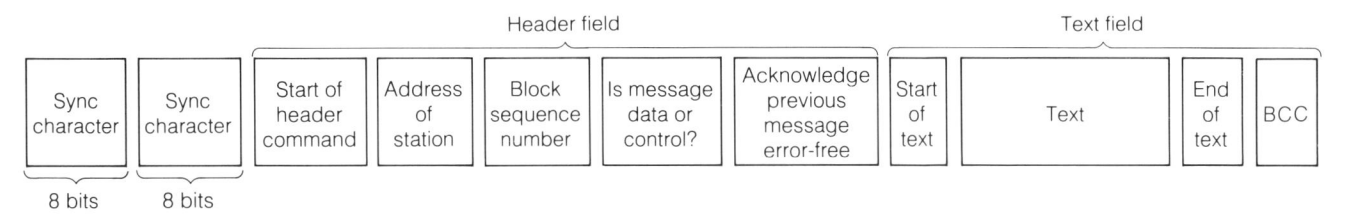

(b) BInary SYNchronous Communications (BISYNC) protocol frame

LSI Protocol-Control Chips

Because of the complexity of synchronous protocols, the housekeeping details often are best handled by a specialized programmable peripheral chip (hardware) rather than programming action (software). The MC6854 Advanced Data Link Controller (ADLC) is a typical example.

The 6854 (shown in simplified form in Figure 21.21) handles SDLC and HDLC bit-oriented protocols and does for smart terminals what the 6850 does for dumb terminals.

When information is sent to a secondary station, the 6854 helps to assemble an HDLC or SDLC frame for transmission and to disassemble a frame upon reception.

The 6854 can also handle loop-mode SDLC data links, popular because of a drastic reduction in hardware and software requirements. In the loop mode, the substations (slave stations) are daisy chained on a single line (a loop) as shown in Figure 21.21b. The data frames sent out on the loop by the 6854 loop controller (master) are relayed from station to station. Any secondary station finding its address in the address field inputs the data from that frame. Future protocol chips will be multilingual and will feature automatic protocol recognition in order to provide transparent communication (operator need not be aware of protocol used).

LOCAL AREA NETWORKS (LANs)

A communication *network* is a multiuser/multifunction collection of various CPU, memory, and data-terminal units dispersed over a medium to wide area. All units making up the network can communicate with each other and with shared data (memory) over coaxial cables using a communication protocol.

The various units making up the network can be arranged in a string, loop, or star configuration (Figure 21.22), or a combination of the three.

The star configuration is used for systems requiring centralized control. The string and loop configurations are often found in distributed control systems, where the cable acts as a bus and each terminal can gain network control as the need arises. Distributed control offers an important advantage: a malfunction in one terminal will not cause the entire network to go down. (Terminals can be "multidropped.")

The final stage of network evolution will produce the *dispersed* processing network. Rather than the top-down hierarchically (master/slave) oriented distributed system, the processing capability is parceled out (dispersed) among many equally accessible multifunction/multiprotocol information stations, all in direct communication.

Channel Access

Channel access to a network (Who gets to use the common line?) is by way of *polling* or *contention* techniques such as token passing and collision detection.

Token passing *Token passing*, often associated with ring networks, is a polling process in which a special "token" word circulates around the loop from node to node. When a node wishes to transmit, it captures and holds the token, giving it exclusive right to the channel. When finished sending its message, the token is placed back into circulation.

Collision detection *Collision detection*, the most popular contention technique, gives each node the ability to detect traffic on the channel. As soon as the channel is quiet, any

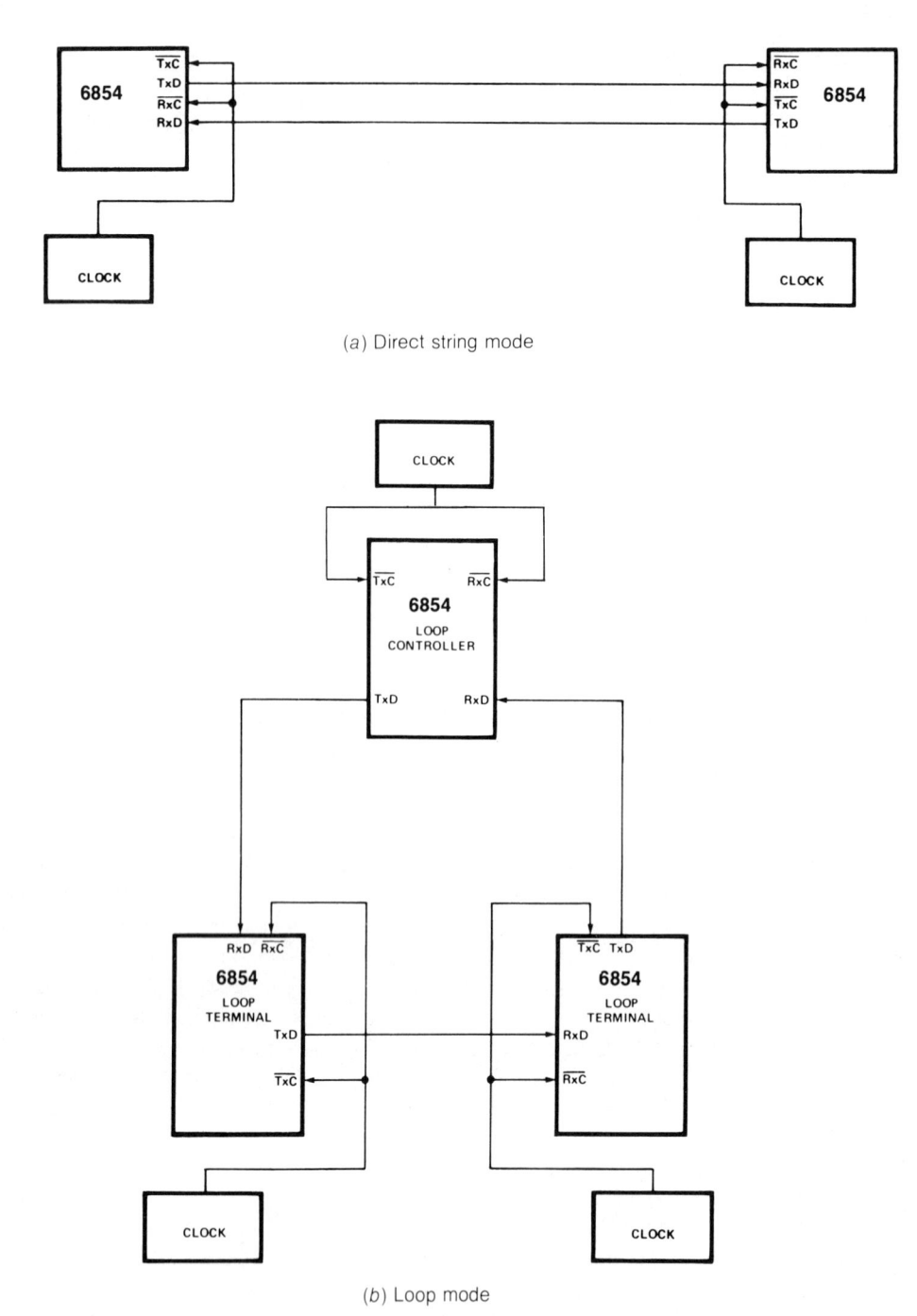

Figure 21.21 Serial communication using the 6854 protocol controller.

(a) Direct string mode

(b) Loop mode

of the nodes can transmit (known as *listen-before-talking*). On those rare occasions when two nodes attempt to begin transmission simultaneously, the messages will collide, resulting in a change in channel energy. When the collision (energy burst) is detected, both transmitters withhold activity for a random period of time, then attempt to transmit again. Since collisions are rare, and information is sent in finite-length *packets* to give fair access to all nodes, collision detection (CD) is a highly efficient form of distributed access.

LAN Standards

The goal of local area networks is to promote universal communication between any and all brands of computers

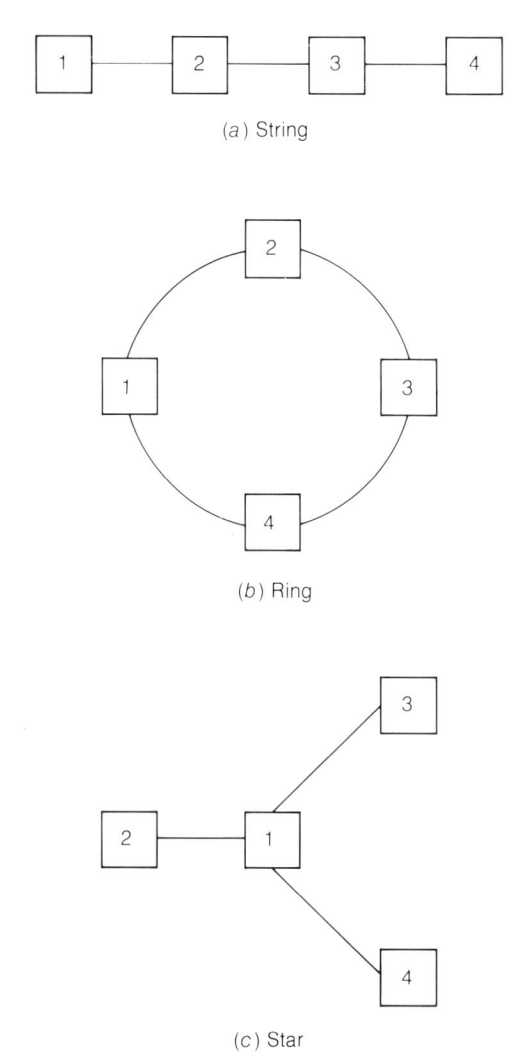

Figure 21.22 The three basic network configurations.

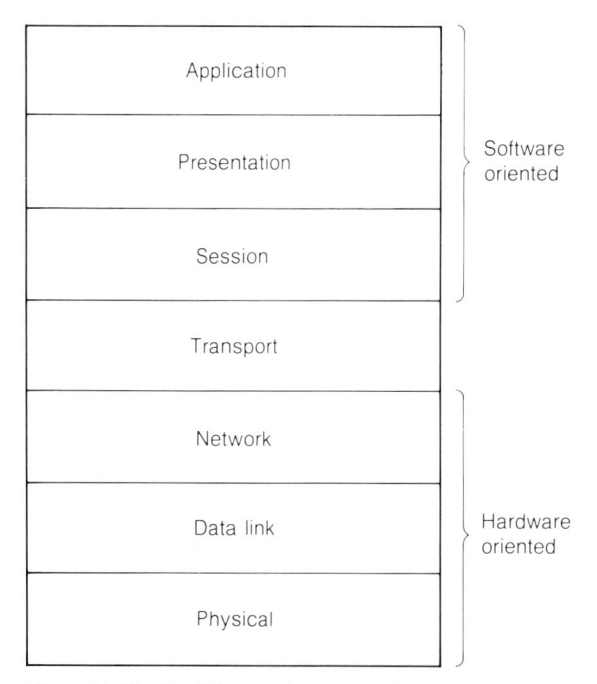

(a) String
(b) Ring
(c) Star

Figure 21.23 The ISO seven-layer model for Open Systems Interconnection (OSI).

(worldwide!). To help meet this goal, the International Standards Organization (ISO) recommended a LAN (also known as *Open Systems Interconnection*) architecture consisting of seven layers (Figure 21.23). The bottom three layers generally define the hardware, the top three specify the software, and the transport layer is the link between hardware and software. The layered approach—in which each layer is independent of the others—allows the network system to be flexible and to easily adapt to new technology and changing standards.

Ethernet

Ethernet is a local serial data-communication network, aimed at the middle ground between long-distance, low-speed networks and specialized short-distance, very-high-speed interconnections. Under joint development by Xerox, Digital Equipment, and Intel, Ethernet uses collision detection to arbitrate the transmission of data packets.

Compatibility is one of the main objectives of Ethernet, which promises to allow almost any intelligent peripheral to communicate with any other, regardless of manufacturer. Such a system will likely find a home in local distributed data processing, electronic mail, and office automation environments, in which bursts of data traffic occur at high peak rates.

Figure 21.24 depicts a typical medium-scale Ethernet configuration, in which eight peripherals communicate over a 50-ohm coaxial cable system at a data rate of 10 million b/s. Each of the two segments, interconnected by a repeater, can be as long as 500 meters. As many as 100 transceivers per segment can be accommodated, with a maximum separation of 2.5 kilometers.

TELECOMMUNICATIONS

The global telephone network is the most extensive and readily available communication system presently in use. It is only natural for computers to look to the telephone system for communication with remote locations.

Modems

The problem with the existing telecommunication network is that the phone lines were developed for human commu-

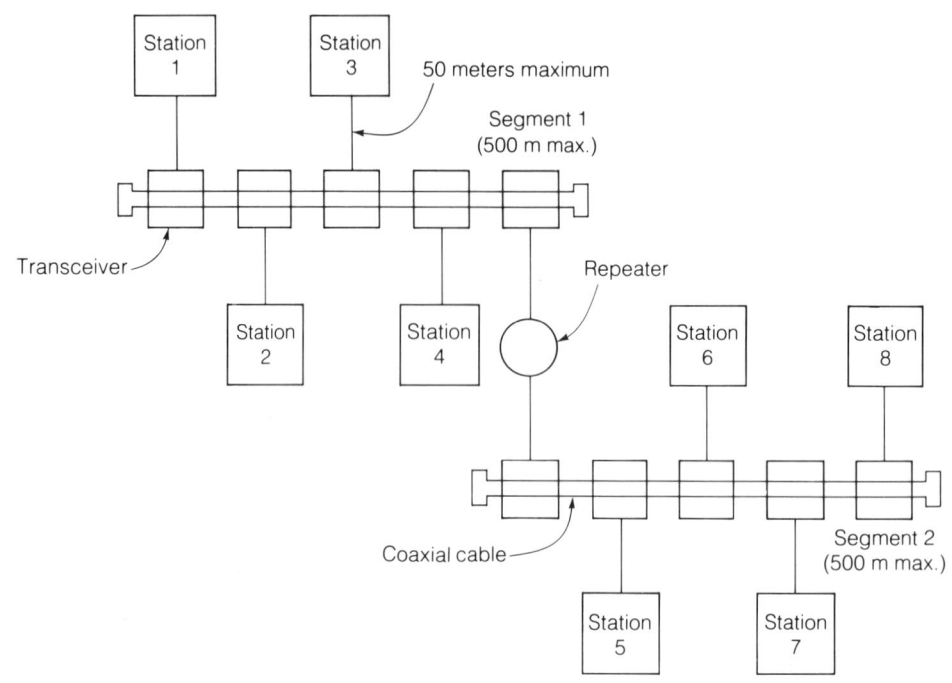

Figure 21.24 Ethernet medium-scale configuration.

nication—which means analog information within a bandwidth of 300 to 3.3 kHz. To condition the signals to flow properly within these limitations, the digital information must first be sent through a *modem* (*mo*dulator/*dem*odulator). A modem is an electronic device for converting digital information to analog form (modulation) for transmission over the telephone network, and to reverse the process upon reception (demodulation).

Using modems, a simple two-station telecommunication system takes on the configuration of Figure 21.25.

Modems use the incoming digital signal to modulate a sine-wave carrier frequency and to demodulate the signal at the other end. As shown in Figure 21.26, modulation can take any of three basic forms: amplitude, frequency, or phase.

Figure 21.27 depicts the two most common telecommunication transmission standards. The Bell 103/113 uses frequency multiplexing to achieve full-duplex operation. However, the narrow bandwidth for each channel limits the transmission rate to approximately 300 bauds. The Bell 202 transmits at a higher baud rate (up to 1800 bauds), but the larger bandwidth limits operation to half-duplex.

Higher-speed modems go beyond the simple *frequency-shift-keying* (FSK) techniques of Figure 21.27 to *phase-shift keying* (PSK). The most popular PSK variation—widely used in 1200 b/s modems—is called *quadrature amplitude modulation* (QAM). This sophisticated technique blends both amplitude and phase modulation to encode 2 bits of data in every state transition. (Since the term *baud* is usually reserved for number of transitions of state, the baud rate of our QAM system is half the bit rate.)

Digital Telecommunications

Until recently, information and voice transmission over telephone lines was entirely an analog operation. However, with

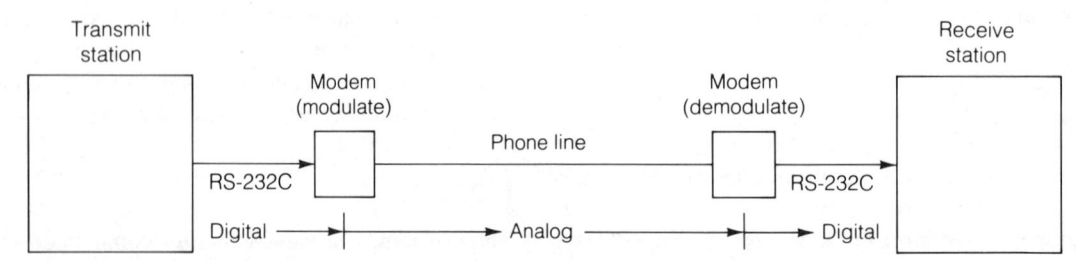

Figure 21.25 The use of modems to communicate by way of phone lines.

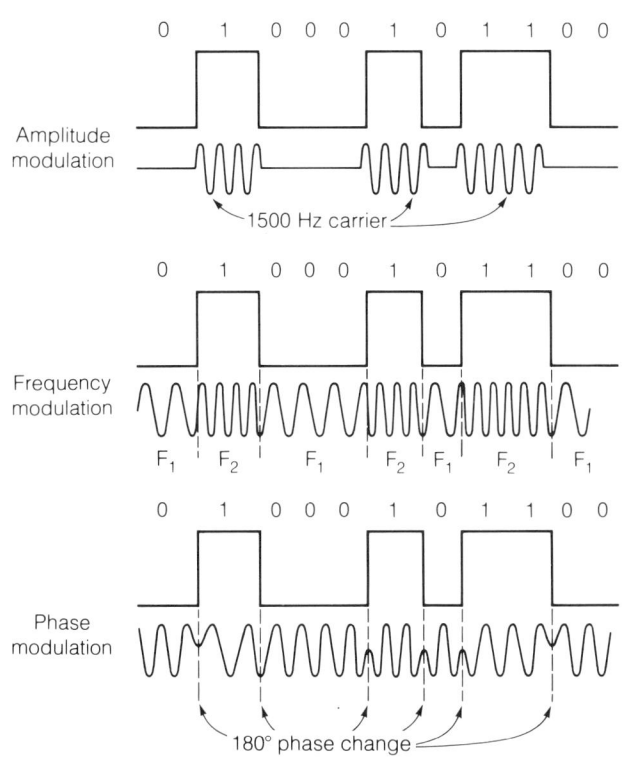

Figure 21.26 Basic telecommunication signal-modulation techniques.

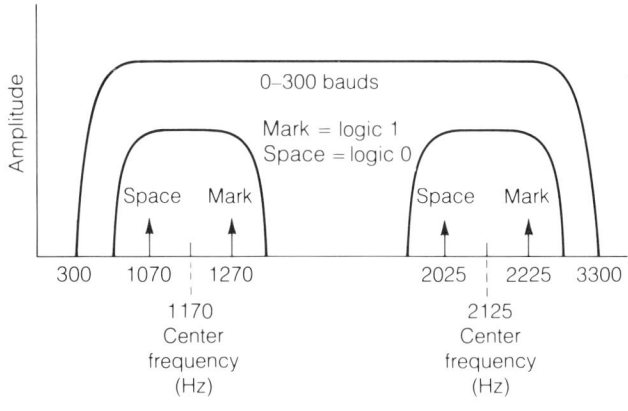

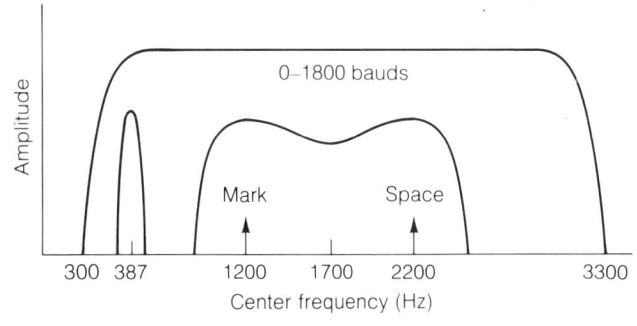

Figure 21.27 Bell serial, binary, asynchronous telecommunication standards based on frequency-shift-keying (FSK) modulation.

the evolution of digital technology and the many advantages it brings—ease of design, precision, low cost, and speed—it was only natural for digital techniques to slowly infiltrate the previously all-analog telephone system. Unfortunately, the high investment in the present analog lines means they cannot be replaced overnight with the more efficient digital channels. Especially hard to replace are the long-distance, narrow-bandwidth voice highways. Therefore, the first digital communication systems have been developed primarily for short distances: toll lines connecting offices, private branch exchanges (PBX), local communication networks (Ethernet), and in general wherever it is economically feasible. Using a technique called *submultiplexing,* in which a voice slot is further subdivided into data-carrying fields, these systems will allow both voice and digital communication on the same line.

Pulse-code modulation (PCM) The type of modulation used by digital telecommunication systems is called *pulse-code modulation.* As shown in Figure 21.28, an input signal is sampled at regular intervals, and each analog voltage is converted to an 8-bit word. The sequence of 8-bit words becomes the serial data stream. Special coding (companding) processes allow 8 bits to represent a full 72 dB of dynamic range.

If 24 analog signals (phones) are sampled in a time-multiplexed scheme, with synchronization and signaling (control) added, you have the basic PCM carrier format of Figure 21.29. This sequence of PCM words, known as the *T1 PCM carrier format,* was developed primarily for interconnecting switching offices. It allows the transmission of 24 time-multiplexed serial channels over a single twisted-pair line. Note that control information for each of the 24 channels is sent by reserving the eighth bit of every sixth frame for signaling; an extra bit is added to each frame to maintain synchronization.

The Codec and PCM filter To efficiently implement the 24-channel T1 PCM carrier format, two new LSI chips have evolved. They are known as the *codec* (*co*der/*dec*oder) and the *PCM line filter* (see Figure 21.30). Their function is to convert an analog voice signal to a digital PCM bit stream at the other end of the line.

Using the 2910 codec and the 2912 PCM filter, a simple two-station telecommunication link takes on the configuration of Figure 21.31a.

The 2912 transmit filter, called an *antialiasing filter,* is used to remove high-frequency components in order to minimize the distortion noise caused by the sampling process. Another filter, also integrated within the 2912 PCM filter, is the *reconstruction filter.* It is used at the receive end to

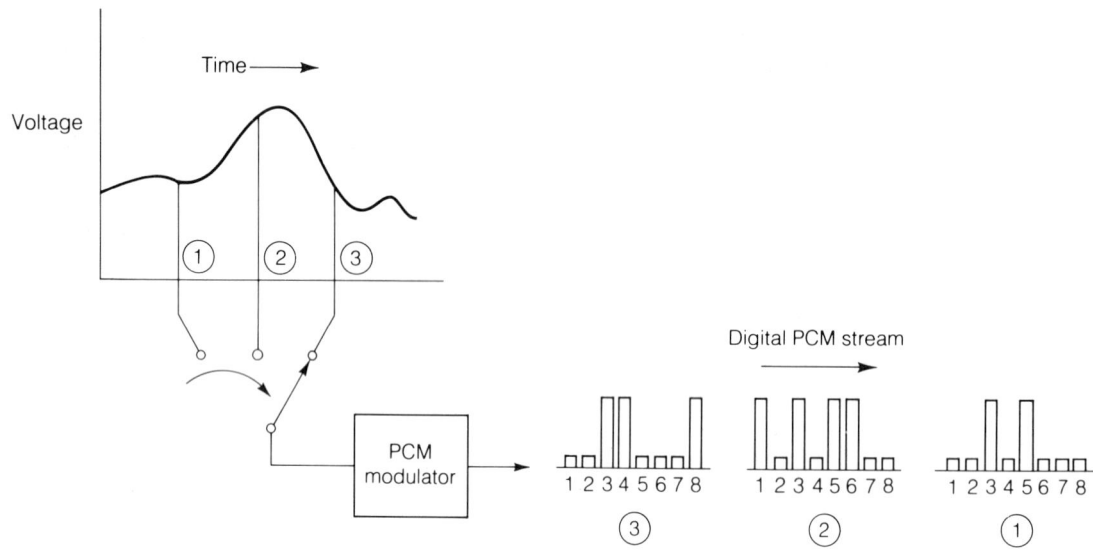

Figure 21.28 Sampled analog voltages converted to serial stream of PCM words.

reconstruct (smooth out) the digital "squared-off" output emitted by the receive codec.

The 2910 codec performs analog-to-digital and digital-to-analog conversions, PCM formatting, companding (nonlinear conversion between analog and digital), and timing.

A typical PCM link and associated waveforms (both time and frequency domain) are shown in Figure 21.31b. Since satisfactory voice reproduction does not require frequency components above approximately 4 kHz, we may safely sample at 8 kHz. (According to sampling theory, if we sample at twice the highest frequency of interest, essentially no information will be lost.)

From transmitter to receiver, the following operations take place:

1. Before transmission begins, an 8-bit word written to the control registers of both transmit and receive codecs assigns the data link to a particular transmit-and-receive time slot.
2. An arbitrary voice signal, consisting of a 2 kHz low-frequency component and a 5 kHz high-frequency component, is transmitted from a telephone set. (As previously stated, the 5 kHz component is unnecessary for adequate voice reproduction and is included simply to determine its effect.)
3. By counting clock cycles relative to the incoming transmit-and-receive frame sync pulse, the codec is able to determine the correct time slot among the 24 channels to transmit a PCM word.
4. Once synchronized to its assigned time channel, the analog signal is filtered to remove the unnecessary 5 kHz component and sampled at the 8 kHz rate by the 2910 codec. Each sample is held in the sample-and-hold block for A/D conversion. (Note that the sum and difference 6 kHz and 10 kHz sidebands produced by the 8K sampling process do not fold back into the 300 Hz to 4 kHz signal band. However, the 5 kHz incoming component, if it had not been removed by the antialiasing filter, would have appeared at 3 kHz in the signal band, causing distortion noise that could not have been removed.) Analog-to-digital conversion is initiated and the corresponding digital word is generated in the appropriate time slot.
5. Every sixth frame the 2910 automatically inserts a special signal bit in the eighth bit position (used for control functions such as dialing information) and a special

Reproduced by permission of Intel Corp.

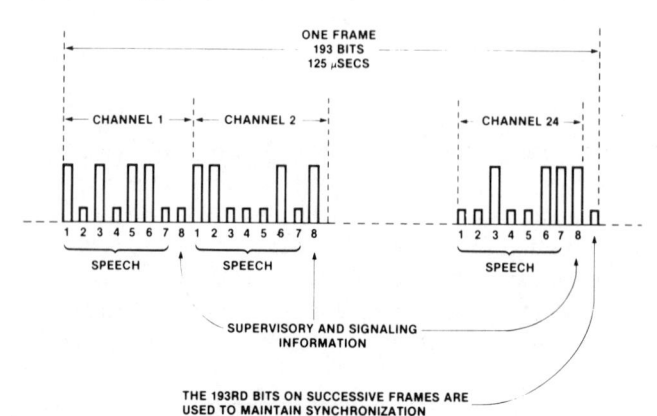

Figure 21.29 PCM carrier format.

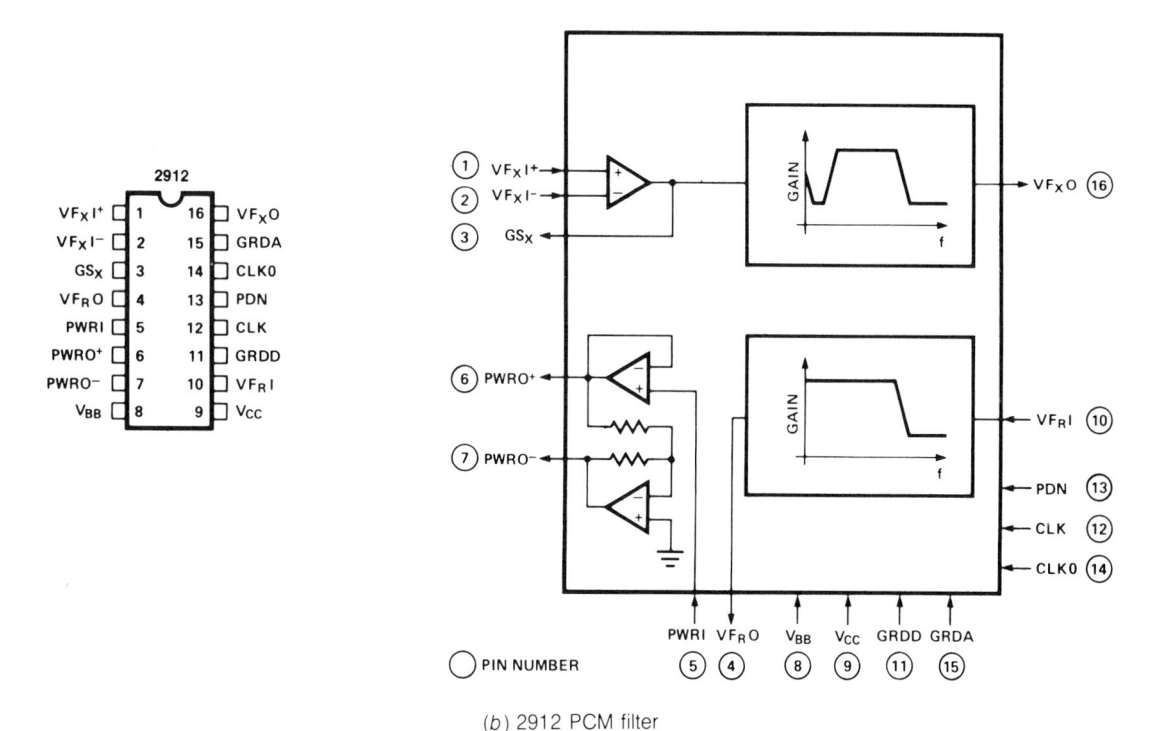

Figure 21.30 Codec and PCM filter block diagrams and pin-outs.

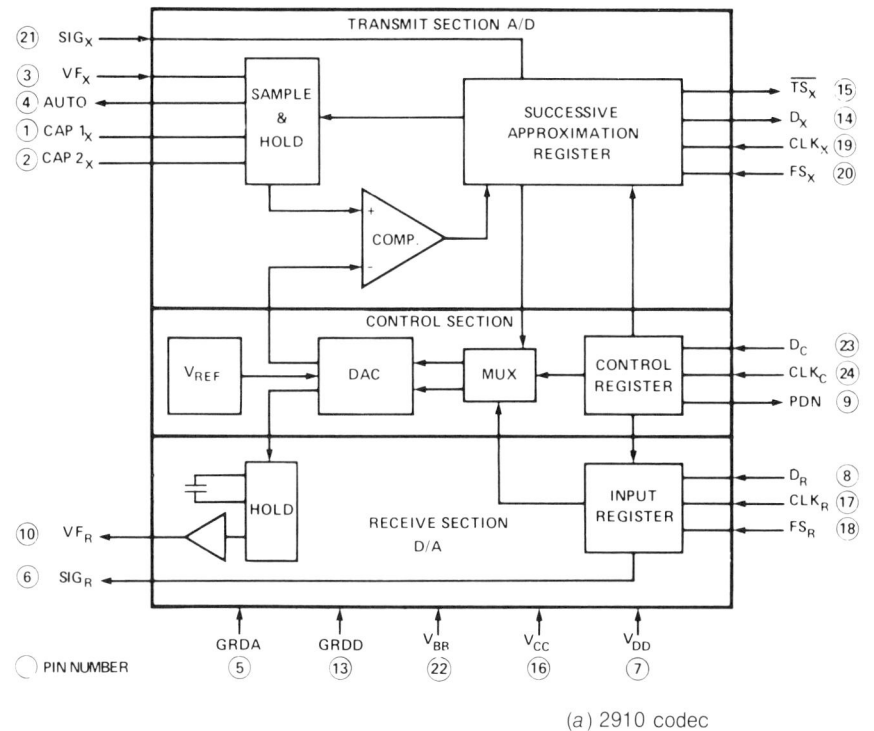

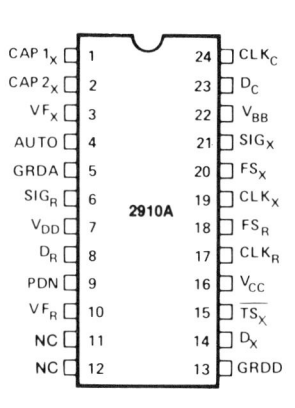

(a) 2910 codec

Reproduced by permission of Intel Corp.

(b) 2912 PCM filter

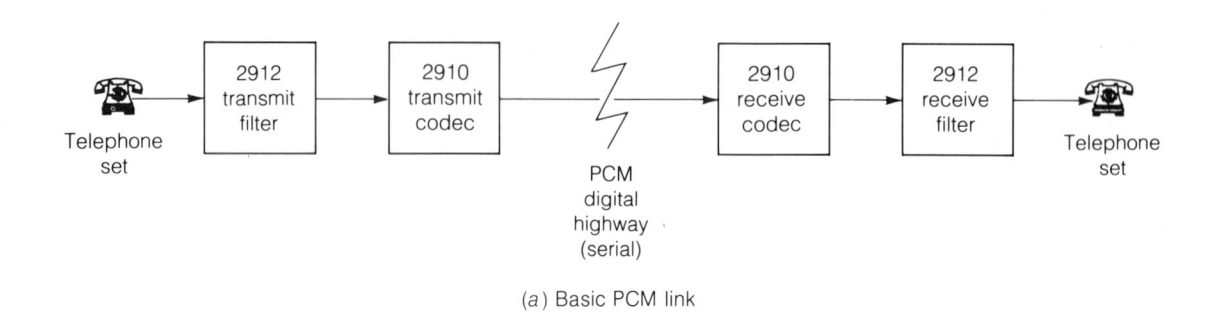

Figure 21.31 A single PCM telephone link using the 2912/2910 filter/codec pair.

sync bit following the entire 24 frames (used for frame identification). (The signal and sync information is obtained from the SIG_x and FS_x input pins to the 2910).

6. The digital information is sent out on the PCM highway and blended in with up to 23 other PCM streams, each assigned to its own unique time slot.
7. When the receive codec at the other end detects the proper time slot, the 8-bit data word is shifted into a serial register. When the register is full, it interrupts the 2910 and a digital-to-analog operation is performed. (Since digital-to-analog conversion takes only a fraction of the time of the A/D operation, DAC conversions can be on an interrupt basis.)
8. The resulting analog signal level is held in a sample-and-hold circuit until released by timing.
9. The "squared off" output of the receive codec is passed through the reconstruction filter where the 6K and 10K aliasing components are removed (both the transmit antialiasing and receive reconstruction filters are contained within the 2912 PCM filter chip, as shown in Figure 21.30).

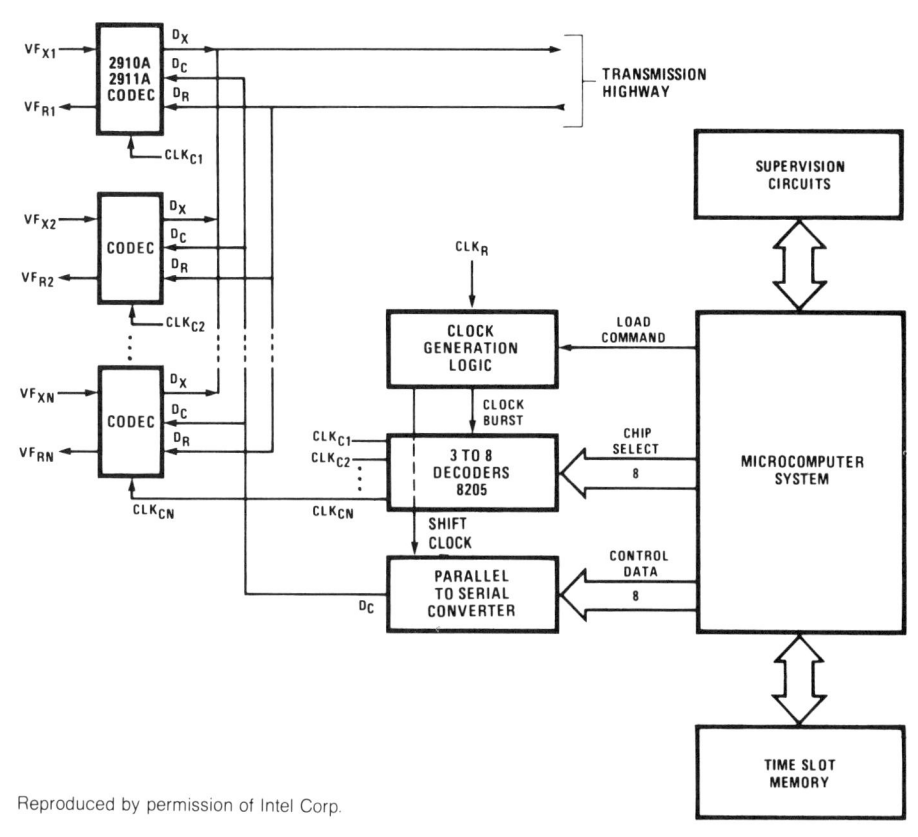

Figure 21.32 Multiplexed telecommunication switching system using codec transmitter/receivers.

10. The original analog signal is recreated (without the unnecessary 5 kHz component, of course) and passed on to the receive telephone.

Figure 21.32 shows how an array of codecs is used to produce a complete intelligent switching system, able to handle up to 256 input phone lines (only 24 can be transmitting simultaneously). When the microprocessor detects an "off-hook" condition, it assigns that codec to an available time slot (by writing an 8-bit code into the codec). At the end of conversation, the codec is taken off the line and placed into a standby condition.

In the future, we can expect the present analog-based phone system to give way gradually to an all-digital network.

FIBER-OPTIC DIGITAL HIGHWAYS

The ever-expanding requirements of modern communication systems are one reason for the development of newer high-speed technologies (silicon on sapphire, Josephson function). The T1 PCM system can transmit information at a respectable 1.5 million bits per second (Mb/s). However, transmission by lightwave carrier over fiber-optic lines can take place at more than 250 Mb/s, with 200 gigabits per second demonstrated in the laboratory (1 gigabit = 10^9 bits).

This wider bandwidth means that a single inexpensive fiber cable can carry as much information as 1000 pairs of copper wire—with high resistance to erosion and total freedom from electromagnetic interference and short circuits.

New low-loss fiber-optic cables, coupled with special high-radiance LEDs, allow repeater stations to be extended from the conventional 1 mile to more than 40 miles. Clearly, the system of Figure 21.33 is the data-transmission highway of the 1980s.

SPEECH SYNTHESIS

The 1980s will also be the decade of the talking computer. As the techniques of speech synthesis reach maturity, a vast array of consumer, industrial, and military products will be communicating with us by way of the spoken word.

At first glance, speech synthesis appears to be a very simple process. Just sample the spoken word at twice the highest frequency of interest (the Nyquist rate) and store the digitized words in memory for later playback. Unfortunately, this direct recording technique is not practical, for synthesizing only a single second of speech would require some 100,000 bits of stored information. Therefore, the race for practical speech synthesis becomes a race to reduce

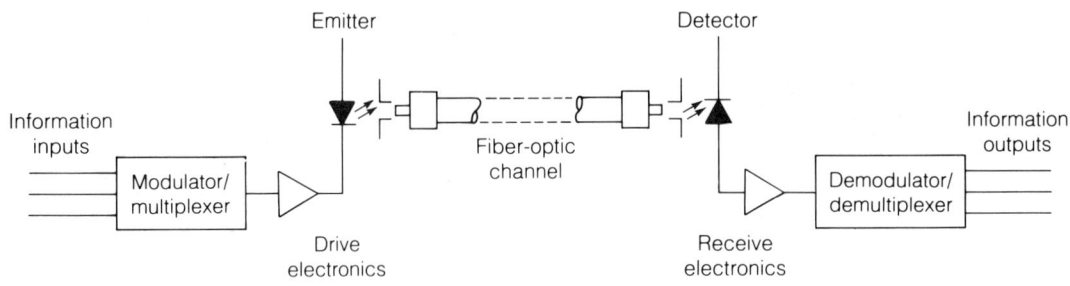

Figure 21.33 Fiber-optic communication link.

the storage requirements—to store in memory only that information absolutely necessary for the realistic reproduction of speech. As we will see, by eliminating unnecessary information in the speech pattern, we can produce one second of human speech with only 400 to 2,000 bits of information. Two general techniques are available for the synthesis of human speech:

- Time-domain synthesis
- Frequency-domain synthesis

The first method is more straightforward. We simply compress and digitize speech wave patterns in the time domain, and store the information sequentially in ROM for later playback through a DAC. The process is diagrammed in Figure

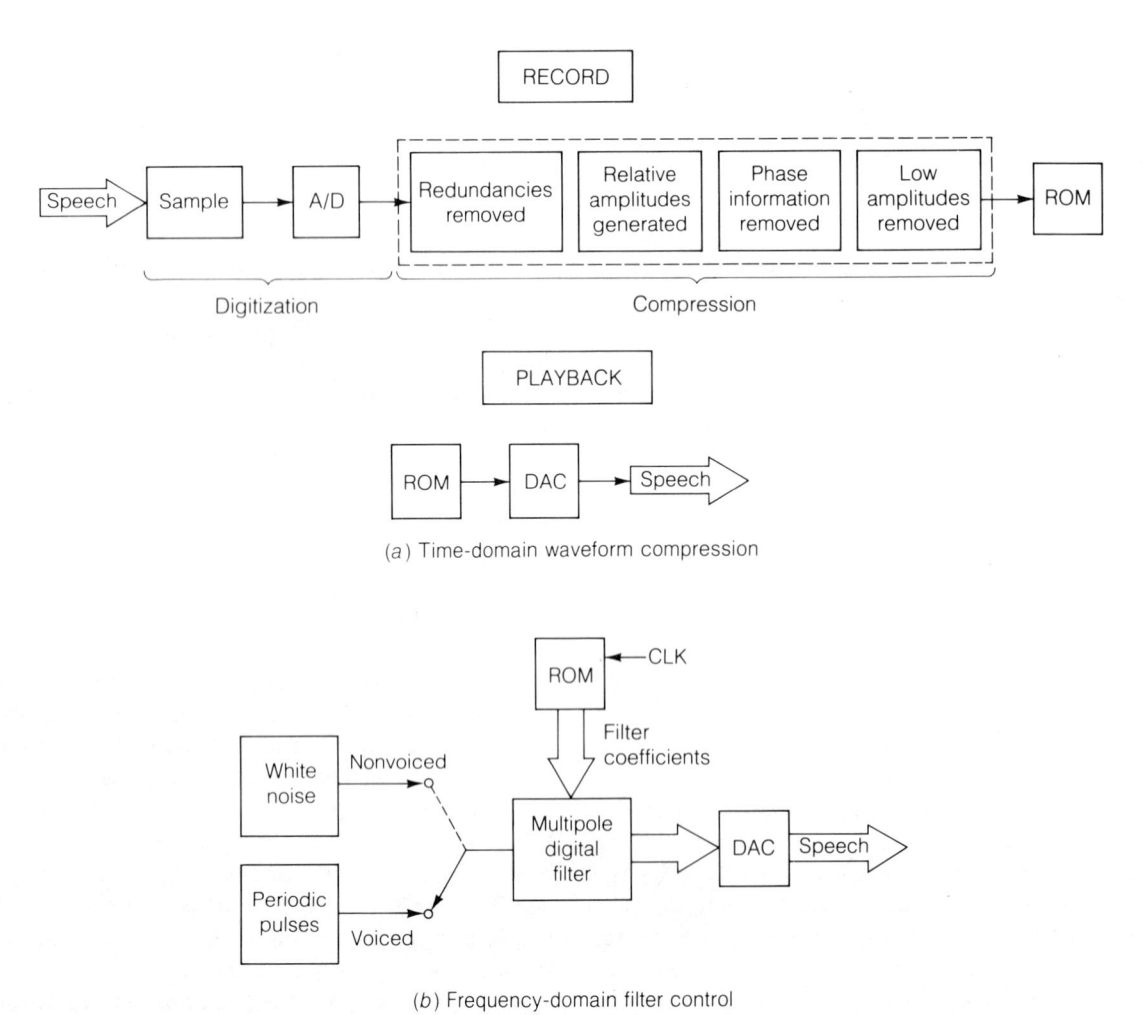

(a) Time-domain waveform compression

(b) Frequency-domain filter control

Figure 21.34 Two popular speech-synthesis techniques.

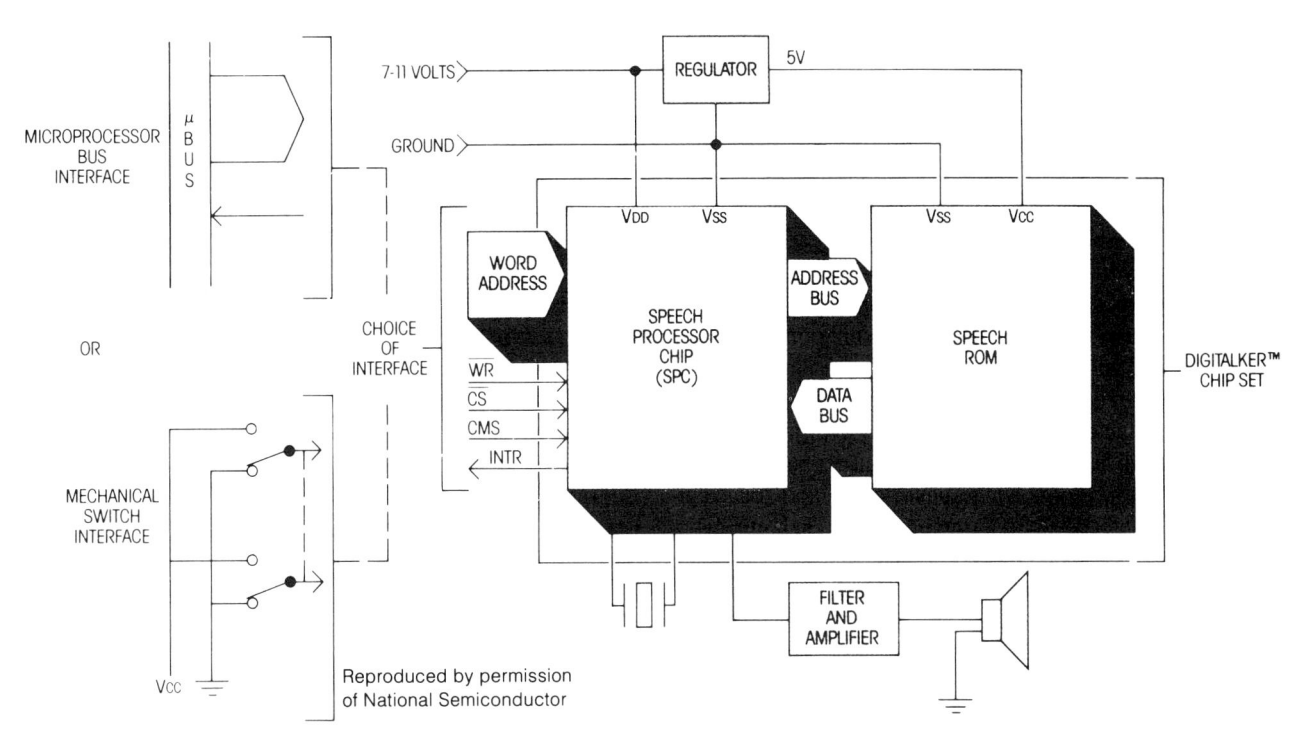

Figure 21.35 The National Semiconductor Digitalker.

21.34a. The speech waveform is sampled at the Nyquist rate, digitized by an A/D converter, and passed through four digital compression processes, eliminating information that is not required for faithful sound reproduction.

The first compression process removes redundant speech elements, and the second process removes absolute amplitude information, leaving only relative amplitude data. Phase (direction) components—which the ear cannot detect—are removed by the third process, and the fourth process removes all low-amplitude components. The hardware for carrying out waveform digitization and compression is simple and straightforward, with little need for sophisticated mathematical calculations and number crunching.

The second method operates in the frequency domain and is true speech synthesis, not merely a modified (compressed) recording of real speech. The most popular frequency-domain technique is called *linear predictive coding* (LPC). To speak a word using LPC, either periodic pulses (for voiced sounds such as "a") or white noise (for unvoiced sounds such as "f" or "s") is generated and passed through a multipole digital filter (Figure 21.34b), whose coefficients are sequentially controlled by parameters stored in ROM.

The filter parameters are obtained from a linear equation that models the human voice tract, allowing a speech sample to be predicted from previous ones and thereby eliminating redundancies.

Another frequency-domain technique reconstructs speech from stored spectral bands of frequencies (called *formants*). Each formant corresponds to a major band of resonant frequencies. An especially promising technique is called *phoneme* synthesis, in which the spectral parameters are derived from basic word sounds. A phoneme represents a simple elemental speech sound, of which there are 38 to 40 in the English language.

Programmable speech-synthesis chip sets are now available from a variety of manufacturers. For example, the Digitalker™ from National Semiconductor (Figure 21.35) uses the compression technique to store up to 256 words of natural-sounding speech. It is designed to interface easily with any popular microprocessor.

Although speech recognition is considerably more difficult than speech synthesis, progress is occurring on this front also. In one technique, the speaker's voice is sampled some 20,000 times a second. The samples are grouped into blocks of approximately 1,000 and each block is converted to the frequency domain (a spectral profile) by a Fourier transformation. The spectral waveform is then compared with samples previously recorded and stored in ROM. Since each spectral block may be compared with thousands of stored patterns, the process is slow, taking some 100 times longer than speech synthesis. However, real-time speech recognition probably will become a reality in this decade.

INTELLIGENT-MACHINE UPDATE

Having mastered the techniques of data communication, our intelligent machine will soon be able to communicate accurately and reliably, using a variety of languages and formats, with any computer in the world. When the human species first developed this ability, it quickly revolutionized our social structure. What an intelligent machine—capable of learning and making decisions—will do with instant access to unlimited information can only be imagined.

QUESTIONS AND PROBLEMS

1. What are the major characteristics of *asynchronous* communications? Of *synchronous* communications?
2. Compare *simplex, half-duplex,* and *full-duplex* transmission.
3. What is the ASCII code sequence for the word *STOP*?
4. When using RS-232C, how is the logic 1 state determined?
5. What is the advantage of using a current loop for communication?
6. Based on the IEEE (GPIB) 488 standard, how does a peripheral transmit data?
7. Write a program to generate an asynchronous data stream without the use of the USART (the serial data stream is emitted directly from a port bit).
8. Develop the assembly-language programs corresponding to the flowcharts of Figure 21.17.
9. What is the purpose of a synchronous protocol?
10. On the 6850, how does the address bus distinguish between data and control registers?
11. Based on Figure 21.14, how would you reset the 6850 via software?
12. When the TDRE status signal goes active, what condition of the 6850 is indicated?
13. When using the SDLC bit-oriented protocol, how do we make sure the flag word does not appear anywhere in the text?
14. When using the Binary Synchronous Communication protocol (BISYNC), how does the receiver determine start of transmission?
15. What is a *modem,* and what is it used for?
16. What type of multiplexing does the Bell 202 format use?
17. What are some of the advantages of communicating in digital rather than analog?
18. How are data encoded when using *pulse-code modulation* (PCM)?
19. When using the T1 PCM carrier format, how many people may use a single digital highway at the same time?
20. What kind of multiplexing does the T1 system use?
21. How does the T1 system detect the "phone off hook" condition?
22. What are the inputs and resulting outputs to a *codec*?
23. What is the purpose of the transmit-and-receive filters within the 2912 PCM filter chip?
24. Redraw the waveforms of Figure 21.31*b*, using 3 kHz and 6 kHz input signals from the transmit phone.
25. What is the major advantage of a fiber-optic digital highway?
26. Name several components of human speech that are unnecessary for faithful reproduction of the spoken word.
27. What instruction is tailor-made for testing status bit 0 (RDRF) of the 6850 during receive polling operations?

chapter 22

Product Development

The major goal in the game of chess—at least in tournament play—is to win the game. A major purpose of studying microcomputers is to help bring microprocessor-based products to market.

A number of steps are involved in product development, from initial conception to final packaging. Only two, however, are of primary interest to the engineer and technician, and they will be the subjects of this chapter: hardware/software development and troubleshooting.

As shown in Figure 22.1, a great deal of interaction between hardware design, software design, and troubleshooting must take place before the final product is perfected and released to the market.

HARDWARE/SOFTWARE DEVELOPMENT

Software on Silicon

To become adept at the "hardware" of chess (the chess pieces and the board) requires perhaps only a day or two. To become adept at the "software" of chess (playing the game) requires a lifetime. Today, hardware/software development is in much the same state. Although hardware costs have dropped dramatically, software costs—because of increased program complexity—have risen just as dramatically. It can easily cost $100,000 of software development time to fill $200 worth of memory.

One solution to the problem is to transfer the software overhead to hardware, that is, *to place the software on silicon*. The first salvos in the battle to swallow up software with complex LSI circuits began with the programmable peripheral chips introduced in Chapter 19. Therefore, perhaps the first step in hardware/software development is to take full advantage of the sophisticated support chips presently on the market. A few typical examples are (those near the top of the list we have already covered):

- 6821 Peripheral Interface Adapter
- 6828 Priority Interrupt Controller
- 6850 Asynchronous Communications Interface Adapter
- 8273 Programmable HDLC/SDLC Controller (Intel)
- 2653 Polynomial Generator Checker (Signetics)
- 2652 Multiprotocol Communications Controller (Signetics)
- SCU-1 Serial Control Unit (Mostek)
- MT8860 Digital Decoder (Mitel)
- SC-01 Speech Synthesizer (Votrax)
- MC6859 Data-Encryption Chip (Motorola)

Each of these chips can greatly reduce the software load of both the CPU and the programmer. In the future, we can expect VLSI technology to place even more software on silicon, eventually integrating the operating system and the high-level language into the hardware.

The feature that makes VLSI a "sky's the limit" technology and that gives it such an exciting potential is the new computer-aided-design (CAD) workstations, which are

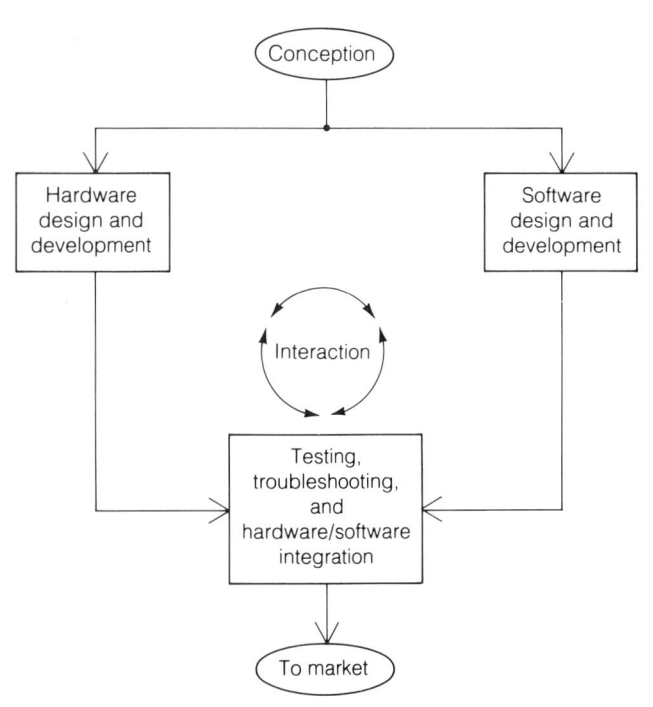

Figure 22.1 Product-development flowchart.

Pascal	Assembly language	Machine code
	LDAA $0, X	$A6
If X > Y then	CMPA $1, X	$00
Z: = X	BCC NEXT	$A1
ELSE Z: = Y;	LDAA $1, X	$01
	NEXT: STAA $2, X	$24
		$A6
		$01
		$A7
		$02

Figure 22.2 High-level, assembly, and machine-language comparison.

rapidly approaching the designer's dream: a slab of purified sand (silicon) and tiny amounts of doping material are entered into one end of the system and, after several sessions at the computer keyboard, a fully functional and tested VLSI custom chip flows from the other end (see the section on CAD/CAM later in this chapter). Not all the system and applications software can be placed on silicon, of course, so sooner or later we must turn to software development.

Software Development

All three software routines in Figure 22.2 are identical. We can see at a glance that the ease of writing and interpreting the programs is ranked from left to right—from high-level to low-level languages (those who are totally unfamiliar with Pascal can probably understand the intent of the single program statement).

Pascal is a high-level language. That is, each statement of a high-level program is formulated to resemble plain conversational English or traditional mathematical symbols and corresponds to several lines of assembly or machine code (typically 8 to 12 lines). We already know the advantages of writing programs in assembly language. A high-level language simply extends the benefits further. When using a high-level language, we can concentrate fully on program concepts and not be concerned at all with hardware-management details. In fact, when writing programs in high-level language, we do not even need to know what microprocessor will ultimately run the program. High-level routines are compact, reliable, easy to modify, and simple to read and understand.

Many types of high-level languages are available. As shown in Figure 22.3, the higher the level, the more they resemble natural human languages. For software development purposes, we will divide all high-level languages into one of two groups: *structured* or *nonstructured*. At the present time, Pascal is the best known structured language, and BASIC is

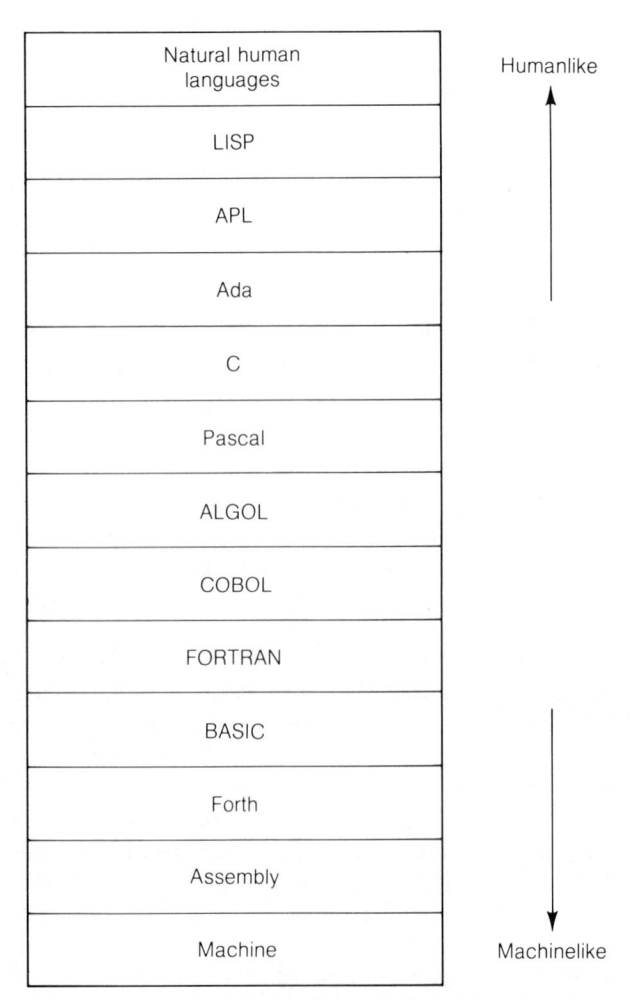

Humanlike ↑
Natural human languages
LISP
APL
Ada
C
Pascal
ALGOL
COBOL
FORTRAN
BASIC
Forth
Assembly
Machine
↓ Machinelike

Figure 22.3 The computer language scale from machine to human.

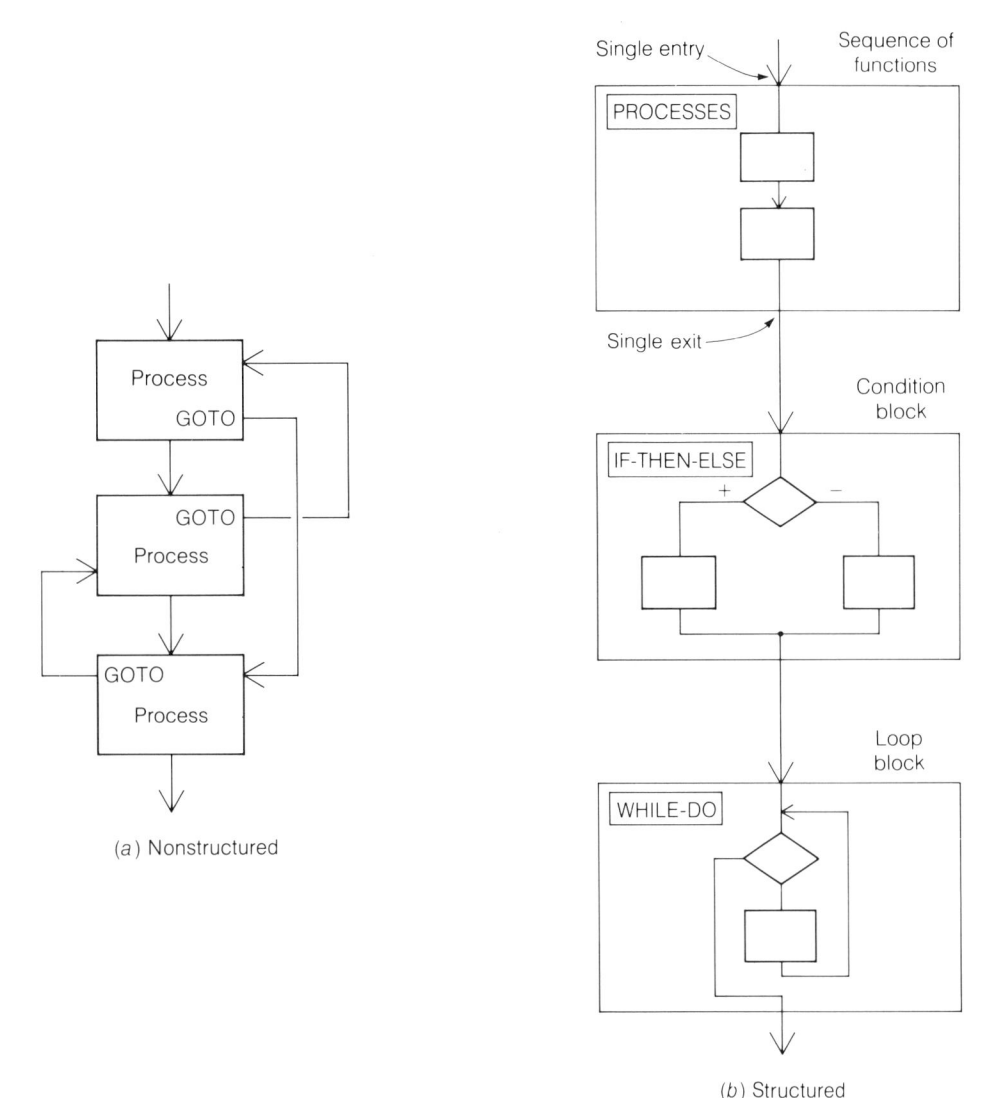

Figure 22.4 Nonstructured and structured programming compared.

the most prominent nonstructured language. (The trend is toward applying structured concepts to normally nonstructured languages.)

Structured/nonstructured programming Pascal, Ada, and FORTRAN 77 are riding the current wave of popularity for structured programming. In the broadest possible terms, structured programming is simply a set of rules yielding programs that are particularly easy to write, test, modify, and read. In other words, a structured program is reliable, readable, and maintainable. More specifically, the term usually refers to the concept of solving a problem (program) by repeatedly breaking it into subproblems (subprograms). Each subprogram or subtask is commonly referred to as a *module* or a *block*. This modular approach is based on a fact long known to programmers, but only recently proven mathematically: programs can be written as a sequence of single-entry/single-exit modules (or blocks) without the need for jumps (GOTOs) between modules. (Structured programming is often called "GOTO-less" programming, even though the concept involves a great deal more.)

The theoretical framework for structured programming is found in the *structure theorem*, first proposed by Corrado Bohm and Guiseppe Jacopini in 1966. According to the structure theorem, each single-entry/single-exit module can be expressed using only three basic building blocks (or constructs): a *process* (simple sequence of statements), a *loop* (WHILE-DO), or a *condition* (IF-THEN-ELSE). Using flowcharts, Figure 22.4 compares structured with nonstructured programming and shows the three basic concepts of structured programming that almost eliminate the need for the GOTO statement. (However, the GOTO statement is still retained as its use is occasionally unavoidable.) More complex structured programs are formulated by nesting and com-combining the three constructs in a variety of ways. Programs written in structured format are known as *proper* programs.

Each basic module of a structured program takes the following general form:

```
(* A program module *)

PROGRAM NAME;
Declarations;
BEGIN
   Statement1;
   Statement2;
   Statement3;
      Etc.;
END.
```

The first line—(* A program module *)—is an optional comment, which is ignored during translation to machine language (compilation). Comments can be placed anywhere in the program as long as they are bracketed by "(* . . . . *)".

The first line of the actual program is always the module name, which assigns an identification word to the program block. Following the name are the declarations. Declarative statements reserve memory locations and identify data types. The *reserved words* BEGIN and END. bracket the list of executable instructions; as with all reserved words, they have special meaning to the compiler and cannot be used elsewhere in the program.

As in assembly-language programming, a typical "real-world" structured high-level program generally consists of a main program, in which each statement CALLs a subroutine (known as a *procedure*). Communication between main program and procedure modules is by way of parameters.

Therefore, a more generalized program module takes the following form:

```
(* Modular program format using procedures *)

PROGRAM NAME;
Global declarations;

PROCEDURE   1stProcedureName(formal parameters);
Local declarations;
BEGIN
   Statement1;
   Statement2;
     Etc.;
END;
```

(Additional procedures)

```
BEGIN (* Main program *)
   1stProcedureName(actual parameters);
   2ndProcedureName(actual parameters);
   3rdProcedureName(actual parameters);
   Etc.;
END.
```

Following the rules of Pascal, all procedure blocks are listed between the main program declarations and the main program block of instructions.

Execution begins with the first statement of the main program. The first procedure is CALLed, and the actual parameters following the procedure name are sent to the procedure for processing. (Following the rules of syntax, spaces are not allowed in the procedure name.) When processing within the CALLed procedure is complete, action returns to the next statement of the main program (another procedure, in our example).

When procedures are nested (CALLed from within another procedure), proper programs of great complexity can be constructed.

Although structured programming does occasionally require more memory capacity, there are many advantages in its use. First of all, since all modules are independent, a large program can be broken down into small, easily managed sections and partitioned out among several programmers (parallel programming). Also, the lack of interaction between the blocks means a given block can be altered safely, without affecting other blocks. And finally, structured programs are easy to maintain and to troubleshoot.

Because structured programming is simply a set of rules, any computer language can be written in either structured or nonstructured format. Even assembly language can be adapted to structured programming by using only subroutines (or macros) and avoiding all jumps. However, the newer languages, such as Pascal and Ada, were developed with structured programming in mind, and they should simplify the job of writing well-structured programs.

One way to contrast structured with nonstructured programming is to make two listings of the same program, one using BASIC, a nonstructured language, and the other using Pascal, a structured language. Based on the very familiar MIMIC-DELAY program, such a comparison is shown in Figure 22.5.

The MIMIC-DELAY Pascal program The MIMIC-DELAY program inports a number and, only for numbers greater than 128, delays the outported response a time period approximately equal to the size of the number. For numbers 128 or below, a zero is outported.

Turning to the structured version first (Figure 22.5a), we

```
(* This modified mimic program delays all input numbers > 128 by
an amount equal to the inported number.  All numbers <= 128 are
blanked out (set to zero) *)

PROGRAM MIMICDELAY;
VAR NUMBER : INTEGER;

PROCEDURE DELAY (N : INTEGER);
VAR I : INTEGER;
BEGIN
  IF N > 128 THEN
    WHILE N > 0 DO
      BEGIN
        N := N - 1;
        I := 100;
        WHILE I > 0 DO
          I := I - 1;
      END
  ELSE
    NUMBER := 0;
END;

BEGIN (* MAIN PROGRAM *)
  WHILE TRUE DO
  BEGIN
    WRITE('GIVE ME A NUMBER ');
    READLN(NUMBER);
    DELAY(NUMBER);
    WRITELN(NUMBER);
  END;
END.
```
(a) Structured pascal

```
10   REM This modified mimic program delays all input numbers
20   REM > 128 by an amount equal to the inported number.
30   REM All numbers <= 128 are blanked out (set to zero).
40   PRINT "Give me a number"
50   INPUT NUM
60   N = NUM
70   IF N > 128 THEN GOTO 100
80   NUM = 0
90   GOTO 160
100  IF N = 0 THEN GOTO 160
110  N = N - 1
120  I = 100
130  IF I = 0 THEN GOTO 100
140  I = I - 1
150  GOTO 130
160  PRINT NUM
170  GOTO 40
```
(b) Nonstructured BASIC

Figure 22.5 The MIMIC-DELAY high-level program.

will see how the systematic and disciplined approach of Pascal makes the routine easier to write and easier to understand.

First, let's turn our attention to the declaration statements, and note that program MIMICDELAY contains three variables: NUMBER, I, and N (a *variable* is a memory location, or "container" into which data can be placed). By declaring all variables, both the reader and the compiler will know the scope of the variable (where it is valid), what variables the program contains, and what type of information can be placed into each variable. As shown, variables "NUMBER" and "I" are declared by placing them after the reserved word VAR (for VARiable) and are typed as integers (1, 4, 128, etc.). That is, only integers may be placed into variables NUMBER and I; any other data type (such as "real" or "string") will give a compiler error. Variable N is a formal parameter (it will receive the actual parameter sent from a main program statement), and therefore is declared and typed by placing it after the procedure name.

By declaring variable NUMBER in the main-program block, it becomes a *global* variable, accessible by all procedure and program modules. By declaring N and I within procedure DELAY, they become *local* variables, accessible only from within procedure DELAY. *By making all variables as local as possible, we are assured that during software development, changes and modifications in one procedure module will not ripple through the program causing unwanted changes elsewhere and that during execution, one procedure's operations will not cause inadvertent changes in another procedure's data.*

Let's follow through the program as it would be executed, starting at the beginning of the main program. Although the main program can include any legal statement, it generally consists of only procedure names, each sending an actual parameter to the CALLed procedure. Three of the four procedures—READLN, WRITE, and WRITELN—are built-in (intrinsic) procedures (they came with the Pascal software package and are pre-declared). The DELAY procedure, of course, we wrote—so it is not intrinsic and must be included in the program.

Execution begins with a CALL of the intrinsic procedure WRITE, which sends the parameter string 'Give me a number' to the procedure for output to the CRT screen (a "string" is a series of characters bracketed by apostrophes and treated as a single unit). READLN, the next procedure, accepts an integer entered by way of the computer keyboard and places the integer in variable NUMBER (the variable name "NUMBER" was sent to the procedure as an "empty box," which was filled with the integer entered from the keyboard). Upon returning from procedure READLN, we CALL procedure DELAY, sending the contents of NUMBER to the procedure and placing them into "container" (memory location) N.

Within the BEGIN/END body of procedure DELAY we find a *decision-making* statement. As written, IF the number inside container N is greater than 128, THEN perform the operation that follows; ELSE, if the number is 128 or less, place a zero in container NUMBER. The operation to be performed if the number is greater than 128 is a nested delay loop, implemented using the WHILE-DO construct. As long as (WHILE) the contents of N is greater than 0, we perform (DO) the statements bracketed by BEGIN/END. Each pass through the outer loop decrements N by 1 and forces us to spin around the inner WHILE-DO loop 100 times (the inner loop actions are not bracketed by BEGIN/END because only a single statement is involved). The strategy is identical to the assembly-language double-nested delay loop of Figure 14.19. Statements such as N := N − 1 are known as *assignment statements,* since an integer equal to one less than the previous contents of N are "assigned to" variable N. (Such a statement, of course, is illegal in algebra, but perfectly okay in high-level programming.)

After completing the DELAY procedure, we return to the WRITELN procedure of the main program. Procedure WRITELN receives the contents of NUMBER (the actual parameter) and writes the integer to the CRT screen, completing the MIMIC process.

The structured version is easy to follow because it reads like a book—*it is English-like and it is modular.* Would you like a brief high-level summary of the program's intent? Look to the main program and there you will find a "Table of Contents," a descriptive list of "Chapter Titles" (procedures) arranged in sequence.

Comparing the structured Pascal program with the nonstructured BASIC program (Figure 22.5*b*), it is obvious at a glance that the structured program is easier to follow, troubleshoot, and maintain. Nonstructured programming, with its numerous jumps (GOTOs) back and forth, is often compared to a plate of spaghetti; structured programming, with its smooth, sequential flow, is like a string of pearls. (To be fair, we should mention that the BASIC program of Figure 22.5*b* is designed to demonstrate nonstructured programming and is not necessarily the way a skilled BASIC programmer would code the problem.)

Of course, this simple MIMIC-DELAY program uses only a tiny fraction of the available power and versatility of the full Pascal language. Numerous textbooks and courses are available on this and other block-structured languages if you want additional information.

Top-Down Software Design

Structured programming—as much a management technique as a technological innovation—often goes hand in hand with *top-down* programming. Top-down programming is a commonsense approach to software design in which the programmer begins at the highest abstract level and works down to the final program statements through a series of successive refinements (really the same idea as structured programming: a problem is solved by breaking it into subproblems). Top-down programming allows the development of a software solution before a single line of code is written. Once a solution to a problem is found at the "top level"— using graphics, structured flowcharts, or pseudocode—it can be coded in any convenient high-level language.

The Warnier-Orr Diagram

The Warnier-Orr diagram is one popular technique for modularizing a program at the top level. Figure 22.6 shows how the MIMIC-DELAY program is broken down (modularized) by Warnier-Orr diagramming. Going from left to right, the program is subdivided hierarchically into smaller and smaller blocks by the use of left-hand braces (the right-hand braces would be redundant). As shown, the MIMIC-DELAY program is first broken up into three modules: "get number," "perform delay," and "output number." Modules "get number" and "perform delay" are further broken down into submodules to be processed sequentially or nested within the larger module. The process continues until each module is small enough to be coded using the three basic constructs (sequential processing, IF-THEN-ELSE decision making, and WHILE-DO looping).

As demonstrated by the MIMIC-DELAY Warnier-Orr diagram, the IF-THEN-ELSE construct is diagrammed by the use of the exclusive-OR and NOT Boolean symbols, and the WHILE-DO construct by writing the number of loops to be performed in parentheses below the block title. Nesting is automatically handled by the placement of the blocks (braces).

When Warnier-Orr diagramming is complete, coding begins at the highest hierarchical level (left side of the diagram).

As is often the case, these high-level block titles become procedure names. Each procedure is then coded by further calling low-level procedures, or by direct coding using combinations of the three basic high-level language constructs.

The inherent block structures of Warnier-Orr diagrams lend themselves perfectly to block-structured languages such as Pascal. Flowcharts, on the other hand, are usually more suited for nonstructured and assembly-language programming. Many other techniques besides Warnier-Orr diagrams are used by professional programmers to modularize complex programs.

Object-Oriented Programming

The next step in structured design is represented by the new object-oriented high-level languages, such as Ada.

Rather than simply modularizing program code in the form of procedures, an object-oriented language modularizes *groups of procedures, and their associated data structures* in a single unit (called an *object* or *package*). Each object is treated as a software "black box" (similar to objects in real life such as a TV set or an automobile), providing a service or function to the outside world with the internal design—the data structures and algorithms—invisible and inaccessible.

A specification or contract defines the interface between objects. *As long as the contract is upheld, changes can be made freely to objects on either side of the interface.*

By clustering both the procedures and their common data structures and specifying only the information required to interface the objects, program design and debugging are greatly enhanced.

Compiler vs Interpreter

Programs written in high-level languages are like poetry because they can be written down as fast as our inspirations come. The computer, however, is a single-minded machine able to absorb commands only in its native tongue of binary. Since translation from high-level statements to binary machine code is a repetitive process following exact rules, it is tailor-made for a computer. The program that accomplishes the translation, known as a *compiler,* is similar in concept to the assembler program used to translate assembly code to machine code. Of course, a compiler is a more complex and sophisticated program, particularly for the structured languages.

There are times, however, when assembly-language programming is preferable to high-level programming. The problem with high-level languages is that the generated code is not as compact as it could be (human beings, given enough time, can usually write more efficient programs consuming less memory space). For example, if a program must fit into the available 2K of ROM space aboard a 6801 single-chip microprocessor, it may be necessary to resort to assembly-language programming to squeeze down a program of 2,055

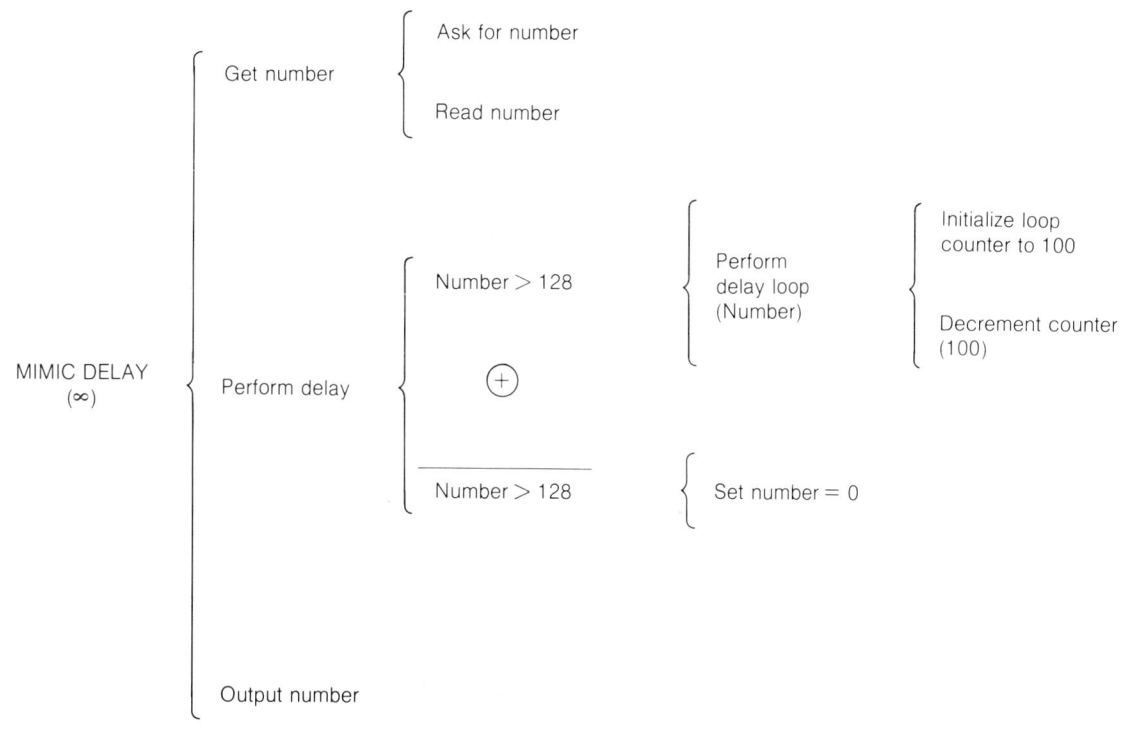

Figure 22.6 MIMIC-DELAY top-down program design using Warnier-Orr diagrams.

words into the available 2,048 memory locations. On the other hand, if there is memory to spare (remember, memory space is relatively inexpensive when compared to software development costs), a high-level language can generate code up to 10 times faster and therefore at lower cost. (Using modular techniques, it is possible to code some modules in assembly language and the remaining in a high-level language. Each module can be separately compiled and linked together to form one main program module.) Processing speed is also a factor in the choice between high-level and assembly-level programming. If an assembled program is shorter than a compiled program, it runs faster—an especially important factor in the fields of telecommunications and real-time process control.

An *interpreter* is closely related to a compiler and often used to execute BASIC. An interpreter translates and executes *each line* of a high-level language program *as it is running;* the compiler translates the *entire* high-level program to object code before execution. Giving instantaneous results, an interpreter is interactive with the programmer and allows for easy program development and error correction. However, it slows down the execution of programs. (In a loop, for example, each line of code would have to be translated on each pass.) Furthermore, since an interpreter must be stored in memory at the time of execution, it requires a great deal more memory than a compiler.

There even exists an in-between system, called a *P-system*. To bring down the expense of writing a separate compiler for each microprocessor on the market, why not partially compile the high-level language *just short of the point where it becomes processor dependent?* This "partially digested" code is called *P-code*. The final translation of the universal P-code (which will run on any machine) down to machine code (which will run on only a specific processor) is done by a relatively inexpensive and simple interpreter—which is unique to each machine. A P-system—partly compiled and partly interpreted—is intermediate in speed between fully compiled code and purely interpreted code. The best-known P-system is UCSD Pascal.

The choice between a compiler, a P-system, or an interpreter, then, depends on the application. If you are using your computer as an intelligent calculator, in which quick answers are a must, an interpreter would be the logical choice. On the other hand, if you are developing a high-speed telecommunication program to load into a 68764 EPROM, the routine would have to be compiled into machine language. Some languages—such as BASIC—even offer the user a choice between an interpreter or a compiler.

TROUBLESHOOTING

It is not unusual for troubleshooting and program debugging to take up 50% of product development time. Troubleshooting, therefore, should be placed on an equal footing with system design. As expected, a number of tools and techniques are available—some designed primarily for software debugging, others aimed at hardware troubleshooting.

First of all, there are very few troubleshooting techniques that do not require a knowledge of the system under test. Random substitution and replacement of parts (known as "shotgunning") is the exception. Although such a technique can be effective in small systems using a limited number of LSI parts (such as the ET-3400A single-board computer), it generally is time-consuming, expensive, and unproductive. At the outset, therefore, we will assume a basic rule of troubleshooting: *To effectively troubleshoot a microcomputer system, we require a fundamental knowledge of microcomputer architecture and processing action*. Quite often, when armed with a good knowledge of the computer system, a simple description of the problem will quickly bring to mind a number of probable causes.

In this chapter we will introduce seven basic troubleshooting techniques, all requiring a knowledge of the system under test. Each technique has its advantages and disadvantages, of course, and part of the troubleshooting art is in selecting the proper tools and techniques to best debug the system at hand. These seven techniques are:

- Static testing
- Software diagnostics
- Single stepping
- Breakpointing
- Signature analysis
- Logic analyzers
- In-circuit emulation

(In-circuit emulation will be covered in the section on development systems.)

Static Testing

Static testing involves the use of dc voltages to stimulate the circuit. It is aimed primarily at locating faults in circuits and components. Since the microprocessor is the controlling device for the system under test, static testing begins with removing the microprocessor and substituting static signals for those normally produced by the microprocessor. By manipulating the dc signals, we can simulate any state or action of the microprocessor (but, of course, at much reduced speed). We can trace signals from the CPU socket to the system peripherals, and we can simulate memory, I/O, and read and write processes. (Static testing is really a form of dc *emulation*, in which we are emulating the actions of the microprocessor.)

The major advantages of static testing are its simplicity and low cost. Testing static voltages is easier than testing dynamic signals, and requires less expensive equipment. Because all signals hold steady, certain types of faults in the circuitry are more easily located. However, static testing cannot uncover timing problems—these require a dynamic analysis of the system, often when running at full speed. Also, static testing is limited in its ability to uncover software-related problems.

Software Diagnostics

Under certain conditions, the computer itself can locate faults within the system (self-diagnostics). The major requirement is that those sections of the hardware/software system required by the diagnostic procedure must be assumed to be working properly. For example, an instruction set diagnostic program may be used to check out only those instructions not used by the program itself.

A popular use of diagnostic programs is to test the system RAM using a diagnostic program stored in ROM. A simple RAM diagnostic routine is shown in Figure 22.7. All ones are written to each cell under test, and then read back out. If an error is found (a zero), the location of the fault is outported. If the RAM system passes the ones test, it is repeated using all zeros.

Many instruments and computer systems (the IBM PC, for example) perform self-diagnostics upon power up. Advanced microprocessors (such as Motorola's 68010 virtual memory processor and Intel's iAPX 432 32-bit microprocessor system) even provide built-in debug services as part of the microcode.

Single Stepping

Single stepping is a way of slowing down computer action for close scrutiny. The operator steps, at any desired speed, from one state to the next, examining the status of the system and comparing the present state with the expected state.

The $\overline{\text{HALT}}$ input is used by the 6800 to freeze the action after each step. Unfortunately, the program can only be halted after each instruction cycle, not after each clock cycle. Furthermore, since the address, R/$\overline{\text{W}}$, and data lines float during a HALT period, all bus information must be saved and displayed during each step (for example, by an output port). To place a HALT state after each instruction cycle, drive the $\overline{\text{HALT}}$ input with a latch circuit such as that of Figure 22.8.

Single stepping by instruction cycles is also accomplished by software, usually included in the monitor program of single-board computers. At the press of a key, the processor completes one instruction cycle and returns to a holding-pattern loop awaiting the next single-step command. At each step, memory locations and internal registers can be examined and modified. As we will see in Chapter 25, the Motorola 68000 16-bit microprocessor offers a special *trace* mode of operation for automatic instruction-cycle single stepping.

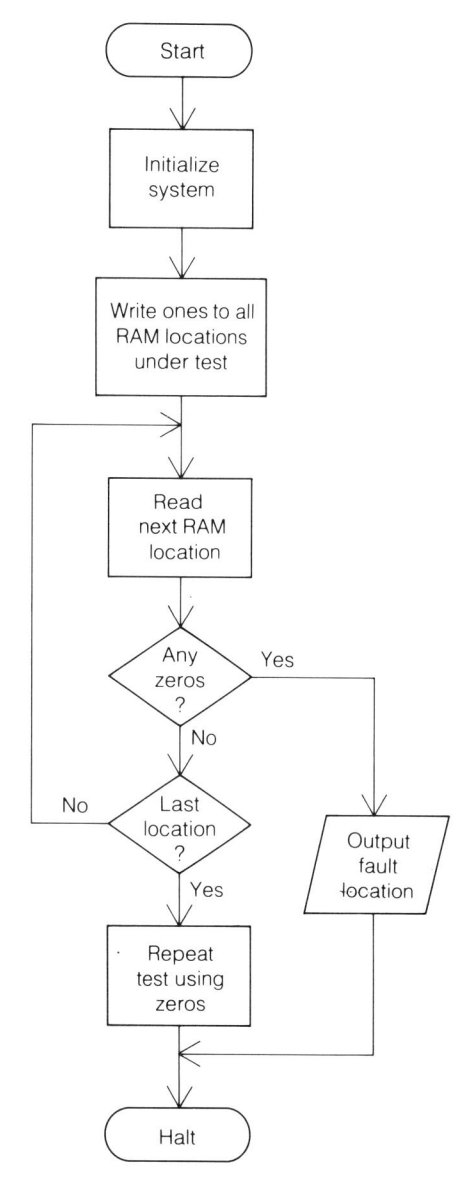

Figure 22.7 High-level diagnostic flowchart for testing RAM.

Breakpointing

The technique of breakpointing also "freezes" computer action, but only at certain predesignated program locations (called *breakpoints*). Between breakpoints, the processor runs at full speed. Breakpointing, therefore, gives the operator a method of quickly homing in on the problem. Once the problem is localized, single stepping may prove productive.

Typically, a breakpoint is installed in a program by substituting a CALL (or software interrupt) instruction at a point where an error is expected to appear. When the processor arrives at the breakpoint, it ceases main-program action and

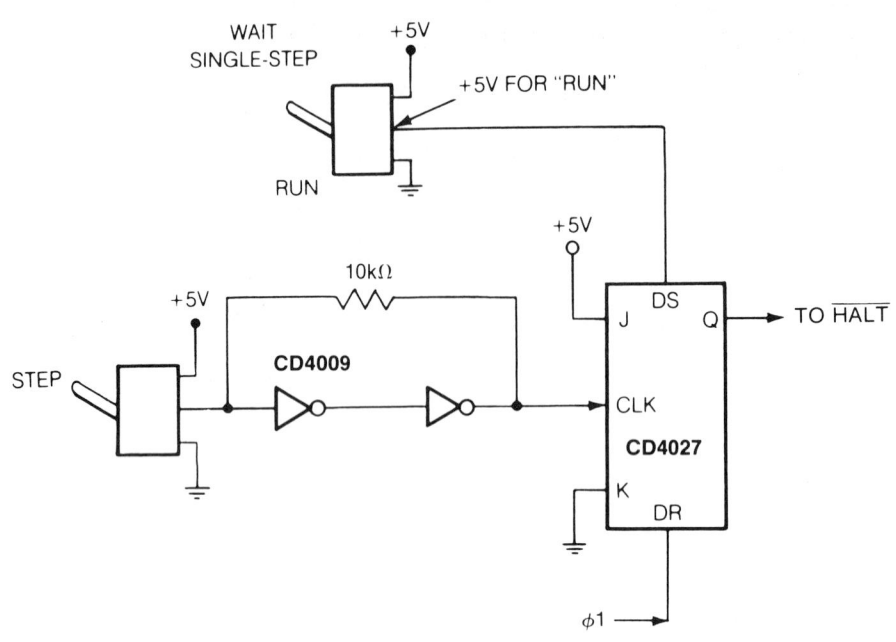

Figure 22.8 Instruction-cycle single-step circuit.

branches to a breakpoint routine, giving the operator an opportunity to examine the system.

Installing a breakpoint can be as simple as the "homemade" technique shown in Figure 22.9. The program shown is designed to produce a musical tone whose pitch is proportional to the size of the inported number. Instead, the routine is generating a constant high-frequency tone, regardless of the number inported. Since the decision-making block is the most crucial, we will place a breakpoint following the conditional branch to check on the state of the system at that point. The breakpoint routine is very simple, and reflects our interest in only the contents of accumulator A (which should be holding a zero at the breakpoint).

When the program is run, from the start to the breakpoint, the breakpoint routine tells us that accumulator A is holding a number one less than the value of the inported number—meaning the routine passed through the delay loop only once. Immediately we see the answer: instead of jumping on zero (BEQ), we should be jumping on *not* zero (BNE). When the change is made, the program operates as intended.

Many computer systems offer built-in breakpoint capability. On the ET-3400A single-board computer, for example, breakpoints are set with the SWI instruction. When the processor arrives at the first breakpoint, it calls the breakpoint routine. Within the breakpoint routine, the operator uses the front panel keys to examine and set memory locations and registers, and to single step through the program. When troubleshooting is complete at the first breakpoint location, the system can be commanded to resume main-program action until the second breakpoint is reached.

Signature Analysis

The signature analyzer of Figure 22.10 is a simple, easy-to-use test instrument for verifying the performance of and locating bugs in a complex microcomputer or digital system.

The idea behind signature analysis is to absorb a long string of serial digital data from a circuit node and then compress it into a short 4-digit "signature." The signature corresponding to each node in the circuit could be labeled on the schematic as shown in Figure 22.11a. A field-service engineer would simply backtrack through a circuit, checking signatures until an error is found. Signature analysis is a portable, field-service technique, especially useful in circuits employing LSI chips, where internal operations are inaccessible.

The technique for compressing a long string of data into a short code we have seen before; it is the cyclic-redundancy-check character (CRCC), borrowed from the telecommunications field. We produce a CRCC by dividing a specified data stream by a polynomial and retaining the remainder. Based on a rather complex mathematical proof, it turns out that feeding data into a pseudorandom binary sequence (PRBS) generator is the same as dividing the data by the characteristic polynomial of the generator. Figure 22.11b shows how a PRBS corresponding to a characteristic polynomial is generated by modulo 2 addition of taps on a 16-bit shift register. When the PRBS is combined with the external data stream, a 4-character CRCC signature is produced.

Figure 22.11c demonstrates the acquisition sequence. Start and stop signals are taken from the system under test, and

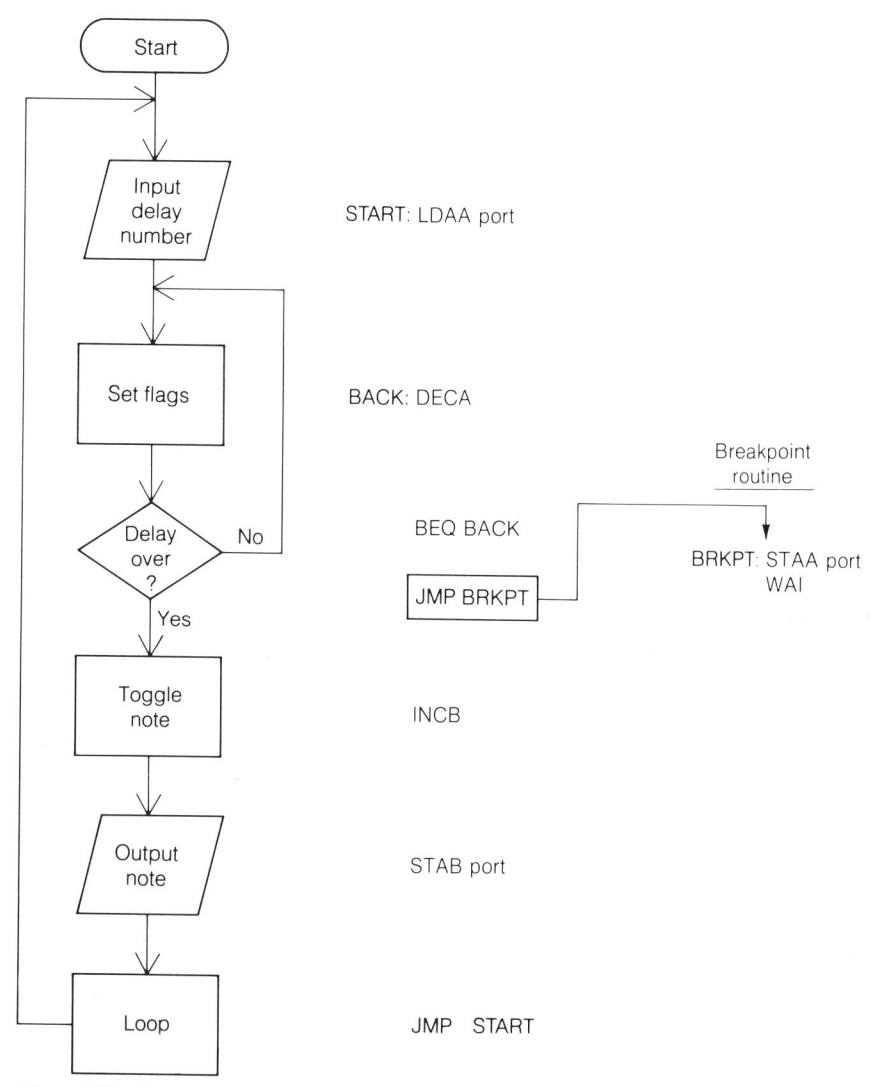

```
                                      START: LDAA port

                                      BACK: DECA

                                                        Breakpoint
                                                         routine
                                      BEQ BACK
                                                        BRKPT: STAA port
                                      JMP BRKPT               WAI

                                      INCB

                                      STAB port

                                      JMP  START
```

Figure 22.9 Using a breakpoint for software debugging.

they provide the data-collection "window" or measurement time period. The start and stop signals can be taken from address or control lines, output ports, or any signals that bracket a unique data stream. During the acquisition sequence, incoming data are sampled at each rising edge of the clock.

The one drawback to signature analysis is that the stimulus required to produce the streams of data had to be designed into the product. However, external-stimulus devices are now coming onto the market to provide the field-service technician with the necessary external-stimulus signals.

Logic Analyzers

As microcomputer systems become more complex, even the most sophisticated oscilloscopes lack the power to ferret out a well-entrenched "bug." Consequently, microcomputer hardware/software debugging has been turned over to the *logic analyzer*, a test instrument specifically designed to operate in the parallel digital environment of the microcomputer.

Basic principles The logic analyzer is to the digital world what the oscilloscope is to the analog world. As with all test instruments, logic analysis is a two-step process: acquisition of data followed by display of data.

In both acquisition and display, a number of basic factors are common to all logic analyzers. Where the various logic analyzers differ is in their *exact* acquisition and display techniques. Using 4-bit data words, Figure 22.12 shows the three facets of data acquisition common to all logic analyzers: threshold detection, clocking and triggering, and sequential storage.

Figure 22.10 The Hewlett-Packard 5004A signature analyzer, used for field troubleshooting of complex microprocessor-based circuits.

Unlike an oscilloscope, the logic analyzer displays logic states (1s and 0s), not continuous analog signals. The threshold-detection circuits classify each bit of an incoming data word as either a logic 0 or a logic 1, depending on its voltage level relative to a threshold. When the threshold is user selectable, data can be acquired from all the popular logic families—TTL, CMOS, ECL.

The clock-trigger section is responsible for strobing the data into the sequential storage medium and for issuing a trigger to either start or end data collection, for viewing either pretrigger or posttrigger information. (When the trigger *initiates* data collection, acquisition is automatically halted when the display RAM is filled.) The trigger is generated by constantly comparing the incoming parallel data words with a user-selectable trigger word. By including a clocked delay in the trigger line, acquisition can be stopped a specific number of clock cycles *after* the trigger word is detected, allowing the trigger word to be positioned anywhere in RAM. Using this delayed-trigger feature, we can select the desired ratio of pre- to post-trigger information to be viewed.

The clock circuit determines the rate at which data are acquired and strobed into the sequential storage medium. The operator can select between two clock sources: a synchronous source from the system under test, or an asynchronous source from an internal clock generator. Generally speaking, logic *state* analysis—in which data words are displayed as sequences of binary, octal, or hexadecimal numbers—requires synchronous sampling; logic *timing* analysis—in which the data words are displayed as continuous waveforms—requires asynchronous sampling. The reason is fundamental. To make sense from a sequence of binary, octal, or hexadecimal numbers, and to avoid skipping or repeating data, those numbers must be correlated with the system under test by way of clock-cycle timing. When viewing waveforms, on the other hand, we must provide good resolution and we must be able to capture randomly occurring glitches. Therefore, we should sample the data asynchronously three to ten times faster than the system under test.

Sequential storage, the final element in data acquisition, is usually accomplished by a high-speed RAM addressed by a counter. In practice, most analyzers store anywhere from 64 to 2,048 words.

Figure 22.13a illustrates the display of data, the second and final step in the logic-analysis process. When data acquisition is complete, the information stored in the sequential-access RAM is displayed in one of two major formats: *state* and *timing*.

The state display, usually generated from information captured synchronously, displays sequential data words in binary, octal, hexadecimal, and sometimes even in mnemonics. The timing display, usually generated from information captured asynchronously, displays the data waveforms in parallel, using up to 16 or more channels.

Occasionally logic analyzers display information pictorially, in the form of a graph or a map (Figure 22.13b). The graph mode plots the binary weight of each word in memory on the Y axis and the position in RAM on the X axis. Since the data are displayed from left to right in the order of collection, the graph highlights the data-flow sequence.

Similar to the graph mode, the map mode breaks down each memory word into two sections, one section forming the X value on the CRT screen; and the other, the Y value. The map mode is often the starting point for troubleshooting a system, since it presents the widest possible overview of system activity. The operator quickly learns the map characteristics of a properly functioning system, and any changes are readily apparent. As we home in on the problem, we may go from map to graph to state to timing modes, each display mode narrowing down the problem area and presenting a more detailed picture of a specific area of program activity.

Now that we are acquainted with the basics of logic analysis, it is time to examine and compare several real-world logic analyzers to see how they have refined the two-step acquisition/delay process to a high level of sophistication, and how each offers unique features and advantages.

Hewlett-Packard 1615A Logic Analyzer The Hewlett-Packard 1615A (Figure 22.14) is a 24-channel (8 for tim-

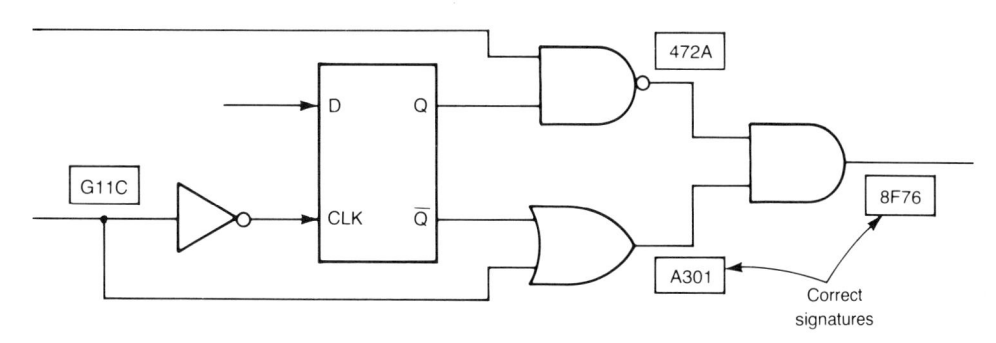

(a) Documenting a schematic for signature-analysis troubleshooting

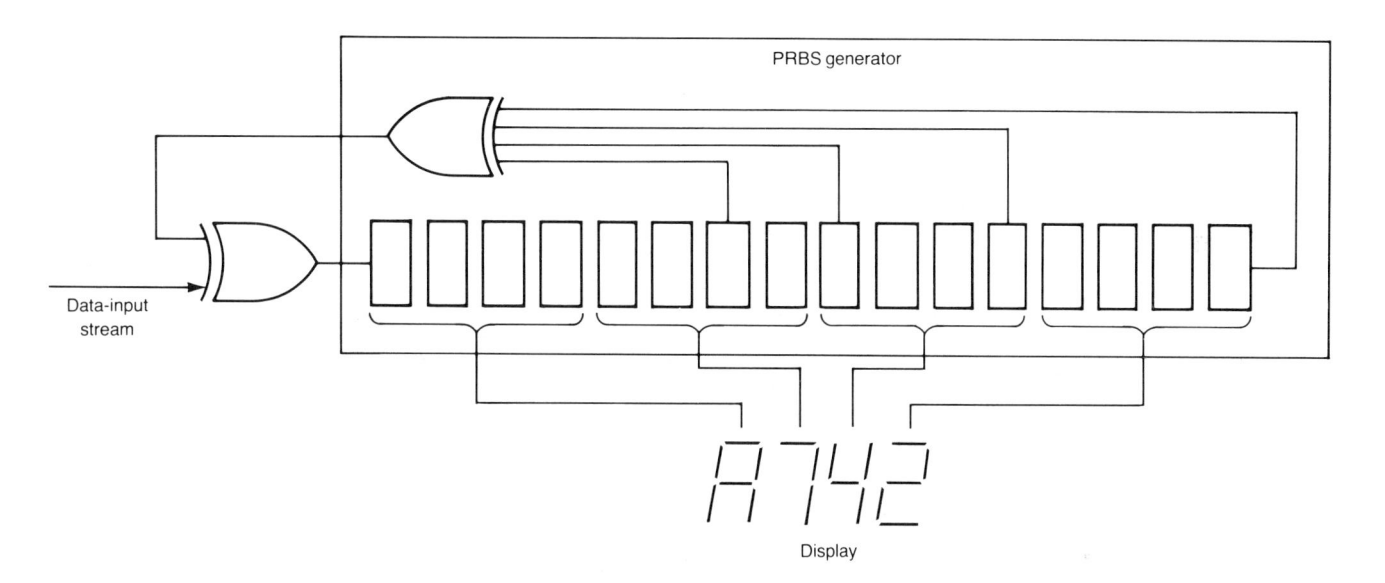

(b) A CRCC signature produced by overlaying the input-data stream with the PseudoRandom Binary Sequence (PRBS) generator

(c) The 5004 A acquisition sequence

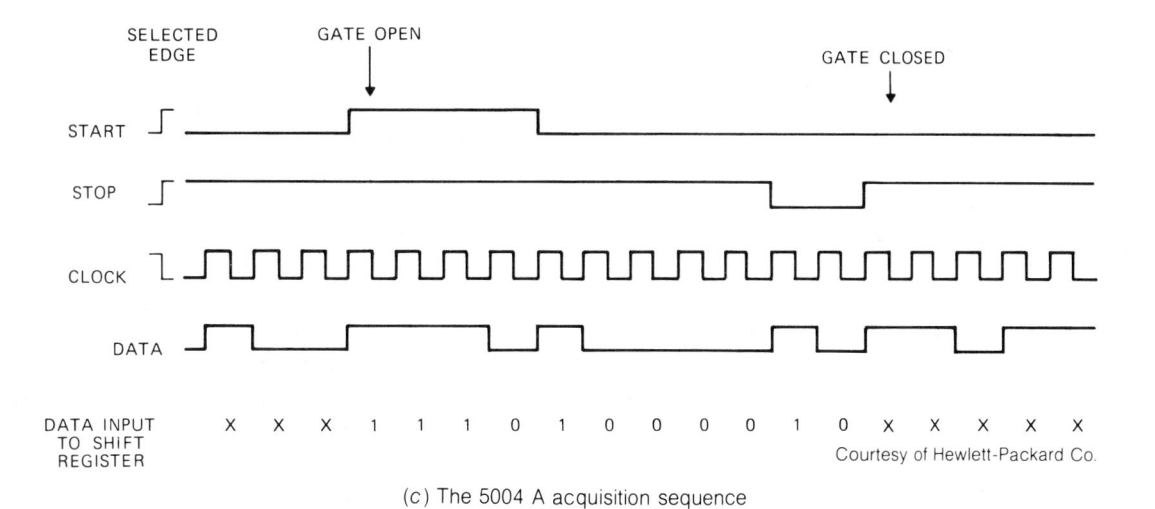

Courtesy of Hewlett-Packard Co.

Figure 22.11 The signature-analysis technique.

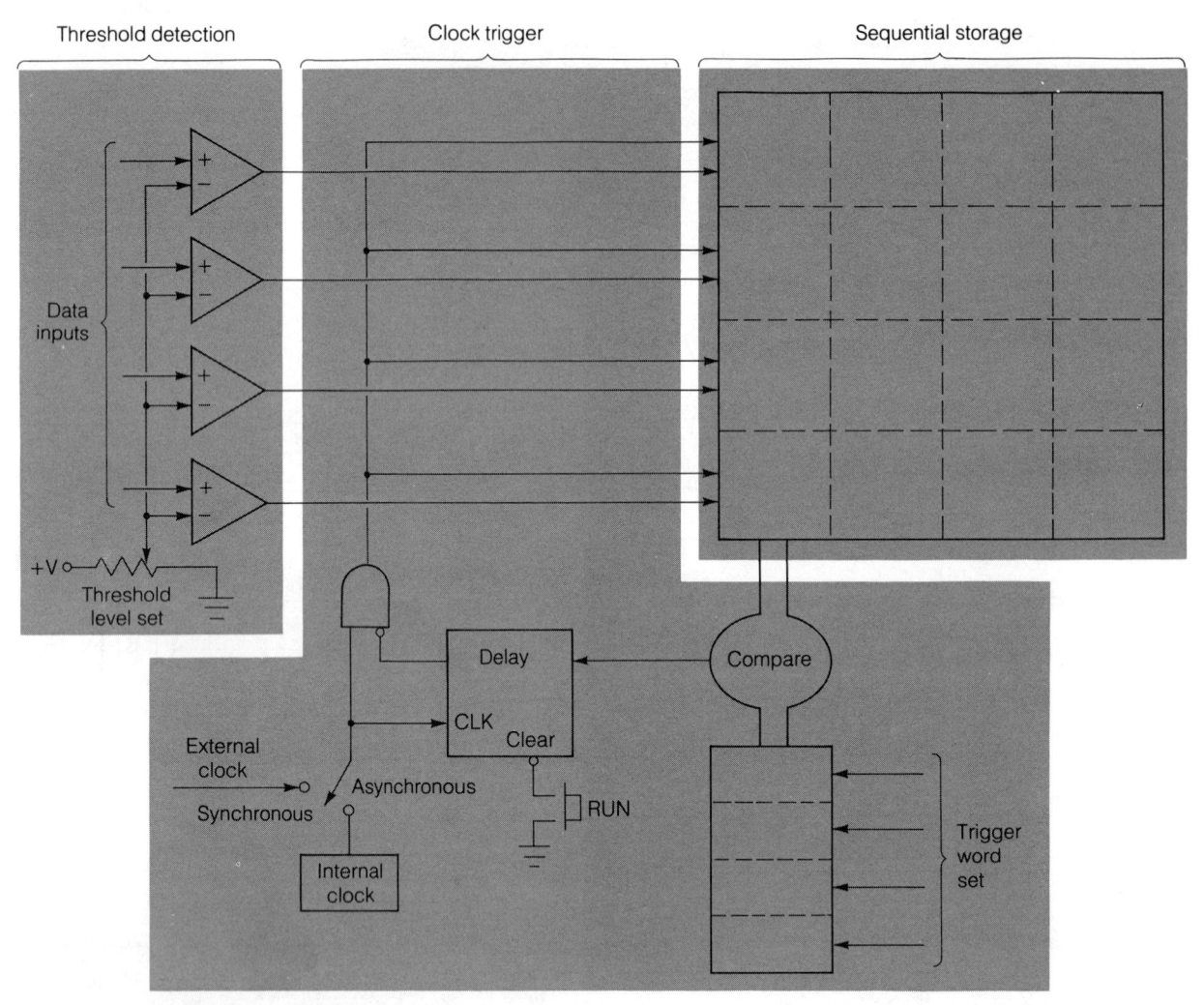

Figure 22.12 The three basic acquisition sections of a logic analyzer.

ing), 20 MHz, synchronous/asynchronous logic analyzer, featuring a 256 × 24 storage RAM, sophisticated glitch detection, and simultaneous state and timing measurements. The 1615A, like all modern logic analyzers, is a multifunctional "menu" analyzer. A menu analyzer allows the user to select acquisition and display parameters by positioning a cursor on the CRT screen.

The 1615A menu includes the *format* and *trace specifications* of Figure 22.15. The overall mode of operation is selected with the format specification, and detailed measurement parameters are selected with the trace specification. Typical format and trace specification parameters include mode of operation (timing, state, or simultaneous), logic polarity, external clock slope, numerical base (binary, octal, hex), and triggering criteria.

The 1615A includes combination, sequential, and delayed triggering—which can even include glitches. Triggering can be initiated with a single pattern of bits, an ORed combination of up to three 8-bit patterns, NOT patterns, glitches, or a combination of glitches and bit patterns.

Of special interest is the simultaneous state and timing mode of operation, selected by way of the format specification. This mode of operation allows the 1615A to monitor 8 bits of timing and 16 bits of state input simultaneously. That is, the same data field can be captured both synchronously for state display (using the external system clock) and asynchronously for timing display (using the internal clock). Thus the relationship between synchronous and asynchronous activities can be examined. For example, asynchronous handshaking signals (timing) can be related to a specific point in program execution (state).

For synchronous problems involving program execution, the basic state mode is selected from the format menu and data are displayed in this mode as a trace listing of binary, octal, or hexadecimal values.

For asynchronous problems involving handshake, I/O,

Figure 22.13 Logic-analysis display.

(a) Major display modes

State display | Timing display

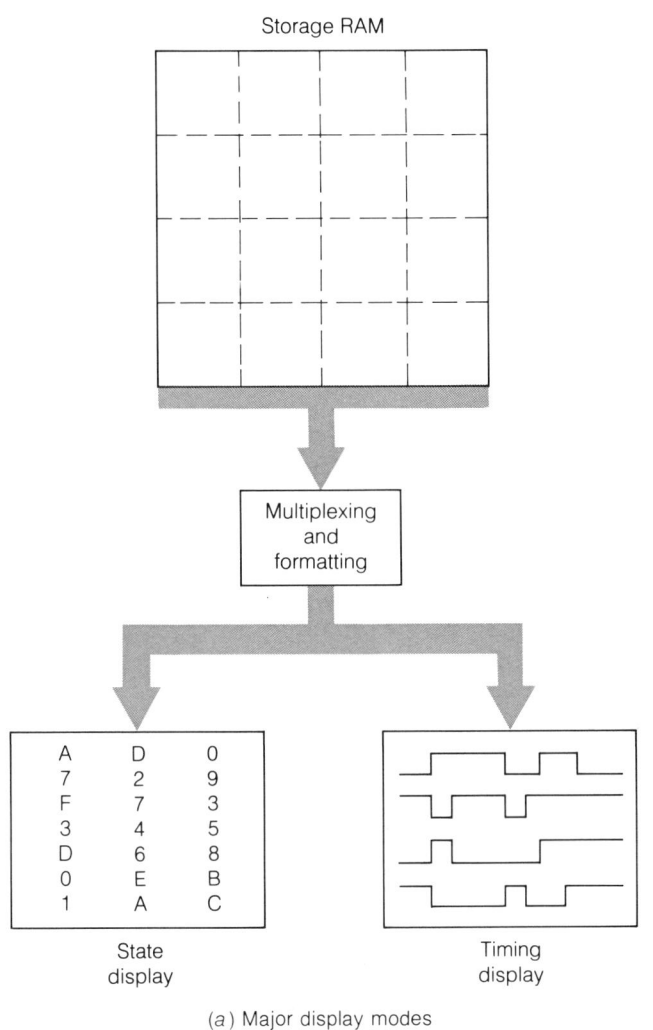

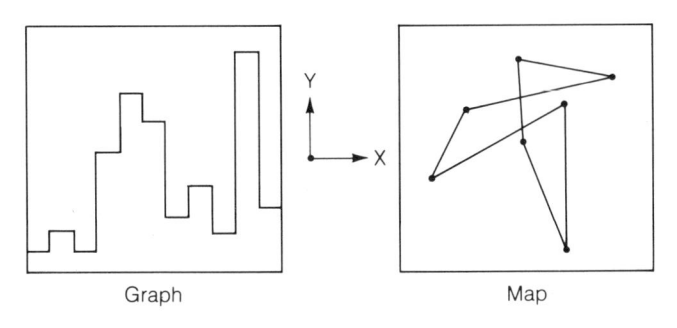

(b) Additional display modes

Graph | Map

timing, and glitch detection, the basic timing mode is selected. Captured data are displayed as a parallel set of timing waveforms (as shown in Figure 22.14). Glitches are displayed as highlighted edges and vertical bars. To zoom in on areas of concern, the timing display can be expanded by a factor of 10.

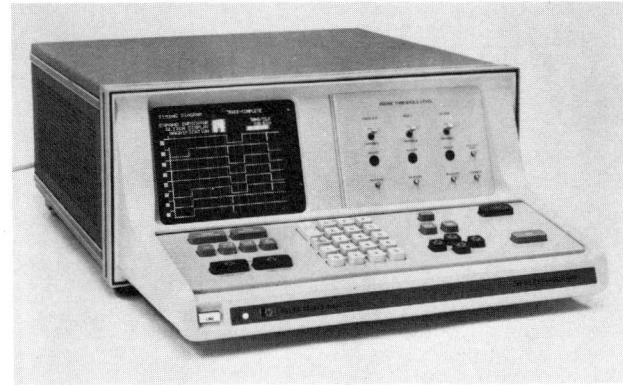

Courtesy of Hewlett-Packard Co.

Figure 22.14 The Hewlett-Packard 1615A logic analyzer.

Tektronix 7D02 Logic Analyzer The Tektronix 7D02 (Figure 22.16) is a 52-channel (8 for timing), 10 MHz, timing/state, synchronous/asynchronous logic analyzer, featuring 256 × 52 acquisition and storage memories, display in disassembled mnemonics, and triggering by programming.

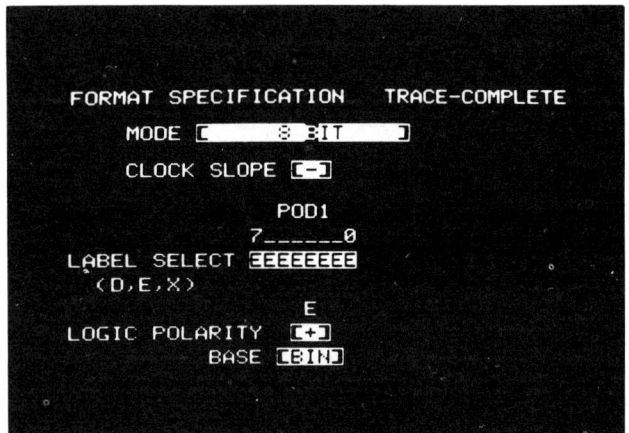

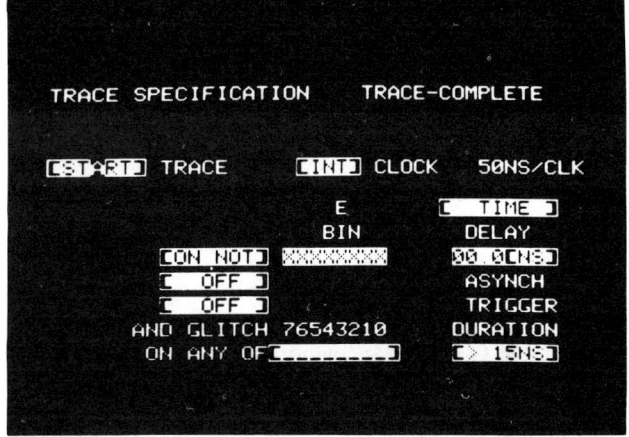

Courtesy of Hewlett-Packard Co.

Figure 22.15 The format and trace specification menus of the 1615A.

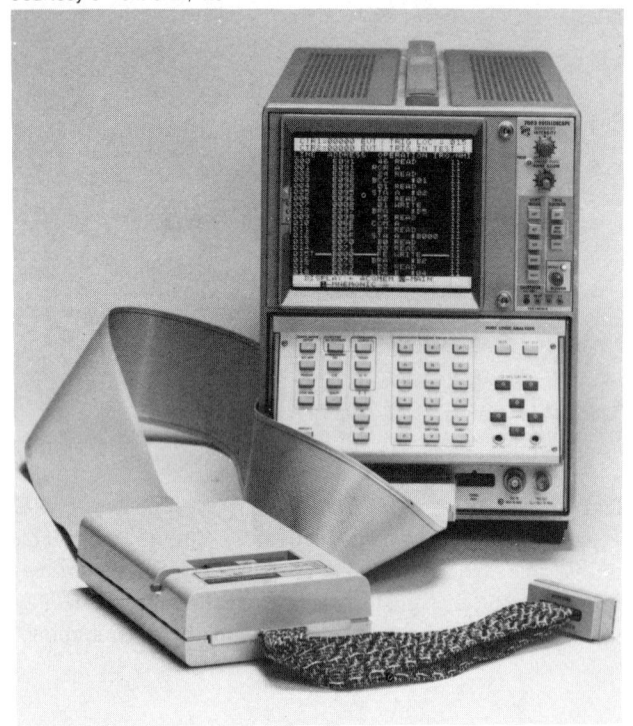

Figure 22.16 The Tektronix 7D02 logic analyzer.

Since many of the features of the 7D02 are similar to those found on other analyzers (such as glitch detection and timing display), we will concentrate on the two unique features offered by the 7D02: the ability to display disassembled mnemonics and trigger generation by user programming (both are state-related functions).

The display of information using disassembled mnemonics is shown in Figure 22.16. Using a special personality module for each microprocessor, the 7D02 converts the machine-language data from the system bus to program mnemonics, just as the original program might have been written (the 7D02 *disassembles* the data). Working from disassembled data greatly speeds up and simplifies hardware/software debugging.

Triggering by programming, the major feature of the 7D02, takes the combinational, sequential, and delayed triggering of conventional analyzers and extends the process to include trigger specification by high-level programming. Instead of triggering on a simple ORed combination of inputs, for example, the user programs a series of tests in a high-level structured language (similar to Pascal), entered via the front panel. IF-THEN-ELSE and GOTO statements allow the programmed tests to include conditional branching. By custom tailoring the data-acquisition resources to the needs of your system, a complex program can be tracked through all its loops and branches in order to arrive at the problem area quickly.

The high-level trigger program consists of a series of tests, with each test built around the IF-THEN DO sequence. *IF defines a test and THEN DO defines a response to the test.* A simple example follows:

TEST 1

1. IF
   1. WR #1
   1. DATA = xx
   1. ADDRESS = 2050
   1. WRITE
1. THEN DO
   1. TRIGGER
      END TEST 1

In simple terms, the program says the following: "*If* the data word in word recognizer register #1 was *written* to address 2050, *then* trigger the acquisition of data." To root out faults hidden deep within a complex program, numerous such tests may be written in sequence, with branching back and forth between the various tests accomplished by way of the GOTO instruction. A single test-program format, as it appears on the 7D02 CRT screen, is shown in Figure 22.17.

We can expect future logic analyzers to become even more sophisticated as they strive to meet the needs of the more complex microprocessing systems of the near future.

DEVELOPMENT SYSTEMS

In today's competitive market, most product development is a "race to the moon." The first manufacturer to market an

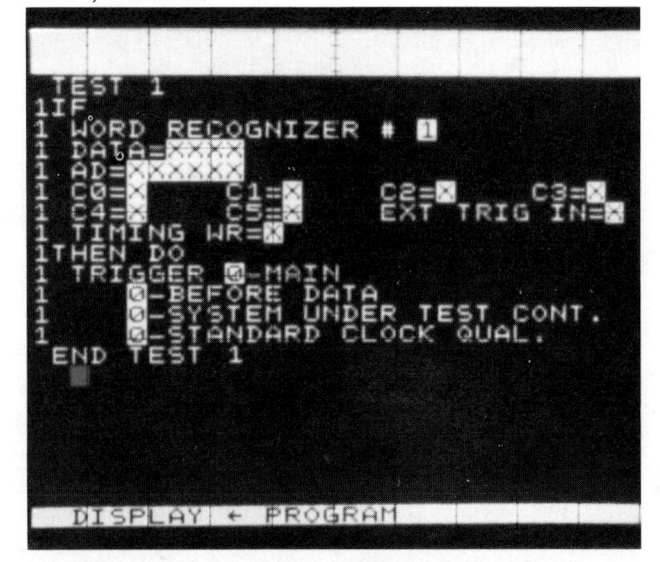

Figure 22.17 A single IF-THEN DO 7D02 trigger format.

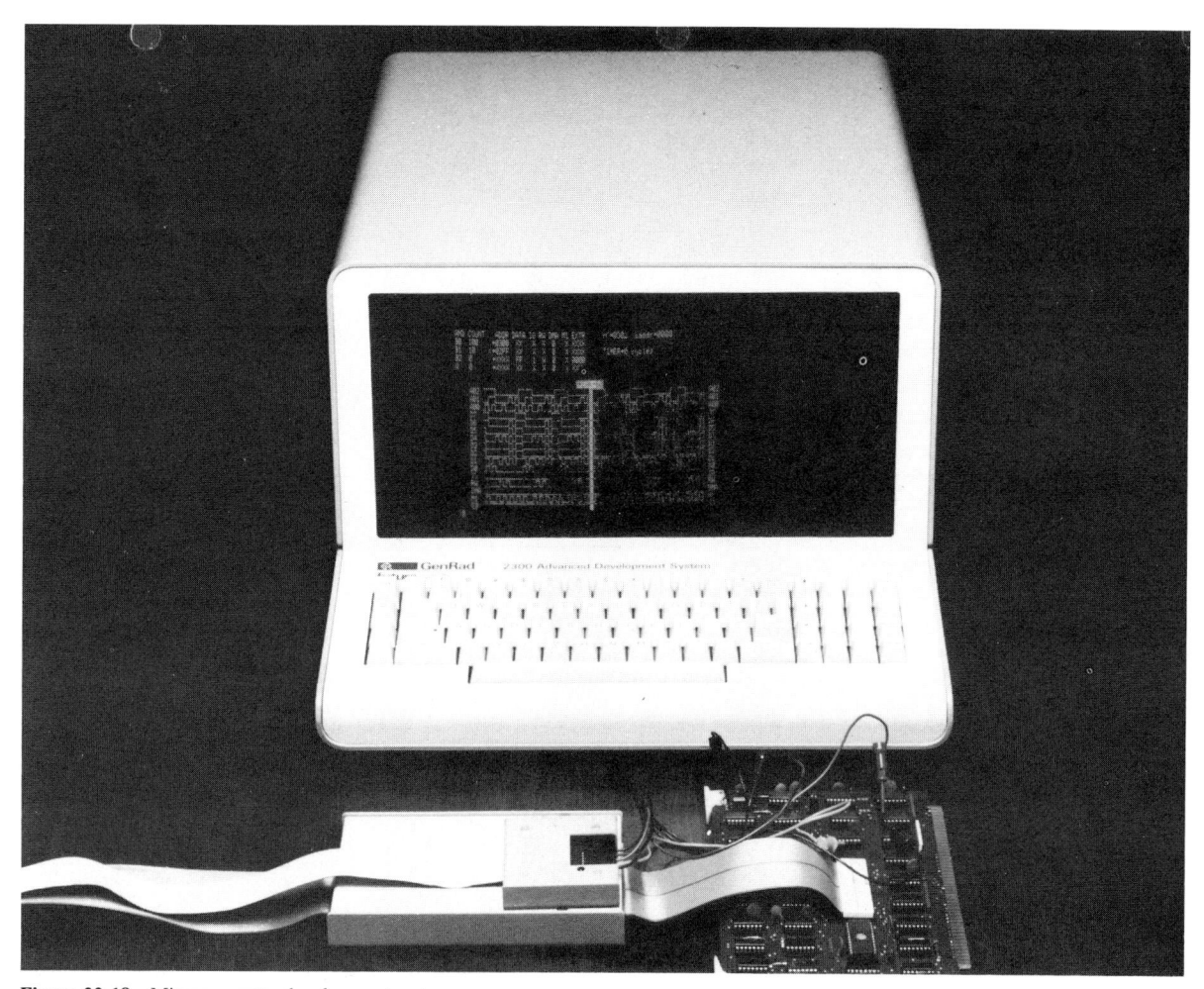

Figure 22.18 Microcomputer development system.

Courtesy of Gen Rad

affordable, quality product wins the race. In this regard, the development system is our most important support tool.

As shown in Figure 22.18, a development system is a complete computer system, designed to aid product development, and usually including a video terminal, two floppy-disk drives, line printer, processing unit, user-available RAM, several serial I/O ports, as well as a number of support programs (usually offered on floppy disk). Although the development system cannot help in the conception of the product, it can greatly aid the remaining aspects of product development (refer to Figure 22.1).

The development system offers a complete computer system on which to write, compile, and store programs. An option—the in-circuit emulator (ICE)—allows us to test and troubleshoot the hardware and to integrate our hardware/software design. By sharing resources with the development system, software/hardware debugging and integration can take place *while the prototype system is under development*.

To summarize, the basic development system allows us to write the software; the emulator option allows us to run the program on the product hardware (sharing resources with the development system if necessary) and to test, troubleshoot, and integrate our system.

Software Development

Since we are using the development system to perform software-design tasks that would otherwise have to be performed by the human brain, it follows that we must load the computer's memory with various programs designed to carry out those development tasks. Such a software-development package includes the following routines:

- Monitor system
- System supervisor

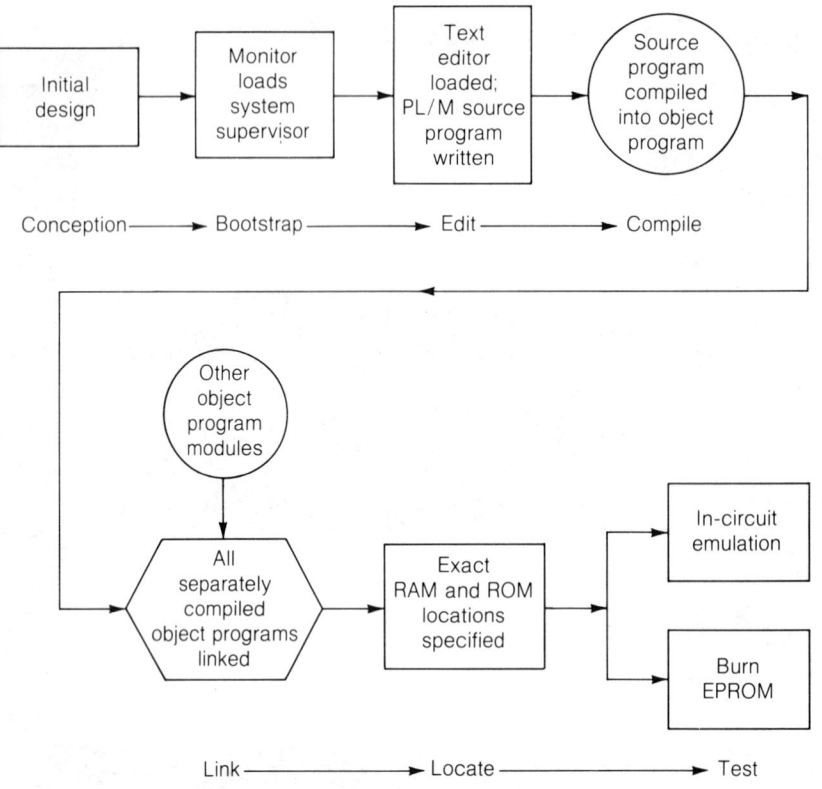

Figure 22.19 The major software design steps of a development system.

- Editor
- Assembler or compiler
- Link
- Locate

Based on these software-development routines, Figure 22.19 flowcharts the software design phase of product development. Moving from left to right, software design proceeds as follows:

1. The development-system *monitor* routine, contained within a ROM built into the development system, handles the initialization of the system when first started. Using the monitor routine, the operator can load the *system supervisor* routine from a floppy disk (the "bootstrap" operation). The system supervisor is the overall management program that allows the user to coordinate all routines and activities involved in the software-development phase. The system supervisor, along with its collection of utility programs, is often called an *operating system*. The supervisor, as well as each utility program, is known as a *file* (a named program). Once loaded into the system RAM, the system supervisor rather than the monitor reads the keyboard commands and data input.

2. Using the system supervisor, the *text editor* utility is called into the system from a file on the floppy disk. The text editor is similar to a word processor in that it allows the programmer to create, modify, and correct source programs (files) from the front console.

3. Once the prototype high-level program (for example, Pascal) has been written, it must be compiled into a binary *object program*. Using the system supervisor, the compiler accepts the high-level source program and translates it into relocatable binary object code (*relocatable*, remember, means the program can be adjusted to run from any address location).

   Also generated by the compilation process is the LIST (LST) file, a major troubleshooting aid. A LIST file takes the source file and numbers the program statements, assigning each a nesting level (how deeply is a given instruction nested inside WHILE-DO loops, for example). Included in the LST file are all syntax errors discovered during compilation. Using an optional attribute appended to the compilation command, the LST file may include the assembly-language formulation of each high-level statement (especially useful when using the 7D02 logic analyzer).

   Figure 22.20 shows the LIST file for our MIMIC-

```
PL/M-86 COMPILER    MIMICDELAY
                                PAGE   1


ISIS-II PL/M-86 V2.1 COMPILATION OF MODULE MIMICDELAY
OBJECT MODULE PLACED IN :F1:ROY.OBJ
COMPILER INVOKED BY:  PLM86 :F1:ROY.SRC



    1           MIMIC$DELAY:
                DO;
    2     1       DECLARE NUMBER BYTE;

    3     1       DELAY:
                  PROCEDURE (N);
    4     2         DECLARE (N,I) BYTE;
    5     2         IF N > 128D THEN
    6     2           DO WHILE N > 0;
    7     3             N = N - 1;
    8     3             I = 100;
    9     3             DO WHILE I > 0;
*** ERROR #105, STATEMENT #9, NEAR 'O',    UNDECLARED IDENTIFIER, BYTE ASSUMED
   10     4               I = I - 1;
   11     4             END;
   12     3           END;
                    ELSE
   13     2           0 = NUMBER;
*** ERROR #29, STATEMENT #13,   ILLEGAL STATEMENT
   14     2       END DELAY;

   15     1       NUMBER = INPUT(1);
   16     1       CALL DELAY(NUMBER);
   17     1       OUTPUT(2) = NUMBER;
   18     1     END MIMIC$DELAY;



MODULE INFORMATION:

    CODE AREA SIZE     = 0050H      80D
    CONSTANT AREA SIZE = 0000H       0D
    VARIABLE AREA SIZE = 0003H       3D
    MAXIMUM STACK SIZE = 0006H       6D
    24 LINES READ
    2 PROGRAM ERROR(S)

END OF PL/M-86 COMPILATION
```

(a) Two syntax errors found

Figure 22.20 The MIMIC-DELAY program LIST file written in PL/M.

```
PL/M-86 COMPILER       MIMICDELAY
                              PAGE   1

ISIS-II PL/M-86 V2.1 COMPILATION OF MODULE MIMICDELAY
OBJECT MODULE PLACED IN :F1:ROY.OBJ
COMPILER INVOKED BY:   PLM86 :F1:ROY.SRC


    1               MIMIC$DELAY:
                      DO;
    2      1          DECLARE NUMBER BYTE;
    3      1          DELAY:
                        PROCEDURE (N);
    4      2            DECLARE (N,I) BYTE;
    5      2            IF N > 128D THEN
    6      2              DO WHILE N > 0;
    7      3                N = N - 1;
    8      3                I = 100;
    9      3                DO WHILE I > 0;
   10      4                  I = I - 1;
   11      4                END;
   12      3              END;
                        ELSE
   13      2              NUMBER = 0;
   14      2          END DELAY;

   15      1          NUMBER = INPUT(1);
   16      1          CALL DELAY(NUMBER);
   17      1          OUTPUT(2) = NUMBER;
   18      1        END MIMIC$DELAY;


MODULE INFORMATION:

    CODE AREA SIZE     = 005FH    95D
    CONSTANT AREA SIZE = 0000H     0D
    VARIABLE AREA SIZE = 0002H     2D
    MAXIMUM STACK SIZE = 0006H     6D
    24 LINES READ
    0 PROGRAM ERROR(S)

END OF PL/M-86 COMPILATION
```

(b) Errors corrected

Figure 22.20 *(continued)*

DELAY program written in PL/M, an Intel-developed structured high-level language similar to Pascal. In Figure 22.20a, the compiler has uncovered two syntax errors. When the errors are corrected (Figure 22.20b), we are ready to proceed. (Identification of the two errors is left as an exercise.)

4. Once an error-free object file is created, the system supervisor calls on the *link* routine to combine all library and separately compiled programs into a single object program. (Remember, a block-structured language—such as Pascal—encourages large programming tasks to be broken up into several modules and written individually.)

5. To complete the software-development process, the programmer, under direction of the system supervisor, calls on the *locate* routine. The locate routine allows the programmer to specify the exact RAM and ROM locations to be reserved for program code, data, and stack operations.

A machine-language program now exists. With the help of the system supervisor, it can be burned into PROM or downloaded into the hardware system under test. For programs and systems of any complexity, it would be very rare indeed if the software were error-free and the hardware devoid of bugs. The next step in the product-development process is to troubleshoot the system and merge the hardware and software efforts.

In-Circuit Emulation is a development-system option that allows hardware/software development to proceed interactively. To accomplish emulation, the microprocessor of the product is removed, and in essence the entire development system is substituted by plugging in a 40-pin cable (see Figure 22.21).

To test the product, the program is run on the product hardware, just as if the original microprocessor were in place. (As far as the product is concerned, the development system/emulator combination acts just like the original microprocessor.) However, the in-circuit emulator does much more than the original microprocessor: it gives the operator a "window" to look inside the system; to examine and alter CPU registers, main memory, and flag values; and to automatically collect and store address, data, and status information for future reference.

A "trace" (block) of collected real-time program information can be displayed as disassembled mnemonics and compared with the LIST file.

Using in-circuit emulation, your program can be single-stepped. Within the single-step mode, the in-circuit emulator runs your program and collects information one instruction cycle at a time. All register and status information may be displayed at the end of each instruction cycle.

The in-circuit emulator can specify breakpoints, based on

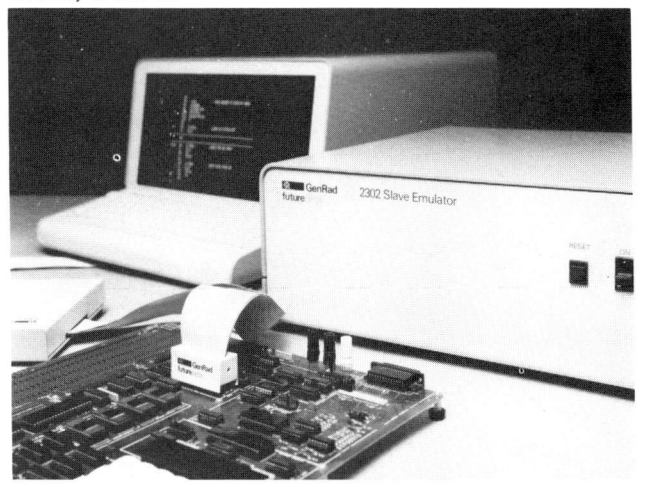

Figure 22.21 In-circuit emulator.

a number of different breakpoint conditions (for example, a specific address). When a breakpoint is encountered, you can display the last several instruction cycles executed and the contents of any memory of processor cell (run a trace).

Of special importance is the ability to use in-circuit emulation at any stage in product development. By borrowing the hardware resources of the development/emulator system, we can even begin testing software before any prototype hardware exists. As our prototype system develops, memory and I/O resources can be shared between emulator and prototype. In the final stages of design, when hardware and software integration is well along, the in-circuit emulator can run extensive diagnostics and product testing. In short, the in-circuit emulator is the "parent of a product," nurturing our prototype system from the earliest stages of implementation through the final phases of checkout.

For the future, the trend is toward shared-resource development systems, able to emulate multiprocessor systems. Figure 22.22 depicts a multistation, multiuser development-system network for hardware and software development, allowing up to eight users to develop products with different processors simultaneously. Looking further into the future, we can expect shared-resource development networks to link all aspects of product development, including design, production, and support.

CAD/CAM

CAD/CAM stands for *computer-aided design/computer-aided manufacturing* and represents the full-scale invasion of the manufacturing industry by the computer.

Initially, CAD stood for little more than *computer-aided drafting*—a computer with two-dimensional graphics. Since then, it has spread into every facet of design, manufacturing, and engineering. CAD/CAM generally falls into one of two categories: mechanical or electrical.

Mechanical CAD/CAM

Although the state of the art in mechanical CAD is solids, the mainstay is the generation of a 3-D wire-frame model (see Figure 22.23). Since the wire-frame model is really a database stored in memory, the model can be mathematically moved, rotated, and manipulated in a variety of ways by simple software commands. Once a database exists, it can be tapped to support all areas of engineering, design, and manufacturing: the production of 2-D mechanical drawings by projection; the matching of separately created parts; the creation of a programmed "tool path" for numerically controlled machines; and the robotics control programs for assembly and manufacturing.

Even initial engineering functions are being integrated into the CAD/CAM process. Called *computer-aided engineering* (CAE), the computer will analyze the wire-frame model, perhaps calculating its mass and thermal properties. Using *finite element modeling* (FEM), in which a complex structure is broken up into a number of small solids, the computer can perform complex stress analysis. When ready for manufacturing, the CAD/CAM system can mathematically "unfold" the structure and develop the outlines for die stamping.

Electrical CAD/CAM

As with mechanical CAD/CAM concepts, its electrical counterpart started as an isolated incident—a computer dig-

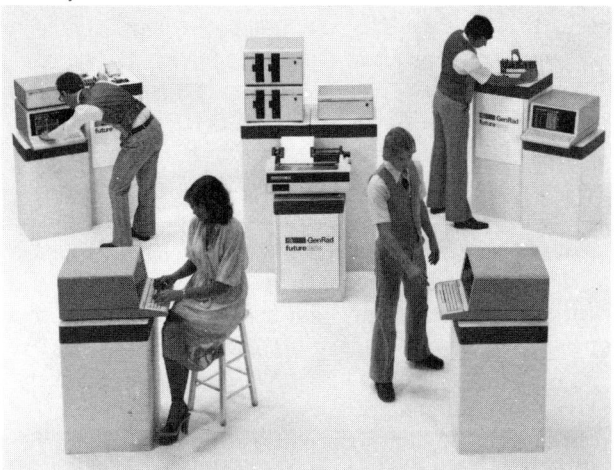

Figure 22.22 The shared-resource development system.

Figure 22-23 CAD system for creating 3-D wire-frame models.

itizing printed-circuit artwork in order to aid the manufacturing process. From this simple beginning it spread rapidly in both directions, from initial engineering (CAE) to final manufacturing (CAM). Using powerful software routines, the CAD system can place the component parts and route the traces for the greatest efficiency (Figure 22.24). And, given this ability, the design of the chips themselves becomes a CAD activity, in which the output is fed to the masking station. Once a circuit is designed, the database can be "postprocessed" to control the drilling of holes in the printed-circuit board, as well as the insertion of components.

With the advent of *engineering workstations,* the engineer can design the schematic, adding and hooking up parts as needed. When the design is finished, it is turned over to a sophisticated circuit simulator for testing and analysis.

Beyond mechanical and electrical product development, CAE/CAD/CAM concepts are spreading into nearly every area of human activity: architecture and plant design, movies and art, and even mapping, where whole countries have been placed on a CAD/CAM system for analysis and planning.

The future of CAD/CAM—in conjunction with graphics and robotics—is nothing short of awesome, for it will soon be hard to imagine marketing a product that was not engineered, designed, and manufactured by a CAD/CAM system.

OPERATING SYSTEMS

In the world of software there are *application* (user's) programs and there are *system* (operating system) programs. For human beings, an *operating system* is the entire nervous-system network that we were born with, while an application program might be, say, "riding a bicycle." Our "operating system" accepts and interprets the high-level command ("ride bicycle"), and marshalls all the resources required to carry out the application task.

The same idea holds in a computer. An application program carries out a dedicated, "real world" task; an operating system runs the user's program, coordinating and controlling the computer and all its peripherals. Therefore, as intro-

Figure 22.24 An electrical CAD/CAM workstation.

duced in Chapter 18, a microcomputer-oriented operating system performs two major functions:

- It manages the resources of the computer system.
- It accepts and carries out high-level commands entered from a keyboard.

Why are operating systems needed? Imagine the "simple" process of printing out a file of information from a floppy disk. Without the intervention of an operating system, the task would be unimaginably difficult and time-consuming for the average user. But with an operating system, one need only type in a high-level command (such as COPY A:PROG TO LP) and the operating system will manage all system resources in carrying out the command.

Since resource management is automatic and therefore "invisible" to the user, the essence of an operating system boils down to the following:

AN OPERATING SYSTEM INTERPRETS AND CARRIES OUT HIGH-LEVEL COMMANDS ISSUED BY THE OPERATOR.

An operating system is therefore often called a *command language*.

Operating systems have evolved into two major categories: those primarily oriented toward developing new software, and those primarily oriented toward efficient execution of application programs. Add new operating-system responsibilities in the areas of multiuser networking and real-time applications, and we see why the operating-system landscape is wide and varied.

Let us briefly review two of the more popular operating systems in use today and see what each has to offer.

CP/M

CP/M (Control Program for Microprocessors) was the first disk-based popular operating system available. First written to run on the 8080 microprocessor, it is a software-development operating system designed for a single user.

CP/M is actually a collection of programs (files) that reside on a *system diskette*. When the computer is turned on, the *resident monitor* in ROM automatically loads (*bootstraps*) the operating system software into internal RAM. The operating system then "takes over," issues a prompt, and monitors the keyboard for high-level commands (a *prompt* is a symbol the system displays when ready for the next command). The typical CP/M prompt is A>, where "A" stands for disk drive A. (A second disk drive, if present, will be labeled "B".) The user can switch between drive A and drive B at any time by typing A: or B:.

To reiterate, *the CP/M system interprets and carries out high-level commands*. Therefore, to understand and use CP/M is to gain a working knowledge of the available commands. A partial list is given below:

TYPE	*ERA
*DIR	DUMP
REN	LOAD
*PIP	ED

Let's briefly review those commands marked with an asterisk. (For a users guide to CP/M, and a complete list of CP/M commands, consult one of the many available CP/M handbooks.)

- *DIR (Display a list of files in the specified drive on the CRT screen.)* The command is:

    A> DIR (CR)   where "CR" = carriage return

    A complete list (directory) of all the files found on the diskette in drive A will be "printed" on the CRT screen.

- *PIP (Copy a file from one disk to another.)* First type:

    A> PIP (CR)

    which executes the program called *PIP.* (Peripheral Interchange Program). Within the PIP program, type:

    A:PROG.TXT = B:PROG.TXT (CR)

    File PROG.TXT in drive B will be copied into drive A and will have the same name.

- *ERA (Delete [erase] a file.)* Suppose we wish to now erase the file in drive B that we saved in drive A. We simply type:

    A> ERA B:PROG.TXT (CR)

Understanding CP/M What actually happens when we enter a typical command such as **A> ERA B:PROG.TXT (CR)**? After the command has been entered, the core supervisor program (which was "booted up" into RAM when the system was turned on) interprets (decodes) the command name "ERA." The supervisor then searches for a utility program called *ERA*. In other words, *the command name (ERA) is also a utility program name*. Once the utility program is found, it is executed, using information supplied after the utility name (i.e., B:PROG.TXT). When finished, control is returned to the supervisor to await the next high-level command.

Some utilities (called "built-in") are pulled into RAM along with the supervisor during the boot operation. Other utilities (called "transient") remain on the system disk and are pulled into RAM only when needed.

UNIX

UNIX, developed by Bell Labs in the early 1970s, has achieved "stardom" because it took the next logical step in operating system design: *it combined the features of a command language (such as CP/M) with the power of a programming language (such as Pascal)*. This combination is known as *the shell*.

Because it combines multi-user features and the hierarchical file system, UNIX is called the operating system of the future. Let's examine a few of UNIX's features in more detail.

Resembling an inverted tree (Figure 22.25), the hierarchical file structure makes it possible to quickly locate a given file among thousands of files. Starting at the top of the tree (the "root"), you work your way down through the layers of file directories from general broad-based categories to more and more specific categories until you locate the correct file.

The shell, as the name implies, is a software "skin" that acts as an interface between the operator and the operating system. A few of the simpler services provided by the shell include the following:

- *Asynchronous processing* allows the system to perform "background" tasks (i.e., compilation) on one file while using the terminal for an unrelated operation.

- *Control flow* uses the high-level IF-THEN-ELSE construct in a chain of operating system commands so different programs (files) can be evoked based on the results of previous program execution. UNIX can therefore take over some of the functions ordinarily done by a high-level program.

- *Wild card* uses the symbols "*" and "?" to perform operations on categories of files. For example, the UNIX command

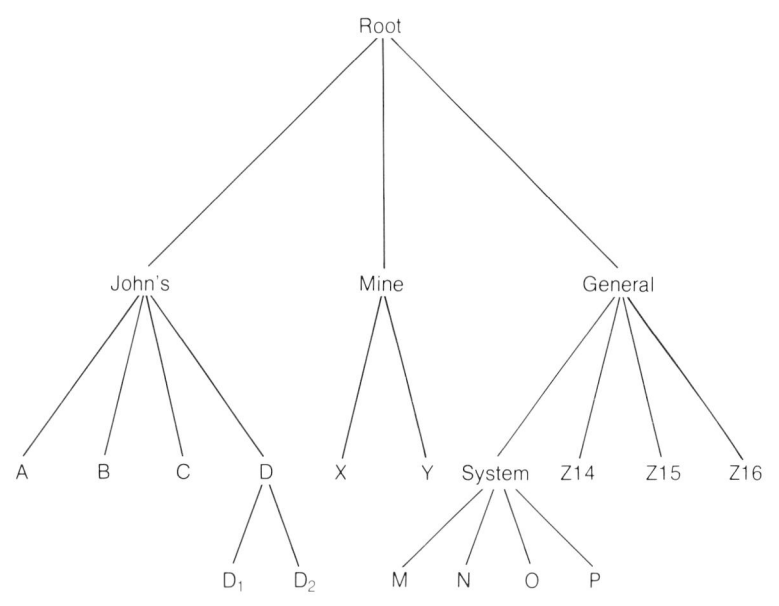

Figure 22.25 The inverted tree structure of the UNIX file system.

rm *.bak (CR)

will delete all files with an extension of bak (backup).

With over 50 commonly used commands, UNIX is not an operating system that can be mastered quickly—as is CP/M. As a result of the proliferation of 16-bit multiuser systems, UNIX or a UNIX-like language may become the standard operating system of the future.

Operating Environments

For some applications, the new *operating environments,* designed to simulate a real desk top, may make conventional operating systems obsolete.

By inputting information from "the mouse" and displaying information in "windows" (separate sections of the CRT screen displaying different applications), new levels of task integration and user interfacing have been achieved. Via the mouse, the cursor is moved to an area on the screen; in this way, new windows can be opened and information can be shifted (as if shifting papers on a desk top) between windows without disturbing the operation of any programs they represent.

Requiring more than 128K of primary memory, operating environments are ambitious software systems, and many versions will battle for marketplace dominance in the coming years.

Real-Time Operating Systems

Operating systems that must respond rapidly to external events are known as *real-time* operating systems. Because external real-world events occur randomly and often simultaneously, interrupt handling and multitasking are primary attributes of a real-time operating system. To provide the necessary high-speed reaction times, many real-time operating system "primitives" (short standard routines) are "embedded" into ROM.

INTELLIGENT-MACHINE UPDATE

With the advent of the development system, computers are (in a sense) developing other computers. How long will it be before the initial *conception* block of Figure 22.1 is also carried out under computer control? Will the computer then be able to reproduce improved copies of itself, *without human intervention*?

QUESTIONS AND PROBLEMS

1. Why are duties normally assigned to software being taken over by peripheral chips (hardware)?
2. What is a *high-level language*?
3. What are the advantages of *top-down programming*?
4. What task is performed by a *compiler*?

5. Why is *assembly-language programming* sometimes preferred over high-level language programming?
6. How does the *single-step circuit* of Figure 22.8 allow the operator to step from one instruction cycle to the next?
7. How can the *breakpoint technique* home in on a problem area faster than single stepping?
8. With regard to signature analysis, what is a *signature* and how is it generated?
9. State the two steps involved in *logic analysis*.
10. Based on the simplified data-acquisition diagram of Figure 22.12, how is a *trigger* generated and what does it do?
11. How does the delay block of Figure 22.12 affect the position of the trigger word in the 4×4 RAM?
12. Why is *state analysis* usually a synchronous process, and *timing analysis* usually an asynchronous process?
13. What is *combinational* and *sequential* triggering?
14. How is information organized when using the *graph* mode of display?
15. What two unique features are offered by the 7D02 logic analyzer?
16. What high-level command defines a 7D02 test?
17. List the hardware components of a development system.
18. What part of the development process is handled by the *in-circuit emulator*?
19. What is the *system supervisor* in a development system?
20. What is the purpose of the *text editor* file? the *locate* file? the *link* file?
21. During in-circuit emulation, how is the prototype product interfaced with the development system?
22. What are the three types of structures used by structured programs?
23. How is the instinctive intelligence of a newborn baby related to a *monitor* program?
24. Compared to a compiler, why is an interpreter inefficient when executing a program with many loops?
25. Replacing an existing ROM/PROM with a software diagnostic ROM/PROM is a popular means of troubleshooting. Write a simple diagnostic routine designed to "exercise" the system of Figure 9.8 (the diagnostic routine will be burned into a 2532 EPROM and substituted for the existing EPROM). Indicate what you would see on the various bus and I/O lines when they are probed by a scope.
26. What do the terms *CAD, CAM,* and *CAE* stand for?
27. In relation to CAD/CAM, what is "postprocessing"?
28. What are the two main functions of an *operating system*?
29. What occurs during a "bootstrap"?
30. In an operating system, what is the relationship between the "supervisor" and the "utilities"?
31. Is CP/M intended for single-user or multiuser operation? UNIX?
32. Why are files particularly easy to locate when using a hierarchical file structure (such as UNIX offers)?
33. What is a *prompt*?
34. Related to CP/M, what do the letters A and B stand for?
35. By researching the literature, list several UNIX commands.
36. Under the UCSD P-system, the Pascal program of Figure 22.5a runs in 8 seconds for an input of 129, and 16 seconds for an input of 255. In contrast, the interpreted BASIC program of Figure 22.5b requires 70 and 140 seconds, respectively, to run. Why is the BASIC program slower? How fast would a fully compiled program run?
37. In the Warnier-Orr diagram of Figure 22.6, what is the meaning of the symbol "∞"?
38. Draw the Warnier-Orr diagram for a program that outputs a musical note whose frequency is proportional to an inported number.
39. By comparing Figures 22.20a and b, and using the error messages listed below (reprinted from the PL/M86 error message table), determine the two syntax errors of Figure 22.20a.

ERROR #29: ILLEGAL STATEMENT
    This may be due to misspelling or missing parts of an otherwise valid statement.
ERROR #105: UNDECLARED IDENTIFIER
    Every identifier must be declared.

40. Referring to Figure 22.20b, how deeply nested is the high-level PL/M statement: I = I − 1;?

chapter 23

The 8-Bit Family of Microprocessors

Biologically, the various species belonging to the same family of the animal kingdom exhibit many more similarities than differences. With a similar anatomy and physiology, experiments run on one family member can often be carried over to others.

The family of 8-bit microprocessors follows the same pattern. The many "species" of 8-bit microprocessors offered by various manufacturers are all different. Yet they all belong to the same family—the family of 8-bit microprocessors—and all have very similar architecture, processing action, and instruction set (indeed, some are direct descendants of others). Once we master a single member of the family—such as the 6800—we have opened the door to all other 8-bit microprocessors, for only a slight change in focus will allow us to design and troubleshoot with almost any 8-bit microprocessor now on the market.

In this chapter we will take a brief look at two additional branches of the 8-bit microprocessor family tree (Figure 23.1), and we will point out how they differ from the Motorola group in architecture, processing action, and instruction set.

THE INTEL GROUP

The Intel 8080 was the pioneer LSI processor—the first 8-bit microprocessor on the market and the one to which all others are compared. It was followed shortly afterward by the 8085, a modified version of the 8080. Following the format of this book we will compare the 8080/8085 with the 6800 by examining differences and similarities in hardware, processing action, and software.

The 8080/8085 Basic Architecture

Figure 23.2 compares the basic architecture of the 8080/8085 with that of the 6800. The major differences show up at a glance.

Clock generation Like the 6800, the 8080 requires an external clock chip (the 8224) for clock generation and signal synchronization. The 8085, on the other hand, integrates the clock function within the microprocessor.

Data multiplexing To make more effective use of the 40 pins, most Intel microprocessors—unlike the 6800—multiplex their data lines. That is, the eight data lines are shared between two sets of time-multiplexed signals. Referring to Figure 23.3, during each 8080 data-transfer cycle, status information first appears on the bus, followed by data. Since the status signals are needed throughout all data-transfer operations, they are latched within the 8228 System Controller by the Status Strobe ($\overline{STSTB}$) pulse. On the 8085, low-level address lines appear first, followed by data. The low-level address information is latched into an 8228 8-bit latch by the action of Address Latch Enable (ALE) and combined with the high-level address lines to generate the full 16-bit address.

Internal registers Unlike the 6800, which is memory oriented, the 8080/8085 offers a collection of general-purpose registers (B, C, D, E, H, and L), in addition to the single accumulator (register A). Although no index register is provided, the HL register pair performs indirect addressing. The WZ register pair is similar to the 6800's MAR. Both are seldom shown on block diagrams.

Memory and I/O control The Motorola and Intel processors differ considerably in the way they interface memory and I/O ports. The Motorola family, we have learned, uses memory-mapped I/O exclusively. The Intel family, on the

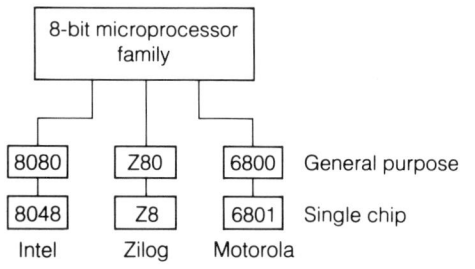

Figure 23.1 Popular members of the 8-bit microprocessor family tree.

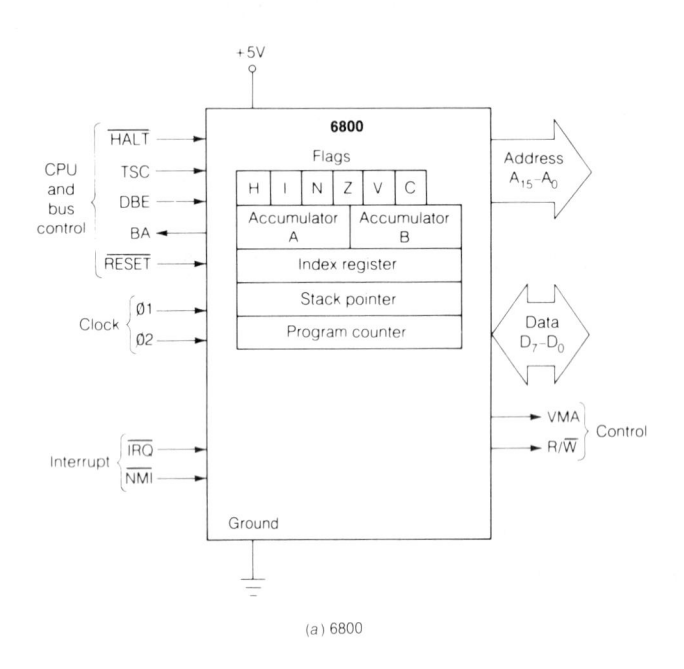

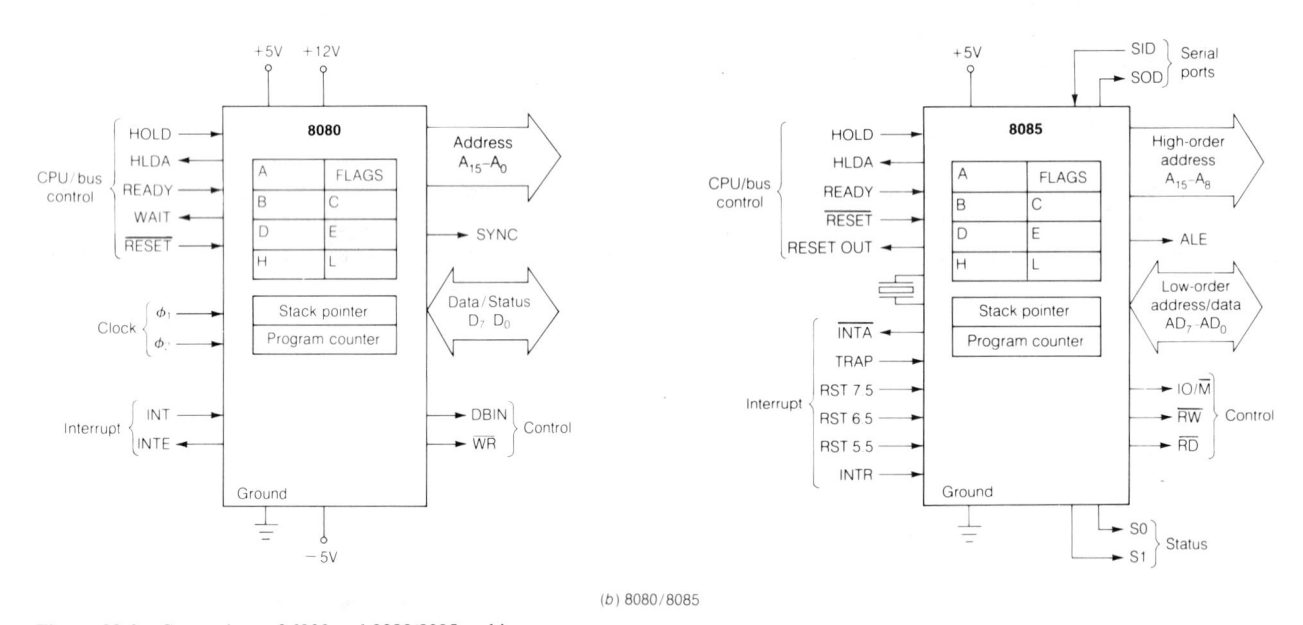

Figure 23.2 Comparison of 6800 and 8080/8085 architecture.

other hand, has adopted *isolated I/O* and has separated the memory space of addresses from the port space of addresses. On the 8080, isolated I/O is accomplished via the control bus by providing separate control lines for memory and for I/O ports (Figure 23.3a). On the 8085, a single line (IO/$\overline{\text{M}}$) distinguishes between the memory space and the port space of addresses. When IO/$\overline{\text{M}}$ is high, the address on the address bus points to an I/O port location; when low, it points to a memory location. Logical combinations of the three control lines ($\overline{\text{RD}}$, $\overline{\text{WR}}$, and IO/$\overline{\text{M}}$) will give the four basic control

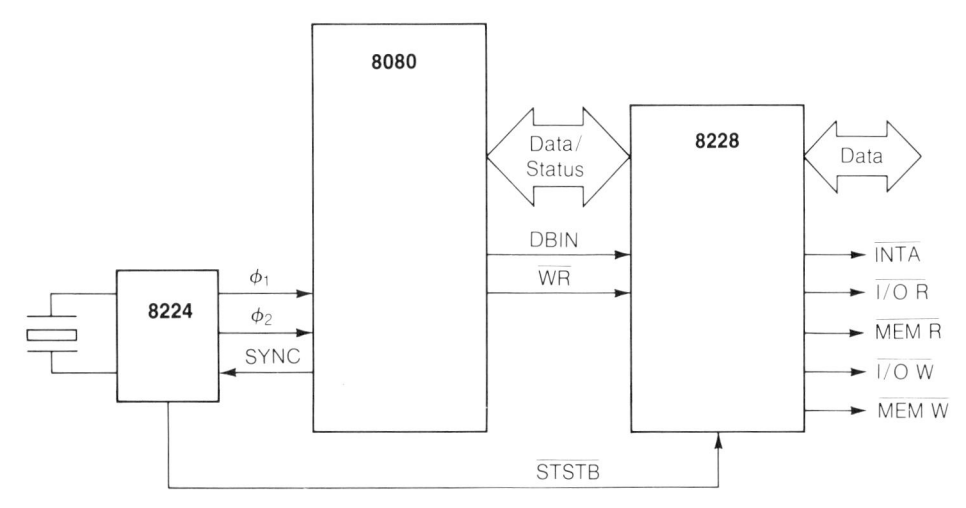

(a) Status information on 8080 sharing data pins

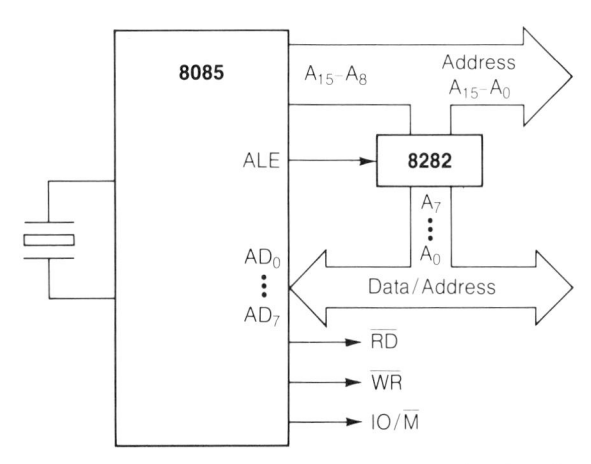

(b) Low-order address information on 8085 sharing data pins

Figure 23.3 Multiplexing the data bus.

processes (I/O read, I/O write, memory read, and memory write). Of course, the Intel processors can switch to a memory-mapped system at any time by simply ignoring the I/O lines (see Figure 23.4). There are, as usual, both advantages and disadvantages to memory-mapped I/O.

Advantages to memory-mapped I/O

- All instructions that operate on ordinary memory locations can now be used with I/O ports. Greater overall flexibility and speed as well as reduced program size are two immediate results.
- The number of processor pins can be reduced without relying on multiplexing. (Or, conversely, the number of features that can be placed within a 40-pin chip is increased.)

Advantages to isolated I/O

- I/O transfers are conceptually easier since only the accumulator and IN- or OUT-port instructions are involved.
- It is often easier to assign port addresses, since compatibility with memory is not required.
- The full 64K address space is in no way affected by I/O addressing.

The 8080/8085 Memory Map

Another difference between the Intel and Motorola 8-bit processors is the position of ROM on a memory map. Because the 6800 RESET and interrupt vectors are contained in page $FF, 6800 ROM must be placed at the very top of the memory map.

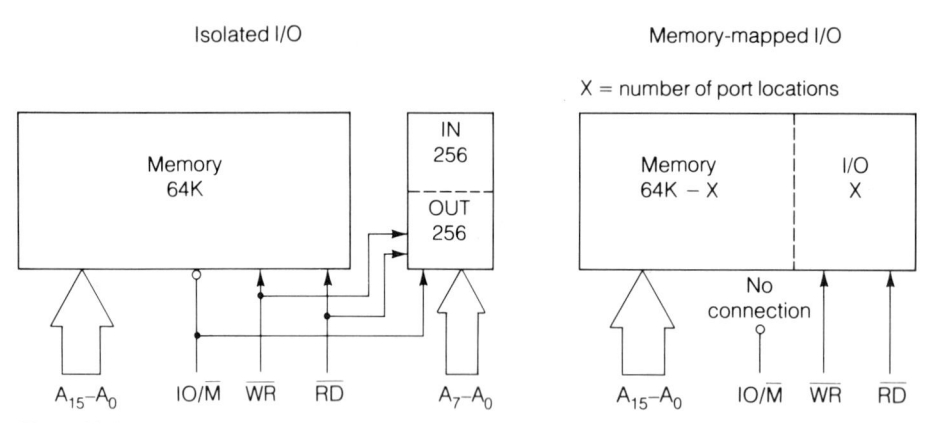

Figure 23.4 Comparison of 8085-based isolated I/O and memory-mapped I/O.

With an 8080/8085 system, on the other hand, a RESET clears the program counter, and all interrupts vector to page zero. Therefore, ROM must start at location 0000H. (As shown, Intel prefers to specify hexadecimal numbers by placing an "H" after the number.)

CPU and Bus Control

Although the CPU and bus control signals appear to be quite different between the 6800 and 8080/8085 (Figure 23.2), they really boil down to the same two functions: DMA control and slow memory interface.

HOLD on the 8080/8085 handles DMA control similarly to $\overline{\text{HALT}}$ on the 6800. When a DMA request is initiated, HOLD is driven high. At the completion of the present instruction, the processor enters a special "idle" state (internal loop). All address, data, and control lines are floated and the HLDA (Hold Acknowledge) handshaking line goes high to inform an external device (DMA controller) that it can take over the system bus and transfer information at high speed. When HOLD is brought back down to zero, the processor exits the DMA state, returns HLDA to zero, and begins processing action from where it left off.

On the 8080/8085, control-line stretching to accommodate slow memories is accomplished by entering another kind of idle state, the WAIT state. When READY (WAIT request) is pulled active low, the processor enters a special internal-loop state in the middle of a machine cycle (on the 8080, the WAIT output signal goes high to acknowledge the WAIT state). However, unlike the HOLD state, all address, data, and control lines remain active, giving the data extra time in which to travel between a slow memory and the CPU.

The Interrupt Structure

The interrupt structure of the 8080/8085 is more complex than that of the 6800 (again refer to Figure 23.2). Because most of the 8080's interrupt structure is contained within the 8085's, we will concentrate on the 8085. As noted, six pins constitute the 8085's interrupt system.

First of all, the 6800 and 8085 differ in the way they generate the interrupt vector (starting address of the ISR). As detailed in Chapter 16, when the 6800 is interrupted, the 16-bit interrupt vector is fetched from two adjacent memory locations and jammed directly into the program counter. The 8085, on the other hand, generates the interrupt vector by fetching a special 1-byte op-code CALL (known as a *restart*) to the instruction register. The CALLed location usually contains a jump to the starting location of the ISR.

The four RST interrupts (RST 5.5, RST 6.5, RST 7.5, and TRAP) generate automatic CALLs to a memory location equal to 8 times the RST number. For example, the RST 6.5 vector is fetched from the memory location equal to 8 times 6.5, or 52D.

The TRAP interrupt input (really an RST 4.5) is similar to the 6800's $\overline{\text{NMI}}$, since it cannot be masked out. As with $\overline{\text{NMI}}$, TRAP is normally reserved for emergencies.

The INT/INTR input on the 8080/8085 has no counterpart in the 6800. When an INT/INTR interrupt is requested, the 8080/8085 enters a special op-code fetch machine cycle, in which control line $\overline{\text{INTA}}$ (generated by the 8228 system controller in an 8080 system) goes active low rather than $\overline{\text{RD}}$ (8085) or $\overline{\text{MEM R}}$ (8080). A special instruction—generally the 1-byte CALL instruction known as *RESTART*—is pulled in from an input port, and "jammed" into the instruction register. The interrupt service routine is CALLed and performed as usual.

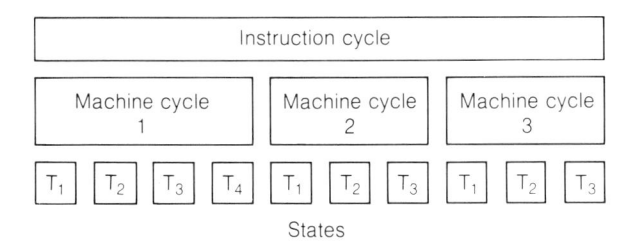

Figure 23.5 Typical 8080/8085 instruction-cycle/machine-cycle/state timing.

8080/8085 Processing Action

Timing cycles As with the 6800, one 8080/8085 instruction is processed in one *instruction cycle*. As seen in Figure 23.5, each instruction cycle in turn is made up of 1 to 5 *machine cycles*. A machine cycle—closely related to a 6800 clock cycle—is required every time a data byte is transferred between a peripheral and the 8080/8085 microprocessor. Obviously, a machine cycle is closely associated with the where/when data-transfer operation. Unlike the 6800, in which the clock cycle and data-transfer cycle are of the same duration, the 8080/8085 machine cycle can be further subdivided into three to five *states* (six for the 8085), where a state is defined as one clock cycle. Although the clock rate of the 8080/8085 is higher than the clock rate of the 6800, it does not translate into higher processing speed since many clock cycles on the 8080/8085 are required to perform the operations carried out by a single 6800 clock cycle. (If all these various cycles seem a little confusing, just remember that a 6800 clock cycle is equivalent to an 8080/8085 machine cycle.)

Data-transfer waveforms The basic where/when data transfer waveforms for the 8080/8085 are shown in Figure 23.6, and compared with the 6800 waveforms. As observed, the 8080/8085 waveforms do not make direct use of the system clock to qualify (time) the data-transfer process.

Processing action example As a final review of 8080/8085 processing action, let's go through the familiar MIMIC sequence step by step, as we did for the 6800 in Chapter 8.

The MIMIC program for the 8080/8085 is shown in Figure 23.7. Placing an arbitrary data word (such as BEH) before the computer's "eyes," the action unfolds as follows (continued reference to Figure 23.8 should be helpful):

- *Step 1:* The starting address of the program (2000H) is placed into the program counter (this is accomplished by the *monitor* program).
- *Step 2:* The program counter points to the first memory location in the program, and a where/when operation fetches the IN-port operation code (DBH) to the instruction register.

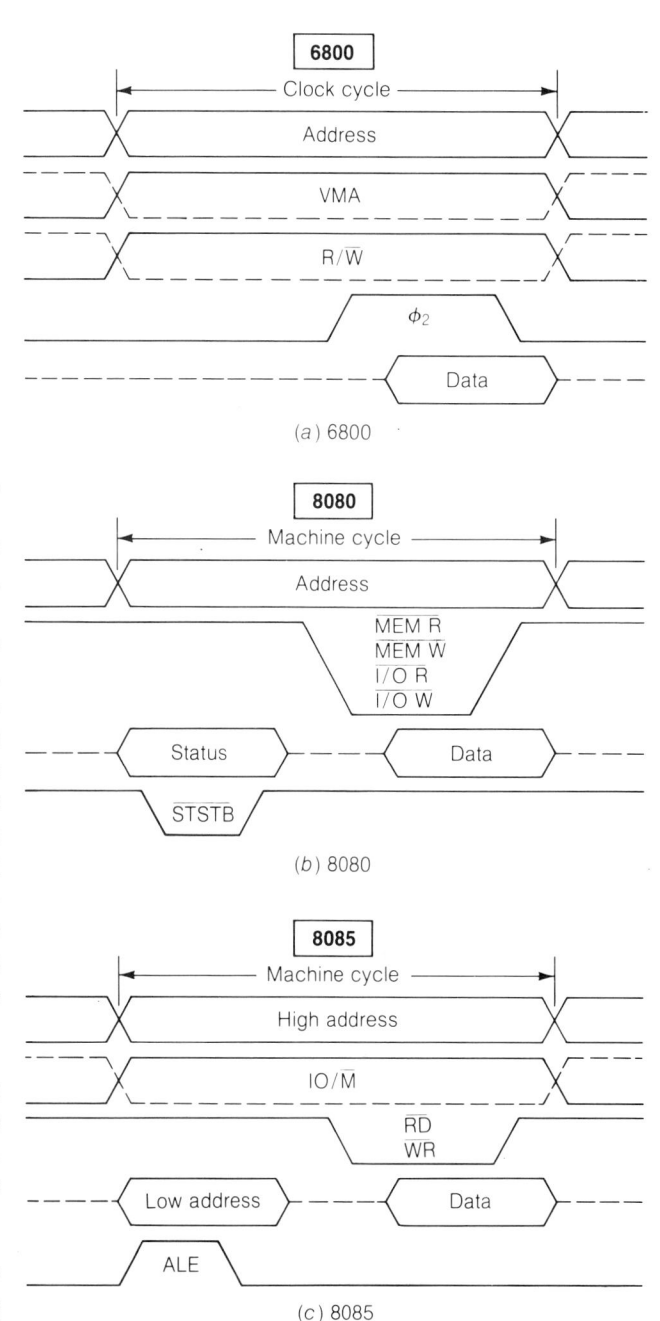

Figure 23.6 A comparison of typical where/when data-transfer waveforms.

- *Step 3:* The IN-port op code is decoded and the proper microprogram selected.
- *Step 4:* The IN-port microprogram directs the program counter to increment to 2001H and another where/when data transfer fetches the port address (40H) to the WZ register pair via the data bus. The 8-bit port address is copied into both the W and Z registers. (The IN- and OUT-port instructions are the only ones in the entire instruction set using an 8-bit address, and the only ones

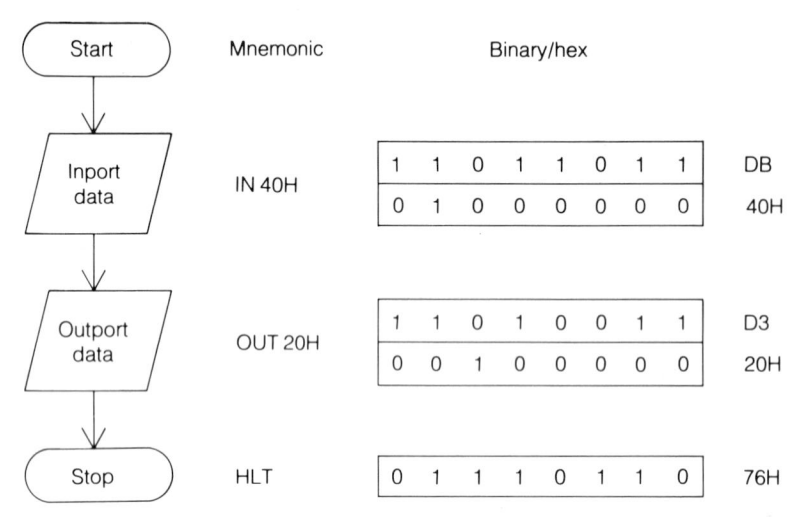

```
Start          Mnemonic           Binary/hex

Inport          IN 40H      | 1 1 0 1 1 0 1 1 |  DB
data                        | 0 1 0 0 0 0 0 0 |  40H

Outport         OUT 20H     | 1 1 0 1 0 0 1 1 |  D3
data                        | 0 0 1 0 0 0 0 0 |  20H

Stop            HLT         | 0 1 1 1 0 1 1 0 |  76H
```

Figure 23.7 The familiar MIMIC program using 8080/8085 instructions.

in which the WZ registers and high-level/low-level address lines are redundant.)

- *Step 5:* The third and final where/when data-transfer operation begins with the port address (4040H) in the WZ register pair "pointing to" the "eyes" of the computer, followed by the data word BEH IN-ported from the outside world to the accumulator.
- *Step 6:* The first instruction complete, timing and control increments the program counter to 2002H and fetches the OUT-port operation code (D3H) to the instruction register.
- *Step 7:* Under direction of the decoded microprogram, the program counter is incremented to 2003H, and the address of the output port (20H) is fetched to the WZ register pair.
- *Step 8:* The port address in the WZ register pair (2020H) points to the "voice" of the computer, and the data in the accumulator (BEH) are transferred to the addressed output port and latched in place.
- *Step 9:* The second instruction complete, the operation code for halt (76H) is fetched to the instruction register, decoded, and computer operation is stopped.

To exit the halt state and repeat the mimic process, we reset the microprocessor, which clears the program counter.

Software—The 8080/8085 Instruction Set

The instruction sets for both the 8080 and the 8085 are nearly identical, consisting of the same basic 72 instruction types. The 8085 instruction set includes two additional instruction types to service the SID (Serial-IN-Data) and SOD (Serial-OUT-Data) 1-bit I/O ports found only on the 8085 (see Figure 23.2), and to perform interrupt status/masking functions for the 8085's special RST interrupts. These 72 (74) types of instructions have been arranged into the same five major groups that we used to study the 6800:

1. Data-transfer group
2. Arithmetic group
3. Logic group
4. Branch group
5. Stack, I/O, machine-control group

The instruction set for the 8080/8085, shown in Figure 23.9, is very similar to the instruction set of the 6800—*until you consider signed-number operations*. Generally speaking, the 8080/8085 instruction set is not designed for efficient signed-number processing, and therefore is not suited for strictly data-processing applications. For example, there is no signed-number overflow-detection flag should the result of an arithmetic operation lie outside the $-128/+127$ signed-number bounds. Furthermore, there is no arithmetic shift-right operation in which the original sign bit is preserved, and the Jump Positive (JP) and Jump Negative (JN) instructions are the only signed-number conditional-branching instructions offered.

The 8080/8085 instruction set contains four addressing modes. As shown below, only the *relative* addressing mode of the 6800 has no counterpart in the 8080/8085 set:

Addressing Modes

8080/8085	6800
Immediate	Immediate
Direct	Extended, Direct
Indirect	Indexed
Register/Not specified	Implied/Inherent
	Relative

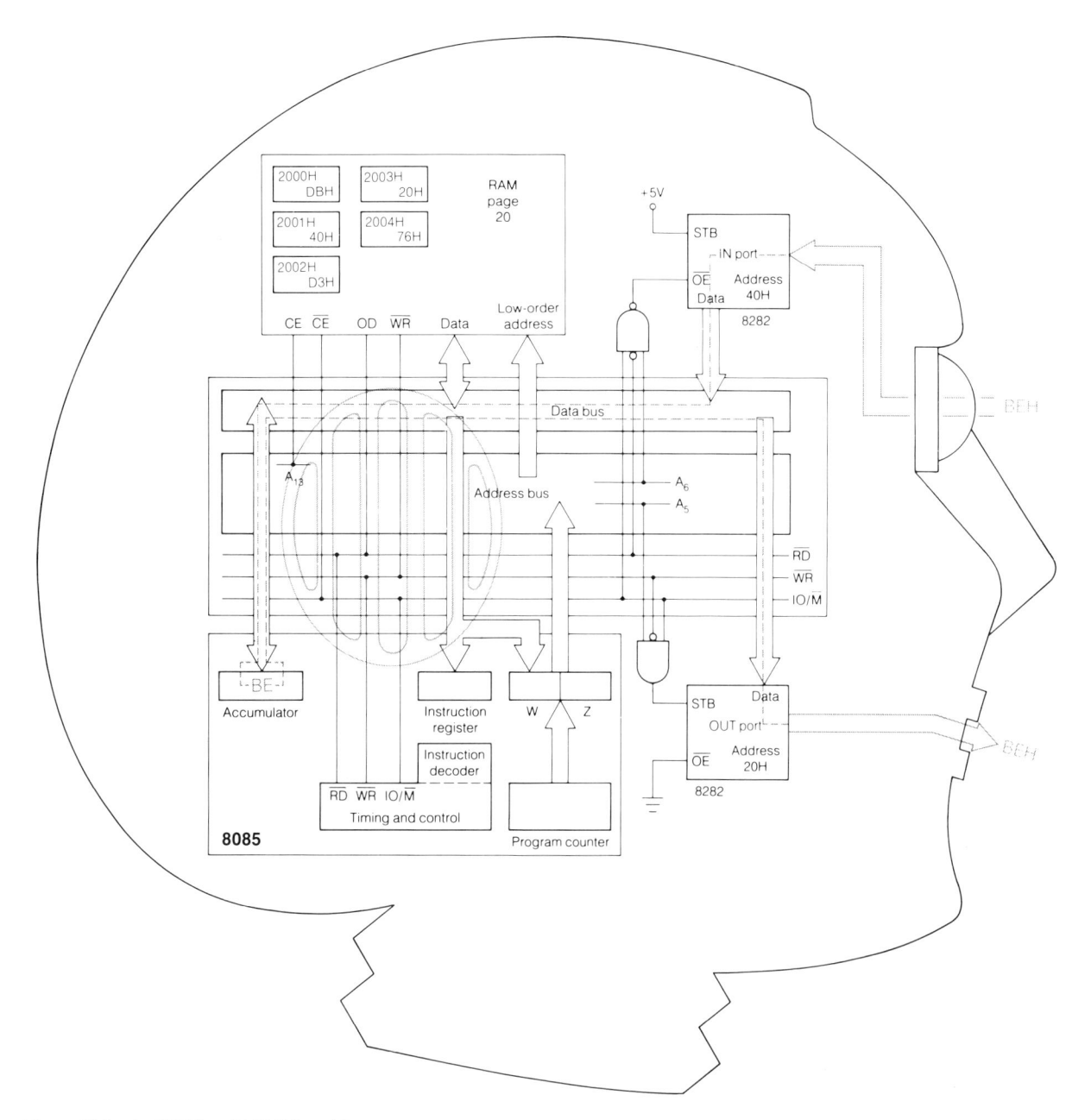

Figure 23.8 An 8085-based MIMIC machine.

The assembly-language mnemonics differ somewhat in structure. Unlike the 6800, each 8080/8085 addressing mode is uniquely specified in the CODE portion of the mnemonic. In the 6800, each addressing mode is specified in the OPERAND portion of the mnemonic. For example, compare below the basic memory-transfer instructions using comparable addressing modes.

Addressing Mode	8080/8085	6800
Immediate	MVI r,data	LDAA #data
Direct	LDA addr	LDAA address
Indirect/Indexed	MOV r,M	LDAA address,X

The 8048 Single-Chip Microcomputer

The 8048 (Figure 23.10) is similar to the Motorola 6801, with an architecture and instruction set tailored for control applications. The 8048 offers 1K × 8 of built-in ROM (expandable to 16K), 64 × 8 of built-in RAM, 27 I/O lines, and an 8-bit timer/event counter. Bit manipulation, BCD operations, conditional branching, and table lookup are emphasized in its instruction set.

One of the newest members of the Intel single-chip family—the 8051—demonstrates the continual upgrade in performance. Its major improvements include 32 programma-

328 Part IV / Applications and Interfacing: Living in a Real World

BRANCH CONTROL GROUP

Jump
- JMP adr C3
- JNZ adr C2
- JZ adr CA
- JNC adr D2
- JC adr DA
- JPO adr E2
- JPE adr EA
- JP adr F2
- JM adr FA
- PCHL E9

Call
- CALL adr CD
- CNZ adr C4
- CZ adr CC
- CNC adr D4
- CC adr DC
- CPO adr E4
- CPE adr EC
- CP adr F4
- CM adr FC

Return
- RET C9
- RNZ C0
- RZ C8
- RNC D0
- RC D8
- RPO E0
- RPE E8
- RP F0
- RM F8

Restart
- RST 0 C7
- RST 1 CF
- RST 2 D7
- RST 3 DF
- RST 4 E7
- RST 5 EF
- RST 6 F7
- RST 7 FF

I/O AND MACHINE CONTROL

Stack Ops
- PUSH B C5
- PUSH D D5
- PUSH H E5
- PUSH PSW F5
- POP B C1
- POP D D1
- POP H E1
- POP PSW F1
- XTHL E3
- SPHL F9

Input/Output
- OUT byte D3
- IN byte DB

Control
- DI F3
- EI FB
- NOP 00
- HLT 76

New Instructions (8085 Only)
- RIM 20
- SIM 30

DATA TRANSFER GROUP

Move
- MOV A,A 7F
- MOV A,B 78
- MOV A,C 79
- MOV A,D 7A
- MOV A,E 7B
- MOV A,H 7C
- MOV A,L 7D
- MOV A,M 7E
- MOV B,A 47
- MOV B,B 40
- MOV B,C 41
- MOV B,D 42
- MOV B,E 43
- MOV B,H 44
- MOV B,L 45
- MOV B,M 46
- MOV C,A 4F
- MOV C,B 48
- MOV C,C 49
- MOV C,D 4A
- MOV C,E 4B
- MOV C,H 4C
- MOV C,L 4D
- MOV C,M 4E
- MOV D,A 57
- MOV D,B 50
- MOV D,C 51
- MOV D,D 52
- MOV D,E 53
- MOV D,H 54
- MOV D,L 55
- MOV D,M 56

Move (cont)
- MOV E,A 5F
- MOV E,B 58
- MOV E,C 59
- MOV E,D 5A
- MOV E,E 5B
- MOV E,H 5C
- MOV E,L 5D
- MOV E,M 5E
- MOV H,A 67
- MOV H,B 60
- MOV H,C 61
- MOV H,D 62
- MOV H,E 63
- MOV H,H 64
- MOV H,L 65
- MOV H,M 66
- MOV L,A 6F
- MOV L,B 68
- MOV L,C 69
- MOV L,D 6A
- MOV L,E 6B
- MOV L,H 6C
- MOV L,L 6D
- MOV L,M 6E
- MOV M,A 77
- MOV M,B 70
- MOV M,C 71
- MOV M,D 72
- MOV M,E 73
- MOV M,H 74
- MOV M,L 75
- XCHG EB

Move immediate
- MVI A, byte 3E
- MVI B, byte 06
- MVI C, byte 0E
- MVI D, byte 16
- MVI E, byte 1E
- MVI H, byte 26
- MVI L, byte 2E
- MVI M, byte 36

Load immediate
- LXI B, dble 01
- LXI D, dble 11
- LXI H, dble 21
- LXI SP, dble 31

Load/Store
- LDAX B 0A
- LDAX D 1A
- LHLD adr 2A
- LDA adr 3A
- STAX B 02
- STAX D 12
- SHLD adr 22
- STA adr 32

ARITHMETIC AND LOGICAL GROUP

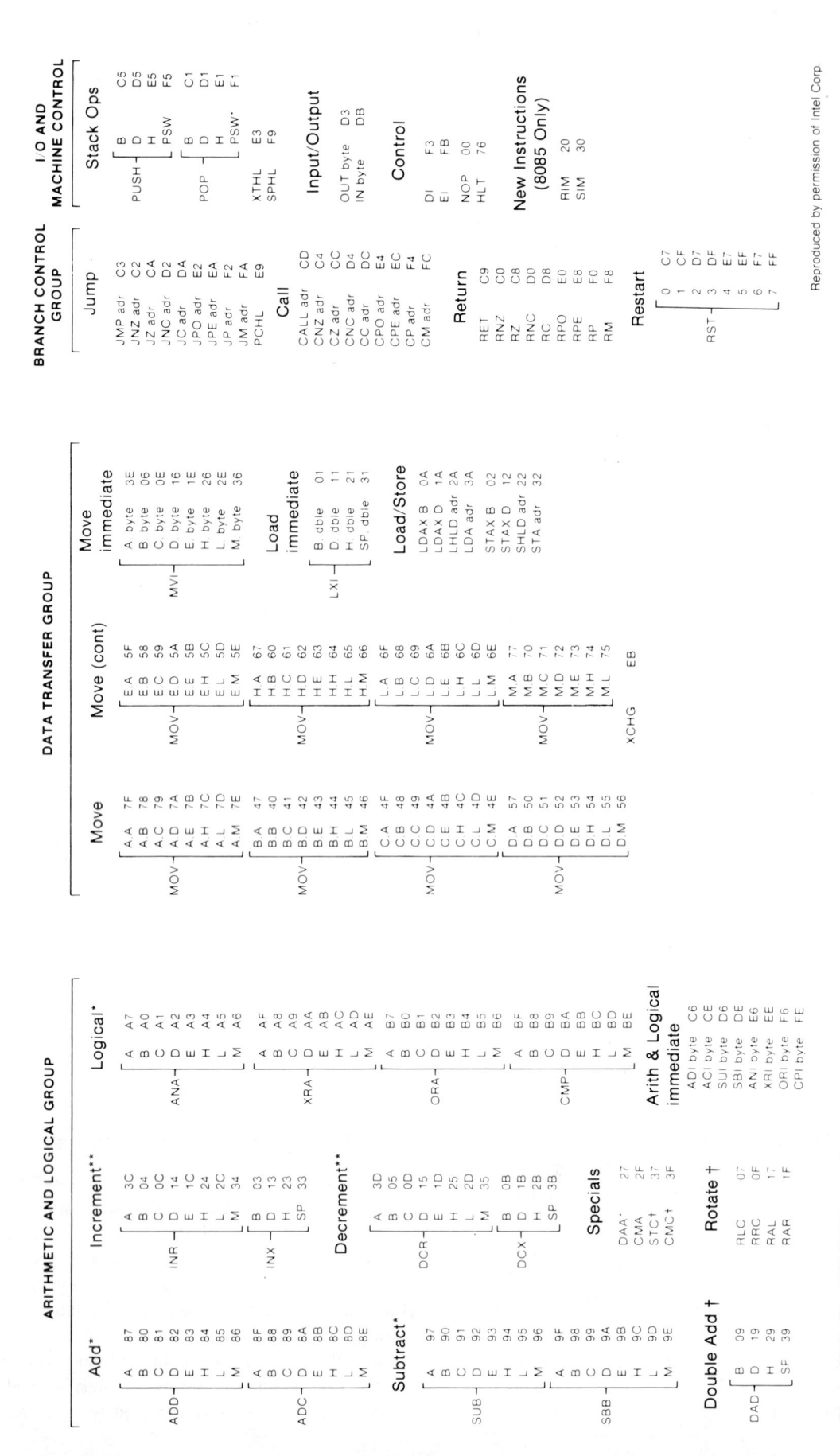

Add*
- ADD A 87
- ADD B 80
- ADD C 81
- ADD D 82
- ADD E 83
- ADD H 84
- ADD L 85
- ADD M 86
- ADC A 8F
- ADC B 88
- ADC C 89
- ADC D 8A
- ADC E 8B
- ADC H 8C
- ADC L 8D
- ADC M 8E

Subtract*
- SUB A 97
- SUB B 90
- SUB C 91
- SUB D 92
- SUB E 93
- SUB H 94
- SUB L 95
- SUB M 96
- SBB A 9F
- SBB B 98
- SBB C 99
- SBB D 9A
- SBB E 9B
- SBB H 9C
- SBB L 9D
- SBB M 9E

Double Add†
- DAD B 09
- DAD D 19
- DAD H 29
- DAD SP 39

Increment**
- INR A 3C
- INR B 04
- INR C 0C
- INR D 14
- INR E 1C
- INR H 24
- INR L 2C
- INR M 34
- INX B 03
- INX D 13
- INX H 23
- INX SP 33

Decrement**
- DCR A 3D
- DCR B 05
- DCR C 0D
- DCR D 15
- DCR E 1D
- DCR H 25
- DCR L 2D
- DCR M 35
- DCX B 0B
- DCX D 1B
- DCX H 2B
- DCX SP 3B

Specials
- DAA* 27
- CMA 2F
- STC† 37
- CMC† 3F

Rotate†
- RLC 07
- RRC 0F
- RAL 17
- RAR 1F

Logical*
- ANA A A7
- ANA B A0
- ANA C A1
- ANA D A2
- ANA E A3
- ANA H A4
- ANA L A5
- ANA M A6
- XRA A AF
- XRA B A8
- XRA C A9
- XRA D AA
- XRA E AB
- XRA H AC
- XRA L AD
- XRA M AE
- ORA A B7
- ORA B B0
- ORA C B1
- ORA D B2
- ORA E B3
- ORA H B4
- ORA L B5
- ORA M B6
- CMP A BF
- CMP B B8
- CMP C B9
- CMP D BA
- CMP E BB
- CMP H BC
- CMP L BD
- CMP M BE

Arith & Logical immediate
- ADI byte C6
- ACI byte CE
- SUI byte D6
- SBI byte DE
- ANI byte E6
- XRI byte EE
- ORI byte F6
- CPI byte FE

Figure 23.9 The 8080/8085 instruction set.

Reproduced by permission of Intel Corp.

ble I/O lines, full-duplex UART, two 16-bit timer/event counters, special Boolean processor, multiply and divide instructions, 4K of ROM, 128 bytes of RAM (externally expandable to 64K), and five-source/two-priority nested interrupts.

8080/8085 Peripheral Chips

As with the 6800, the 8080/8085 family offers a seemingly endless variety of peripheral chips. A few of the more common are listed below next to their comparable Motorola versions.

	Intel	Motorola
PIA	8255A	6821
Interrupt Controller	8259	6828
U(S)ART	8251A	6850
Timer	8253	6840
CRT Controller	8275	6835

THE ZILOG GROUP

After the 8080 was developed, the design team at Intel split—some staying at Intel to develop the 8085, and others moving to Zilog to develop the Z80. As expected, with similar architecture and instruction set, the 8085 and Z80 show the effects of their common 8080 ancestry.

The Z80 Basic Architecture

Figure 23.11 compares the basic architecture of the Z80 side by side with the 8085 and 6800. Like the 6800, the Z80 does not multiplex its address or data lines. Therefore, all 16 address and 8 bidirectional data lines are fully decoded and ready to tie directly into the system bus.

Like the 8085 and 6800, the Z80 requires only a single 5-volt dc supply. However, on Z80 and 6800 systems, the clock must be supplied externally, while the 8085 has integrated all clock circuitry, requiring only an external crystal.

As seen in Figure 23.11, the 8085 internal registers are a subset of the expanded Z80 register set. The basic register and flag set of the 8085 are duplicated to provide two sets of internal registers (register storage is often preferred over memory storage because of its faster access time). The interrupt-vector register (I) and memory-refresh register (R) are not found on either the 6800 or 8080/8085 processors.

Memory and I/O Control

The four control signals of the Z80 ($\overline{MREQ}$, $\overline{IORQ}$, $\overline{RD}$, and $\overline{WR}$) are designed to drive an isolated I/O system. Figure

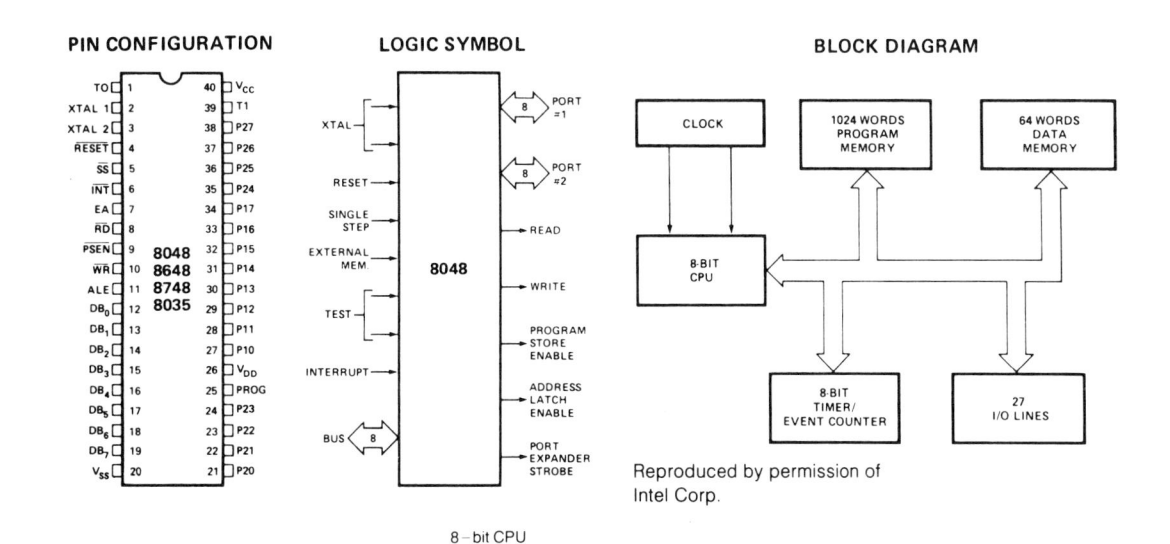

Figure 23.10 Basic architecture, pin-out, and major features of the 8048.

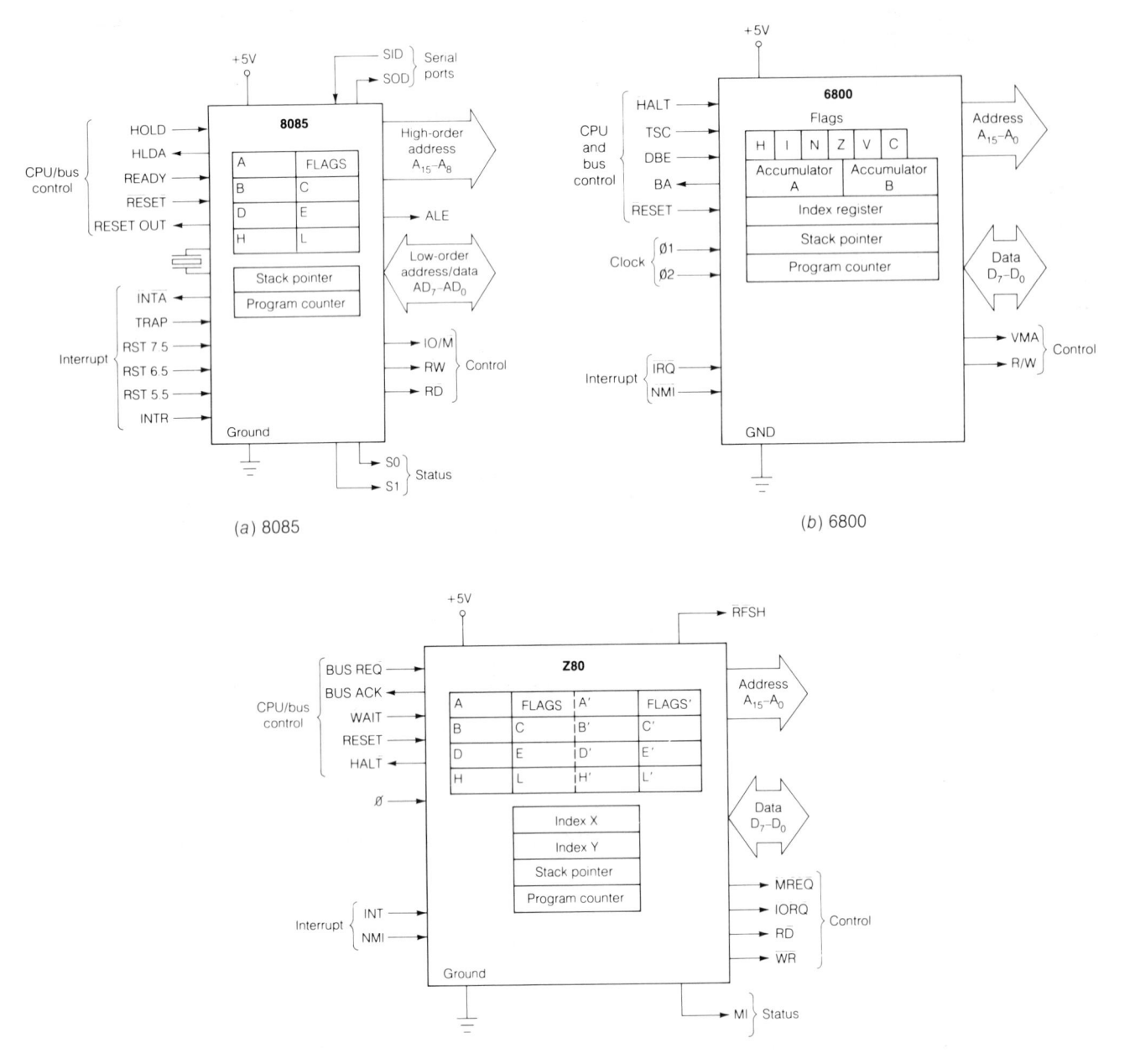

Figure 23.11 Comparison of 8085, 6800, and Z80 architecture.

23.12 shows the interfacing circuitry for each of the four basic data-transfer operations.

6800	Z80	8080/8085
TSC/DBE	WAIT	READY
HALT	BUSREQ	HOLD
BA	BUSACK	HLDA
RESET	RESET	RESET

CPU and Bus Control

As shown below (also refer to Figure 23.11), the CPU and bus-control signals all have direct counterparts on 8080/8085 and 6800 systems (HALT indicates the Z80 has executed a HALT instruction):

Interrupts

Two pins in the Z80 ($\overline{\text{INT}}$ and $\overline{\text{NMI}}$) are reserved for interrupt processing. All but one of the features of the interrupt system have counterparts in the 8085 system.

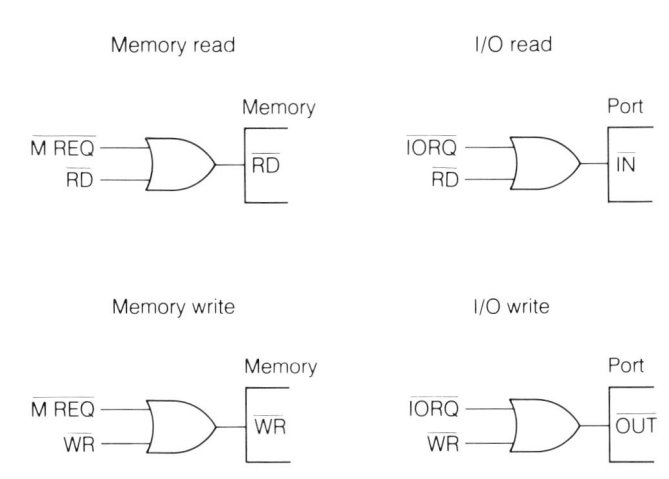

Figure 23.12 Z80 data-transfer control.

- $\overline{NMI}$ *(Non-Maskable Interrupt)* $\overline{NMI}$ is similar to the 8085's TRAP—it has the highest priority and cannot be masked out or disabled. When $\overline{NMI}$ is recognized, it performs a restart vectored interrupt to location 0066H.
- $\overline{INT}$ *(Interrupt)* With three possible modes of operation, the $\overline{INT}$ input of the Z80 is more complex than the INTR of the 8085. Each of the three modes is selected by software execution of the IM0, IM1, or IM2 instruction.

Mode 0 is similar to the INTR input of the 8085, and initiates a RESTART jam into the instruction register from external circuitry. Mode 1, set by the IM1 instruction, turns the $\overline{INT}$ input into an 8085-type RST 7 input, causing an automatic RESTART vector to location 0038H with no external circuitry required.

Mode 2, the most powerful of the three modes, is not represented on the 8085 or 6800. Mode 2 allows up to 128 interrupt vectors to *anywhere* in memory. To form the 16-bit interrupt vector, the Z80 combines an 8-bit low-order address with an 8-bit high order address supplied by the contents of the interrupt-vector register. Mode 2 is usually implemented by placing a vector table of up to 256 locations in memory at the page indicated by the I register. The table has up to 128 two-byte entries, with each entry representing the starting location of an interrupt-service routine. When a mode 2 interrupt is requested, the 8-bit value pulled from external circuitry is merged with the contents of the I register to point to a location within the vector table. The PC is loaded with the contents of the selected vector-table location, effectively causing a jump to the interrupt-service routine.

Memory Refresh

From the standpoint of the external circuitry, refreshing dynamic memory is basically a counting operation. A 6- or 7-bit row address is sent to the memory, along with a refresh-enable pulse. When that row of memory cells has been refreshed, the counter is incremented and the process repeated. In a Z80 system, the memory-refresh register (R) contains the 6- or 7-bit row address, while $\overline{RFSH}$ and $\overline{MREQ}$ (when both are simultaneously low) constitute the refresh-enable signal, informing the memory that the least significant 7 bits of the address bus contain the contents of the R register. Register R is automatically incremented after each refresh operation.

Z80 Timing

Driven by a 2.5 to 4 MHz clock, the basic clock speed of the Z80 is similar to the 8085. The basic state, machine-cycle, instruction-cycle breakdown is also very similar to that of the 8085, reflecting their common lineage.

Addressing Modes

The addressing modes available to the Z80 programmer exceed those available to the 8085 programmer. As shown in the following list, however, all but three (those starred) have counterparts in an 8085 system:

Z80	8085 counterpart
immediate	immediate
extended immediate	16-bit immediate
implied	(present but undefined)
register	register
register indirect	register indirect
extended	direct
modified page zero	restart
*relative	
*indexed	
*bit	

Relative and *indexed addressing* are similar to those used by the 6800; *bit addressing* can be used with any of the previous addressing modes to set, reset, or test any bit of any register or memory location.

The Z80 Instruction Set

The 158 instruction types making up the Z80 instruction set include the 8080 instruction set as a subset. Besides all the 8080 instructions, it features block transfers of data between memory and I/O, additional arithmetic instructions for efficient data processing, and bit operations on any location in memory. Although it is not possible to review all 86 new instructions, a few examples will show the extent of the Z80 instructions available.

332 Part IV / Applications and Interfacing: Living in a Real World

LDIR

| 1 | 1 | 1 | 0 | 1 | 1 | 0 | 1 |
| 1 | 0 | 1 | 1 | 0 | 0 | 0 | 0 |

H 20 L 00 → Source block 2000 ... 20FF → Destination block 3000 ... 30FF ← D 30 E 00

B 01 C 00

(a) LDIR block-transfer process

RES 5, (IY + 40H)

| 1 | 1 | 1 | 1 | 1 | 1 | 0 | 1 |
| 1 | 1 | 0 | 0 | 1 | 0 | 1 | 1 |

} Op-code

| 0 | 1 | 0 | 0 | 0 | 0 | 0 | 0 |

} Displacement

| 1 | 0 | 1 | 0 | 1 | 1 | 1 | 0 |

—— Bit 5 address

DJNZ e

| 0 | 0 | 0 | 1 | 0 | 0 | 0 | 0 |

Memory map

2000 Index
+ 0040 Displacement
———
2040

Location 2040, Bit 5 = 0

B = B − 1 → Yes → B ≠ 0 ? → No   DJNZ e

(c) A single-instruction delay loop using the DJNZ e instruction

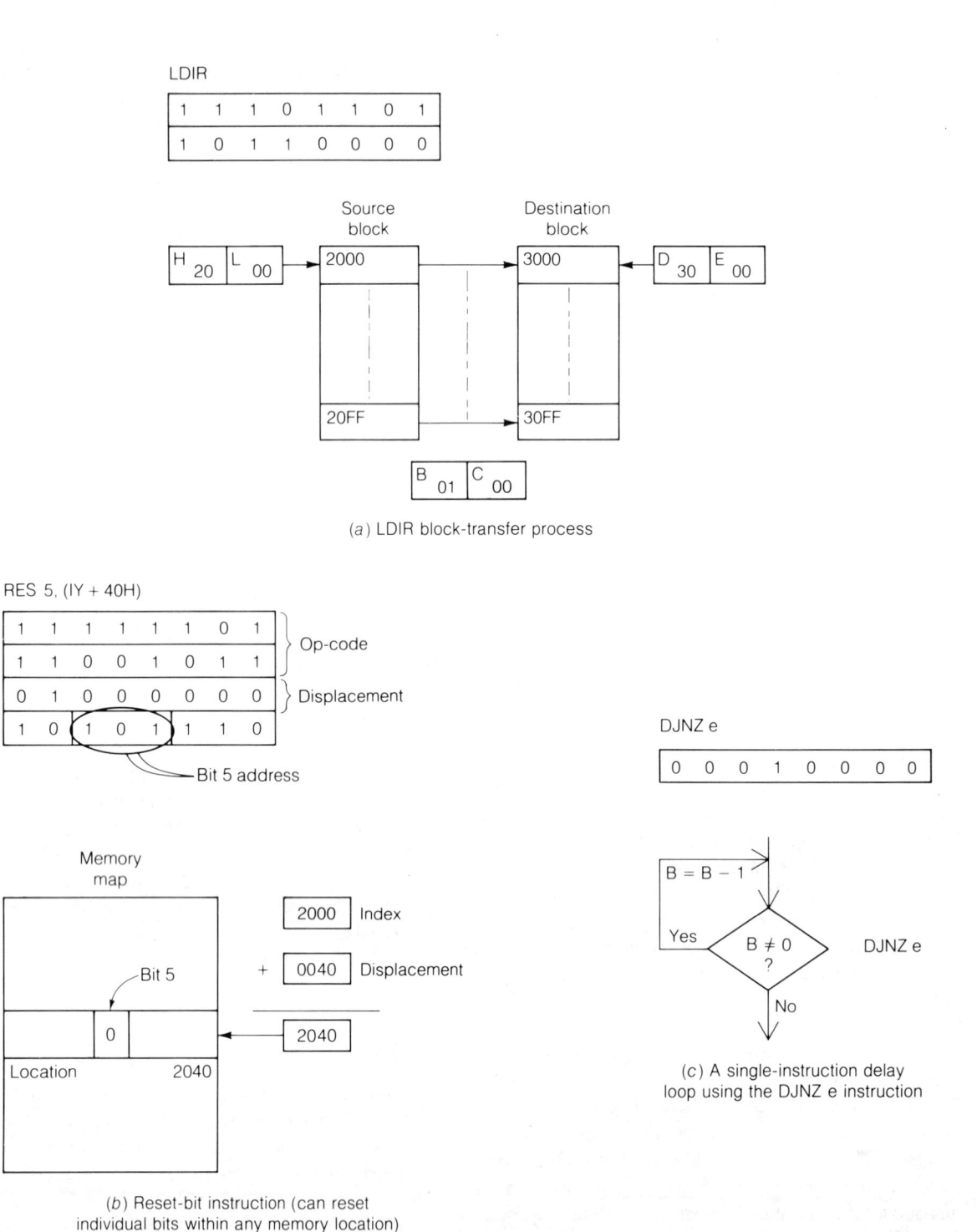

(b) Reset-bit instruction (can reset individual bits within any memory location)

Figure 23.13 Typical Z80 instruction types not found in the 8080/8085 and 6800 instruction sets.

Example 1 By entering into a repetitive loop, the Load-Increment-Repeat (LDIR) instruction transfers a *block* of data (from 1 to 64K bytes) from one area in memory to another area in memory, one byte at a time. Before using this instruction, three register pairs must be preset: register pair HL is initialized to the starting address of the source block, register pair DE to the starting address of the destination block, and register pair BC initialized to the number of bytes to be transferred. Assuming one page of data is to be transferred from memory page 20H to memory page 30H, Figure 23.13a shows the coded instruction and pertinent registers.

Example 2 The RES b, (IX + d) instruction resets a selected bit within the contents of a memory location specified by indexed addressing. For example, if bit 5 of memory location 2040 is to be reset, the process is as shown in Figure 23.13b.

Example 3 The Decrement and Jump on Nonzero (DJNZ e) instruction (Figure 23.13c) combines the decrement and JNZ processes, and implements a delay loop with just a single instruction. The DJNZ e instruction automatically decrements the B register, jumping to itself if the result is nonzero. When B is decremented to zero, control passes to the next instruction in sequence.

The Z8 Microcomputer

The Z8 is Zilog's entry in the single-chip field. Like the 6801 and 8048, the Z8 emphasizes those features particularly well suited for real-time control applications: fast instruction execution, fast interrupt response, on-chip I/O ports, and a 47-member instruction set weighted in favor of bit manipulation, conditional branching, table lookup, and BCD operations.

Figure 23.14 reveals the major architectural features of the Z8. For stand-alone operation, it offers 2K of internal ROM, 128 bytes of RAM, 32 I/O lines, a 144-byte register file, and two timer/counters. Of special interest is the on-chip asynchronous receiver/transmitter (UART), designed to reduce the software overhead for serial data-communication applications.

Further enhancing its image as a single-chip microcomputer, the Z8 blends in features of the programmable peripheral chip. By designating 16 locations of the internal register file as status and control registers, the Z8 can be *self-programmed* to assume a number of configurations, ranging from a stand-alone microcomputer, to a traditional microprocessor with up to 124K of external memory, to a parallel processing element in a multiprocessing system. The four I/O ports, for example, can be configured under program control to provide timing, status, address outputs (for system expansion), and serial or parallel I/O with or without handshake.

A number of versions of the Z8, including a 64-pin development version, complete the Z8 single-chip field.

BIT-SLICE PROCESSORS

Although not part of the 8-bit microprocessor family tree, bit-slice processors are mentioned because they represent an alternative to the basic, general-purpose, fixed-word-size microprocessor (such as those discussed in this chapter).

The original impetus for a bit-slice configuration was the need for higher and higher speed. Ultrahigh-speed processors generally must be fashioned from bipolar or ECL technology. However, these technologies are of low density and high power dissipation—properties that do not lend themselves to large-scale integration. The solution is to construct the CPU from individual building blocks called *bit-slice chips*. Typically based on a 4-bit format, each bit slice is a section of a complete arithmetic/logic unit along with its multiplexers and data paths. The control logic and microinstruction ROM are provided separately. By combining these bit slices in parallel, a computer structure of nearly any word size can be constructed. Since bit-slice processors usually are dedicated to a specific task, the microprograms (and therefore the instruction set) are also custom designed by the user.

Because of the availability and low cost of general-purpose microprocessors, few applications can justify the added expense of the bit-slice custom-design approach.

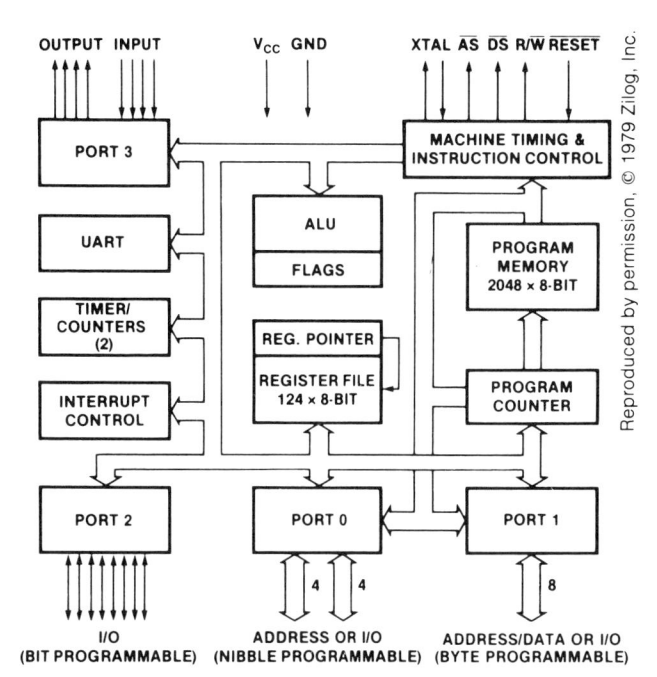

Figure 23.14 The Z8 internal block diagram.

INTELLIGENT-MACHINE UPDATE

Showing a high degree of similarity, all 8-bit microprocessors belong to the same family. Although one particular member of the family may be better suited for a specific application, in general a system can be designed around any 8-bit microprocessor. But, as we have seen in this book, a microcomputer and a human being also show a great deal of similarity. As computer and medical technology improve, will these two beings—microprocessor and human—gradually merge into a single life form?

QUESTIONS AND PROBLEMS

1. Name several hardware features that all microprocessors have in common.
2. What information is multiplexed with the data on an 8080 data bus? On an 8085 data bus?
3. Which one of the 8080/8085's internal register pairs performs indirect addressing?
4. What register pair within the 8080/8085 is similar to the 6800's MAR?
5. Name several advantages of *isolated I/O*.
6. What are the states of the IO/$\overline{\text{M}}$, $\overline{\text{RD}}$, and $\overline{\text{WR}}$ 8085 control lines during a memory read? During an I/O write?
7. Why is ROM in an 8080/8085 system placed at the bottom (lowest memory location) of the memory map (opposite from that of the 6800)?
8. How is a DMA request made to an 8080/8085 processor?
9. On an 8080/8085, what signal input is used when interfacing a slow memory?
10. What are the differences between a HOLD state and a WAIT state on an 8080/8085 system?
11. List the steps that take place from start to finish when an RST 6.5 interrupt is requested on an 8085.
12. How does an 8085 implement a non-maskable interrupt (NMI)?
13. On an 8080/8085 system, what occurs during a *machine cycle*?
14. During an 8085 data transfer, what two signals time the actual flow of data from source to destination?
15. What 6800 addressing mode is not found in the 8080/8085 instruction set?
16. In general terms, how do the 8080/8085 mnemonics distinguish one addressing mode from another? How does this compare to the 6800?
17. Interface an 8282 input port to a Z80 bus system.
18. How do we set up the Z80 for DMA activities?
19. In a Z80 mode 2 interrupt, how is the starting address of the interrupt-service routine determined?
20. What is the difference between *relative* and *indexed* addressing?
21. What Z80 instruction combines both the flag setting and the conditional branch into a single instruction?
22. What is a *bit slice*?

chapter 24

Putting It All Together: An Application

The human race has survived and prospered because it has used its unique tools—hands and brain—to overcome and shape the environment. From the wheel to the space shuttle, the application of our special structure has changed the way we live.

The computer must also prove its worth by application—by solving real-world problems and by performing a variety of tasks efficiently and reliably. Usually these are tasks that we do not wish to do at all or that a computer can do better. One such task is the subject of this chapter: a microprocessor-controlled lunar-landing simulator. Emphasizing control rather than data processing, the system will be taken from initial conception to block-level design, leaving the final hardware design and machine-language program as a laboratory project.

LUNAR-LANDING SIMULATOR

The computer is an ideal simulation device, for training can take place without expensive equipment or the threat of disaster if a mistake is made. Our project involves the simulation of a landing on the moon by controlling a small model of the lunar landing vehicle (LLV). This application will be more challenging than most, for the system must operate at moderate speed in real time and must perform some rather complex mathematical calculations.

Hardware Design

Our hardware design (Figure 24.1) adopts the data-acquisition technique of Chapter 18 (Figure 18.11) and shows the use of a stepper motor to control altitude without resorting to complex feedback paths. Our throttle level and gravitational reference are both input from simple potentiometers (giving us the ability to simulate landing under varying gravitational loads). A pink-noise generator simulates thrust (in this case, the generation of thrust noise is more easily handled by hardware). Note that port A handles five output signals and one input signal, a combination easily accommodated by properly programming port A's data direction register (DDRA). The use of a single register to hold several pieces of data is called *packing*.

Software Design

Our moon-landing simulator program consists of two major parts:

- Calculation of velocity from input thrust and gravity
- Use of velocity parameters to generate the required stepper-motor waveforms

From Chapter 20, we know that, if the inputs to a four-phase stepper motor are properly matched to the bit positions of the output port, the generation of stepper-motor waveforms reduces to a simple series of rotate operations (Figure 24.2). The direction of rotation controls the direction of velocity (up or down), and the delay number sent to the delay loop controls the velocity by specifying the time interval between rotate operations. By continually updating the velocity and direction parameters, the velocity of the LLV can be controlled accurately (the parameters are passed from the math routine to the stepper-motor routine).

Generating the correct velocity parameters to send to the stepper-motor routine is more challenging, for simulating flight dynamics—even in one dimension—requires some advanced mathematics.

To convert thrust and gravity into altitude, we must process the steps indicated by Figure 24.3. The thrust of the lunar lander's engines is subtracted from the force of gravity (weight of the LLV), and, after the mass of the vehicle is divided out, the resulting net acceleration is *integrated* to give the velocity of the LLV. (If we normalize out the effects of mass during system calibration, the divide step is not required.)

To complete our software development, it is clear we must first understand the concept of integration.

Integration (a part of calculus) is closely related to *multiplication*. In fact, multiplication is a special form of integration. To see the difference, consider the following simple problem:

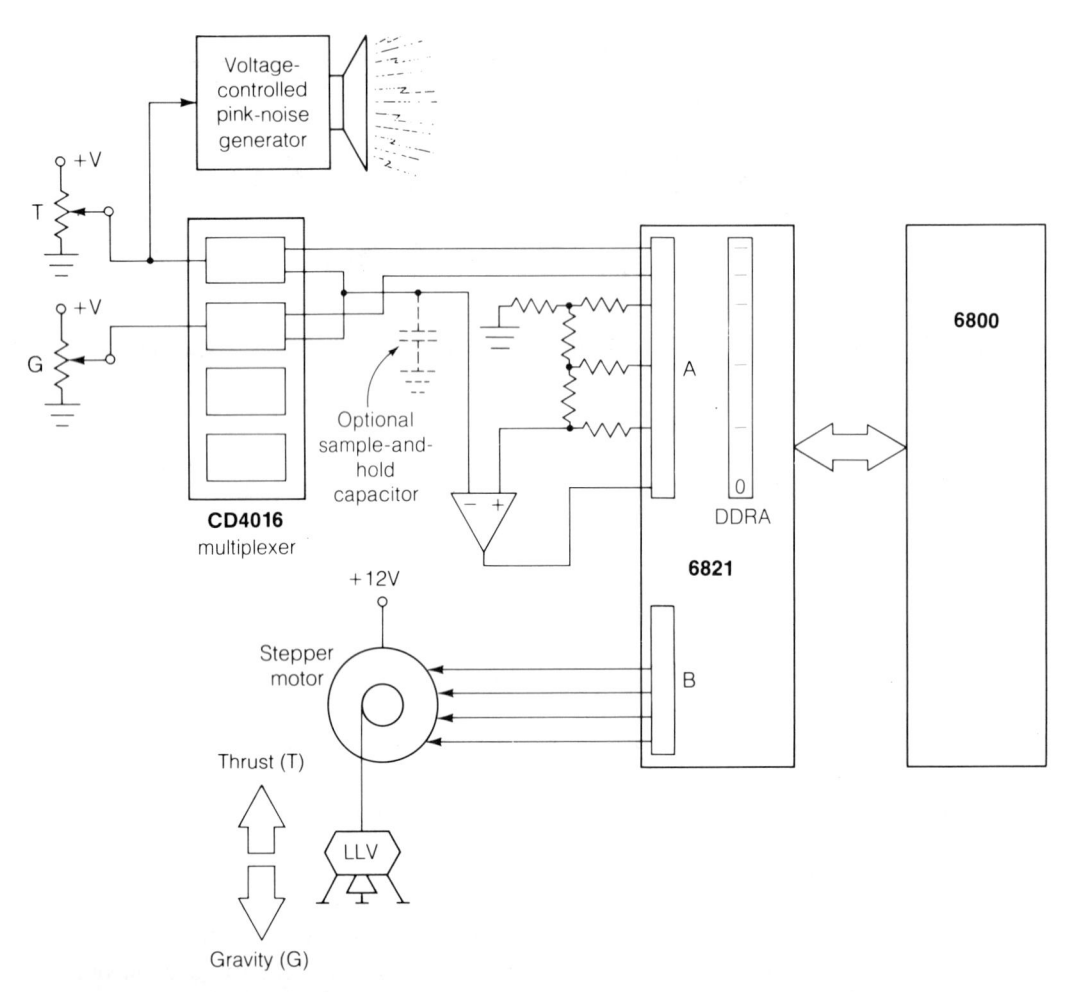

Figure 24.1 Hardware design for lunar-landing simulator.

If we travel 50 miles per hour (mi/h) for 3 hours, how far will we have gone?

The answer—150 miles—is obtained by the mathematical process of multiplication. That is, we multiply the speed (50 mi/h) by the time (3 hours) to obtain the distance (150 miles):

Distance = velocity × time
150 miles = 50 mi/h × 3 hours

The same problem can also be solved graphically as shown in Figure 24.4. If velocity and time are plotted as the y and x axes of a two-dimensional coordinate system, the solution to the problem (150) is represented by the area of the rectangle bounded by the 50 mi/h and 3-hour points. Or, to use more precise terminology, the answer is equal to the *area under the velocity curve*.

Now we will make one seemingly small change in the original problem, and the whole nature of the solution will change. This time, the velocity does not remain constant over the 3-hour period, but becomes a *variable*. How do we "multiply" velocity and time when velocity is a variable? The answer is: we must *integrate*. Below we compare the symbolism of integration with that of simple multiplication. If velocity can be expressed as a mathematical function of time, the problem can be solved using the methods of calculus:

Multiplication (velocity is a constant)	*Integration* (velocity is a variable)
$D = V \times t$	$D = \int_{o}^{t} V(t)\,dt$
$150 = 50 \times 3$	

Fortunately, for those unfamiliar with the mathematical techniques of integration, there is an alternative: the graphical method using the area under the curve. If velocity varies according to the curve of Figure 24.5a, what graphical quantity is equal to the distance traveled? The answer, of course, is *the area under the velocity curve*. When the velocity turns negative, as it does at the $3\frac{1}{2}$-second point, then the generated

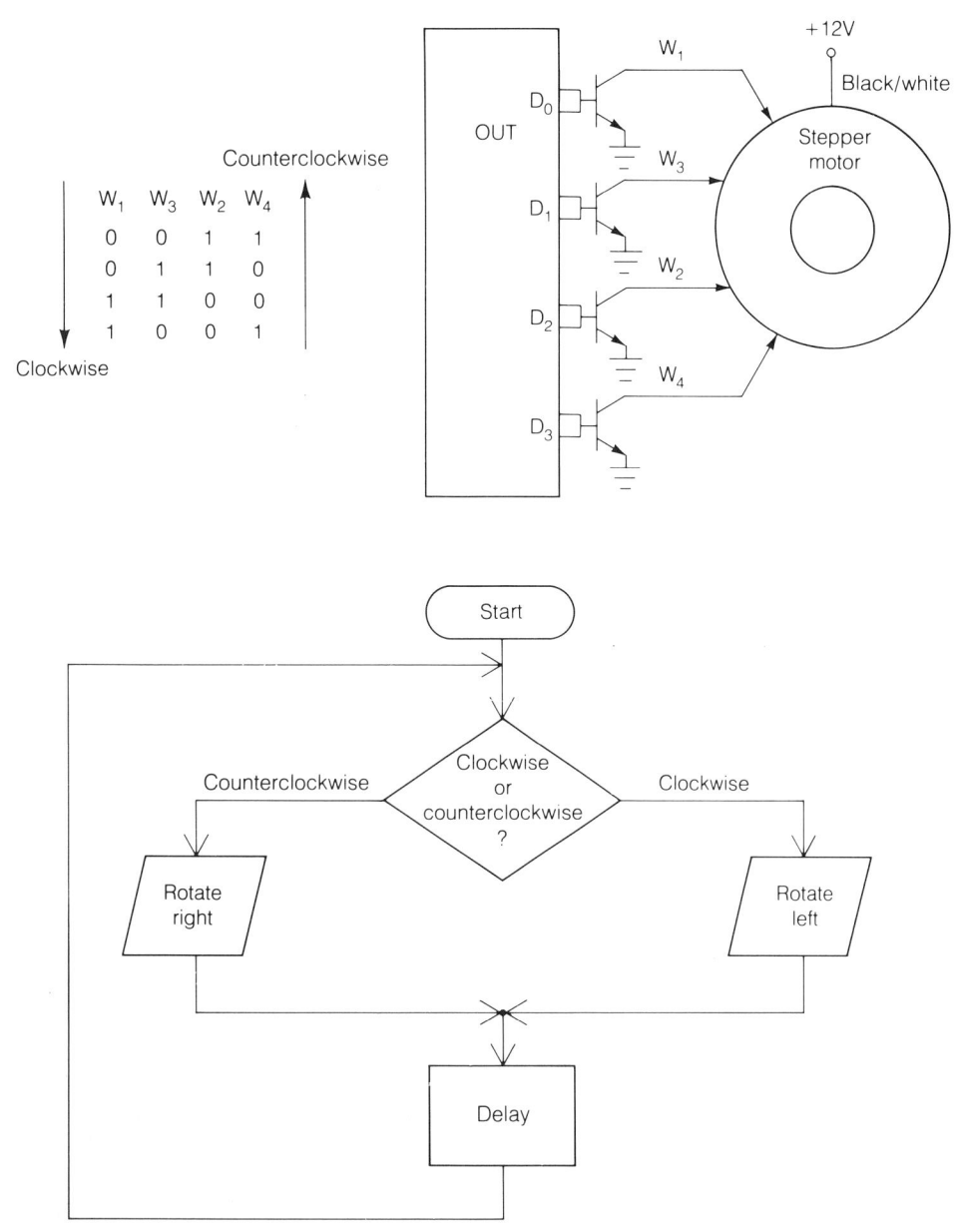

Figure 24.2 Stepper-motor control.

area is also negative and must be subtracted from the positive area above the *x* axis. Since the velocity of our lunar lander will be both positive and negative, we will use signed numbers to handle the situation.

But how can we determine the area under an *analog* curve by calculations on a *digital* computer? Figure 24.5b shows us how—by approximating the curve with a series of thin rectangular elements. By adding the areas of the rectangular elements, we can approximate the area of the total curve.

If the points are sampled one second apart, as shown, then the area under a velocity/time curve (the distance) can be calculated by simply adding together the velocity values (height) of each elemental area. If we sample more often, say four times per second, then the velocity values of each element must be divided by 4 (shift right two times) in order to obtain the proper area. (The divide step can also be normalized out when the system is scaled and calibrated.)

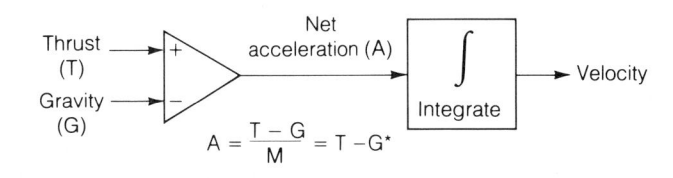

$$A = \frac{T - G}{M} = T - G^*$$

*Mass has been normalized to 1

Figure 24.3 Calculating velocity from thrust and gravity.

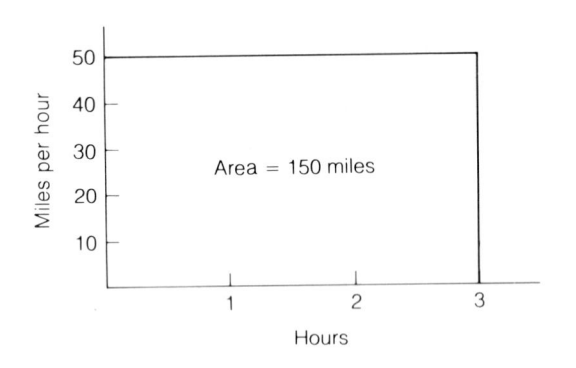

Figure 24.4 Graphical method of multiplying.

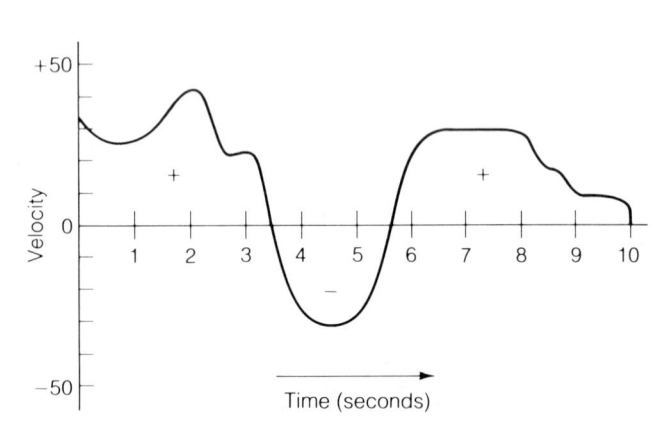

150 miles = 50 miles/hour × 3 hours

(a) Calculating distance when velocity is a variable

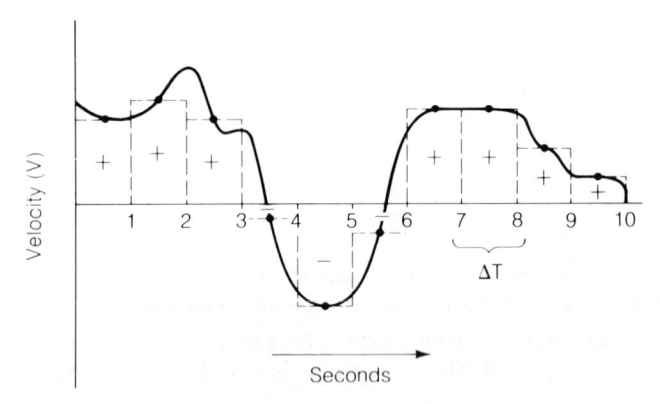

(b) Approximating the area under the curve by summing incremental elements

$$D = \sum_{0}^{10} V\Delta T = \sum_{0}^{10} V$$

If $\Delta T = 1$

Figure 24.5 Integration techniques for a computer.

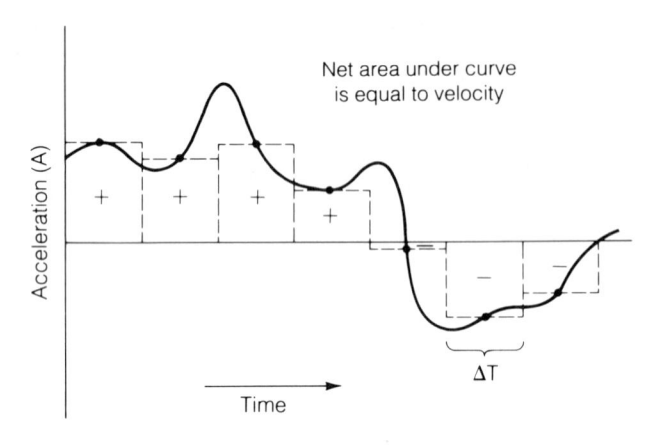

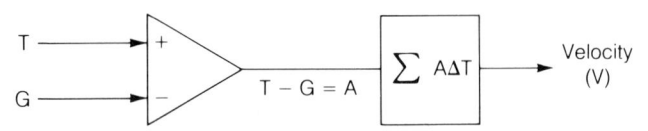

Figure 24.6 Approximating velocity from thrust and gravity.

Again we subtract the negative elements (negative velocity) from the positive elements (positive velocity).

We now have all the mathematical expertise to calculate velocity from acceleration (rather than distance from velocity as we have been doing) and complete our velocity routine. By definition, *velocity is equal to acceleration multiplied by time,* but that is true only if acceleration is a constant. In our situation, since we can vary the thrust of the LLV, the net acceleration most certainly is not a constant—so we must integrate. But integration, we know, can be approximated by a summation (we sum together the small incremental elements of acceleration/time). The mathematical calculations are shown in Figure 24.6.

Converting the mathematics into a computer routine is easy, for we calculate the real-time velocity by keeping a running (cumulative) total of the sampled acceleration values. That is, as each thrust/gravitation reference level is sampled in real time, the calculated acceleration value is added to a *cumulative-total register.* The contents of the cumulative-total register at any time equals the present LLV velocity. (Effects of the sampling rate are normalized out during calibration.) Since we are using signed numbers, we automatically know both the direction and the magnitude. Converting our ideas into a flowchart (Figure 24.7), the second major part (module) of our lunar-lander program is documented.

The final software-development task is to integrate (combine) the two software routines into a single processing system, remembering that each routine *independently* obeys strict timing standards:

• The stepper-motor routine must rotate the waveform out-

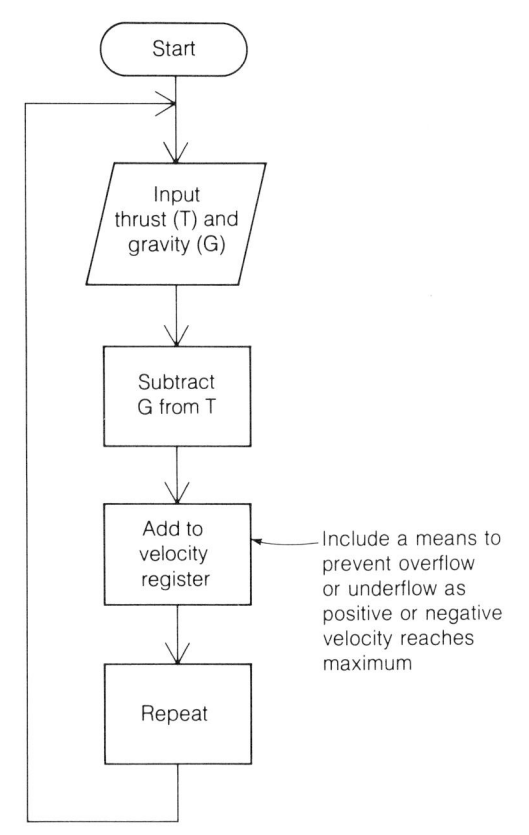

Figure 24.7 Math-routine flowchart for calculation of velocity from thrust and gravity.

Flowchart: Start → Input thrust (T) and gravity (G) → Subtract G from T → Add to velocity register (Include a means to prevent overflow or underflow as positive or negative velocity reaches maximum) → Repeat (loops back to Start).

puts at a rate dependent on the velocity parameter sent to the delay block.

- The velocity routine—which calculates the velocity from the acceleration using the summation technique—requires the computer to sample the thrust and gravitational reference inputs at regular intervals (four times each second in our case).

The following are three ways in which we may approach the problem of processing the two independent routines on a single microcomputer system (Figure 24.8):

1. We may adopt a purely software approach, remaining in the stepper-motor routine and dropping out after each $\frac{1}{4}$ second to perform a single math routine (velocity update).
2. We can interrupt the stepper-motor routine at the 4 Hz rate, passing to the math routine at the required intervals.
3. We can turn over the stepper-motor processes to a slave processor, sending updated velocity information at the 4 Hz rate.

Method 1 would be difficult to implement because the amount of time spent in the stepper-motor routine would depend on the velocity parameter. Method 3 involves a slave processor—a technique with which we are not all that familiar. Therefore, method 2—the interrupt method—appears to be the best choice.

Using the interrupt technique, a 555 timer, running at 4 Hz, will interrupt the computer and allow the thrust and gravitational reference values to be sampled at regular intervals and the velocity to be updated at the 4 Hz rate. (The small amount of interrupt time spent in the math routine will not significantly affect the stepper-motor timing.)

Our complete hardware/software design is given in Figure 24.9. The final system design is left as an exercise. (Appendix V offers several suggestions and comments for fully implementing the lunar-landing simulator design.)

Modifications and Improvements

In real life an LLV has a limited amount of fuel aboard and must be landed before the fuel is expended. We assume the rate at which the fuel is consumed is proportional to the thrust. Therefore, to simulate the effects of fuel consumption, subtract the incremental thrust inputs (or fraction thereof) from a register holding an initial fuel value. When the fuel runs out, we inhibit the thrust input and the vehicle goes into free fall. In addition to varying the gravitational pull, we can allow the total amount of on-board fuel to be set at various levels to vary the skill factor. Of course, it would be helpful to display the fuel level as it is consumed.

As time goes by and fuel is consumed, the LLV becomes lighter and the thrust is more effective in producing acceleration. To simulate this action, we can add increasing values to the thrust input as the fuel is consumed (a high degree of simulation accuracy here requires advanced mathematics).

If we wish to output the LLV velocity at the time of impact (to determine the probable LLV damage and passenger injury), we may include a sensor at the surface impact point. An interrupt would cause the contents of the velocity register to be displayed at the time of impact. As an alternative, we could integrate the velocity to produce the distance. When the distance register equals zero, we would stop stepper-motor action and output the contents of the velocity register.

Many other modifications are possible—including two-dimensional motion—as we strive for greater and greater simulation accuracy.

INTELLIGENT-MACHINE UPDATE

By performing a variety of tasks—often more efficiently than its human counterparts—our intelligent machine has proven its worth. Like a band of sorcerers, microprocessors will now fan out across the land, taking each passive and stoic machine they come across—from an airplane to a zoom lens—and infusing it with the magic of intelligence.

(a) Software method

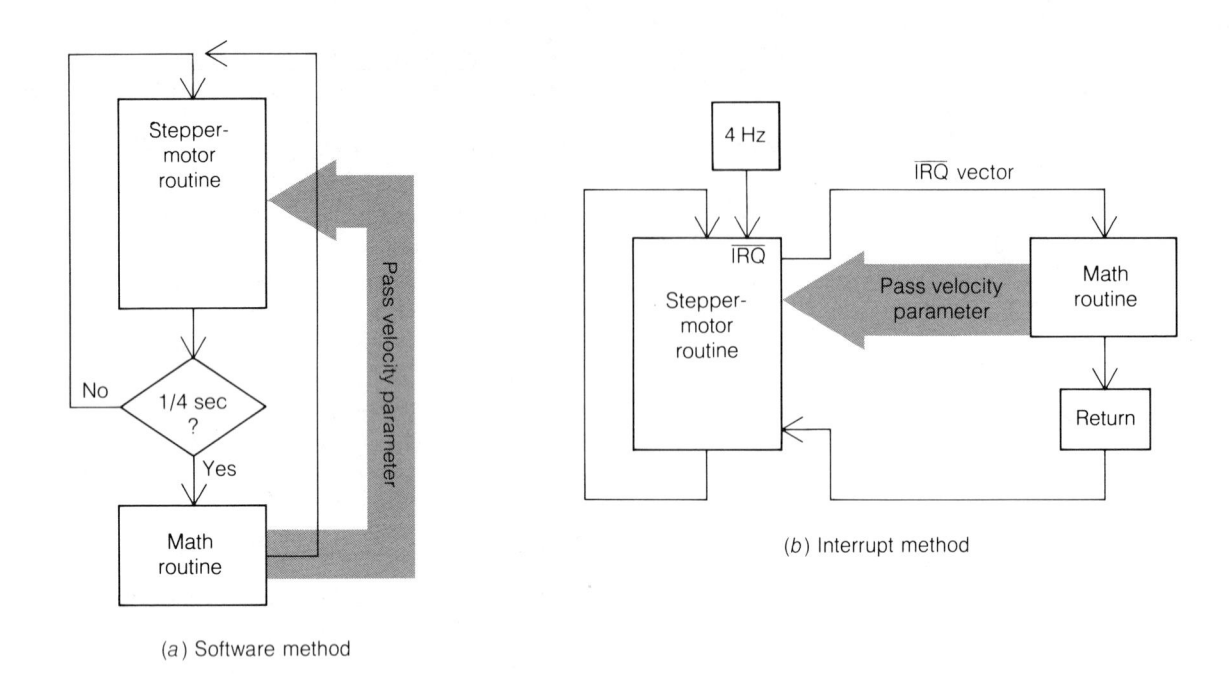

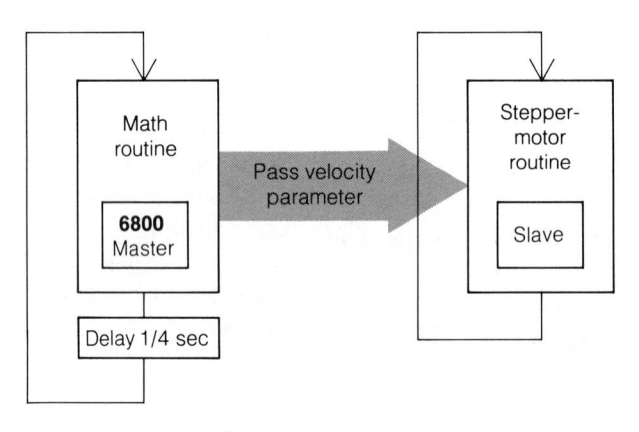

(b) Interrupt method

(c) Slave processor method

Figure 24.8 Three methods of processing two independent routines on a single processing system.

QUESTIONS AND PROBLEMS

1. Why did we choose to design our LLV system around a microprocessor rather than use combinational logic?
2. What are the two major components of a data-acquisition system?
3. Why does a stepper motor not require feedback?
4. Design a simple pink-noise generator circuit using the junction noise of a reverse-biased, open-collector transistor.
5. What is the difference between *multiplication* and *integration*?
6. What determines the theoretical accuracy of the summation approximation of an integral?
7. Why must the numbers used in our velocity calculation of the LLV be *signed* numbers?
8. What three techniques are available for combining two routines that have independent timing requirements?
9. Complete the hardware/software design of the lunar-landing simulator and test your design in the laboratory.

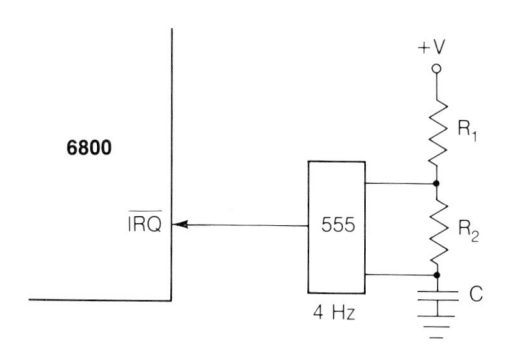

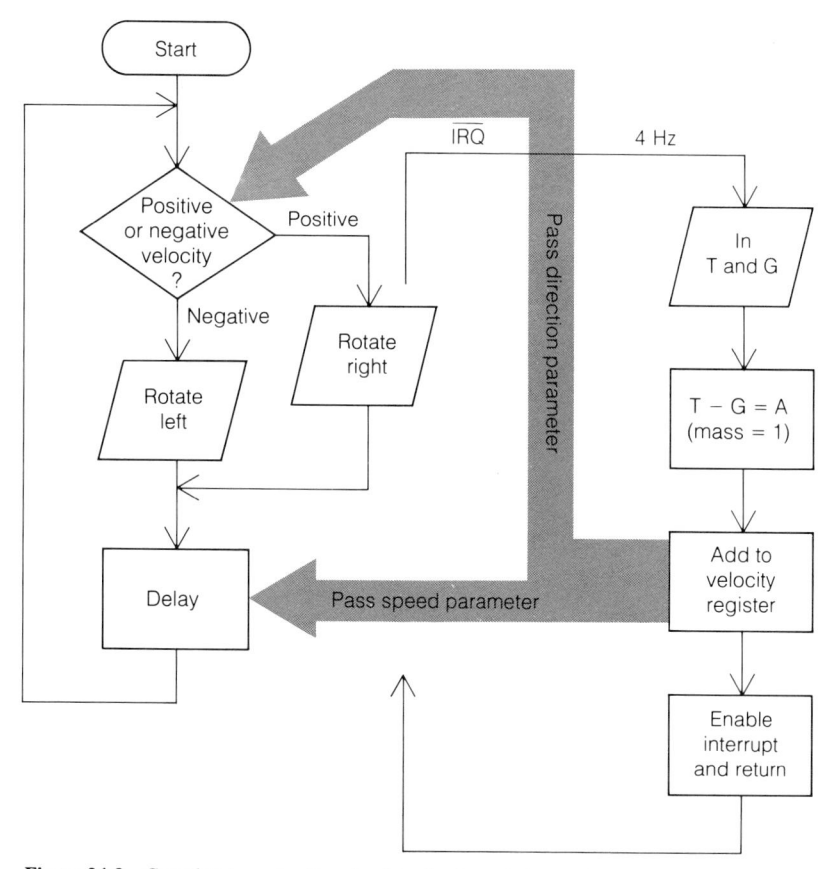

Figure 24.9 Complete lunar-landing simulator hardware/software design.

part V

Advanced Processors: The Newest Generation

Human development has reached a nearly level stage, or plateau, in the history of life. The human brain has not changed, at least in gross size, in the past 100,000 years. However, development of *intelligence* has not ended on earth, for *artificial intelligence*—the intelligence of the computer—is growing at a staggering pace, and there is no natural limit in sight.

In Part V we will introduce one of the more recent products of computer evolution: the 68000 16-bit microprocessor.

chapter 25

The 68000 16-Bit Microprocessor

The human mind is a living archaeological site. The deeper we go into the human brain, the farther back into history we travel—150 million years, to the oldest and most primitive brain structure, when mammals were just emerging. Such a system is hierarchical and parallel in nature. The outer, most recently developed cerebral cortex controls the higher-level abstract and most generalized processes, and sets system goals and priorities; the inner, most ancient levels handle simultaneously (in parallel) the detailed and specific actions that carry out the system goals.

Also hierarchical and parallel in nature are the 16-bit microprocessors. At the core of a 16-bit microprocessor we find remnants of the 8-bit architecture and instruction set. As we move away from the core, we find a complex multiprocessing system, specifically designed to operate from hierarchical code generated by a high-level language.

Add improved architecture and high-speed processing action, and we find in 16-bit microprocessors the beginnings of the fifth generation computer: high throughput, hierarchical in both hardware and software, and capable of parallel operation.

In this chapter we will examine the Motorola 68000 16-bit microprocessor. We will find that the 68000 has achieved a quantum jump in overall performance, and has expanded into areas once the sole property of minicomputers and mainframe computers.

THE 68000 AT A GLANCE

Comparing the architecture and pin-out of the 68000 side by side with the 6800 (Figure 25.1), it is easy to see why the 68000 provides an order-of-magnitude increase in overall performance.

The most evident features of the 68000 are its 16-bit data bus and 24-bit address bus, giving it a 16-megabyte *direct* addressing range—256 times greater than the 6800.

A brief look at the 19 internal registers will tell us a lot about the flexibility and power of the 68000. The eight 32-bit data registers (D_0 through D_7) can be used for byte (8-bit), word (16-bit), and long word (32-bit) operations. The eight address registers are used for based and indexed *indirect* addressing as well as for additional stack pointers (to avoid interference with mathematical operations, the condition flags are not changed by operations upon the address registers). The *status register* (Figure 25.2) is divided into two sections: a *system byte* holding interrupt mask bits and privilege state indicators, and a *user byte* holding flags for conditional branching.

The instruction set of the 68000 (Figure 25.3) offers 56 basic instruction types, including the usual data movement, arithmetic/logic, branch, and system-control operations. The instruction set is supported by 14 addressing modes and 5 basic data types. Interrupt requests are serviced by a multilevel interrupt structure, with 255 vector locations available.

Throughput is enhanced by arithmetic/logic units operating in parallel, one performing address calculations (calculating the effective address) and the other performing data calculations. Also increasing performance is the *prefetch queue*, which "looks ahead" and fetches future instructions during data bus "dead time" (it attempts to have available as much instruction information as possible before execution).

Fifth-generation concepts are inherent in the hardware of the 68000. The consistent architecture (highly regular and general with few special cases), multiple registers and stacks, and large addressing range provide for efficient processing of code compiled from a high-level modular language such as Pascal. In other words, the 68000 was designed for programmers as well as for hardware designers.

Parallel processing—another fifth-generation concept—is fully supported by built-in bus arbitration logic for multiple processors and shared resources.

68000 BUS INTERFACING

The 64 I/O signals of the 68000 are functionally grouped as shown in Figure 25.1. Let us briefly go over each of the nine groups.

Address Group

We know that 24 binary numbers are required to address 16 megabytes, yet the 68000 has only 23 address pins, labeled

Chapter 25 / The 68000 16-Bit Microprocessor **345**

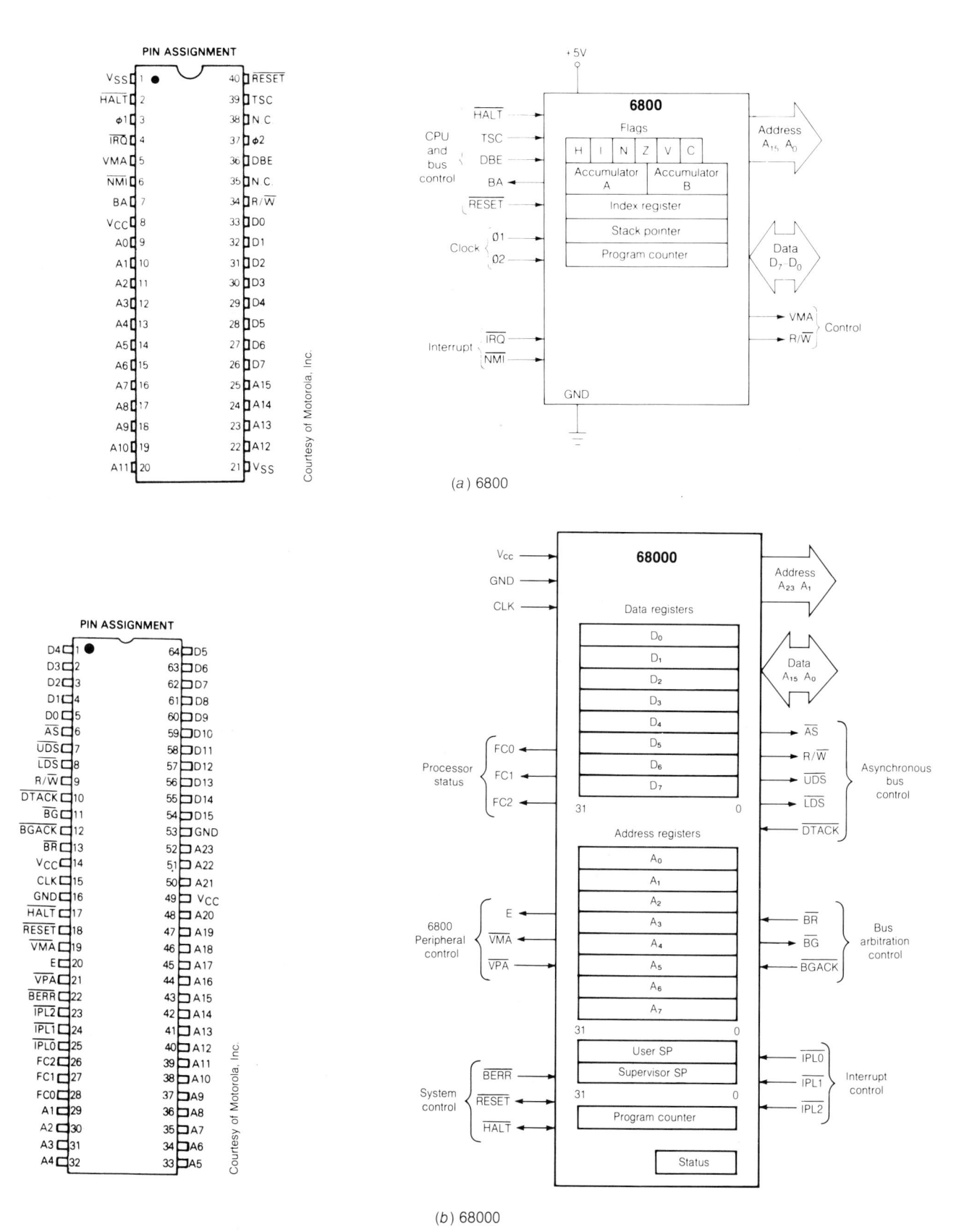

(a) 6800

(b) 68000

Figure 25.1 Comparison of 6800 and 68000 architecture and pin-out.

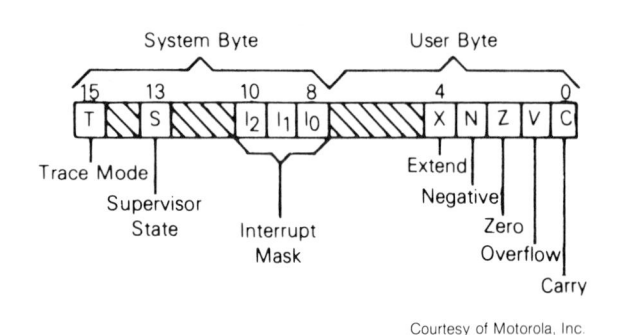

Figure 25.2 The 68000 status register, showing the system byte and user byte.

A_1 through A_{23}. Where is address line A_0? The answer is, A_0 is used internally to generate the $\overline{UDS}$ (Upper Data Strobe) and $\overline{LDS}$ (Lower Data Strobe) output control signals. When we see how data is organized in memory, we will know why.

Think of the 16-megabyte addressing space of the 68000 as consisting of 8 mega*words*. As shown in Figure 25.4, each word begins on an even address. However, for flexibility—especially when interfacing older 8-bit 6800 peripherals—it is essential that the 68000 be able to address individual bytes (either high order or low order) as well as whole words. That is where $\overline{LDS}$ and $\overline{UDS}$ come in. Addressing any byte or word in memory works as follows: First, address lines A_1 through A_{23} go active, essentially pointing to a word location.

- To access the lower byte of the addressed word, $\overline{LDS}$ goes active low.
- To access the upper byte of the addressed word, $\overline{UDS}$ goes active low.
- To access the entire word, both $\overline{UDS}$ and $\overline{LDS}$ go active low.

As demonstrated for the two 64K × 8 memory modules of Figure 25.5, the physical memory system for the 68000 is organized as bytewide memory units paired off to form words. When $\overline{LDS}$ goes active low, the low order unit is activated; when $\overline{UDS}$ goes active low, the high-order unit is activated; and when both $\overline{LDS}$ and $\overline{UDS}$ go active low, both units are activated simultaneously.

The Data Group

The 16 lines (D_0 through D_{15}) interfacing the data bus are standard bidirectional, three-state general purpose data paths, able to transfer and accept data in either word or byte length.

Asynchronous Bus Control Group

Along with the familiar R/$\overline{W}$ control signal (read when high; write when low) and the $\overline{LDS}/\overline{UDS}$ signals introduced earlier, are two new control signals unique to the 68000: Address Strobe ($\overline{AS}$) and Data Transfer Acknowledge ($\overline{DTACK}$). They are simple handshaking signals, used for asynchronous data transfers. Their main purpose is to allow the mixing of slow and fast memories or peripherals, with the processor automatically transferring each byte or word at the fastest rate possible.

Mnemonic	Description
ABCD	Add Decimal with Extend
ADD	Add
AND	Logical And
ASL	Arithmetic Shift Left
ASR	Arithmetic Shift Right
B$_{CC}$	Branch Conditionally
BCHG	Bit Test and Change
BCLR	Bit Test and Clear
BRA	Branch Always
BSET	Bit Test and Set
BSR	Branch to Subroutine
BTST	Bit Test
CHK	Check Register Against Bounds
CLR	Clear Operand
CMP	Compare
DB$_{CC}$	Test Condition, Decrement and Branch
DIVS	Signed Divide
DIVU	Unsigned Divide

Mnemonic	Description
EOR	Exclusive Or
EXG	Exchange Registers
EXT	Sign Extend
JMP	Jump
JSR	Jump to Subroutine
LEA	Load Effective Address
LINK	Link Stack
LSL	Logical Shift Left
LSR	Logical Shift Right
MOVE	Move
MOVEM	Move Multiple Registers
MOVEP	Move Peripheral Data
MULS	Signed Multiply
MULU	Unsigned Multiply
NBCD	Negate Decimal with Extend
NEG	Negate
NOP	No Operation
NOT	One's Complement
OR	Logical Or

Mnemonic	Description
PEA	Push Effective Address
RESET	Reset External Devices
ROL	Rotate Left without Extend
ROR	Rotate Right without Extend
ROXL	Rotate Left with Extend
ROXR	Rotate Right with Extend
RTE	Return from Exception
RTR	Return and Restore
RTS	Return from Subroutine
SBCD	Subtract Decimal with Extend
S$_{CC}$	Set Conditional
STOP	Stop
SUB	Subtract
SWAP	Swap Data Register Halves
TAS	Test and Set Operand
TRAP	Trap
TRAPV	Trap on Overflow
TST	Test
UNLK	Unlink

Courtesy of Motorola, Inc.

Figure 25.3 The 68000 instruction set.

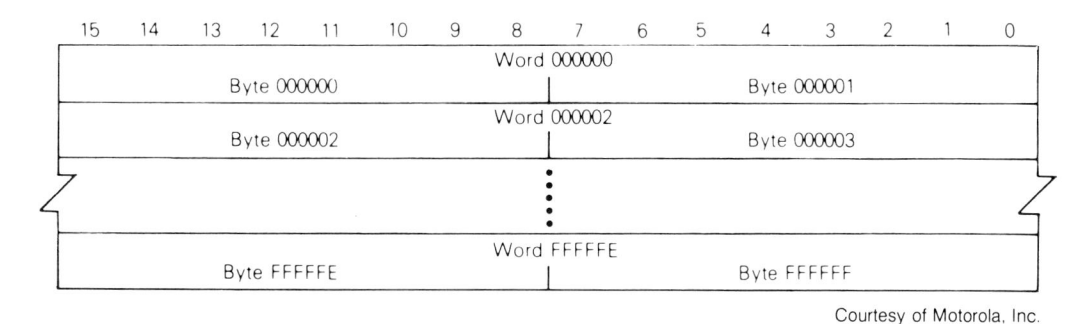

Figure 25.4 68000 byte/word organization in memory.

Bus Arbitration Control

The 68000 encourages the design of multiprocessor systems using a shared bus. In order to determine which device will be the bus master (have exclusive "rights" to the shared bus), the various devices must "talk to each other" by way of the three bus-arbitration control signals. The handshaking sequence is as follows:

- When a device wishes to be master, it sends a Bus Request (BR) to all other devices that could be bus masters.
- Upon receiving the request, the current master eventually responds by pulling Bus Grant (BG) low, informing the requester that it will release bus control.
- When the requester becomes the master, it informs the multiprocessor system by asserting Bus Grant Acknowledge (BGACK).

To mediate fairly between the devices and allow for priority, the bus grant signal may be routed through a priority-encoded network or master scheduler. Any arbitration technique can be used as long as the basic handshaking protocol is obeyed.

Interrupt Control Group

As we learned earlier, an interrupt is an unexpected subroutine CALL. With the 68000, however, the process is more complex than with the 6800.

An interrupt is requested by placing a binary 0 to 7 into the three pins IPL0, IPL1, and IPL2. The interrupt number is checked against the current 3-bit mask in the status register. If the requested priority number is greater than the mask contents, the interrupt is accepted. A copy of the status register is saved, and the processor initiates a special Interrupt Acknowledge read cycle to fetch the interrupt vector

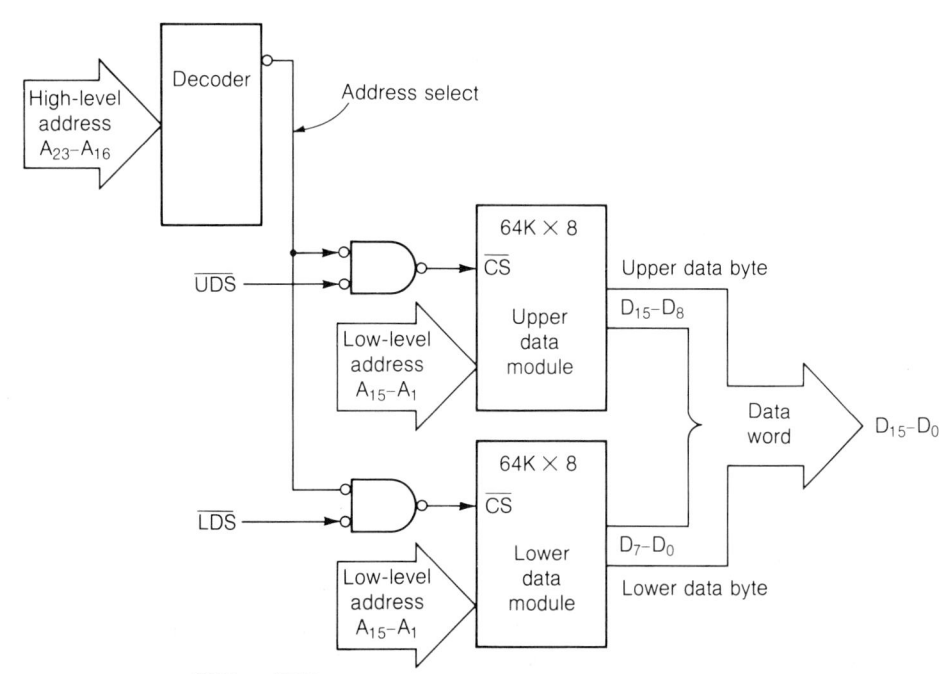

Figure 25.5 Using $\overline{LDS}$ and $\overline{UDS}$ to address individual bytes as well as whole words.

Vector Number(s)	Address Dec	Address Hex	Address Space	Assignment
0	0	000	SP	Reset: Initial SSP
—	4	004	SP	Reset: Initial PC
2	8	008	SD	Bus Error
3	12	00C	SD	Address Error
4	16	010	SD	Illegal Instruction
5	20	014	SD	Zero Divide
6	24	018	SD	CHK Instruction
7	28	01C	SD	TRAPV Instruction
8	32	020	SD	Privilege Violation
9	36	024	SD	Trace
10	40	028	SD	Line 1010 Emulator
11	44	02C	SD	Line 1111 Emulator
12*	48	030	SD	(Unassigned, reserved)
13*	52	034	SD	(Unassigned, reserved)
14*	56	038	SD	(Unassigned, reserved)
15	60	03C	SD	Uninitialized Interrupt Vector
16-23*	64	04C	SD	(Unassigned, reserved)
	95	05F		—
24	96	060	SD	Spurious Interrupt
25	100	064	SD	Level 1 Interrupt Autovector
26	104	068	SD	Level 2 Interrupt Autovector
27	108	06C	SD	Level 3 Interrupt Autovector
28	112	070	SD	Level 4 Interrupt Autovector
29	116	074	SD	Level 5 Interrupt Autovector
30	120	078	SD	Level 6 Interrupt Autovector
31	124	07C	SD	Level 7 Interrupt Autovector
32-47	128	080	SD	TRAP Instruction Vectors
	191	0BF		—
48-63*	192	0C0	SD	(Unassigned, reserved)
	255	0FF		—
64-255	256	100	SD	User Interrupt Vectors
	1023	3FF		—

Figure 25.6 68000 exception (interrupt, TRAP, and trace) vector assignments.

Courtesy of Motorola, Inc.

number from an external source. A vector number is an 8-bit number which, when multiplied by 4, gives the memory location of the interrupt vector. As shown by the *exception vector map* of Figure 25.6, the 8-bit vector number points to 1-of-256 interrupt vectors (ISR memory locations). The processor then proceeds as usual, saving the program counter and status register on the stack. The selected interrupt vector is loaded into the program counter, and execution of the interrupt-handling routine begins. A Return from Interrupt instruction at the end of the service routine restores the processor to its pre-interrupt condition. Priority level 7 (all IPL inputs zero) provides the "non-maskable interrupt" capability.

If the Valid Peripheral Address (VPA) input is pulled active low prior to the Interrupt Acknowledge cycle, the processor will "autovector," automatically generating vector numbers 25 through 31 corresponding to the interrupt vector number requested.

System Control

The 68000 $\overline{\text{HALT}}$ input is similar to that of the 6800. When pulled active low, the processor will enter an inactive state, floating all address, data, and control lines. DMA activity can then begin.

When both $\overline{\text{HALT}}$ and $\overline{\text{RESET}}$ are driven low, a total system reset is requested. The processor responds by reading the reset vector into the program counter and performing the reset routine. In addition to the hardware $\overline{\text{RESET}}$, a reset instruction is available which only activates the RESET bidirectional output line, allowing the software to reset the external system to a known state, but to continue internal processing activity.

Bus Error ($\overline{\text{BERR}}$) is an interruptlike peripheral input that warns the processor when a problem exists with the current execution cycle. A typical problem might be the failure of a return handshaking pulse from an external device. In response to the $\overline{\text{BERR}}$ input, the processor loads the Bus Error interrupt vector into the program counter and initiates the bus error handler routine. If $\overline{\text{BERR}}$ and $\overline{\text{HALT}}$ are activated simultaneously, the processor will rerun the operation.

MC6800 Peripheral Control

Because the marketplace dictated a strong need for the 68000 to interface with 6800 devices, this special ability was designed into the 68000. First of all, a portion of the 68000 memory space is set aside for 6800 peripherals. When communication with a 6800-type device is to take place, high-level addressing asserts the Valid Peripheral Address (VPA) signal. The powerful 68000 then "turns into" a 6800 (at least as far as interfacing is concerned), slowing down the 10 MHz clock speed by a factor of 10, and activating the VMA and E signals (the E output line takes on the function of the ϕ_2 clock on the 6800).

Processor Status

The three function codes indicate the type of processor cycle currently underway. For example, the special Interrupt Acknowledge cycle is indicated by a high on all three lines.

Power and Clock

The 68000 is driven by the standard +5 and ground dc power inputs and an external 4 to 12.5 MHz clock (depending on the version of the 68000).

The 68000 Read and Write Cycles

Referring to Figure 25.7, the standard read and write cycles require 8 clock pulses. Early in each cycle, the function codes (FC0, FC1, and FC2), address bits A_1 through A_{23}, and R/$\overline{\text{W}}$ line go active to "point to" a memory-mapped location and specify a read or write operation. After the address has had time to stabilize, AS, $\overline{\text{UDS}}$, and $\overline{\text{LDS}}$ go active to specify a valid address, a byte, or word operation, and to provide the basic data-transfer timing pulse that was supplied by the ϕ_2 signal on the 6800. After a time equal to the access time of the peripheral (read) or the time required to store the data (write), the selected device asserts Data Transfer Acknowledge (DTACK). For slow memories (long access times), if DTACK does not occur before the end of state 4, wait states (see Figure 25.7) are automatically inserted to give the data time to flow.

Courtesy of Motorola, Inc.

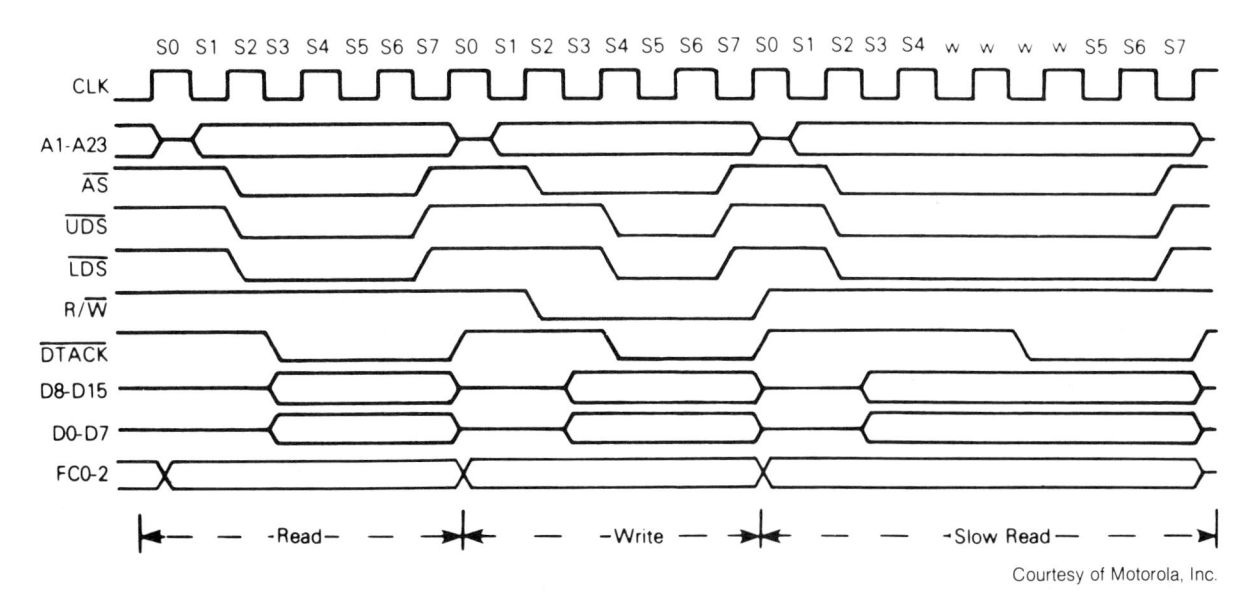

Figure 25.7 68000 read and write cycle timing for fast and slow memory.

PRIVILEGE STATES

To provide a degree of security and protection—an important part of any complex computer system—the 68000 offers two states of privilege: the "user" state or the "supervisor" state.

The *supervisor* state is the highest state of privilege, and is entered by setting the S-bit of the status register high. All instructions are executable from the supervisor state and all resources are available. When in the *user* state (S bit = 0), certain instructions are privileged and cannot be executed. These include STOP, RESET, and all instructions that modify the status register (the supervisor state can be entered by way of an interrupt or RESET).

In general, application programs execute in the user state, and the operating system executes in the supervisor state. Using the function code outputs (FC0, FC1, and FC2), an external memory management unit can control access between user and system memory spaces.

EXCEPTION PROCESSING

Exception processing refers to any state that lies outside the normal processing associated with the execution of instructions. This includes *TRAPs* and *tracing,* in addition to the already familiar *interrupts*. Within the exception vector map of Figure 25.6 are interrupt vectors, TRAP vectors, and a trace vector. Therefore, the three are closely related.

The TRAP vectors listed in the exception vector map include a variety of internally generated interrupt vectors in response to exceptional conditions. For example, any attempt to divide by 0 will trigger a #5 TRAP (see Figure 25.6), essentially calling the divide-by-0 handling routine. Note the location of the RESET vector at the very bottom of the memory map, rather than at the very top as with the 6800.

If the T-bit in the supervisor portion of the status register is set, a *trace exception* is initiated and the trace vector is jammed into the program counter *after each instruction*. Under direction of the trace handler routine (written by the programmer), the operator can single-step through a program, checking for errors.

THE 68000 INSTRUCTION SET

The instruction set of the 68000 is built on equivalents to the 6800 instruction set. The most important new operations include:

- Multiple register operations
- Effective address operations
- Multiprecision arithmetic
- Instructions for multiprocessor operation
- TRAP generating instructions
- High-level-language-oriented instructions

The instruction set includes approximately 1000 forms of machine-level instructions. These 1000 instructions are specifically chosen to translate efficiently into assembly or high-level code. That is, at the assembly level, there are only 56 basic instruction types. (For example, all the old LOAD, STORE, PUSH, and PULL instructions of the 6800 are rolled into one powerful and flexible MOVE instruction.) As with the 6800 instructions, we can get a fairly good idea of the instruction's intent by simply looking at the "verb" content of each mnemonic. These are listed below according to groups. Most of the 68000 instruction types are immediately recognizable from a knowledge of the 6800 system.

Data Movement	*Arithmetic*	*Logical*
Move	Add	AND
Exchange	Clear	OR
Link	Compare	Exclusive-OR
Push	Divide	NOT
Swap	Extend	
	Multiply	
	Negate	
	Subtract	
	Test	

Shift/Rotate	*Bit Manipulation*	*BCD Operations*
Shift	Test	Add
Rotate	Clear	Subtract
	Change	Negate

Program Control	*System Control*
Branch	AND status
Jump	EOR status
Test	Load status
Set	Move
Return	Check
	Store
	Reset
	Return
	Stop
	Trap

To give us an idea of the increased scope of the 68000 instruction set, we will take a brief look at several instruction types that have no direct counterpart in the 6800 repertoire of instructions:

- *DBcc (Test Condition, Decrement, and Branch)* is an indication of things to come in future instruction sets, for it implements the common high-level-language loop statement shown below (one that ends after a certain number of iterations *or* when a given condition is reached) with a single instruction:

WHILE counter > 0 OR Value = 6 DO

- *LEA (Load Effective Address)* transfers the *address* of a memory byte to a specified address register. LEA is useful for setting up pointers for string operations.
- *LINK (Link and Allocate)* allocates stack area in order to facilitate parameter passing during recursive subroutine calls (recursive routines are those that call themselves). LINK also simplifies the process of writing modular programs that use local variables.
- *MOVEM (Move Multiple Registers)* is a block transfer instruction that transfers selected registers to or from consecutive memory locations.
- *Scc (Set According to Condition)* helps to implement high-level-language Boolean-variable processing by setting a specified memory location TRUE (all ones) or FALSE (all zeros) depending on a tested condition.
- *TAS (Test and Set)* uses a *semaphore* to determine the availability of shared resources in a multiprocessor system (a semaphore represents the status of a shared resource). Using a special read-modify-write bus cycle, TAS tests the semaphore to determine if a shared resource is busy. If the resource is available, TAS automatically sets the semaphore to notify other processors that the shared resource is now in use and is unavailable.

68000 Addressing Modes

The 68000 offers 14 addressing modes arranged into 6 basic groups (Figure 25.8). It is the purpose of an addressing mode to locate the data on which to perform the function commanded by the op-code portion of the instruction. In general, the data address is made up of any combination of three components: the displacement, the contents of a data register, and the contents of an address register. The displacement is part of the instruction itself, and the data and address registers are specified by instruction coding. Figure 25.9 diagrams the addressing process using representative modes from each of the six basic types of addressing.

To explain why there are so many memory-addressing modes, we must recall a major design goal of the 68000: the efficient translation of high-level language into machine code. For example, when implementing the high-level statement **C(J) := X** (which means "Jth element in the C array becomes X"), it would be convenient to use the "address register + displacement" mode of addressing. The address index would point to the starting location of the array, and the displacement would locate the Jth element into the array.

Mode
Register Direct Addressing
Data Register Direct
Address Register Direct
Absolute Data Addressing
Absolute Short
Absolute Long
Program Counter Relative Addressing
Relative with Offset
Relative with Index and Offset
Register Indirect Addressing
Register Indirect
Postincrement Register Indirect
Predecrement Register Indirect
Register Indirect with Offset
Indexed Register Indirect with Offset
Immediate Data Addressing
Immediate
Quick Immediate
Implied Addressing
Implied Register

Courtesy of Motorola, Inc.

Figure 25.8 The 14 addressing modes of the 68000 grouped into six basic types.

Instruction Coding—An Example

Although an assembler or compiler will normally be called upon to form each machine-level instruction, we will hand-assemble one instruction to show what is involved.

Problem: Write a machine-language instruction to ADD the contents of data register D_0 to memory location $0010A0, placing the answer back into data register D_0.

The general form of this two-word instruction is given in Figure 25.10, along with several tables that we will use to fill in the various fields of the instruction. The Effective Address (EA) is simply a memory address represented by the addition of displacement and register contents as directed by the instruction.

Arbitrarily selecting the *Register Indirect with Offset* addressing mode and assuming address register 3 holds $00001000, Figure 25.11a shows how the instruction is coded, and Figure 25.11b shows how the 24-bit physical address is calculated from the displacement and contents of the address register. When the instruction is run, the contents of memory location $0010A0 will be added to the contents of data register D_0, and the results placed back into data register D_0.

THE 68000 FAMILY

No general-purpose microprocessor can stand alone. The 68000 in particular, if it is to exhibit fifth-generation char-

352 Part V / Advanced Processors: The Newest Generation

(a) Register direct addressing — Op code → Operand (Data or address register)

(b) Absolute data addressing — Op code, Next word → Operand (Memory location)

(c) Program counter relative addressing — Op code, Displacement; Program counter + Displacement → Operand (Memory location)

(d) Register indirect addressing — Op code, Displacement; Address register + Displacement → Operand (Memory location)

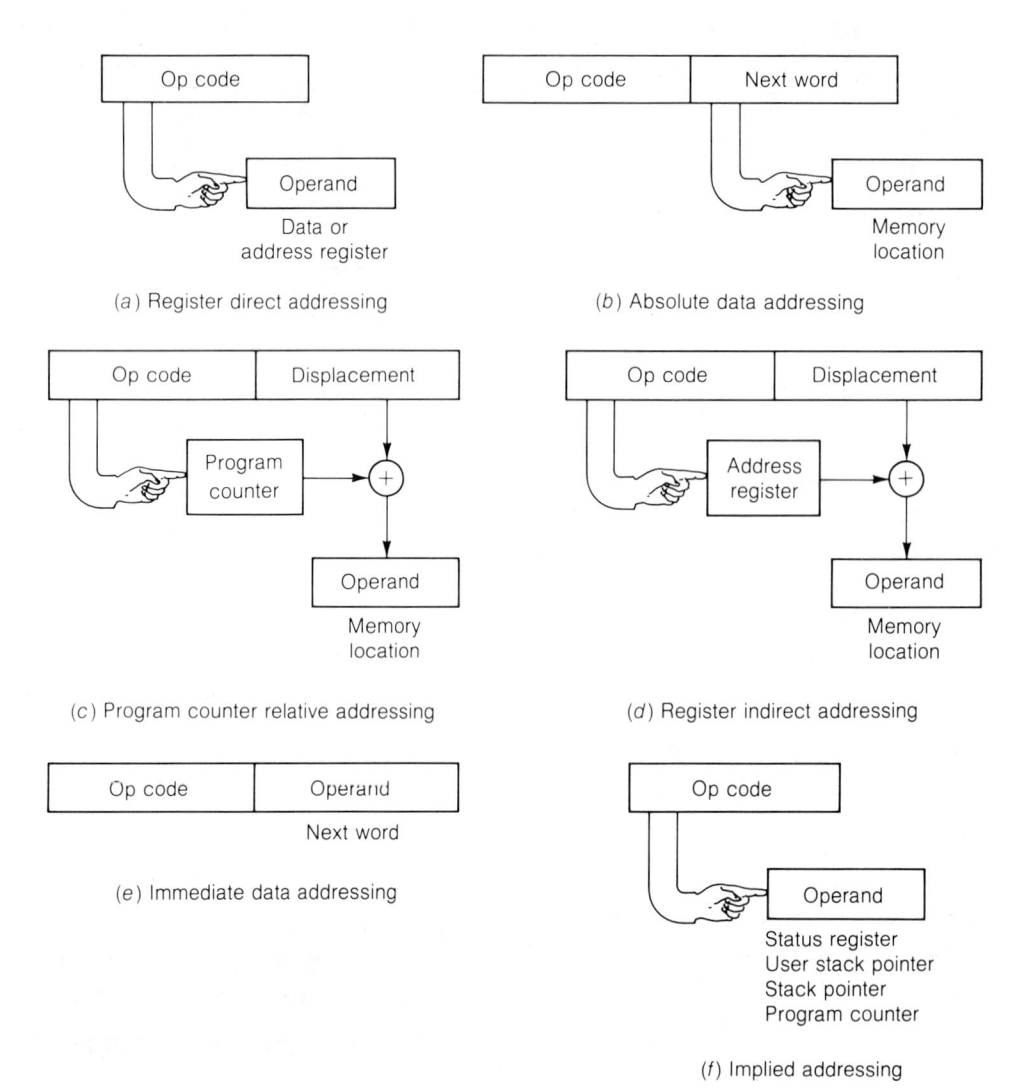

(e) Immediate data addressing — Op code, Operand (Next word)

(f) Implied addressing — Op code → Operand (Status register, User stack pointer, Stack pointer, Program counter)

Figure 25.9 Representative examples of the six basic addressing-mode types.

Add Binary (ADD)

Instruction Format:

15	14	13	12	11 10 9	8 7 6	5 4 3	2 1 0
1	1	0	1	Register	Op-Mode	Effective Address Mode	Register

Instruction Fields:

Register field — Specifies any of the eight data registers.
Op-Mode field —

Byte	Word	Long	Operation
000	001	010	(<Dn>)+(<ea>)→<Dn>
100	101	110	(<ea>)+(<Dn>)→<ea>

Effective Address field — Determines addressing mode:
  a. If the location specified is a source operand, then all addressing modes are allowed as shown:

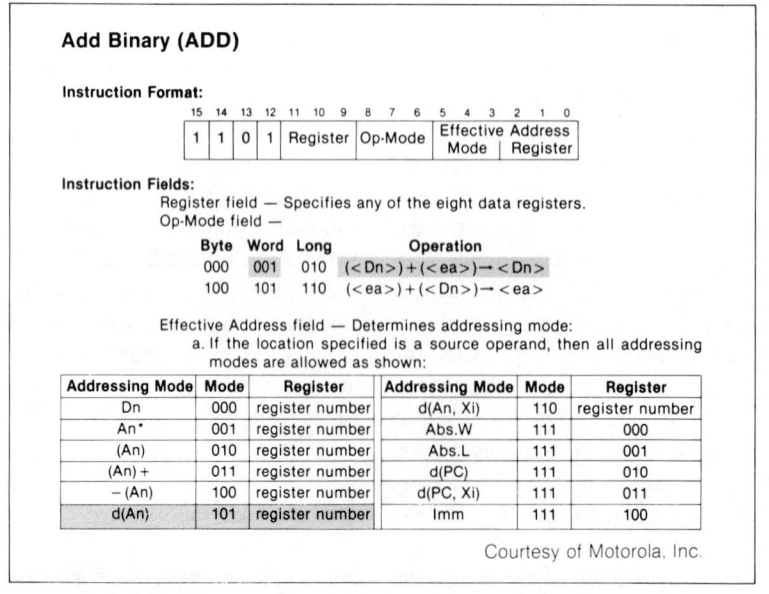

Addressing Mode	Mode	Register	Addressing Mode	Mode	Register
Dn	000	register number	d(An, Xi)	110	register number
An*	001	register number	Abs.W	111	000
(An)	010	register number	Abs.L	111	001
(An)+	011	register number	d(PC)	111	010
−(An)	100	register number	d(PC, Xi)	111	011
d(An)	101	register number	Imm	111	100

Courtesy of Motorola, Inc.

Figure 25.10 The ADD instruction format.

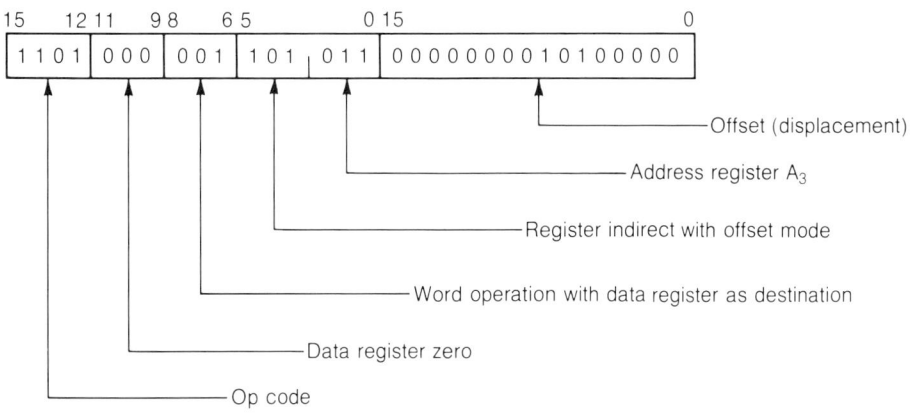

```
  15    12 11   9 8   6 5     0 15                            0
 ┌──────┬─────┬─────┬───┬─────┬────────────────────────────────┐
 │1 1 0 1│0 0 0│0 0 1│1 0 1│0 1 1│0 0 0 0 0 0 0 0 1 0 1 0 0 0 0 0│
 └──────┴─────┴─────┴───┴─────┴────────────────────────────────┘
```

— Offset (displacement)
— Address register A₃
— Register indirect with offset mode
— Word operation with data register as destination
— Data register zero
— Op code

(a) Instruction coding

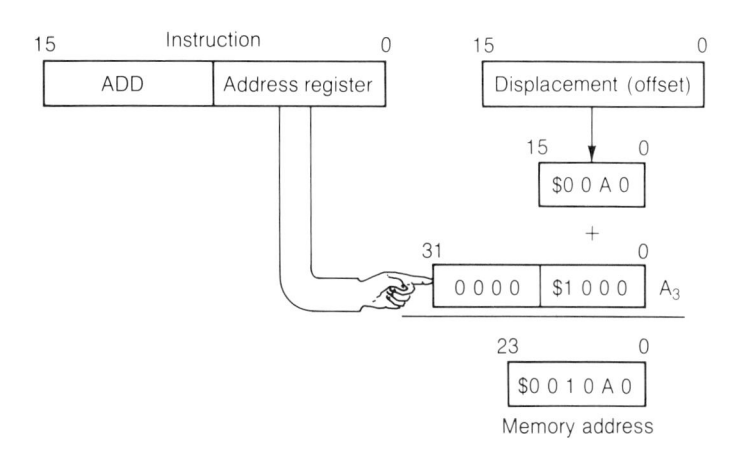

(b) Generating the memory address

Figure 25.11 Example of instruction "Add contents of memory location $0010A0 to data register D₀."

acteristics of speed, modularity, and parallel operation, must be supported by a large and varied family of peripherals.

The 68000 "family photo" is shown in Figure 25.12. Let us briefly focus on several of the more prominent members of the 68000 family.

- *The 68008 reduced data bus 68000* matches the power and versatility of the 16-bit 68000 with the design and cost benefits of an 8-bit microprocessor. With a reduced address bus (1 Mbyte addressing range) and external 8-bit data bus, the pin size is reduced to 48. As a result of complete code compatibility with the 68000, programs developed for the 68000 can run on the 68008 without modification.

- *The 68881 floating-point coprocessor* uses eight 80-bit floating-point data registers to perform all the mathematical functions of the proposed IEEE floating-point standard, including transcendental functions (logs, trig functions, exponentials, etc.). The 68881 coprocessor is designed to interface with the advanced 32-bit 68020 microprocessor.

- *The 68120 intelligent peripheral controller* is a special-purpose single-chip microcontroller (similar to the 6801) specifically designed to be a slave I/O processor to a master 68000. With its own local bus supporting up to 64K of RAM, and its simple interface to a master 68000 for the purpose of trading high-level commands and status information, it clearly implements a simple fifth-generation hierarchical model.

- *The 68451 memory management unit* (MMU) is the "security and protection" interface between the 68000 and the memory space. For each memory access, it accepts a function code and an address from the 68000. The function code specifies the address space (supervisor or user, for example), and the address specifies a location within the selected space.

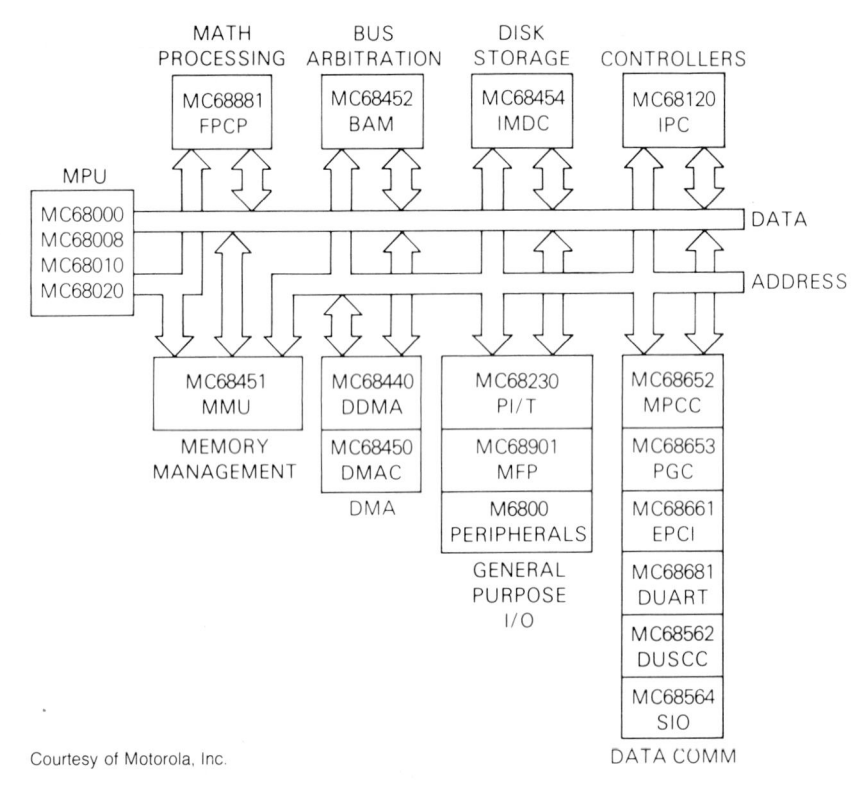

Figure 25.12 The 68000 family of microprocessors and peripherals.

INTELLIGENT-MACHINE UPDATE: A FINAL WORD

Bionics, the science of designing systems modeled after living organisms, has borne fruit many times since its inception 20 years ago. To increase the speed of oceangoing vessels, we study the flexible skin of the porpoise; to develop antifreeze solutions of great durability, we study the blood of the penguin; and to increase our knowledge of navigation, we study the amazing feats of migratory birds. To build better computers, then, perhaps we should study the human brain—the most complex entity in the known universe.

Consider the ordinary honeybee. Endowed with only 900 neurons, it can communicate with other members of the hive; navigate by polarized sunlight; simulate the guidance and flight-control system required for powered flight; sense the smallest changes in its light, sound, smell, magnetic, and electric environment; produce and care for its young; build structures of great geometric design and strength; and meanwhile maintain its required bodily functions. Can *we* do as well with 900 logic gates and other components? Indeed, can we do as well with 900 LSI circuits? From honeybee to human being, what secrets of computer power lie hidden within the animals that share our planet?

Considering the accomplishments of the honeybee, with a brain no bigger than a grain of salt, is it any wonder that the power of the human brain—with its 10 billion neurons—far surpasses that of the computer? Yet, what is significant is not that the human brain far outclasses the computer of today, but that the computer is evolving much faster. Nearly every advance in computer technology introduced in this book—from RAM and ROM to cybernetics and distributed processing—has its counterpart in the human brain. Already the circuits from which we fashion our computers are as small as those of the brain—and they are much faster. But the computer is constrained to the step-by-step processing of logical and mathematical processes. The brain, on the other hand, is global in nature (holographic), processing and synthesizing information in a complex hierarchical, parallel network. However, is this not also the direction we are now taking with the distributed parallel-processing capability of the 68000?

It appears that once again the computer is traveling in the same evolutionary direction as the human mind. Would it not be far faster and more efficient to unlock the secrets of the human brain and apply the knowledge revealed to the evolving computer?

This is a subject for the twenty-first century.

QUESTIONS AND PROBLEMS

1. What is *parallel processing*?
2. Name several features of the 68000 that are responsible for its high performance (speed).
3. What signal sent by a slow peripheral to the 68000 will stretch the read or write cycle?
4. Why is pin A_0 missing on the 68000?
5. What timing signals on the 68000 take the place of the 6800 ϕ_2 clock?
6. When accessing a *byte* at location $1000C1, what are the states of $\overline{UDS}$ and $\overline{LDS}$?
7. Name two fifth-generation concepts found in 68000 architecture.
8. Which of the 19 registers of Figure 25.1b can be used as index registers?
9. How is the 6800 non-maskable interrupt ($\overline{NMI}$) implemented on the 68000?
10. How are automatic interrupt vectors generated in a 68000 system?
11. What signal to the 68000 will place the processor in the floating DMA state?
12. Name one function of the processor status pins.
13. How many of the 68000 instructions are accessible while in a *supervisor* state?
14. What is a *TRAP*?
15. What is a *trace*?
16. At the assembly level, how does the 68000 instruction set encourage efficient coding?
17. How would the instruction of Figure 25.11a change if the contents of memory location $0010B7 was added to data register D_3, and the result placed back in register D_3 (address register A_6 holds $001013)?
18. Why is it a good idea to provide a set of address registers in which the condition codes (flags) are not affected by operations upon the address register set?

Glossary

access time the time span from the start of the read cycle to when valid data are available at the output pins.

accumulator the primary data register within the CPU—holds the initial and final results of a number of processor operations.

active low the initiation of an action when a signal—normally high—goes low.

address a block of data specifying a memory or port location.

addressing mode a particular way of specifying the operand of an instruction.

algorithm a precisely defined set of steps for solving a problem.

aliasing noise distortion due to the sampling process.

analog a continuum of levels representing magnitudes.

archival storage long-term storage in a permanent storage medium.

arithmetic/logic unit (ALU) the portion of computer hardware that performs arithmetic and logic operations.

artificial intelligence (AI) the study of computer techniques to simulate the intellectual capabilities of humans.

ASCII (American Standard Code for Information Interchange) a 7-bit code widely used for information interchange.

assembler a computer program used to translate symbolic language into machine language.

assembly-language program a program written using mnemonics and listed in four fields: code, operand, label, and comment.

asynchronous the events of operations are not controlled by a common master clock.

backup memory high-capacity, high-reliability, but slow memory system; backup memory is usually sequential in nature.

bank switching the use of output-port lines as additional high-level address lines, thereby creating memory banks.

baud the number of code elements transmitted per second (often equal to 1 bit/second).

benchmark program a routine used to evaluate the relative performance of computers.

bidirectional information flow taking place in both directions.

binary coded decimal (BCD) a number system in which each nibble represents a coded decimal character.

BISYNC (Binary Synchronous Communication) an IBM communication protocol for half-duplex operations.

bit manipulation the software setting or resetting of individual selected bits within the total word.

bit slice the building block (usually 4 bits) used to construct custom-designed microcomputers of any word size.

branch a departure from normal sequential program flow.

breakpoint a point in the program at which processing is interrupted in order to allow analysis of the system state.

buffer a device that offers a high-input impedance and low-output impedance to isolate a circuit while providing driving power; also a register used to hold temporary information.

bus a set of conducting elements forming a common connection between many circuit elements.

bus contention two circuits transmitting onto a common bus at the same time.

Butterworth filter a filter having a flat response up to the breakpoint.

byte 8 bits.

bytewide memory memory units in which each addressable location stores a byte.

CAD/CAM (computer-aided design/computer-aided manufacturing) using a computer to aid in the design and manufacturing of mechanical and electronic systems.

central processing unit (CPU) an LSI circuit (such as a general-purpose microprocessor) that combines the ALU, control unit, and internal data registers.

character generator a preprogrammed ROM used to generate symbols in a dot-matrix video display.

charge-coupled device (CCD) a serial array of MOS gates, forming a high-speed, serial-shift register.

clock cycle an internal cycle used by Motorola microprocessors for data transfer and any required internal operations.

closed loop a "circular" system whereby the output is continuously fed back to the input.

COBOL (Common Business-Oriented Language) a high-level language specifically designed for the data-processing industry.

codec (coder/decoder) used in PCM systems to perform digital-to-analog and analog-to-digital conversions.

communication protocol a set of rules and conventions governing information flow.

compiler a programming system that accepts high-level programs and converts them to machine-language programs.

controller a unit that operates automatically to regulate a system.

coprocessor a processor that must operate in conjunction with an independent processor, relying on the independent processor for instruction fetching.

current loop the transmission of serial data by changes in current along a closed path linking receiver and transmitter.

cybernetics the science of communication and control.

cycle stealing a DMA process where information is transferred at least once each instruction cycle when the data bus is unused.

cyclic-redundancy-check character (CRCC) the remainder term when a data polynomial is divided by a generator polynomial; the CRCC is transmitted along with the data and used for error checking.

DAC digital-to-analog converter.

daisy chain an interrupt technique whereby the interrupt acknowledge is hardware-propagated through the peripherals, looking for the highest-priority interrupt request.

damping the reduction of oscillatory tendencies.

data acquisition a system used to collect data, usually involving multiplexing of multiple analog inputs and conversion to digital.

data transfer a process that moves information between CPU and external device by use of a where/when operation.

debouncing the process of producing a single output for each activation of a mechanical switch.

decision choosing one path among many.

decoded addressing an address technique that makes use of decoders to allow all possible combinations of the high-level lines.

deposit to place the program into memory.

development system a computer system designed to aid the development of microprocessor-based systems; it allows the user to write and edit programs, test them in real time, and make modifications to the system.

direct memory access a process whereby the processor is halted; its address, data, and control lines are floated; and external circuitry transfers data between peripherals at high speed.

disk controller the interface electronics between floppy or Winchester disk and CPU.

disk operating system (DOS) an operating system whose system files are usually stored on floppy or Winchester disk.

diskette the Mylar-based recording system of a floppy-disk system.

displacement the amount by which the data location differs from a reference location.

distributed processing the use of intelligent peripherals to scatter the processing load among satellite stations.

duplex two-way communication (full duplex is simultaneous two-way communication).

dynamic memory a memory that stores information capacitively and requires regular recharging of capacitor states.

ECC error checking and correcting.

ECL emitter-coupled logic.

editor an interactive program that allows users to write programs and make changes and corrections.

EE-PROM a PROM erasable by electrical methods.

emulation the ability of one system to imitate the actions of another, while allowing analysis of the system.

EPROM a PROM erasable by ultraviolet light.

ergonomics the science that seeks to adapt work or working conditions to suit the worker.

examine determine the contents of a memory or register location.

execution the part in the processing of an instruction in which a command is carried out.

feedback the return of part of the output of a system back to the input.

FILO (first in/last out) the sequence of data flow to the stack; the last data byte in is the first out.

firmware a cross between hardware and software—programs stored in ROM.

flag flip-flop used to signal the occurrence of a specific condition.

floating point a number convention appropriate for large numbers in which the data bits are separated into fraction and exponent.

flowchart a graphical representation of a program, using block symbols to represent functions.

FORTRAN (formula translation) an early high-level language used for scientific applications.

foldback memory when a page of memory is addressed by more than one high-level address; linear addressing results in foldback memory.

formatting a predetermined arrangement of words used to allow for synchronization, identification, and error checking.

frequency-shift-keyed (FSK) modulation a form of frequency modulation in which a logic 0 is represented by one frequency and a logic 1 by another.

gate array (master slices) a semicustom MSI to VLSI array of basic logic elements, offering a wide variety of circuit elements and interconnections.

GCR (group-coded recording) a coding scheme that eliminates the timing pulse by coding each nibble into a 5-bit word prior to floppy or Winchester storage.

generator polynomial a specifically chosen polynomial designed to generate the CRCC when divided into the data polynomial.

GPIB (general-purpose interface bus) a parallel communication standard used to interconnect instruments and devices.

graphics the technique of placing nontextual images on a CRT screen by computer processing action.

handshaking a request/acknowledge set of back-and-forth signals used to coordinate data flow in asynchronous systems.

hard-sectored the correct sector of a floppy diskette is located by the use of 32 sector holes arranged about the diskette.

hardware the physical components of a computer system.

high-level address lines those lines that interface the memory module's CE inputs and select the desired module from the others in the system.

high-level flowchart a flowchart in which each block stands for a large number of instructions.

high-level language a computer language that generally uses English-like statements for each instruction; each instruction corresponds to a number of machine-code instructions.

hysteresis the difference between the turn-on threshold and the turn-off threshold, after turn-on.

ICE in-circuit emulation.

independent processor a processor that executes its program independently of other processors.

index register a register holding a memory address and used by certain instructions as a reference to locate a specific memory location.

input/output (I/O) hardware devices allowing data to flow between the computer system and the outside world.

instruction a computer command that can be decoded and used to direct a process.

instruction cycle the time required to fetch and execute one instruction.

instruction fetch to bring the operation code and operand into the CPU.

instruction lookahead (prefetching) future instructions fetched during execution of present instructions.

instruction register the register that holds the fetched op code.

instruction set the list of instruction types recognized by a given microprocessor.

integration a concept of calculus similar to multiplication, but used when the multiplicand is a variable rather than a constant.

interrupt an unscheduled request for special CPU action.

interrupt I/O the input or output of data under interrupt control.

interrupt-service routine the program used to service the needs of the interrupting device.

interrupt vector an interrupt whereby the processor automatically calls a specific memory location.

invisible subtraction a subtraction in which the answer is inhibited from going to the accumulator (the compare instruction subtracts invisibly).

ISO International Standards Organization.

isolated I/O a computer system in which memory is distinguished from I/O ports.

Kansas City standard the frequency-shift-keyed (FSK) encoding technique for cassette recorders.

LAN local area network.

label used in programming as a representation of an address.

large-scale integration (LSI) more than 1,000 transistor equivalents integrated on a single chip of silicon.

linear addressing an addressing technique that assigns each memory module to its own unique high-level address line.

logic analyzer a device used to test and troubleshoot microprocessor-based equipment; the acquisition of data is controlled by a number of user-selectable parameters, and the display of data can be in state, timing, or other modes.

logic array a semicustom array of logic elements fabricated on a single MSI base and usually exhibiting a sum-of-products format.

loop a repeating sequence of instructions.

low-level address lines those lines that feed the memory's address pins and are used to select a particular memory location within the selected memory module.

low-level flowchart a flowchart in which each flowchart block represents a very small number of instructions.

lunar landing vehicle (LLV) a spacecraft module designed to land on the moon.

machine cycle an internal cycle used by Intel microprocessors for data transfer and any required internal CPU operations.

machine language the lowest-level computer language, written in binary or hexadecimal.

magnetic bubbles small areas of reverse magnetism that can store logic data and can be propagated through the magnetic medium by external magnetic fields.

masking a form of bit manipulation in which the bits—when properly set or reset—inhibit an action.

memory-address register (MAR) the register used to hold the address of a data word (in the 8080/8085, the MAR is known as the WZ register pair).

memory cell that unit of memory holding a single bit of data.

memory hierarchy ranked categories of memory, from primary to secondary to backup.

memory map a listing of all memory programs showing address assignments.

memory-mapped I/O a computer system in which I/O ports are treated as memory locations.

memory segmentation the subdividing of the total memory space into smaller areas.

microcomputer a small-scale computer system, consisting of CPU, memory, and I/O, often dedicated to a specific purpose and usually using LSI blocks.

microprocessor an LSI component usually integrating the CPU and ALU on a single chip; single-chip microprocessors place all components on one chip.

microprogram the sequential list of subinstructions (microcode) stored within the CPU and used to carry out each main-program command.

minicomputer a small, general-purpose computer, between the microcomputer and mainframe (large-scale) computer in scale; minicomputers usually employ a high-level language.

mnemonic a shorthand English-like symbol for an instruction type.

mode control selecting the overall configuration of a system (often by writing a mode-control word to an internal register).

modem (modulator/demodulator) an interface device that performs the modulation and demodulation functions in a communication link.

monitor program a program in ROM used to perform a variety of functions, such as deposit, examine, and error checking; the monitor program gives the computer its initial "intelligence" upon startup.

multilevel interrupt structure more than one vectored interrupt input.

multiple precision numbers requiring two or more bytes for storage.

multiprocessing use of more than one independent processor in order to process programs concurrently.

multitasking allowing more than one user or program to share a computer system, often by time-sharing.

negative feedback the returned output signal opposes the input (the returned signal is out of phase with the input).

nesting a loop or subroutine placed within another loop or subroutine.

network an interconnecting system of terminals and computer components.

nibble 4 bits (2 nibbles make a byte).

nonmaskable interrupt an interrupt input that cannot be disabled.

object program a program written in binary or hexadecimal machine language.

operand the quantity on which the operation is performed.

operating system a group of programs that manages the resources of the system and frees the user to concentrate on other tasks.

operation code (op code) the part of the instruction that initiates specific actions when decoded.

page a 256 × 8 block of memory.

PAL programmable array logic.

parallel information processed and moved about in multibit units.

parallel processing the processing of more than one program at a time by more than one processor.

parameter a variable required by a given subroutine; also a constant changed by the programmer to control a program.

phoneme an elemental unit of speech.

PLA programmable logic array.

polling the periodic sampling of a control line (for example, to determine if a peripheral requires servicing); polling is used in programmed I/O operations.

POP the process of removing register or flag data from the stack.

port the interface between the computer system and the outside world.

positive feedback the returned output signal reinforces the input (the returned signal is in phase with the input).

primary memory memory fast enough to keep up with the speed of the microprocessor; primary memory achieves its speed through the property of random access.

priority ranking the interrupt input lines according to the highest need for interrupt processing.

program counter a sequencing 16-bit register, holding the consecutive addresses of the stored program.

programmable peripheral chip a multifunctional IC whose characteristics are programmed under software control.

programmable read-only memory (PROM) a user-programmable ROM.

programmed I/O the input or output of data under software control.

programming placing a sequential list of instructions into the computer's memory.

pseudo-instruction an instruction that gives information for proper program development, but is not itself executed.

pulse-code modulation (PCM) a modulation scheme in which the analog signal is sampled periodically and each level converted to digital and transmitted.

push the process of adding register or flag data to the stack.

quasi-static RAM a dynamic RAM with all refreshing circuitry on chip.

random access each memory location can be accessed in the same amount of time.

read to transfer information *to* the CPU.

reenterable describing a routine that can be shared by several other routines.

relative addressing an addressing mode in which the location of the data is known relative to the location of the instruction.

relocatable program a program that may be stored and executed from many areas in memory.

robotics adding artificial intelligence to computer-controlled machines in order to simulate human activities.

ROM read only memory, usually nonvolatile DIP.

sampled-data system making measurements of a function at periodic intervals.

scratchpad memory an internal, easily accessible array of registers for holding intermediate data and addresses.

secondary memory medium-capacity, medium-speed memory, usually quasi-sequential in structure.

sequential (serial) access single-file storage and transmission of data.

signature analysis the conversion of serial data streams to hexadecimal characters (signatures); comparing the actual signature to the expected signature provides a means of troubleshooting the system.

signed numbers a convention that uses the most significant bit (sign bit) to specify positive or negative numbers (1 for negative, 0 for positive); the remaining bits are used to determine the magnitude.

sign magnitude a number convention using the sign bit for a positive or negative number, but always storing the magnitude in true (not 2's complement) form.

simplex transmission one-way communication.

single-chip microcontroller a single-chip microprocessor, including I/O and RAM, and specifically configured for control applications.

single-step to process a program by hand, one step at a time.

soft-sectored the correct sector of a floppy disk is identified by software reading of timing and address information included with every sector.

software computer programs.

source listing the original program written in assembly or high-level language.

stack a block of successive memory locations used to store return addresses and register and flag information during subroutine processing.

stack pointer a register used to point to the most recent data stored in the stack or the next piece of data to be removed.

state equal to one clock cycle, the smallest unit of time in the 8080/8085 system.

state (data domain) display display of data in binary, octal, or hex format.

static memory a memory device requiring only dc voltages to power its operation.

status register a register used to hold information relative to the present state of the system.

stepper motor a motor in which rotation takes place in discrete steps under control of pulses.

stored program the concept of storing the instructions along with the data.

streaming data flow continuous data flow onto a tape system, eliminating the starts and stops.

strobed-output mode an output technique using double buffering to speed data flow.

structured programming the technique of writing programs in blocks, with each block independent and jumps not allowed back and forth between blocks.

subroutine a routine that is part of another routine, but placed at a different memory location.

super-large-scale integration (SLSI) approximately 100,000 transistor equivalents integrated on a single chip of silicon.

synchronous the events or operations take place in step with a common master clock.

throughput the total amount of information processed in a specified time.

time multiplexing the time-sharing of a circuit or system.

timing display display of data in waveform format.

top-down programming program development by moving from the general to the specific—from the high-level conceptual to the low-level instructional stage.

transducer a device that converts analog states (temperature, pressure, etc.) to electrical signals.

tristate circuit a circuit especially designed to transmit information onto a bus; it can transmit the standard logic 1 or 0 states, or it can be floated to allow another circuit to transmit onto the bus.

tunneling quantum-mechanical penetration of an otherwise unsurmountable energy barrier.

two's (2's) complement a number format used in signed-number operations, and equal to the 1's complement + 1 (1's complement is equal to an inversion of all bits).

UART (universal asynchronous receiver/transmitter) a device used to interface a parallel CPU or data terminal to a serial asynchronous communication network.

USART (universal synchronous/asynchronous receiver/transmitter) a device used to interface a parallel CPU or data terminal to a serial synchronous or asynchronous communication network.

very-large-scale integration (VLSI) more than 50,000 transistor equivalents integrated on a single chip of silicon.

virtual memory the automatic page swapping of memory between primary and secondary memories.

volatile memory that loses data when power is removed (nonvolatile memory retains data when power is removed).

Winchester disk a medium-to-high capacity, high-reliability, hard-disk system that features a sealed-disk environment to allow the read/write head to "fly" very close to the surface of the recording medium.

word a 16-bit piece of data, as distinguished from the 8-bit byte.

write to transfer information *from* the CPU.

appendix I

Dictionary of Executable Instructions

ABA — Add Accumulator B to Accumulator A

Operation: ACCA ← (ACCA) + (ACCB)

Description: Adds the contents of ACCB to the contents of ACCA and places the result in ACCA.

Condition Codes:
- H: Set if there was a carry from bit 3; cleared otherwise.
- I: Not affected.
- N: Set if most significant bit of the result is set; cleared otherwise.
- Z: Set if all bits of the result are cleared; cleared otherwise.
- V: Set if there was two's complement overflow as a result of the operation; cleared otherwise.
- C: Set if there was a carry from the most significant bit of the result; cleared otherwise.

Addressing Modes, Execution Time, and Machine Code (hexadecimal/octal/decimal):

Addressing Modes	Execution Time (No. of cycles)	Number of bytes of machine code	HEX.	OCT.	DEC.
Inherent	2	1	1B	033	027

ADC — Add with Carry

Operation: ACCX ← (ACCX) + (M) + (C)

Description: Adds the contents of the C bit to the sum of the contents of ACCX and M, and places the result in ACCX.

Condition Codes:
- H: Set if there was a carry from bit 3; cleared otherwise.
- I: Not affected.
- N: Set if most significant bit of the result is set; cleared otherwise.
- Z: Set if all bits of the result are cleared; cleared otherwise.
- V: Set if there was two's complement overflow as a result of the operation; cleared otherwise.
- C: Set if there was a carry from the most significant bit of the result; cleared otherwise.

Addressing Modes, Execution Time, and Machine Code (hexadecimal/octal/decimal):
(DUAL OPERAND)

Addressing Modes	Execution Time (No. of cycles)	Number of bytes of machine code	HEX.	OCT.	DEC.
A IMM	2	2	89	211	137
A DIR	3	2	99	231	153
A EXT	4	3	B9	271	185
A IND	5	2	A9	251	169
B IMM	2	2	C9	311	201
B DIR	3	2	D9	331	217
B EXT	4	3	F9	371	249
B IND	5	2	E9	351	233

ADD — Add Without Carry

Operation: ACCX ← (ACCX) + (M)

Description: Adds the contents of ACCX and the contents of M and places the result in ACCX.

Condition Codes:
- H: Set if there was a carry from bit 3; cleared otherwise.
- I: Not affected.
- N: Set if most significant bit of the result is set; cleared otherwise.
- Z: Set if all bits of the result are cleared; cleared otherwise.
- V: Set if there was two's complement overflow as a result of the operation; cleared otherwise.
- C: Set if there was a carry from the most significant bit of the result; cleared otherwise.

Addressing Modes, Execution Time, and Machine Code (hexadecimal/octal/decimal):
(DUAL OPERAND)

Addressing Modes	Execution Time (No. of cycles)	Number of bytes of machine code	HEX.	OCT.	DEC.
A IMM	2	2	8B	213	139
A DIR	3	2	9B	233	155
A EXT	4	3	BB	273	187
A IND	5	2	AB	253	171
B IMM	2	2	CB	313	203
B DIR	3	2	DB	333	219
B EXT	4	3	FB	373	251
B IND	5	2	EB	353	235

AND — Logical AND

Operation: ACCX ← (ACCX) · (M)

Description: Performs logical "AND" between the contents of ACCX and the contents of M and places the result in ACCX. (Each bit of ACCX after the operation will be the logical "AND" of the corresponding bits of M and of ACCX before the operation.)

Condition Codes:
- H: Not affected.
- I: Not affected.
- N: Set if most significant bit of the result is set; cleared otherwise.
- Z: Set if all bits of the result are cleared; cleared otherwise.
- V: Cleared.
- C: Not affected.

Addressing Modes, Execution Time, and Machine Code (hexadecimal/octal/decimal):

Addressing Modes	Execution Time (No. of cycles)	Number of bytes of machine code	HEX.	OCT.	DEC.
A IMM	2	2	84	204	132
A DIR	3	2	94	224	148
A EXT	4	3	B4	264	180
A IND	5	2	A4	244	164
B IMM	2	2	C4	304	196
B DIR	3	2	D4	324	212
B EXT	4	3	F4	364	244
B IND	5	2	E4	344	228

ASL
Arithmetic Shift Left

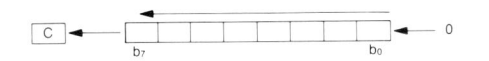

Operation:

$$C \leftarrow \boxed{} \leftarrow 0$$
$$b_7 b_0$$

Description: Shifts all bits of the ACCX or M one place to the left. Bit 0 is loaded with a zero. The C bit is loaded from the most significant bit of ACCX or M.

Condition Codes:
- H: Not affected.
- I: Not affected.
- N: Set if most significant bit of the result is set; cleared otherwise.
- Z: Set if all bits of the result are cleared; cleared otherwise.
- V: Set if, after the completion of the shift operation, EITHER (N is set and C is cleared) OR (N is cleared and C is set); cleared otherwise.
- C: Set if, before the operation, the most significant bit of the ACCX or M was set; cleared otherwise.

Addressing Modes, Execution Time, and Machine Code (hexadecimal/octal/decimal):

Addressing Modes	Execution Time (No. of cycles)	Number of bytes of machine code	HEX.	OCT.	DEC.
A	2	1	48	110	072
B	2	1	58	130	088
EXT	6	3	78	170	120
IND	7	2	68	150	104

ASR
Arithmetic Shift Right

Operation:

$$\boxed{} \rightarrow C$$
$$b_7 b_0$$

Description: Shifts all bits of ACCX or M one place to the right. Bit 7 is held constant. Bit 0 is loaded into the C bit.

Condition Codes:
- H: Not affected.
- I: Not affected.
- N: Set if the most significant bit of the result is set; cleared otherwise.
- Z: Set if all bits of the result are cleared; cleared otherwise.
- V: Set if, after the completion of the shift operation, EITHER (N is set and C is cleared) OR (N is cleared and C is set); cleared otherwise.
- C: Set if, before the operation, the least significant bit of the ACCX or M was set; cleared otherwise.

Addressing Modes, Execution Time, and Machine Code (hexadecimal/octal/decimal):

Addressing Modes	Execution Time (No. of cycles)	Number of bytes of machine code	HEX.	OCT.	DEC.
A	2	1	47	107	071
B	2	1	57	127	087
EXT	6	3	77	167	119
IND	7	2	67	147	103

BCC
Branch if Carry Clear

Operation: PC ← (PC) + 0002 + Rel if (C) = 0

Description: Tests the state of the C bit and causes a branch if C is clear.

See BRA instruction for further details of the execution of the branch.

Condition Codes: Not affected.

Addressing Modes, Execution Time, and Machine Code (hexadecimal/octal/decimal):

Addressing Modes	Execution Time (No. of cycles)	Number of bytes of machine code	HEX.	OCT.	DEC.
REL	4	2	24	044	036

BCS
Branch if Carry Set

Operation: PC ← (PC) + 0002 + Rel if (C) = 1

Description: Tests the state of the C bit and causes a branch if C is set.

See BRA instruction for further details of the execution of the branch.

Condition Codes: Not affected.

Addressing Modes, Execution Time, and Machine Code (hexadecimal/octal/decimal):

Addressing Modes	Execution Time (No. of cycles)	Number of bytes of machine code	HEX.	OCT.	DEC.
REL	4	2	25	045	037

BEQ
Branch if Equal

Operation: PC ← (PC) + 0002 + Rel if (Z) = 1

Description: Tests the state of the Z bit and causes a branch if the Z bit is set.

See BRA instruction for further details of the execution of the branch.

Condition Codes: Not affected.

Addressing Modes, Execution Time, and Machine Code (hexadecimal/octal/decimal):

Addressing Modes	Execution Time (No. of cycles)	Number of bytes of machine code	HEX.	OCT.	DEC.
REL	4	2	27	047	039

BGE
Branch if Greater than or Equal to Zero

Operation: PC ← (PC) + 0002 + Rel if (N) $\oplus$ (V) = 0

i.e. if (ACCX) ≥ (M)
(Two's complement numbers)

Description: Causes a branch if (N is set and V is set) OR (N is clear and V is clear).

If the BGE instruction is executed immediately after execution of any of the instructions CBA, CMP, SBA, or SUB, the branch will occur if and only if the two's complement number represented by the minuend (i.e. ACCX) was greater than or equal to the two's complement number represented by the subtrahend (i.e. M).

See BRA instruction for details of the branch.

Condition Codes: Not affected.

Addressing Modes, Execution Time, and Machine Code (hexadecimal/octal/decimal):

Addressing Modes	Execution Time (No. of cycles)	Number of bytes of machine code	HEX.	OCT.	DEC.
REL	4	2	2C	054	044

BGT
Branch if Greater than Zero

Operation: PC ← (PC) + 0002 + Rel if (Z) + [(N) $\oplus$ (V)] = 0

i.e. if (ACCX) > (M)
(two's complement numbers)

Description: Causes a branch if [Z is clear] AND [(N is set and V is set) OR (N is clear and V is clear)].

If the BGT instruction is executed immediately after execution of any of the instructions CBA, CMP, SBA, or SUB, the branch will occur if and only if the two's complement number represented by the minuend (i.e. ACCX) was greater than the two's complement number represented by the subtrahend (i.e. M).

See BRA instruction for details of the branch.

Condition Codes: Not affected.

Addressing Modes, Execution Time, and Machine Code (hexadecimal/octal/decimal):

Addressing Modes	Execution Time (No. of cycles)	Number of bytes of machine code	HEX.	OCT.	DEC.
REL	4	2	2E	056	046

BHI
Branch if Higher

Operation: PC ← (PC) + 0002 + Rel if (C) + (Z) = 0

i.e. if (ACCX) > (M)
(unsigned binary numbers)

Description: Causes a branch if (C is clear) AND (Z is clear).

If the BHI instruction is executed immediately after execution of any of the instructions CBA, CMP, SBA, or SUB, the branch will occur if and only if the unsigned binary number represented by the minuend (i.e. ACCX) was greater than the unsigned binary number represented by the subtrahend (i.e. M).

See BRA instruction for details of the execution of the branch.

Condition Codes: Not affected.

Addressing Modes, Execution Time, and Machine Code (hexadecimal/octal/decimal):

Addressing Modes	Execution Time (No. of cycles)	Number of bytes of machine code	HEX.	OCT.	DEC.
REL	4	2	22	042	034

BIT
Bit Test

Operation: (ACCX) · (M)

Description: Performs the logical "AND" comparison of the contents of ACCX and the contents of M and modifies condition codes accordingly. Neither the contents of ACCX or M operands are affected. (Each bit of the result of the "AND" would be the logical "AND" of the corresponding bits of M and ACCX.)

Condition Codes:
- H: Not affected.
- I: Not affected.
- N: Set if the most significant bit of the result of the "AND" would be set; cleared otherwise.
- Z: Set if all bits of the result of the "AND" would be cleared; cleared otherwise.
- V: Cleared.
- C: Not affected.

Addressing Modes, Execution Time, and Machine Code (hexadecimal/octal/decimal):

Addressing Modes	Execution Time (No. of cycles)	Number of bytes of machine code	HEX.	OCT.	DEC.
A IMM	2	2	85	205	133
A DIR	3	2	95	225	149
A EXT	4	3	B5	265	181
A IND	5	2	A5	245	165
B IMM	2	2	C5	305	197
B DIR	3	2	D5	325	213
B EXT	4	3	F5	365	245
B IND	5	2	E5	345	229

BLE
Branch if Less than or Equal to Zero

Operation: PC ← (PC) + 0002 + Rel if (Z) ⊕ [(N) ⊕ (V)] = 1
i.e. if (ACCX) ≤ (M)
(two's complement numbers)

Description: Causes a branch if [Z is set] OR [(N is set and V is clear) OR (N is clear and V is set)].

If the BLE instruction is executed immediately after execution of any of the instructions CBA, CMP, SBA, or SUB, the branch will occur if and only if the two's complement number represented by the minuend (i.e. ACCX) was less then or equal to the two's complement number represented by the subtrahend (i.e. M).

See BRA instruction for details of the branch.

Condition Codes: Not affected.

Addressing Modes, Execution Time, and Machine Code (hexadecimal/octal/decimal):

Addressing Modes	Execution Time (No. of cycles)	Number of bytes of machine code	HEX.	OCT.	DEC.
REL	4	2	2F	057	047

BLS
Branch if Lower or Same

Operation: PC ← (PC) + 0002 + Rel if (C) ⊕ (Z) = 1
i.e. if (ACCX) ≤ (M)
(unsigned binary numbers)

Description: Causes a branch if (C is set) OR Z is set).

If the BLS instruction is executed immediately after execution of any of the instructions CBA, CMP, SBA, or SUB, the branch will occur if and only if the unsigned binary number represented by the minuend (i.e. ACCX) was less than or equal to the unsigned binary number represented by the subtrahend (i.e. M).

See BRA instruction for details of the execution of the branch.

Condition Codes: Not affected.

Addressing Modes, Execution Time, and Machine Code (hexadecimal/octal/decimal):

Addressing Modes	Execution Time (No. of cycles)	Number of bytes of machine code	HEX.	OCT.	DEC.
REL	4	2	23	043	035

BLT
Branch if Less than Zero

Operation: PC ← (PC) + 0002 + Rel if (N) ⊕ (V) = 1
i.e. if (ACCX) < (M)
(two's complement numbers)

Description: Causes a branch if (N is set and V is clear) OR (N is clear and V is set).

If the BLT instruction is executed immediately after execution of any of the instructions CBA, CMP, SBA, or SUB, the branch will occur if and only if the two's complement number represented by the minuend (i.e. ACCX) was less than the two's complement number represented by the subtrahend (i.e. M).

See BRA instruction for details of the branch.

Condition Codes: Not affected.

Addressing Modes, Execution Time, and Machine Code (hexadecimal/octal/decimal):

Addressing Modes	Execution Time (No. of cycles)	Number of bytes of machine code	HEX.	OCT.	DEC.
REL	4	2	2D	055	045

BMI
Branch if Minus

Operation: PC ← (PC) + 0002 + Rel if (N) = 1

Description: Tests the state of the N bit and causes a branch if N is set.
See BRA instruction for details of the execution of the branch.

Condition Codes: Not affected.

Addressing Modes, Execution Time, and Machine Code (hexadecimal/octal/decimal):

Addressing Modes	Execution Time (No. of cycles)	Number of bytes of machine code	HEX.	OCT.	DEC.
REL	4	2	2B	053	043

BNE
Branch if Not Equal

Operation: PC ← (PC) + 0002 + Rel if (Z) = 0

Description: Tests the state of the Z bit and causes a branch if the Z bit is clear.
See BRA instruction for details of the execution of the branch.

Condition Codes: Not affected.

Addressing Modes, Execution Time, and Machine Code (hexadecimal/octal/decimal):

Addressing Modes	Execution Time (No. of cycles)	Number of bytes of machine code	HEX.	OCT.	DEC.
REL	4	2	26	046	038

BPL
Branch if Plus

Operation: PC ← (PC) + 0002 + Rel if (N) = 0

Description: Tests the state of the N bit and causes a branch if N is clear.
See BRA instruction for details of the execution of the branch.

Condition Codes: Not affected.

Addressing Modes, Execution Time, and Machine Code (hexadecimal/octal/decimal):

Addressing Modes	Execution Time (No. of cycles)	Number of bytes of machine code	HEX.	OCT.	DEC.
REL	4	2	2A	052	042

BRA
Branch Always

Operation: PC ← (PC) + 0002 + Rel

Description: Unconditional branch to the address given by the foregoing formula, in which R is the relative address stored as a two's complement number in the second byte of machine code corresponding to the branch instruction.

Note: The source program specifies the destination of any branch instruction by its absolute address, either as a numerical value or as a symbol or expression which can be numerically evaluated by the assembler. The assembler obtains the relative address R from the absolute address and the current value of the program counter PC.

Condition Codes: Not affected.

Addressing Modes, Execution Time, and Machine Code (hexadecimal/octal/decimal):

Addressing Modes	Execution Time (No. of cycles)	Number of bytes of machine code	HEX.	OCT.	DEC.
REL	4	2	20	040	032

BSR
Branch to Subroutine

Operation:
PC ← (PC) + 0002
↓ (PCL)
SP ← (SP) − 0001
↓ (PCH)
SP ← (SP) − 0001
PC ← (PC) + Rel

Description: The program counter is incremented by 2. The less significant byte of the contents of the program counter is pushed into the stack. The stack pointer is then decremented (by 1). The more significant byte of the contents of the program counter is then pushed into the stack. The stack pointer is again decremented (by 1). A branch then occurs to the location specified by the program.

See BRA instruction for details of the execution of the branch.

Condition Codes: Not affected.

Addressing Modes, Execution Time, and Machine Code (hexadecimal/octal/decimal):

Addressing Modes	Execution Time (No. of cycles)	Number of bytes of machine code	HEX.	OCT.	DEC.
REL	8	2	8D	215	141

BVC
Branch if Overflow Clear

Operation: PC ← (PC) + 0002 + Rel if (V) = 0
Description: Tests the state of the V bit and causes a branch if the V bit is clear.
See BRA instruction for details of the execution of the branch.
Condition Codes: Not affected.

Addressing Modes, Execution Time, and Machine Code (hexadecimal/octal/decimal):

Addressing Modes	Execution Time (No. of cycles)	Number of bytes of machine code	HEX.	OCT.	DEC.
REL	4	2	28	050	040

BVS
Branch if Overflow Set

Operation: PC ← (PC) + 0002 + Rel if (V) = 1
Description: Tests the state of the V bit and causes a branch if the V bit is set.
See BRA instruction for details of the execution of the branch.
Condition Codes: Not affected.

Addressing Modes, Execution Time, and Machine Code (hexadecimal/octal/decimal):

Addressing Modes	Execution Time (No. of cycles)	Number of bytes of machine code	HEX.	OCT.	DEC.
REL	4	2	29	051	041

CBA
Compare Accumulators

Operation: (ACCA) − (ACCB)
Description: Compares the contents of ACCA and the contents of ACCB and sets the condition codes, which may be used for arithmetic and logical conditional branches. Both operands are unaffected.
Condition Codes:
H: Not affected.
I: Not affected.
N: Set if the most significant bit of the result of the subtraction would be set; cleared otherwise.
Z: Set if all bits of the result of the subtraction would be cleared; cleared otherwise.
V: Set if the subtraction would cause two's complement overflow; cleared otherwise.
C: Set if the subtraction would require a borrow into the most significant bit of the result; clear otherwise.

Addressing Modes, Execution Time, and Machine Code (hexadecimal/octal/decimal):

Addressing Modes	Execution Time (No. of cycles)	Number of bytes of machine code	HEX.	OCT.	DEC.
INHERENT	2	1	11	021	017

CLC
Clear Carry

Operation: C bit ← 0
Description: Clears the carry bit in the processor condition codes register.
Condition Codes:
H: Not affected.
I: Not affected.
N: Not affected.
Z: Not affected.
V: Not affected.
C: Cleared.

Addressing Modes, Execution Time, and Machine Code (hexadecimal/octal/decimal):

Addressing Modes	Execution Time (No. of cycles)	Number of bytes of machine code	HEX.	OCT.	DEC.
INHERENT	2	1	0C	014	012

CLI
Clear Interrupt Mask

Operation: I bit ← 0
Description: Clears the interrupt mask bit in the processor condition codes register. This enables the microprocessor to service an interrupt from a peripheral device if signalled by a high state of the "Interrupt Request" control input.
Condition Codes:
H: Not affected.
I: Cleared.
N: Not affected.
Z: Not affected.
V: Not affected.
C: Not affected.

Addressing Modes, Execution Time, and Machine Code (hexadecimal/octal/decimal):

Addressing Modes	Execution Time (No. of cycles)	Number of bytes of machine code	HEX.	OCT.	DEC.
INHERENT	2	1	0E	016	014

CLR
Clear

Operation: ACCX ← 00
or: M ← 00
Description: The contents of ACCX or M are replaced with zeros.
Condition Codes:
H: Not affected.
I: Not affected.
N: Cleared
Z: Set
V: Cleared
C: Cleared

Addressing Modes, Execution Time, and Machine Code (hexadecimal/octal/decimal):

Addressing Modes	Execution Time (No. of cycles)	Number of bytes of machine code	HEX.	OCT.	DEC.
A	2	1	4F	117	079
B	2	1	5F	137	095
EXT	6	3	7F	177	127
IND	7	2	6F	157	111

CLV
Clear Two's Complement Overflow Bit

Operation: V bit ← 0
Description: Clears the two's complement overflow bit in the processor condition codes register.
Condition Codes:
H: Not affected.   Z: Not affected.
I: Not affected.   V: Cleared.
N: Not affected.   C: Not affected.

Addressing Modes, Execution Time, and Machine Code (hexadecimal/octal/decimal):

Addressing Modes	Execution Time (No. of cycles)	Number of bytes of machine code	HEX.	OCT.	DEC.
INHERENT	2	1	0A	012	010

CMP
Compare

Operation: (ACCX) − (M)
Description: Compares the contents of ACCX and the contents of M and determines the condition codes, which may be used subsequently for controlling conditional branching. Both operands are unaffected.
Condition Codes:
H: Not affected.
I: Not affected.
N: Set if the most significant bit of the result of the subtraction would be set; cleared otherwise.
Z: Set if all bits of the result of the subtraction would be cleared; cleared otherwise.
V: Set if the subtraction would cause two's complement overflow; cleared otherwise.
C: Carry is set if the absolute value of the contents of memory is larger than the absolute value of the accumulator; reset otherwise.

Addressing Modes, Execution Time, and Machine Code (hexadecimal/octal/decimal):
(DUAL OPERAND)

Addressing Modes	Execution Time (No. of cycles)	Number of bytes of machine code	HEX.	OCT.	DEC.
A IMM	2	2	81	201	129
A DIR	3	2	91	221	145
A EXT	4	3	B1	261	177
A IND	5	2	A1	241	161
B IMM	2	2	C1	301	193
B DIR	3	2	D1	321	209
B EXT	4	3	F1	361	241
B IND	5	2	E1	341	225

COM
Complement

Operation: ACCX ← = (ACCX) = FF − (ACCX)
or: M ← = (M) = FF − (M)
Description: Replaces the contents of ACCX or M with its one's complement. (Each bit of the contents of ACCX or M is replaced with the complement of that bit.)
Condition Codes:
H: Not affected.
I: Not affected.
N: Set if most significant bit of the result is set; cleared otherwise.
Z: Set if all bits of the result are cleared; cleared otherwise.
V: Cleared.
C: Set.

Addressing Modes, Execution Time, and Machine Code (hexadecimal/octal/decimal):

Addressing Modes	Execution Time (No. of cycles)	Number of bytes of machine code	HEX.	OCT.	DEC.
A	2	1	43	103	067
B	2	1	53	123	083
EXT	6	3	73	163	115
IND	7	2	63	143	099

365

CPX
Compare Index Register

Operation: (IXL) - (M - 1)
(IXH) - (M)

Description: The more significant byte of the contents of the index register is compared with the contents of the byte of memory at the address specified by the program. The less significant byte of the contents of the index register is compared with the contents of the next byte of memory, at one plus the address specified by the program. The Z bit is set or reset according to the results of these comparisons, and may be used subsequently for conditional branching.

The N and V bits, though determined by this operation, are not intended for conditional branching.

The C bit is not affected by this operation.

Condition Codes:
- H: Not affected.
- I: Not affected.
- N: Set if the most significant bit of the result of the subtraction from the more significant byte of the index register would be set; cleared otherwise.
- Z: Set if all bits of the results of both subtractions would be cleared; cleared otherwise.
- V: Set if the subtraction from the more significant byte of the index register would cause two's complement overflow; cleared otherwise.
- C: Not affected.

Addressing Modes, Execution Time, and Machine Code (hexadecimal/octal/decimal):

Addressing Modes	Execution Time (No. of cycles)	Number of bytes of machine code	HEX.	OCT.	DEC.
IMM	3	3	8C	214	140
DIR	4	2	9C	234	156
EXT	5	3	BC	274	188
IND	6	2	AC	254	172

DAA
Decimal Adjust ACCA

Operation: Adds hexadecimal numbers 00, 06, 60, or 66 to ACCA, and may also set the carry bit, as indicated in the following table:

State of C-bit before DAA (Col. 1)	Upper Half-byte (bits 4-7) (Col. 2)	Initial Half-carry H-bit (Col.3)	Lower Half-byte (bits 0-3) (Col. 4)	Number Added after by DAA (Col. 5)	State of C-bit after DAA (Col. 6)
0	0-9	0	0-9	00	0
0	0-8	0	A-F	06	0
0	0-9	1	0-3	06	0
0	A-F	0	0-9	60	1
0	9-F	0	A-F	66	1
0	A-F	1	0-3	66	1
1	0-2	0	0-9	60	1
1	0-2	0	A-F	66	1
1	0-3	1	0-3	66	1

Note: Columns (1) through (4) of the above table represent all possible cases which can result from any of the operations ABA, ADD, or ADC, with initial carry either set or clear, applied to two binary-coded-decimal operands. The table shows hexadecimal values.

Description: If the contents of ACCA and the state of the carry-borrow bit C and the half-carry bit H are all the result of applying any of the operations ABA, ADD, or ADC to binary-coded-decimal operands, with or without an initial carry, the DAA operation will function as follows.

Subject to the above condition, the DAA operation will adjust the contents of ACCA and the C bit to represent the correct binary-coded-decimal sum and the correct state of the carry.

Condition Codes:
- H: Not affected.
- I: Not affected.
- N: Set if most significant bit of the result is set; cleared otherwise.
- Z: Set if all bits of the result are cleared; cleared otherwise.
- V: Not defined.
- C: Set or reset according to the same rule as if the DAA and an immediately preceding ABA, ADD, or ADC were replaced by a hypothetical binary-coded-decimal addition.

Addressing Modes, Execution Time, and Machine Code (hexadecimal/octal/decimal):

Addressing Modes	Execution Time (No. of cycles)	Number of bytes of machine code	HEX.	OCT.	DEC.
INHERENT	2	1	19	031	025

DEC
Decrement

Operation: ACCX ← (ACCX) - 01
or: M ← (M) - 01

Description: Subtract one from the contents of ACCX or M.

The N, Z, and V condition codes are set or reset according to the results of this operation.

The C bit is not affected by the operation.

Condition Codes:
- H: Not affected.
- I: Not affected.
- N: Set if most significant bit of the result is set; cleared otherwise.
- Z: Set if all bits of the result are cleared; cleared otherwise.
- V: Set if there was two's complement overflow as a result of the operation; cleared otherwise. Two's complement overflow occurs if and only if (ACCX) or (M) was 80 before the operation.
- C: Not affected.

Addressing Modes, Execution Time, and Machine Code (hexadecimal/octal/decimal):

Addressing Modes	Execution Time (No. of cycles)	Number of bytes of machine code	HEX.	OCT.	DEC.
A	2	1	4A	112	074
B	2	1	5A	132	090
EXT	6	3	7A	172	122
IND	7	2	6A	152	106

DES
Decrement Stack Pointer

Operation: SP ← (SP) - 0001

Description: Subtract one from the stack pointer.

Condition Codes: Not affected.

Addressing Modes, Execution Time, and Machine Code (hexadecimal/octal/decimal):

Addressing Modes	Execution Time (No. of cycles)	Number of bytes of machine code	HEX.	OCT.	DEC.
INHERENT	4	1	34	064	052

DEX
Decrement Index Register

Operation: IX ← (IX) - 0001

Description: Subtract one from the index register.

Only the Z bit is set or reset according to the result of this operation.

Condition Codes:
- H: Not affected.
- I: Not affected.
- N: Not affected.
- Z: Set if all bits of the result are cleared; cleared otherwise.
- V: Not affected.
- C: Not affected.

Addressing Modes, Execution Time, and Machine Code (hexadecimal/octal/decimal):

Addressing Modes	Execution Time (No. of cycles)	Number of bytes of machine code	HEX.	OCT.	DEC.
INHERENT	4	1	09	011	009

EOR
Exclusive OR

Operation: ACCX ← (ACCX) ⊕ (M)

Description: Perform logical "EXCLUSIVE OR" between the contents of ACCX and the contents of M, and place the result in ACCX. (Each bit of ACCX after the operation will be the logical "EXCLUSIVE OR" of the corresponding bit of M and ACCX before the operation.)

Condition Codes:
- H: Not affected.
- I: Not affected.
- N: Set if most significant bit of the result is set; cleared otherwise.
- Z: Set if all bits of the result are cleared; cleared otherwise.
- V: Cleared
- C: Not affected.

Addressing Modes, Execution Time, and Machine Code (hexadecimal/octal/decimal):

Addressing Modes	Execution Time (No. of cycles)	Number of bytes of machine code	HEX.	OCT.	DEC.
A IMM	2	2	88	210	136
A DIR	3	2	98	230	152
A EXT	4	3	B8	270	184
A IND	5	2	A8	250	168
B IMM	2	2	C8	310	200
B DIR	3	2	D8	330	216
B EXT	4	3	F8	370	248
B IND	5	2	E8	350	232

INC
Increment

Operation: ACCX ← (ACCX) + 01
or: M ← (M) + 01
Description: Add one to the contents of ACCX or M.

The N, Z, and V condition codes are set or reset according to the results of this operation.

The C bit is not affected by the operation.

Condition Codes:
- H: Not affected.
- I: Not affected.
- N: Set if most significant bit of the result is set; cleared otherwise.
- Z: Set if all bits of the result are cleared; cleared otherwise.
- V: Set if there was two's complement overflow as a result of the operation; cleared otherwise. Two's complement overflow will occur if and only if (ACCX) or (M) was 7F before the operation.
- C: Not affected.

Addressing Modes, Execution Time, and Machine Code (hexadecimal/octal/decimal):

Addressing Modes	Execution Time (No. of cycles)	Number of bytes of machine code	HEX.	OCT.	DEC.
A	2	1	4C	114	076
B	2	1	5C	134	092
EXT	6	3	7C	174	124
IND	7	2	6C	154	108

INS
Increment Stack Pointer

Operation: SP ← (SP) + 0001
Description: Add one to the stack pointer.
Condition Codes: Not affected.

Addressing Modes, Execution Time, and Machine Code (hexadecimal/octal/decimal):

Addressing Modes	Execution Time (No. of cycles)	Number of bytes of machine code	HEX.	OCT.	DEC.
INHERENT	4	1	31	061	049

INX
Increment Index Register

Operation: IX ← (IX) + 0001
Description: Add one to the index register.

Only the Z bit is set or reset according to the result of this operation.

Condition Codes:
- H: Not affected.
- I: Not affected.
- N: Not affected.
- Z: Set if all 16 bits of the result are cleared; cleared otherwise.
- V: Not affected.
- C: Not affected.

Addressing Modes, Execution Time, and Machine Code (hexadecimal/octal/decimal):

Addressing Modes	Execution Time (No. of cycles)	Number of bytes of machine code	HEX.	OCT.	DEC.
INHERENT	4	1	08	010	008

JMP
Jump

Operation: PC ← numerical address
Description: A jump occurs to the instruction stored at the numerical address. The numerical address is obtained according to the rules for EXTended or INDexed addressing.
Condition Codes: Not affected.

Addressing Modes, Execution Time, and Machine Code (hexadecimal/octal/decimal):

Addressing Modes	Execution Time (No. of cycles)	Number of bytes of machine code	HEX.	OCT.	DEC.
EXT	3	3	7E	176	126
IND	4	2	6E	156	110

JSR
Jump to Subroutine

Operation:
Either: PC ← (PC) + 0003 (for EXTended addressing)
or: PC ← (PC) + 0002 (for INDexed addressing)
Then:
↓ (PCL)
SP ← (SP) - 0001
↓ (PCH)
SP ← (SP) - 0001
PC ← numerical address

Description: The program counter is incremented by 3 or by 2, depending on the addressing mode, and is then pushed onto the stack, eight bits at a time. The stack pointer points to the next empty location in the stack. A jump occurs to the instruction stored at the numerical address. The numerical address is obtained according to the rules for EXTended or INDexed addressing.

Condition Codes: Not affected.

Addressing Modes, Execution Time, and Machine Code (hexadecimal/octal/decimal):

Addressing Modes	Execution Time (No. of cycles)	Number of bytes of machine code	HEX.	OCT.	DEC.
EXT	9	3	BD	275	189
IND	8	2	AD	255	173

LDA
Load Accumulator

Operation: ACCX ← (M)
Description: Loads the contents of memory into the accumulator. The condition codes are set according to the data.

Condition Codes:
- H: Not affected.
- I: Not affected.
- N: Set if most significant bit of the result is set; cleared otherwise.
- Z: Set if all bits of the result are cleared; cleared otherwise.
- V: Cleared.
- C: Not affected.

Addressing Modes, Execution Time, and Machine Code (hexadecimal/octal/decimal):
(DUAL OPERAND)

Addressing Modes	Execution Time (No. of cycles)	Number of bytes of machine code	HEX.	OCT.	DEC.
A IMM	2	2	86	206	134
A DIR	3	2	96	226	150
A EXT	4	3	B6	266	182
A IND	5	2	A6	246	166
B IMM	2	2	C6	306	198
B DIR	3	2	D6	326	214
B EXT	4	3	F6	366	246
B IND	5	2	E6	346	230

LDS
Load Stack Pointer

Operation:
SPH ← (M)
SPL ← (M+1)

Description: Loads the more significant byte of the stack pointer from the byte of memory at the address specified by the program, and loads the less significant byte of the stack pointer from the next byte of memory, at one plus the address specified by the program.

Condition Codes:
- H: Not affected.
- I: Not affected.
- N: Set if the most significant bit of the stack pointer is set by the operation; cleared otherwise.
- Z: Set if all bits of the stack pointer are cleared by the operation; cleared otherwise.
- V: Cleared.
- C: Not affected.

Addressing Modes, Execution Time, and Machine Code (hexadecimal/octal/decimal):

Addressing Modes	Execution Time (No. of cycles)	Number of bytes of machine code	HEX.	OCT.	DEC.
IMM	3	3	8E	216	142
DIR	4	2	9E	236	158
EXT	5	3	BE	276	190
IND	6	2	AE	256	174

LDX
Load Index Register

Operation: IXH ← (M)
IXL ← (M + 1)

Description: Loads the more significant byte of the index register from the byte of memory at the address specified by the program, and loads the less significant byte of the index register from the next byte of memory, at one plus the address specified by the program.

Condition Codes:
- H: Not affected.
- I: Not affected.
- N: Set if the most significant bit of the index register is set by the operation; cleared otherwise.
- Z: Set if all bits of the index register are cleared by the operation; cleared otherwise.
- V: Cleared.
- C: Not affected.

Addressing Modes, Execution Time, and Machine Code (hexadecimal/octal/decimal):

Addressing Modes	Execution Time (No. of cycles)	Number of bytes of machine code	HEX.	OCT.	DEC.
IMM	3	3	CE	316	206
DIR	4	2	DE	336	222
EXT	5	3	FE	376	254
IND	6	2	EE	356	238

LSR
Logical Shift Right

Operation: 0 → [b7 ... b0] → C

Description: Shifts all bits of ACCX or M one place to the right. Bit 7 is loaded with a zero. The C bit is loaded from the least significant bit of ACCX or M.

Condition Codes:
- H: Not affected.
- I: Not affected.
- N: Cleared.
- Z: Set if all bits of the result are cleared; cleared otherwise.
- V: Set if, after the completion of the shift operation, EITHER (N is set and C is cleared) OR (N is cleared and C is set); cleared otherwise.
- C: Set if, before the operation, the least significant bit of the ACCX or M was set; cleared otherwise.

Addressing Modes, Execution Time, and Machine Code (hexadecimal/octal/decimal):

Addressing Modes	Execution Time (No. of cycles)	Number of bytes of machine code	HEX.	OCT.	DEC.
A	2	1	44	104	068
B	2	1	54	124	084
EXT	6	3	74	164	116
IND	7	2	64	144	100

NEG
Negate

Operation: ACCX ← − (ACCX) = 00 − (ACCX)
or: M ← − (M) = 00 − (M)

Description: Replaces the contents of ACCX or M with its two's complement. Note that 80 is left unchanged.

Condition Codes:
- H: Not affected.
- I: Not affected.
- N: Set if most significant bit of the result is set; cleared otherwise.
- Z: Set if all bits of the result are cleared; cleared otherwise.
- V: Set if there would be two's complement overflow as a result of the implied subtraction from zero; this will occur if and only if the contents of ACCX or M is 80.
- C: Set if there would be a borrow in the implied subtraction from zero; the C bit will be set in all cases except when the contents of ACCX or M is 00.

Addressing Modes, Execution Time, and Machine Code (hexadecimal/octal/decimal):

Addressing Modes	Execution Time (No. of cycles)	Number of bytes of machine code	HEX.	OCT.	DEC.
A	2	1	40	100	064
B	2	1	50	120	080
EXT	6	3	70	160	112
IND	7	2	60	140	096

NOP
No Operation

Description: This is a single-word instruction which causes only the program counter to be incremented. No other registers are affected.

Condition Codes: Not affected.

Addressing Modes, Execution Time, and Machine Code (hexadecimal/octal/decimal):

Addressing Modes	Execution Time (No. of cycles)	Number of bytes of machine code	HEX.	OCT.	DEC.
INHERENT	2	1	01	001	001

ORA
Inclusive OR

Operation: ACCX ← (ACCX) ○ (M)

Description: Perform logical "OR" between the contents of ACCX and the contents of M and places the result in ACCX. (Each bit of ACCX after the operation will be the logical "OR" of the corresponding bits of M and of ACCX before the operation).

Condition Codes:
- H: Not affected.
- I: Not affected.
- N: Set if most significant bit of the result is set; cleared otherwise.
- Z: Set if all bits of the result are cleared; cleared otherwise.
- V: Cleared.
- C: Not affected.

Addressing Modes, Execution Time, and Machine Code (hexadecimal/octal/decimal):
(DUAL OPERAND)

Addressing Modes	Execution Time (No. of cycles)	Number of bytes of machine code	HEX.	OCT.	DEC.
A IMM	2	2	8A	212	138
A DIR	3	2	9A	232	154
A EXT	4	3	BA	272	186
A IND	5	2	AA	252	170
B IMM	2	2	CA	312	202
B DIR	3	2	DA	332	218
B EXT	4	3	FA	372	250
B IND	5	2	EA	352	234

PSH
Push Data Onto Stack

Operation: ↓ (ACCX)
SP ← (SP) − 0001

Description: The contents of ACCX is stored in the stack at the address contained in the stack pointer. The stack pointer is then decremented.

Condition Codes: Not affected.

Addressing Modes, Execution Time, and Machine Code (hexadecimal/octal/decimal):

Addressing Modes	Execution Time (No. of cycles)	Number of bytes of machine code	HEX.	OCT.	DEC.
A	4	1	36	066	054
B	4	1	37	067	055

PUL
Pull Data from Stack

Operation: SP ← (SP) + 0001
↑ ACCX

Description: The stack pointer is incremented. The ACCX is then loaded from the stack, from the address which is contained in the stack pointer.

Condition Codes: Not affected.

Addressing Modes, Execution Time, and Machine Code (hexadecimal/octal/decimal):

Addressing Modes	Execution Time (No. of cycles)	Number of bytes of machine code	HEX.	OCT.	DEC.
A	4	1	32	062	050
B	4	1	33	063	051

ROL
Rotate Left

Operation: C ← [b7 ... b0] ← C

Description: Shifts all bits of ACCX or M one place to the left. Bit 0 is loaded from the C bit. The C bit is loaded from the most significant bit of ACCX or M.

Condition Codes:
- H: Not affected.
- I: Not affected.
- N: Set if most significant bit of the result is set; cleared otherwise.
- Z: Set if all bits of the result are cleared; cleared otherwise.
- V: Set if, after the completion of the operation, EITHER (N is set and C is cleared) OR (N is cleared and C is set); cleared otherwise.
- C: Set if, before the operation, the most significant bit of the ACCX or M was set; cleared otherwise.

Addressing Modes, Execution Time, and Machine Code (hexadecimal/octal/decimal):

Addressing Modes	Execution Time (No. of cycles)	Number of bytes of machine code	HEX.	OCT.	DEC.
A	2	1	49	111	073
B	2	1	59	131	089
EXT	6	3	79	171	121
IND	7	2	69	151	105

ROR — Rotate Right

Operation:

```
C → [ b7 ............ b0 ] → C
```

Description: Shifts all bits of ACCX or M one place to the right. Bit 7 is loaded from the C bit. The C bit is loaded from the least significant bit of ACCX or M.

Condition Codes:
- H: Not affected.
- I: Not affected.
- N: Set if most significant bit of the result is set; cleared otherwise.
- Z: Set if all bits of the result are cleared; cleared otherwise.
- V: Set if, after the completion of the operation, EITHER (N is set and C is cleared) OR (N is cleared and C is set); cleared otherwise.
- C: Set if, before the operation, the least significant bit of the ACCX or M was set; cleared otherwise.

Addressing Modes, Execution Time, and Machine Code (hexadecimal/octal/decimal):

Addressing Modes	Execution Time (No. of cycles)	Number of bytes of machine code	HEX.	OCT.	DEC.
A	2	1	46	106	070
B	2	1	56	126	086
EXT	6	3	76	166	118
IND	7	2	66	146	102

RTI — Return from Interrupt

Operation:
- SP ← (SP) + 0001, ↑CC
- SP ← (SP) + 0001, ↑ACCB
- SP ← (SP) + 0001, ↑ACCA
- SP ← (SP) + 0001, ↑IXH
- SP ← (SP) + 0001, ↑IXL
- SP ← (SP) + 0001, ↑PCH
- SP ← (SP) + 0001, ↑PCL

Description: The condition codes, accumulators B and A, the index register, and the program counter, will be restored to a state pulled from the stack. Note that the interrupt mask bit will be reset if and only if the corresponding bit stored in the stack is zero.

Condition Codes: Restored to the states pulled from the stack.

Addressing Modes, Execution Time, and Machine Code (hexadecimal/octal/decimal):

Addressing Modes	Execution Time (No. of cycles)	Number of bytes of machine code	HEX.	OCT.	DEC.
INHERENT	10	1	3B	073	059

RTS — Return from Subroutine

Operation:
- SP ← (SP) + 0001
- ↑PCH
- SP ← (SP) + 0001
- ↑PCL

Description: The stack pointer is incremented (by 1). The contents of the byte of memory, at the address now contained in the stack pointer, are loaded into the 8 bits of highest significance in the program counter. The stack pointer is again incremented (by 1). The contents of the byte of memory, at the address now contained in the stack pointer, are loaded into the 8 bits of lowest significance in the program counter.

Condition Codes: Not affected.

Addressing Modes, Execution Time, and Machine Code (hexadecimal/octal/decimal):

Addressing Modes	Execution Time (No. of cycles)	Number of bytes of machine code	HEX.	OCT.	DEC.
INHERENT	5	1	39	071	057

SBA — Subtract Accumulators

Operation: ACCA ← (ACCA) − (ACCB)

Description: Subtracts the contents of ACCB from the contents of ACCA and places the result in ACCA. The contents of ACCB are not affected.

Condition Codes:
- H: Not affected.
- I: Not affected.
- N: Set if most significant bit of the result is set; cleared otherwise.
- Z: Set if all bits of the result are cleared; cleared otherwise.
- V: Set if there was two's complement overflow as a result of the operation.
- C: Carry is set if the absolute value of accumulator B plus previous carry is larger than the absolute value of accumulator A; reset otherwise.

Addressing Modes, Execution Time, and Machine Code (hexadecimal/octal/decimal):

Addressing Modes	Execution Time (No. of cycles)	Number of bytes of machine code	HEX.	OCT.	DEC.
INHERENT	2	1	10	020	016

SBC — Subtract with Carry

Operation: ACCX ← (ACCX) − (M) − (C)

Description: Subtracts the contents of M and C from the contents of ACCX and places the result in ACCX.

Condition Codes:
- H: Not affected.
- I: Not affected.
- N: Set if most significant bit of the result is set; cleared otherwise.
- Z: Set if all bits of the result are cleared; cleared otherwise.
- V: Set if there was two's complement overflow as a result of the operation; cleared otherwise.
- C: Carry is set if the absolute value of the contents of memory plus previous carry is larger than the absolute value of the accumulator; reset otherwise.

Addressing Modes, Execution Time, and Machine Code (hexadecimal/octal/decimal):
(DUAL OPERAND)

Addressing Modes	Execution Time (No. of cycles)	Number of bytes of machine code	HEX.	OCT.	DEC.
A IMM	2	2	82	202	130
A DIR	3	2	92	222	146
A EXT	4	3	B2	262	178
A IND	5	2	A2	242	162
B IMM	2	2	C2	302	194
B DIR	3	2	D2	322	210
B EXT	4	3	F2	362	242
B IND	5	2	E2	342	226

SEC — Set Carry

Operation: C bit ← 1

Description: Sets the carry bit in the processor condition codes register.

Condition Codes:
- H: Not affected.
- I: Not affected.
- N: Not affected.
- Z: Not affected.
- V: Not affected.
- C: Set.

Addressing Modes, Execution Time, and Machine Code (hexadecimal/octal/decimal):

Addressing Modes	Execution Time (No. of cycles)	Number of bytes of machine code	HEX.	OCT.	DEC.
INHERENT	2	1	0D	015	013

SEI — Set Interrupt Mask

Operation: I bit ← 1

Description: Sets the interrupt mask bit in the processor condition codes register. The microprocessor is inhibited from servicing an interrupt from a peripheral device, and will continue with execution of the instructions of the program, until the interrupt mask bit has been cleared.

Condition Codes:
- H: Not affected.
- I: Set.
- N: Not affected.
- Z: Not affected.
- V: Not affected.
- C: Not affected.

Addressing Modes, Execution Time, and Machine Code (hexadecimal/octal/decimal):

Addressing Modes	Execution Time (No. of cycles)	Number of bytes of machine code	HEX.	OCT.	DEC.
INHERENT	2	1	0F	017	015

SEV — Set Two's Complement Overflow Bit

Operation: V bit ← 1

Description: Sets the two's complement overflow bit in the processor condition codes register.

Condition Codes:
- H: Not affected.
- I: Not affected.
- N: Not affected.
- Z: Not affected.
- V: Set.
- C: Not affected.

Addressing Modes, Execution Time, and Machine Code (hexadecimal/octal/decimal):

Addressing Modes	Execution Time (No. of cycles)	Number of bytes of machine code	HEX.	OCT.	DEC.
INHERENT	2	1	0B	013	011

STA — Store Accumulator

Operation: M ← (ACCX)

Description: Stores the contents of ACCX in memory. The contents of ACCX remains unchanged.

Condition Codes:
- H: Not affected.
- I: Not affected.
- N: Set if the most significant bit of the contents of ACCX is set; cleared otherwise.
- Z: Set if all bits of the contents of ACCX are cleared; cleared otherwise.
- V: Cleared.
- C: Not affected.

Addressing Modes, Execution Time, and Machine Code (hexadecimal/octal/decimal):

Addressing Modes	Execution Time (No. of cycles)	Number of bytes of machine code	HEX.	OCT.	DEC.
A DIR	4	2	97	227	151
A EXT	5	3	B7	267	183
A IND	6	2	A7	247	167
B DIR	4	2	D7	327	215
B EXT	5	3	F7	367	247
B IND	6	2	E7	347	231

STS — Store Stack Pointer

Operation:
M ← (SPH)
M + 1 ← (SPL)

Description: Stores the more significant byte of the stack pointer in memory at the address specified by the program, and stores the less significant byte of the stack pointer at the next location in memory, at one plus the address specified by the program.

Condition Codes:
- H: Not affected.
- I: Not affected.
- N: Set if the most significant bit of the stack pointer is set; cleared otherwise.
- Z: Set if all bits of the stack pointer are cleared; cleared otherwise.
- V: Cleared.
- C: Not affected.

Addressing Modes, Execution Time, and Machine Code (hexadecimal/octal/decimal):

Addressing Modes	Execution Time (No. of cycles)	Number of bytes of machine code	HEX.	OCT.	DEC.
DIR	5	2	9F	237	159
EXT	6	3	BF	277	191
IND	7	2	AF	257	175

STX — Store Index Register

Operation:
M ← (IXH)
M + 1 ← (IXL)

Description: Stores the more significant byte of the index register in memory at the address specified by the program, and stores the less significant byte of the index register at the next location in memory, at one plus the address specified by the program.

Condition Codes:
- H: Not affected.
- I: Not affected.
- N: Set if the most significant bite of the index register is set; cleared otherwise.
- Z: Set if all bits of the index register are cleared; cleared otherwise.
- V: Cleared.
- C: Not affected.

Addressing Modes, Execution Time, and Machine Code (hexadecimal/octal/decimal):

Addressing Modes	Execution Time (No. of cycles)	Number of bytes of machine code	HEX.	OCT.	DEC.
DIR	5	2	DF	337	223
EXT	6	3	FF	377	255
IND	7	2	EF	357	239

SUB — Subtract

Operation: ACCX ← (ACCX) − (M)

Description: Subtracts the contents of M from the contents of ACCX and places the result in ACCX.

Condition Codes:
- H: Not affected.
- I: Not affected.
- N: Set if most significant bit of the result is set; cleared otherwise.
- Z: Set if all bits of the result are cleared; cleared otherwise.
- V: Set if there was two's complement overflow as a result of the operation; cleared otherwise.
- C: Set if the absolute value of the contents of memory are larger than the absolute value of the accumulator; reset otherwise.

Addressing Modes, Execution Time, and Machine Code (hexadecimal/octal/decimal):
(DUAL OPERAND)

Addressing Modes	Execution Time (No. of cycles)	Number of bytes of machine code	HEX.	OCT.	DEC.
A IMM	2	2	80	200	128
A DIR	3	2	90	220	144
A EXT	4	3	B0	260	176
A IND	5	2	A0	240	160
B IMM	2	2	C0	300	192
B DIR	3	2	D0	320	208
B EXT	4	3	F0	360	240
B IND	5	2	E0	340	224

SWI — Software Interrupt

Operation:
PC ← (PC) + 0001
↓ (PCL), SP ← (SP)−0001
↓ (PCH), SP ← (SP)−0001
↓ (IXL), SP ← (SP)−0001
↓ (IXH), SP ← (SP)−0001
↓ (ACCA), SP ← (SP)−0001
↓ (ACCB), SP ← (SP)−0001
↓ (CC), SP ← (SP)−0001
I ← 1
PCH ← (n−0005)
PCL ← (n−0004)

Description: The program counter is incremented (by 1). The program counter, index register, and accumulator A and B, are pushed into the stack. The condition codes register is then pushed into the stack, with condition codes H, I, N, Z, V, C going respectively into bit positions 5 thru 0, and the top two bits (in bit positions 7 and 6) are set (to the 1 state). The stack pointer is decremented (by 1) after each byte of data is stored in the stack.

The interrupt mask bit is then set. The program counter is then loaded with the address stored in the software interrupt pointer at memory locations (n−5) and (n−4), where n is the address corresponding to a high state on all lines of the address bus.

Condition Codes:
- H: Not affected.
- I: Set.
- N: Not affected.
- Z: Not affected.
- V: Not affected.
- C: Not affected.

Addressing Modes, Execution Time, and Machine Code (hexadecimal/octal/decimal):

Addressing Modes	Execution Time (No. of cycles)	Number of bytes of machine code	HEX.	OCT.	DEC.
INHERENT	12	1	3F	077	063

TAB — Transfer from Accumulator A to Accumulator B

Operation: ACCB ← (ACCA)

Description: Moves the contents of ACCA to ACCB. The former contents of ACCB are lost. The contents of ACCA are not affected.

Condition Codes:
- H: Not affected.
- I: Not affected.
- N: Set if the most significant bit of the contents of the accumulator is set; cleared otherwise.
- Z: Set if all bits of the contents of the accumulator are cleared; cleared otherwise.
- V: Cleared.
- C: Not affected.

Addressing Modes, Execution Time, and Machine Code (hexadecimal/octal/decimal):

Addressing Modes	Execution Time (No. of cycles)	Number of bytes of machine code	HEX.	OCT.	DEC.
INHERENT	2	1	16	026	022

TAP
Transfer from Accumulator A to Processor Condition Codes Register

Operation: CC ← (ACCA)

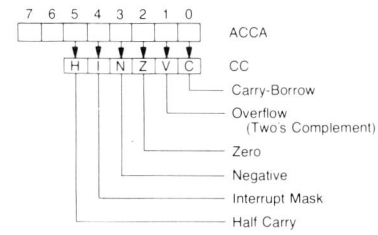

Bit Positions

```
 7 6 5 4 3 2 1 0
             ACCA
    H I N Z V C   CC
              └─ Carry-Borrow
            └─── Overflow (Two's Complement)
          └───── Zero
        └─────── Negative
      └───────── Interrupt Mask
    └─────────── Half Carry
```

Description: Transfers the contents of bit positions 0 thru 5 of accumulator A to the corresponding bit positions of the processor condition codes register. The contents of accumulator A remain unchanged.

Condition Codes: Set or reset according to the contents of the respective bits 0 thru 5 of accumulator A.

Addressing Modes, Execution Time, and Machine Code (hexadecimal/octal/decimal):

Addressing Modes	Execution Time (No. of cycles)	Number of bytes of machine code	HEX.	OCT.	DEC.
INHERENT	2	1	06	006	006

TBA
Transfer from Accumulator B to Accumulator A

Operation: ACCA ← (ACCB)

Description: Moves the contents of ACCB to ACCA. The former contents of ACCA are lost. The contents of ACCB are not affected.

Condition Codes:
- H: Not affected.
- I: Not affected.
- N: Set if the most significant accumulator bit is set; cleared otherwise.
- Z: Set if all accumulator bits are cleared; cleared otherwise.
- V: Cleared.
- C: Not affected.

Addressing Modes, Execution Time, and Machine Code (hexadecimal/octal/decimal):

Addressing Modes	Execution Time (No. of cycles)	Number of bytes of machine code	HEX.	OCT.	DEC.
INHERENT	2	1	17	027	023

TPA
Transfer from Processor Condition Codes Register to Accumulator A

Operation: ACCA ← (CC)

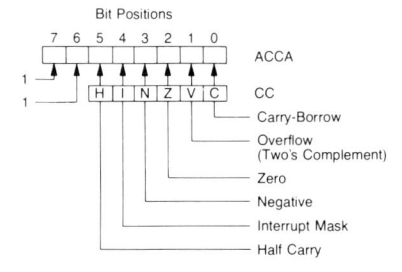

Bit Positions

```
 7 6 5 4 3 2 1 0
             ACCA
 1 1 H I N Z V C   CC
              └─ Carry-Borrow
            └─── Overflow (Two's Complement)
          └───── Zero
        └─────── Negative
      └───────── Interrupt Mask
    └─────────── Half Carry
```

Description: Transfers the contents of the processor condition codes register to corresponding bit positions 0 thru 5 of accumulator A. Bit positions 6 and 7 of accumulator A are set (i.e. go to the "1" state). The processor condition codes register remains unchanged.

Condition Codes: Not affected.

Addressing Modes, Execution Time, and Machine Code (hexadecimal/octal/decimal):

Addressing Modes	Execution Time (No. of cycles)	Number of bytes of machine code	HEX.	OCT.	DEC.
INHERENT	2	1	07	007	007

TST
Test

Operation: (ACCX) − 00
(M) − 00

Description: Set condition codes N and Z according to the contents of ACCX or M.

Condition Codes:
- H: Not affected.
- I: Not affected.
- N: Set if most significant bit of the contents of ACCX or M is set; cleared otherwise.
- Z: Set if all bits of the contents of ACCX or M are cleared; cleared otherwise.
- V: Cleared.
- C: Cleared.

Addressing Modes, Execution Time, and Machine Code (hexadecimal/octal/decimal):

Addressing Modes	Execution Time (No. of cycles)	Number of bytes of machine code	HEX.	OCT.	DEC.
A	2	1	4D	115	077
B	2	1	5D	135	093
EXT	6	3	7D	175	125
IND	7	2	6D	155	109

TSX
Transfer from Stack Pointer to Index Register

Operation: IX ← (SP) + 0001

Description: Loads the index register with one plus the contents of the stack pointer. The contents of the stack pointer remain unchanged.

Condition Codes: Not affected.

Addressing Modes, Execution Time, and Machine Code (hexadecimal/octal/decimal):

Addressing Modes	Execution Time (No. of cycles)	Number of bytes of machine code	HEX.	OCT.	DEC.
INHERENT	4	1	30	060	048

TXS
Transfer From Index Register to Stack Pointer

Operation: SP ← (IX) − 0001

Description: Loads the stack pointer with the contents of the index register, minus one. The contents of the index register remain unchanged.

Condition Codes: Not affected.

Addressing Modes, Execution Time, and Machine Code (hexadecimal/octal/decimal):

Addressing Modes	Execution Time (No. of cycles)	Number of bytes of machine code	HEX.	OCT.	DEC.
INHERENT	4	1	35	065	053

WAI
Wait for Interrupt

Operation:
PC ← (PC) + 0001
↓ (PCL), SP ← (SP)−0001
↓ (PCH), SP ← (SP)−0001
↓ (IXL), SP ← (SP)−0001
↓ (IXH), SP ← (SP)−0001
↓ (ACCA), SP ← (SP)−0001
↓ (ACCB), SP ← (SP)−0001
↓ (CC), SP ← (SP)−0001

Condition Codes: Not affected.

Description: The program counter is incremented (by 1). The program counter, index register, and accumulators A and B, are pushed into the stack. The condition codes register is then pushed into the stack, with condition codes H, I, N, Z, V, C going respectively into bit positions 5 thru 0, and the top two bits (in bit positions 7 and 6) are set (to the 1 state). The stack pointer is decremented (by 1) after each byte of data is stored in the stack.

Execution of the program is then suspended until an interrupt from a peripheral device is signalled, by the interrupt request control input going to a low state.

When an interrupt is signalled on the interrupt request line, and provided the I bit is clear, execution proceeds as follows. The interrupt mask bit is set. The program counter is then loaded with the address stored in the internal interrupt pointer at memory locations (n-7) and (n-6), where n is the address corresponding to a high state on all lines of the address bus.

Condition Codes:
- H: Not affected.
- I: Not affected until an interrupt request signal is detected on the interrupt request control line. When the interrupt request is received the I bit is set and further execution takes place, provided the I bit was initially clear.
- N: Not affected.   V: Not affected.
- Z: Not affected.   C: Not affected.

Addressing Modes, Execution Time, and Machine Code (hexadecimal/octal/decimal):

Addressing Modes	Execution Time (No. of cycles)	Number of bytes of machine code	HEX.	OCT.	DEC.
INHERENT	9	1	3E	076	062

appendix II

6800 Instruction Set—Motorola Classifications

TABLE 1 — HEXADECIMAL VALUES OF MACHINE CODES

00	·		40	NEG	A		80	SUB	A	IMM	C0	SUB	B	IMM
01	NOP		41	·			81	CMP	A	IMM	C1	CMP	B	IMM
02	·		42	·			82	SBC	A	IMM	C2	SBC	B	IMM
03	·		43	COM	A		83	·			C3	·		
04	·		44	LSR	A		84	AND	A	IMM	C4	AND	B	IMM
05	·		45	·			85	BIT	A	IMM	C5	BIT	B	IMM
06	TAP		46	ROR	A		86	LDA	A	IMM	C6	LDA	B	IMM
07	TPA		47	ASR	A		87	·			C7	·		
08	INX		48	ASL	A		88	EOR	A	IMM	C8	EOR	B	IMM
09	DEX		49	ROL	A		89	ADC	A	IMM	C9	ADC	B	IMM
0A	CLV		4A	DEC	A		8A	ORA	A	IMM	CA	ORA	B	IMM
0B	SEV		4B	·			8B	ADD	A	IMM	CB	ADD	B	IMM
0C	CLC		4C	INC	A		8C	CPX	A	IMM	CC	·		
0D	SEC		4D	TST	A		8D	BSR		REL	CD	·		
0E	CLI		4E	·			8E	LDS		IMM	CE	LDX		IMM
0F	SEI		4F	CLR	A		8F	·			CF	·		
10	SBA		50	NEG	B		90	SUB	A	DIR	D0	SUB	B	DIR
11	CBA		51	·			91	CMP	A	DIR	D1	CMP	B	DIR
12	·		52	·			92	SBC	A	DIR	D2	SBC	B	DIR
13	·		53	COM	B		93	·			D3	·		
14	·		54	LSR	B		94	AND	A	DIR	D4	AND	B	DIR
15	·		55	·			95	BIT	A	DIR	D5	BIT	B	DIR
16	TAB		56	ROR	B		96	LDA	A	DIR	D6	LDA	B	DIR
17	TBA		57	ASR	B		97	STA	A	DIR	D7	STA	B	DIR
18	·		58	ASL	B		98	EOR	A	DIR	D8	EOR	B	DIR
19	DAA		59	ROL	B		99	ADC	A	DIR	D9	ADC	B	DIR
1A	·		5A	DEC	B		9A	ORA	A	DIR	DA	ORA	B	DIR
1B	ABA		5B	·			9B	ADD	A	DIR	DB	ADD	B	DIR
1C	·		5C	INC	B		9C	CPX		DIR	DC	·		
1D	·		5D	TST	B		9D	·			DD	·		
1E	·		5E	·			9E	LDS		DIR	DE	LDX		DIR
1F	·		5F	CLR	B		9F	STS		DIR	DF	STX		DIR
20	BRA	REL	60	NEG		IND	A0	SUB	A	IND	E0	SUB	B	IND
21	·		61	·			A1	CMP	A	IND	E1	CMP	B	IND
22	BHI	REL	62	·			A2	SBC	A	IND	E2	SBC	B	IND
23	BLS	REL	63	COM		IND	A3	·			E3	·		
24	BCC	REL	64	LSR		IND	A4	AND	A	IND	E4	AND	B	IND
25	BCS	REL	65	·			A5	BIT	A	IND	E5	BIT	B	IND
26	BNE	REL	66	ROR		IND	A6	LDA	A	IND	E6	LDA	B	IND
27	BEQ	REL	67	ASR		IND	A7	STA	A	IND	E7	STA	B	IND
28	BVC	REL	68	ASL		IND	A8	EOR	A	IND	E8	EOR	B	IND
29	BVS	REL	69	ROL		IND	A9	ADC	A	IND	E9	ADC	B	IND
2A	BPL	REL	6A	DEC		IND	AA	ORA	A	IND	EA	ORA	B	IND
2B	BMI	REL	6B	·			AB	ADD	A	IND	EB	ADD	B	IND
2C	BGE	REL	6C	INC		IND	AC	CPX		IND	EC	·		
2D	BLT	REL	6D	TST		IND	AD	JSR		IND	ED	·		
2E	BGT	REL	6E	JMP		IND	AE	LDS		IND	EE	LDX		IND
2F	BLE	REL	6F	CLR		IND	AF	STS		IND	EF	STX		IND
30	TSX		70	NEG		EXT	B0	SUB	A	EXT	F0	SUB	B	EXT
31	INS		71	·			B1	CMP	A	EXT	F1	CMP	B	EXT
32	PUL	A	72	·			B2	SBC	A	EXT	F2	SBC	B	EXT
33	PUL	B	73	COM		EXT	B3	·			F3	·		
34	DES		74	LSR		EXT	B4	AND	A	EXT	F4	AND	B	EXT
35	TXS		75	·			B5	BIT	A	EXT	F5	BIT	B	EXT
36	PSH	A	76	ROR		EXT	B6	LDA	A	EXT	F6	LDA	B	EXT
37	PSH	B	77	ASR		EXT	B7	STA	A	EXT	F7	STA	B	EXT
38	·		78	ASL		EXT	B8	EOR	A	EXT	F8	EOR	B	EXT
39	RTS		79	ROL		EXT	B9	ADC	A	EXT	F9	ADC	B	EXT
3A	·		7A	DEC		EXT	BA	ORA	A	EXT	FA	ORA	B	EXT
3B	RTI		7B	·			BB	ADD	A	EXT	FB	ADD	B	EXT
3C	·		7C	INC		EXT	BC	CPX		EXT	FC	·		
3D	·		7D	TST		EXT	BD	JSR		EXT	FD	·		
3E	WAI		7E	JMP		EXT	BE	LDS		EXT	FE	LDX		EXT
3F	SWI		7F	CLR		EXT	BF	STS		EXT	FF	STX		EXT

TABLE 2 — ACCUMULATOR AND MEMORY OPERATIONS

OPERATIONS	MNEMONIC	IMMED OP ~ #	DIRECT OP ~ #	INDEX OP ~ #	EXTND OP ~ #	IMPLIED OP ~ #	BOOLEAN/ARITHMETIC OPERATION (All register labels refer to contents)	COND CODE REG 5 4 3 2 1 0 H I N Z V C
Add	ADDA	8B 2 2	9B 3 2	AB 5 2	BB 4 3		A + M → A	↕ • ↕ ↕ ↕ ↕
	ADDB	CB 2 2	DB 3 2	EB 5 2	FB 4 3		B + M → B	↕ • ↕ ↕ ↕ ↕
Add Acmltrs	ABA					1B 2 1	A + B → A	↕ • ↕ ↕ ↕ ↕
Add with Carry	ADCA	89 2 2	99 3 2	A9 5 2	B9 4 3		A + M + C → A	↕ • ↕ ↕ ↕ ↕
	ADCB	C9 2 2	D9 3 2	E9 5 2	F9 4 3		B + M + C → B	↕ • ↕ ↕ ↕ ↕
And	ANDA	84 2 2	94 3 2	A4 5 2	B4 4 3		A · M → A	• • ↕ ↕ R •
	ANDB	C4 2 2	D4 3 2	E4 5 2	F4 4 3		B · M → B	• • ↕ ↕ R •
Bit Test	BITA	85 2 2	95 3 2	A5 5 2	B5 4 3		A · M	• • ↕ ↕ R •
	BITB	C5 2 2	D5 3 2	E5 5 2	F5 4 3		B · M	• • ↕ ↕ R •
Clear	CLR			6F 7 2	7F 6 3		00 → M	• • R S R R
	CLRA					4F 2 1	00 → A	• • R S R R
	CLRB					5F 2 1	00 → B	• • R S R R
Compare	CMPA	81 2 2	91 3 2	A1 5 2	B1 4 3		A − M	• • ↕ ↕ ↕ ↕
	CMPB	C1 2 2	D1 3 2	E1 5 2	F1 4 3		B − M	• • ↕ ↕ ↕ ↕
Compare Acmltrs	CBA					11 2 1	A − B	• • ↕ ↕ ↕ ↕
Complement, 1's	COM			63 7 2	73 6 3		M̄ → M	• • ↕ ↕ R S
	COMA					43 2 1	Ā → A	• • ↕ ↕ R S
	COMB					53 2 1	B̄ → B	• • ↕ ↕ R S
Complement, 2's	NEG			60 7 2	70 6 3		00 − M → M	• • ↕ ↕ ① ②
(Negate)	NEGA					40 2 1	00 − A → A	• • ↕ ↕ ① ②
	NEGB					50 2 1	00 − B → B	• • ↕ ↕ ① ②
Decimal Adjust, A	DAA					19 2 1	Converts Binary Add. of BCD Characters into BCD Format	• • ↕ ↕ ↕ ③
Decrement	DEC			6A 7 2	7A 6 3		M − 1 → M	• • ↕ ↕ ④ •
	DECA					4A 2 1	A − 1 → A	• • ↕ ↕ ④ •
	DECB					5A 2 1	B − 1 → B	• • ↕ ↕ ④ •
Exclusive OR	EORA	88 2 2	98 3 2	A8 5 2	B8 4 3		A ⊕ M → A	• • ↕ ↕ R •
	EORB	C8 2 2	D8 3 2	E8 5 2	F8 4 3		B ⊕ M → B	• • ↕ ↕ R •
Increment	INC			6C 7 2	7C 6 3		M + 1 → M	• • ↕ ↕ ⑤ •
	INCA					4C 2 1	A + 1 → A	• • ↕ ↕ ⑤ •
	INCB					5C 2 1	B + 1 → B	• • ↕ ↕ ⑤ •
Load Acmltr	LDAA	86 2 2	96 3 2	A6 5 2	B6 4 3		M → A	• • ↕ ↕ R •
	LDAB	C6 2 2	D6 3 2	E6 5 2	F6 4 3		M → B	• • ↕ ↕ R •
Or, Inclusive	ORAA	8A 2 2	9A 3 2	AA 5 2	BA 4 3		A + M → A	• • ↕ ↕ R •
	ORAB	CA 2 2	DA 3 2	EA 5 2	FA 4 3		B + M → B	• • ↕ ↕ R •
Push Data	PSHA					36 4 1	A → M_SP, SP − 1 → SP	• • • • • •
	PSHB					37 4 1	B → M_SP, SP − 1 → SP	• • • • • •
Pull Data	PULA					32 4 1	SP + 1 → SP, M_SP → A	• • • • • •
	PULB					33 4 1	SP + 1 → SP, M_SP → B	• • • • • •
Rotate Left	ROL			69 7 2	79 6 3		M ⟲	• • ↕ ↕ ⑥ ↕
	ROLA					49 2 1	A ⟲	• • ↕ ↕ ⑥ ↕
	ROLB					59 2 1	B ⟲	• • ↕ ↕ ⑥ ↕
Rotate Right	ROR			66 7 2	76 6 3		M ⟳	• • ↕ ↕ ⑥ ↕
	RORA					46 2 1	A ⟳	• • ↕ ↕ ⑥ ↕
	RORB					56 2 1	B ⟳	• • ↕ ↕ ⑥ ↕
Shift Left, Arithmetic	ASL			68 7 2	78 6 3		M	• • ↕ ↕ ⑥ ↕
	ASLA					48 2 1	A	• • ↕ ↕ ⑥ ↕
	ASLB					58 2 1	B	• • ↕ ↕ ⑥ ↕
Shift Right, Arithmetic	ASR			67 7 2	77 6 3		M	• • ↕ ↕ ⑥ ↕
	ASRA					47 2 1	A	• • ↕ ↕ ⑥ ↕
	ASRB					57 2 1	B	• • ↕ ↕ ⑥ ↕
Shift Right, Logic	LSR			64 7 2	74 6 3		M	• • R ↕ ⑥ ↕
	LSRA					44 2 1	A	• • R ↕ ⑥ ↕
	LSRB					54 2 1	B	• • R ↕ ⑥ ↕
Store Acmltr	STAA		97 4 2	A7 6 2	B7 5 3		A → M	• • ↕ ↕ R •
	STAB		D7 4 2	E7 6 2	F7 5 3		B → M	• • ↕ ↕ R •
Subtract	SUBA	80 2 2	90 3 2	A0 5 2	B0 4 3		A − M → A	• • ↕ ↕ ↕ ↕
	SUBB	C0 2 2	D0 3 2	E0 5 2	F0 4 3		B − M → B	• • ↕ ↕ ↕ ↕
Subtract Acmltrs	SBA					10 2 1	A − B → A	• • ↕ ↕ ↕ ↕
Subtr. with Carry	SBCA	82 2 2	92 3 2	A2 5 2	B2 4 3		A − M − C → A	• • ↕ ↕ ↕ ↕
	SBCB	C2 2 2	D2 3 2	E2 5 2	F2 4 3		B − M − C → B	• • ↕ ↕ ↕ ↕
Transfer Acmltrs	TAB					16 2 1	A → B	• • ↕ ↕ R •
	TBA					17 2 1	B → A	• • ↕ ↕ R •
Test, Zero or Minus	TST			6D 7 2	7D 6 3		M − 00	• • ↕ ↕ R R
	TSTA					4D 2 1	A − 00	• • ↕ ↕ R R
	TSTB					5D 2 1	B − 00	• • ↕ ↕ R R

LEGEND:
- OP Operation Code (Hexadecimal);
- ~   Number of MPU Cycles;
- #   Number of Program Bytes;
- +   Arithmetic Plus;
- −   Arithmetic Minus;
- ·   Boolean AND;
- M_SP Contents of memory location pointed to be Stack Pointer;
- +   Boolean Inclusive OR;
- ⊕   Boolean Exclusive OR;
- M̄   Complement of M;
- →   Transfer Into;
- 0   Bit = Zero;
- 00 Byte = Zero;

CONDITION CODE SYMBOLS:
- H   Half-carry from bit 3;
- I   Interrupt mask
- N   Negative (sign bit)
- Z   Zero (byte)
- V   Overflow, 2's complement
- C   Carry from bit 7
- R   Reset Always
- S   Set Always
- ↕   Test and set if true, cleared otherwise
- •   Not Affected

CONDITION CODE REGISTER NOTES:
(Bit set if test is true and cleared otherwise)

1. (Bit V) Test: Result = 10000000?
2. (Bit C) Test: Result = 00000000?
3. (Bit C) Test: Decimal value of most significant BCD Character greater than nine?
   (Not cleared if previously set.)
4. (Bit V) Test: Operand = 10000000 prior to execution?
5. (Bit V) Test: Operand = 01111111 prior to execution?
6. (Bit V) Test: Set equal to result of N⊕C after shift has occurred.

TABLE 3 — INDEX REGISTER AND STACK POINTER INSTRUCTIONS

POINTER OPERATIONS	MNEMONIC	IMMED OP ~ #	DIRECT OP ~ #	INDEX OP ~ #	EXTND OP ~ #	IMPLIED OP ~ #	BOOLEAN/ARITHMETIC OPERATION	COND. CODE REG. 5 4 3 2 1 0 H I N Z V C
Compare Index Reg	CPX	8C 3 3	9C 4 2	AC 6 2	BC 5 3		$X_H - M, X_L - (M+1)$	• • ① ① ② •
Decrement Index Reg	DEX					09 4 1	$X - 1 \to X$	• • • ① • •
Decrement Stack Pntr	DES					34 4 1	$SP - 1 \to SP$	• • • • • •
Increment Index Reg	INX					08 4 1	$X + 1 \to X$	• • • ① • •
Increment Stack Pntr	INS					31 4 1	$SP + 1 \to SP$	• • • • • •
Load Index Reg	LDX	CE 3 3	DE 4 2	EE 6 2	FE 5 3		$M \to X_H, (M+1) \to X_L$	• • ③ ③ R •
Load Stack Pntr	LDS	8E 3 3	9E 4 2	AE 6 2	BE 5 3		$M \to SP_H, (M+1) \to SP_L$	• • ③ ③ R •
Store Index Reg	STX		DF 5 2	EF 7 2	FF 6 3		$X_H \to M, X_L \to (M+1)$	• • ③ ③ R •
Store Stack Pntr	STS		9F 5 2	AF 7 2	BF 6 3		$SP_H \to M, SP_L \to (M+1)$	• • ③ ③ R •
Indx Reg → Stack Pntr	TXS					35 4 1	$X - 1 \to SP$	• • • • • •
Stack Pntr → Indx Reg	TSX					30 4 1	$SP + 1 \to X$	• • • • • •

① (Bit N) Test: Sign bit of most significant (MS) byte of result = 1?
② (Bit V) Test: 2's complement overflow from subtraction of ms bytes?
③ (Bit N) Test: Result less than zero? (Bit 15 = 1)

TABLE 4 — JUMP AND BRANCH INSTRUCTIONS

OPERATIONS	MNEMONIC	RELATIVE OP ~ #	INDEX OP ~ #	EXTND OP ~ #	IMPLIED OP ~ #	BRANCH TEST	COND. CODE REG. 5 4 3 2 1 0 H I N Z V C
Branch Always	BRA	20 4 2				None	• • • • • •
Branch If Carry Clear	BCC	24 4 2				$C = 0$	• • • • • •
Branch If Carry Set	BCS	25 4 2				$C = 1$	• • • • • •
Branch If = Zero	BEQ	27 4 2				$Z = 1$	• • • • • •
Branch If ≥ Zero	BGE	2C 4 2				$N \oplus V = 0$	• • • • • •
Branch If > Zero	BGT	2E 4 2				$Z + (N \oplus V) = 0$	• • • • • •
Branch If Higher	BHI	22 4 2				$C + Z = 0$	• • • • • •
Branch If ≤ Zero	BLE	2F 4 2				$Z + (N \oplus V) = 1$	• • • • • •
Branch If Lower Or Same	BLS	23 4 2				$C + Z = 1$	• • • • • •
Branch If < Zero	BLT	2D 4 2				$N \oplus V = 1$	• • • • • •
Branch If Minus	BMI	2B 4 2				$N = 1$	• • • • • •
Branch If Not Equal Zero	BNE	26 4 2				$Z = 0$	• • • • • •
Branch If Overflow Clear	BVC	28 4 2				$V = 0$	• • • • • •
Branch If Overflow Set	BVS	29 4 2				$V = 1$	• • • • • •
Branch If Plus	BPL	2A 4 2				$N = 0$	• • • • • •
Branch To Subroutine	BSR	8D 8 2					• • • • • •
Jump	JMP		6E 4 2	7E 3 3		See Special Operations	• • • • • •
Jump To Subroutine	JSR		AD 8 2	BD 9 3			• • • • • •
No Operation	NOP				01 2 1	Advances Prog. Cntr. Only	• • • • • •
Return From Interrupt	RTI				3B 10 1		①
Return From Subroutine	RTS				39 5 1		• • • • • •
Software Interrupt	SWI				3F 12 1	See Special Operations	• • • • • •
Wait for Interrupt *	WAI				3E 9 1		• ② • • • •

*WAI puts Address Bus, R/W, and Data Bus in the three state mode while VMA is held low.

① (All) Load Condition Code Register from Stack. (See Special Operations)
② (Bit 1) Set when interrupt occurs. If previously set, a Non Maskable Interrupt is required to exit the wait state.

TABLE 5 — CONDITION CODE REGISTER INSTRUCTIONS

OPERATIONS	MNEMONIC	IMPLIED OP ~ #	BOOLEAN OPERATION	COND. CODE REG. 5 4 3 2 1 0 H I N Z V C
Clear Carry	CLC	0C 2 1	$0 \to C$	• • • • • R
Clear Interrupt Mask	CLI	0E 2 1	$0 \to I$	• R • • • •
Clear Overflow	CLV	0A 2 1	$0 \to V$	• • • • R •
Set Carry	SEC	0D 2 1	$1 \to C$	• • • • • S
Set Interrupt Mask	SEI	0F 2 1	$1 \to I$	• S • • • •
Set Overflow	SEV	0B 2 1	$1 \to V$	• • • • S •
Acmltr A → CCR	TAP	06 2 1	$A \to CCR$	①
CCR → Acmltr A	TPA	07 2 1	$CCR \to A$	• • • • • •

R = Reset
S = Set
• = Not affected

① (ALL) Set according to the contents of Accumulator A.

appendix III

6800 Instruction Set— Author Classification

DATA-TRANSFER GROUP

LDA	Load Accumulator
LDS	Load Stack Pointer
LDX	Load Index Register
STA	Store Accumulator
STS	Store Stack Register
STX	Store Index Register
TAB	Transfer Accumulators
TAP	Transfer Accumulators to Condition Codes Register
TBA	Transfer Accumulators
TPA	Transfer Condition Codes Register to Accumulator
TSX	Transfer Stack Pointer to Index Register
TXS	Transfer Index Register to Stack Pointer

LOGICAL GROUP

AND	Logical AND
ORA	Inclusive OR Accumulator
EOR	Exclusive OR
COM	Complement
CMP	Compare
CBA	Compare Accumulators
CPX	Compare Index Registers
LSR	Logical Shift Right
ROL	Rotate Left
ROR	Rotate Right
TST	Test
BIT	Bit Test

ARITHMETIC GROUP

ABA	Add Accumulators
ADC	Add with Carry
ADD	Add
SUB	Subtract
SBA	Subtract Accumulators
SBC	Subtract with Carry
DAA	Decimal Adjust
DEC	Decrement
DES	Decrement Stack Pointer
DEX	Decrement Index Register
INC	Increment
INS	Increment Stack Pointer
INX	Increment Index Register
ASL	Arithmetic Shift Left
ASR	Arithmetic Shift Right
NEG	Negate
CLR	Clear

BRANCH GROUP

JMP	Jump
JSR	Jump to Subroutine
BCC	Branch if Carry Clear
BCS	Branch if Carry Set
BEQ	Branch if Equal to Zero
BGE	Branch if Greater or Equal Zero
BGT	Branch if Greater than Zero
BHI	Branch if Higher
BLE	Branch if Less or Equal
BLS	Branch if Lower or Same
BLT	Branch if Less than Zero
BMI	Branch if Minus
BNE	Branch if Not Equal to Zero
BPL	Branch if Plus
BRA	Branch Always
BSR	Branch to Subroutine
BVC	Branch if Overflow Clear
BVS	Branch if Overflow Set
RTI	Return from Interrupt
RTS	Return from Subroutine
SWI	Software Interrupt

STACK AND MACHINE-CONTROL GROUP

PSH	Push Data
PUL	Pull Data
NOP	No Operation
CLC	Clear Carry
CLI	Clear Interrupt Mask
SEC	Set Carry
SEI	Set Interrupt Mask
SEV	Set Overflow
WAI	Wait for Interrupt
CLR	Clear

appendix IV

6800 Instruction Set—Cycle-by-Cycle Operation

TABLE 6 — INHERENT MODE CYCLE-BY-CYCLE OPERATION

Address Mode and Instructions	Cycles	Cycle #	VMA Line	Address Bus	R/$\overline{W}$ Line	Data Bus
ABA DAA SEC ASL DEC SEI ASR INC SEV CBA LSR TAB CLC NEG TAP CLI NOP TBA CLR ROL TPA CLV ROR TST COM SBA	2	1	1	Op Code Address	1	Op Code
		2	1	Op Code Address + 1	1	Op Code of Next Instruction
DES DEX INS INX	4	1	1	Op Code Address	1	Op Code
		2	1	Op Code Address + 1	1	Op Code of Next Instruction
		3	0	Previous Register Contents	1	Irrelevant Data (Note 1)
		4	0	New Register Contents	1	Irrelevant Data (Note 1)
PSH	4	1	1	Op Code Address	1	Op Code
		2	1	Op Code Address + 1	1	Op Code of Next Instruction
		3	1	Stack Pointer	0	Accumulator Data
		4	0	Stack Pointer − 1	1	Accumulator Data
PUL	4	1	1	Op Code Address	1	Op Code
		2	1	Op Code Address + 1	1	Op Code of Next Instruction
		3	0	Stack Pointer	1	Irrelevant Data (Note 1)
		4	1	Stack Pointer + 1	1	Operand Data from Stack
TSX	4	1	1	Op Code Address	1	Op Code
		2	1	Op Code Address + 1	1	Op Code of Next Instruction
		3	0	Stack Pointer	1	Irrelevant Data (Note 1)
		4	0	New Index Register	1	Irrelevant Data (Note 1)
TXS	4	1	1	Op Code Address	1	Op Code
		2	1	Op Code Address + 1	1	Op Code of Next Instruction
		3	0	Index Register	1	Irrelevant Data
		4	0	New Stack Pointer	1	Irrelevant Data
RTS	5	1	1	Op Code Address	1	Op Code
		2	1	Op Code Address + 1	1	Irrelevant Data (Note 2)
		3	0	Stack Pointer	1	Irrelevant Data (Note 1)
		4	1	Stack Pointer + 1	1	Address of Next Instruction (High Order Byte)
		5	1	Stack Pointer + 2	1	Address of Next Instruction (Low Order Byte)

Note 1. If device which is addressed during this cycle uses VMA, then the Data Bus will go to the high impedance three-state condition. Depending on bus capacitance, data from the previous cycle may be retained on the Data Bus.

Note 2. Data is ignored by the MPU.

Note 3. While the MPU is waiting for the interrupt, Bus Available will go high indicating the following states of the control lines: VMA is low; Address Bus, R/$\overline{W}$, and Data Bus are all in the high impedance state.

TABLE 6 — INHERENT MODE CYCLE-BY-CYCLE OPERATION (CONTINUED)

Address Mode and Instructions	Cycles	Cycle #	VMA Line	Address Bus	R/W Line	Data Bus
WAI	9	1	1	Op Code Address	1	Op Code
		2	1	Op Code Address + 1	1	Op Code of Next Instruction
		3	1	Stack Pointer	0	Return Address (Low Order Byte)
		4	1	Stack Pointer − 1	0	Return Address (High Order Byte)
		5	1	Stack Pointer − 2	0	Index Register (Low Order Byte)
		6	1	Stack Pointer − 3	0	Index Register (High Order Byte)
		7	1	Stack Pointer − 4	0	Contents of Accumulator A
		8	1	Stack Pointer − 5	0	Contents of Accumulator B
		9	1	Stack Pointer − 6 (Note 3)	1	Contents of Cond. Code Register
RTI	10	1	1	Op Code Address	1	Op Code
		2	1	Op Code Address + 1	1	Irrelevant Data (Note 2)
		3	0	Stack Pointer	1	Irrelevant Data (Note 1)
		4	1	Stack Pointer + 1	1	Contents of Cond. Code Register from Stack
		5	1	Stack Pointer + 2	1	Contents of Accumulator B from Stack
		6	1	Stack Pointer + 3	1	Contents of Accumulator A from Stack
		7	1	Stack Pointer + 4	1	Index Register from Stack (High Order Byte)
		8	1	Stack Pointer + 5	1	Index Register from Stack (Low Order Byte)
		9	1	Stack Pointer + 6	1	Next Instruction Address from Stack (High Order Byte)
		10	1	Stack Pointer + 7	1	Next Instruction Address from Stack (Low Order Byte)
SWI	12	1	1	Op Code Address	1	Op Code
		2	1	Op Code Address + 1	1	Irrelevant Data (Note 1)
		3	1	Stack Pointer	0	Return Address (Low Order Byte)
		4	1	Stack Pointer − 1	0	Return Address (High Order Byte)
		5	1	Stack Pointer − 2	0	Index Register (Low Order Byte)
		6	1	Stack Pointer − 3	0	Index Register (High Order Byte)
		7	1	Stack Pointer − 4	0	Contents of Accumulator A
		8	1	Stack Pointer − 5	0	Contents of Accumulator B
		9	1	Stack Pointer − 6	0	Contents of Cond. Code Register
		10	0	Stack Pointer − 7	1	Irrelevant Data (Note 1)
		11	1	Vector Address FFFA (Hex)	1	Address of Subroutine (High Order Byte)
		12	1	Vector Address FFFB (Hex)	1	Address of Subroutine (Low Order Byte)

Note 1. If device which is addressed during this cycle uses VMA, then the Data Bus will go to the high impedance three-state condition. Depending on bus capacitance, data from the previous cycle may be retained on the Data Bus.
Note 2. Data is ignored by the MPU.
Note 3. While the MPU is waiting for the interrupt, Bus Available will go high indicating the following states of the control lines: VMA is low; Address Bus, R/W, and Data Bus are all in the high impedance state.

TABLE 7 — IMMEDIATE MODE CYCLE-BY-CYCLE OPERATION

Address Mode and Instructions	Cycles	Cycle #	VMA Line	Address Bus	R/W Line	Data Bus
ADC EOR ADD LDA AND ORA BIT SBC CMP SUB	2	1	1	Op Code Address	1	Op Code
		2	1	Op Code Address + 1	1	Operand Data
CPX LDS LDX	3	1	1	Op Code Address	1	Op Code
		2	1	Op Code Address + 1	1	Operand Data (High Order Byte)
		3	1	Op Code Address + 2	1	Operand Data (Low Order Byte)

TABLE 8 — DIRECT MODE CYCLE-BY-CYCLE OPERATION

Address Mode and Instructions	Cycles	Cycle #	VMA Line	Address Bus	R/W̄ Line	Data Bus
ADC EOR ADD LDA AND ORA BIT SBC CMP SUB	3	1	1	Op Code Address	1	Op Code
		2	1	Op Code Address + 1	1	Address of Operand
		3	1	Address of Operand	1	Operand Data
CPX LDS LDX	4	1	1	Op Code Address	1	Op Code
		2	1	Op Code Address + 1	1	Address of Operand
		3	1	Address of Operand	1	Operand Data (High Order Byte)
		4	1	Operand Address + 1	1	Operand Data (Low Order Byte)
STA	4	1	1	Op Code Address	1	Op Code
		2	1	Op Code Address + 1	1	Destination Address
		3	0	Destination Address	1	Irrelevant Data (Note 1)
		4	1	Destination Address	0	Data from Accumulator
STS STX	5	1	1	Op Code Address	1	Op Code
		2	1	Op Code Address + 1	1	Address of Operand
		3	0	Address of Operand	1	Irrelevant Data (Note 1)
		4	1	Address of Operand	0	Register Data (High Order Byte)
		5	1	Address of Operand + 1	0	Register Data (Low Order Byte)

Note 1. If device which is address during this cycle uses VMA, then the Data Bus will go to the high impedance three-state condition. Depending on bus capacitance, data from the previous cycle may be retained on the Data Bus.

TABLE 9 — EXTENDED MODE CYCLE-BY-CYCLE

Address Mode and Instructions	Cycles	Cycle #	VMA Line	Address Bus	R/W̄ Line	Data Bus
STS STX	6	1	1	Op Code Address	1	Op Code
		2	1	Op Code Address + 1	1	Address of Operand (High Order Byte)
		3	1	Op Code Address + 2	1	Address of Operand (Low Order Byte)
		4	0	Address of Operand	1	Irrelevant Data (Note 1)
		5	1	Address of Operand	0	Operand Data (High Order Byte)
		6	1	Address of Operand + 1	0	Operand Data (Low Order Byte)
JSR	9	1	1	Op Code Address	1	Op Code
		2	1	Op Code Address + 1	1	Address of Subroutine (High Order Byte)
		3	1	Op Code Address + 2	1	Address of Subroutine (Low Order Byte)
		4	1	Subroutine Starting Address	1	Op Code of Next Instruction
		5	1	Stack Pointer	0	Return Address (Low Order Byte)
		6	1	Stack Pointer 1	0	Return Address (High Order Byte)
		7	0	Stack Pointer 2	1	Irrelevant Data (Note 1)
		8	0	Op Code Address + 2	1	Irrelevant Data (Note 1)
		9	1	Op Code Address + 2	1	Address of Subroutine (Low Order Byte)
JMP	3	1	1	Op Code Address	1	Op Code
		2	1	Op Code Address + 1	1	Jump Address (High Order Byte)
		3	1	Op Code Address + 2	1	Jump Address (Low Order Byte)
ADC EOR ADD LDA AND ORA BIT SBC CMP SUB	4	1	1	Op Code Address	1	Op Code
		2	1	Op Code Address + 1	1	Address of Operand (High Order Byte)
		3	1	Op Code Address + 2	1	Address of Operand (Low Order Byte)
		4	1	Address of Operand	1	Operand Data
CPX LDS LDX	5	1	1	Op Code Address	1	Op Code
		2	1	Op Code Address + 1	1	Address of Operand (High Order Byte)
		3	1	Op Code Address + 2	1	Address of Operand (Low Order Byte)
		4	1	Address of Operand	1	Operand Data (High Order Byte)
		5	1	Address of Operand + 1	1	Operand Data (Low Order Byte)
STA A STA B	5	1	1	Op Code Address	1	Op Code
		2	1	Op Code Address + 1	1	Destination Address (High Order Byte)
		3	1	Op Code Address + 2	1	Destination Address (Low Order Byte)
		4	0	Operand Destination Address	1	Irrelevant Data (Note 1)
		5	1	Operand Destination Address	0	Data from Accumulator
ASL LSR ASR NEG CLR ROL COM ROR DEC TST INC	6	1	1	Op Code Address	1	Op Code
		2	1	Op Code Address + 1	1	Address of Operand (High Order Byte)
		3	1	Op Code Address + 2	1	Address of Operand (Low Order Byte)
		4	1	Address of Operand	1	Current Operand Data
		5	0	Address of Operand	1	Irrelevant Data (Note 1)
		6	1/0 (Note 2)	Address of Operand	0	New Operand Data (Note 2)

Note 1. If device which is addressed during this cycle uses VMA, then the Data Bus will go to the high impedance three-state condition. Depending on bus capacitance, data from the previous cycle may be retained on the Data Bus.

Note 2. For TST, VMA = 0 and Operand data does not change.

TABLE 10 — RELATIVE MODE CYCLE-BY-CYCLE OPERATION

Address Mode and Instructions	Cycles	Cycle #	VMA Line	Address Bus	R/W̄ Line	Data Bus
BCC BHI BNE BCS BLE BPL BEQ BLS BRA BGE BLT BVC BGT BMI BVS	4	1	1	Op Code Address	1	Op Code
		2	1	Op Code Address + 1	1	Branch Offset
		3	0	Op Code Address + 2	1	Irrelevant Data (Note 1)
		4	0	Branch Address	1	Irrelevant Data (Note 1)
BSR	8	1	1	Op Code Address	1	Op Code
		2	1	Op Code Address + 1	1	Branch Offset
		3	0	Return Address of Main Program	1	Irrelevant Data (Note 1)
		4	1	Stack Pointer	0	Return Address (Low Order Byte)
		5	1	Stack Pointer − 1	0	Return Address (High Order Byte)
		6	0	Stack Pointer − 2	1	Irrelevant Data (Note 1)
		7	0	Return Address of Main Program	1	Irrelevant Data (Note 1)
		8	0	Subroutine Address	1	Irrelevant Data (Note 1)

Note 1. If device which is addressed during this cycle uses VMA, then the Data Bus will go to the high impedance three-state condition. Depending on bus capacitance, data from the previous cycle may be retained on the Data Bus.

TABLE 11 — INDEXED MODE CYCLE-BY-CYCLE

Address Mode and Instructions	Cycles	Cycle #	VMA Line	Address Bus	R/W̄ Line	Data Bus
INDEXED						
JMP	4	1	1	Op Code Address	1	Op Code
		2	1	Op Code Address + 1	1	Offset
		3	0	Index Register	1	Irrelevant Data (Note 1)
		4	0	Index Register Plus Offset (w/o Carry)	1	Irrelevant Data (Note 1)
ADC EOR ADD LDA AND ORA BIT SBC CMP SUB	5	1	1	Op Code Address	1	Op Code
		2	1	Op Code Address + 1	1	Offset
		3	0	Index Register	1	Irrelevant Data (Note 1)
		4	0	Index Register Plus Offset (w/o Carry)	1	Irrelevant Data (Note 1)
		5	1	Index Register Plus Offset	1	Operand Data
CPX LDS LDX	6	1	1	Op Code Address	1	Op Code
		2	1	Op Code Address + 1	1	Offset
		3	0	Index Register	1	Irrelevant Data (Note 1)
		4	0	Index Register Plus Offset (w/o Carry)	1	Irrelevant Data (Note 1)
		5	1	Index Register Plus Offset	1	Operand Data (High Order Byte)
		6	1	Index Register Plus Offset + 1	1	Operand Data (Low Order Byte)
STA	6	1	1	Op Code Address	1	Op Code
		2	1	Op Code Address + 1	1	Offset
		3	0	Index Register	1	Irrelevant Data (Note 1)
		4	0	Index Register Plus Offset (w/o Carry)	1	Irrelevant Data (Note 1)
		5	0	Index Register Plus Offset	1	Irrelevant Data (Note 1)
		6	1	Index Register Plus Offset	0	Operand Data
ASL LSR ASR NEG CLR ROL COM ROR DEC TST INC	7	1	1	Op Code Address	1	Op Code
		2	1	Op Code Address + 1	1	Offset
		3	0	Index Register	1	Irrelevant Data (Note 1)
		4	0	Index Register Plus Offset (w/o Carry)	1	Irrelevant Data (Note 1)
		5	1	Index Register Plus Offset	1	Current Operand Data
		6	0	Index Register Plus Offset	1	Irrelevant Data (Note 1)
		7	1/0 (Note 2)	Index Register Plus Offset	0	New Operand Data (Note 2)
STS STX	7	1	1	Op Code Address	1	Op Code
		2	1	Op Code Address + 1	1	Offset
		3	0	Index Register	1	Irrelevant Data (Note 1)
		4	0	Index Register Plus Offset (w/o Carry)	1	Irrelevant Data (Note 1)
		5	0	Index Register Plus Offset	1	Irrelevant Data (Note 1)
		6	1	Index Register Plus Offset	0	Operand Data (High Order Byte)
		7	1	Index Register Plus Offset + 1	0	Operand Data (Low Order Byte)
JSR	8	1	1	Op Code Address	1	Op Code
		2	1	Op Code Address + 1	1	Offset
		3	0	Index Register	1	Irrelevant Data (Note 1)
		4	1	Stack Pointer	0	Return Address (Low Order Byte)
		5	1	Stack Pointer − 1	0	Return Address (High Order Byte)
		6	0	Stack Pointer − 2	1	Irrelevant Data (Note 1)
		7	0	Index Register	1	Irrelevant Data (Note 1)
		8	0	Index Register Plus Offset (w/o Carry)	1	Irrelevant Data (Note 1)

Note 1. If device which is addressed during this cycle uses VMA, then the Data Bus will go to the high impedance three-state condition. Depending on bus capacitance, data from the previous cycle may be retained on the Data Bus.

Note 2. For TST, VMA = 0 and Operand data does not change.

appendix V

Design Suggestions for Lunar-Landing Simulator

The following suggestions and comments pertain to the design of the lunar-landing simulator of Chapter 24.

- To avoid premature overflow (or underflow) of the velocity register, we have limited the thrust and gravity to the 0–7 range by including only three outputs in the A/D DAC of Figure 24.1. If the gravity is set at a typical value of 3, then the maximum-thrust situation results in 4 (7 − 3) being added to the cumulative-velocity register at the interrupt rate. At the 4 Hz interrupt rate, 16 (4 × 4) would be added to the cumulative-velocity register each second. From a standing start it would therefore require 8 seconds to reach maximum velocity (128/16)—a realistic situation.
- Use the technique of Figure 17.8 to prevent overflow or underflow of cumulative total register.
- The speed parameter sent to the delay block of the stepper-motor routine (see Figure 24.2) must be in true form. Furthermore, the larger the speed parameter, the smaller the velocity. The parameter generated by the math routine, however, is in 2's complement form for negative numbers and is directly proportional to true speed. Therefore, to properly condition the speed parameter, we take the 2's complement of all negative velocities (which automatically converts the speed to true form and strips away the sign bit of 1) and subtract the result from 127.
- To calibrate the system, choose a stepper-motor pulley size that gives the desired maximum vertical speed when rotating at the maximum rate.

INDEX

Access time, 37
Ada, 297
Addition,
    BCD, 206–207
    of signed numbers, 116–118
Addressing:
    basic concepts, 18–19, 31–36, 42
    bank switching, 36
    coincident selection, 31, 42
    foldback, 37
    high level, 32–36
    indexed, 110, 122
    linear vs decoded, 18–19, 34–36
    mapping RAM, 36
    modes, 107–111, 351
    relative, 139
ALU, 6, 80–82
American National Standards Institute (ANSI), 72
    floating point standard, 208–209
American Standard Code for Information Interchange (ASCII), 270–271
Analog-to-digital, 219–222
ANSI (*see* American National Standards Institute)
Arithmetic instructions, 6, 81, 115–126
Arithmetic/logic unit, 6, 81
ASCII, 270–271
Assembler, machine, 142–145, 153, 162, 177–180, 195, 210–211
Assembly-language programming, 140–145
Asynchronous communication, 214, 269–270
    serial transmission format, 269–270
    6850 Asynchronous Communication Interface Adapter (ACIA), 274–281

Babbage, Charles, 2
Backup storage devices, 24–25, 70–74
    audio cassette, 72–73
    definition of, 24–25
    half-inch magnetic tape, 71
    hybrid (secondary/backup) systems, 73
    optical, 73
    quarter-inch magnetic tape, 71
    recording modes, 58–60
    streaming tape, 70–71
    video cassette, 73
BASIC, programming language, 296–297, 300
BCD addition, 206–207
Bit manipulation, 132–135
Bit-slice processors, 333

Boole, George, 2
Boolean instructions, 127–137
Boolean, formulae for condition codes, 149
Bootstrap, disk loading, 144, 312
Branch, instructions:
    conditional, 147–162, 203–206
    unconditional, 138–140
Breakpointing, 303–304
    with in-circuit emulation, 315
Bubble memory, 67–69
Bus, 10–15
    buffering, 14
    interfacing, 18–20, 32–36, 240–242, 244, 248–249, 279–281, 344–348
    Multibus (IEEE-796), 13
    receivers, 14
    S-100 (IEEE-696), 12
    STD, 13
    transceivers, 14
    transmitters, 14
    VERSAbus, 14

Cache memory, 26
CAD (Computer-aided design), 51, 54, 315–316
CALL instruction, 167–169
    when to CALL, 174–175
Cassette recording, 72–73
Central processing unit (CPU), 76–82
Centronics, handshaking standard, 215–216, 240–245
Character generation, 227–228
Charge-coupled device, 69–70
Clock, 94–95
    6875 clock generator, 94–95
Clock cycle, 6800, 96–97
CMOS, 39, 54
COBOL (Common Business-Oriented Language), 4
Codec (coder/decoder), 287–291
Collision detection, 283–284
Communication (*see* Data Communication)
Comunication protocols, 282–283
Compare instruction, 155–158
Compiler, 301–302
Computer-aided design (CAD), 51, 54, 315–316
Controllers, 252–268
    disk drive, 71
    moon-landing simulator, 335–339
    single-chip, 255–262

Controller sequencer (CON), 79
CPU, 6, 76–82
CRC (*see* Error detection)
Current loop, 272–273
Cybernetics, 252
Cycle stealing, 98

Daisy chain, 191–192
Damping, 252–253
Data acquisition, 233
Data communication, 269–294
    Asynchronous Communication Interface Adapter (ACIA), 274–281
    codec, 287–291
    current loop, 272–273
    fiberoptics, 291
    GPIB, 273–274
    local area networks (LANs), 283–285
    modems, 285–286
    protocols, 282–283
    RS-232C, 271–272
    simplex/duplex, 240
    standards, 271–273
    speech synthesis, 291–293
    telecommunications, 285–291
Data logger, 233
Data structures, 209–210
Data-transfer, 16–18
    instructions, 106–114
Debouncing (interrupt), 193–194
Decision-making, 147, 151
    greater-than/less-than, 155–157
Delay loop, 158–159
Development systems, 310–315
Digital-to-analog (DAC), 217–219
Disk drive controller, 71
Direct addressing, 108–109
Display:
    multiplexed, 225
    touch-screen, 224
    video, 227–228
Division, 202
DMA I/O, 216–217
DMA request, 98
Double precision, 200
Duplex transmission, 240
Dynamic RAM, 40–42

ECC (*see under* Error detection)
EE-PROM, 48
ENIAC, 3

384 Index

EPROM, 45–48
Erasable Programmable Read-Only Memory (EPROM), 45–48
   access times, 47
Error detection:
   cyclic redundancy checking (CRC), 60–61
   Error checking and correcting (ECC), 61–63
Ethernet, 285
Extended addressing, 109–110, 122

Feedback, 252–253
Fiber-optics, 291
FILO (first in/last out), 171
Flags, 147–148, 202–206
Floating-point numbers, 208–209
Floppy-disk systems, 63–65
   error detection, 60–63
   formatting, 60
   RAM disk, 65
Flowchart, 85
   high level vs low level, 122–123
Foldback memory, 36
Formatting, floppy disk, 60, 64
FORTRAN, 4
Fractions, 207

Gate arrays, 52–54
General-Purpose Interface Bus (GPIB), 273–274
GPIB (IEEE 488), 273–274
Graphics, 228–232
   software, 231–233
   turtle, 232–233

Handshaking, 214–216
   Centronics standard, 215–216, 240–245
Heathkit, ET-3400A trainer, 19, 195–196
High-level languages, 296–301

Immediate addressing, 107–108
In-circuit emulation (ICE), 314–315
Indexed addressing, 110, 122
Inherent addressing, 110–111
Instruction cycle, definition of, 96
Instruction register, 79
Instruction set, 84–85
   addressing modes, 107–111
   arithmetic group, 115–126
   branch group, 138–162, 167–169, 203–206
   data-transfer group, 106–114
   logical group, 127–137
   PUSH/PULL, 172–174
   shift and rotate, 129–131
   test and bit test, 153–155
Intel, microprocessors of, 321–329
Integration, mathematical, 335–338
Interfacing, bus:
   ACIA (6850), 279–281
   memory, 32–36
   PIA (6820), 240–242, 244
   PIC (6828), 248–249
   ports, 18–20
   68000, 344–348
Interpreter, 301–302
Interrupt I/O, 216, 281
Interrupts, 184–198
   daisy chain, 191–192
   debouncing, 193–194
   EA3400A trainer, 195–196
   interrupt I/O, 216
   masking, 192–193
   multiple, 189–192

priority, 189–192
scanned, 189
6828 Priority Interrupt Controller, 245–250
68000, 350
SWI instruction, 186–187
vector map, 188–189
vectored, 189–191
WAI instruction, 187–188
Z-80, 330–331
Isolated I/O, 18, 322–323

Jump:
   conditional, 147–162, 203–206
   unconditional, 138–140
   subroutine, 167–169

Kansas City Standard, 72
Keyboard entry, 222–224

Label, in assembly-language programming, 141
Languages:
   assembly, 140–145
   high level, 4, 231–232, 296–302
Large-scale integration (LSI), 4
Link, 211, 233–234, 314
LIFO (Last-in/first-out), 171
Local area networks (LANs), 283–285
Locate, 211, 233, 314
Logic analysis, 305–310
   HP1615A, 306–309
   Tektronix 7D02, 309–310
Logic arrays, 51–55
   gate arrays, 52–54
   PAL/PLA, 52–53
   standard cell, 54–55
Logical instructions, 127–137
Loops, 138–140
   delay, 158–159
   using indexed addressing, 161–162

Machine assembly update, 142–145, 153, 162, 177–180, 195, 210–211, 233–234
MACRO, 177–180
Magnetic tape, 70–74
   audio-cassette, 72–73
   half-inch, 71
   quarter-inch, 71
MAR (Memory-address register), 87–88
Masking:
   bit manipulation, 132–135
   interrupt, 192–193
Memory:
   access time, 37
   addressing, 28–37
   arrays, 32–36
   backup, 24, 70–74
   bubble, 67–69
   cache, 26
   cassette, 72–73
   charge-coupled, 69–70
   CMOS, 39, 54
   DMA, 98
   dynamic, 40–42
   floppy disk, 63–65
   foldback, 37
   hierarchy, 24–27
   magnetic-core RAM, 42–43
   map, 26
   mapped I/O, 18, 321–323
   nonvolatile static, 48–50
   optical, 37–38, 73
   performance, 37–39

pin-out standards, 50–51
primary, 24–25, 28–56
quasi-static, 42
RAM disk, 65
recording modes, 58–60
random access (RAM), 24, 28
read only (ROM), 28, 43–50
secondary, 24–25, 57–70
sequential, 24
static RAM, 28–39, 48–50
virtual, 26
Winchester disk, 65–67
Memory-mapped I/O, 18, 321–323
Microcode, 79–80
Microcomputer, definition of, 1
Microcontroller, 255–262
   6801, 255–260
Microprocessor:
   bit-slice, 333
   central processing unit (CPU), 76–82
   definition of, 1
   history of, 2–4
   operation of, 76–82, 91–94
   single chip, 2, 255–262
   68000, 344–353
   vs logic arrays, 55
   waveforms, 97
Mimic program, 85–92
Mnemonic, 86
Modems, 285–286
Modes, addressing, 107–111
Monitor, 227, 311–312
Moon-landing simulator, 335–339
Motorola:
   6800 family, 99–103
   68000 family, 351–353
Mouse, 225
Multibus, 13
Multiple-precision numbers, 200
Multiplexing, 10, 225
Multiplication, 200–202
Multiprocessing, 344, 347, 351
Music, computer, 162

Negative numbers, 116–118, 202–206
Nesting:
   delay loops, 159
   interrupts, 192
   subroutines, 172
Networks, local area, 283–285
Neumann, John von, 3

Object program, 144–145, 312
Operand, 5, 77, 93
Operating system, 316–319
   CP/M, 318–319
   real-time, 319
   UNIX, 318–319
Operation code (op code), 5, 77, 135
Optical storage, 73

PAL (programmable array logic), 52–53
Parallel processing, 267
Parameter, 175–180, 299–300
Pascal, 232, 297–301
Pascal, Blaise, 2
PCM, 287–291
Peripheral Interface Adapter (PIA), 239–245
PLA (programmable logic array), 52–53
PL/M (Programming Language/Micro),
Ports:
   instructions, 87–88

interfacing, 16–23, 88
simple I/O, 16–23
Primary memory, 24, 28–56
   CMOS, 39, 54
   dynamic RAM, 40–42
   magnetic-core RAM, 42–43
   quasi-static RAM, 42
   read-only (ROM), 28, 43–50
   static RAM, 28–39, 48–50
Priority Interrupt Controller, 245–250
Procedures, 232, 299–300
Product development, 295–320
   CAD/CAM, 315–316
   development system, 310–315
   operating systems, 316–319
   software, 296–302
   troubleshooting, 302–314, 314–315
Program counter, 78
Programmed I/O, 216
Programmable peripheral chips, 237–251
   6821 Peripheral Interface Adapter, 239–245
   6828 Priority Interrupt Controller, 245
   6850 Asynchronous Communications Interface Adapter (ACIA), 274–281
Programmable read-only memory (PROM), 45–50
   bipolar, 48
   CMOS, 48
   EE-PROM (electrically erasable PROMs), 48
   EPROM (UV erasable programmable read-only memory), 45–48
   68764, 46–47
Programmed I/O, 216
Programming:
   assembly language, 140–145
   BASIC, 296–297, 300
   Pascal, 232, 296–301
   structured, 296–301
   top-down, 300–301
PROM (*see* Programmable read-only memory)
Protocols, communication, 282–283
PULL process, 172–174
Pulse-code modulation (PCM), 287
PUSH process, 172–174

RAM (*see* Random-access memory)
RAM disk, 65
Random-access memory (RAM),
   access time, 37
   core, 42–43
   dynamic, 40–42
   magnetic core, 42–43
   nonvolatile static, 48–50

optical, 37–38
pin-out standards, 50–51
PROM, 45–50
quasi-static, 42
RAM disk, 65
RAM/ROM system, 51
6665A (64K × 1) dynamic RAM, 40
6810 (128 × 8) RAM, 32–37
68764 (8K × 8) EPROM, 46–48
static, 28–39, 45–50
2114 (1K × 4) RAM, 32–37
2816 (2K × 8) EE-PROM, 48
Read-only memory (ROM), 28, 43–50
   factory-programmed ROM, 44–45
   PROM, 45–48
Reasoning, using the conditional branch, 147–162
Reentrant, 192
Relative addressing, 139
Reset, 99
Return instruction, 169–171
Robotics, 262–267
ROM (*see* Read-only memory)
Rotate instructions, 129–131
RS-232C, 271–273

S-100 Bus (IEEE-696), 12
Searching, program for, 209–210
Secondary memory, 24, 57–70
   bubble, 67–69
   charge coupled, 69–70
   definition of, 24
   error detection and correction, 60–63
   floppy disk, 63–65
   formatting, 60
   RAM disk, 65
   recording modes, 58–60
   Winchester disk, 65–67
Shift instructions, 129–131
Signature analysis, 304–305
Sign magnitude, 117–118
Signed numbers, 116–118, 202–206
   signed number conditional branch instructions, 203–206
   subtraction, 116–118
Single-chip microcomputers, 2, 255–262
Single-stepping, 303
Sorting, 209–210
Source program, 140, 312
Speech synthesis, 291–293
Stacks, 168, 171
   LIFO/FILO, 171

Stepper motor, 260–262
Stored-program computer, 3–4, 77
Streaming tape, 70–71
Strings, 210
Structured programming, 296–301
Structure theorem, 297
Subroutines, 167–183
   parameters, 175–177, 299–300
Subtraction, signed numbers, 116–118
Successive approximation, in A/D, 220
Synchronous communication, 214, 269

Table lookup, 210
Telecommunications, 285–291
   codec (coder/decoder), 287–291
   digital, 286–291
   fiberoptics, 291
Time multiplexing, 10
Timing, cycles:
   clock, 94–98
   instruction, 96
   program, 159–160
Token passing, 283
Top-down programming, 300–301
Touch-screen display, 224
Tristate circuits, 11
   6882B, 12, 16
Troubleshooting, 302–310
   breakpointing, 303–304
   in-circuit emulation, 314–315
   logic analysis, 305–310
   signature analysis, 304–305
   single-stepping, 303
   software diagnostics, 303
   static testing, 302—303
TTY (teletype), serial transmission standard, 269
Two's complement, 116–118

UART (Universal Asynchronous Receiver/Transmitter), 274–281

Vectored interrupt, 189–191
Video, 227–228
   displays, 229–231
Virtual memory, 26
VLSI (Very large scale integration), 1, 51

Warnier-Orr Diagram, 300–301
Winchester disk, 65–67

Zilog Corp., microprocessors of, 329–333